AMC WHITE MOUNTAIN GUIDE

Twenty-fifth edition

*A guide to trails in the mountains
of New Hampshire and adjacent
parts of Maine.*

APPALACHIAN MOUNTAIN CLUB
BOSTON, MASSACHUSETTS

Cover Photograph: Dick Smith

Copyright © 1992 Appalachian Mountain Club

EDITIONS
First Edition 1907, Second Edition 1916, Third Edition 1917
Fourth Edition 1920, Fifth Edition 1922, Sixth Edition 1925
Seventh Edition 1928, Eighth Edition 1931, Ninth Edition 1934
Tenth Edition 1936, Eleventh Edition 1940, Twelfth Edition 1946
Thirteenth Edition 1948, Fourteenth Edition 1952, Fifteenth Edition 1955
Sixteenth Edition 1960, Seventeenth Edition 1963, Eighteenth Edition 1966
Nineteen Edition 1969, Twentieth Edition 1972,
Twenty-First Edition 1976, Twenty-Second Edition 1979
Twenty-Third Edition 1983, Twenty-Fourth Edition 1987
Twenty-Fifth Edition 1992

Library of Congress Cataloging-in-Publication Data
Appalachian Mountain Club.
    AMC White Mountain Guide : a guide to trails in the mountains
of New Hampshire and adjacent parts of Maine / Appalachian
Mountain Club.—25th ed.
        p.   cm.
    Includes index.
    ISBN 1-878239-12-0
    1. Hiking—White Mountains (N.H. and Me.)—Guidebooks.
2. Trails—White Mountains (N.H. and Me.)—Guidebooks.
3. White Mountains (N.H. and Me.)—Guidebooks. I. Title.
II. Title: White Mountain Guide.
GV199.42.W47A67   1992
917.42'2—dc20   92–7545
                                                        CIP

**Due to changes in conditions, use of the
information in this book
is at the sole risk of the user.**

Printed in the United States of America.

Printed on recycled paper.

10 9 8 7 6 5 4   94 95 96 97

Contents

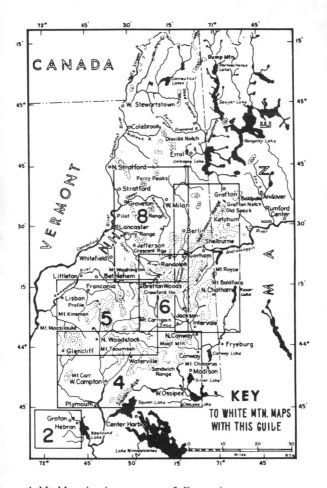

KEY TO WHITE MTN. MAPS WITH THIS GUIDE

1. Mt. Monadnock
2. Mt. Cardigan
3. (No map)
4. Chocorua-Waterville

5. Franconia
6. Mt. Washington Range
7. Carter-Mahoosuc
8. Pilot Range

To the Owner of this Book

This book aims for complete coverage of hiking trails located in the White Mountain National Forest (WMNF) in New Hampshire and Maine, and also includes descriptions of the more important trails outside the national forest in New Hampshire, with a small amount of coverage of immediately adjoining parts of Maine. For other regions in Maine, consult the *AMC Maine Mountain Guide*. No attempt is made to cover any kind of skiing (alpine, downhill, or cross-country), although several cross-country (ski-touring) trails are mentioned where they happen to cross hiking trails. Rock climbs are not described in this book, since they require special techniques and equipment and should be undertaken only by roped parties under qualified leaders, due to the high degree of danger to inexperienced or insufficiently equipped climbers or groups.

The mountains themselves may seem virtually changeless, but the lands of the White Mtns. are constantly subjected to the powerful forces of nature and the pervasive effects of contact with human visitors and management policies. Since change is therefore the rule, no source of information can be perfectly trustworthy, and a guidebook to this region can never be more than a record of the way things were at a given moment in time. Though great care has been taken to make this book as accurate as possible, it will be a useful tool only if its owner employs constant good judgment and vigilance. In the woods we are visitors who must accept that this environment can only be partly adapted to our convenience, and we must make up the difference by adapting our behavior as circumstances demand.

While trails vary greatly in the amount of use they receive and the ease with which they can be followed, it cannot be emphasized too strongly that there is almost no trail that might not be closed unexpectedly or suddenly become obscure or hazardous under certain conditions. Trails can be rerouted or abandoned or closed by landowners. Signs are stolen or fall from their posts. Storms may cause blowdowns or landslides, which can obliterate a trail for an entire climbing season or longer. Trails may not be cleared of fallen trees and brush until late summer, and not all trails are cleared every year. Logging operations can cover trails with slash and add a bewildering network of new roads. In addition, even momentary inattention to trail markers, particularly arrows at sharp turns or signs at junctions, or misinterpretation of signs or guidebook descriptions, can cause hikers to become separated from all but the most heavily traveled paths or at least lead them into what may be a much longer or more difficult route. So please remember that this book is an aid to planning, not a substitute for careful observation and good judgment.

As a consequence, all the trail-maintaining organizations, including the AMC, reserve the right to discontinue any trail without notice, and expressly disclaim any legal responsibility for the condition of any trail. Most organizations give priority to heavily used trails, so quite often rarely used trails do not receive as much attention, and following them may require great care.

We request your help in keeping the *White Mountain Guide* accurate; new editions are published at intervals of about four years. This book belongs to the entire hiking community, not just to the AMC and the people who produce it. If you encounter a problem with a trail, or with a map or description in this book, please let us know. The comments of a person who is inexperienced or unfamiliar with a trail are often particularly useful. Any comments or corrections can be sent to the *White Mountain Guide,* AMC, 5 Joy St., Boston MA 02108.

TRIP PLANNING

The descriptions in this book are intended to apply in the conditions that are usually encountered during the normal hiking season, which runs approximately from Memorial Day to Columbus Day. In some years ice or snowdrifts may remain at higher elevations until the end of May, and possibly much later in some of the major ravines and other places such as Mahoosuc Notch. When snow or ice is present, trails are often far more difficult to follow, and usually far more arduous, or even dangerous, to hike on. Winterlike conditions can occur above treeline in any month of the year. Even in midsummer, hikers above treeline should be prepared for cold weather with a wool sweater, hat, mittens, and a wind parka, which will give comfort on sunny but cool days and protection against sudden storms. Spring and fall are particularly difficult seasons in the mountains, since the weather may be pleasant in the valleys and brutal on the summits and ridges. A great number of the serious incidents in the mountains occur in the spring and fall, when hikers deceived by mild conditions at home or even at trailheads may find themselves facing severe, perhaps life-threatening, weather hazards.

Plan your trip schedule with safety in mind. Consider the strength of your party, and the general strenuousness of the trip: the overall distance, the amount of climbing, and the roughness of the terrain. Get a weather report, but be aware of the fact that most forecasts are not intended to apply to the mountain region; a day that is sunny and pleasant in the lowlands may be inclement in the mountains. The National Weather Service in Concord NH (603-225-5191) issues a recreational forecast for the White Mtn. region and broadcasts it by short-wave radio each morning approximately from 5 A.M. to 10 A.M.; this forecast is posted at Pinkham Notch Visitor Center at about 8 A.M. Plan to finish your hike with daylight to spare (days grow shorter rapidly in late summer and fall). Hiking after dark, even with flashlights (which frequently fail), makes finding trails more difficult and crossing streams hazardous. Let someone else know where you will be hiking, and do not let inexperienced people get separated from the group. Many unpaved roads are not passable until about Memorial Day, and the WMNF closes many of its roads with locked gates from November to May; many trips are much longer when the roads are not open because hikers must park farther away from the actual trailhead.

FOLLOWING TRAILS

Hikers should always carry a compass and carefully keep track of their approximate location on the map. The maps included with this guide are topographic maps (maps with the shape of the terrain represented by contour lines). They are designed as an aid to planning trips and following well-established trails, and for determining a reasonable course of action in an emergency. They therefore cover fairly large areas, which necessarily limits the amount of detail that can be shown on them. In particular, on trails that closely follow streams, it is often impossible to show accurately the number and location of crossings; the text of the trail's description should be consulted for this information. Due to this limited detail, these maps are not generally suitable for following obscure trails or for bushwhacks (planned trips away from trails). See introduction for information on more detailed maps, which necessarily cover much smaller areas, published by the United States Geological Survey (USGS).

The best compass for hiking is the protractor type: a circular, liquid-filled compass that turns on a rectangular, clear plastic base. Excellent compasses of this type, with leaflets that give ample instructions for their use, are available for less than $10. Such a compass is easily set to the bearing you wish to follow, and then it is a simple matter of keeping the compass needle aligned to north and following the arrow on the base. More sophisticated and expensive compasses have features designed for special applications that are often not useful in the woods; these are normally harder to use and apt to cause confusion in an emergency situation. Directions of the compass given in the text are based on true north instead of magnetic north, unless otherwise specified. There is a deviation of 16 to 17 degrees between true north and magnetic north in the White Mtns. This means that true north will be about 17 degrees to the right of (clockwise from) the compass's north needle. If you take a bearing from a map, you should add 17 degrees to the bearing when you set your compass. On the maps included with this guide, the black lines that run from bottom to top are aligned with true north and south. The diagonal, light-brown lines on the Mt. Washington map (map 6) are aligned with magnetic north and south, the direction that the compass needle will point.

In general, trails are maintained to provide a clear pathway while protecting the environment by minimizing erosion and other damage. Some may offer rough and difficult passage. Most hiking trails are marked with paint on trees or rocks, though some still only have axe blazes cut into trees. The trails that compose the Appalachian Trail through the White Mtns. are marked with vertical, rectangular white paint blazes throughout. Side trails off the Appalachian Trail (AT) are usually marked with blue paint. Other trails are marked in other colors, the most popular being yellow. Except for the Appalachian Trail and its side trails, and trails maintained by certain clubs such as the Chocorua Mountain Club (CMC) and the Wonalancet Outdoor Club (WODC) the color of blazing has no significance and may change without notice; therefore blaze color is not a reliable means of distinguishing particular trails from intersecting ones. Above timberline, cairns (piles of rocks) mark the trails. Where hikers have trodden out the vegetation, the footway is usually visible except when it is covered by snow or by fallen leaves. In winter, signs at trailheads and intersections and blazes also are often covered by snow. Trails following or crossing logging roads require special care at intersections in order to distinguish the trail from diverging roads, particularly since blazing is usually very sparse along the road. Around shelters or campsites, well-trodden paths may lead in all directions, so look for signs and paint blazes.

If you lose a trail and it is not visible to either side, it is usually best to backtrack right away to the last mark seen and look again from there; this will be made much easier if you carefully note each trail marking and keep track of where and how long ago you saw the most recent one. Even when you cannot immediately find the trail, it is a serious but not a desperate situation. Few people become truly lost in the White Mtns.; a moment's reflection and five minutes with the map will show that you probably know at least your approximate location and the direction to the nearest road, if nothing else. Most cases in which a person has become lost for any length of time involve panic and aimless wandering, so the most important first step is to take a break, make an inventory of useful information, decide on a course of action and stick to it. (The caution against allowing inexperienced persons to become separated from a group should be repeated here since they are most likely to panic and wander aimlessly. Make sure also that all party members are familiar with the route of the trip and the names of the trails to be used, so that if any do become separated they will have some prospect of rejoining the group.) If you have carefully kept track of your location on the map, it will usually be possible to find a nearby stream, trail, or road to which a compass course may be followed. Most distances are short enough (except in the north country, north of NH 110) that it is possible, in the absence of alternatives, to reach a highway in half a day, or at most in a whole day, simply by going downhill, carefully avoiding any dangerous cliffs (which will normally be found in areas where the map's contour lines are unusually close together), until you come upon a river or brook. The stream should then be followed downward.

WHAT TO CARRY

Good things to have in your pack for a summer day hike in the White Mtns., include a guidebook, maps, filled water bottle (ordinary plastic soft drink bottles work well, or you can purchase water bottles), compass, knife (good-quality stainless steel, since ordinary steel rusts very quickly), rain gear, windbreaker, wool sweater(s), wool hat and mittens, waterproof matches, enough food for your usual needs plus extra high-energy foods in reserve (such as dried fruit or candy), first-aid supplies (including personal medicines, aspirin, adhesive bandages, gauze, and antiseptic), needle and thread, safety pins, nylon cord, trash bag, toilet paper, and a (small) flashlight with extra batteries and a spare bulb. Wear comfortable hiking boots. Blue jeans, sweatshirts, and other cotton clothes are popular but, once wet, dry very slowly and may be uncomfortable; in adverse weather conditions they often become a serious drain on a cold and tired hiker's heat reserves. Wool keeps much of its insulation value even when wet, and it (or one of several modern synthetic materials) is indispensable for hikers who want to visit places from which return to civilization might require substantial time and effort if weather conditions deteriorate. Not only do hats, mittens, and other such gear provide safety in adverse conditions, but they also allow you to enjoy the summits in comfort on those occasional crisp, clear, cold days when the views are particularly fine.

MOUNTAIN HAZARDS

In emergencies, call the toll-free NH State Police number (800-852-3411) or Pinkham Notch Visitor Center (603-466-2727).

Hypothermia, the most serious danger to hikers in the White Mtns., is the loss of ability to preserve body heat because of injury, exhaustion, lack of sufficient food, and inadequate or wet clothing. Most of the dozens of deaths on Mt. Washington have resulted from hypothermia. It is important to understand that a person does not "freeze to death," since death occurs at a body temperature of about 80° F. Most cases occur in temperatures above freezing; the most dangerous weather conditions involve rain, with wind, with temperatures below 50° F. The symptoms include uncontrolled shivering, impaired speech and movement, lowered body temperature, and drowsiness. Death can result, unless the victim (who will not understand the situation due to impaired mental function) is rewarmed. In mild cases the victim should be given dry clothing and placed in a sleeping bag (perhaps with someone else in it to provide body heat), then quick-energy food, and, when fully conscious, something warm (not hot) to drink. In severe cases only prompt hospitalization offers reasonable hope for recovery. It is not unusual for a victim to resist treatment and even combat rescuers. It should therefore be obvious that prevention of hypothermia is the only truly practical course. Uncontrollable shivering should be regarded as an absolute evidence of hypothermia; this shivering will eventually cease on its own, but that is merely the sign that the body has given up the struggle and is sinking toward death.

Lightning is another serious hazard, particularly on the Presidential and Franconia ranges and on any bare ridge or summit. In the White Mtns., the best course of action is to avoid the dangerous places when thunderstorms are likely, and to go down the mountain to shelter in thick woods as quickly as possible if you detect an unexpected "thumper." Most thunderstorms occur when a cold front passes, or on very warm days; those produced by cold fronts are typically more sudden and violent. Weather forecasts that mention cold fronts or predict temperatures much above 80° F in the lowlands and valleys should arouse concern.

Many people believe that the most risky part of hiking in the White Mtns. is the drive to the trailhead, and the recent rapid increase in New Hampshire's moose population has added a significant new hazard. During the first nine months of 1991, collisions between moose and automobiles caused the deaths of four people and more than 160 moose. The great majority of these collisions occur in the period from early May to the middle of July, when the moose leave the woods to avoid the black flies and to seek out the road salt that has accumulated in ditches near highways. Motorists need to be aware of the seriousness of the problem, particularly at night when these huge, dark animals are both active and very difficult to see. Instinct often causes them to face an auto rather than run from it, and they are also apt to cross the road suddenly just as a car approaches. It is thus safest to assume that moose will behave in the most inconvenient manner possible. Otherwise they probably constitute little threat to hikers on foot, though it would be wise to give bulls a wide berth during the fall mating season.

Bears are common but tend to keep well out of sight. Since the closing of many of the town dumps in the north country, some bears have become a nuisance and even a hazard at some popular campsites; any bear that has lost its natural fear of humans and gotten used to living off us is extremely dangerous. Careful protection of food at campsites is mandatory; it must never be kept overnight in a tent. Deer-hunting season (with guns) is in November, when you'll probably see many more hunters than deer. Most hunters usually stay fairly close to roads. However, avoid wearing brown or anything that might give a hunter the impression of the flash of white of a white-tail deer running away. Wearing hunter's orange clothing is strongly recommended.

There are no poisonous snakes in the White Mtns. Mosquitoes and black flies are the woodland pests most frequently encountered by hikers. Mosquitoes are worst throughout the summer in low, wet areas, and black flies are most bloodthirsty in June and early July; at times these winged pests can make life in the woods virtually unbearable. Fishermen's head-nets can be useful. The most effective repellents are based on the active ingredient diethyl-meta-toluamide, generally known as "deet," but there are growing doubts about its safety, and there are other effective repellents available. Hikers should probably apply repellents with "deet" to clothing rather than skin where possible, and avoid using them on small children.

Unfortunately, cars parked at trailheads are frequently targets of break-ins, so never leave valuables or expensive equipment in the car while you are off hiking, particularly overnight.

BROOK CROSSINGS

Rivers and brooks are often crossed without bridges, and it is usually possible to jump from rock to rock; a hiking staff or stick is a great aid to balance. Use caution; several fatalities have resulted from hikers (particularly solo hikers) falling on slippery rocks and, suffering an injury that rendered them unconscious, causing them to drown in relatively shallow streams. If you need to wade across (which is often the safer course), wear your boots, but not necessarily socks. Note that many crossings that may only be a nuisance in summer may be a serious obstacle in cold weather, when your feet and boots *must* be kept dry. Higher waters, which can turn innocuous brooks into virtually uncrossable torrents, occur in the spring as snow melts, or after heavy rainstorms, particularly in the fall when trees drop their leaves and take up less water. Avoid trails with potentially dangerous stream crossings during these high-water periods. If you are cut off from roads by swollen streams, it is better to make a long detour, even if you need to wait and spend a night in the woods. Rushing current can make wading extremely hazardous, and several deaths have resulted. Flood waters may subside within a few hours, especially in small brooks. It is particularly important not to camp on the far side of a brook from your exit point if the crossing is difficult and heavy rain is predicted.

DRINKING WATER

The pleasure of quaffing a cup of water fresh from a pure mountain spring is one of the traditional attractions of the mountains. Unfortunately, in many mountain regions, including the White Mtns., the presence of cysts of the intestinal parasite *giardia lamblia* in water sources is thought to be common, though difficult to prove. It is impossible to be completely sure whether a given source is safe, no matter how clear the water or remote the location. The safest course is for day hikers to carry their own water, and for those who use sources in the woods to treat the water before drinking it. A conservative practice is to boil water for 20 min. or to use an iodine-based disinfectant. Several effective types of fine-mesh filters are also available. Chlorine-based products, such as

Halazone, are ineffective in water that contains organic impurities. All water purification chemicals tend to deteriorate quickly in the pack. Remember to allow extra contact time (and use twice as many tablets) if the water is very cold. The symptoms of giardiasis are severe intestinal distress and diarrhea, but such discomforts can have many other causes, making the disease difficult to diagnose accurately. The principal cause of the spread of this noxious ailment in the woods is probably careless disposal of human waste, so keep it at least 200 ft. away from water sources. If there are no toilets nearby, dig a hole 6 to 8 in. deep (but not below the organic layer of the soil) for a latrine and cover it completely after use. The bacteria in the organic layer of the soil will decompose the waste naturally. Many people unknowingly carry the giardia parasites, which are sometimes present in municipal water supplies and frequently do not produce symptoms. Some authorities feel that the disease is more likely to be spread by fellow party members than by contaminated water. For this reason it would be advisable to be scrupulous about washing hands after answering calls of nature.

DISTANCES AND TIMES

The distances and times that appear in the tables at the end of trail descriptions are cumulative from the starting point at the head of each table. All trails in this book have been measured with a surveyor's wheel within the past few years. Minor inconsistencies sometimes occur when measured distances are rounded, and the distances given often differ from those on trail signs.

There is no reliable method for estimating hiking times, since hikers travel at different speeds and react differently to the variety of trail conditions that occur in the White Mtns. In order to give inexperienced hikers a rough basis for planning, estimated times have been calculated for this book by allowing a half-hour for each mile of distance or 1000 ft. of climbing. No attempt has been made to adjust these times for the difficulties of specific trails, since fine-tuning an inherently limited method would probably only lead to greater unjustified reliance on it. In many cases, as hikers gain experience, they find that they usually require a fairly predictable percentage of book time to hike most trails, but eventually they are almost certain to encounter a significant exception. Therefore, all hikers using this book should be well aware of the limitations of the time-estimating formula, and should always regard book times with a critical eye and check each trail description thoroughly for trail conditions that might increase the given times. Keep in mind that hiking times will vary with steep or rough trails, for hikers with heavy packs, or for large groups, particularly with inexperienced hikers. Average descent times also vary; times for descending are given in this book only for segments of ridgecrest trails that have substantial descents in both directions. In winter, travel on a packed trail may be faster than in summer, but with heavy packs or in deep snow it may take two or three times the summer estimate.

FIRE REGULATIONS

Campfire permits are no longer required in the WMNF, but hikers who build fires are still legally responsible for any damage they may cause. Fires are not permitted on state land except at explicitly designated sites, and on private land the owner's permission is required. During periods when there is a high risk of forest fires, the forest supervisor may temporarily close the entire WMNF against public entry. Such general closures apply only as long as the dangerous conditions prevail. Other forest lands throughout New Hampshire or Maine may be closed during similar periods through proclamation by the respective governors. These special closures are given wide publicity so that local residents and visitors alike may realize the danger of fires in the woods.

PROTECTING THE BEAUTY OF THE MOUNTAINS

Please use special care above timberline. Extreme weather and a short growing season make the vegetation in these areas especially fragile. Footsteps can destroy the toughest natural cover, so please try to stay on the trail or walk on rocks. And, of course, don't camp above timberline—it is illegal and very damaging to alpine vegetation.

Once every campsite had a dump, and many trails became unsightly with litter. Now visitors are asked to bring trash bags and carry out everything—food, paper, glass, cans—they carry in. Cooperation with the "carry in/carry out" program has been outstanding, resulting in a great decrease in trailside litter over the past few years; in fact, some hikers even carry out more than they carried in. We hope you will join in the effort. Your fellow backcountry users will appreciate it.

A FINAL NOTE

Hiking is a sport of self-reliance. Its high potential for adventure and relatively low level of regulation have been made possible by the dedication of most hikers to the values of prudence and independence. This tradition of self-reliance imposes an obligation on each of us: At any time we may have to rely on our own ingenuity and judgment, aided by map and compass, to reach our goals or even make a timely exit from the woods. While the penalty for error rarely exceeds an unplanned and uncomfortable night in the woods, more serious consequences are possible. Most hikers find satisfaction in obtaining the knowledge and skills that free them from blind dependence on the next blaze or trail sign, and enable them to walk in the woods with confidence and assurance. Those who learn the skills of getting about in the woods, the habits of studious acquisition of information before the trip and careful observation while in the woods, soon find that they have earned "Freedom of the Hills".

The AMC requests that those who use the trails, shelters, and campsites heed the rules (especially those having to do with camping) of the WMNF, NH Division of Parks (NHDP), and the Society for the Protection of New Hampshire Forests (SPNHF). The same consideration should be shown to private land owners. In many cases the privileges enjoyed by hikers today could be withdrawn if rules and conditions are not observed. Trails must not be cut in the WMNF without the approval of the forest supervisor, nor elsewhere without consent of the owners and definite provision for maintenance.

The trails that we use and enjoy are only in part the product of government agencies and public nonprofit organizations; there is ultimately no "they" responsible for providing the hiking public with a variety of interesting, convenient, well-maintained trails. Many trails are cared for by one dedicated person, or a small group. Funds for trail work are scarce, and unless hikers contribute both time and money to trail maintenance, the diversity of trails available to the public is almost certain to decline. Every hiker can make some contribution to the improvement of the trails, if nothing more than pushing a blowdown off the trail rather than walking around it. These trails belong to us, and without our participation in their care they will languish. (Write to AMC Trails, Pinkham Notch Visitor Center, Box 298, Gorham NH 03581, for more information on trail maintenance.)

Introduction

According to Ticknor's *White Mountains*, published in 1887, the higher peaks "seem to have received the name of White Mtns. from the sailors off the coast, to whom they were a landmark and a mystery lifting their crowns of brilliant snow against the blue sky from October until June."

CLIMATE AND VEGETATION

The climate gets much cooler, windier, and wetter at higher elevations. The summit of Mt. Washington is under cloud cover about 55 percent of the time. On an average summer afternoon, the high temperature on the summit is only about 52° F (11° C); in the winter, about 15° F (-9° C). The record low temperature is -46° F. Average winds throughout the day and night are 26 mph in summer and 44 mph in winter. Winds have gusted over 100 mph in every month of the year, and set the world record of 231 mph on April 12, 1934. During the storm of February 24–26, 1969, the observatory recorded a snowfall of 97.8 in. Within a 24-hour period during that storm, a total of 49.3 in. was recorded, a record for the mountain and for all weather observation stations in the United States.

The forest in the White Mtns. is of two major types: northern hardwood forest (birch, beech, and maple), found at elevations of less than about 3000 ft., and the boreal forest (spruce, fir, and birch), found from about 3000 ft. to the timberline. At low elevations, oaks and white pines may be seen, and hemlocks are found in some deep valleys; red pines may grow up to about elevations of 2000 ft. in ledgy areas. Above the timberline is the "krummholz," the gnarled and stunted trees that manage to survive wherever there is a bit of shelter from the violent winds, and the tiny wildflowers, some of which are extremely rare. Hikers are encouraged to be particularly careful in their activities above treeline, as the plants that grow there already have to cope with the severity of the environment. For information about these trees and plants, consult *Trees and Shrubs of Northern New England*, published by the SPNHF, and the *Field Guide to Mountain Flowers of New England* and *At Timberline*, both published by the AMC.

MAPS

Detailed maps are available from the USGS for most of the United States, including all of New Hampshire and Maine. These are published in rectangles of several standard sizes called quadrangles ("quads"). Most areas in the regions covered in this guide are now covered by the recent, more detailed 7.5-minute quads—some in metric format—which have largely replaced the old 15-minute quads. Although topography on the newer maps is excellent, some recent maps are very inaccurate in showing the locations of some trails. These maps can be obtained at a number of local outlets and from USGS Map Sales, Federal Center, Box 25286, Denver CO 80225. Index maps showing the available USGS quads in any state (specify states) and an informative pamphlet entitled "Topographic Maps" are available free on request from the USGS.

Extra copies of AMC maps may be purchased at the AMC's Boston and Pinkham Notch offices and at some book and outdoor equipment stores. Other maps of specific areas of the White Mtns. are mentioned in the relevant individual sections of this guide.

CAMPING

Those who camp overnight in the backcountry tend to have more of an impact on the land than day hikers. In the past, some popular sites suffered misuse and began to resemble disaster areas, as campers left piles of trash and devastated the surrounding trees by stripping them for firewood. For this reason, backpackers should take great care to minimize their effect on the mountains by practicing low-impact camping and making conscious efforts to preserve the natural forest. One alternative is to camp in well-prepared, designated sites; the popular ones are supervised by caretakers. The other alternative has come to be called clean camping: to disperse camping over a wide area, out of sight of trails and roads, and to camp with full respect for wilderness values. Repeated camping on one site compacts the soil and makes it difficult for vegetation to survive. The objective of clean camping is to leave no trace of one's presence, so that the site will not be reused before it has a chance to recover.

There are more than fifty backcountry shelters and tent sites in the White Mtn. area, open on a first-come, first-served basis. Some sites have summer caretakers who collect an overnight fee to help defray maintenance expenses. Most sites have shelters, a few have only tent platforms, and some have both. Shelters are intended as overnight accommodations for persons carrying their own bedding and cooking supplies. The more popular shelters are often full, so be prepared to camp off the trail in your own tent or tarp at a legal site. Make yourself aware of regulations and restrictions prior to your trip. Unless you plan carefully, it is quite possible to find yourself far from any legal, practical campsite with night swiftly approaching.

If you camp away from established sites, look for a spot more than 200 ft. from the trail and from any surface water, and observe local Restricted Use Area (RUA) rules. Bring all needed shelter, including whatever poles, stakes, ground insulation, and cord you need. Try to choose a clear, level site for pitching your tent. Use a compass, and check landmarks carefully to find your way to and from your campsite. Do not cut boughs or branches for bedding. Avoid clearing vegetation and never make a ditch around the tent. Wash your dishes and yourself well away from streams, ponds, and springs. Heed the rules of neatness, sanitation, and fire prevention, and carry out everything—food, paper, glass, cans, etc.—that you carry in (and whatever trash less-thoughtful campers may have left). Food should not be kept in your tent; if possible, hang it from a tree—well down from a high, sturdy branch and well away from the tree trunk—to protect it from raccoons and bears.

In some camping areas, a human browse line where people have gathered firewood over the years is quite evident: Limbs are gone from trees, the ground is devoid of deadwood, and vegetation has been trampled as people scoured the area for the smallest burnable twig. The use of portable backpacking stoves is mandatory in popular areas, and is encouraged elsewhere to prevent damage to vegetation. Operate stoves with great caution—fuels can be explosive. Wood campfires should not be made unless there is ample dead and down wood available near your site; never cut green trees. Make such fires in safe, sheltered places and not in leaves or rotten wood, or against logs, trees, or stumps. Before you build a fire, clear a space at least 5 ft. in radius of all flammable material down to the mineral soil. Do not leave a fire unattended in any circumstances. Completely extinguish all fires with earth or water before you leave a campsite, even temporarily. Restore the campfire site to as natural an appearance as possible before leaving the campsite.

Roadside Campgrounds

The WMNF operates a number of roadside campgrounds with limited facilities; fees are charged. Consult the

WMNF offices for details. Many of these campgrounds are full on summer weekends. Reservations for sites at some WMNF campgrounds can be made through MIST-IX (800-283-CAMP). Several NH state parks also have campgrounds located conveniently for hikers in the White Mtns. and other parts of the state. No reservations can be made at state campgrounds. For details on state parks and campgrounds, contact the Office of Vacation Travel, Box 856, Concord NH 03301 (603-271-2665). Brochures on state parks and state and private campgrounds are usually available at NH highway rest areas throughout the normal camping season.

Camping Regulations

Trailside camping is really practical only within the WMNF, with a few limited exceptions, such as the established campsites on the Appalachian Trail. The laws of the states of Maine and New Hampshire require that permission be obtained from the owner to camp on private land, and that permits be obtained to build campfires anywhere outside the WMNF, except at officially designated campsites. Camping and campfires are not permitted in NH state parks except in campgrounds.

Overnight camping is permitted in almost all of the WMNF. To limit or prevent some of the adverse impacts of concentrated, uncontrolled camping, the US Forest Service (USFS) has adopted regulations for a number of areas in the WMNF that are threatened by overuse and misuse. The objective of the RUA program is not to hinder backpackers and campers, but to disperse their use of the land so that people can enjoy themselves in a clean and attractive environment without causing deterioration of natural resources. By protecting the plants, water, soil, and wildlife of the White Mtns., these restrictions should help to provide a higher quality experience for all visitors. Because hikers and backpackers have cooperated with RUA rules, many areas once designated as RUAs have recovered and are no longer under formal restrictions. However, common sense and self-imposed restrictions are still necessary to prevent damage.

Stated briefly, the 1991 RUA rules prohibit camping and wood or charcoal fires above timberline (where trees are less than 8 ft. in height), or within a specified distance of certain roads, trails, streams, and other locations, except at designated sites. Some of these restrictions are in force throughout the year and others only from May 1 to November 1. Stoves are permitted, even for day use. This guide provides information on RUAs as of 1991 in each relevant section, but since the list of restricted areas changes from year to year, hikers should contact the USFS in Laconia NH (603-524-6450) or any Ranger District office for up-to-date information.

WINTER CLIMBING

Snowshoeing and cross-country skiing on White Mtn. trails and peaks have steadily become more popular in the last decade. Increasing numbers of hikers have discovered the beauty of the woods in winter, and advances in clothing and equipment have made it possible for experienced winter travelers to enjoy great comfort and safety. The greatest danger is that winter climbing begins to look too easy and too safe, while snow, ice, and weather conditions are constantly changing, and a relatively trivial error of judgment may have grave, even fatal, consequences. Conditions can vary greatly from day to day, and from trail to trail, so much more experience is required to foresee and avoid dangerous situations in winter than in summer. Trails are frequently difficult or impossible to follow, and navigation skills are hard to learn in adverse weather conditions (as anyone who has tried to read a map in a blizzard can attest). Breaking trail on snowshoes can be strenuous and exhausting work. Some trails go through areas that may pose a severe avalanche hazard. In a whiteout above tree-line, it may be almost impossible to tell the ground from the sky, and hikers frequently become disoriented.

Winter conditions on the lower trails in the White Mtns. may require only snowshoes or skis and some warm clothing. Even so, summer hiking boots are usually inadequate, flashlight batteries fail quickly (a headlamp with battery pack works better), and water in canteens freezes unless wrapped in a sock or sweater. The winter hiker needs good physical conditioning and must dress carefully in order to avoid overheating and excessive per-spiration, which soaks clothing and soon leads to chilling. Cotton clothes are useful only as long as they can be kept perfectly dry (an impossible task, thus the winter climbers' maxim, "cotton kills"); only wool and some of the newer synthetics retain their insulating values when wet. Fluid intake must increase, as dehydration can be a serious problem in the dry winter air.

Above timberline, conditions often require specialized equipment, and also skills and experience of a different magnitude. The conditions on the Presidential Range in winter are as severe as any in North America, south of the mountains of Alaska and the Yukon Territory. On the summit of Mt. Washington in winter, winds average 44 mph, and daily high temperatures average 15° F. There are few calm days, and even on an average day conditions will probably be too severe for any but the most experi-enced and well-equipped climbers. The Mt. Washington Observatory routinely records wind velocities in excess of 100 mph, and temperatures are often far below zero. The combination of high wind and low temperature has such a cooling effect that the worst conditions on Mt. Washing-ton are approximately equal to the worst reported in Antarctica, despite the much greater cold in the latter region. Extremely severe storms can develop suddenly and unexpectedly. But the most dangerous aspect of winter in the White Mtns. is the extreme variability of the weather: It is not unusual for a cold, penetrating, wind-driven rain to be followed within a few hours by a cold front that brings below-zero temperatures and high winds.

No book can begin to impart all the knowledge necessary to cope safely with the potential for such brutal conditions, but helpful information can be found in *Winterwise: A Backpacker's Guide*, by John M. Dunn (1988, Adirondack Mountain Club), which despite its title is also quite useful for those primarily interested in winter dayhiking, and in the *AMC Guide to Winter Camping*, by Stephen Gorman (1991, Appalachian Mountain Club). Hikers who are interested in extending their activities into the winter season are strongly advised to seek out organized parties with leaders who have extensive winter experience. Each year the AMC and the Adirondack Mountain Club operate a week-long winter school that exposes participants to techniques and equipment for safe winter travel. The AMC and several of its chapters also sponsor numerous workshops on evenings and weekends, in addition to introductory winter hikes and regular winter schedules through which participants can gain experience. Information on such activities can be obtained from the AMC information center at the Boston headquarters at 5 Joy Street.

WHITE MOUNTAIN NATIONAL FOREST

Most of the higher White Mtns. are within the White Mountain National Forest (WMNF), which was established under the Weeks Act and now comprises about 770,000 acres, of which about 47,000 acres are in Maine and the rest in New Hampshire. It is important to remember that this is not a national *park,* but a national *forest;* parks are established primarily for preservation and recreation, while national forests are managed for multiple uses. In the administration of national forests maintains the following objectives are considered: recreation development, timber production, watershed protection, and wildlife propagation. It is the policy of the USFS to manage logging operations so that trails, streams, camping places, and other spots of public interest are protected. Mtn. recreation has been identified as the most important resource in the WMNF. The boundaries of the WMNF are usually marked wherever they cross roads or trails, usually by red-painted corner posts and blazes. Hunting and fishing are permitted in the WMNF under the state laws; state licenses are required. Organized groups, including nonprofit organizations, must apply for an Outfitter-Guide Permit if they conduct trips on WMNF land for which they charge any kind of fee; contact any WMNF office for details. The WMNF administration offers much informational literature that is available free of charge at the Forest Supervisor's Office in Laconia, the Ranger District offices (list below), and other information centers.

The national Wilderness Preservation system, which included the Great Gulf, was established in 1964 with passage of the Wilderness Act. The Presidential Range–Dry River Wilderness, the Pemigewasset Wilderness, the Sandwich Range Wilderness, and the Caribou–Speckled Mountain a total of about 115,000 acres of designated wilderness in the WMNF—about 15 percent of its area. Regulations for these areas prohibit logging and road building, as well any use of mechanized equipment or vehicles, including bicycles. It should be noted that wilderness areas are established by an act of Congress, and not simply by USFS administrative action, though the recommendations of the USFS are a critical part of the process of selecting areas for Congressional designation. Management of these areas in accordance with guidelines contained in the Wilderness Act is entrusted to the USFS. Most important is the protection of the natural environment, and among other qualities that the USFS is charged with preserving is the opportunity for visitors to enjoy solitude and challenge within this natural environment. As a consequence, for example, "structures for user convenience" such as shelters are not permitted in designated Wilderness. In general, Wilderness visitors should look forward to a rougher, wilder, more primitive experience than in other parts of the WMNF, and should expect USFS regulations to emphasize the preservation of Wilderness qualities even when substantial inconvenience to hikers results. Those who are mainly looking for a pleasant hiking experience in scenic surroundings should look elsewhere—there are many wild, beautiful places outside of designated Wilderness. It is one of the ironies of Wilderness protection that such designation often draws crowds of people who believe they can enjoy a true Wilderness experience simply by visiting a piece of land with this official certification, and as a result the wildness that caused the area to be designated as Wilderness is severely compromised.

The USFS has also established nine Scenic Areas in the WMNF to preserve lands of outstanding or unique natural beauty: Gibbs Brook, Nancy Brook, Greeley Ponds, Pinkham Notch, Lafayette Brook, Rocky Gorge, Lincoln Woods, Sawyer Pond, and Snyder Brook. Furthermore, camping is restricted in many areas under the Restricted Use Area (RUA) program to protect vulnerable areas from damage. To preserve the rare alpine plants of the Mt. Washington Range and other significant and uncommon ecosystems within the entire WMNF, rules prohibit the removal of any tree, shrub, or plant without written permission. Cultural sites and artifacts on public lands are also protected by federal law. If you discover such remains, please leave them undisturbed.

WMNF Offices and Ranger Districts (R. D.s)

The Androscoggin and Saco Ranger District offices have sometimes been open seven days a week in the summer, occasionally with evening hours. Otherwise, the offices are open during normal business hours.

Forest Supervisor, PO Box 638, Laconia NH 03247. (On North Main St., across railroad tracks from downtown section). Tel. 603-528-8721; TDD (for hearing impaired) 603-528-8722.

Ammonoosuc R. D., Trudeau Rd., Bethlehem NH 03574. (Just north of US 3 opposite Gale River Rd.). Tel. 603-869-2626.

Androscoggin R. D., 80 Glen Rd., Gorham NH 03581. (At south end of town along NH 16). Tel. 603-466-2713.

Evans Notch R. D., RD 2, Box 2270, Bethel ME 04217. (On US 2 easet of Bethel village). Tel. 207-834-2134.

Pemigewasset R. D., RFD 3, Box 15, Rte. 175, Plymouth NH 03264. (From I-93 Exit 25, turn left uphill, bear left at fork at top of hill onto NH 175 [north], then on left in 1 mi.). Tel. 603-536-1310.

Saco R. D., RFD 1, Box 94, Conway NH 03818 (On Kancamagus Highway just west of NH 16). Tel. 603-447-5448; TDD 603-447-1989.

THE APPALACHIAN TRAIL (AT)

This footpath runs over 2000 mi. from Springer Mtn. in Georgia to Katahdin in Maine, and traverses the White Mtns. for about 170 mi. in a southwest to northeast direction, from Hanover NH to Grafton Notch in ME. Its route traverses many of the major peaks and ranges of the White Mtns., following many historic and scenic trails. Except for a few short segments between Hanover and Glencliff, the trails that make up the AT in the White

Mtns. are all described in this book. In each section of this Guide through which the AT passes, its route through the section is described in a separate paragraph near the beginning. Information on the Appalachian Trail and the several guidebooks that cover its entire length can be obtained from the Appalachian Trail Conference, PO Box 236, Harpers Ferry WV 25425.

With the passage of the National Trails System Act by Congress on October 2, 1968, the AT became the first federally protected footpath in this country and was officially designated the Appalachian National Scenic Trail. Under this act the Appalachian Trail is administered primarily as a footpath by the Secretary of Interior in consultation with the Secretary of Agriculture and representatives of the states through which it passes. In addition, an Advisory Council for the Appalachian National Scenic Trail was appointed by the Secretary of the Interior. It includes representatives of each of the states and the several hiking clubs recommended by the Appalachian Trail Conference.

SOCIETY FOR THE PROTECTION OF NEW HAMPSHIRE FORESTS

This organization has worked since 1901 to protect the mountains, forests, wetlands, and farmlands of New Hampshire, and to encourage wise forestry practices. It owns Lost River in Kinsman Notch, a substantial reservation on Monadnock, and a number of other lands. In cooperation with the AMC, it protects and maintains the Monadnock–Sunapee Greenway. Its headquarters building in Concord NH was designed as a showcase of the latest techniques in energy conservation. For membership information, contact the SPNHF, 54 Portsmouth St., Concord NH 03301 (603-224-9945).

ABBREVIATIONS

The following abbreviations are used in trail descriptions.

hr.	hour(s)
min.	minutes(s)
mph	miles per hour
in.	inch(es)
ft.	foot, feet
km.	kilometer(s)
yd.	yard(s)
est.	estimated
AMC	Appalachian Mountain Club
AT	Appalachian Trail
CMC	Chocorua Mountain Club
CTA	Chatham Trails Association
CU	Camp Union
DOC	Dartmouth Outing Club
HA	Hutmen's Association
JCC	Jackson Conservation Commission
MMVSP	Mt. Madison Volunteer Ski Patrol
NHDP	New Hampshire Division of Parks
PEAOC	Phillips Exeter Academy Outing Club
RMC	Randolph Mountain Club
SLA	Squam Lakes Association
SPNHF	Society for the Protection of New Hampshire Forests
SSOC	Sub Sig Outing Club
USFS	United States Forest Service
USGS	United States Geological Survey
WMNF	White Mountain National Forest
WODC	Wonalancet Outdoor Club
WVAIA	Waterville Valley Athletic and Improvement Association

The Nancy Pond Trail is currently maintained by Camp Pasquaney, and Camp Mowglis maintains several trails in the Cardigan area.

NEW ENGLAND TRAIL CONFERENCE

The New England Trail Conference was organized in 1917 to develop the hiking possibilities of New England and to coordinate the work of local organizations. The conference serves as a clearinghouse for information about trail maintenance and use both for organized groups and for individuals. The annual meeting of this organization is held in the spring, when representatives of mountaineering and outing clubs from all over New England meet for a full program of reports, talks, and illustrated lectures on mountain climbing, hiking, trails, and shelters. All sessions are open to the public. For information, contact the secretary, Forrest House, 33 Knollwood Drive, East Longmeadow MA 01028.

WHITE MOUNTAIN GUIDEBOOK COMMITTEE

Editor
Eugene S. Daniell III

Associate Editor
Jon Burroughs

Chairman, AMC Communications Committee
Dave Van Note

SECTION 1
Mt. Washington
and the Southern Ridges

This section includes the summit of Mt. Washington and
the major ridges that run south from it, which constitute
the southern portion of the Presidential Range. It is bounded on the north by the Mt. Washington Cog Railway and
the Mt. Washington Auto Rd., on the east by NH 16, on
the south by US 302, and on the west by US 302 and the
Base Road. The northern portion of the Presidential
Range, including Mts. Clay, Jefferson, Adams, and Madison, and the Great Gulf, is covered in Section 2 of this
book. Many of the trails described in Section 2 also provide routes to Mt. Washington. The AMC Mt. Washington Range map (map 6) covers this entire section.

Three major ridges run southwest or south from Mt.
Washington, separated by deep river valleys from each
other and from the ranges to the west and east. The most
impressive ridge is formed by the Southern Peaks, running
southwest from Mt. Washington and ending abruptly at
the cliffs of Mt. Webster that overlook Crawford Notch,
including (from northeast to southwest) Mts. Monroe,
Franklin, Eisenhower, Pierce (also known as Clinton),
Jackson, and Webster. On the northwest, the headwaters
of the Ammonoosuc River (a Connecticut River tributary)
flow across the Fabyan Plain, which separates the Southern Peaks from the much lower Cherry--Dartmouth Range.
The Dry River begins in Oakes Gulf high on Mt. Washington, and runs to the Saco River below Crawford Notch
through a deep valley between the Southern Peaks and the
Montalban Ridge. The Montalban Ridge is the longest of
all Mt. Washington's subsidiary ridges, extending about

15 mi. from the summit; it first runs south over Boott Spur, Mt. Isolation, Mt. Davis, Stairs Mtn., Mt. Resolution, and Mt. Parker, then swings east to Mts. Langdon, Pickering, and Stanton, the low peaks above the intervales of Bartlett and Glen near the confluence of the Rocky Branch and Saco River. The Bemis Ridge is a significant spur running from Mt. Resolution southwest over Mt. Crawford, then south to Hart Ledge, which overlooks the great bend in the Saco. East of the Montalbans lies the Rocky Branch of the Saco River, and to the east of that stream rises the Rocky Branch Ridge, a long, wide-spreading assortment of humps and flat ridges running south from Boott Spur via Slide Peak, with no noteworthy summit except Iron Mtn. at the far south end. Still farther east the Ellis River flows down from Pinkham Notch, with NH 16 running through the valley and the ridges of Wild-cat Mtn. on the opposite side.

In this section the Appalachian Trail follows the entire Webster Cliff Trail from Crawford Notch to its intersection with the Crawford Path near the summit of Mt. Pierce, then follows the Crawford Path to the summit of Mt. Washington. On the way it also crosses the summits of Mts. Webster, Jackson, and Pierce, and passes near Mts. Eisenhower, Franklin, and Monroe. From Mt. Washington, it descends to the Gulfside Trail (see Section 2) via the Trinity Heights Connector. Then, after passing over the ridge of the Northern Peaks (although missing most of the summits) and through the Great Gulf—areas covered in Section 2—it returns to Section 1 at the Mt. Washington Auto Road and follows the Old Jackson Road to Pinkham Notch Visitor Center and NH 16.

MOUNTAIN SAFETY

Caution: Mt. Washington has a well-earned reputation as the most dangerous small mountain in the world. Storms increase in violence with great rapidity toward the summit. The highest wind velocity ever recorded at any surface weather station (231 mph on April 12, 1934) was attained on Mt. Washington. Judged by the windchill temperatures, the worst conditions on Mt. Washington are approximately equal to the worst reported from Antarctica, although actual temperatures on Mt. Washington are not as low. If you begin to experience difficulty due to the weather, remember that the worst is yet to come, and turn back, without shame, before it is too late. (This warning applies as well to all peaks above timberline, particularly the Northern Peaks.) Each hiker should carry, as a bare minimum, a good rain suit with a hood (or equivalent outfit) that will also protect from wind, an extra sweater, a wool hat, and mittens.

Ascents of the mountain in winter are sometimes easy enough to lull inexperienced hikers into false confidence, but the worst conditions are inconceivably brutal and can materialize with little warning. Safe ascent of the mountain in winter requires much warm clothing, some special equipment, and experienced leadership. From Columbus Day to Memorial Day, no building is open to provide shelter or refuge to hikers.

Inexperienced hikers sometimes misjudge the difficulty of climbing Mt. Washington by placing too much emphasis on the relatively short distance from the trailheads to the summit. To a person used to walking around the neighborhood, the trail distance of 4 mi. or so sounds rather tame. But the most important factor in the difficulty of the trip is the altitude gain of about 4000 ft. from base to summit. To a person unused to mountain trails, and in less than excellent physical condition, this unrelenting uphill grind can be grueling and intensely discouraging. If you are not an experienced hiker or a trained athlete, you will almost certainly enjoy the ascent of Mt. Washington a great deal more if you build up to it with easier climbs.

Carry a compass and take care to stay on the trails, and in bad weather favor the main trails with their large, yellow-topped cairns over the less-used connecting trails that are often far less clearly marked. If you become lost above treeline in a dense fog or a white out, there is no completely satisfactory course of action in this situation, since the objective is to get below treeline, with or without a trail. The weather exposure is generally worse to the west whereas cliffs are more prevalent in the ravines to the east. If you know where the nearest major trail should be, then it is probably best to try to find it. If you have adequate clothing, it may be best to find a scrub patch and shelter yourself in it. In the absence of alternatives, take note that the cog railway on one slope and the Mt. Washington Auto Road on another make a crooked line from west to east. Remember which side of the mountain you are on, and walk clockwise or counter-clockwise to the closer of the two, skirting the heads of ravines; sooner or later you will strike the road or the railroad, landmarks that are difficult to miss in even the darkest night or the thickest fog, unless they are concealed by snowdrifts. Given a choice, aim for the auto road, as the railroad is on the side of the mountain that faces the prevailing winds.

Whether, as is often stated, Mt. Washington has the worst weather in the world, or at least in North Amierca, is subject ot debate. But the dozens of people who have died on its slopes in the last century furnish adequate proof that the weather is vicious enough to kill those who are foolish enough to challenge the mountain at its worst. This needless loss of life has been due, almost without exception, to the failure of robust but incautious hikers to realize that winterlike storms of incredible violence occur frequently, even during the summer months. Winds of hurricane force exhaust even the strongest hiker, and cold rain driven horizontally by the wind penetrates clothing and drains heat from the body. Temperatures in the 30s and low 40s can be even more dangerous than those below freezing, since rain penetrates and soaks clothing much more rapidly than snow, although at colder temperatures sleet and freezing rain on rocks can further obstruct a attempt to return to safety.

As the victim's body temperature falls, brain function quickly deteriorates; this is one of the first, and most insidious, effects of excessive heat loss (hypothermia). Eventually the victim loses coordination, staggers, and then falls, numb and dazed, never to rise again. At this point, even immediate access to the best medical treatment obtainable will not assure the victim's survival. Prevention is the only sure cure. Those who misjudge conditions and their own endurance almost always get away with their mistakes, and thus many are lulled into overconfidence. The mountain spares most fools, but now and then it claims one or two without mercy.

All water sources in this heavily used area should be suspected of being unfit to drink; the safest course is to avoid drinking from trailside sources. Water is available at the Sherman Adams summit building during the months that it is open, roughly from Memorial Day to Columbus Day.

SUMMIT BUILDINGS

No hotel or overnight lodging for the public is available on the summit of Mt. Washington. From Columbus Day to Memorial Day no buildings are open to hikers for shelter or refuge. The new summit building, named in honor of former Governor Sherman Adams and operated by the NH Division of Parks and Recreation during the summer season (mid-May to mid-October), has food service, a pack room, a souvenir shop, public rest rooms, telephone, and a post office. It houses the Mt. Washington Observatory, the Mt. Washington Museum, and facilities for park personnel.

The first Summit House on Mt. Washington was built in 1852. The oldest building still standing on the summit is the Tip Top House, a hotel first built in 1853 and rebuilt after it suffered a fire in 1915. It is now owned by the State of New Hampshire and is part of the Mt. Washington State Park. Plans call for restoring this stone building at a future date, but its eventual use has not yet been decided, and at present it is closed to all but park use. The second Summit House, 1873–1908, was destroyed by fire.

There are several other buildings on the summit of Mt. Washington, all closed to the general public. The Yankee Building, built in 1941 to house transmitter facilities for the first FM station in northern New England, is now leased by WMTW-TV and houses two-way radio equipment for various state, federal, and local organizations. The transmitter building and powerhouse for WMTW-TV and WHOM-FM, built in 1954 and designed to withstand winds of 300 mph, provides living quarters for station personnel and houses television and microwave equipment. The Stage Office, built in 1975 to replace a similar building constructed in 1908, is owned by the Mt. Washington Auto Road Company.

MT. WASHINGTON OBSERVATORY

There has been a year-round weather observatory on Mt. Washington from 1870 to 1886, and from 1932 to the present. The present observatory is operated by a non-profit corporation, and individuals from the general public are invited to become members and contribute to the support of its important work. For details contact the Mt. Washington Observatory, Membership Secretary, 1 Washington St., Gorham NH 03581.

THE MT. WASHINGTON AUTO ROAD

This road from the Glen House site on NH 16 to the summit, often called the Carriage Rd., was constructed in 1855-61. Automobiles are charged a toll at the foot of the mountain. With long zigzags and an easy grade, the Auto Rd. climbs the prominent northeast ridge named for Benjamin Chandler, who died of hypothermia on the upper part in 1856. Hiking on the road is not forbidden, but despite easier grades and smoother footing than hiking trails, the distance is long and the competition with automobile traffic is annoying and potentially dangerous. In winter, ruts from official snow vehicle traffic and severe icing and drifting make it a less pleasant and more difficult route than might be anticipated. The emergency shelters that were formerly located along the upper part of the road have been removed.

Because of the continual theft and destruction of trail signs, these are often placed on the trails at some distance from the Auto Rd. The names of some trails are painted on rocks at the point where they leave the road.

The Auto Rd. leaves NH 16 opposite the Glen House site (1600 ft.), crosses the Peabody River, and starts the long climb. Just above the 2-mi. mark, after sharp curves right and then left, the Appalachian Trail crosses; to the south, it follows the Old Jackson Road (now a foot trail) past junctions with the Nelson Crag Trail and the Raymond Path to Pinkham Notch Visitor Center; to the north it follows the Madison Gulf Trail toward the Great Gulf and the Northern Peaks. Lowe's Bald Spot, a fine viewpoint about 0.3 mi. from the road, is reached by an easy hike on the Madison Gulf Trail and a side path.

The Auto Rd. continues to treeline, passing to the left of the site of the Halfway House (3840 ft.), and soon swings around the Horn, skirting a prominent shoulder, known as the Ledge, where there is a fine view to the north. A short distance above there, the Chandler Brook

Trail descends into the Great Gulf on the right, and soon the route used by snow vehicles in winter diverges right.

Just above the 5-mi. mark, on the right exactly at the sharp turn, there are some remarkable folded strata in the rocks beside the road. Here, near Cragway Spring, the lower section of the Nelson Crag Trail enters on the left; the upper section leaves on the same side a few yards above. At about 5.5 mi., the road passes through the patch of high scrub in which Dr. B. L. Ball survived two nights in a winter storm in October 1855. A short distance above the 6-mi. mark, where the winter route rejoins, the Wamsutta Trail descends on the right to the Great Gulf, and the Alpine Garden Trail diverges left. The trenchlike structures near the road are the remains of the old Glen House Bridle Path, built in 1853. The road soon makes a hairpin turn and circles the left edge of a lawn known as the Cow Pasture, where the Huntington Ravine Trail enters on the left and the remains of an old corral are visible on the right a little farther along. Beyond the 7-mi. post, the Cog Railway approaches and runs above the road on the right; near the tracks, just below the summit, the Bourne monument stands at the spot where Lizzie Bourne perished in September 1855 at the age of 23, the second recorded death on the mountain. The Tuckerman Ravine Trail enters on the left just below the parking-lot complex, and the summit buildings are reached by a wooden stairway at about 8 mi.

THE MT. WASHINGTON COG RAILWAY

The Mt. Washington Cog Railway, an unusual artifact of nineteenth-century engineering with a fascinating history, was completed in 1869. Its maximum grade, 13.5 in. to the yard, is equaled by only one other railroad (excluding funicular roads), that on Pilatus in the Alps. The location of the Base Station is called Marshfield, in honor of

Sylvester Marsh, an inventor of meat-packing machinery who was the chief promoter and builder of the railway, and Darby Field, leader of the first recorded ascent of Mt. Washington in 1642. When the cog railway is in operation, walking on the track is not permitted; at other times it is a poor walking route. A new public parking area is located on the Base Rd. about 0.5 mi. west of Marshfield. Hikers who wish to visit or park at the base station itself should expect to pay an admission fee.

The cog railway ascends a minor westerly ridge in a nearly straight line to the treeline, which is reached near the trestle called Jacob's Ladder (4800 ft.). This trestle, standing as much as 30 ft. above the mountainside, is the steepest part of the railroad. After crossing the shoulder toward Mt. Clay, the line curves right and runs close to the edge of the Great Gulf; there is a fine view across the Gulf toward the Northern Peaks from the vicinity of the Gulf Tank (5600 ft.). It is 3 mi. from Marshfield to the summit, and trains ascend in about 1 hr. 10 min.

SKIING IN THE MT. WASHINGTON AREA

A number of cross-country ski trails have been constructed near Pinkham Notch Visitor Center, which has become a center for the sport. In addition, a number of the summer trails are suitable for ski-touring. Information on these trails can be obtained at the camp's Trading Post.

The slopes of Tuckerman Ravine and the snowfields on and near the summit cone are famous for the opportunities they offer for alpine skiing. The skiing season on the Tuckerman headwall starts around the beginning of March and may last into June in some seasons. The ravine area and the John Sherburne Ski Trail are patrolled by the USFS and the Mt. Washington Volunteer Ski Patrol. Warning notices about sections that are unsafe because of ice or possible avalanche danger are posted in the shelter area. Skiing areas in the ravine, and also those in the Gulf of Slides or on any part of the mountain above timberline, are subject to wide temperature variations within short periods of time. The difference between corn snow and ice, or between bathing suits and parkas, may be an hour, or even less, when clouds roll in or the afternoon sun drops behind a shoulder of the mountain, so skiers should prepare accordingly. There is a sun deck at Hermit Lake, but no longer a warming room open to the public.

The Tuckerman Ravine Trail affords an easy ascent route on foot since it is normally well packed, but skiing downhill on it is prohibited because of the hazard to hikers. Skiers should descend from Tuckerman Ravine on the John Sherburne Ski Trail (WMNF). This trail—named for John H. Sherburne, Jr., whose efforts contributed greatly to its establishment—leaves the south end of the parking lot at Pinkham Notch Visitor Center at the same point as the Gulf of Slides Ski Trail. It ascends by a zigzag course always to the left (south) of the Tuckerman Ravine Trail and the Cutler River to the foot of the Little Headwall of the ravine, above the shelter area, where it ends. It is 10 to 50 ft. wide, and although the slope is suitable for expert and intermediate skiers at some points, less expert skiers can negotiate this trail.

The Gulf of Slides, which is situated somewhat similarly to Tuckerman Ravine, receives a large volume of snow that remains in the ravine, so open-slope skiing is possible well into the spring (April and May). Its slopes, though less severe than those in Tuckerman, are more uniform and subject to frequent avalanches. The Gulf of Slides Ski Trail leaves the south end of the parking lot at Pinkham Notch Visitor Center at the same point as the John Sherburne Ski Trail, and ascends west 2200 ft. in about 2.5 mi. to the bowl of the Gulf of Slides.

The Old Jackson Road is a good run for skiers of all abilities. It drops 650 ft. and can be run in 30 min. The ascent takes 1 hr. Skiers should use the old trail instead of the relocation; enter the Old Jackson Road below the 2-mi. mark, about 0.2 mi. below where the relocation and the Madison Gulf Trail meet at the Auto Rd. There are other trails in the region north of Pinkham Notch Visitor Center specifically designed for skiing.

The Mt. Washington Auto Rd. is not usually suitable for skiing due to windblown bare and icy spots and ruts from snow vehicle traffic. The areas between the top of the Tuckerman headwall and the summit cone, and on Chandler Ridge near the 6-mi. mark on the Auto Rd., afford good spring skiing at all levels of skill, but are hard to reach because of their elevation and more exposed to bad weather.

GEOGRAPHY

Mt. Washington (6288 ft.), the highest peak east of the Mississippi River and north of the Carolinas, was seen from the ocean as early as 1605. Its first recorded ascent was in June 1642 by Darby Field of Exeter NH and one or two Algonkian natives, who may have reached the summit by way of the Southern Peaks, though no conclusive case can be made for any of the several reasonably practical routes, since only two rather meager, second-hand accounts of this expedition have survived. The mountain has a long and varied history of activity, having been the site of hotels, a road and a railway, a weather observatory, a daily newspaper, a radio station and a television station, and an assortment of auto, foot, and ski races. *The Story of Mt. Washington,* by F. Allen Burt, treats the fascinating (and frequently unusual) human history of the mountain in great detail, while Peter Randall's *Mount Washington* is a shorter and less detailed handbook of human and natural history.

Mt. Washington is a broad, massive mountain with great ravines cut deep into its steep sides, leaving buttress ridges that reach up through the timberline and support the great upper plateau. The timberline occurs at an elevation of 4500 to 5000 ft., depending on the degree of exposure to the mountain's fierce weather. The upper plateau, which varies in elevation from 5000 to 5500 ft., bears comparatively gentle slopes interspersed with lawns— wide, grassy areas strewn with rocks. The summit cone, covered with fragments of rock and almost devoid of vegetation, rises steeply above this plateau. The upper part of the mountain has a climate similar to that of northern Labrador, and its areas of alpine tundra support a fascinating variety of plant and animal life adapted to the extreme conditions of the alpine environment. Many of these species are found only on other high mountaintops or in the tundra many hundreds of miles farther north, and a few plants are found only or primarily on the Presidential Range. The alpine plants in particular have attracted many professional and amateur scientists (including Henry David Thoreau), and many of the features of the mountain are named for early botanists, such as Manasseh Cutler, Jacob Bigelow, Francis Boott, William Oakes, and Edward Tuckerman. Hikers should take great care not to damage the plant life in these areas, as their struggle for survival is already severe. Avoid unnecessary excursions away from the trails, and step on rocks rather than vegetation wherever possible. The AMC publishes the *AMC Field Guide to Mtn. Flowers of New England*, an illustrated guide to all plants that normally grow above or near treeline, and *At Timberline*, a handbook that covers geology and animal life as well as plants. The NH Department of Resources and Economic Development (PO Box 856, Concord NH 03301) publishes booklets on geology intended for the general public; the Presidential Range area is covered by *The Geology of the Mt. Washington Quadrangle* and *The Geology of the Crawford Notch Quadrangle.*

The slopes of Mt. Washington are drained by tributaries of three major rivers: the Androscoggin, the Connecticut, and the Saco. The high, massive Northern Peaks (see Section 2) continue the rocky alpine terrain of Mt. Washington to the north and northeast in an arc that encloses the Great Gulf, the largest glacial cirque in the White Mtns. (A glacial cirque is a landform that results when a glacier excavates a typical V-shaped brook valley with a narrow floor and fairly uniform slopes, turning it into the classic U-shaped cirque with its broad, fairly flat floor and almost vertical walls.

Moving clockwise from the Great Gulf around the east side of the mountain, Chandler Ridge (by which the Mt. Washington Auto Rd. ascends the upper part of the mountain) passes over the small peak of Nelson Crag before merging into the summit cone; this ridge divides the Great Gulf from the great ravines of the east face: Huntington Ravine, the Ravine of Raymond Cataract, and Tuckerman Ravine, which is one of the finest examples of the glacial cirque. Chandler Ridge also forms the north boundary of the lawn that lies at the foot of the summit cone just above the three eastern ravines, which is called the Alpine Garden for its colorful displays of alpine flowers in late June.

The steep eastern slopes of the mountain bear several notable waterfalls. Raymond Cataract falls through a series of wild and beautiful cascades in the Ravine of Raymond Cataract, but brush has covered a former footway, so the cataract can only be reached by those intrepid explorers who are skilled in off-trail travel. Crystal Cascade is easily reached from Pinkham Notch Visitor Center by a walk of about 0.4 mi. on the Tuckerman Ravine Trail. Glen Ellis Falls, located deep in the Ellis River valley, can be easily reached from the parking area on NH 16, 0.8 mi. south of Pinkham Notch Visitor Center, by a gravel path with rock steps and handrails that passes under the highway through a tunnel and reaches the falls in 0.3 mi. The main fall is 70 ft. high, and below it are several pools and smaller falls.

Boott Spur, the great southeast shoulder of Mt. Washington, forms the south wall of Tuckerman Ravine and the north wall of the Gulf of Slides, and the flat ridge connecting it with the cone of Mt. Washington bears Bigelow Lawn, the largest of the Presidential Range lawns. Both the Montalban Ridge and the Rocky Branch Ridge descend from Boott Spur and quickly drop below treeline, continuing south in thick woods with occasional open summits. Oakes Gulf, at the headwaters of the Dry River, lies west of Boott Spur and east of Mt. Monroe. The Southern Peaks, running southwest from Mt. Washington, form the second most prominent ridge in the range (after the Northern Peaks), dropping to the treeline slowly and rising above it again several times before the final descent into the woods below Mt. Pierce. The Mt. Washington Cog Railway ascends the unnamed ridge between the less spectacular ravines of the western face, Ammonoosuc Ravine and Burt Ravine, which lie between the Southern Peaks and the Northern Peaks.

Day trips to the summit of Mt. Washington can be made by a great variety of routes, but the vast majority of climbers use only a very few trails. From the west, the mountain is most frequently ascended from the parking area (2500 ft.) on the Base Rd. near the Cog Railway base station by the Ammonoosuc Ravine Trail and the Crawford Path, or by the Jewell and Gulfside trails (see Section 2), or by a loop using both routes. The Ammonoosuc Ravine Trail has a long, very steep section but offers the shelter of Lakes of the Clouds Hut, just above treeline, if a storm arises. The Jewell Trail provides an easier ascent or descent, but reaches the Gulfside Trail high on the slope of Mt. Clay, a more dangerous place in bad weather. Both of these routes are used heavily. Because of the very high elevation (3000 ft.) of its trailhead on the Jefferson Notch Road, the Caps Ridge Trail is frequently used for a one-day hike to Mt. Washington, in combination with the Gulfside Trail and the Cornice (see Section 2). It offers fine scenery and the opportunity to also climb Mt. Jefferson with little extra effort, but this longer, rougher route to Mt. Washington is more exposed to bad weather and saves no exertion despite its higher start. The Boundary Line Trail (see Section 2) connects the Base Rd. parking area with the Jefferson Notch Rd,, and thus makes possible loop trips involving the Caps Ridge Trail and the Ammonoosuc Ravine or Jewell trails.

Most hikers ascend from the east. The Tuckerman Ravine Trail from Pinkham Notch Visitor Center (2000 ft.) is by far the most popular route, affording what is probably the easiest ascent of Mt. Washington, with moderate grades for most of its length and spectacular views of the ravine. In the spring and fall this trail is often closed by the WMNF because of dangerous snow or ice conditions; notice of its closure is posted at Pinkham Notch Visitor Center. In this case the Lion Head Trail is usually the best alternative route. The Lion Head Trail runs along the prominent Lion Head buttress north of Tuckerman Ravine; an older route of this trail, closed for summer hiking due to severe erosion, is the most popular and least dangerous route of ascent in winter. Routes other than the Tuckerman Ravine Trail are all somewhat longer, or steeper, or both, but have good views and are less crowded.

The Southern Presidentials form a great ridge that extends about 8 mi. southwest from the summit of Mt. Washington to the Webster Cliffs above Crawford

Notch. The Ammonoosuc River lies to the northwest, and the Dry River to the southeast. The summits on this ridge decrease in elevation from northeast to southwest.

Mt. Monroe (5384 ft.), the highest, is a sharply pointed pyramid that rises abruptly from the flat area around the Lakes of the Clouds, with a secondary summit, a small crag sometimes called Little Monroe (5207 ft.), on its west ridge. The summit, crossed by the Mount Monroe Loop, is completely above treeline, and affords fine views of the deep chasm of Oakes Gulf on the east, the beautiful Lakes of the Clouds, and the nearby summit of Mt. Washington. The flat region between Mt. Monroe and the Lakes of the Clouds supports a bountiful number of alpine plants, making it the most significant and most vulnerable habitat in the White Mtns. Part of this area is closed to all public entry due to damage caused in the past by hikers coming to admire these plants, which can withstand the full violence of above-treeline weather but not the tread of hikers' boots.

Mt. Franklin (5004 ft.) is a rather flat shoulder of Monroe that appears impressive only when seen from below, in the Franklin-Eisenhower Col. Its summit, whose exact location (and even existence) is not entirely obvious, lies a short distance east of the Crawford Path and commands an excellent view straight down into Oakes Gulf.

Mt. Eisenhower (4761 ft.), previously called Mt. Pleasant, was renamed after the former president's death. While there is a good deal of scrub on the lower slopes of this dome-shaped mountain, the top is completely bald. Its summit is crossed by the Mount Eisenhower Loop.

Mt. Pierce (4310 ft.) was named for Franklin Pierce, the only president born in New Hampshire, by act of the NH Legislature in 1913. Although this name appears on all USGS maps it was not universally accepted, and the mountain's former name, Mt. Clinton, persists in the Mt.

Clinton Rd. and the Mount Clinton Trail, which ascends the southeast slopes of the mountain. Mt. Pierce is wooded almost to the top of its flat summit on the west, but a broad open area on the east side affords fine views. Its summit lies on the Webster Cliff Trail just above its junction with the Crawford Path.

Mt. Jackson (4052 ft.), named for NH State Geologist Charles Jackson (not for President Andrew Jackson), has a square, ledgy summit with steep sides and a flat top, affording possibly the finest views overall among the Southern Peaks. Its summit is crossed by the Webster Cliff Trail and is also reached by the Jackson branch of the Webster–Jackson Trail.

Mt. Webster (3910 ft.), once called Notch Mtn., was renamed for Daniel Webster, the great orator, US Senator from New Hampshire, and Secretary of State. The summit is crossed by the Webster Cliff Trail, which is intersected by the Webster branch of the Webster–Jackson Trail not far from the top.

To the southeast of the Southern Peaks lies the Dry River, running down the central valley of the Presidential–Dry River Wilderness. This river has also been called the Mt. Washington River, but Dry River has won the battle, possibly because of the irony of the name. The Dry River runs from Oakes Gulf to the Saco through a deep, narrow, steep-walled ravine. Though in a dry season the flow is meager, with lots of rocks lying uncovered, its watershed has extremely rapid runoff and its sudden floods are legendary: They have killed hikers. No other logging railroad constructed in the White Mtns. had as many river crossings in so short a distance as the railroad that was built up this valley, and no other logging railroad ever had all its trestles swept away by floods so quickly after ceasing operation.

Access to the Dry River area has always been somewhat difficult, and ascents of the Southern Peaks from this side is relatively arduous, but since the Wilderness was established by law and the number of wilderness-seeking visitors increased sharply, the WMNF has made access somewhat easier by eliminating many river crossings through trail relocations and the construction of a bridge. However, it is still an area where visitors need to keep a careful watch on the weather and take account of any substantial rainfall.

The Montalban Ridge extends southward from Boott Spur, forming the longest subsidiary ridge in the Presidential Range, running for about 15 mi. between the Rocky Branch on the east and the Dry River and Saco River on the west. At Mt. Resolution the main ridge curves to the east along the Saco Valley, while the short Bemis Ridge carries the line of the upper ridge south to the great bend in the Saco. The peaks of the Montalban Ridge, in order from the north, include Mt. Isolation (4005 ft.), Mt. Davis (3840 ft.), Stairs Mtn. (3460 ft.), Mt. Resolution (3428 ft.), Mt. Parker (3015 ft.), Mt. Langdon (2423 ft.), Mt. Pickering (1942 ft.), and Mt. Stanton (1748 ft.). The peaks of the Bemis Ridge include Mt. Crawford (3129 ft.), Mt. Hope (2520 ft.), and Hart Ledge (2040 ft.). Cave Mtn. (1460 ft.), a low spur of the range near Bartlett village, is much better known for the cave on its south face than for its summit.

The views from the summits of Mts. Isolation, Davis, and Crawford are among the finest in the White Mtns., and Mts. Resolution and Parker also offer excellent outlooks. The Giant Stairs are a wild and picturesque feature of the region, offering a spectacular view from the top of the cliff that forms the upper stair. These two great step-like ledges at the south end of the ridge of Stairs Mtn. are regular in form and visible from many points. A third, similar cliff, sometimes called the Back Stair, lies east of the main summit but has no trail. Mt. Stanton and Mt. Pickering are wooded but have frequent open ledges that afford interesting views in various directions.

All of the peaks named above are reached by well-maintained trails, except Mt. Hope and Hart Ledge. Mt. Hope is heavily wooded and very seldom climbed. The fine cliff of Hart Ledge rises more than 1000 ft. above the meadows at the great bend in the Saco River just above Bartlett and affords commanding views to the east, west, and south. There is no regular trail, but intrepid bushwhackers may follow the road west along the north side of the river, passing under the cliffs, then climb up the slope well to the west of the cliffs.

East of the Montalban Ridge, across the Rocky Branch and west of the Ellis River, lies the Rocky Branch Ridge. This heavily wooded ridge runs south from Gulf Peak, and is sharply defined for about 3 mi., then flattens out. It has no important peaks. Iron Mtn. (2716 ft.), is a small mountain near Jackson with a fine north outlook and a magnificent open ledge at the top of its south cliff. It is the most prominent summit on the long ridge between the Rocky Branch and the Ellis River, which begins as the Rocky Branch Ridge but becomes broad and poorly defined long before it reaches Iron Mtn.

HUTS, SHELTERS, AND CAMPING

Note: No hotel or overnight lodging for the public is available on the summit of Mt. Washington. No camping is permitted above treeline in summer. In winter, camping is permitted where there is two feet or more of snow, but not on frozen bodies of water

HUTS

For current information on AMC huts, Pinkham Notch Visitor Center, or Crawford Notch Hostel, contact the Reservations, Pinkham Notch Visitor Center, Box 298, Gorham NH 03581 (603-466-2727).

Pinkham Notch Visitor Center (AMC)

Pinkham Notch Visitor Center is a unique mountain facility in the heart of the WMNF. This camp, originally built in 1920 and greatly enlarged since then, is located on NH 16 practically at the height-of-land in Pinkham Notch, about 20 mi. north of Conway and 11 mi. south of Gorham. It is also 0.8 mi. north of Glen Ellis Falls and 0.5 mi. south of the base of the Wildcat Mountain Ski Area. Pinkham Notch Visitor Center offers food and lodging to the public throughout the year and is managed similarly to the AMC huts. The Reservations number is 603-466-2727. Concord Trailways offers daily bus service to and from South Station in Boston, and the AMC operates a hiker shuttle bus during the summer.

The Joe Dodge Lodge, which accommodates more than one hundred guests in rooms with double beds or two, three, or four bunks, also offers a library that commands a spectacular view of the nearby Wildcat Ridge, and a living room where accounts of the day's activities can be shared next to an open fireplace. The center features a sixty-five–seat conference room equipped with audiovisual facilities.

The Trading Post, a popular meeting place for hikers, has been a center of AMC educational and recreational activities since 1920. Weekend workshops, seminars, and lectures are conducted throughout the year. The building houses a dining room, an information desk, and a mountain store where equipment and guidebooks are available. The pack-room downstairs is open 24 hours a day for hikers to stop in, relax, shower, and repack their gear.

Pinkham Notch Visitor Center is the most important trailhead on the east side of Mt. Washington, and free public parking is available, although sleeping in cars is not permitted. The Tuckerman Ravine Trail, the Lost Pond Trail, and the Old Jackson Road all start at the camp, giving access to many more trails, and a number of walking trails have been constructed for shorter trips in the Pinkham vicinity. Among these are the Crew-Cut Trail, George's Gorge Trail, Liebeskind's Loop, and the Square Ledge Trail. There are also several ski-touring trails; for information consult personnel at the Visitor Center Trading Post.

Crawford Notch Hostel (AMC)

Low-cost, self-service lodging for those willing to provide their own meals is available in historic Crawford Notch. Guests must supply food and sleeping bags; cooking facilities and equipment are provided. The hostel is an excellent choice for families and small groups, and is a convenient base for a wide range of hiking trips and other outdoor activities. The main hostel building, the recently renovated Shapleigh studio, has accommodations for twenty-four people in two bunkrooms, along with toilet facilities, showers, and a complete kitchen with stove, refrigerator, and sinks. It is heated in fall, winter, and spring. Two adjacent cabins, heated by wood stoves, accommodate eight persons each; cabin guests are welcome to use all hostel facilities. There is a caretaker in residence. The hostel is open to the public, and AMC members receive a discount. Overnight lodging is available year-round. Reservations are encouraged.

Lakes of the Clouds Hut (AMC)

The original stone hut, greatly enlarged since, was built in 1915. It is located on a shelf near the foot of Mt. Monroe about 50 yd. west of the larger lake at an elevation of about 5050 ft. It is reached by the Crawford Path or the Ammonoosuc Ravine Trail, and has accommodations for ninety guests. The hut is open to the public from June to mid-September, and closed at all other times. Space for backpackers is available at a lesser cost. A refuge room in the cellar is left open in the winter for emergency use only.

Mizpah Spring Hut (AMC)

The newest of the AMC huts was completed in 1965 and is located at about 3800 ft. elevation on the site formerly occupied by the Mizpah Spring Shelter, at the junction of the Webster Cliff Trail and the Mount Clinton Trail, near the Mizpah Cutoff. The hut accommodates sixty guests, with sleeping quarters in eight rooms containing from four to ten bunks. This hut is open to the public from mid-May to mid-October. There are tentsites nearby (caretaker, fee charged).

CAMPING

Presidential Range–Dry River Wilderness

In this area, camping and fires are prohibited above treeline (where trees are less than 8 ft. tall), and within 200 ft. of any trail except at designated sites. No campsite can be used by more than ten persons at any one time. Many shelters have been removed, and the remaining ones will be dismantled when major maintenance is required; do not count on using any of these shelters.

Restricted Use Areas

The WMNF has established a number of Restricted Use Areas (RUAs) where camping and wood or charcoal fires are prohibited, in some areas throughout the year and in others only from May 1 to November 1. The specific areas are under continual review, and areas are added to or subtracted from the list in order to provide the greatest amount of protection to areas subject to damage by excessive camping, while imposing the lowest level of restrictions possible. A general list of RUAs follows, but you should obtain a map of current RUAs from the WMNF.

(1) Camping is not permitted above treeline (where trees are less than 8 ft. tall) except in winter, and then only where there is at least two feet of snow and not on

frozen bodies of water. The point where the restricted area begins is marked on most trails with small signs, but the absence of such signs should not be construed as proof of the legality of a site.

(2) No camping is permitted within $1/4$ mi. of most facilities such as huts, cabins, shelters, or tentsites, except at the facility itself.

(3) No camping is permitted within 200 ft. of certain trails. In 1991, designated trails included the Ammonoosuc Ravine Trail.

(4) In Tuckerman and Huntington ravines (Cutler River drainage), camping is prohibited throughout the year except at the Hermit Lake Shelters; the Hermit Lake tentsites are available in winter only. The Hermit Lake Shelters are lean-tos open to the public. Overnight use is limited to the eighty-six spaces in the shelters. Ten tentsites for forty people are available between December 1 and April 1. Tickets for shelter space (nontransferable and nonrefundable) must be purchased at Pinkham Notch Visitor Center in person (first come, first served) for a nominal fee, for a maximum of seven consecutive nights. Users may no longer kindle charcoal or wood fires; people intending to cook must bring their own small stoves. Day visitors and shelter users alike are required to carry out all their own trash and garbage. No receptacles are provided. This operating policy is under continual review, so it can change from time to time. Information is available at the caretaker's residence. There is no warming room open to the public, and refreshments are not available.

Crawford Notch State Park

No camping is permitted in Crawford Notch State Park except at the public Dry River Campground (fee charged).

Established Trailside Campsites

Mizpah Tentsite (AMC) has seven tent platforms at Mizpah Spring Hut. In summer there is a caretaker, and a fee is charged.

Lakes of the Clouds Hut (AMC) has limited space available for backpackers at a substantially lower cost than the normal hut services.

Rocky Branch Shelter #1 and Tentsite (WMNF) is located near the junction of the Rocky Branch and Stairs Col trails, just outside the Presidential Range–Dry River Wilderness.

Mt. Langdon Shelter (WMNF) is located at the junction of the Mt. Langdon and Mt. Stanton trails, at the edge of the Presidential Range–Dry River Wilderness.

Rocky Branch Shelter #2 (WMNF) is located at the junction of the Rocky Branch and Isolation trails, within the Presidential Range–Dry River Wilderness. Following the established policy for management of wilderness, this shelter will be removed when major maintenance is required.

Dry River Shelter #3 (WMNF) is located on the Dry River Trail, 6.3 mi. from US 302, within the Presidential Range–Dry River Wilderness. This shelter will be removed when major maintenance is required.

Resolution Shelter (AMC) is located on a spur path that leaves the Davis Path at its junction with the Mount Parker Trail, within the Presidential Range–Dry River Wilderness. The water source is scanty in dry seasons. This shelter will be removed when major maintenance is required.

THE TRAILS

Tuckerman Ravine Trail (WMNF)

This trail to the summit of Mt. Washington from NH 16 at Pinkham Notch Visitor Center is probably the most popular route of ascent on the mountain. From Pinkham Notch Visitor Center, it uses a rocky tractor road to the floor of Tuckerman Ravine. From there to the top of the headwall it is a well-graded path, steady but not excessively steep. Its final section ascends the cone of Mt. Washington steeply over fragments of rock. In the spring and fall the WMNF often closes the section of trail on the headwall because of snow and ice, and notice is posted at Pinkham Notch Visitor Center. In these circumstances, the Lion Head Trail is usually the most convenient alternative route. In winter the headwall is often impassable except for experienced and well-equipped snow and ice climbers, and it is frequently closed by the WMNF even to such climbers because of avalanche hazard.

The trail starts behind the trading post at Pinkham Notch Visitor Center, and the Old Jackson Road diverges right in 50 yd. Be careful to avoid numerous side paths, including the Blanchard Ski Trail, in this area. In 0.3 mi. it crosses a bridge to the south bank of Cutler River, begins its moderate but relentless climb, and soon passes a side path leading 20 yd. right to the best viewpoint to Crystal Cascade. At a sharp curve to the right 0.4 mi. from Pinkham Notch Visitor Center, the Boott Spur Trail leaves on the left. At 1.3 mi, the Huntington Ravine Trail diverges on the right. At 1.5 mi. the trail crosses a tributary, then at 1.6 mi, the main branch, of the Cutler River at 1.7 mi. the unsigned Huntington Ravine Fire Rd., which is the easiest route to Huntington Ravine in winter but offers very rough footing on some parts in summer, leaves on the right. At 2.1 mi. the Raymond Path enters on the right at a point when the Tuckerman trail turns sharp left. At a crossroads at 2.3 mi. the Boott Spur Link leaves on the left, and the Lion Head Trail leaves on the right directly opposite. In another 0.1 mi. the trail reaches the buildings at the floor of Tuckerman Ravine near Hermit Lake. The cliff on the right is called Lion Head and the more distant crags on the left are the Hanging Cliffs of Boott Spur.

The main trail keeps to the right (north) of the main stream and ascends a well-constructed footway into the upper floor of the ravine, and finally, at the foot of the headwall, bears right and ascends a steep slope where the Snow Arch can be found on the left in the spring and early summer. In the spring the snowfield above the Snow Arch usually extends across the trail, and the trail is often closed. Some snow may persist in the ravine until late summer. The arch (which does not always form) is carved by a stream of snow melt-water that flows under the snowfield. *Caution:* Do not approach too near the arch and under no circumstances cross or venture beneath it, since sections weighing many tons may break off at any moment, and one death and several narrow escapes have occurred. When ascending the headwall, be careful not to kick rocks loose so that they begin to roll; this may put hikers below you in serious danger.

Turning sharp left at the top of the debris slope and traversing under a cliff, the trail emerges from the ravine and climbs almost straight west up a grassy, ledgy slope with ledges. At 3.4 mi., a short distance above the top of the headwall, the Alpine Garden Trail diverges right. At Tuckerman Junction, on the lower edge of Bigelow Lawn at 3.6 mi., the Tuckerman Crossover leads almost straight ahead (southwest) to the Crawford Path near the Lakes of the Clouds Hut; the Southside Trail diverges from the Tuckerman Crossover in 30 yd. and leads west, skirting the cone to the Davis Path; and the Lawn Cutoff leads left (south) toward Boott Spur. The Tuckerman Ravine Trail turns sharp right and ascends the steep rocks, marked by cairns and paint on ledges. At 3.8 mi., at Cloudwater Spring about one-third of the way up the cone, the Lion Head Trail re-enters on the right. The Tuckerman trail continues to ascend to the Auto Rd. a few yards below the lower parking area, from which wooden stairways lead to the summit area.

Tuckerman Ravine Trail (map 6:F9)

Distances from Pinkham Notch Visitor Center

> *to* Boott Spur Trail: 0.4 mi., 20 min.
> *to* Huntington Ravine Trail: 1.3 mi., 1 hr. 10 min.
> *to* Raymond Path: 2.1 mi., 1 hr. 50 min.
> *to* Lion Head Trail and Boott Spur Link: 2.3 mi., 2 hr. 5 min.
> *to* Hermit Lake shelters: 2.4 mi., 2 hr. 10 min.
> *to* Snow Arch: 3.1 mi., 2 hr. 50 min.
> *to* Alpine Garden Trail: 3.4 mi., 3 hr. 15 min.
> *to* Tuckerman Junction: 3.6 mi., 3 hr. 30 min.
> *to* Lion Head Trail (upper junction): 3.8 mi., 3 hr. 45 min.
> *to* Mt. Washington summit: 4.2 mi. (6.8 km.), 4 hr. 15 min.

Lion Head Trail (AMC)

The Lion Head Trail follows the steep-ended ridge that forms the north wall of Tuckerman Ravine, aptly named for its appearance from points in Pinkham Notch north of Pinkham Notch Visitor Center. The trail begins and ends on the Tuckerman Ravine Trail and thus provides an alternative route to the summit of Mt. Washington, although much steeper in parts. It is an especially important alternative when the Tuckerman Ravine Trail over the headwall is closed because of snow or ice hazards. An older route of the trail, closed to summer hiking, it is considered the least dangerous route to the summit of Mt. Washington in winter conditions, and is the most frequently used winter ascent route. The signs and markings are changed at the beginning and end of the winter season to ensure that climbers take the proper route for prevailing conditions.

The Lion Head Trail diverges right from the Tuckerman Ravine Trail 2.3 mi. from Pinkham Notch Visitor Center and 0.1 mi. below Hermit Lake, opposite the foot of the Boott Spur Link. Running north, it passes a side path on the left to one of the Hermit Lake shelters and crosses the outlet of Hermit Lake. In 0.1 mi. the winter route diverges left, and the summer trail soon begins to climb the steep slope by switchbacks, scrambling up several small ledges with very rough footing and reaching treeline at 0.4 mi. It then bears left and ascends an open slope; the winter route rejoins at 0.7 mi., just below the lower Lion Head. (The winter route is 0.2 mi. shorter.) The trail continues to the upper Lion Head at 0.9 mi., then runs mostly level, with impressive views from the open spur, until it crosses the Alpine Garden Trail at 1.1 mi. After passing through a belt of scrub, it ascends to the Tuckerman Ravine Trail, which it enters at Cloudwater Spring about one-third of the way up the cone of Mt. Washington, about 0.4 mi. and 600 ft. below the summit.

Lion Head Trail (map 6:F9)

Distances from lower junction with Tuckerman Ravine Trail

> *to* Alpine Garden Trail: 1.1 mi. (1.8 km.), 1 hr. 15 min.
> *to* upper junction with Tuckerman Ravine Trail: 1.6 mi. (2.5 km.), 1 hr. 45 min.

Distance from Pinkham Notch Visitor Center

> *to* summit (via summer route and Tuckerman Ravine Trail): 4.1 mi. (7.0 km.), 4 hr. 10 min.

Huntington Ravine Trail (AMC)

Caution: This may be the most difficult regular hiking trail in the White Mtns. Many of the ledges demand proper use of handholds for safe passage, and extreme caution must be exercised at all times. Although experienced hikers who are reasonably comfortable on steep rock will probably encounter little difficulty when conditions are good, the exposure on several of the steepest ledges is likely to prove extremely unnerving to novices and to those who are uncomfortable in steep places. Persons encumbered with large or heavy packs may experience great difficulty in some places. This trail is very dangerous when wet or icy, and its use for descent is strongly discouraged. Since retreat under unfavorable conditions can be extremely difficult and hazardous, never venture beyond the Fan in deteriorating conditions or when weather on the Alpine Garden is likely to be severe. During late fall, winter, and early spring, this trail (and any part of the ravine headwall) should be attempted only by those with complete technical ice-climbing training and equipment. In particular, the ravine must *not* be regarded as a feasible escape route from the Alpine Garden in severe winter conditions.

The trail diverges right from the Tuckerman Ravine Trail 1.3 mi. from Pinkham Notch Visitor Center. In 0.2 mi. it crosses the Cutler River and, at 0.3 mi., the brook that drains Huntington Ravine. At 0.5 mi. it goes straight across the Raymond Path, a junction that might not be well signed. It crosses the Huntington Ravine Fire Rd. and then climbs to meet it again, turning left on the road; at this junction a fine view of the ravine can be obtained by following the road about 100 yd. in the opposite direction. Above this point the trail and road separate, rejoin, or cross several times; the junctions are not always well marked, but both routes lead to the same objective and the major advantage of the trail is somewhat better footing. At 1.3 mi. the first-aid cache in the floor of the ravine is reached. Just beyond here there are some interesting boulders near the path whose tops afford good views of the ravine. Beyond the scrubby trees is a steep slope covered with broken rock, known as the Fan, whose tip lies at the foot of the deepest gully. To the left of this gully are precipices; the lower is called the Pinnacle.

After passing through the boulders, the path ascends to the left side of the Fan and, marked by yellow blazes on the rocks, crosses the talus diagonally. It then turns left and ascends in scrub along the north (right) side of the Fan to its tip at 1.8 mi., crossing a small brook about two-thirds of the way up. The trail then recrosses the brook and immediately attacks the rocks to the right of the main gully, climbing about 650 ft. in 0.3 mi. The route up the headwall follows the line of least difficulty and should be followed carefully over the ledges, which are dangerous, especially when wet. The first pitch above the Fan—a large, fairly smooth, steeply sloping ledge— is probably the most difficult scramble on the trail. Above the first ledges the trail climbs steeply through scrub and over short sections of rock, with some fairly difficult scrambles. About two-thirds of the way up it turns sharp left at a promontory with a good view, then continues to the top of the headwall where it crosses the Alpine Garden Trail at 2.1 mi. From this point it ascends moderately, crossing the Nelson Crag Trail at 2.3 mi., and reaches the Mt. Washington Auto Rd. just below the 7-mi. mark, 1.1 mi. below the summit.

Huntington Ravine Trail (map 6:F9)

Distances from Tuckerman Ravine Trail

    to Raymond Path: 0.5 mi., 30 min.

    to first-aid cache in ravine floor: 1.3 mi., 1 hr. 15 min.

    to Alpine Garden Trail crossing: 2.1 mi., 2 hr. 20 min.

    to Auto Rd.: 2.4 mi. (3.8 km.), 2 hr. 35 min.

Distance from Pinkham Notch Visitor Center

    to Mt. Washington summit (via Tuckerman Ravine, Huntington Ravine, and Nelson Crag trails): 4.3 mi. (6.9 km.), 4 hr. 20 min.

Nelson Crag Trail (AMC)

This trail, which now runs to the summit of Mt. Washington, begins on the Old Jackson Road at a point 1.7 mi.

from Pinkham Notch Visitor Center and 0.2 mi. from the Auto Rd. It is an attractive trail, rather lightly used, though fairly steep in the lower part and greatly exposed to weather in the upper part.

Leaving the Old Jackson Road, this trail follows and soon crosses a small brook, then climbs steadily, soon becoming quite steep. At about 1.1 mi. it rises out of the scrub, emerging on the crest of Chandler Ridge, from which there is an unusual view of Pinkham Notch in both directions. From this point the trail is above treeline and very exposed to the northwest winds. It then bears northwest, climbs moderately over open ledges, and joins the Auto Rd. near Cragway Spring (unreliable), at the sharp turn about 0.3 mi. above the 5-mi. mark. A few yards above, the trail again diverges left from the Auto Rd. and climbs steeply to the crest of the ridge. It passes over Nelson Crag, crosses the Alpine Garden Trail, then swings left and follows a relocated route across the Huntington Ravine Trail and up the rocks to Ball Crag (6106 ft.), and finally runs across the Auto Rd. and the Cog Railway to the summit. To descend on this trail, start by going down the walkway on the lower side of the summit building.

Nelson Crag Trail (map 6:F9)

Distances from Old Jackson Road

> *to* the Auto Rd. near Cragway Spring: 1.5 mi., 1 hr. 50 min.
>
> *to* Huntington Ravine Trail: 2.5 mi., 2 hr., 50 min.
>
> *to* the summit of Mt. Washington: 3.3 mi. (5.3 km.), 3 hr. 25 min.

Boott Spur Trail (AMC)

This trail runs from the Tuckerman Ravine Trail near Pinkham Notch Visitor Center to the Davis Path near the summit of Boott Spur. It follows the long ridge that forms the south wall of Tuckerman Ravine and affords fine views. Grades are mostly moderate, but the trail is above treeline and thus exposed to weather for a considerable distance.

The trail diverges left from the Tuckerman Ravine Trail at a sharp right turn 0.4 mi. from Pinkham Notch Visitor Center, about 150 yd. above the side path to Crystal Cascade. It crosses the John Sherburne Ski Trail, climbs through a ledgy area, crosses a tiny brook, and climbs steeply up a crevice in a ledge to the ridgecrest. At 0.5 mi., after a slight descent, there is a sharp right turn where a side trail (left) leads in 50 yd. down to a restricted view east. The trail passes through some interesting woods, crosses a moist region, and then ascends northwest up a steeper slope toward a craggy shoulder. Halfway up this section, a side trail leads left 100 yd. to a small brook (last water). At the ridgecrest, 1.0 mi. from the Tuckerman Ravine Trail, the main trail turns left and a side trail leads right (east) 25 yd. to an interesting though restricted outlook to Huntington Ravine. The trail continues upward at moderate grades, reaching a ledgy ridgecrest that affords some views, and at 1.7 mi. a side trail on the right leads in 30 yd. to Ravine Outlook, which provides an excellent view of Tuckerman Ravine and of Lion Head directly in front of the summit of Mt. Washington.

The main trail emerges from the scrub at 1.9 mi., soon bears left and angles up the slope to Split Rock, which you can pass through or go around, at 2.0 mi. The trail then turns right, passes through a final patch of fairly high scrub, and rises steeply over two minor humps to a broad, flat ridge, where, at 2.2 mi., Boott Spur Link descends on the right to the Tuckerman Ravine Trail near Hermit Lake. Above this point the trail follows the ridge, which consists of a series of steplike levels and steep slopes. The views of the ravine are excellent, particularly where the path skirts the dangerous Hanging Cliff, 1500 ft. above Hermit Lake. After passing just to the right (north) of the summit of the Spur, the trail ends at the Davis Path.

Boott Spur Trail (map 6:F9)

Distances from Tuckerman Ravine Trail
>   *to* Ravine Outlook: 1.7 mi., 1 hr. 45 min.
>   *to* Split Rock: 2.0 mi., 2 hr.
>   *to* Boott Spur Link: 2.2 mi., 2 hr. 20 min.
>   *to* Davis Path junction: 2.9 mi. (4.7 km.), 3 hr.

Distances from Pinkham Notch Visitor Center
>   *to* Davis Path junction: 3.4 mi., 3 hr. 25 min.
>   *to* Mt. Washington summit (via Davis and Crawford paths): 5.4 mi. (8.7 km.), 4 hr. 50 min.

Boott Spur Link (AMC)

This steep but interesting trail climbs the south wall of Tuckerman Ravine, connecting the main floor of the Ravine with the upper part of Boott Spur. It leaves the Tuckerman Ravine Trail on the south 2.3 mi. from Pinkham Notch Visitor Center and 0.1 mi. below Hermit Lake, opposite the foot of the Lion Head Trail. It immediately crosses two branches of Cutler River and the John Sherburne Ski Trail, then climbs straight up the slope very steeply through woods and scrub, with rapidly improving views back into the Ravine. It continues to climb steeply over open rocks to the crest of Boott Spur, where it meets the Boott Spur Trail.

Boott Spur Link (map 6:F9)

Distance from Tuckerman Ravine Trail
>   *to* Boott Spur Trail: 0.6 mi. (1.0 km.), 45 min.

Gulf of Slides Ski Trail (WMNF)

This trail leads from Pinkham Notch Visitor Center on NH 16 into the Gulf of Slides, a ravine somewhat similar to Tuckerman Ravine but far less well-known and crowded than its illustrious neighbor on the other side of Boott Spur. While this trail is not specifically maintained as a summer hiking trail and may be wet in spots, it still provides an interesting route to a relatively secluded valley. This is a dead-end trail, so hikers must enter and return by the same route.

This trail leaves the south end of the parking lot at Pinkham Notch Visitor Center in common with the John Sherburne Ski Trail. In a short distance it turns left where the Blanchard Ski Trail continues straight, crosses Cutler River and a smaller side channel on bridges, and immediately turns left where the Sherburne Trail turns right. After crossing a branch of New River on a bridge, it bears right along this stream, passes a junction where the Avalanche Brook Ski Trail diverges left, recrosses the stream, and climbs moderately up into the Gulf of Slides, staying mostly well to the north of New River. At 1.9 mi. it swings left where the Graham Ski Trail (marked by can tops) goes right. At 2.2 mi. it passes a first-aid cache, ascends roughly for a short distance, then descends for a short distance to the headwaters of New River near the base of the steep slopes of the ravine's headwall. Soon the trail reaches the base of ski trails leading into the major gullies and ends.

Gulf of Slides Ski Trail (map 6:F9–G9)
Distance from Pinkham Notch Visitor Center
   to Gulf of Slides: 2.5 mi. (4.0 km.), 2 hr. 15 min.

Glen Boulder Trail (AMC)
This trail runs from NH 16 to the Davis Path 0.4 mi. below Boott Spur. It is rough in parts, but reaches treeline and views relatively quickly.

The trail leaves the west side of NH 16 at the Glen Ellis Falls parking area. It ascends gradually for about 0.4 mi. to the base of a small cliff, then climbs around to the right of the cliff and meets the Direttissima, which enters from the right (north) from Pinkham Notch Visitor Center. Here the trail turns sharp left (south) and soon passes a short branch trail that leads left to an outlook on the brink of a cliff, which commands a fine view of Wildcat Mtn. and Pinkham Notch. The main trail turns west, rises gradually, then steepens. At 0.8 mi. it crosses the Avalanche Brook Ski Trail, which is marked with blue plastic markers and is not maintained for hiking. The Glen Boulder Trail soon reaches the north bank of a brook draining the minor ravine south of the Gulf of Slides. After following the brook, which soon divides, the trail then turns southwest and crosses both branches. It is level for 200 yd., then rapidly climbs the northeast side of the spur through evergreens, giving views of the minor ravine and spur south of the Gulf of Slides. Leaving the trees, it climbs over open rocks and, at 1.6 mi., reaches the Glen Boulder, an immense rock perched on the end of the spur that is a familiar landmark for travelers through Pinkham Notch. The view is wide, from Chocorua around to Mt. Washington, and is particularly fine of Wildcat Mtn.

From the boulder the trail climbs steeply up the open ridgecrest to its top at 2.0 mi., re-enters high scrub and ascends moderately. At 2.3 mi. a side trail descends right about 60 yd. to a fine spring. The main trail continues to Gulf Peak (sometimes called Slide Peak), the rather insignificant peak heading the Gulf of Slides, at 2.6 mi. It then turns north and descends slightly, leaving the scrub, and runs entirely above treeline—greatly exposed to the weather—to the Davis Path just below a minor crag.

Glen Boulder Trail (map 6:F9)

Distances from Glen Ellis Falls parking area on NH 16

> *to* The Direttissima: 0.4 mi., 25 min.
>
> *to* Avalanche Brook Ski Trail: 0.8 mi., 45 min.
>
> *to* Glen Boulder: 1.6 mi., 1 hr. 40 min.
>
> *to* Slide Peak: 2.6 mi., 2 hr. 45 min.
>
> *to* Davis Path junction: 3.2 mi. (5.2 km.), 3 hr. 15 min.
>
> *to* Boott Spur Trail (via Davis Path): 3.7 mi., 3 hr. 40 min.

to Mt. Washington summit (via Davis and Crawford paths): 5.7 mi. (9.2 km.), 5 hr.

The Direttissima (MMVSP)

For hikers desiring access to the Glen Boulder Trail from Pinkham Notch Visitor Center, this nearly level trail eliminates a road walk on NH 16. It begins about 0.2 mi. south of Pinkham Notch Visitor Center, just south of the highway bridge over the Cutler River, indicated by a sign at the edge of the woods. Marked by paint blazes, the trail turns sharp left about 30 yd. into the woods and follows a cleared area south. It turns slightly west at the end of this clearing and winds generally south, crossing a small brook, skirts through the upper (west) end of a gorge, and then crosses the gorge on a bridge at 0.5 mi. The trail continues past an excellent viewpoint looking down the Notch, passes along the top of a cliff and then the bottom of a cliff, and ends at the Glen Boulder Trail.

The Direttissima (map 6:F9–G9)
Distance from NH 16 near Cutler River bridge
   to Glen Boulder Trail: 1.0 mi. (1.6 km.), 40 min.

Alpine Garden Trail (AMC)

This trail leads from the Tuckerman Ravine Trail to the Mt. Washington Auto Rd. through the grassy lawn called the Alpine Garden, forming a convenient link between the trails on the east side of the mountain. Although its chief value is its beauty, it also forms part of various routes for those who do not wish to visit the summit. It is completely above treeline and exposed to bad weather, although it is on the mountain's east side, which is usually somewhat sheltered.

The tiny alpine flowers here are best seen in late June. Especially prominent in this area are the five-petaled, white Diapensia, the bell-shaped, pink-magenta Lapland Rosebay, and the very small, pink flowers of the Alpine

Azalea. (See the AMC's *Field Guide to Mountain Flowers of New England* and *At Timberline: A Nature Guide to the Mountains of the Northeast*.) No plants should ever be picked or otherwise damaged. Hikers are urged to stay on trails or walk very carefully on rocks so as not to kill the fragile alpine vegetation.

The trail diverges right from the Tuckerman Ravine Trail a short distance above the ravine headwall, about 0.2 mi. below Tuckerman Junction. It leads northeast, bearing toward Lion Head, and crosses the Lion Head Trail. Beyond this crossing the trail leads generally north until it ends at the road. It traverses the Alpine Garden and crosses a tiny stream that is the headwater of Raymond Cataract. (This water may be contaminated by drainage from the summit buildings.) The trail soon approaches the top of Huntington Ravine and crosses the Huntington Ravine Trail. Here, a little off the trail, there is a fine view of this impressive ravine. Rising to the top of the ridge, the trail crosses the Nelson Crag Trail, then descends and soon enters the old Glen House Bridle Path, constructed in 1853, whose course is still plain although it was abandoned over a century ago. In a short distance the Alpine Garden Trail turns left and in a few yards enters the Auto Rd. a short distance above the 6 mi. mark and opposite the upper terminus of the Wamsutta Trail.

Alpine Garden Trail (map 6:F9)
Distances from Tuckerman Ravine Trail
    to Lion Head Trail: 0.3 mi., 10 min.
    to Huntington Ravine Trail: 1.2 mi., 45 min.
    to Nelson Crag Trail: 1.4 mi., 50 min.
    to Auto Rd. junction: 1.8 mi. (2.9 km.), 1 hr.

Southside Trail (AMC)
This trail forms a link between Tuckerman Ravine and the Crawford Path and Westside Trail. It diverges right (west) from Tuckerman Crossover about 30 yd. south-

west of the Tuckerman Ravine Trail at Tuckerman Junction and, skirting the southwest side of Mt. Washington's summit cone, enters the Davis Path near its junction with the Crawford Path.

Southside Trail (map 6:F9)
Distance from Tuckerman Junction
    to Davis Path: 0.3 mi. (0.5 km.), 10 min.

Tuckerman Crossover (AMC)

This trail connects Tuckerman Ravine with Lakes of the Clouds Hut. It is totally above treeline, and crosses a high ridge where there is much exposure to westerly winds. It leaves the Tuckerman Ravine Trail left (southwest) at Tuckerman Junction, where the latter trail turns sharp right to ascend the cone. It rises gradually across Bigelow Lawn, crosses the Davis Path, then descends moderately to the Crawford Path, which it meets along with the Camel Trail a short distance above the upper Lake of the Clouds. Turning left on the Crawford Path, the Lakes of the Clouds Hut is reached in 0.2 mi.

Tuckerman Crossover (map 6:F9)
Distances from Tuckerman Junction
    to Crawford Path: 0.8 mi. (1.3 km.), 25 min.
    to Lakes of the Clouds Hut (via Crawford Path): 1.0 mi. (1.6 km.), 30 min.

Lawn Cutoff (AMC)

This trail provides a direct route between Tuckerman Junction and Boott Spur, entirely above treeline. It leaves the Tuckerman Ravine Trail at Tuckerman Junction and leads south across Bigelow Lawn to the Davis Path about 0.5 mi. north of Boott Spur.

Lawn Cutoff (map 6:F9)
Distance from Tuckerman Junction
    to Davis Path: 0.4 mi. (0.6 km.), 15 min.

Camel Trail (AMC)

This trail, connecting Boott Spur with the Lakes of the Clouds Hut, is named for ledges on Boott Spur that resemble a kneeling camel when seen against the skyline.

This is the right-hand trail of the two that diverge right (east) from the Crawford Path 0.2 mi. northeast of Lakes of the Clouds Hut (the Tuckerman Crossover is the left of the diverging trails). It ascends easy, grassy slopes, crosses the old location of the Crawford Path, and continues in a straight line across the level stretch of Bigelow Lawn. It aims directly toward the ledges that form the camel, passes under the camel's nose, and joins the Davis Path about 200 yd. northwest of the Lawn Cutoff.

Camel Trail (map 6:F9)

Distance from Crawford Path
    to Davis Path: 0.7 mi. (1.1 km.), 30 min.

Westside Trail (WMNF)

This trail was partially constructed by pioneer trail-maker J. Rayner Edmands; many segments are paved with carefully placed stones. It is wholly above timberline, and is very much exposed to the prevailing west and northwest winds. However, by avoiding the summit of Mt. Washington, it saves about 0.7 mi. in distance and 600 ft. in elevation between points on the Northern Peaks and those on the Crawford Path.

The trail diverges left from the Crawford Path, where the latter path begins to climb the steep part of the Mt. Washington summit cone. It skirts the cone, climbing for 0.6 mi. at an easy grade, then descends moderately, crosses under the Mt. Washington Cog Railway, and soon ends at the Gulfside Trail.

Westside Trail (map 6:F9)

Distance from Crawford Path
    to Gulfside Trail: 0.9 mi. (1.4 km.), 30 min.

Trinity Heights Connector (NHDP)

This trail allows the Appalachian Trail to make a loop over the summit of Mt. Washington; formerly the true summit was a side trip, albeit very short, from the AT, so technically the AT did not pass over it. Trinity Heights is a name formerly used for the summit region. From the true summit (marked by a large sign), the path runs generally northwest over the rocks to the Gulfside Trail less than 0.1 mi. from its junction with the Crawford Path.

Trinity Heights Connector (map 6:F9)
Distance from true summit of Mt. Washington
   to Gulfside Trail: 0.2 mi. (0.3 km.), 5 min.

Raymond Path (AMC)

This trail, one of the older paths in the region, leaves Old Jackson Road about 0.3 mi. from the Auto Rd. and 1.7 mi. from Pinkham Notch Visitor Center, about 100 yd. south of the beginning of the Nelson Crag Trail, and ends at the Tuckerman Ravine Trail about 0.3 mi. below Hermit Lake. Its grades are mostly easy to moderate.

The trail diverges from Old Jackson Road, crosses several small branches of the Peabody River, climbing moderately to the crest of a small ridge at 0.8 mi., where there is an excellent view to Lion Head and Boott Spur. It then descends moderately for a short distance to a small mossy brook, then begins to ascend easily, crossing Nelson Brook at 1.2 mi. and the Huntington Ravine Trail at 1.8 mi. From here it drops down a steep bank to cross the brook that drains Huntington Ravine. Soon it crosses the brook coming from the Ravine of Raymond Cataract (sign) and then the Huntington Ravine Fire Rd., then climbs rather steeply 0.3 mi. to the Tuckerman Ravine Trail.

Raymond Path (map 6:F9)
Distances from Old Jackson Road
   to Huntington Ravine Trail: 1.8 mi., 1 hr. 20 min.

to Tuckerman Ravine Trail: 2.4 mi. (3.9 km.), 1 hr. 50 min.

to Hermit Lake (via Tuckerman Ravine Trail): 2.7 mi., 2 hr.

Old Jackson Road (AMC)

This trail runs north from Pinkham Notch Visitor Center to the Mt. Washington Auto Rd., is part of the Appalachian Trail, and is blazed in white.

The trail diverges right from the Tuckerman Ravine Trail about 50 yd. from the trailhead at the rear of the trading post. After about 0.3 mi. the Blanchard and Connie's Way ski trails cross, and at 0.4 mi. the Link Ski Trail enters right just before a bridge and the Crew-Cut Trail leaves right (east) just after the bridge. Soon the Old Jackson Road begins to ascend more steeply, crossing a small brook running in an interesting gorge with a waterfall. The trail climbs to a flat region at the headwater of the Peabody River where, at 0.9 mi., George's Gorge Trail leaves right (east). (This junction may be incorrectly signed Liebeskind's Loop.) After a while, the Old Jackson Road descends slightly, crosses several small brooks, and then at a larger brook makes a sharp left turn uphill. After a short, steep climb it turns right and runs nearly level. At 1.7 mi. the Raymond Path leaves on the left, and in another 100 yd., just after a small brook is crossed, the Nelson Crag Trail leaves on the left. Continuing north, the trail climbs slightly up an interesting little rocky hogback, passes through an old gravel pit, and meets the Auto Rd. just above the 2-mi. mark, opposite the Madison Gulf Trail.

Old Jackson Road (map 6:F9)

Distance from Pinkham Notch Visitor Center

to Mt. Washington Auto Rd.: 1.9 mi. (3.1 km.), 1 hr. 20 min.

Crew-Cut Trail (MMVSP)

The Crew-Cut Trail leaves the Old Jackson Road on the right about 0.4 mi. from Pinkham Notch Visitor Center, just after a stream crossing and just before the Old Jackson Road starts to climb steeply. It is called Brad's Trail on some signs.

After crossing a stony, dry brook bed it runs generally east-northeast, crossing two small brooks. On the east bank of the second brook, at 0.2 mi., the George's Gorge Trail leaves left. The Crew-Cut Trail continues generally northeast, rising gradually up the slope through open woods and crossing several gullies. It skirts southeast of the steeper rocky outcroppings until, about 0.5 mi. from the Old Jackson Road, Liebeskind's Loop enters left, coming down from George's Gorge Trail. The spur path to Lila's Ledge, which affords fine views, leaves Liebeskind's Loop less than 0.1 mi. from this junction. The Crew-Cut Trail passes under the base of a cliff, turns right and descends steeply over a few small ledges and through open woods until it passes east of a small, high-level bog formed by an old beaver dam. Shortly thereafter, it crosses a small stream and Connie's Way Ski Trail, and goes through open woods again, emerging at the top of the grassy slope on NH 16 almost exactly opposite the south end of the Wildcat Ski Area parking lot.

Crew-Cut Trail (map 6:F9–F10)
Distance from Old Jackson Road
  to NH 16: 1.0 mi. (1.6 km.), 35 min.

George's Gorge Trail (MMVSP)

This trail leaves the Crew-Cut Trail to the left 0.2 mi. from the Old Jackson Road, on the east bank of a small brook (the infant Peabody River), and leads up the brook, steeply in places, passing Chudacoff Falls, and then swings rather sharply away from the brook. Liebeskind's Loop leaves on the right at 0.5 mi., and George's

Gorge Trail then climbs nearly to the top of a knob and descends west to the Old Jackson Road in the flat section near its halfway point, 0.9 mi. from Pinkham Notch Visitor Center. (This junction may be incorrectly signed Liebeskind's Loop.)

George's Gorge Trail (map 6:F9–F10)
Distance from Crew-Cut Trail
    to Old Jackson Road: 0.8 mi. (1.3 km.), 45 min.

Liebeskind's Loop (MMVSP)

Liebeskind's Loop makes possible a loop hike (using the Crew-Cut, George's Gorge, Loop, and Crew-Cut trails) without resorting to returning either by NH 16 or by the steep section of the Old Jackson Road. This loop hike is best made in the sequence referred to above, since the Gorge is more interesting on the ascent and the Loop is more interesting on the descent.

Liebeskind's Loop leaves right (east) near the high point of the George's Gorge Trail, 0.2 mi. from Old Jackson Road, and descends to a swampy flat, then rises through a spruce thicket to the top of a cliff, where there is a fine lookout with a good view down Pinkham Notch. Here the trail turns left and runs along the edge of the cliff, finally descending by an easy zigzag in a gully to a beautiful open grove of birches. The trail continues east, descending through two gorges and skirting the east end of rises until it finally climbs a ridge to its crest. Here a spur trail leads left 0.1 mi. to Lila's Ledge, which affords excellent views of Pinkham Notch and the eastern slope of Mt. Washington. Liebeskind's Loop then descends on the other side of the ridge to join the Crew-Cut Trail, which can then be followed back to the starting point.

Liebeskind's Loop (map 6:F9–F10)
Distance from George's Gorge Trail
    to Crew-Cut Trail: 0.6 mi. (1.0 km.), 20 min.

Crawford Path (WMNF)

Caution: Parts of this trail are dangerous in bad weather. Several hikers have died on the Crawford Path through failure to observe proper precautions. Below Mt. Eisenhower there are a number of ledges exposed to the weather, but they are scattered and shelter is usually available in nearby scrub. From the Eisenhower-Franklin Col the trail runs completely above treeline, exposed to the full force of all storms. The most dangerous part of the path is the section on the cone of Mt. Washington, beyond Lakes of the Clouds Hut. Always carry a compass and study the map before starting. If trouble arises on or above Mt. Monroe, take refuge at Lakes of the Clouds Hut or go down the Ammonoosuc Ravine Trail. The path is well marked with large cairns topped by yellow-painted rocks, and in poor visibility great care should be exercised to stay on it, since many of the other paths in the vicinity are much less clearly marked. If you lose the path in bad weather and cannot find it again after diligent effort, you should travel west, descending into the woods and following streams downhill to the roads. On the southeast, toward the Dry River valley, nearly all the slopes are more precipitous, the river crossings are potentially dangerous, and the distance to a highway is much greater.

This trail is considered to be the oldest continuously maintained footpath in America. The first section, a trail leading up Mt. Pierce (Mt. Clinton), was cut in 1819 by Abel Crawford and his son Ethan Allen Crawford. In 1840 Thomas J. Crawford, a younger son of Abel, converted the footpath into a bridle path, but more than a century has passed since its regular use for ascents on horseback ended. The trail still follows the original path, except for the section between Mt. Monroe and the Westside Trail, which was relocated to take it off the windswept ridge and down to the shelter at Lakes of the

Clouds. From Mt. Pierce to the summit of Mt. Washington, the Crawford Path is part of the Appalachian Trail and blazed in white.

The south trailhead is on US 302 opposite the Crawford House site. The former parking area just west of the trailhead has been closed, and the principal parking area at this end is now on Mt. Clinton Rd. near its junction with US 302, at a newly constructed lot from which the Crawford Connector, a spur path 0.2 mi. long, leads to the Crawford Path.

The following description of the path is in the northbound direction (toward Mt. Washington). See below for a description of the path in the reverse direction.

Leaving US 302, the trail soon passes a short side trail to a view of a small flume in Gibbs Brook, and at 0.2 mi. the Crawford Conenctor from the new parking lot enters on the left.

Crawford Cliff Spur. At this junction there is also a side trail that leads left to Crawford Cliff. This side path immediately crosses Gibbs Brook and follows it to a small flume and pool. It climbs steeply above the brook, then turns left at an old sign, becomes very rough, and reaches a ledge with an outlook over Crawford Notch and the Willey Range, 0.4 mi. (20 min.) from the Crawford Path.

The main trail continues along the south bank of Gibbs Brook, and at 0.4 mi. a side path leads 40 yd. left to Gibbs Falls. Soon the trail passes an information sign for the Gibbs Brook Scenic Area, and climbs moderately but steadily. At about 1 mi. from US 302, the trail climbs away from the brook and angles up the side of the valley. At 1.7 mi. the Mizpah Cutoff diverges east for Mizpah Spring Hut. The Crawford Path continues to ascend at easy to moderate grades, crossing several small brooks, then reaches its high point on the shoulder of Mt. Pierce and runs almost level, breaking into the open with fine views, and at 2.9 mi. reaches its junction with the Webster Cliff Trail, which leads right (south) to the summit of Mt. Pierce in about 0.1 mi.

From Mt. Pierce to Mt. Eisenhower the path runs through patches of scrub and woods with many open ledges that give magnificent views in all directions. Cairns and the marks of many feet on the rocks indicate the way. The path winds generally northeast, fairly near the poorly defined crest of the broad ridge, which is composed of several rounded humps. At 3.6 mi. the trail crosses a small brook in the col, then ascends mostly on ledges to the junction with the Mount Eisenhower Loop, which diverges left at 4.1 mi. The trip over this summit adds only 0.2 mi. and 300 ft. of climbing to the trip, and the view is excellent in good weather. The Crawford Path continues right and runs nearly level through scrub on the southeast side of the mountain; this is the better route in bad weather. The Mount Eisenhower Loop rejoins the Crawford Path on the left at 4.6 mi., just above the sag between Mt. Eisenhower and Mt. Franklin, on a ledge that overlooks Red Pond, a small pool of stagnant water. The Edmands Path has been relocated and now enters the Mount Eisenhower Loop near this junction, rather than entering the Crawford Path directly a short distance farther along as it used to do.

At 4.8 mi. the Mount Eisenhower Trail from the Dry River enters right. The Crawford Path then begins the ascent of the shoulder called Mt. Franklin, first moderately, then steeply for a short distance near the top. At 5.3 mi. the trail reaches the relatively level shoulder and continues past an unmarked path at 5.8 mi. that leads right 130 yd. to the barely noticeable summit of Mt. Franklin, from which there are excellent views, particularly into Oakes Gulf. At 6.1 mi. the Mount Monroe Loop diverges left to cross both summits of Monroe, affording excellent views. It is about the same length as the parallel section of the Crawford Path but requires about 350 ft. more climbing. The Crawford Path is safer in bad weather, since it is much less exposed to the weather. The Crawford Path continues along the edge of the precipice that forms the northwest wall of Oakes Gulf, then follows a relocated section, passing an area that has been closed to public entry to preserve an endangered species of plant. The area between the two ends of the Mount Monroe Loop is one of great fragility and botanical importance. The most scrupulous care is required on the part of visitors in order to protect this area. At 6.7 mi. the Mount Monroe Loop rejoins on the left, and the path descends easily to Lakes of the Clouds Hut.

The Ammonoosuc Ravine Trail diverges left at the corner of the hut and in another 30 yd. the Dry River Trail diverges right. The Crawford Path crosses the outlet of the larger lake and passes between it and the second lake, where the Camel Trail to Boott Spur and the Tuckerman Crossover to Tuckerman Ravine diverge right. The path then ascends moderately on the northwest side of the ridge, always some distance below the crest. The Davis Path, which here follows the original location of the Crawford Path, enters at 7.7 mi., at the foot of the Mt. Washington summit cone. In another 50 yd. the Westside Trail, a short-cut to the Northern Peaks, diverges left. The Crawford Path runs generally north, switching back and forth as it climbs the steep cone through a trench in the rocks. At the plateau west of the summit, it meets the Gulfside Trail at 8.0 mi., then turns right, passes through the old corral in which saddle horses from the Glen House were once kept, and from there ascends to the summit.

Crawford Path (map 6:G8–F9)

Distances from US 302 near Crawford House site
  to Mizpah Cutoff: 1.7 mi., 1 hr. 40 min.
  to Webster Cliff Trail: 2.9 mi., 2 hr. 35 min.

to south end of Mount Eisenhower Loop: 4.1 mi., 3
    hr. 25 min.
to Mount Eisenhower Trail: 4.8 mi., 3 hr. 50 min.
to Lakes of the Clouds Hut: 6.8 mi., 5 hr. 10 min.
to Westside Trail: 7.7 mi., 5 hr. 55 min.
to Gulfside Trail: 8.0 mi., 6 hr. 20 min.
to Mt. Washington summit: 8.2 mi. (13.2 km.), 6 hr.
    30 min.

Crawford Path (WMNF) *[in reverse]*

Descending from the summit of Mt. Washington, the
path lies on the right (north) side of the railroad track.
After passing between the buildings it leads generally
northwest; avoid random side paths toward the south.
Shortly it reaches a junction with the Gulfside Trail and
turns sharp left, then zigzags downward through a trench
in the rocks. At 0.5 mi. the Westside Trail enters right
and in another 50 yd. the Davis Path diverges left. The
Crawford Path now descends moderately on the northwest side of the ridge well below the crest, and the Tuckerman Crossover and the Camel Trail enter on the left
just before the trail reaches the Lakes of the Clouds. It
then passes between the lakes, and reaches Lakes of the
Clouds Hut at 1.4 mi., where the Dry River Trail enters
on the left and the Ammonoosuc Ravine Trail enters on
the right.

The Crawford Path now climbs up to the base of Mt.
Monroe, where the north end of the Mount Monroe Loop
diverges right to cross both summits of Monroe, affording excellent views. It is about the same length as the
parallel section of the Crawford Path but requires about
350 ft. more climbing. The Crawford Path is safer in bad
weather, as it is much less exposed to the weather. It circles around the foot of this sharp peak, following a relocated section past an area that has been closed to public
entry to preserve an endangered species of plant. The

area between the two ends of the Mount Monroe Loop is one of great fragility and botanical importance. To protect this area, the most scrupulous care is required on the part of visitors. The Crawford Path continues along the edge of the precipice that forms the northwest wall of Oakes Gulf, the Mount Monroe Loop rejoins on the right, and the main path continues along the flat ridge, passing an unmarked path at 2.4 mi. that leads left 130 yd. to the barely noticeable summit of Mt. Franklin, from which there are excellent views, particularly into Oakes Gulf. At 2.9 mi. the trail drops off the end of the shoulder, then descends moderately to the sag, passing the Mount Eisenhower Trail on the left at 3.4 mi. The Mount Eisenhower Loop leaves on the right at 3.6 mi. on a small ledge overlooking Red Pond, a small pool of stagnant water. The Edmands Path has been relocated and now enters the Mount Eisenhower Loop near this junction, rather than entering the Crawford Path directly as it used to do. The trip over Mt. Eisenhower adds only 0.2 mi. and 300 ft. of climbing to the trip, and the view is excellent in good weather. The Crawford Path bears left and runs nearly level through scrub on the southeast side of the mountain; this is the better route in bad weather.

The Mount Eisenhower Loop rejoins on the right at 4.1 mi., and the Crawford Path descends on ledges to cross a small brook in the col, then climbs moderately to the junction with the Webster Cliff Trail at 5.3 mi., on an open ledge just below the summit of Mt. Pierce. From here the trail soon enters the scrub and then full woods, descends moderately past the Mizpah Cutoff at 6.5 mi., and continues through the Gibbs Brook Scenic Area. At a junction 0.2 mi. before the Crawford Path reaches US 302 opposite the Crawford House site, the side path to Crawford Cliff (see above) diverges right, and the Crawford Connector also diverges right and runs 0.2 mi. to the new parking area on Mt. Clinton Rd. near its junction with US 302.

Crawford Path (map 6:G8–F9)

Distances from the summit of Mt. Washington

   to Gulfside Trail: 0.2 mi., 5 min.

   to Westside Trail: 0.5 mi., 15 min.

   to Lakes of the Clouds Hut: 1.4 mi., 40 min.

   to Mount Eisenhower Trail: 3.4 mi., 1 hr. 45 min.

   to south end of Mount Eisenhower Loop: 4.1 mi., 2 hr. 10 min.

   to Webster Cliff Trail: 5.3 mi., 2 hr. 50 min.

   to Mizpah Cutoff: 6.5 mi., 3 hr. 30 min.

   to US 302: 8.2 mi. (13.2 km.), 4 hr. 20 min.

Mount Eisenhower Loop (AMC)

This short trail parallels the Crawford Path, climbing over the bare, flat summit of Mt. Eisenhower, which provides magnificent views. It diverges from the Crawford Path 4.1 mi. from US 302 at the south edge of the summit dome, climbs easily for 0.1 mi., then turns sharp left in a flat area and ascends to the summit at 0.4 mi. It then descends moderately to a ledge overlooking Red Pond, then drops steeply over ledges, passes through a grassy sag just to the left of Red Pond, and finally climbs briefly past a junction with the Edmands Path on the left to rejoin the Crawford Path on a small, rocky knob.

Mount Eisenhower Loop (map 6:G8)

Distances from south junction with Crawford Path

   to summit of Mt. Eisenhower: 0.4 mi., 20 min.

   to north junction with Crawford Path: 0.8 mi. (1.2 km.), 35 min.

Mount Monroe Loop (AMC)

This short trail runs parallel to the Crawford Path and passes over the summits of Mt. Monroe and Little Monroe. The views are fine but these summits are very exposed to the weather. The trail diverges from the Crawford Path 6.1 mi. from US 302 and quickly ascends the minor crag called Little Monroe, then descends into the shallow, grassy sag beyond. It then climbs steeply to the summit of Mt. Monroe at 0.4 mi., follows the northeast ridge to the end of the shoulder, and drops sharply to the Crawford Path 0.1 mi. south of Lakes of the Clouds Hut.

Mount Monroe Loop (map 6:F9)

Distances from south junction with Crawford Path

   to summit of Mt. Monroe: 0.4 mi., 20 min.

   to north junction with Crawford Path: 0.7 mi. (1.1 km.), 30 min.

Ammonoosuc Ravine Trail (WMNF)

The Ammonoosuc Ravine Trail runs from the Base Rd. to Lakes of the Clouds Hut, following the headwaters of the Ammonoosuc River with many falls, cascades, and pools as well as superb views from its upper section. This trail is the most direct route to Lakes of the Clouds Hut, and the best route in bad weather, since it lies in woods or scrub except for the last 200 yd. to the hut. The section above Gem Pool is extremely steep and rough, and is likely to prove quite arduous for many hikers, particularly those with limited trail-walking experience; it is also somewhat tricky to descend this section because of the steep terrain and slippery rocks. Together with the upper section of the Crawford Path, this trail provides the shortest route to Mt. Washington from the west. It can also be reached on foot from the Jefferson Notch Rd. via the Boundary Line Trail (see Section 2).

The trail begins at a parking lot on the Base Rd., about 1 mi. east of its junction with the Mt. Clinton Rd. and the Jefferson Notch Rd. It follows a path through the woods, crossing Franklin Brook at 0.3 mi., then passing over a double pipeline as it skirts around the Base Station area. It joins the old route of the trail (the Base Station is 0.3 mi. to the left) at the edge of the Ammonoosuc River at 1.0 mi. after a slight descent, and bears right along the river, following the old route for the rest of the way. It ascends mostly by easy grades, with some rough footing, crossing Monroe Brook at 1.7 mi., and at 2.1 mi. it crosses the outlet of Gem Pool, a beautiful pool at the foot of a cascade.

Now the very steep, rough ascent begins. At 2.3 mi. a side path (sign) leads right about 80 yd. to a spectacular viewpoint at the foot of the gorge. Above this point the main brook falls about 600 ft. down a steep trough in the mountainside at an average angle of 45 degrees. Another brook a short distance to the north does the same, and these two spectacular water slides meet at the foot of the gorge, forming a pool at the base. The main trail continues its steep ascent, passes an outlook over the cascades to the right of the trail, and at 2.5 mi. crosses the main brook on flat ledges at the head of the highest fall, a striking viewpoint. The grade now begins to ease, and the trail crosses several brooks as ledges become more frequent and the scrub becomes smaller and more sparse. At 3.0 mi. the trail emerges from the scrub and follows a line of cairns directly up some rock slabs (which are slippery when wet), passes through one last patch of scrub, and reaches the Crawford Path at the south side of Lakes of the Clouds Hut.

Ammonoosuc Ravine Trail (map 6:F8–F9)
Distances from the Base Road parking lot
    to Gem Pool: 2.1 mi., 1 hr. 30 min.
    to brook crossing on flat ledges: 2.5 mi., 2 hr. 10 min.
    to Lakes of the Clouds Hut: 3.1 mi. (5.0 km.), 2 hr. 55 min.

Edmands Path (WMNF)
The Edmands Path leads from the Mt. Clinton Rd. to the Mount Eisenhower Loop near its junction with the Crawford Path, just south of the Eisenhower-Franklin Col. It provides the shortest route to the summit of Mt. Eisen-

hower, and an easy access to the middle portion of the Crawford Path. The last 0.2-mi. segment before the Crawford Path junction is very exposed to northwest winds and, although short, could pose problems in bad weather. The ledgy brook crossings in the upper part of the trail are treacherous in icy conditions. J. Rayner Edmands, the pioneer trail-maker, relocated and reconstructed this trail in 1909. The rock cribbing and paving in the middle and upper sections of the trail testify to the infinite pains that Edmands took to construct a trail with constant comfortable grades over rather difficult terrain. Most of his work has survived the weather and foot traffic of many decades well, and the trail retains probably the best grade and footing of any comparable trail in the White Mtns. It is nearly always comfortable, and almost never challenging.

The path leaves the east side of the Mt. Clinton Rd. at a new parking lot 2.3 mi. north of the Crawford House site. It runs nearly level across two small brooks, then at 0.4 mi. it crosses Abenaki Brook and turns sharp right onto an old logging road on the far bank. At 0.7 mi. the trail diverges left off the old road and crosses a wet area. Soon it begins to climb steadily, undulating up the west ridge of Mt. Eisenhower, carefully searching out the most comfortable grades. At 2.2 mi. the trail swings left and angles up the mountainside on a footway supported by extensive rock cribbing, then passes through a little stone gateway. At 2.5 mi. it crosses a small brook running over a ledge, and soon the grade becomes almost level as the trail contours around the north slope of Mount Eisenhower, affording excellent views out through the trees. At 2.8 mi. it breaks into the open, crosses the nose of a ridge on a footway paved with carefully placed stones, and reaches the Mt. Eisenhower Loop a few yards from the Crawford Path.

Edmands Path (map 6:G8)

Distances from Mt. Clinton Road

   to stone gateway: 2.2 mi., 2 hr. 5 min.

   to Mount Eisenhower Loop junction: 3.0 mi. (4.9 km.), 2 hr. 40 min.

Webster-Jackson Trail (AMC)

This trail connects US 302 at the Crawford Depot information center with the summits of both Mt. Webster and Mt. Jackson, and provides the opportunity for an interesting loop trip, since the two summits are linked by the Webster Cliff Trail.

The trail, blazed in blue, leaves the east side of US 302 0.1 mi. south of the Crawford Depot and 0.1 mi. north of the Gate of the Notch. It runs through a clearing, enters the woods, and passes the side path leading right to Elephant Head at 0.1 mi. from US 302.

Elephant Head Spur. Elephant Head is an interesting ledge that forms the east side of the Gate of the Notch, with veins of white quartz in the gray rock providing a remarkable likeness to an elephant's head. The path runs through the woods parallel to the highway at an easy grade, then ascends across the summit of the knob and descends 40 yd. to the top of the ledge that overlooks Crawford Notch with fine views, 0.2 mi. (10 min.) from the Webster-Jackson Trail.

The main trail runs along the south bank of Elephant Head Brook, well above the stream, then turns right, away from the brook, at 0.2 mi. The trail continues up the slope, crosses Little Mossy Brook at 0.3 mi., and continues in the same general direction, nearly level stretches alternating with sharp pitches. At 0.6 mi. from US 302 a side path leads right 60 yd. to Bugle Cliff, a massive ledge overlooking Crawford Notch, where the view is well worth the slight extra effort required; but if there is ice present, exercise extreme caution. The main trail rises fairly steeply and crosses Flume Cascade Brook at 0.9 mi. At 1.4 mi., within sound of Silver Cascade Brook, the trail divides, the left branch for Mt. Jackson and the right (straight ahead) for Mt. Webster.

Mt. Webster. The Webster (right) branch immediately descends steeply to Silver Cascade Brook, crosses it just below a beautiful cascade and pool, then bears left and climbs steeply up the bank. The trail then climbs steadily south 1.0 mi., meeting the Webster Cliff Trail on the high plateau northwest of the summit of Mt. Webster, 2.4 mi. from US 302. The ledgy summit of Mt. Webster, with an excellent view of Crawford Notch and the mountains to the west and south, is 0.1 mi. right (south); turn left to reach Mt. Jackson.

Mt. Jackson. The Jackson (left) branch ascends gradually until it comes within sight of Silver Cascade Brook, then begins to climb moderately. About 0.5 mi. above the junction, it crosses three branches of the brook in quick succession. At 1.0 mi. from the junction it passes Tisdale Spring (unreliable, often scanty and muddy), a short distance below the base of the rocky cone. The trail soon swings right and ascends steep ledges to the open summit, 2.6 mi. from US 302.

Webster-Jackson Trail (map 6:C8)

Distances from US 302

to Elephant Head side path: 0.1 mi., 5 min.

to Bugle Cliff: 0.6 mi., 35 min.

to Flume Cascade Brook: 0.9 mi., 45 min.

to Mt. Webster–Mt. Jackson fork: 1.4 mi., 1 hr. 10 min.

to Webster Cliff Trail (via Webster branch): 2.4 mi., 2 hr. 15 min.

to summit of Mt. Webster (via Webster Cliff Trail): 2.5 mi. (4.1 km.), 2 hr. 20 min.

to summit of Mt. Jackson (via Jackson branch): 2.6 mi. (4.2 km.), 2 hr. 25 min.

for loop trip over summits of Webster and Jackson (via Webster Cliff Trail): 6.5 mi. (10.5 km.), 4 hr. 30 min.

Webster Cliff Trail (AMC)

This trail, a part of the Appalachian Trail, leaves the east side of US 302 opposite the road to Willey House Station, about 1 mi. south of the Willey House Recreation Area at the Willey House site. It ascends along the edge of the spectacular cliffs that form the east wall of Crawford Notch, then leads over Mts. Webster, Jackson, and Pierce to the Crawford Path 0.1 mi. north of Mt. Pierce.

From US 302, it runs nearly east 0.1 mi. to a bridge across the Saco River. Then the trail climbs steadily up the south end of the ridge, winding up the steep slope, growing steeper as it approaches the cliffs, and swinging more to the north. At 1.8 mi. from US 302 it reaches the first open ledge, and from here on, as the trail ascends the ridge with easier grades, there are frequent outlook ledges giving ever-changing perspectives of the notch and the mountains to the south and west. At 2.4 mi. a ledge affords a view straight down to the State Park buildings, and at 3.3 mi. the jumbled, ledgy summit is reached.

The trail then descends north, and in 0.1 mi. the Webster branch of the Webster-Jackson Trail from Crawford Depot on US 302 enters left. The Webster Cliff Trail swings east and crosses numerous wet gullies, finally ascending the steep, ledgy cone of Mt. Jackson, reaching the summit at 4.7 mi., where the Jackson branch of the Webster-Jackson Trail enters left.

The trail leaves the summit of Mt. Jackson toward Mt. Pierce, following a line of cairns running north, and descends the ledges at the north end of the cone quite rapidly into the scrub, then enters and winds through open alpine meadows. At 5.2 mi., where a side path leads right 40 yd. to an outlook, the trail turns sharp left and drops into the woods. It continues up and down along the ridge toward Mt. Pierce, then descends gradually to the junction at 6.3 mi. with the Mizpah Cutoff, which leads left (west) to the Crawford Path. At 6.4 mi. Mizpah Spring Hut (which also has tentsites) is reached, and the Mount Clinton Trail to the Dry River diverges right (southeast) diagonally down the hut clearing. Continuing west of the hut, the trail ascends very rapidly, passes an outlook toward Mt. Jackson, and reaches an open ledge with good views at 6.6 mi. The grade lessens, and after a sharp right turn in a ledgy area the trail reaches the summit of the southwest knob of Mt. Pierce, which affords a view of the summit of Mt. Washington rising over Mt. Pierce. The trail descends into a sag and ascends easily through scrub to the summit of Mt. Pierce at 7.2 mi., where it comes into the open. It then descends moderately in the open in the same direction (northeast) about 150 yd. to its junction with the Crawford Path.

Webster Cliff Trail (map 6:G8)

Distances from US 302

> *to* first open ledge: 1.8 mi., 1 hr. 50 min.
> *to* summit of Mt. Webster: 3.3 mi., 3 hr.
> *to* summit of Mt. Jackson: 4.7 mi., 4 hr.
> *to* Mizpah Spring Hut: 6.4 mi., 4 hr. 50 min.
> *to* Crawford Path: 7.3 mi. (11.7 km.), 5 hr. 35 min.

Mizpah Cutoff (AMC)

This short trail provides a direct route from US 302 near the AMC Crawford Notch Hostel to Mizpah Spring Hut. It diverges right (east) from the Crawford Path 1.7 mi. from US 302, climbs the ridge at a moderate grade, passes through a fairly level area, and descends slightly to join the Webster Cliff Trail 0.1 mi. south of Mizpah Spring Hut.

Mizpah Cutoff (map 6:G8)

Distance from Crawford Path
   to Mizpah Spring Hut: 0.7 mi. (1.1 km.), 30 min.

Distance from US 302
   to Mizpah Spring Hut (via Crawford Path and Mizpah Cutoff): 2.4 mi. (3.9 km.), 2 hr. 10 min.

Saco Lake Trail (AMC)

This very short trail makes a loop around the east shore of Saco Lake, beginning and ending on US 302. It starts opposite the AMC Crawford Notch Hostel and ends after crossing the dam at the south end of Saco Lake. In addition to being an attractive short walk, it provides an alternative to part of the road walk between beginning points of the Crawford Path and Webster-Jackson Trail.

Saco Lake Trail (map 6:G8)

Distance from north junction with US 302
   to south junction with US 302: 0.3 mi. (0.5 km.), 10 min.

Dry River Trail (WMNF)

The Dry River Trail is the main trail from US 302 up the Dry River Valley and through Oakes Gulf to Lakes of the Clouds Hut, giving access to Mt. Washington, the Southern Peaks, and the upper portion of the Montalban Ridge. It is almost entirely within the Presidential Range–Dry River Wilderness. The first 5 mi. roughly follows the route of an old logging railroad, although the river and its tributaries have eradicated much of the old roadbed, and the relocations cut to eliminate the numerous, potentially hazardous river crossings have bypassed much of the remaining grade. The few river crossings that remain can be very difficult when water is high. The trail is somewhat rougher than most similar valley trails elsewhere in the White Mtns. Dry River shelters #1 and #2 have been removed; Dry River Shelter #3 will be removed when major maintenance is required.

The trail leaves the east side of US 302, 0.3 mi. north of the entrance to Dry River Campground and 2.6 mi. south of the Willey House site. From the highway the trail follows a wide wood road, generally northeast, for 0.5 mi. to its junction with the bed of the old logging railroad. From here the trail follows the railroad bed, enters the Wilderness Area at 0.7 mi., and leaves the railroad grade sharp left at 0.9 mi., staying on the west side of the river (the railroad crossed it). A pleasant pool lies just downstream from this point. The trail climbs over a low bluff, rejoins the roadbed, then leaves it again and climbs over a higher bluff, where there is a restricted but beautiful outlook up the Dry River to Mt. Washington, Mt. Monroe, and the headwall of Oakes Gulf. At 1.7 mi. the trail crosses the Dry River on a suspension bridge, and continues up the east bank, occasionally using portions of the old railroad grade. At 2.9 mi. it turns sharp right off the railroad grade where the Mount Clinton Trail diverges left to ascend to Mizpah Spring Hut. At 4.2 mi. it makes a sharp turn away from the river, then turns left and continues along the bank at a higher level. At 4.9 mi. the trail crosses Isolation Brook, turns right along the bank, and in 60 yd. the Isolation Trail diverges right.

The Dry River Trail continues straight along the high river bank and passes a cleared outlook over the river; at 5.2 mi. the Mount Eisenhower Trail diverges sharp left from the Dry River Trail and descends the steep bank to cross the river. The Dry River Trail continues along the east bank, passing at 5.4 mi. a side path (sign) that leads down left 40 yd. to the attractive pool at the foot of Dry River Falls. The top of the falls, with an interesting pothole, can also be reached from here. At 5.6 mi. the trail crosses the river to the west side; the crossing is normally fairly easy, but could be a problem at high water. At 6.3 mi. Dry River Shelter #3 is passed. In another 60 yd. the trail crosses a major tributary of Dry River at the confluence, and continues along the bank of the main stream, gradually rising higher above the river.

At 7.4 mi. the trail begins to swing away from the river, which has been at least audible to this point, and gradually climbs into Oakes Gulf. After it crosses a small ridge and descends sharply on the other side, views begin to appear, although the trail remains well sheltered in the scrub. At 8.7 mi. there is a good outlook perch just to the right of the trail. Then the trail climbs out of the scrub, turns left and crosses a small brook at a right angle. At 9.1 mi. the trail turns sharp right from the gully it formerly ascended, where signs forbid public entry into the area formerly crossed by the trail. (The closed area is the habitat of an endangered plant species.) The trail continues to climb, passing the Wilderness Area boundary sign in a patch of scrub, and reaches the height-of-land on the southwest ridge of Mt. Washington at 9.4 mi. It then descends to the larger of the Lakes of the Clouds, follows its south edge, and ends at Lakes of the Clouds Hut.

Dry River Trail (map 6:H8–F9)

Distances from US 302

> *to* suspension bridge: 1.7 mi., 1 hr. 5 min.
> *to* Mount Clinton Trail: 2.9 mi., 1 hr. 50 min.
> *to* Isolation Trail: 4.9 mi., 3 hr. 15 min.
> *to* Mount Eisenhower Trail: 5.2 mi., 3 hr. 25 min.
> *to* Dry River Shelter #3: 6.3 mi., 4 hr. 15 min.
> *to* Lakes of the Clouds Hut: 9.6 mi. (15.5 km.), 7 hr.

Mount Clinton Trail (WMNF)

This trail connects the lower part of the Dry River to Mizpah Hut and the southern part of the Southern Peaks. This trail is almost entirely within the Presidential Range–Dry River Wilderness. *Caution:* The crossing of Dry River near its junction with the Dry River Trail can vary from an easy skip over the stones to a waist-high ford in a torrent, and there may be no safe way across.

The trail diverges left from the Dry River Trail 2.9 mi. from US 302, and immediately crosses the Dry River. On the west side of the river it follows a short stretch of old railroad grade, then swings left up the bank of a major tributary, following an old logging road at a moderate grade much of the way. At 0.5 mi. the trail crosses this brook for the first of seven times, and scrambles up a washed-out area on the other bank. At 1.2 mi. the trail turns sharp left off the road and descends to the brook, crosses at a ledgy spot, and soon regains the road on the other side. It follows close to the brook, crossing many tributaries as well as the main brook, to the seventh crossing at 1.8 mi. Above an eroded section where a small brook has taken over the road, walking on the old road becomes very pleasant, and the Dry River Cutoff enters on the right at 2.5 mi. From here the trail ascends past a large boulder to the Wilderness Area boundary at 2.9 mi., and soon enters the clearing of Mizpah Spring Hut, where it joins the Webster Cliff Trail.

Mount Clinton Trail (map 6:G8)
Distances from Dry River Trail
    to Dry River Cutoff: 2.5 mi., 2 hr.
    to Mizpah Spring Hut: 3.0 mi. (4.8 km.), 2 hr. 25 min.

Mount Eisenhower Trail (WMNF)
This trail connects the middle part of the Dry River Valley to the Crawford Path at the Eisenhower-Franklin Col. Its grades are mostly easy to moderate and it extends above treeline for just a short distance on the ridge top. This trail is almost entirely within the Presidential Range–Dry River Wilderness.

The trail diverges left from the Dry River Trail about 5.2 mi. from US 302, and descends steeply on a former route of the Dry River Trail through an area with many side paths; take care to stay on the proper trail. The trail crosses Dry River (may be difficult or impassable at high water), and follows the bank downstream. At 0.2 mi. it joins its former route and bears right up a rather steep logging road. The Dry River Cutoff diverges left at 0.3 mi., and soon the grade eases. The Mount Eisenhower Trail generally leads north, keeping a bit to the west of the crest of the long ridge that runs south from a point midway between Mts. Franklin and Eisenhower. At 1.3 mi. it passes through a blowdown patch with views of Mt. Pierce, and from here on there are occasional views to the west from the edge of the ravine. At 1.8 mi. it turns sharp right, then left, and soon ascends more steeply for a while. At 2.4 mi. the trail finally gains the crest of the ridge, and winds among rocks and scrub, passing the Wilderness Area boundary 50 yd. before reaching the Crawford Path, 0.2 mi. north of the north end of the Mount Eisenhower Loop in the Eisenhower-Franklin Col.

Mount Eisenhower Trail (map 6:G8)
Distances from Dry River Trail
>   to Dry River Cutoff: 0.3 mi., 15 min.
>   to Crawford Path: 2.7 mi. (4.3 km.), 2 hr. 20 min.

Dry River Cutoff (AMC)

This trail connects the middle part of the Dry River Valley to Mizpah Spring Hut and the southern section of the Southern Peaks. Grades are mostly easy with some moderate sections. This trail is entirely within the Presidential Range–Dry River Wilderness.

The trail diverges left from the Mount Eisenhower Trail 0.3 mi. from the latter trail's junction with the Dry River Trail. In 0.1 mi. it crosses a substantial brook after a slight descent, then turns sharp left and climbs the bank, crosses a tributary, then swings back and climbs above the bank of the tributary. It crosses several branches of the tributary and gains the height-of-land on the southeast ridge of Mt. Pierce at 1.3 mi., then runs almost on the level to its junction with the Mount Clinton Trail at 1.7

mi. Mizpah Spring Hut is 0.5 mi. to the right from this junction via the Mount Clinton Trail.

Dry River Cutoff (map 6:G8)
Distance from Mount Eisenhower Trail
   to Mount Clinton Trail: 1.7 mi. (2.8 km.), 1 hr. 15 min.

Davis Path (AMC)
The Davis Path, constructed by Nathaniel P. T. Davis in 1844, was the third bridle path leading up Mt. Washington. It was in use until 1853 or 1854, but soon after became impassable, and eventually went out of existence until it was reopened as a foot trail in 1910. The sections leading up Mt. Crawford and Stairs Mtn. give some idea of the magnitude of the task Davis performed. The resolution that enabled Davis to push forward with this apparently hopeless task was the inspiration for the naming of Mt. Resolution. The trail lies almost entirely within the Presidential Range–Dry River Wilderness.

This path leaves US 302 on the west side of the Saco River at a paved parking lot near the Notchland Inn, 5.6 mi. south of the Willey House site in Crawford Notch State Park. It follows the bank of the river about 200 yd. upstream to the suspension footbridge (Bemis Bridge). Beyond the east end of the bridge, the trail passes through private land. It continues straight east across an overgrown field near a camp, then turns left into a path along a power line, crossing a small brook and turning right along its bank. Soon the path reaches a dry brook and turns east, entering the woods on a logging road along the brook bed, and then crosses the brook at a point where there may be running water upstream, soon recrosses it, and begins to climb away from it, shortly entering the WMNF and the Wilderness area. At 0.9 mi. the trail turns sharp right and soon enters the old, carefully graded bridle path and begins to ascend the steep ridge between Mt. Crawford and Mt. Hope by zigzags. Attaining the crest at 1.9 mi., the Davis Path follows this ridge north, mounting over bare ledges with good outlooks, particularly to Carrigain and Tripyramid.

At 2.2 mi. from US 302, at the foot of a large, sloping ledge, a side trail diverges left and climbs 0.3 mi. to the bare, peaked summit of Mt. Crawford at 2.5 mi., from which there is a magnificent view of Crawford Notch, the Dry River Valley, and the surrounding ridges and peaks.

From this junction the path turns northeast, descends slightly to the col between the peak of Mt. Crawford and its ledgy, domelike east knob (sometimes called Crawford Dome), and resumes the ascent. It soon passes over a ledgy shoulder of Crawford Dome, with good views back to the impressive little peak of Mt. Crawford, and dips to the Crawford-Resolution Col. Leaving this col, the path runs north, rises slightly, and keeps close to the same level along the steep west side of Mt. Resolution. The Mount Parker Trail, which diverges right (east) at 3.7 mi., leads in about 0.6 mi. to open ledges near the summit of Mt. Resolution and continues to the Mount Langdon Trail and Bartlett village. Fine views can be obtained from open ledges by ascending this trail for a bit more than 0.1 mi., hikers can enjoy fine views. A trail that branches left at this junction descends steeply about 120 yd. to the AMC Resolution Shelter, an open camp with room for eight, situated on a small branch of Sleeper Brook. (WMNF policies call for removal of this shelter whenever major maintenance is required.) Ordinarily there is water just behind the shelter, but in dry seasons it may be necessary to go down the brook a short distance. In most seasons, this is the first water after the brook at the base of the climb up from the Saco Valley; in dry seasons it may be the last water available on the trail unless you descend well down one of the branches of the Isolation Trail, since all of the water sources near the ridge-crest are unreliable.

At 4.0 mi. the path passes just west of Stairs Col, which lies between Mt. Resolution and Stairs Mtn. Here the Stairs Col Trail to the Rocky Branch diverges right. The path now veers northwest, passing west of the precipitous Giant Stairs, ascending gradually along a steep mountainside, then zigzagging northeast toward the flat top of Stairs Mtn. As the path turns sharp left shortly before reaching the top of the slope, a branch trail leads right a few steps to the "Down-look," a good viewpoint at the brink of a cliff. At the top of the climb, 4.4 mi. from US 302, a branch trail leads right (southeast) 0.2 mi. past the summit to the top of the Giant Stairs, where there is an inspiring view.

The Davis Path continues down the north ridge of Stairs Mtn. for 1.0 mi., then runs east in a col for about 0.1 mi. Turning north again and crossing a small brook (watch for this turn), it passes over a small rise and descends into another col. The path next begins to ascend the long north and south ridge of Mt. Davis, keeping mostly to the west slopes. At 6.1 mi. there is a small spring on the right, and at 6.5 mi. a small brook is crossed. At 8.5 mi. a branch trail diverges right (east) 0.2 mi. to the summit of Mt. Davis, which commands perhaps the finest view on the Montalban Ridge, and one of the best in the mountains. The main path now descends to the col between Mt. Davis and Mt. Isolation, where it crosses a small brook, and then ascends Mt. Isolation. At 9.7 mi. a spur path (which is signed, but easily missed) diverges left at a ledgy spot, leading in 125 yd. to the summit of Mt. Isolation. The open summit provides magnificent views in all directions.

At 10.5 mi. the path leads past the site of the former Isolation Shelter, and at 10.6 mi. the east branch of the Isolation Trail enters right from the Rocky Branch Valley. Water can be obtained by going down the Isolation Trail to the right (east); decent water (which must be treated for drinking) may be a considerable distance down. The path continues to climb steadily, and the west branch of the Isolation Trail descends left to the Dry River Valley at 10.9 mi. The trail passes over a hump and runs through a sag at 11.5 mi., then ascends to treeline at 12.1 mi. From here the trail runs above treeline and completely exposed to the weather. At 12.5 mi. the Glen Boulder Trail joins on the right just below a small crag, and at 13.0 mi. the path passes just west of the summit of Boott Spur (5500 ft.), and the Boott Spur Trail to AMC Pinkham Notch Visitor Center diverges right (east).

Turning northwest, the path leads along the almost level ridges of Boott Spur and crosses Bigelow Lawn. At 13.6 mi. the Lawn Cutoff diverges right to Tuckerman Junction, and, 200 yd. farther on, the Camel Trail diverges left (west) to the Lakes of the Clouds Hut. At 14.0 mi. the Davis Path begins to follow the original location of the Crawford Path and crosses the Tuckerman Crossover, and in about 0.3 mi. is joined on the right by the Southside Trail. At 14.4 mi. the Davis Path enters the present Crawford Path, which climbs to the summit of Mt. Washington.

Davis Path (map 6:H8–F9)
Distances from parking area near US 302

> *to* Mt. Crawford spur path: 2.2 mi., 2 hr. 5 min.
>
> *to* Mount Parker Trail: 3.7 mi., 3 hr.
>
> *to* Stairs Col Trail: 4.0 mi., 3 hr. 10 min.
>
> *to* Giant Stairs spur path: 4.4 mi., 3 hr. 35 min.
>
> *to* Mt. Davis spur path: 8.5 mi., 6 hr.
>
> *to* Mt. Isolation spur path: 9.7 mi., 6 hr. 40 min.
>
> *to* Isolation Trail, east branch: 10.6 mi., 7 hr. 20 min.
>
> *to* Isolation Trail, west branch: 10.9 mi., 7 hr. 45 min.
>
> *to* Glen Boulder Trail: 12.5 mi., 8 hr. 55 min.
>
> *to* Boott Spur Trail: 13.0 mi., 9 hr. 20 min.
>
> *to* Lawn Cutoff: 13.6 mi., 9 hr. 35 min.
>
> *to* Crawford Path: 14.4 mi. (23.2 km.), 10 hr. 10 min.
>
> *to* Lakes of the Clouds Hut (via Camel Trail): 14.4 mi., 10 hr.

to Mt. Washington summit (via Crawford Path): 15.0
mi. (24.1 km.), 10 hr. 45 min.

Stairs Col Trail (AMC)

This trail connects the Rocky Branch Valley with Stairs
Col on the Davis Path, providing, in particular, the easiest route to the Giant Stairs. Note that there is usually
water in small streams in the upper part of this trail, but
very little on the Davis Path. This trail is almost entirely
within the Presidential Range–Dry River Wilderness.

It leaves the Rocky Branch Trail on the left opposite
the Rocky Branch Shelter #1 area, and follows an old
railroad siding 50 yd. It then turns sharp left, crosses a
swampy area, and climbs briefly to a logging road where
it enters the Dry River Wilderness Area. From here nearly to Stairs Col, the trail follows logging roads along the
ravine of Lower Stairs Brook, becoming quite steep at
1.3 mi. and crossing the headwaters of the brook at about
1.5 mi., where it enters a birch glade. The trail becomes
gradual as it approaches Stairs Col, then it crosses this
ferny pass below the cliffs of Stairs Mtn. and continues
down the west side a short distance to meet the Davis
Path. Turn right for the Giant Stairs.

Stairs Col Trail (map 6:H9)
Distance from Rocky Branch Trail
    to Davis Path junction: 1.8 mi. (2.9 km.), 1 hr. 45 min.

Rocky Branch Trail (WMNF)

The valley of the Rocky Branch of the Saco River lies
between the two longest subsidiary ridges of Mt. Washington: the Montalban Ridge to the west and the Rocky
Branch Ridge to the east. In the upper part of the valley,
the forest is still recovering from fires that swept the
slopes in 1914–16; the lack of mature trees, particularly
conifers, is evident in many areas. The northeast terminus of the trail is located at a paved parking lot on NH 16
about 5 mi. north of Jackson, just north of the highway

bridge over the Ellis River. The Jericho (south) trailhead is reached by following the Jericho Rd. (FR 27), called Rocky Branch Rd. by the USFS, which leaves US 302 just east of the bridge over the Rocky Branch, 1 mi. west of the junction of US 302 and NH 16. The Jericho Rd. is asphalt for about 1 mi., then a good gravel road for another 3.4 mi. to the beginning of the trail. There are four river crossings between the junctions with the Stairs Col Trail and the Isolation Trail, and one just beyond the Isolation Trail junction; these crossings are wide, and are difficult and possibly dangerous at high water.

At the northeast terminus, on NH 16 below Pinkham Notch, the trail leaves the north end of the parking lot (avoid a gravel road that branches left just below the parking lot) and climbs moderately on an old logging road. At about 0.5 mi. the Avalanche Brook Ski Trail enters from the left and leaves on the right at 0.7 mi. At 1.3 mi. the trail swings left away from the bank of a small brook, and continues to ascend, then turns sharp left at 1.8 mi. and follows an old, very straight road on a slight downhill grade. After about 0.5 mi. on this road, it swings gradually right and climbs moderately, following a brook part way, and reaches the Dry River Wilderness Area boundary just east of the ridge top. Passing the almost imperceptible height-of-land at 2.8 mi., the trail follows a short bypass to the left of a very wet area and runs almost level, then descends easily, with small brooks running in and out of the trail. At 3.5 mi. the trail begins to swing left, descends gradually to the Rocky Branch and follows it downstream for a short distance, then crosses it at 3.7 mi. This crossing may be very diffi- cult, and the trail can be difficult to follow from this crossing for travelers going toward NH 16, since it is poorly marked and there are well-beaten side paths to campsites; the main trail first parallels the river heading upstream and then swings gradually away from the river

on a well-defined old road. (*Note:* If you are climbing to
Mt. Isolation from NH 16, and the river is high, you can
avoid two crossings by bushwhacking upstream along
the east side of the river for 0.4 mi., since the Isolation
Trail soon crosses back to the east bank.) On the west
bank of the river at the crossing is the junction with the
Isolation Trail, which turns right (north), following the
river bank on the old railroad grade.

The Rocky Branch Trail turns left following the old
railroad grade at this junction, and passes Rocky Branch
Shelter #2 in 60 yd. (USFS Wilderness policies call for
removal of this shelter whenever major maintenance is
required.) The trail then runs generally south along the
west bank for about 2.4 mi., at times on the old railroad
grade, then follows the grade, crossing the river four
times. These crossings are difficult at high water, but it
may be practical to avoid some or all—particularly the
upstream pair, which are a bit more than 0.1 mi. apart,
while the downstream pair are 0.4 mi. apart—by bushwhacking along the west bank. Passing out of the Wilderness Area, the trail reaches a junction at 7.8 mi. with the
Stairs Col Trail on the right and a spur path 20 yd. farther
on the left that leads 60 yd. to WMNF Rocky Branch
Shelter #1 and tentsite. Continuing south along the river
on the railroad grade, the trail eventually enters a new
gravel logging road and follows it for another 0.4 mi. to
Jericho Rd., crossing the river and Otis Brook on logging
road bridges just before reaching its south terminus. In
the reverse direction, where the new road swings to the
left about 0.4 mi. from Jericho Rd., the trail continues
straight ahead on the old grade, which looks like an old
grassy road.

Rocky Branch Trail (map 6:G10–H9)
Distances from parking lot off NH 16
    to height-of-land: 2.8 mi., 2 hr. 20 min.
    to Isolation Trail: 3.7 mi., 2 hr. 50 min.

to Stairs Col Trail: 7.8 mi., 4 hr. 50 min.
to Jericho Rd.: 9.8 mi. (15.8 km.), 5 hr. 50 min.

Isolation Trail (WMNF)

This trail links the Dry River Valley (Dry River Trail), the Montalban Ridge (Davis Path), and the Rocky Branch Valley (Rocky Branch Trail). It lies entirely within the Presidential Range–Dry River Wilderness.

The trail diverges from the Rocky Branch Trail just north of Rocky Branch Shelter #2 (which will be removed when major maintenance is required), at the point where the Rocky Branch Trail turns east to cross the river. The Isolation Trail follows the river north on what is left of the old railroad grade, crossing the river at 0.4 mi. At 0.7 mi. the trail turns sharp right off the railroad grade, climbs briefly, then follows a logging road that runs high above the river. The trail crosses the river three more times; the next two are only 70 yd. apart, and so can be fairly easily avoided. The last crossing comes at 1.7 mi., after which the trail climbs easily along a tributary, reaching the Davis Path at 2.6 mi. after passing through an area of confusing side paths where the trail must be followed with care.

Coinciding with the Davis Path, it climbs steadily north for about 0.3 mi., then turns left off the Davis Path, runs level for 0.2 mi., then descends moderately southwest into the Dry River Valley. At 4.3 mi. the trail reaches a branch of the Dry River and follows its northwest bank on an old logging road disrupted by numerous small slides, then ends at the Dry River Trail, 4.9 mi. from US 302.

Isolation Trail (map 6:G9–G8)

Distances from Rocky Branch Trail
to fourth crossing of the Rocky Branch: 1.7 mi., 1 hr. 10 min.
to Davis Path, south junction: 2.6 mi., 1 hr. 50 min.
to Davis Path, north junction: 2.9 mi., 2 hr. 10 min.

to branch of Dry River: 4.3 mi., 2 hr. 50 min.

to Dry River Trail: 5.3 mi. (8.6 km.), 3 hr. 20 min.

Distances from Rocky Branch Trail at parking area on NH 16

to Isolation Trail: 3.8 mi., 2 hr. 50 min.

to Davis Path, south junction: 6.4 mi., 4 hr. 40 min.

to Mt. Isolation (via Davis Path): 7.3 mi. (11.8 km.), 5 hr. 15 min.

Mount Langdon Trail (WMNF)

This trail runs from the road on the north side of the Saco near Bartlett village to the Mt. Langdon Shelter, meeting both the Mount Parker Trail and the Mount Stanton Trail, and thus giving access to both the higher and lower sections of the Montalban Ridge. Note that this trail does not get particularly close to the summit of Mt. Langdon, which is crossed by the Mount Stanton Trail.

From the four corners of the junction of US 302 and the Bear Notch Rd. in Bartlett village, follow the road that leads north across a bridge over the Saco to an intersection at 0.4 mi. The trail begins almost straight ahead; there are two entrances that very soon converge (no sign). The trail follows a fairly recent gravel logging road, and at 0.3 mi. the path to Cave Mtn. diverges left, marked by the word "cave" painted on a rock, which is hard to see unless you are looking for it. The road gradually becomes older and less evident. The trail crosses a good-sized brook at 1.0 mi. and climbs more steadily, bearing sharp right twice as the road fades away.

The Mount Langdon Trail crosses Oak Ridge at 2.2 mi. and descends, sharply at times, to the Oak Ridge–Mt. Parker Col, where it bears right at 2.5 mi. at the junction with the Mount Parker Trail. The Mount Langdon Trail then descends gradually to the WMNF Mt. Langdon Shelter, capacity eigh, where this trail and the Mount Stanton Trail both end. Some care is required in following the trail near the shelter. Water may be found in a brook 60 yd. from the shelter on the Mount Stanton Trail, although in dry weather the brook may have to be followed downhill.

Mount Langdon Trail (map 6:H9)

Distances from the road on the north bank of the Saco River

    to Mount Parker Trail: 2.5 mi., 2 hr.

    to Mt. Langdon Shelter: 2.9 mi. (4.7 km.), 2 hr. 15 min.

    to high point on Mt. Langdon (via Mount Stanton Trail): 3.7 mi., 2 hr. 55 min.

Mount Parker Trail (SSOC)

This pleasant, rugged, lightly used trail passes several excellent viewpoints, and provides access from Bartlett to Mt. Parker, Mt. Resolution, the Stairs Col area, and the upper Montalban Ridge. It is almost entirely within the Presidential–Dry River Wilderness. *Caution:* There is no reliable water.

This trail begins in the Oak Ridge–Mt. Parker Col 2.5 mi. from Bartlett, continuing straight ahead to the north where the Mt. Langdon Trail turns right (east). It climbs moderately with many switchbacks through beech and oak woods, descends briefly, and then continues its winding ascent to the open summit of Mt. Parker at 1.4 mi., where there are excellent views.

Continuing north, the trail follows the long ridge between Mt. Parker and Mt. Resolution and passes over three bumps, alternating between spruce woods and semi-open ledges with restricted views. It then runs along the west and south slopes of the remainder of the ridge until it reaches the southeast corner of Mt. Resolution, where it turns sharp right and zigzags up to the col between the main summit ridge and a southerly knob at 3.2 mi. Here a branch trail leads left 0.1 mi. to this open knob, where there are excellent views. Beyond this junction the trail winds along the flat top of Mt. Resolution until it reaches a large cairn on an open ledge with excellent views at 3.8 mi. The true summit is probably just above this cairn; there is another knob of almost equal elevation about 0.1 mi. east-northeast, with excellent views north but no path. From the cairn the trail descends into a gully where it crosses a small, sluggish brook (water unreliable), then heads down northwest over fine open ledges and finally drops steeply to the Davis Path, opposite the branch trail to Resolution Shelter.

Mount Parker Trail (map 6:H9)
Distances from Mount Langdon Trail

to summit of Mt. Parker: 1.4 mi., 1 hr. 15 min.

to branch trail to open southerly knob: 3.2 mi., 2 hr. 25 min.

to high point on Mt. Resolution: 3.8 mi., 2 hr. 50 min.

to Davis Path junction: 4.3 mi. (6.8 km.), 3 hr.

Mount Stanton Trail (SSOC)

This trail passes over the low eastern summits of the Montalban Ridge, and affords many views from scattered ledges. To reach the east trailhead (the west trailhead is at Mt. Langdon Shelter), leave the north side of US 302 1.8 mi. west of its junction with NH 16 in Glen and a short distance east of the bridge over the Saco River. Follow a paved road west about 0.2 mi., then bear right on Oak Ridge Drive, and almost immediately turn sharp right on Hemlock Drive. At a crossroads 0.6 mi. from US 302 turn right, and trailhead is on the left side of this road (limited parking). This is an area of new home construction; the turns at road junctions are well marked with unobtrusive signs.

In 100 yd. the trail passes to the right of a red-blazed WMNF boundary corner, and at 0.3 mi. turns sharp left with yellow blazes where the red-blazed WMNF boundary continues straight ahead. The trail climbs steeply at times, but there are gentler sections, and the outlooks from White's Ledge begin at about 0.8 mi. The trail climbs steeply again after passing a large boulder on the right of the trail, and at 1.2 mi. it turns sharp right on a ledge as climbing becomes easier. At 1.4 mi. it passes within 15 yd. of the summit of Mt. Stanton. The summit area is covered with a fine stand of red (Norway) pines, and there are good views from nearby scattered ledges.

The trail descends to the Stanton-Pickering col, ascends steadily, crosses a ledgy ridge and descends slightly, then climbs again and at 2.1 mi. passes 30 yd. to the right of the summit of Mt. Pickering. It then leads to ledges on a slightly lower knob, where there are excellent views. The trail descends to a minor col, then crosses over several interesting small humps sometimes called the Crippies. These humps have scattered outlook ledges, and the best view is from the fourth and last Crippie, which is crossed at 3.3 mi.

After the last Crippie the trail may be less well cleared and harder to follow. It descends somewhat along the north side of the ridge toward Mt. Langdon, then climbs north moderately with a few steep pitches, passing an outlook to Carter Dome, Carter Notch, and Wildcat Mtn. At 4.5 mi. the trail passes about 35 yd. to the right of the summit of Mt. Langdon, which is wooded and viewless, then descends easily to a gravel slope, turns right, and continues downward to a brook that is crossed 60 yd. east of Mt. Langdon Shelter, where the Mount Stanton Trail ends.

Mount Stanton Trail (map 6:H10–H9)
Distances from the trailhead off Hemlock Drive
> *to* high point on Mt. Stanton: 1.4 mi., 1 hr. 15 min.
> *to* high point on Mt. Pickering: 2.1 mi., 1 hr. 50 min.
> *to* fourth Crippie: 3.3 mi., 2 hr. 35 min.
> *to* high point on Mt. Langdon: 4.5 mi., 3 hr. 35 min.

to Mount Langdon Trail at Mt. Langdon Shelter: 5.3
  mi. (8.5 km.), 4 hr.

Cave Mountain Path

This mountain, remarkable for the shallow cave near its
wooded summit, is easily reached from Bartlett by following the Mount Langdon Trail for 0.3 mi. to a path that
forks left, signed only by a rock with the word "cave"
painted on it (watch for it carefully). In 0.3 mi. this branch
trail leads up a steep gravel slope to the cave. A faint trail
to the right of the cave leads, after a short scramble, to the
top of the cliff in which the cave is located, where there is
a good view of Bartlett and the Saco River.

Cave Mountain Path (map 6:H9)
Distances from Mount Langdon Trail
  to cave: 0.3 mi., 20 min.
  to outlook: 0.4 mi., 25 min.

Winniweta Falls Trail (WMNF)

This trail provides easy access to an interesting waterfall.
It leaves the west side of NH 16, 3 mi. north of the bridge
over the Ellis River in Jackson. It fords the wide bed of
the Ellis River, often a rather shallow stream but difficult
to cross in moderate flow and potentially dangerous at
high water. On the far bank, it bears right onto a ski trail
(sign, reading "Ellis River Trail"), and follows a logging
road up the north bank of Miles Brook, from which the
Ellis River Ski Trail soon diverges. At an arrow, the path
turns left from the road and soon reaches the falls.

Winniweta Falls Trail (map 6:G10)
Distance from NH 16
  to Winniweta Falls: 0.9 mi. (1.4 km.), 40 min.

Iron Mountain Trail (JCC)

The summit of this mountain is wooded, with somewhat
restricted views, but an outlook on the north side and the

south cliffs provide very attractive views for relatively little effort. To the east of the cliffs are some abandoned iron mines. A prominent easterly ridge, on which there was once a trail, descends almost to NH 16, ending in a cliff called Duck's Head, near the Iron Mountain House. Reach the trail by leaving NH 16 in Jackson, next to the golf links and nearly opposite the red covered bridge, and following a road prominently signed Green Hill Rd. At 1.2 mi. the pavement ends, and at 1.4 mi. FR 325 bears right. Bear left here; the road (FR 119) becomes fairly steep, a bit rough, and very narrow (be prepared to back up if required for other cars to pass). At 2.7 mi. from NH 16, swing left at a sign as the road ahead becomes very poor, and park in a small designated field behind the house of the Hayes Farm (now a summer residence).

The trail crosses the field, passes through a narrow band of trees, and crosses a second field, entering the woods at the top edge. The path climbs steadily and the footing is good. At 0.6 mi. there is a side path right 20 yd. to a fine outlook up the Rocky Branch Valley to Mt. Washington, with the Southern Presidentials visible over the Montalban Ridge. The main trail continues to the summit at 0.8 mi., where there are remains of the former fire tower and a rickety wooden tower. The trail descends steadily along a rocky ridge, dropping about 300 ft., then crosses several humps in thick woods. At 1.5 mi. a faintly marked side path descends left 0.2 mi. and 250 ft. to the old mines (tailings, water-filled shaft, tunnel), while the main trail ascends in a short distance to ledges and the edge of the cliffs, where there are wide views to the south and west.

Iron Mountain Trail (map 6:H10)

Distances from Hayes Farm

   to summit of Iron Mtn.: 0.8 mi., 50 min.
   to south cliffs: 1.6 mi. (2.6 km.), 1 hr. 15 min.

SECTION 2
The Northern Peaks and the Great Gulf

This section covers the high peaks of Mt. Washington's massive northern ridge, which curves north and then northeast like a great arm embracing the magnificent glacial cirque called the Great Gulf. This ridge runs for 5 mi. with only slight dips below the 5000 ft. elevation, and each of the three main peaks rises at least 500 ft. above the cols. The AMC Mt. Washington Range map (map 6) covers the entire area. The RMC publishes a map of the Randolph Valley and Northern Peaks, printed on plastic-coated paper, and a guidebook, *Randolph Paths*, which you can obtain from the Randolph Mountain Club (RMC), Randolph NH 03570. The map covers the dense trail network on the northern slope of this region with much greater detail and clarity than map 6, and it is highly recommended for people who want to explore some of the attractive, less crowded paths in this section. The RMC maintains a considerable number of paths on the Northern Peaks; many of these paths are used very lightly and are wilder and rougher than most trails in the WMNF. They are also less plainly marked, cleared, and trampled out, so they may not be suitable for the inexperienced; but adventurous hikers with good trail-following skills will find them a delightful alternative to the heavily used principal routes on the range. Many of these paths also provide opportunities for less strenuous, varied walks to the many waterfalls and other interesting places on the lower slopes of the range.

Caution: The peaks and higher ridges of this range are nearly as exposed to the elements as Mt. Washington, and should be treated with the same degree of respect and caution. Severe wintry storms can occur at any time of the year, and many hikers have died in this area from failure to observe the basic principles of safety. In addition, all of the major peaks are strenuous climbs by even the easiest routes. The distances quoted may not seem long to a novice, but there is only one route to a major peak, the Caps Ridge Trail to Mt. Jefferson, that involves less than 3000 ft. of climbing, and that route is not at all easy; although it is relatively short, it is also quite steep with numerous scrambles on ledges that a person unfamiliar with mountain trails might find daunting. Most routes to the summits involve 4000 to 4500 ft. of climbing, roughly equal to the ascent of Mt. Washington, due to the lower elevations of the major trailheads. The substantial amount of effort required to climb these peaks, together with the threat of sudden and violent storms, should make the danger of overextending yourself quite apparent.

The first trail to be built on the Northern Peaks was probably the Stillings Path, cut about 1852 primarily for transporting building materials from Randolph to the summit of Mt. Washington; in 1860 or 1861 a partial trail was made over the peaks to Mt. Washington, of which some sections still exist. Lowe's Path was cut in 1875–1876, the branch path through King Ravine was made in 1876, and the Osgood Path was opened in 1878. Many trails were constructed between 1878 and the beginning of lumbering in about 1902, but this network was greatly damaged by lumbering, and some trails were obliterated. The more important ones have since been restored.

In this section, the Appalachian Trail follows the Gulfside Trail from its junction with the Trinity Heights Connector near the summit of Mt. Washington to Madison Hut. It then follows the Osgood Trail over Mt. Madison and down into the Great Gulf, proceeding to the Auto Rd. via the Osgood Cutoff, Great Gulf Trail (for a very short distance), and Madison Gulf Trail.

GEOGRAPHY

The upper part of the mass of the Northern Peaks is covered with rock fragments; above 5000 ft. there are no trees and little scrub. The southeast side of the range is dominated by the Great Gulf and the two smaller cirques that branch off from it, Jefferson Ravine and Madison Gulf; the two Jefferson "knees," fairly prominent buttresses truncated by the Great Gulf, are the only ridges of note. Many ridges and valleys radiate from this range on the north and west sides, the most important being, from north to south: on Mt. Madison, the Osgood Ridge, Howker Ridge, Bumpus Basin, Gordon Ridge, and the ravine of Snyder Brook, which is shared with Mt. Adams; on Mt. Adams, Durand Ridge, King Ravine, Nowell Ridge, Cascade Ravine, the Israel Ridge, and Castle Ravine, which is shared with Mt. Jefferson; on Mt. Jefferson, the Castellated Ridge and the Ridge of the Caps; and an unnamed but conspicuous ridge extending westerly from Mt. Clay. The Great Gulf, Bumpus Basin, King Ravine, and Castle Ravine are glacial cirques, a landform that results when a glacier excavates a typical V-shaped brook valley with a narrow floor and fairly uniform slopes, turning it into the classic U-shaped cirque with its broad, fairly flat floor and almost vertical walls.

The Great Gulf is the largest cirque in the White Mtns., lying between Mt. Washington and the Northern Peaks and drained by the West Branch of the Peabody River. The headwall, bounded on the south by the slopes of Mt. Washington and on the west by the summit ridge of Mt. Clay, rises from 1100 to 1600 ft. above a bowl-shaped valley enclosed by steep walls that extend east for about 3.5 mi. The gulf then continues as a more open valley about 1.5 mi. farther east. The glacial action that formed the Great Gulf and its tributary gulfs is believed to have occurred mainly prior to the most recent ice age. The views from its walls and from points on its floor are among the best in New England, and steep slopes and abundant water result in a great number of cascades. The first recorded observation of the Great Gulf was by Darby Field in 1642, and the name probably had its origin in 1823 in a casual statement of Ethan Allen Crawford, who, having lost his way in cloudy weather, came to "the edge of a great gulf." J. W. Robbins, a botanist, visited the region in 1829, but it was little known until Benjamin F. Osgood blazed the first trail, from the Osgood Trail to the headwall, in 1881.

Mt. Clay (5541 ft.) is the first peak on the ridge north of Mt. Washington. Strictly speaking it is only a shoulder, comparable to Boott Spur on the southeast ridge of its great neighbor, since it rises barely 150 ft. above the connecting ridge. But it offers superb views from the cliffs that drop away practically at the summit to form the west side of the Great Gulf headwall.

Mt. Jefferson (5712 ft.) has three summits a short distance apart, in line northwest and southeast, with the highest in the middle. Perhaps the most striking view is down the Great Gulf with the Carter Range beyond; the best views of the gulf are obtained from points on the Gulfside Trail to the north of the summit. There are other fine views, most notably those to Mt. Washington and the other Northern Peaks, to the Fabyan Plain on the southwest, and down the broad valley of the Israel on the northwest. The Castellated Ridge, sharpest and most salient of the White Mtn. ridges, extends northwest, forming the southwest wall of Castle Ravine. The view of the "Castles" from US 2 near the village of Bowman is unforgettable. The Ridge of the Caps, similar in formation but less striking, extends to the west. Jefferson's "knees," the two eastern ridges that are cut off abruptly by the Great Gulf, have precipitous wooded slopes and gently sloping tops. South of the peak of Mt. Jefferson lies a smooth, grassy plateau called Monticello Lawn

(5400 ft.). In addition to its share of the Great Gulf proper, Jefferson's slopes are cut by two other prominent glacial cirques: Jefferson Ravine, a branch of the Great Gulf northeast of the mountain, and Castle Ravine, drained by a branch of Israel River, on the north. The boundary between these two cirques is the narrow section of the main Northern Presidential ridge that runs from Jefferson through Edmands Col to Mt. Adams.

Mt. Adams (5774 ft.), second highest of the New England summits, has a greater variety of interesting features than any other New England mountain except Katahdin: its sharp, clean-cut profile; its large area above treeline; its inspiring views, the finest being across the Great Gulf to Mts. Washington, Jefferson, and Clay; its great northern ridges, Durand sharp and narrow, Nowell massive and broad-spreading; its four glacial cirques, King Ravine and the three that it shares with its neighbors, the Great Gulf, Madison Gulf, and Castle Ravine. Mt. Adams also has several lesser summits and crags, of which the two most prominent are Mt. Sam Adams (5594 ft.), a rather flat mass to the west, and Mt. Quincy Adams (5410 ft.), a sharp, narrow shark-fin ridge to the north.

Mt. Madison (5367 ft.) is the farthest northeast of the high peaks of the Presidential Range, remarkable for the great drop of over 4000 ft. to the river valleys east and northeast from its summit. The drop to the Androscoggin at Gorham (4580 ft. in about 6.5 mi.) is probably the closest approach in New England, except at Katahdin, of a major river to a high mountain. The views south and southwest to the neighboring Presidential peaks and into the Great Gulf are excellent. The distant view is cut off in these directions, though Chocorua is visible.

Edmands Col (4938 ft.), named for pioneer trailmaker J. Rayner Edmands, lies between Mt. Adams and Mt. Jefferson, and Sphinx Col (4959 ft.) lies between Mt. Jefferson and Mt. Clay. The col between Mt. Adams and

Mt. Madison has an elevation of about 4890 ft., so there is a range of only about 70 ft. between the lowest and highest of the three major cols on this ridge. In the unnamed Adams-Madison Col lies Star Lake, a small, shallow body of water among jagged rocks, with impressive views, particularly up to Mt. Madison and Mt. Quincy Adams.

Pine Mtn. (2410 ft.) is a small peak lying to the northeast, between Mt. Madison and the great bend of the Androscoggin River at Gorham. Though low compared to its lofty neighbors, it is a rugged mountain with a fine cliff on the southeast side, and offers magnificent, easily attained views of its Northern Presidential neighbors and of the mountains and river valleys to the north and east.

HUTS, SHELTERS, AND CAMPING
HUTS
Madison Hut (AMC)
In 1888, at Madison Spring (4800 ft.), a little north of the Adams–Madison Col, the AMC built a stone hut that was later demolished. The present hut, rebuilt and improved after a fire in 1940, accommodates fifty guests on a coed basis and is open to the public from June to mid-September. It is located 6.0 mi. from the summit of Mt. Washington via the Gulfside Trail, and 6.8 mi. from Lakes of the Clouds Hut via the Gulfside Trail, Westside Trail, and Crawford Path. In bad weather the best approach (or exit) is via the Valley Way, which is sheltered to within a short distance of the hut. Nearby points of interest include Star Lake and the Parapet, a crag overlooking Madison Gulf.

For current information contact ANC Reservations, Pinkham Notch Visitor Center, Box 298, Gorham NH 03581 (603-466-2727).

CAMPING

Great Gulf Wilderness

In this area, camping and fires are prohibited above tree-line (where trees are less than 8 ft. tall), except in winter, where snow cover is at least two feet (and then never on frozen bodies of water) or within 200 ft. of any trail except at designated sites, and within one-quarter mile of Spaulding Lake. Camping is prohibited on the Great Gulf Trail south of its junction with the Sphinx Trail. No more than ten persons may use any particular campsite at any one time, and hiking groups may not exceed ten persons. All former shelters have been removed.

Restricted Use Areas

The WMNF has established a number of Restricted Use Areas (RUAs) where camping and wood or charcoal fires are prohibited from May 1 to November 1. The specific areas are under continual review, and areas are added to or subtracted from the list in order to provide the greatest amount of protection to areas subject to damage by excessive camping, while imposing the lowest level of restrictions possible. A general list of RUAs follows, but hikers should obtain a map of current RUAs from the WMNF.

(1) Camping is not permitted above treeline (where trees are less than 8 ft. tall) except in winter, and even then it is allowed only on sites that are covered with at least two feet of snow and not located on frozen bodies of water. Small signs mark the points where the restricted area begins on most trails, but the absence of such signs should not be construed as proof of the legality of a site.

(2) No camping is permitted within one-quarter mile of most facilities such as huts, cabins, shelters, or tentsites, except at the facility itself.

(3) No camping is permitted within 200 ft. of certain trails. In 1991, designated trails included the Valley Way south of its junction with the Scar Trail.

Established Trailside Campsites

The Log Cabin (RMC), first built about 1890, and totally rebuilt in 1985, is located at a spring at 3300 ft. altitude, beside Lowe's Path at the junction with the Cabin-Cascades Trail. The cabin is partially enclosed, and is open to the public. A fee is charged, and there is room for about ten guests. The cabin has no stove, and no wood fires are permitted in the area. Guests are required to leave the cabin clean and carry out all trash.

The Perch (RMC) is an open log shelter located at about 4300 ft. on the Perch Path between the Randolph Path and Israel Ridge Path, but much closer to the former. It is open to the public and accommodates eight. There are also four tent platforms at the site; the caretaker at Gray Knob often visits to collect the overnight fee.

Crag Camp (RMC) is situated at the edge of King Ravine near the Spur Trail at about 4200 ft. It is open to the public. A fee is charged. It is an enclosed cabin, supplied with cooking utensils and a gas stove in the summer, with room for about fourteen guests. A caretaker maintains it during July and August. Wood fires are not allowed in the area. Hikers are required to limit groups to ten and stays to two nights. All trash must be carried out.

Gray Knob (Town of Randolph and RMC) is an enclosed, winterized cabin on Gray Knob Trail at its junction with Hincks Trail, near Lowe's Path, at about 4400 ft. It is open to the public. A fee is charged. Gray Knob has room for twelve guests and is supplied with a gas stove and cooking utensils in the summer. There is a caretaker year round. Rules are the same as for Crag Camp.

These RMC shelters are all Restricted Use Areas, and no camping is allowed within one-quarter mile except at the shelters and tent platforms. Fees should be mailed to the Randolph Mountain Club, Randolph NH 03570, if they are not collected by the caretakers. Any infraction of rules or acts of vandalism should be reported to the above address.

Osgood Campsite (WMNF) is located near the junction of the Osgood Trail and Osgood Cutoff (which is on the Appalachian Trail).

ACCESS ROADS AND PARKING

Important access roads in this section are the Pinkham B Rd. (also called Dolly Copp Rd.), Jefferson Notch Rd., and the Base Rd. Pinkham B Rd. runs from US 2 at the west foot of the hill between Gorham and Randolph, over the notch between Pine Mtn. and Mt. Madison, to NH 16 about 4.5 mi. south of Gorham. Dolly Copp Campground is located on this road near NH 16. Jefferson Notch Rd. runs from the Valley Rd. in Jefferson (which in turn runs between US 2 and NH 115), through the notch between Mt. Jefferson and the Dartmouth Range, to the Base Rd., which runs from US 302 at Bretton Woods to the Base Station of the Cog Railway at Marshfield. Directly across the Base Rd. from Jefferson Notch Rd. is the Mt. Clinton Rd., which runs south to the Crawford House site. Jefferson Notch Rd., a good gravel road, is open in summer and early fall, but since it reaches the highest point of any public through road in NH (3008 ft. at Jefferson Notch), snow and mud disappear late in the spring and ice returns early. Drive with care, since the road is winding and narrow in places, and watch for logging trucks. The southern half is in better condition than the north, which is sound but very rough. The high point in the notch is about 5.5 mi. from the Valley Rd. on the north, and 3.4 mi. from the Base Rd. on the south.

The most important parking areas are at Pinkham Notch Visitor Center; at a newly constructed area on NH 16 1.5 mi. south of Dolly Copp Campground; at Randolph East, on Pinkham B (Dolly Copp) Rd. near US 2; at Appalachia, on US 2 about 1 mi. west of Pinkham B Rd.; at Lowe's Store on US 2 (nominal fee charged); and at Bowman, on US 2 about 1 mi. west of Lowe's Store. (Randolph East, Appalachia, and Bowman owe their names and locations to their former status as stations on the railroad line.) The highest points from which to climb the Northern Peaks, not including the summit of Mt. Washington, are Jefferson Notch Rd. at the Caps Ridge Trail (3008 ft.); the parking lot on the Base Rd., 1.1 mi. east of the Jefferson Notch Rd. for the Jewell Trail (2500 ft.); and the Pinkham B Rd., also called Dolly Copp Rd., at the Pine Link (1650 ft.).

THE TRAILS

Gulfside Trail (WMNF)

This trail leads from Madison Hut to the summit of Mt. Washington. It threads the principal cols, avoiding the summits of the Northern Peaks, offering extensive, ever-changing views. Its altitudes range from about 4800 ft. close to the hut, to 6288 ft. on the summit of Mt. Washington. The name Gulfside was given by J. Rayner Edmands who, starting in 1892, located and built the greater part of the trail, sometimes following trails that had existed before. All but about 0.8 mi. of the trail was once a graded path, and parts were paved with carefully placed stones—work cut short by Edmands's death in 1910. The whole trail is part of the Appalachian Trail, except for a very short segment at the south end.

The trail is well marked with large cairns, each topped with a yellow-painted stone, and, though care must be used, it can often be followed even in dense fog. The trail is continuously exposed to the weather, and dangerously high winds and low temperatures may occur with little warning at any season of the year. If such storms threaten serious trouble on the Gulfside Trail, do not attempt to ascend the Mt. Washington summit cone, where conditions are usually far worse. If you are not close to the huts at Madison Spring or at Lakes of the Clouds, descend into one of the ravines on a trail if possible, or without trail if necessary. A night of discomfort in the woods is better than exposure on the heights, which may prove fatal. Slopes on the Great Gulf (southeast) side are more sheltered, but generally steeper and farther from highways. It is particularly important not to head toward Edmands Col in deteriorating conditions; there is no easy trail out in bad weather, and the emergency refuge was removed in 1982. There is no substitute for studying the map carefully and understanding the hazards and options before setting out on the ridge.

The following description of the path is in the southbound direction (toward Mt. Washington). See below for a description of the path in the reverse direction.

Part I. Madison Hut–Edmands Col

The trail begins about 30 yd. from Madison Hut at a junction with the Valley Way and Star Lake Trail, leads southwest through a patch of scrub, then aims to the right (north) of Mt. Quincy Adams and ascends its steep, open north slope. At the top of this slope, on the high plateau between King Ravine and Mt. Quincy Adams, it is joined from the right by the Air Line, which has just been joined by the King Ravine Trail. Here there are striking views back to Mt. Madison, and into King Ravine at the Gateway a short distance down on the right. The Gulfside and Air Line coincide for less than 100 yd., then the Air Line branches left toward the summit of Mt. Adams. Carefully placed stones pave much of the Gulfside Trail for about the next 0.5 mi. It rises moderately southwest, then steepens, and at 0.9 mi. from the hut reaches a grassy lawn in the saddle (5520 ft.) between Mt. Adams and Mt. Sam Adams. Here several trails intersect at a spot called Thunderstorm Junction, where there is a massive cairn that once stood about 10 ft. high. Entering the junction on the right is the Great Gully Trail, coming up across the slope from the southwest corner of King Ravine. Here, also, the Gulfside is crossed by Lowe's Path, ascending from Lowe's Store on US 2 to the summit of Mt. Adams. About 100 yd. down Lowe's Path, the Spur Trail branches right for Crag Camp. The summit of Mt. Adams is about 0.3 mi. from the junction (left), via Lowe's Path; a round trip to the summit requires about 25 min.

An unofficial trail, known as the White Trail because its cairns are topped with white rocks, runs from Thunderstorm Junction to the summit of Mt. Sam Adams, and then follows its south ridge to the Gulfside at the point where the Israel Ridge Path enters from US 2. Sam Adams is an interesting viewpoint, well worth a visit, but in good weather the cairned path is not necessary, since the route over the rocks between Sam Adams and either starting point is quite plain. In addition, the Sam Adams ridge is much more exposed to the wind and weather than the Gulfside, and the cairns are neither prominent enough nor close enough together to be followed reliably when visibility is poor.

Continuing southwest from Thunderstorm Junction and beginning to descend, the Gulfside Trail passes a junction on the left with the Israel Ridge Path, which ascends a short distance to Lowe's Path and then to Mt. Adams. For about 0.5 mi. the Gulfside Trail and Israel Ridge Path coincide, passing Peabody Spring (unreliable water source) just to the right in a small, grassy flat; more reliable water is located just beyond, at the base of a conspicuous boulder a bit to the left of the path. Soon the trail climbs easily across a small ridge, where the Israel

Ridge Path diverges right, at 1.5 mi. from Madison Hut. A small pool called Storm Lake lies near this junction in wet weather. The Gulfside bears left toward the edge of Jefferson Ravine, and, always leading toward Mt. Jefferson, descends southwest along the narrow ridge that divides Jefferson Ravine from Castle Ravine, near the edge of the southeast cliffs, from which there are fine views into the Great Gulf. This part of the Gulfside was never graded. The trail reaches Edmands Col at 2.2 mi. from the hut, with 3.8 mi. to go to Mt. Washington.

At Edmands Col (4930 ft.) is a bronze tablet in memory of J. Rayner Edmands, who made most of the graded paths on the Northern Peaks. Gulfside Spring (reliable) is 30 yd. south of the col, and Spaulding Spring (reliable) is about 0.2 mi. north near the Castle Ravine Trail. The emergency shelter once located at this col has been dismantled, and none of the trails leaving this area is a particularly satisfactory escape route in bad weather. From the col, the Edmands Col Cutoff leads south, entering scrub almost immediately, affording the quickest route to this rough form of shelter in dangerous weather; it then continues about 0.5 mi. to the Six Husbands Trail leading down to the Great Gulf, but it is very rough, and the Six Husbands Trail is fairly difficult to descend, making it a far less than ideal escape route unless the severity of the weather leaves no choice. The Randolph Path leads north into the Randolph valley, running above treeline with great exposure to northwest winds for over 0.5 mi.; branching from this path about 0.1 mi. north of the col are the Cornice, a very rough trail leading west entirely above treeline to the Castle Trail, and the Castle Ravine Trail, which descends steeply over very loose talus and may be hard to follow, but is nevertheless probably the fastest, safest route to civilization unless it is too dangerous to cross through Edmands Col.

Part II. Edmands Col–Sphinx Col

South of Edmands Col the Gulfside Trail ascends steeply over rough rocks, with Jefferson Ravine on the left. It passes flat-topped Dingmaul Rock, from which there is a good view down the ravine, with Mt. Adams on the left. About 100 yd. beyond, the Mount Jefferson Loop branches right and leads 0.4 mi. to the summit of Mt. Jefferson (5715 ft.). The views from the summit are excellent, and the Loop is only slightly longer than the parallel section of the Gulfside, though it requires about 300 ft. of extra climbing and about 10 min. more hiking time.

The path now rises less steeply. It crosses the Six Husbands Trail and soon reaches its greatest height on Mt. Jefferson, about 5400 ft. Curving southwest and descending a little, it crosses Monticello Lawn, a comparatively smooth, grassy plateau. Here the Mount Jefferson Loop rejoins the Gulfside about 0.3 mi. from the summit. A short distance beyond the edge of the lawn the Cornice enters right from the Caps Ridge Trail. The Gulfside descends to the south, and from one point there is a view of the Sphinx down the slope to the left. A few yards north of the low point in Sphinx Col, the Sphinx Trail branches left (east) into the Great Gulf through a grassy passage between ledges. Sphinx Col is 3.7 mi. from Madison Hut, with 2.3 mi. left to the summit of Mt. Washington. In bad weather, a fairly quick descent to sheltering scrub can be made via the Sphinx Trail, though once treeline is reached this trail becomes rather steep and difficult.

Part III. Sphinx Col–Mt. Washington

From Sphinx Col the path leads toward Mt. Washington, and soon the Mount Clay Loop diverges left to climb over the summits of Mt. Clay, with impressive views into the Great Gulf. This Loop adds about 300 ft. of climbing and 10 min.; the distance is about the same. The Gulfside Trail is slightly easier and passes close to a spring, but misses the best views. It bears right from the junction with the Mount Clay Loop, runs south and climbs moderately, angling up the west side of Mt. Clay. About 0.3 mi. above Sphinx Col, a loop leads to water a few steps down to the right. The side path continues about 30 yd. farther to Greenough Spring (more reliable), then rejoins the Gulfside about 100 yd. above its exit point. The Gulfside continues its moderate ascent, and the Jewell Trail from the Base Rd. enters from the right at 4.6 mi. From this junction the ridgecrest of Mt. Clay can be reached by a short scramble up the rocks without trail. The Gulfside swings southeast and soon descends slightly to the Clay-Washington col (5380 ft.), where the Mount Clay Loop rejoins it from the left. A little to the east is the edge of the Great Gulf, with fine views, especially of the east cliffs of Mt. Clay.

The path continues southeast, rising gradually on Mt. Washington. About 0.1 mi. above the col, the Westside Trail branches right, crosses the Cog Railway, and leads to the Crawford Path and Lakes of the Clouds Hut. The Gulfside continues southeast between the Cog Railway on the right and the edge of the Gulf on the left. If you lose the path, you can follow the railway to the summit. At the extreme south corner of the Gulf, the Great Gulf Trail joins the Gulfside from the left, 5.5 mi. from Madison Hut. Here the Gulfside turns sharp right, crosses the railway, and continues west to the plateau just west of the summit. Here it passes a junction with the Trinity Heights Connector, a link in the Appalachian Trail, which branches left and climbs for 0.2 mi. to the true summit of Mt. Washington. In another 0.1 mi. the Gulfside joins the Crawford Path just below (north of) the old corral, and the two trails turn left and coincide to the summit.

Gulfside Trail (map 6:F9)

Distances from Madison Hut

    to Air Line: 0.3 mi., 20 min.

    to Thunderstorm Junction: 0.9 mi., 50 min.

to Israel Ridge Path, north junction: 1.0 mi., 55 min.

to Israel Ridge Path, south junction: 1.5 mi., 1 hr. 5 min.

to Edmands Col: 2.2 mi., 1 hr. 30 min.

to to Mount Jefferson Loop, north end: 2.4 mi., 1 hr. 40 min.

to Six Husbands Trail: 2.7 mi., 1 hr. 50 min.

to Mount Jefferson Loop, south end: 3.1 mi., 2 hr. 5 min.

to Cornice: 3.2 mi., 2 hr. 10 min.

to Sphinx Trail: 3.7 mi., 2 hr. 25 min.

to Mount Clay Loop, north end: 3.8 mi., 2 hr. 30 min.

to Jewell Trail: 4.6 mi., 3 hr.

to Mount Clay Loop, south end: 4.9 mi., 3 hr. 15 min.

to Westside Trail: 5.0 mi., 3 hr. 25 min.

to Great Gulf Trail: 5.5 mi., 3 hr. 50 min.

to Trinity Heights Connector: 5.7 mi., 4 hr. 5 min.

to Crawford Path: 5.8 mi. (9.3 km.), 4 hr. 5 min.

to Mt. Washington summit (via Crawford Path): 6.0 mi. (9.7 km.), 4 hr. 20 min.

to Lakes of the Clouds Hut (via Westside Trail and Crawford Path): 6.8 mi., 4 hr. 25 min.

GULFSIDE TRAIL (WMNF) [in reverse]

Part I. Mt. Washington–Sphinx Col

Descending from the summit of Mt. Washington, coinciding with the Crawford Path, the trail is on the right (north) side of the railroad track. After passing between the buildings it leads generally northwest; avoid random side paths toward the south. Shortly it reaches its departure from the Crawford Path, just below the remains of an old corral, and turns sharp right. In 0.1 mi. it passes a junction with the Trinity Heights Connector, a link in the Appalachian Trail, which branches right and climbs for 0.2 mi. to the true summit of Mt. Washington. It then descends steadily, crossing the railroad, and at 0.5 mi., as the Gulfside turns sharp left at the extreme south corner of the Great Gulf, the Great Gulf Trail joins on the right. The Gulfside continues northwest between the Cog Railway on the left and the edge of the Gulf on the right. At 1.0 mi., the Westside Trail branches left, crosses the Cog Railway, and leads to the Crawford Path and Lakes of the Clouds Hut. The Gulfside descends gradually to the Clay-Washington Col (5380 ft.), where the Mount Clay Loop diverges right to traverse the summit of Mt. Clay, with impressive views into the Great Gulf. This Loop adds about 300 ft. of climbing and 10 min.; the distance is about the same. The Gulfside Trail is slightly easier and passes close to a spring, but misses the best views. A little to the east at this col is the edge of the Great Gulf, with fine views, especially of the east cliffs of Mt. Clay.

After a slight ascent, the Gulfside begins to angle down the west side of Mt. Clay, and the Jewell Trail from the Base Rd. enters from the left at 1.4 mi. From this junction the ridgecrest of Mt. Clay can be reached by a short scramble up the rocks without trail. About 0.3 mi. above Sphinx Col, a loop leads left to Greenough Spring (reliable), then rejoins the Gulfside about 100 yd. below its exit point. As the grade levels approaching Sphinx Col, the Mount Clay Loop rejoins on the right. At Sphinx Col, it is 2.3 mi. from Mt. Washington and 3.7 mi. to Madison Hut. In bad weather, a fairly quick descent to sheltering scrub can be made via the Sphinx Trail, though once treeline is reached this trail becomes rather steep and difficult.

Part II. Sphinx Col–Edmands Col

A few yards north of the low point in Sphinx Col, the Sphinx Trail branches right (east) into the Great Gulf through a grassy passage between ledges. The Gulfside ascends to the north, and from one point there is a view of the Sphinx down the slope to the right. The Cornice enters left from the Caps Ridge Trail a short distance before the Gulfside begins to cross Monticello Lawn, a

comparatively smooth, grassy plateau. Here the Mount
Jefferson Loop branches left and leads 0.3 mi. to the
summit of Mt. Jefferson (5715 ft.). The views from the
summit are excellent, and the Loop is only slightly
longer than the parallel section of the Gulfside, though it
requires about 300 ft. of extra climbing and about 10
min. more hiking time.

The path now turns northeast and rises less steeply. It
crosses the Six Husbands Trail after reaching its greatest
height on Mt. Jefferson, about 5400 ft., then descends
moderately to the point where the Mount Jefferson Loop
rejoins on the left about 0.3 mi. from the summit. The
trail descends steeply north over rough rocks, with Jefferson Ravine on the right, and about 100 yd. beyond, it
passes flat-topped Dingmaul Rock, from which there is a
good view down the ravine, with Mt. Adams on the left.
The trail reaches Edmands Col at 3.8 mi. from Mt.
Washington, with 2.2 mi. to go to Madison Hut.

At Edmands Col (4930 ft.) is a bronze tablet in memory of J. Rayner Edmands, who made most of the graded
paths on the Northern Peaks. Gulfside Spring (reliable) is
30 yd. south of the col, and Spaulding Spring (reliable) is
about 0.2 mi. north near the Castle Ravine Trail. The
emergency shelter once located at this col has been dismantled, and none of the trails leaving this area is a particularly satisfactory escape route in bad weather. From
the col, the Edmands Col Cutoff leads south, entering
scrub almost immediately, affording the quickest route to
this rough form of shelter in dangerous weather; it then
continues about 0.5 mi. to the Six Husbands Trail leading down to the Great Gulf, but it is very rough, and the
Six Husbands Trail is fairly difficult to descend, making
it a far less than ideal escape route unless the severity of
the weather leaves no choice. The Randolph Path leads
north into the Randolph Valley, running above treeline
with great exposure to northwest winds for over 0.5 mi.;

branching from this path about 0.1 mi. north of the col are the Cornice, a very rough trail leading west entirely above treeline to the Castle Trail, and the Castle Ravine Trail, which descends steeply over very loose talus and may be hard to follow, but is nevertheless probably the fastest, safest route to civilization unless it is too dangerous to cross through Edmands Col.

Part III. Edmands Col–Madison Hut

Leaving Edmands Col, the Gulfside climbs moderately along the edge of Jefferson Ravine, ascending northeast along the narrow ridge that divides Jefferson Ravine from Castle Ravine near the edge of the southeast cliffs, from which there are fine views into the Great Gulf. This part of the Gulfside was never graded. About 0.7 mi. above Edmands Col, the trail reaches the crest of a small ridge, where the Israel Ridge Path enters left. Near this junction in wet weather there is a small pool called Storm Lake. For about 0.5 mi. the Gulfside Trail and Israel Ridge Path coincide, passing reliable water at the base of a conspicuous boulder just to the right of the path; Peabody Spring (unreliable water source) is just beyond on the left in a small, grassy flat. The Gulfside Trail continues to ascend and, as it levels out on a grassy lawn in the saddle (5520 ft.) between Mt. Adams and Mt. Sam Adams, the Israel Ridge Path diverges right and ascends a short distance to Lowe's Path and then to Mt. Adams.

In another 0.1 mi. several trails intersect at a spot called Thunderstorm Junction where there is a massive cairn that once stood about 10 ft. high. Entering the junction on the left is the Great Gully Trail, coming up across the slope from the southwest corner of King Ravine. Here, also, the Gulfside is crossed by Lowe's Path, ascending from Lowe's Store on US 2 to the summit of Mt. Adams. About 100 yd. down Lowe's Path, the Spur Trail branches right for Crag Camp. The summit of Mt. Adams is about

0.3 mi. from the junction (right), via Lowe's Path; a round trip to the summit requires about 25 min.

An unofficial trail, known as the White Trail because its cairns are topped with white rocks, runs from Thunderstorm Junction to the summit of Mt. Sam Adams, and then follows its south ridge to the Gulfside at the point where the Israel Ridge Path enters from US 2. Sam Adams is an interesting viewpoint; in good weather the route over the rocks between Sam Adams and either starting point is quite plain without the cairns. In addition, the Sam Adams ridge is much more exposed to the wind and weather than the Gulfside, and the cairns are neither prominent enough nor close enough together to be followed reliably when visibility is poor.

From Thunderstorm Junction the Gulfside descends northeast, gradually at first, and enters a section about 0.5 mi. long that is paved with carefully placed stones. At the end of this section, on the high plateau between King Ravine and Mt. Quincy Adams, the Air Line enters on the right, descending from Mt. Adams, and the trails coincide for less than 100 yd. Then the Air Line branches left at the top of the steep, open north slope of Mt. Quincy Adams, and just below this junction the King Ravine Trail branches left from the Air Line. Here there are striking views ahead to Mt. Madison, and into King Ravine at the Gateway a short distance down on the left. The Gulfside then descends the slope and passes through a patch of scrub to a junction with the Valley Way and Star Lake Trail about 30 yd. from Madison Hut.

Gulfside Trail (map 6:F9)
Distances from the summit of Mt. Washington
    to Crawford Path junction: 0.2 mi., 5 min.
    to Trinity Heights Connector: 0.3 mi., 10 min.
    to Great Gulf Trail: 0.5 mi., 15 min.
    to Westside Trail: 1.0 mi., 30 min.
    to Mount Clay Loop, south end: 1.1 mi., 35 min.

to Jewell Trail: 1.4 mi., 45 min.

to Mount Clay Loop, north end: 2.2 mi., 1 hr. 5 in.

to Sphinx Trail: 2.3 mi., 2 hr. 10 min.

to Cornice: 2.8 mi., 1 hr. 35 min.

to Mount Jefferson Loop, south end: 2.9 mi., 1 hr. 40 min.

to Six Husbands Trail: 3.3 mi., 1 hr. 55 min.

to Mount Jefferson Loop, north end: 3.6 mi., 2 hr. 5 min.

to Edmands Col: 3.8 mi., 2 hr. 10 min.

to Israel Ridge Path, south junction: 4.5 mi., 2 hr. 40 min.

to Israel Ridge Path, north junction: 5.0 mi., 3 hr.

to Thunderstorm Junction: 5.1 mi., 3 hr. 5 min.

to Air Line: 5.6 mi., 3 hr. 20 min.

to Madison Hut: 6.0 mi., 3 hr. 35 min.

Distance from Lakes of the Clouds Hut

to Madison Hut (via Westside Trail, Crawford Path, and Gulfside Trail): 6.8 mi., 4 hr. 25 min.

Mount Jefferson Loop (AMC)

This trail diverges right (west) from the Gulfside Trail 0.2 mi. south of Edmands Col, and climbs steeply almost straight up the slope. Just below the summit, the Six Husbands Trail enters on the left, then the Castle Trail enters on the right, and soon the junction with Caps Ridge Trail is reached at the base of the summit crag. The true summit is 40 yd. right (west) on the Caps Ridge Trail. The Mount Jefferson Loop then descends to rejoin the Gulfside Trail on Monticello Lawn.

Mount Jefferson Loop (map 6:F9)

Distances from north junction with Gulfside Trail

to summit of Mt. Jefferson: 0.4 mi., 25 min.

to south junction with Gulfside Trail: 0.7 mi. (1.1 km.), 35 min.

Mount Clay Loop (AMC)

This trail diverges left (east) from the Gulfside Trail about 0.1 mi. south of Sphinx Col, and ascends a somewhat steep, rough slope to the ragged ridge crest. The views into the Great Gulf from the brink of the east cliffs are excellent. After crossing the summit and passing over several slightly lower knobs, the trail descends easily to the flat col between Mt. Clay and Mt. Washington, where it rejoins the Gulfside Trail.

Mount Clay Loop (map 6:F9)
Distances from north junction with Gulfside Trail
  to summit of Mt. Clay: 0.5 mi., 30 min.
  to north junction with Gulfside Trail: 1.2 mi. (1.9 km.), 55 min.

Edmands Col Cutoff (RMC)
This important link, connecting the Gulfside Trail and Randolph Path at Edmands Col with the Six Husbands Trail, makes possible a quick escape from Edmands Col into plentiful, sheltering scrub on the lee side of Mt. Jefferson; it also provides a route to civilization through the Great Gulf via Six Husbands Trail, and although this route is long, with a steep, rough, and rather difficult descent, it may be the safest escape route from the vicinity of Edmands Col in severe weather. Footing on this trail is very rough and rocky. It lies almost entirely within the Great Gulf Wilderness.

Leaving Edmands Col, the trail passes Gulfside Spring in 70 yd., then begins a rough scramble over rockslides and through scrub, marked by cairns. The trail is generally almost level, but has many small rises and falls over minor ridges and gullies. It affords good views to the Great Gulf and out to the east. It ends at the Six Husbands Trail 0.3 mi. below that trail's junction with the Gulfside Trail.

Edmands Col Cutoff (map 6:F9)
Distance from Edmands Col
  to Six Husbands Trail: 0.5 mi. (0.8 km.), 20 min.

Cornice (RMC)

This trail diverges west from the Randolph Path near Spaulding Spring, 0.1 north of the Gulfside Trail in Edmands Col, where the Castle Ravine Trail also diverges from the Randolph Path. It crosses the Castle Trail and the Caps Ridge Trail, and returns to the Gulfside at Monticello Lawn. From Edmands Col to the Caps Ridge Trail it is extremely rough, with a lot of tedious and strenuous rock hopping, which is very hard on knees and ankles. Note that his climb may take considerably more time than the estimates below. As a route from Edmands Col to the Caps Ridge Trail, the Cornice saves a little climbing compared to the route over the summit of Jefferson, but is much longer, requires more exertion, and is just as exposed to the weather. This makes its value as a bad-weather route very questionable. But it does offer some interesting views, and it provides an excellent shortcut from the Caps Ridge Trail to the Gulfside south of Mt. Jefferson.

The Cornice leaves the Randolph Path, crossing a small grassy depression where there may be no perceptible footway until it climbs the rocky bank on the other side. It ascends moderately over large rocks, passing above a rock formation that resembles the Loch Ness monster, and circles around the north and west sides of Mt. Jefferson, crossing the Castle Trail above the Upper Castle. It intersects the Caps Ridge Trail above the Upper Cap, turns left (east) up the Caps Ridge Trail about 20 yd., then diverges right (south) and climbs gradually with improved footing to the Gulfside Trail just below Monticello Lawn.

Cornice (map 6:F9)

Distances from Randolph Path

to Castle Trail: 0.6 mi., 25 min.

to Caps Ridge Trail: 1.3 mi., 45 min.

to Gulfside Trail junction: 1.8 mi. (2.9 km.), 1 hr. 10 min.

Randolph Path (RMC)

This graded path extends southwest from the Pinkham B (Dolly Copp) Rd. near Randolph Village, over the slopes of Mt. Madison and Mt. Adams, to the Gulfside Trail in Edmands Col between Mt. Adams and Mt. Jefferson. In addition to providing a route from Randolph to Edmands Col, it crosses numerous other trails along the way, and thus constitutes an important linking trail between them. Some sections are heavily used and well beaten, while others bear very little traffic and must be followed with care. J. Rayner Edmands built the trail from 1893 to 1899; parts of it were reconstructed in 1978 as a memorial to Christopher Goetze, an active RMC member and former editor of *Appalachia,* the AMC's journal.

The path begins at the parking space on the Pinkham B Rd. known as Randolph East, 0.2 mi. south of US 2 and 0.3 mi. west of the Boston and Maine Railroad crossing. Coinciding with the Howker Ridge Trail, it bears sharp left and crosses the railroad tracks, and 30 yd. beyond turns right (west) where the Howker Ridge Trail diverges left (southeast). The Randolph Path runs along the south edge of the power line clearing for about 0.3 mi., then swings southwest. Soon it enters a logging road, turns right and follows it for about 150 yd., then leaves it on the right though continuing to parallel it for a while. It crosses the Sylvan Way at 0.7 mi., and at 1.4 mi. it reaches Snyder Brook, where the Inlook Trail and Brookside join on the left. The Brookside and the Randolph Path cross the brook together on a bridge, then the Brookside diverges right and leads down to the Valley Way. After a short climb the Randolph Path crosses the Valley Way, and soon after that joins the Air Line, coincides with it for 20 yd., then leaves it on the right.

At 1.9 mi. the Short Line enters right; by this shortcut route it is 1.3 mi. to US 2 at Appalachia. The Short Line coincides with the Randolph Path for 0.4 mi., then branches left for King Ravine. The Randolph Path descends slightly and crosses Cold Brook on Sanders Bridge, and the Cliffway diverges right just beyond. At 3.1 mi. it crosses the King Ravine Trail at its junction with the Amphibrach, a junction called the Pentadoi. The Randolph Path continues across Spur Brook on ledges just below some interesting pools and cascades, and beyond the brook the Spur Trail diverges left. The Randolph Path climbs around the nose of a minor ridge and becomes steeper. Soon the Log Cabin Cutoff diverges right and runs 0.2 mi. to the Log Cabin; and in another 0.2 mi. an unmaintained branch of the Log Cabin Cutoff descends steeply and directly from the Randolph Path to the Log Cabin.

At 3.9 mi. from Randolph East, Lowe's Path is crossed and the grade moderates as the trail angles up the steep west side of Nowell Ridge. At 4.7 mi. good outlooks begin to appear, providing particularly notable views of the Castles nearby and Mt. Lafayette in the distance to the southwest. At about 5.0 mi. the Perch Path crosses, leading left (north) to the Gray Knob Trail and right (south) to The Perch and Israel Ridge Path, crossing a small brook on the Perch Path about 60 yd. south of the Randolph Path. Above this junction the Randolph Path rises due south through high scrub. At 5.4 mi. the Gray Knob Trail from Crag Camp and Gray Knob enters left at about the point where the Randolph Path rises out of the high scrub. In another 70 yd. the Israel Ridge Path enters right (west), ascending from US 2, and the trails coincide for about 150 yd., then the Israel Ridge Path branches left for Mt. Adams in an area where views to Jefferson and the Castles are particularly fine. From this point the Randolph Path is nearly level to its end at Edmands Col, curving around the head of Castle Ravine, offering continuous excellent views. It is above treeline, much exposed to the weather, and visible for a long distance ahead. Near Edmands Col is Spaulding Spring (reliable water source), in a small grassy depression on the right, which the Castle Ravine Trail from US 2 comes up through and the Cornice to the Caps and Castles crosses. In 0.1 mi. more the Randolph Path joins the Gulfside Trail in Edmands Col.

Randolph Path (map 6:E9–F9)

Distances from Randolph East parking area

> *to* Valley Way: 1.5 mi., 1 hr. 5 min.
>
> *to* Air Line: 1.6 mi., 1 hr. 10 min.
>
> *to* Short Line, north junction: 1.9 mi., 1 hr. 30 min.
>
> *to* King Ravine Trail and Amphibrach: 3.1 mi., 2 hr. 25 min.
>
> *to* Lowe's Path: 3.9 mi., 3 hr. 5 min.
>
> *to* Perch Path: 5.0 mi., 4 hr.
>
> *to* Israel Ridge Path, north junction: 5.4 mi., 4 hr. 30 min.
>
> *to* Edmands Col and Gulfside Trail: 6.1 mi. (9.8 km.), 4 hr. 55 min.
>
> *to* Mt. Washington summit (via Gulfside Trail and Crawford Path): 9.9 mi., 7 hr. 45 min.

The Link (RMC)

This path links the Appalachia parking area and the trails to Mt. Madison with the trails ascending Mt. Adams and Mt. Jefferson. It connects with the Amphibrach, Cliffway, Lowe's Path, and Israel Ridge Path, and the Castle Ravine, Emerald, Castle, and Caps Ridge trails. The section between the Caps Ridge and Castle trails, although very rough, makes possible a circuit of the Caps and the Castles from Jefferson Notch Rd. It is graded as far as Cascade Brook. Much of the trail is very lightly used, and must be followed with care.

The Link, coinciding with the Amphibrach, diverges right from the Air Line 100 yd. south of Appalachia, just after entering the woods beyond the power line clearing, and runs west, fairly close to the edge of this clearing. At

0.6 mi. it enters a logging road and bears left; then Beechwood Way diverges left, and, just east of Cold Brook, Sylvan Way enters left. Cold Brook is crossed at 0.7 mi. on the Memorial Bridge, where there is a fine view upstream to Cold Brook Fall, which can be reached in less than 100 yd. by Sylvan Way or by a spur from the Amphibrach. Memorial Bridge is a memorial to J. Rayner Edmands, Eugene B. Cook, and other pioneer pathmakers: King, Gordon, Lowe, Watson, Peek, Hunt, Nowell, and Sargent. Just west of the brook the Amphibrach diverges left and the Link continues straight ahead.

The Link then follows old logging roads southwest with gradually increasing grades and occasional wet footing. At 2.0 mi. the Cliffway leads left (east) to viewpoints on Nowell Ridge, and the Link swings to the south and climbs at easy grades, crossing Lowe's Path at 2.7 mi. It crosses the north branch of the Mystic Stream at 3.1 mi. and the main Mystic Stream, in a region of small cascades, at 3.3 mi. It soon curves left, rounds the western buttress of Nowell Ridge, and, running southeast nearly level, enters Cascade Ravine on the mountainside high above the stream. At 4.0 mi. it enters the Israel Ridge Path coming up on the right from US 2, and the trails coincide for 50 yd., then the Israel Ridge Path diverges sharp left for Mt. Adams, passing Cabin-Cascades Trail in about 60 yd. The Link continues straight from this junction, descending sharply to Cascade Brook, which it crosses on a large flat ledge at the top of the largest cascade where there are fine views down the valley. This crossing may be difficult at high water. The trail makes a steep and very rough climb up the bank of the brook, then swings right, and the grade eases and the footing gradually improves as it rounds the tip of Israel Ridge and runs generally south into Castle Ravine.

At 5.1 mi. the Link joins the Castle Ravine Trail, with which it coincides while the two trails pass Emerald

Trail and cross Castle Brook, then at 5.4 mi. the Link diverges sharp right and ascends steeply west, angling up the southwest wall of Castle Ravine. At 6.0 mi. it crosses the Castle Trail below the first Castle at about 4050 ft., then runs south, generally descending gradually, over a very rough pathway with countless treacherous roots, rocks, and hollows that are very tricky and tedious to negotiate. At 6.5 mi. the trail crosses a gravelly slide with good views, and at 7.0 mi. it crosses a fair-sized brook flowing over mossy ledges. At 7.6 mi. it turns sharp left uphill and in 50 yd. reaches the Caps Ridge Trail 1.1 mi. above the Jefferson Notch Rd., about 100 yd. above the famous ledge with the potholes and the fine view up to Jefferson.

The Link (map 6:E9–F8)

Distances from Appalachia parking area

 to Memorial Bridge: 0.7 mi., 25 min.

 to Cliffway: 2.0 mi., 1 hr. 25 min.

 to Lowe's Path: 2.7 mi., 1 hr. 55 min.

 to Israel Ridge Path: 4.0 mi., 2 hr. 45 min.

 to Castle Ravine Trail, lower junction: 5.1 mi., 3 hr. 25 min.

 to Castle Trail: 6.0 mi., 4 hr. 20 min.

 to Caps Ridge Trail: 7.6 mi. (12.2 km.), 5 hr. 20 min.

Great Gulf Trail (WMNF)

This trail begins at the new parking area on NH 16, about 1.5 mi. south of its junction with Pinkham B (Dolly Copp) Rd. near Dolly Copp Campground. It follows the West Branch of the Peabody River through the Great Gulf, climbs up the headwall, and ends at a junction with the Gulfside Trail 0.5 mi. below the summit of Mt. Washington. Ascent on the headwall is steep and rough. Except for the first 1.6 mi. it lies in the Great Gulf Wilderness; camping is prohibited above the junction with the Sphinx Trail.

Leaving the new parking lot, the trail descends slightly to cross the Peabody River on a bridge, then ascends to a junction at 0.3 mi. with the former route from Dolly Copp Campground, now called the Great Gulf Link Trail. The Great Gulf Trail turns sharp left here and follows a logging road along the northwest bank of the West Branch of the Peabody River, at first close to the stream and later some distance away from it. An alternate route of the trail for skiing diverges right at 0.6 mi. and rejoins at 1.0 mi., where the main trail turns sharp left. At 1.6 mi. the Hayes Copp Ski Trail diverges right, the Great Gulf Trail soon crosses into the Wilderness, and the Osgood Trail diverges right at 1.8 mi.; Osgood Campsite is 0.9 mi. from here via the Osgood Trail. The Great Gulf Trail returns to the West Branch and follows it fairly closely for 0.7 mi., then climbs to the high gravelly bank called the Bluff, where there is a good view of the gulf and the mountains around it. The trail follows the edge of the Bluff, then at 2.7 mi. the Osgood Cutoff (which is part of the Appalachian Trail) continues straight ahead while the Great Gulf Trail descends sharp left; for a short distance this trail is also part of the Appalachian Trail. In 50 yd. it crosses Parapet Brook on a bridge, then climbs to the crest of the little ridge that separates Parapet Brook from the West Branch, where the Madison Gulf Trail (as recently relocated) enters right, coming down from the vicinity of Madison Hut through Madison Gulf. The two trails coincide for a short distance, descending to cross the West Branch on a suspension bridge and ascending the steep bank on the south side. Here, the Madison Gulf Trail branches left, taking the Appalachian Trail with it, while the Great Gulf Trail turns right, leading up the south bank of the river past Clam Rock, a huge boulder on the left, at 3.1 mi.

At 3.9 mi. the Great Gulf Trail crosses Chandler Brook, and on the far bank the Chandler Brook Trail diverges left and ascends to the Mt. Washington Auto Rd. The Great Gulf Trail continues close to the river, passing in sight of the mouth of the stream that issues from Jefferson Ravine on the north, to join the Six Husbands Trail (right) and Wamsutta Trail (left) at 4.5 mi. At 5.2 mi. the trail climbs up ledges beside a cascade and continues past numerous other attractive cascades in the next 0.2 mi. After crossing over to the northwest bank of the West Branch (may be difficult), it soon crosses the brook that descends from Sphinx Col and at 5.6 mi. reaches the junction where the Sphinx Trail, leading to the Gulfside Trail, diverges right. Camping is prohibited above this junction. The Great Gulf Trail soon crosses again to the southeast bank of the West Branch, passing waterfalls, including Weetamoo, considered the finest in the Gulf. There are remarkable views down the Gulf to Mt. Adams and Mt. Madison. The trail crosses an eastern tributary and, after a slight ascent, reaches Spaulding Lake (4250 ft.) at 6.5 mi. from NH 16 and about 1.3 mi. by trail from the summit of Mt. Washington.

The Great Gulf Trail continues on the east side of the lake, and a little beyond begins to ascend the steep headwall. The trail runs south and then southeast, rising 1600 ft. in about 0.5 mi. over fragments of stone, many of which are loose. The way may be poorly marked, because snow slides may sweep away cairns, but paint blazes are usually visible on the rocks. The trail generally curves a little to the left until within a few yards of the top of the headwall, then, bearing slightly right, emerges from the gulf and ends at the Gulfside Trail near the Cog Railway. From here it is 0.5 mi. to the summit of Mt. Washington by the Gulfside Trail.

Great Gulf Trail (map 6:F10–F9)

Distances from new parking area on NH 16
  to Osgood Trail: 1.8 mi., 1 hr. 10 min.
  to Osgood Cutoff: 2.7 mi., 1 hr. 50 min.

   to Madison Gulf Trail, south junction: 2.8 mi., 1 hr. 55 min.

   to Six Husbands and Wamsutta trails: 4.5 mi., 3 hr. 15 min.

   to Sphinx Trail: 5.6 mi., 4 hr.

   to Spaulding Lake: 6.5 mi., 4 hr. 45 min.

   to Gulfside Trail junction: 7.3 mi., 6 hr.

   to Mt. Washington summit (via Gulfside Trail and Crawford Path): 7.8 mi. (12.6 km.), 6 hr. 25 min.

Great Gulf Link Trail (WMNF)

This trail was formerly a segment of the Great Gulf Trail. It leaves Dolly Copp Campground at the south end of the main camp road, which is a dead end. The trail enters the woods, and in 0.1 mi. turns sharp left onto an old logging road that has cross-country ski markers in both directions. It follows the logging road south along the west bank of the Peabody River, passing some interesting pools, and at 0.7 mi. it passes a junction with a branch of the Hayes Copp Ski Trail on the right. It ends at a junction with the Great Gulf Trail, which comes in on the left from the parking lot on NH 16 and continues straight ahead into the Gulf.

Great Gulf Link Trail (map 6:F10)

Distance from Dolly Copp Campground

   to Great Gulf Trail: 1.0 mi., 35 min.

Madison Gulf Trail (AMC)

This trail begins on the Mt. Washington Auto Rd. a little more than 2 mi. from the Glen House site, opposite the Old Jackson Road, and descends gently to the West Branch, where it meets the Great Gulf Trail. It then ascends along Parapet Brook to the Parapet, a point 0.3 mi. from Madison Hut. From the Auto Rd. to its departure from the Great Gulf Trail, the Madison Gulf Trail is part of the Appalachian Trail and therefore blazed in white; the rest is blazed in blue. It lies almost entirely within the Great Gulf Wilderness.

Caution: The section of this trail on the headwall of Madison Gulf is one of the most difficult in the White Mtns., passing over several ledge outcrops, bouldery areas, and a chimney with loose rock. The steep slabs may be slippery when wet, and several ledges require scrambling and the use of handholds—hikers with a short reach may have great trouble reaching the handholds on the ledges. Stream crossings may be very difficult in wet weather. The trail is not recommended for the descent, or for hikers with heavy packs, or or in wet weather. Allow extra time, and do not start up the headwall late in the day. The ascent of the headwall may require several hours more than the estimated time; parties often fail to reach the hut before dark on account of slowness on the headwall.

This trail is well marked, well protected from storms, and has plenty of water. Combined with the Old Jackson Rd., it is the shortest route (7.1 mi.) from Pinkham Notch Visitor Center to Madison Hut via the Great Gulf, but not usually the easiest; there are several reasonable alternative routes, none of them without problems. The route via the Osgood Cutoff and Osgood Trail, 7.5 mi. long, is steep in parts, but has no hard brook crossings or difficult scrambles; however, it is very exposed to weather in the upper part, even if the rough but more sheltered Parapet Trail is used to bypass the summit of Mt. Madison. The route via the Buttress Trail is 8.4 mi. long, and has two significant brook crossings and somewhat more weather exposure than Madison Gulf Trail, though substantially less than the Osgood-Parapet route. In any event, there is no way to avoid the 0.3 mi. walk to the hut across the windswept col between Madison and Adams, except by going over the summit of Madison where conditions may well be much worse. Therefore, the choice of route comes down to a trade off among the factors of distance, weather exposure, brook crossings, and rock scrambles; hikers must consider which factors they feel better prepared to deal with, taking current and expected conditions into account. For many hikers the Madison Gulf Trail is the best choice only in very severe weather, and in such conditions the necessity of crossing from the Parapet to the hut may make the entire project too risky.

The trail leaves the Auto Rd. above the 2-mi. mark, opposite the Old Jackson Road junction. In 0.2 mi. a side path branches right in a little pass west of Lowe's Bald Spot and climbs 0.1 mi. to this little ledgy summit, an excellent viewpoint. The Madison Gulf Trail bears left and ascends over a ledge with a limited view, descends rapidly for a short distance, then gently, crossing many small brooks. The trail curves into the valley of the West Branch of the Peabody River and continues descending gently until it meets the Great Gulf Trail on the south bank at 2.1 mi. The two trails now run together, descending the steep bank to the West Branch, crossing a suspension bridge to the north bank, and climbing to the crest of the little ridge that divides Parapet Brook from the West Branch. Here the Great Gulf Trail continues straight ahead, leading to NH 16 or to the Osgood Trail for Mt. Madison and Madison Hut via the Osgood Cutoff. The Madison Gulf Trail (recently relocated) turns left up the narrow ridge and continues between the two streams until it enters its former route near the bank of Parapet Brook at 2.5 mi. At 2.8 mi. it crosses one channel of the divided brook, runs between the two for 0.1 mi., then crosses the other to the northeast bank. It follows the brook bank for a little way, then turns right, away from the brook, then turns left and ascends along the valley wall at a moderate grade, coming back to the brook at the mouth of the branch stream from Osgood Ridge. From here it follows Parapet Brook rather closely, and at 3.5 mi. crosses the brook for the first of three times in less than 0.5 mi., ascending to the lower floor of the Gulf where it reaches Sylvan Cascade, at 4.1 mi.

The Madison Gulf Trail then ascends to the upper floor of the Gulf, where it crosses numerous small brooks. From the floor it rises gradually to Mossy Slide at the foot of the headwall, then ascends very rapidly alongside a stream, which becomes partly hidden among the rocks as the trail climbs. The trail then climbs very steeply, with some difficult scrambles, on the headwall of the gulf. It emerges on the rocks at treeline and it bears right, then climbs moderately to its junction with the Parapet Trail. For the Parapet (0.1 mi.) and Madison Hut (0.3 mi.), turn left; for the Osgood Trail, turn right.

Madison Gulf Trail (map 6:F9)

Distances from Mt. Washington Auto Road

to Great Gulf Trail: 2.1 mi., 1 hr. 10 min.

to foot of Madison Gulf headwall at Sylvan Cascade: 4.1 mi., 2 hr. 55 min.

to Parapet Trail: 4.8 mi. (7.7 km.), 3 hr. 45 min.

to Madison Hut (via Parapet and Star Lake trails): 5.2 mi., 4 hr.

Distance from Pinkham Notch Visitor Center

to Madison Hut (via Old Jackson Road and Madison Gulf, Parapet, and Star Lake trails): 7.1 mi. (11.4 km.), 5 hr. 10 min.

Chandler Brook Trail (AMC)

This wild, rough, and beautiful trail passes many cascades as it climbs from the Great Gulf Trail to the Auto Rd. just above the 4-mi. post. It lies almost entirely within the Great Gulf Wilderness. It diverges south from the Great Gulf Trail 3.9 mi. from NH 16, just above its crossing of Chandler Brook, and follows the brook rather closely, crossing three times, passing fine waterfalls that can be seen from the trail. From the last crossing the course is southeast, rising over a jumbled mass of stones and keeping west of interesting rock formations. The trail enters the Auto Rd. near a ledge of white quartz at the Horn, 0.3 mi. above the 4-mi. post. (Descending, look for this white ledge, which is close to the Auto Rd. The trail is marked by cairns here and is visible from the road.)

Chandler Brook Trail (map 6:F9)

Distance from Great Gulf Trail

    to Mt. Washington Auto Rd.: 0.9 mi. (1.4 km.), 1 hr. 10 min.

Wamsutta Trail (AMC)

This wild, rough, and beautiful trail begins on the Great Gulf Trail and ascends to the Auto Rd. opposite the Alpine Garden Trail, with which it provides routes to Tuckerman Junction, Lakes of the Clouds Hut, and other points to the south. It is almost entirely within the Great Gulf Wilderness. The trail was named for Wamsutta, the first of six successive husbands of Weetamoo, a queen of the Pocasset tribe, for whom a beautiful waterfall in the Great Gulf is named.

Leaving the Great Gulf Trail opposite the Six Husbands Trail, 4.5 mi. from NH 16, the trail crosses a small stream, then ascends gradually. Soon it climbs the very steep and rough northerly spur of Chandler Ridge. Passing a quartz ledge on the right, the trail continues steeply to a small, open promontory on the crest of the spur, which offers a good view, at 0.9 mi. It then ascends gradually through woods, passing a spring on the right. Continuing along the ridgecrest at a moderate grade, the trail emerges at treeline and climbs to a point near the top end of the winter shortcut of the Auto Rd. After turning right along this road, the trail ends in another 100 yd. at the Auto Rd. just above the 6-mi. post.

Wamsutta Trail (map 6:F9)

Distances from Great Gulf Trail

    to outlook on promontory: 0.9 mi., 1 hr. 5 min.

to Mt. Washington Auto Rd.: 1.7 mi. (2.7 km.), 1 hr. 55 min.

Sphinx Trail (AMC)

This wild, beautiful, and very rough trail runs from the Great Gulf Trail below Spaulding Lake to the Gulfside Trail in Sphinx Col, between Mt. Jefferson and Mt. Clay. The trail is important because it affords the quickest escape route for anyone overtaken by storm in the vicinity of Sphinx Col. It diverges east from the Gulfside Trail 40 yd. north of the Clay-Jefferson col, through a grassy, rock-walled corridor, and descends to the Great Gulf Trail. Once below the col, the hiker is quickly protected from the rigor of west and northwest winds. For a considerable part of its length, it climbs very steeply; there is a long section of very slippery rocks in a brook bed, very tedious particularly on the descent, and some of the scrambles on the ledges in the upper part are challenging. The trail's name is derived from the profile of a rock formation seen from just below the meadow where water is found. It lies almost entirely within the Great Gulf Wilderness.

The trail branches northwest from the Great Gulf Trail near the crossing of the brook that descends from between Mt. Clay and Mt. Jefferson, 5.6 mi. from NH 16. It soon turns due west and ascends close to the brook, first gradually, then very steeply, passing several attractive cascades and pools. For about 100 yd. it runs directly in the brook bed, where the rocks are extremely slippery. At 0.6 mi., at the foot of a broken ledge with several small streams cascading over it, the trail turns left away from the brook and angles up across two more small brooks, then climbs a small chimney where views out from the scrub start to appear, and scrambles up ledges with several difficult rock pitches. About 100 yd. above the chimney, after a slight descent, the trail crosses a small meadow where there is usually water just downhill from the trail, under a rock north of the trail. The trail then climbs steeply up a rocky cleft, ascends easily over the crest of a small rocky ridge and descends into a slight sag, and finally climbs to the Gulfside just north of Sphinx Col at the end of a grassy passage at the base of a rock wall.

Sphinx Trail (map 6:F9)

Distance from Great Gulf Trail
   to Gulfside Trail: 1.1 mi. (1.7 km.), 1 hr. 15 min.

Six Husbands Trail (AMC)

This wild, very rough trail provides magnificent views of the inner part of the Great Gulf. It diverges from the Great Gulf Trail 4.5 mi. from NH 16, opposite the Wamsutta Trail, and climbs up the north knee of Jefferson, crosses the Gulfside, and ends at the Mount Jefferson Loop a short distance northeast of the summit. It is very steep and is not recommended for descent except to escape bad conditions above treeline. Up to the Gulfside Trail junction, it lies entirely within the Great Gulf Wilderness. The name honors the six successive husbands of Weetamoo, queen of the Pocasset tribe.

Leaving the Great Gulf Trail, it descends directly across the West Branch, avoiding side paths along the stream. In times of high water this crossing may be very difficult, but there may be a better crossing upstream. The trail climbs easily northward across a low ridge to join Jefferson Brook, the stream that flows from Jefferson Ravine, and ascends along its southwest bank. At 0.5 mi. the Buttress Trail branches right and crosses the stream. The Six Husbands Trail swings away from the brook (last sure water) and soon runs through an area containing many large boulders. Soon it begins to attack the steep main buttress, the north knee of Jefferson, passing two boulder caves. At 1.0 mi. it ascends a steep ledge on a pair of ladders, then climbs under an overhanging ledge on a second pair, with a tricky spot at the top that may be dangerous if wet or icy. In another 100 yd. it reaches a promontory with a fine view, and begins a moderately difficult scramble up the crest of a rocky ridge. At 1.3 mi. the trail reaches the top of the knee approximately at treeline, and the grade moderates. Cairns mark the trail across the bare stretches. At 1.7 mi. the Edmands Col Cutoff branches right, leading in 0.5 mi. to Edmands Col, and the trail becomes steeper as it begins to climb the cone of Mt. Jefferson. Soon it passes over a talus slope that is usually covered well into July by a great drift of snow, conspicuous for a considerable distance from viewpoints to the east. Marked by cairns, the trail crosses the Gulfside Trail and continues west toward the summit of Mt. Jefferson, joining the Mount Jefferson Loop 0.1 mi. below the summit.

Six Husbands Trail (map 6:F9)

Distances from Great Gulf Trail junction

　to Buttress Trail: 0.5 mi., 20 min.

　to Edmands Col Cutoff: 1.7 mi., 1 hr. 45 min.

　to Gulfside Trail: 2.0 mi., 2 hr. 5 min.

　to Mount Jefferson Loop: 2.3 mi. (3.6 km.), 2 hr. 25 min.

Buttress Trail (AMC)

This trail leads from the Six Husbands Trail to the Star Lake Trail near Madison Hut, and it is the most direct route from the upper part of the Great Gulf to Madison Hut. It is mostly sheltered until it nears the hut, and grades are moderate; in bad weather, or for hikers with heavy packs, or for descending, it is probably the best route from the lower part of the Gulf to the hut, in spite of the greater length (see Madison Gulf Trail, the principal alternative, for a discuttion of the options). It lies almost entirely within the Great Gulf Wilderness.

The trail diverges north from the Six Husbands Trail, 0.5 mi. from the Great Gulf Trail, and immediately crosses Jefferson Brook (last sure water), the brook that flows out of Jefferson Ravine. It bears right (east) in 0.1 mi., and climbs diagonally across a steep slope of large, loose, angular fragments of rock (be careful not to dislodge the loose rocks). At the top of this talus slope there is a spectacular view up the Great Gulf, and to the steep buttress of Jefferson's north knee rising nearby across a small valley. The trail continues east, rising gradually along a steep, wooded slope, then at 0.5 mi. it reaches a ridge corner and swings left (north) and runs across a gently sloping upland covered with trees, passing a spring (reliable water source) on the left at 1.0 mi. At 1.2 mi. the trail passes through a boulder cave formed by a large boulder across the path, then reaches the foot of a steep ledge, swings left, and climbs it. At 1.4 mi. the trail swings right after passing between two ledges; the ledge on the right provides a fine view. The trail now ascends less steeply on open rocks above the scrub line, crosses a minor ridge, and descends moderately. After passing under an overhanging rock, it re-enters high scrub that again provides shelter almost all the way to the junction with the Star Lake Trail, which is reached in the gap between the Parapet and Mt. Quincy Adams, just southwest of Star Lake, 0.3 mi. from Madison Hut.

Buttress Trail (map 6:F9)

Distances from Six Husbands Trail junction

   to Star Lake Trail: 1.9 mi. (3.1 km.), 1 hr. 50 min.
   to Madison Hut (via Star Lake Trail): 2.2 mi. (3.6 km.), 2 hr.

Osgood Trail (AMC)

This trail runs from the Great Gulf Trail, 1.8 mi. from the new Great Gulf Wilderness parking area on NH 16, up the southeast ridge of Mt. Madison to the summit, then down to Madison Hut. Built by B. F. Osgood in 1878, this is the oldest trail now in use to the summit of Mt.

Madison. Above the Osgood Cutoff it is part of the
Appalachian Trail. The section of the trail that formerly
ran from the Great Gulf Trail to the Mt. Washington
Auto Rd. has been abandoned. The Osgood Trail begins
in the Great Gulf Wilderness, but for most of its length it
is just outside the boundary (in fact, it constitutes the
northern section of the eastern boundary of the Great
Gulf Wilderness).

The trail leaves the Great Gulf Trail and ascends at an
easy to moderate grade. At 0.3 mi. the trail crosses a
small brook, follows it, recrosses, and bears away from it
to the left. At 0.8 mi. the Osgood Cutoff comes in from
the left, and a spur path leads right over a small brook
(last sure water) and continues about 100 yd. to the
Osgood Campsite. From this junction to Madison Hut,
the Osgood Trail is part of the Appalachian Trail.

At 1.4 mi. the trail begins to climb a very steep section,
then at about 1.6 mi. it gradually but steadily becomes less
steep, and the grade is easy by the time the trail emerges
on the crest of Osgood Ridge at treeline at 2.1 mi. Ahead,
on the crest of the ridge, ten or twelve small, rocky peaks
curve to the left in a crescent toward the summit of Mt.
Madison; the trail, marked by cairns, follows this ridgecrest. At 2.8 mi. from the Great Gulf Trail, the Osgood
Trail reaches Osgood Junction in a small hollow. Here, the
Daniel Webster–Scout Trail enters on the right, ascending
from Dolly Copp Campground, and the Parapet Trail
diverges left on a level path marked by cairns and passes
around the south side of the cone of Madison with little
change of elevation, making a very rough but comparatively sheltered route to Madison Hut.

From Osgood Junction the Osgood Trail climbs over a
prominent crag, crosses a shallow sag, and starts up the
east ridge of Madison's summit cone, where it is soon
joined on the right by the Howker Ridge Trail. Hikers
planning to descend on the Howker Ridge Trail must take

care to distinguish the trail from beaten side paths that lead back to the Osgood Trail. The Osgood Trail ascends to the summit of Mt. Madison at 3.3 mi., where the Watson Path enters on the right, then follows the crest of the ridge past several large cairns, drops off to the left (south), and descends westward just below the ridgecrest and above the steep slopes falling off into Madison Gulf on the left. Soon it crosses to the north side of the ridge and descends steeply, and, 30 yd. before it reaches Madison Hut, the Pine Link joins on the right.

Osgood Trail (map 6:F10–F9)

Distances from Great Gulf Trail

    to Osgood Cutoff: 0.8 mi., 45 min.

    to Osgood Junction: 2.8 mi., 2 hr. 55 min.

    to Mt. Madison summit: 3.3 mi., 3 hr. 25 min.

    to Madison Hut: 3.8 mi. (6.1 km.), 3 hr. 40 min.

Osgood Cutoff (AMC)

This link trail, a part of the Appalachian Trail, provides a convenient shortcut from the Great Gulf and Madison Gulf trails to the Osgood Trail. It is entirely within the Great Gulf Wilderness. The trail leaves the Great Gulf Trail on the Bluff, continuing straight where the Great Gulf Trail makes a sharp left to descend to Parapet Brook, and climbs moderately for 0.2 mi. to its former junction with the Madison Gulf Trail. Then it makes a sharp right and runs nearly on contour east across several brooks to the Osgood Trail at its junction with the spur path to Osgood Campsite, where there is reliable water.

Osgood Cutoff (map 6:F9)

Distance from Madison Gulf Trail

   to Osgood Trail: 0.6 mi. (1.0 km.), 25 min.

Daniel Webster–Scout Trail (WMNF)

This trail, cut in 1933 by Boy Scouts from the Daniel Webster Council, leads from Dolly Copp Campground to the Osgood Trail at Osgood Junction, 0.5 mi. below the summit of Mt. Madison. It begins on the main camp-ground road 0.9 mi. south of the campground entrance on the Pinkham B (Dolly Copp) Rd., with adequate parking available about 0.1 mi. farther, on the left. For most of its length its grades are moderate and its footing is some-what rocky but not unusually rough; however, the upper part of this trail is very steep and much exposed to the weather.

The trail starts out through a section of open woods with some very large trees, soon crosses the Hayes Copp Ski Trail (here a grassy logging road), and swings north-west almost to the bank of Culhane Brook. Veering away from the brook just before reaching it, the trail climbs moderately up the north slope of Madison, mostly angling upward, carefully avoiding a more direct assault on the steeper parts of the mountainside. At 2.0 mi. it reaches the base of a little buttress, where the forest changes abruptly from hardwoods to evergreens, and winds steeply up the buttress to its top. It switchbacks upward a bit farther, then resumes its moderate ascent, angling northwest across the steep slope, becoming steeper and rockier. At 2.9 mi. it begins a very steep and rough climb nearly straight up the slope with ever-increasing amounts of talus and decreasing amounts of scrub, where views begin to appear and improve. At 3.2 mi. the trail reaches treeline and moderates somewhat, though it is still steep. As it approaches the ridgecrest, it turns left and ascends directly up the slope for the last 100 yd. to Osgood Junction and the Osgood Trail.

Daniel Webster–Scout Trail (map 6:F10–F9)
Distances from Dolly Copp Campground

    to foot of little buttress: 2.0 mi., 1 hr. 45 min.

    to Osgood Junction: 3.5 mi., 3 hr. 35 min.

    to Mt. Madison summit (via Osgood Trail): 4.1 mi., 4 hr. 10 min.

Parapet Trail (AMC)

This trail, marked with cairns and blue paint, runs at a roughly constant elevation around the south side of the Mt. Madison summit cone, from the Osgood Trail at Osgood Junction to the Star Lake Trail between the Parapet and Madison Hut. Although above timberline and extremely rough, particularly in its eastern one-third, in bad weather the Parapet Trail is mostly sheltered from the northwest winds. The rocks can be very slippery, the trail may be hard to follow if visibility is poor, and the extra effort of rock hopping more than expends the energy saved by avoiding the climb of about 300 ft. over the summit of Mt. Madison. Therefore it is probably a useful bad weather route only if strong northwest or west winds are a major part of the problem.

From Osgood Junction the trail rises very slightly marked by cairns across the open rocks; take care to distinguish its cairns from those ascending the ridgecrest on the right, which belong to the Osgood Trail. At 0.8 mi. the Madison Gulf Trail enters left at the bottom of a little gully, and the Parapet Trail ascends a ledge and then makes a sharp right turn at 0.9 mi., where a spur path leads left 30 yd. onto the Parapet, a ledge that commands excellent views over the Great Gulf and Madison Gulf to the mountains beyond. The Parapet Trail then runs north, passing above Star Lake, and joins the Star Lake Trail 0.1 mi. south of Madison Hut.

Parapet Trail (map 6:F9)

Distances from Osgood Junction

    to Madison Gulf Trail: 0.8 mi., 30 min.

    to Star Lake Trail: 1.0 mi. (1.5 km.), 35 min.

    to Madison Hut (via Star Lake Trail): 1.1 mi., 40 min.

Pine Link (AMC)

The Pine Link ascends Mt. Madison from the highest point of the Pinkham B (Dolly Copp) Rd., leaving on the west side of the road 2.4 mi. from US 2 and 1.9 mi. from NH 16, directly opposite the private road to the Horton Center on Pine Mtn. It is an interesting trail that provides an unusual variety of views from its outlook ledges, and also from the section above treeline on Madison's northwest slope. Combined with the upper part of the Howker Ridge Trail, it provides a very scenic loop. In general it is only moderately steep and rough, but the part above the treeline is continuously exposed to the full force of northwest winds for about 0.7 mi. This part might also be very difficult to follow if visibility is poor, and it requires a considerable amount of fairly strenuous rock hopping.

The trail first ascends the northwest slope of a spur of Howker Ridge, climbing by a series of short, steep pitches interspersed with level sections. At 1.0 mi. it crosses a flat, swampy area and ascends another steep pitch, then climbs to the ridgecrest of the spur and follows it. At 1.7 mi. it passes an outlook with good views from the south side of the trail, the result of a 1968 fire. At 1.9 mi., just before the trail descends into a sag, a spur path leads left 20 yd. to a bare crag with lovely views up to Madison and out to the Carters. At 2.4 mi., after a fairly long section of trail that has a brook running in and out of it, the Pine Link turns right and joins the Howker Ridge Trail in a shady little glen. Turning left at this junction, the Pine Link coincides with the Howker Ridge Trail. The two trails pass over a ledgy minor knob (a Howk) that offers a good view and then descend from the ledge down a steep cleft to a wet sag. After passing a small cave on the right of the trail, the Pine Link branches right at 2.8 mi. at the foot of the most prominent Howk. This fine viewpoint is only about 0.1 mi. above the junction and is well worth a visit. From the junction the Pink Link runs nearly level across a wet area, then rises moderately on the slope above Bumpus Basin, crossing several small brooks. Climbing out of the scrub at 3.3 mi., it runs above tree-

line with fine views and great exposure. After crossing
the Watson Path at 3.5 mi. (0.3 mi. below the summit of
Mt. Madison), the Pine Link descends gradually, often
over large rocks, to the Osgood Trail 30 yd. from Madison Hut.

Pine Link (map 6:E10–F9)

Distances from Pinkham B (Dolly Copp) Road

   to Howker Ridge Trail, lower junction: 2.4 mi., 2 hr.
     20 min.

   to Watson Path: 3.5 mi., 3 hr. 30 min.

   to Madison Hut: 4.0 mi. (6.5 km.), 3 hr. 45 min.

Howker Ridge Trail (RMC)

This wild, rough, very scenic trail leads from the
Pinkham B (Dolly Copp) Rd. at the Randolph East parking area, 0.2 mi. south of US 2, to the Osgood Trail near
the summit of Mt. Madison. It is an interesting trail with
a great variety of attractive scenery and woods, offering
excellent outlooks at different altitudes and passing three
fine cascades. Howker Ridge is the long, curving northeast ridge of Mt. Madison that partly encloses the deep,
bowl-shaped valley called Bumpus Basin. The trail follows the crest of the ridge, on which there are four little
peaks called the Howks.

    Coinciding with the Randolph Path, the trail bears
sharp left and quickly crosses the railroad tracks, and 30
yd. beyond diverges left (southeast) where the Randolph
Path turns right (west). It crosses a recent logging road
near a yarding area, and then enters a shallow gully and
turns right, going up through it. At 0.4 mi. it reaches the
bank of Bumpus Brook and follows it, passing Stairs Fall,
a cascade on a tributary that enters Bumpus Brook directly across from the viewpoint. The trail continues along the
brook, passing Devil's Kitchen and other interesting pools
and cascades. At Coosauk Fall the Sylvan Way enters on
the right, and in less than 0.1 mi. the Kelton Trail diverges

on the right. At 1.0 mi. the Howker Ridge Trail crosses Bumpus Brook at the foot of Hitchcock Fall, then climbs steeply up the bank on the other side, levels off, descends slightly, and reaches a junction with a spur trail that leads right 40 yd. to the Bear Pit, a natural cleft in the ledge that forms a traplike box. The main trail climbs steeply through conifer woods, then moderates, reaching a rocky shoulder and descending into a sag. It resumes climbing and passes over a ledgy ridgecrest called Blueberry Ledge—now too overgrown to produce many blueberries—then continues up the ridge. It climbs steeply at first and then moderately as it approaches the crest of the first Howk, a long, narrow, densely wooded ridge capped by a number of small peaks. Following the ridge at easy grades, the trail passes a good though limited outlook ahead to Mt. Madison and crosses the ledgy but viewless summit of the first Howk at 2.3 mi., then descends steeply for a short distance. After crossing through a long, fairly level sag, the trail climbs seriously again, and at 3.0 mi. it passes over the ledgy summit of the second Howk, where there are fine views, especially into Bumpus Basin. Descending into the woods again, it passes through the shady glen where the Pine Link enters on the left; water is available less than 100 yd. down this trail.

From this junction the two trails coincide for 0.3 mi., ascending over one of a group of several small, ledgy knobs that constitute the third Howk, affording another good view. Descending a steep cleft to a wet sag, the trail passes a small cave to the right of the trail and then ascends to a junction where the Pine Link branches right. Bearing slightly left, the Howker Ridge Trail climbs rather steeply up ledges to the open summit of the highest, most prominent Howk (4315 ft.) at 3.6 mi., where there are good views in all directions. The trail descends back into the scrub, climbs over another minor crag, and passes through one last patch of high scrub before breaking out above treeline for good. The ensuing section of trail is very exposed to northwest winds and may be difficult to follow in poor visibility; however, if you lose the trail in conditions that do not require descent below treeline, it is easy enough to reach the Osgood Trail simply by climbing up to the ridgecrest, as the Osgood Trail follows that crest closely. From treeline the trail climbs steeply up the rocks, generally angling a bit to the left, aiming for the notch between the most prominent visible crag and the lower crag to its left. As it approaches the ridgecrest, it turns more to the right, heading for the most prominent visible crag, and strikes the Osgood Trail about 100 yd. above a small sag and 0.2 mi. below the summit of Mt. Madison.

On the descent, at the junction of the Howker Ridge and Osgood trails, take care to avoid beaten paths that lead back into the Osgood Trail. On leaving the junction, keep well to the left, descending only slightly, until you see the RMC sign a short distance down the path.

Howker Ridge Trail (map 6:E9–F9)
Distances from Pinkham B (Dolly Copp) Road

to Hitchcock Fall: 1.0 mi., 50 min.

to first Howk: 2.3 mi., 2 hr. 15 min.

to Pine Link, lower junction: 3.1 mi., 3 hr.

to Osgood Trail: 4.2 mi. (6.8 km.), 4 hr. 15 min.

to Mt. Madison summit (via Osgood Trail): 4.5 mi., 4 hr. 20 min.

Kelton Trail (RMC)

This path runs from the Howker Ridge Trail just above Coosauk Fall to the Brookside just below Salmacis Fall, from which the Watson Path and Valley Way can be quickly reached. It passes several fine outlooks, notably the Upper Inlook.

The trail branches right from the Howker Ridge Trail about 0.7 mi. from the Pinkham B (Dolly Copp) Rd. It climbs to Kelton Crag, with some steep, slippery sections, then ascends toward the fingerlike north spur of Gordon Ridge, reaching an upper crag at the edge of a very old burn. From both crags there are restricted views; there is usually water between them on the right. Ascending, with good views east, the trail reaches the Overlook at the edge of the old burn, and runs west to the Upper Inlook where the Inlook Trail enters right from Dome Rock. The Kelton Trail then runs south, nearly level but rough in places, through dense woods. It crosses Gordon Rill (reliable water source) and Snyder Brook, and enters the Brookside 0.1 mi. below the foot of Salmacis Fall.

Kelton Trail (map 6:E9)
Distances from Howker Ridge Trail
>   *to* Kelton Crag: 0.3 mi., 20 min.
>   *to* Inlook Trail: 0.8 mi., 1 hr.
>   *to* the Brookside: 1.7 mi. (2.7 km.), 1 hr. 25 min.

Inlook Trail (RMC)
This path ascends the ridge that leads northwest from the end of the fingerlike north spur of Gordon Ridge, and offers excellent views from the brink of the line of cliffs that overlook Snyder Brook and culminate in Dome Rock. It begins at the junction of the Randolph Path and the Brookside on the east bank of Snyder Brook, and ascends steeply at the start, soon reaching the first of several "inlooks" up the valley of Snyder Brook to Mt. John Quincy Adams and Mt. Adams. After passing Dome Rock, which offers an excellent view north from the tip of the finger, the trail continues up to the Upper Inlook near the crest of the finger, where it ends at its junction with the Kelton Trail.

Inlook Trail (map 6:E9)
Distances from Randolph Path
>   *to* Dome Rock: 0.6 mi., 45 min.
>   *to* Kelton Trail: 0.7 mi. (1.1 km.), 50 min.

The Brookside (RMC)

This trail follows Snyder Brook from the Valley Way, at the point where it leaves the brook 0.9 mi. from the Appalachia parking area, to the Watson Path 100 yd. south of Bruin Rock, offering views of many cascades and pools. It continues straight where the Valley Way turns right uphill about 30 yd. above its junction with the Beechwood Way, and after a short washed-out section the Randolph Path joins on the right. The trails cross Snyder Brook together on a bridge, then the Randolph Path turns left, the Inlook Trail leaves straight ahead, and the Brookside turns right up the bank of the brook. At 0.3 mi. the Brookside recrosses the brook, and climbs along the west bank at a moderate grade, rising well above the brook, with occasional views through the trees to cliffs on the valley wall on the other side of the brook. Returning gradually to brook level, it comes to the junction with the Kelton Trail, which enters from the left at 1.2 mi. The trail becomes steeper and rougher, and runs close to the brook, passing Salmacis Fall and continuing along a wild and beautiful part of the brook, with cascades and mossy rocks in a beautiful forest. It then climbs away from the brook and finally ascends sharply to the Watson Path 100 yd. south of Bruin Rock.

The Brookside (map 6:E9)

Distance from the Valley Way
   to Watson Path: 1.7 mi. (2.7 km.), 1 hr. 30 min.

Watson Path (RMC)

The old Watson Path, completed by L. M. Watson in 1882, originally led from the Ravine House to the summit of Mt. Madison. The present path begins at the Scar Trail, leads across the Valley Way to Bruin Rock, and then follows the original route to the summit. It is an interesting route to Mt. Madison, but it is steep and rough, and, on the slopes above treeline, fully exposed to the northwest winds. The cairns above treeline are not very prominent, and the trail may be hard to follow when visibility is poor.

Branching from the Scar Trail 0.3 mi. from the Valley Way, it runs level, turning sharp left at 0.1 mi. and crossing the Valley Way at 0.2 mi., 2.4 mi. from the Appalachia parking area. This first section is seldom used and is rather difficult to follow. After crossing the Valley Way, the trail continues at an easy grade to Bruin Rock—a large, flat-topped boulder on the west bank of Snyder Brook, and in another 100 yd. the Brookside enters on the left. In another 80 yd. the Lower Bruin branches to the right toward the Valley Way, and the Watson Path crosses the brook at the foot of Duck Fall, and soon attacks the steep flank of Gordon Ridge on a very steep and rough footway. At 1.0 mi. the trail emerges from the scrub onto the grassy, stony back of the ridge. It crosses Pine Link at 1.4 mi. and ascends to the summit of Mt. Madison over rough and shelving stones.

Watson Path (map 6:E9–F9)

Distances from Scar Trail

    to Valley Way: 0.2 mi., 5 min.

    to Pine Link: 1.4 mi., 1 hr. 40 min.

    to Mt. Madison summit: 1.7 mi. (2.7 km.), 2 hr.

Distance from Appalachia parking area

    to Mt. Madison summit (via Valley Way and Watson Path): 4.1 mi. (6.6 km.), 4 hr. 10 min.

Valley Way (WMNF)

This is the most direct and easiest route from the Appalachia parking area to Madison Hut, well sheltered almost to the door of the hut. In bad weather it is the safest route to or from the hut.

The trail, with the Air Line, begins at Appalachia, and crosses the railroad to a fork where the Valley Way leads left and the Air Line right across the power line location into the woods. Just into the woods, the Maple Walk diverges left, and at 0.2 mi. Sylvan Way crosses. The trail enters the WMNF at 0.3 mi., and at 0.5 mi. the Fallsway comes in on the left, soon leaving left for Tama Fall and the Brookbank, then reentering the Valley Way in a few yards—a short but worthwhile loop.

The Valley Way leads nearer Snyder Brook and is soon joined from the right by Beechwood Way. About 30 yd. above this junction the Brookside continues straight, while the Valley Way turns right and climbs 100 yd. to the crossing of the Randolph Path at 0.9 mi. It then climbs at a comfortable grade high above Snyder Brook. At 2.1 mi. the Scar Trail branches right, leading to the Air Line via Durand Scar, an excellent outlook on the Scar Loop only about 0.2 mi. above the Valley Way, well worth the small effort required to visit it. At 2.4 mi. the Watson Path crosses, leading left to the summit of Mt. Madison. The Valley Way angles up the rather steep slopes of Durand Ridge considerably above the stream. At 2.8 mi. the Lower Bruin enters left, coming up from Bruin Rock and Duck Fall. At 3.1 mi. a path formerly led to Valley Way Campsite, which may be re-opened if sanitation problems can be solved; at present camping on the site is prohibited. Soon the trail passes a spring to the right of the trail. At 3.3 mi. the Upper Bruin branches steeply right, leading in 0.2 mi. to the Air Line at the lower end of the Knife-edge.

Now the Valley Way steepens and approaches nearer to Snyder Brook. High up in the scrub, the path swings right away from the brook, then swings back toward the stream and emerges from the scrub close to the stream, reaching a junction with the Air Line Cutoff 50 yd. below the hut, and ending in another 10 yd. at a junction with the Gulfside and Star Lake trails.

Valley Way (map 6:E9–F9)

Distances from Appalachia parking area

> *to* Randolph Path crossing: 0.9 mi., 45 min.
> *to* Watson Path crossing: 2.4 mi., 2 hr. 5 min.
> *to* Upper Bruin junction: 3.3 mi., 3 hr. 5 min.
> *to* Madison Hut: 3.8 mi. (6.1 km.), 3 hr. 40 min.
> *to* Mt. Madison summit (via Osgood Trail): 4.2 mi. (6.8 km.), 4 hr. 10 min.

Lower Bruin (RMC)

This short trail branches right from the Watson Path on the west bank of Snyder Brook, where the Watson Path crosses the brook at Duck Fall. It ascends rapidly, passes through a campsite area, turns right uphill away from the brook, turns left and continues to climb rather steeply, then becomes gradual and ends at the Valley Way. When following the trail in the reverse direction, be sure to turn left into the campsite area rather than following a beaten path down to the brook.

Lower Bruin (map 6:E9)

Distance from Watson Path

> *to* Valley Way: 0.2 mi. (0.3 km.), 15 min.

Upper Bruin (RMC)

This short but steep trail branches right from the Valley Way 3.3 mi. from Appalachia and climbs to the Air Line near treeline, 3.1 mi. from Appalachia.

Upper Bruin (map 6:E9)

Distance from Valley Way

> *to* Air Line: 0.2 mi. (0.3 km.), 15 min.

Air Line (AMC)

This trail, completed in 1885, is the shortest route to Mt. Adams from a highway. It runs from the Appalachia parking area up Durand Ridge to the summit. The middle section is rather steep, and the sections on the knife-edged crest of Durand Ridge and above treeline are very exposed to weather but afford magnificent views.

The trail, in common with the Valley Way, begins at Appalachia and crosses the railroad to the power line clearing, where the Air Line leads right and Valley Way left. In 40 yd., just after the Air Line enters the woods, the Link and the Amphibrach diverge right. The Air Line crosses Sylvan Way at 0.2 mi. and Beechwood Way and Beechwood Brook at 0.6 mi. At 0.8 mi. from Appalachia the Short Line diverges right, and at 0.9 mi. the Air Line enters the Randolph Path, coincides with it for 15 yd., then diverges left uphill. At 1.6 mi. there may be water in a spring 30 yd. left (east) of the path (sign). From here the path becomes very steep for 0.5 mi., then eases up and reaches an old clearing known as Camp Placid Stream (unreliable water source) at 2.4 mi., where the Scar Trail enters left, coming up from the Valley Way.

At 3.0 mi. the Air Line emerges from the scrub, and at 3.1 mi. the Upper Bruin comes up left from the Valley Way. The Air Line now ascends over the bare, ledgy crest of Durand Ridge known as the Knife-edge, passing over crags that drop off sharply into King Ravine on the right and descend steeply but not precipitously into Snyder Glen on the left. At 3.2 mi., just south of the little peak called Needle Rock, the Chemin des Dames comes up from King Ravine. The trail now climbs steadily up the ridge toward Mt. Adams. From several outlooks along the upper part of this ridge, you can look back down the ridge for a fine example of the difference between the U-shaped glacial cirque of King Ravine on the left (west), and the ordinary V-shaped brook valley of Snyder Brook on the right (east). At 3.5 mi. the Air Line Cutoff leads left (southeast) 0.2 mi. through the scrub to Madison Hut, which is visible from this junction in clear weather. Water is available on this branch not far from the main path.

The Air Line now departs a little from the edge of the ravine, going left of the jutting crags at the ravine's southeast corner, and rises steeply. Since there is no single well-beaten footway in this section, the trail might be hard to follow in poor visibility. At 3.7 mi. it passes the Gateway of King Ravine, and the King Ravine Trail diverges right and plunges between two crags into that gulf. Here there is a striking view of Mt. Madison. In 60 yd. the path enters the Gulfside Trail, turns right, and coincides with it for 70 yd. on the high plateau at the head of the ravine. Then the Air Line diverges to the left (southwest), passing northwest of Mt. John Quincy Adams, up a rough route over large, angular stones to the summit of Mt. Adams, where it meets Lowe's Path and the Star Lake Trail.

Air Line (map 6:E9–F9)
Distances from Appalachia parking area
>   *to* Randolph Path: 0.9 mi., 50 min.
>   *to* Scar Trail: 2.4 mi., 2 hr. 25 min.
>   *to* Chemin des Dames: 3.2 mi., 3 hr. 10 min.
>   *to* Air Line Cutoff: 3.5 mi., 3 hr. 30 min.
>   *to* Gulfside Trail: 3.7 mi., 3 hr. 45 min.
>   *to* Mt. Adams summit: 4.3 mi. (6.9 km.), 4 hr. 25 min.
>   *to* Madison Hut (via Air Line Cutoff): 3.7 mi. (6.0 km.), 3 hr. 40 min.

Scar Trail (RMC)
This trail runs from the Valley Way 2.1 mi. from Appalachia to the Air Line at Camp Placid Stream, an old clearing 2.4 mi. from Appalachia. It provides a route to Mt. Adams that includes the spectacular views from Durand Ridge while avoiding the steepest section of the Air Line, and also has excellent outlooks of its own.

The trail ascends moderately and divides 0.2 mi. above the Valley Way. The Scar Loop, an alternative route to the right, climbs up a natural ramp between two sections of rock face, turns sharp left, and 40 yd. above the loop junction reaches Durand Scar, which commands excellent views both up and down the valley of Snyder Brook; those up to Adams and Madison are especially fine. The Loop then scrambles up the ledge, passes another fine outlook up the Snyder Brook valley, and descends slightly to rejoin the main path.

The main Scar Trail bears left at the loop junction. In 0.1 mi. it turns sharp right as the Watson Path diverges left, then climbs across a small brook to the upper loop junction where the Scar Loop re-enters. From here the trail winds its way up the mountainside to the Air Line with mostly moderate grades and good footing.

Scar Trail (map 6:E9)

Distances from Valley Way

to Durand Scar (via Scar Loop): 0.2 mi., 15 min.

to Watson Path (via main trail): 0.3 mi., 20 min.

to Air Line (via either route): 1.0 mi. (1.6 km.), 1 hr.

Distance from Appalachia parking area

to Mt. Adams summit (via Valley Way, Scar Trail or Scar Loop, and Air Line): 5.1 mi., 4 hr. 50 min.

Air Line Cutoff (AMC)

This short trail provides a direct route, sheltered by scrub, from the Air Line high on Durand Ridge to the Valley Way just below Madison Hut.

Air Line Cutoff (map 6:F9)

Distance from Air Line

to Madison Hut: 0.2 mi. (0.3 km), 10 min.

Star Lake Trail (AMC)

This trail leads from Madison Hut to the summit of Mt. Adams, much of the way angling up the steep southeast side of Mt. John Quincy Adams. It is often more sheltered from the wind than the Air Line, but it is steep and rough, especially in the upper part where it rock-hops a great deal of large talus and then tackles some fairly challenging rock scrambles on the steep section just below the summit ridge. It may also be difficult to follow on descent.

The trail runs south from the hut, rising gently, and at 0.2 mi. the Parapet Trail branches to the left, passing east of Star Lake, leading to the Parapet and to the Madison Gulf and Osgood trails. The Star Lake Trail passes along the west shore of the lake, and beyond it at 0.3 mi. the Buttress Trail diverges left and descends to the Great Gulf. The Star Lake Trail ascends southwest on the steep southeast slope of Mt. Quincy Adams, leaving the scrub and passing a good spring below the trail. It becomes progressively steeper and rougher as it angles up the rocky slope, and the rocks become larger and require more strenuous hopping. Coming to the crest of a minor easterly ridge, it turns right and climbs steeply with some fairly difficult scrambles to the top of the shoulder, then ascends moderately along the ridgecrest to the summit, where it meets Lowe's Path and the Air Line.

Star Lake Trail (map 6:F9)
Distances from Madison Hut
    to Buttress Trail: 0.3 mi., 10 min.
    to Mt. Adams summit: 1.0 mi. (1.6 km.), 1 hr.

Short Line (RMC)
This graded path, leading from the Air Line to the King Ravine Trail below Mossy Fall, was built in 1899–1901 by J. Rayner Edmands. It offers direct access to the Randolph Path and to King Ravine from the Appalachia parking area.

The Short Line branches right from the Air Line 0.8 mi. from Appalachia. At 0.5 mi. it unites with the Randolph Path, coincides with it for 0.4 mi., then branches left and leads south up the valley of Cold Brook toward

King Ravine, keeping a short distance east of the stream. At 2.7 mi. from Appalachia, the path joins the King Ravine Trail just below Mossy Fall.

Short Line (map 6:E9)

Distances from Air Line junction

    to Randolph Path, lower junction: 0.5 mi., 30 min.
    to Randolph Path, upper junction: 0.9 mi., 50 min.
    to King Ravine Trail: 1.9 mi. (3.1 km,), 1 hr. 40 min.

King Ravine Trail (RMC)

Charles E. Lowe built this branch from Lowe's Path through King Ravine in 1876. It is very steep and rough on the headwall of the ravine, but is one of the most spectacular trails in the White Mtns., offering an overwhelming variety of wild and magnificent scenery. It is not a good trail to descend, on account of steep, rough, slippery footing, and extra time should be allowed in either direction due to the roughness—and the views. The trip to the floor of the ravine is well worth the effort even if you do not ascend the headwall.

The King Ravine Trail diverges left from Lowe's Path 1.8 mi. from US 2, and rises over a low swell of Nowell Ridge. At 0.8 mi. it crosses Spur Brook below some cascades, and in another 0.1 mi. it crosses the Randolph Path at its junction with the Amphibrach, a spot called the Pentadoi. Skirting the east spur of Nowell Ridge, it enters King Ravine and descends slightly, crosses a western branch of Cold Brook, goes across the lower floor of the ravine, and crosses the main stream. At 1.7 mi., near the foot of Mossy Fall (last sure water), it is joined by the Short Line, the usual route of access from the Appalachia parking area. Just above this fall, Cold Brook, already a good-sized stream, gushes from beneath the boulders that have fallen into the ravine.

So far the path has been fairly gradual, but in the next 0.3 mi. it rises about 500 ft. and gains the upper floor of the ravine (3700 ft). The grandeur of the views of the ravine from the jumbled rocks that the trail passes around warrants the trip to this area, even if you do not intend to continue up the headwall. The Chemin des Dames, leading very steeply up to the Air Line, branches sharp left at 2.1 mi. The King Ravine Trail turns sharp right here and then divides in another 10 yd. The main trail, called the Subway, leads right from this junction; it is one of the celebrated features of White Mtn. trails, very strenuous, winding through boulder caves, over and under boulders ranging up to the size of a small house. The path to the left, called the Elevated, avoids some of the main boulder caves and is thus much easier, and also offers some good views of the ravine. The paths rejoin after 220 yd. on the Subway or 140 yd. on the Elevated, and soon the Great Gully Trail diverges right, then the King Ravine Trail divides again. Left is the main trail, and right is a loop path—about 30 yd. shorter than the main trail—that leads to boulder caves near the foot of the headwall, which have ice throughout the year. After the paths rejoin at about 2.4 mi. from Lowe's Path, the ascent of the headwall begins. It is very steep and rough, rising about 1100 ft. in 0.5 mi. over large blocks of rock marked with paint, climbing to the Gateway where the trail issues from the ravine between two crags and immediately joins the Air Line, just below its junction with the Gulfside Trail. From the Gateway there is a striking view of Mt. Madison. Madison Hut is in sight, and can be reached by taking the Gulfside Trail left. The summit of Mt. Adams is 0.6 mi. away via the Air Line.

King Ravine Trail (map 6:E9–F9)
Distances from Lowe's Path

    to Randolph Path: 0.9 mi., 40 min.

    to Short Line: 1.7 mi., 1 hr. 10 min.

    to foot of King Ravine headwall: 2.4 mi., 1 hr. 55 min.

    to Air Line: 2.9 mi. (4.7 km.), 2 hr. 45 min.

Chemin des Dames (RMC)

This trail leads from the floor of King Ravine up its east wall and joins the Air Line just above treeline. It is the shortest route out of the ravine, but is nevertheless very steep and rough, climbing about 800 ft. in 0.4 mi. over gravel and talus, some of which is loose; it is also a very difficult trail to descend.

Leaving the King Ravine Trail, it winds through scrub and boulders to the east side of the ravine, where it climbs steeply over talus through varying amounts of scrub, permitting plentiful though not constant views. About halfway up the steep slope it passes through a boulder cave. Above this there are many fine views out across King Ravine and up to the towering crags of Durand Ridge. High up the trail angles to the right across the top of a small slide and along the base of a rock face, reaching the Air Line in a shallow little col.

Chemin des Dames (map 6:E9–F9)

Distance from King Ravine Trail
   to Air Line junction: 0.4 mi. (0.6 km.), 40 min.

Great Gully Trail (RMC)

This wild and beautiful trail provides an alternative route between the floor of King Ravine and the Gulfside Trail, reaching the latter at Thunderstorm Junction. It is extremely steep and rough, and, like the other trails in the ravine, especially difficult to descend. It is lightly used and marked, and must be followed with great care. It has one particularly difficult scramble, and should not be attempted in wet or icy conditions.

Leaving the King Ravine Trail just past the point where the Subway and Elevated rejoin, the Great Gully Trail leads across a region damaged by an avalanche and at 0.3 mi. reaches the brook, but does not cross it. At the base of an attractive high cascade the trail turns right, away from the brook, and climbs up rock to the spine of a narrow ridge and to a promontory with a spectacular view. The trail then passes under an overhanging rock on a ledge with a high, sheer drop close by on the left, forcing the faint of heart to crawl on their bellies, dragging their packs behind them. After negotiating this pitch the climber is rewarded with a fine view of the cascade, and the trail turns sharp right and climbs to another viewpoint, then crosses the brook above the cascade at a spot where *Arnica mollis*, an herb of the aster family that Thoreau sought on his trips to the mountains, grows in profusion. The trail continues to climb steeply to treeline, then begins to moderate, running almost due south across a grassy area marked by cairns that might be hard to follow in poor visibility, meeting the Gulfside and Lowe's Path at Thunderstorm Junction.

Great Gully Trail (map 6:F9)
Distance from King Ravine Trail
   to Gulfside Trail: 1.0 mi. (1.6 km.), 1 hr. 20 min.

The Amphibrach (RMC)
This trail runs from the Appalachia parking area to Memorial Bridge, then swings south and parallels Cold Brook to the five-way junction with the Randolph Path and King Ravine Trail known as the Pentadoi. The trail takes its unusual name from the marking that was used when it was first made, about 1883: three blazes—short, long, and short. It is a good alternative approach to King Ravine or to any point reached via the Randolph Path or the Link; and also, via the Beechwood Way, to points reached by the Short Line, the Air Line, or the Valley Way. Its moderate grade and relative smoothness make it comparatively less difficult when descent after dark is necessary. It is, in fact, one of the kindest trails to the feet in this region.

The Amphibrach, coinciding with the Link, diverges right from the Air Line 100 yd. south of Appalachia, just after entering the woods beyond the power line clearing, and runs west, fairly close to the edge of this clearing. At 0.6 mi. it enters a logging road and bears left, then Beechwood Way diverges left, and, just east of Cold Brook, Sylvan Way enters left. Cold Brook is crossed at 0.7 mi. on the Memorial Bridge, where there is a fine view upstream to Cold Brook Fall that can be reached in less than 100 yd. by Sylvan Way or by a spur from the Amphibrach. Memorial Bridge is a memorial to J. Rayner Edmands, Eugene B. Cook, and other pioneer pathmakers: King, Gordon, Lowe, Watson, Peek, Hunt, Nowell, and Sargent. Just west of the brook the Amphibrach diverges left and the Link continues straight ahead.

The Amphibrach now follows the course of Cold Brook, ascending west of the stream but generally not in sight of the water. In 20 yd. from the junction a side trail branches left 50 yd. to the foot of Cold Brook Fall. Soon the Amphibrach enters the WMNF. At 1.8 mi. the Monaway crosses, leading right to the Cliffway and left to Coldspur Ledges, pleasant flat ledges at the confluence of Cold and Spur brooks reached about 80 yd. from this junction. The Amphibrach soon crosses Spur Brook on the rocks and then bears away to the left (east), ascending the tongue of land between the two brooks, climbing moderately. At 2.2 mi. it crosses the Cliffway, which leads right (west) less than 0.2 mi, to picturesque Spur Brook Falls, and, becoming a bit rougher, it continues upward to join the King Ravine Trail a few steps below the Pentadoi.

The Amphibrach (map 6:E9)
Distances from Appalachia parking area

　to Memorial Bridge: 0.7 mi., 25 min.

　to Monaway: 1.8 mi., 1 hr. 20 min.

　to Randolph Path and King Ravine Trail: 2.6 mi. (4.2 km.), 2 hr. 10 min.

Cliffway (RMC)

This path runs from the Link, 2.0 mi. from the Appalachia parking area, crossing the Amphibrach, to the Randolph Path, 2.1 mi. from Appalachia. Many of its former viewpoints from the cliffs and ledges of the low swell of Nowell Ridge are now overgrown, but White Cliff still offers an excellent view of the Randolph Valley and the Pliny and Crescent ranges to the north. The trail has generally easy grades, but it is very lightly used and marked, and great care is required to follow it.

Leaving the Link, the Cliffway climbs gradually to White Cliff, where it turns sharp right. Here the Ladderback Trail diverges left along the cliff top, connecting to the Monaway. At 1.0 mi. the Cliffway crosses overgrown Bog Ledge, where a tantalizing view of King Ravine barely filters through the trees, then descends sharply for a short distance and turns left through a boggy area where the path is rather obscure. It then turns sharp left again and soon meets the Monaway at the edge of overgrown King Cliff. The Monaway continues straight, while the Cliffway turns sharp right and drops down a small broken ledge that resembles a ruined stairway, then runs nearly level across a moist area to Spur Brook at the base of picturesque Spur Brook Fall. It then climbs beside the fall, crosses Spur Brook above the fall, and runs across the Amphibrach to the Randolph Path at the west end of Sanders Bridge over Cold Brook.

Cliffway (map 6:E9)

Distances from the Link

 to White Cliff: 0.7 mi., 30 min.

 to Spur Brook Fall: 1.7 mi., 1 hr.

 to Randolph Path: 2.1 mi. (3.4 km.), 1 hr. 15 min.

Monaway (RMC)

This short link trail affords the shortest route from the Randolph area to the Cliffway at White Cliff or King

Cliff. It crosses the Amphibrach just below that trail's crossing of Spur Brook. At this junction, a short segment of the Monaway leads east downhill about 80 yd. to pleasant Coldspur Ledges at the confluence of Cold and Spur brooks. The main part of the Monaway runs west uphill at a moderate grade, passes a junction on the right at 0.3 mi. with the Ladderback Trail to White Cliff, then swings south along the brink of overgrown King Cliff and meets the Cliffway, which turns left to Spur Brook Fall and continues straight to Bog Ledge and White Cliff.

Monaway (map 6:E9)
Distance from the Amphibrach
    to Cliffway: 0.4 mi. (0.6 km.), 20 min.

Ladderback Trail (RMC)

This short link trail—named for Ladderback Rock, a large boulder in the woods—connects the Monaway to the Cliffway at White Cliff, permitting a short loop hike including White Cliff and the overgrown Bog Ledge and King Cliff. It is rough and must be followed with great care. As it approaches White Cliff it turns sharp left and Along the Brink, a path only 20 yd. long, diverges straight ahead and parallels the Ladderback Trail to White Cliff a few steps closer to the brink.

Ladderback Trail (map 6:E9)
Distance from Cliffway
    to Monaway: 0.2 mi. (0.4 km.), 5 min.

Spur Trail (RMC)

This trail leads from the Randolph Path, just above its junction with the King Ravine Trail, to Lowe's Path just below Thunderstorm Junction. It ascends the east spur of the Nowell Ridge near the west edge of King Ravine, passing Crag Camp (cabin). At several points below treeline there are superb outlooks into King Ravine, and above treeline views into King Ravine and up to Madison and Adams are continuous and excellent. The upper part is very exposed to weather.

The Spur Trail diverges south from the Randolph Path about 100 yd. west of its junction with the King Ravine Trail, on the west bank of Spur Brook, and climbs rather steeply along Spur Brook past attractive cascades and pools. At 0.2 mi. a short branch path leads left 90 yd. to Chandler Fall, where the brook runs down a steep, smooth slab of rock. At 0.3 mi. the Hincks Trail to Gray Knob (cabin) diverges right, and the Spur Trail crosses to the east side of the brook, the last water until Crag Camp. It ascends the spur that forms the west wall of King Ravine, passing a 10-yd. side path left to the Upper Crag, a good outlook to the ravine and Mts. Madison and Adams. At 0.9 mi. it crosses the deck of Crag Camp and soon passes the junction on the right with the Gray Knob Trail, which leads west 0.4 mi. to Gray Knob.

The trail continues to climb quite steeply up the ridge, but not so near the edge of the ravine. At 1.1 mi. a side path (sign, hard to see on the descent) leads left 100 yd. to Knight's Castle, a spectacular perch high up on the ravine wall. Here the Spur Trail passes into high scrub, and in another 0.2 mi. it breaks out above treeline, commanding excellent views; those to King Ravine are better in the lower portion, while those to Madison and Adams are better higher up. The grade moderates as it joins Nowell Ridge, ascending well to the east of the crest, and merges with Lowe's Path 100 yd. below the Gulfside Trail at Thunderstorm Junction.

Spur Trail (map 6:E9–F9)

Distances from Randolph Path

 to Crag Camp: 0.9 mi., 1 hr. 5 min.

 to Lowe's Path: 2.0 mi. (3.2 km.), 2 hr. 15 min.

 to Mt. Adams summit (via Lowe's Path): 2.4 mi., 2 hr. 35 min.

Hincks Trail (RMC)

This short link trail connects the Spur Trail and Randolph Path to Gray Knob (cabin). It is fairly steep and rough. It diverges right from the Spur Trail immediately before its crossing of Spur Brook, about 0.3 mi. above the Randolph Path. Soon it comes to the edge of Spur Brook near a pleasant little cascade over mossy rocks, then winds rather steeply up the valley, passing through several patches of woods damaged by wind, to Gray Knob.

Hincks Trail (map 6:E9–F9)

Distance from Spur Trail

  to Gray Knob: 0.7 mi. (1.1 km.), 50 min.

Gray Knob Trail (RMC)

This trail connects three of the four RMC camps (Crag Camp, Gray Knob, and the Perch) with each other, and also links the upper parts of the Spur Trail and Lowe's, Randolph, and Israel Ridge paths, affording in particular a route from Crag Camp and Gray Knob to Edmands Col without loss of elevation. Grades are mostly easy but the footing is frequently rough, and south of Lowe's Path it has substantial weather exposure, although some sheltering scrub is usually fairly close by.

Leaving the Spur Trail 50 yd. above Crag Camp, it soon works around a jutting ledge at a ridge corner on log bridges, then passes a side path on the right leading down 25 yd. to a good piped spring. Soon after passing a spring (left), it ascends a short pitch to Gray Knob cabin (left) at 0.4 mi., where the Hincks Trail enters on the right. The Gray Knob Trail then runs almost level, passing a short spur right to an outlook up to the crag for which the cabin is named, continues past the Quay, a short-cut path on the right that runs 50 yd. to Lowe's Path at a fine outlook ledge, and crosses Lowe's Path at 0.5 mi. Almost immediately it enters scrub of variable height, offering a mixture of shelter and weather exposure with nearly constant views, and begins to climb moderately. At 0.8 mi. the Perch Path diverges right. The Gray Knob Trail continues to climb moderately up the slope, then levels off and runs nearly on contour to the Randolph Path just before its junction with the Israel Ridge Path.

Gray Knob Trail (map 6:E9–F9)
Distances from Spur Trail
    to Lowe's Path: 0.5 mi., 20 min.
    to Randolph Path: 1.7 mi. (2.7 km.), 1 hr. 10 min.

Perch Path (RMC)

This path runs from the Gray Knob Trail across the Randolph Path and past the Perch to the Israel Ridge Path. It diverges right from the Gray Knob Trail 0.3 mi. south of Lowe's Path, descends moderately and crosses the Randolph Path at 0.3 mi., then soon passes a small brook and the Perch and runs nearly level to the Israel Ridge Path at a sharp curve.

Perch Path (map 6:F9)
Distances from Gray Knob Trail
    to the Perch: 0.4 mi., 10 min.
    to Israel Ridge Path junction: 0.5 mi. (0.8 km.), 15 min.

Lowe's Path (AMC)

This trail, cut in 1875–1876 by Charles E. Lowe and Dr. William G. Nowell from Lowe's house in Randolph to the summit of Mt. Adams, is the oldest of the mountain trails that begin from the Randolph Valley. It begins on the south side of US 2, 100 yd. west of Lowe's Store, where cars may be parked for a small fee. It is perhaps the easiest way to climb Mt. Adams, with mostly moderate grades, good footing, and excellent views, but it still has considerable exposure to weather in the part above treeline.

Leaving US 2, Lowe's Path follows a broad wood road for 100 yd., then diverges right at a sign giving the history of the trail. It passes through a logged area, crosses the railroad track and then the power lines, and ascends through woods at a moderate grade, heading at first southwest and then southeast, crossing several small brooks. At 1.7 mi. the Link crosses, and at 1.8 mi. the King Ravine Trail branches left. Lowe's Path continues to ascend, and at 2.4 mi. it passes just to the right of the Log Cabin. Here the Log Cabin Cutoff runs left 0.2 mi. to the Randolph Path, and the Cabin-Cascades Trail to the Israel Ridge Path in Cascade Ravine leaves on the right. Water is always available at the Log Cabin and midway between the cabin and treeline. The path now begins to ascend more seriously, and after crossing the Randolph Path at 2.7 mi. it climbs steeply up to the crest of Nowell Ridge, then moderates. At an outlook ledge at 3.2 mi., the short path called the Quay diverges left to Gray Knob Trail, and 30 yd. farther the Gray Knob Trail crosses; the cabin at Gray Knob is 0.1 mi. left (east) by either route.

Soon the trail breaks out of the scrub, and from here on it is above treeline and very exposed to wind, with maginficent views. At 4.1 mi., after the steady ascent up Nowell Ridge, the trail reaches the crag known as Adams 4 (5355 ft.), descends into a little sag, then rises moderately again, keeping to the left (east) of Mt. Sam Adams. The Spur Trail joins on the left 100 yd. below Thunderstorm Junction, the major intersection with the Gulfside at 4.4 mi., where the Great Gully Trail also enters on the left. Lowe's Path climbs moderately up the jumbled rocks of the Mt. Adams summit cone, passing the junction where the Israel Ridge Path enters right at 4.6 mi. Climbing almost due east, it reaches the summit of Mt. Adams at 4.8 mi., where it meets the Air Line and Star Lake Trail.

Lowe's Path (map 6:E9–F9)

Distances from US 2 near Lowe's Store
to the Link: 1.7 mi., 1 hr. 25 min.

to King Ravine Trail: 1.8 mi., 1 hr. 30 min.
to Log Cabin: 2.4 mi., 2 hr. 10 min.
to Randolph Path: 2.7 mi., 2 hr. 25 min.
to Gray Knob Trail: 3.2 mi., 3 hr. 10 min.
to Adams 4 summit: 4.1 mi., 4 hr.
to Gulfside Trail: 4.4 mi., 4 hr. 20 min.
to Mt. Adams summit: 4.8 mi. (7.7 km.), 4 hr. 35 min.

Cabin-Cascades Trail (RMC)

One of the earliest AMC trails (1881), the Cabin-Cascades Trail leads from the Log Cabin on Lowe's Path to the Israel Ridge Path near the cascades on Cascade Brook, descending almost all the way. It is generally rough with one rather steep, very rough section.

The trail begins at Lowe's Path 2.4 mi. from US 2, opposite the Log Cabin. It runs gradually downhill, with minor ups and downs, crossing the Mystic Stream at 0.3 mi. At 0.7 mi. it enters Cascade Ravine and descends a steep pitch, passing a rocky outlook with a good view to the Castles and Mt. Bowman rising over Israel Ridge. It then begins the final steep, rough descent to Cascade Brook, ending at the Israel Ridge Path just above its upper junction with the Link. The first and highest cascade can be reached by descending on the Israel Ridge path 60 yd. to the Link, then following it downward to the left another 60 yd. to the ledges at the top of the cascade. The second cascade can be seen by following the Israel Ridge Path about 150 yd. upward.

Cabin-Cascades Trail (map 6:E9–F9)
Distance from Lowe's Path
    to Israel Ridge Path: 1.0 mi. (1.6 km.), 30 min.

Israel Ridge Path (RMC)

This trail runs to the summit of Mt. Adams from the Castle Trail, 1.3 mi. from US 2 at Bowman (1.0 mi. west of Lowe's Store). It was constructed as a graded path by J.

Rayner Edmands beginning in 1892. Although hurricanes and slides have severely damaged the original trail, and there have been many relocations, the upper part is still one of the most beautiful of the Randolph trails. Some brook crossings may be difficult in high water.

From Bowman follow the Castle Trail for 1.3 mi. Here, the Israel Ridge Path branches left and at 0.1 mi. crosses to the east bank of the Israel River. It follows the river, then turns left up the bank at 0.4 mi., where the Castle Ravine Trail diverges right and continues along the river. The Israel Ridge Path bears southeast up the slope of Nowell Ridge into Cascade Ravine, and at 1.2 mi. the Link enters left. The trails coincide for 50 yd., and then the Link diverges right to cross Cascade Brook. The highest of the cascades can be reached by following this trail 60 yd. downhill to the right. In another 60 yd. the Cabin-Cascades Trail enters left from the Log Cabin. The Israel Ridge Path now enters virgin growth. From this point to treeline, the forest has never been disturbed by lumbering, though slides and windstorms have done much damage.

The path continues to ascend on the north side of Cascade Brook to the head of the second cascade at 1.4 mi., where it crosses the brook, turns right downstream for a short distance, then turns left and climbs. It climbs steeply up Israel Ridge, sometimes also called the Emerald Tongue, which rises between Cascade and Castle ravines. At 2.2 mi. the path turns sharp left (east) where the Emerald Trail diverges right to descend steeply into Castle Ravine. Emerald Bluff, a remarkable outlook to the Castles and Castle Ravine that is well worth a visit, can be reached from this junction in less than 0.2 mi. by following the Emerald Trail and a spur path that turns right before the main trail begins its steep descent. The Israel Ridge Path angles up a rather steep slope, then turns right at 2.4 mi. where the Perch Path enters left (east), 0.1 mi. from the Perch. The main path ascends south to treeline, where it joins the Randolph Path at 2.8 mi. The junction of the Gray Knob Trail with the Randolph Path is 80 yd. to the left (north) at this point. For 0.1 mi. the Israel Ridge and Randolph paths coincide, then the Israel Ridge Path branches to the left and, curving east, ascends the southwest ridge of Mt. Adams and joins the Gulfside Trail at 3.3 mi., near Storm Lake. It coincides with the Gulfside for 0.5 mi., running northeast past Peabody Spring to the Adams–Sam Adams Col. At 3.8 mi., with the cairn at Thunderstorm Junction in sight ahead, the Israel Ridge Path branches right from the Gulfside Trail, and at 3.9 mi. enters Lowe's Path, which leads to the summit of Mt. Adams at 4.1 mi. The cairns between the Gulfside Trail and Lowe's Path are rather sketchy, so in poor visibility it might be better to follow Lowe's Path from Thunderstorm Junction to the summit.

Israel Ridge Path (map 6:E8–F9)

Distances from Castle Trail

>   *to* Castle Ravine Trail: 0.4 mi., 20 min.
>   *to* the Link: 1.2 mi., 1 hr. 5 min.
>   *to* Perch Path: 2.4 mi., 2 hr. 25 min.
>   *to* Randolph Path, lower junction: 2.8 mi., 2 hr. 55 min.
>   *to* Gulfside Trail: 3.3 mi., 3 hr. 20 min.
>   *to* Mt. Adams summit: 4.1 mi. (6.7 km.), 4 hr.
>   *to* Edmands Col (via Randolph Path): 3.5 mi., 3 hr. 15 min.

Emerald Trail (RMC)

This steep, rough, wild trail connects Israel Ridge Path with the Castle Ravine Trail, passing Emerald Bluff, a fine viewpoint to the Castles and Castle Ravine. The short section between Israel Ridge Path and Emerald Bluff is uncharacteristically gradual and easy. The path is lightly used and blazed, and must be followed with care. Emerald Bluff can be visited from US 2 by a wild, scenic loop hike using the Castle Ravine Trail, Emerald Trail, and Israel Ridge Path.

The trail leaves the combined Castle Ravine Trail and Link 0.2 mi. from their lower junction and descends slightly across a channel of Castle Brook, then climbs a very steep and rough slope. As the trail levels off on the crest of Israel Ridge just south of Emerald Bluff, it turns sharp right. Here a side path turns left and leads 50 yd. to the viewpoint on Emerald Bluff. The main trail runs at easy grades to the Israel Ridge Path 0.2 mi. below its junction with the Perch Path.

Emerald Trail (map 6:F9)
Distances from Castle Ravine Trail and the Link
    to Emerald Bluff: 0.5 mi., 40 min.
    to Israel Ridge Path: 0.6 mi. (1.0 km.), 45 min.

Castle Ravine Trail (RMC)
This scenic, challenging trail diverges from the Israel Ridge Path 1.7 mi. from US 2 at Bowman and leads through wild and beautiful Castle Ravine to the Randolph Path near Edmands Col. While it is reasonably well sheltered except for the highest section, parts of the trail are very rough, especially where it crosses unstable talus on the headwall, which makes footing extremely poor for descending or when the rocks are wet. It is lightly used and marked, and must be followed with great care. Some of the brook crossings may be very difficult at moderate to high water, and the ravine walls are very steep, making rapid flooding likely during heavy rain. Nevertheless, consider it seriously as a potential escape route from Edmands Col in bad weather.

From Bowman follow the Castle Trail and the Israel Ridge Path to a point 1.7 mi. from Bowman. Here the Israel Ridge Path turns left up a slope, while the Castle Ravine Trail leads straight ahead near the river. It crosses to the west bank (difficult at high water, and not easy at other times) and soon reaches a point abreast of the Forks of Israel, where Cascade and Castle brooks unite to form Israel River. The trail crosses to the east bank, passes a cascade, and recrosses to the west bank. In general, it follows the route of an old logging road, now almost imperceptible. After entering Castle Ravine, the trail crosses to the east bank and climbs at a moderate grade well above the brook. At 1.5 mi. the Link enters from the left, and the two trails coincide, passing at 1.7 mi. the junction with the Emerald Trail left (north) from Israel Ridge. After crossing to the southwest side of the brook in a tract of enchanted cool virgin forest beloved of *Musca nigra,* the Link diverges right for the Castle Trail at 1.8 mi. while the Castle Ravine Trail continues up the ravine close to the brook, crossing it several times and once using its bed for a short distance. It recrosses Castle Brook near the foot of the headwall, close to where the stream emerges from under the mossy boulders that have fallen into the ravine, then winds through a rocky area where you can often hear the water running underground. The trail turns left and mounts the steep slope, and at 2.1 mi. it passes under Roof Rock, a large, flat-bottomed boulder that would provide some shelter in a rainstorm.

Rising very steeply southeast, with very rough footing, the trail soon winds up a patch of bare rocks, marked by small cairns and dashes of paint, where there are good views up to the Castles and down the valley northward to the Pliny Range. It re-enters the scrub at a large cairn, and in 100 yd. it re-emerges from the scrub at the foot of a steep slope of very loose rock (use extreme care when descending). It climbs very steeply to the top of the headwall, marked by cairns and paint on rocks, then ascends gradually in a grassy little valley with little evident footway and sparsely placed cairns, passing Spaulding Spring and joining the Randolph Path (sign) on the rocks to the left of the grassy valley, 0.1 mi. north of Edmands Col.

To descend, follow the Randolph Path north from Edmands Col to the grassy valley, then descend along it until you find the line of cairns leading down the headwall.

Castle Ravine Trail (map 6:F8–F9)
Distances from Israel Ridge Path

to the Link, lower junction: 1.5 mi., 1 hr. 15 min.

to Roof Rock: 2.1 mi., 1 hr. 50 min.

to Randolph Path: 2.8 mi. (4.5 km.), 2 hr. 50 min.

Castle Trail (AMC)

This trail follows the narrow, serrated ridge that runs northwest from Mt. Jefferson, providing magnificent views in a picturesque setting. The part that traverses the Castles is rough with some difficult rock scrambles. In bad weather it can be a dangerous trail due to long and continuous exposure to the northwest winds. The original path was constructed in 1883–1884, but most of it has since been relocated.

The Castle Trail begins at Bowman on US 2, 3 mi. west of the Appalachia parking area and 4.2 mi. east of the junction of US 2 and NH 115. Park on the north side of the railroad, cross the track, and follow the right-hand driveway for 150 yd. to where the trail enters woods on the right (signs). The trail circles left, crosses a power line, and at 0.4 mi. crosses the Israel River (may be difficult at high water) at the site of an old bridge.

At 1.3 mi. the Israel Ridge Path branches left (east) toward the brook. The last sure water is a short distance along this trail. The Castle Trail continues to rise above the brook on the northeast flank of Mt. Bowman, and at 1.5 mi. it turns sharp right, away from the brook. Now climbing up the slope at a steeper angle, it ascends a long series of rock steps, passes a very large boulder on the left at 2.2 mi., and becomes much steeper for the next 0.3 mi. At 2.5 mi., it enters a blowdown area near the crest of the ridge connecting Mt. Bowman and the Castellated Ridge and becomes almost level. Soon it ascends easily with excellent footing through open woods with abundant ferns, and gradually becomes steeper again as it climbs the main ridge below the Castles to a shoulder with a sharp, ragged crest. Here it winds along the steep slopes near the ridgecrest to a little gap at 3.5 mi., where the Link crosses, coming up from Castle Ravine on the left and leading to the Caps Ridge Trail on the right.

The ridge becomes very narrow and the trail becomes steep and rough with some fairly difficult scrambles. After passing over two ledges with a good outlook from each, it reaches treeline and climbs to the foot of the first and most impressive Castle (4458 ft.), composed of a pair of pillars, at 3.8 mi. The view is superb. The trail leads on past a slightly higher but less impressive, Castle, then runs through a small col filled with scrub that would provide reasonable shelter in a storm, and continues to ascend over several higher but lesser crags as the Castellated Ridge blends into the main mass of Mt. Jefferson. At 4.5 mi., the Cornice crosses, leading northeast to the Randolph Path near Edmands Col and south to the Caps Ridge and Gulfside trails. The Castle Trail ascends moderately over the rocks and joins the Mount Jefferson Loop in a small flat area just north of the summit crag.

Castle Trail (map 6:E8–F9)
Distances from Bowman
>   *to* Israel Ridge Path: 1.3 mi., 50 min.
>   *to* the Link junction: 3.5 mi., 3 hr.
>   *to* first Castle: 3.8 mi., 3 hr. 20 min.
>   *to* Mt. Jefferson summit: 5.0 mi. (8.1 km.), 4 hr. 35 min.

Caps Ridge Trail *(AMC)*
The Caps Ridge Trail makes a direct ascent of Mt. Jefferson from the height-of-land on the Jefferson Notch Rd. at an elevation of 3008 ft., the highest trailhead on a public

through road in the White Mtns. This makes it possible to ascend Mt. Jefferson with much less climbing than on any other trail to a Presidential peak over 5000 ft., except for a few trails that begin high on the Mt. Washington Auto Rd. However, the Caps Ridge Trail is steep and rough with numerous ledges that require rock scrambling and are slippery when wet, and the upper part is very exposed to weather. Therefore the route is more strenuous than might be expected from the relatively small distance and elevation gain. (It is not easier to ascend Mt. Washington via the Caps Ridge Trail than via the Jewell Trail, because the descent from Monticello Lawn to Sphinx Col mostly cancels out the advantage of the higher start.)

The trail leaves the Jefferson Notch Rd. at a parking area and crosses a wet section on log bridges, then ascends steadily up the lower part of the ridge. At 1.0 mi. there is an outcrop of granite on the right that provides a fine view, particularly of the summit of Jefferson and the Caps Ridge ahead. There are several potholes in this outcrop; such potholes are normally formed only by torrential streams. Such streams occur on high ridges like the Ridge of the Caps only during the melting of a glacier, so these potholes indicate to geologists that the continental ice sheet once covered this area.

About 100 yd. beyond this outcrop, the Link enters from the left, providing a nearly level but rough 1.6 mi. link to the Castle Trail just below the Castles, making possible a very scenic though strenuous loop over the Caps and Castles. The Caps Ridge Trail follows the narrow crest of the ridge, becoming steeper and rougher as it climbs up into scrub, and views become more and more frequent. At 1.5 mi. the trail reaches the lowest Cap (4422 ft.) after a steep scramble up ledges, and the trail is entirely in the open from here on. The trail continues very steeply up the ridge to the highest Cap (4830 ft.) at 1.9 mi., then continues to climb steeply as the ridge blends into the summit mass. At 2.1 mi. the Cornice enters left, providing a very rough route to the Castle Trail and Edmands Col, and then diverges right in 20 yd., providing an easy shortcut to Monticello Lawn and points to the south. The Caps Ridge Trail continues east, keeping a little south of the crest of the ridge, to the summit of Mt. Jefferson, then descends east 40 yd. to the base of the little summit cone, where it meets the Mount Jefferson Loop just above its junctions with the Castle and Six Husbands trails.

Caps Ridge Trail (map 6:F8–F9)

Distances from Jefferson Notch Road

> *to* the Link: 1.1 mi., 55 min.
>
> *to* lower Cap: 1.5 mi., 1 hr. 25 min.
>
> *to* upper Cap: 1.9 mi., 1 hr. 50 min.
>
> *to* Cornice: 2.1 mi., 2 hr. 5 min.
>
> *to* Mt. Jefferson summit: 2.5 mi., 2 hr. 40 min.
>
> *to* junction with Mount Jefferson Loop: 2.6 mi. (4.1 km.), 2 hr. 45 min.
>
> *to* Gulfside Trail (via Cornice): 2.5 mi., 2 hr. 25 min.
>
> *to* Mt. Washington summit (via Cornice and Gulfside Trail): 5.2 mi., 4 hr. 30 min.

Boundary Line Trail (WMNF)

This trail connects the Jefferson Notch Rd., 1.4 mi. south of the Caps Ridge Trail, to the new parking area on the Base Rd., 1.1 mi. from its junction with the Jefferson Notch Rd. It thus provides a shortcut between the bases of the Caps Ridge Trail and the Jewell Trail or the Ammonoosuc Ravine Trail (Section 1), though it is lightly marked and must be followed with care. It diverges left (north) from the Jewell Trail 0.4 mi. from the Base Rd. parking lot and runs north, nearly level, closely following the straight boundary line between two unincorporated townships. At 0.5 mi. it crosses Clay Brook and continues to its end at the Jefferson Notch Rd.

Boundary Line Trail (map 6:F8)

Distance from Jewell Trail
   to Jefferson Notch Rd.: 0.9 mi. (1.4 km.), 30 min.

Distance from Base Road parking area
   to Caps Ridge Trail (via Jewell Trail and Jefferson
      Notch Rd.): 2.7 mi., 1 hr. 35 min.

Jewell Trail (WMNF)

This trail begins at the new parking area on the Base Rd.,
climbs the unnamed ridge that leads west from Mt. Clay,
and ends at the Gulfside Trail high on the west slope of
Mt. Clay, 0.3 mi. north of the Clay-Washington Col and
1.4 mi. north of the summit of Mt. Washington. The
grade is constant, but seldom steep, there are no rock
scrambles, and the footing is generally very good. It provides the easiest route to Mt. Washington from the west,
with a great length of ridge above treeline with fine
views but full exposure to the weather, and no shelter
between the summit and treeline. In bad weather, or if
afternoon thunderstorms threaten, it is safer to descend
via the Lakes of the Clouds Hut and the Ammonoosuc
Ravine Trail, despite the steep and slippery footing on
the latter trail; descent by the Jewell Trail is much easier.
The trail is named for Sergeant W. S. Jewell, an observer
for the Army Signal Corps on Mt. Washington, who perished on the Greeley expedition to the Arctic in 1884.

   The Jewell Trail enters the woods directly across the
road from the parking area, crosses the Ammonoosuc
River at 0.1 mi., then swings northeast and ascends at an
easy grade. At 0.4 mi. the Boundary Line Trail diverges
left, while the Jewell Trail ascends the crest of the low
ridge between the Ammonoosuc River and Clay Brook,
joining the old route of the trail at 1.0 mi. The old path
can be followed right 0.4 mi. to the Base Station. From
the junction the main trail descends slightly to Clay
Brook, crosses on a footbridge, then climbs northeast by

long switchbacks. At 2.0 mi. it passes through a blow-down patch at the edge of the steep wall of Burt Ravine, where there are interesting though limited views. It then swings somewhat to the north side of the ridge and climbs east, staying well below the ridgecrest until near the treeline. Reaching treeline at about 3.0 mi., it zigzags at a moderate grade up the ridgecrest, which quickly becomes less prominent and blends into the slope of Mt. Clay. At 3.5 mi. the trail swings to the right away from what remains of the ridge and angles up the slope at an easy grade to the Gulfside Trail. For Mt. Washington, follow the Gulfside right. For Mt. Clay, scramble up the rocks above the junction.

Jewell Trail (map 6:F8–F9)
Distances from Base Road parking area
  to Clay Brook crossing: 1.1 mi., 45 min.
  to Gulfside Trail: 3.7 mi. (5.9 km.), 3 hr. 20 min.
  to Mt. Washington summit (via Gulfside Trail): 5.1 mi., 4 hr. 30 min.

Pine Mountain Road
This trail uses the private automobile road to the Horton Center on Pine Mtn. most of the way to the summit of Pine Mtn. The road begins a little northwest of the highest point of the Pinkham B (Dolly Copp) Rd., 2.4 mi. from US 2 and 1.9 mi. from NH 16, and opposite the foot of Pine Link. It is closed to public vehicular use and has a locked gate, but may be used as a foot trail to the summit. Hikers should watch for automobiles descending on this road. The Ledge Trail, a foot trail over the top of the south cliff, diverges from the road and runs to the summit; it is frequently used to make a loop over the summit. The views from the summit are good, both to the much higher surrounding peaks and to the valleys of the Androscoggin, Moose, and Peabody rivers. The Douglas Horton Center, a center for renewal and education oper-

ated by the NH Conference of the United Church of
Christ (Congregational), occupies a tract of 100 acres on
the summit. The center (not open to the public) consists
of six buildings and an outdoor chapel on the more precipitous northeast peak. Although camping is not permitted, day hikers are welcome to enjoy the views.

The road runs northeast from Pinkham B Rd. across
the col and winds up the south and west flanks of the
mountain. At 0.9 mi. the Ledge Trail branches right to
climb around the south cliff and on to the summit. About
1.6 mi. from Pinkham B Rd., the trail turns off the gravel
road on the right and follows the old tractor road, which
swings south past a spur on the left to a northeast outlook
and ascends easily to the summit, where it meets the
Ledge Trail.

Pine Mountain Road (map 6:E10)
Distances from Pinkham B Rd.
   to Ledge Trail: 0.9 mi., 35 min.
   to summit: 2.0 mi. (3.2 km.), 1 hr. 25 min.
   for loop via Ledge Trail with return via Pine Moun-
      tain Rd.: 3.5 mi., 2 hr. 10 min.

Ledge Trail (WMNF)

This trail runs to the summit of Pine Mtn. from the Pine
Mountain Trail (private road, closed to public vehicles),
making possible an attractive loop with a sporty ascent
past excellent views and an easy return. It diverges from
the Pine Mountain Rd. 0.9 mi. from the Pinkham B
(Dolly Copp) Rd., runs under the south cliff and then
climbs up to the east of the cliff to its top, with beautiful
views to the south and west. It then continues to meet the
Pine Mountain Trail at the summit.

Ledge Trail (map 6:E10)
Distance from Pine Mountain Road
   to summit: 0.6 mi. (1.0 km.), 35 min.

Town Line Brook Trail (RMC)

This good but steep path gives access to Triple Falls from Pinkham B (Dolly Copp) Rd., 1.4 mi. southeast of the railroad crossing. These three beautiful cascades on Town Line Brook are named Proteus, Erebus, and Evans. The watershed is steep and the rainwater runs off very rapidly, so the falls should be visited during or immediately after a rain.

Town Line Brook Trail (map 6:E10)
Distance from Pinkham B (Dolly Copp) Road
    to the end of the path above Triple Falls: 0.2 mi. (0.3 km.), 15 min.

Sylvan Way (RMC)

The Sylvan Way leads from the Link and Amphibrach at Memorial Bridge, 0.7 mi. from the Appalachia parking area, over Snyder Brook to the Howker Ridge Trail at Coosauk Fall. Leaving Memorial Bridge, after 80 yd. it turns left away from Cold Brook at the base of Cold Brook Fall, where a beaten path continues ahead up the brook. Sylvan Way crosses Beechwood Way at 0.1 mi., Air Line at 0.6 mi., and Valley Way 100 yd. farther. At 0.7 mi., within a space of 30 yd., Maple Walk enters left, Fallsway crosses, Sylvan Way crosses Snyder Brook on ledges 60 yd. above Gordon Fall, and the Brookbank crosses. From here Sylvan Way ascends gradually, crossing Randolph Path at 1.1 mi. and continuing to the Howker Ridge Trail.

Sylvan Way (map 6:E9)
Distance from Memorial Bridge
    to Howker Ridge Trail: 1.7 mi. (2.7 km.), 1 hr.

Fallsway (RMC)

Fallsway is an alternative route to the first 0.6 mi. of the Valley Way, following close to Snyder Brook and passing several falls. From the east end of the Appalachia parking area it goes east for 60 yd., then turns right on a gravel road and crosses the railroad and power lines. Here the Brookbank diverges left as Fallsway enters the woods and continues straight ahead. At 0.2 mi. from Appalachia, the path reaches Snyder Brook and soon passes Gordon Fall, where Gordon Fall Loop diverges right. In 60 yd. Sylvan Way crosses and Maple Walk enters right as the trail continues up the brook in hemlock woods. Lower and Upper Salroc Falls are passed, and soon Fallsway enters Valley Way at 0.6 mi., below Tama Fall. In 30 yd. Fallsway leaves Valley Way and passes Tama Fall, where Brookbank enters, and in another 80 yd. Fallsway ends at the Valley Way.

Fallsway (map 6:E9)

Distance from Appalachia parking area

　　to Valley Way junction above Tama Fall: 0.7 mi. (1.2 km.), 30 min.

Brookbank (RMC)

Brookbank diverges from Fallsway near the railroad and rejoins Fallsway above Tama Fall. It leaves Fallsway at the edge of the woods just beyond the power lines, 0.1 mi. from the Appalachia parking lot, and runs parallel to the railroad for about 0.1 mi., then crosses Snyder Brook, turns sharp right (south), and enters the woods. It runs up the east side of the brook, passing Gordon Fall, Sylvan Way, Upper and Lower Salroc Falls, and Tama Fall. Above Tama Fall it recrosses the brook and re-enters Fallsway.

Brookbank (map 6:E9)

Distance from lower junction with Fallsway

　　to upper junction with Fallsway: 0.7 mi. (1.2 km.), 30 min.

Maple Walk (RMC)

The Maple Walk diverges left from Valley Way a few yards from the Appalachia parking area and passes a junction where Gordon Fall Loop diverges left and in 70 yd. reaches Fallsway at Gordon Fall. Maple Walk then runs to the junction of Fallsway and Sylvan Way just above Gordon Fall.

Maple Walk (map 6:E9)

Distance from Valley Way
   to Sylvan Way and Fallsway: 0.2 mi. (0.3 km.), 5 min.

Beechwood Way (RMC)

This path runs from the Link and Amphibrach 0.6 mi. from Appalachia to the Valley Way 0.9 mi. from Appalachia, just below its junctions with the Brookside and the Randolph Path. It follows a good logging road with moderate grades. It leaves the Amphibrach, crosses Sylvan Way in 100 yd. and then the Air Line at 0.6 mi., and ends at the Valley Way.

Beechwood Way (map 6:E9)

Distance from Amphibrach
   to Valley Way: 0.8 mi. (1.3 km.), 40 min.

SECTION 3
The Franconia, Twin, and Willey Ranges

The central region of the White Mtns. is a great wooded area studded with beautiful peaks, with no through highways and only a few gravel roads near the edges. The vast expanses of unbroken forest compensate for mountains that are, except for the Franconia Range and the cliffs of Mt. Bond, generally less rugged than the Presidentials. The region is bordered on the west and northwest by US 3 (and I-93), on the north by US 302, on the east by NH 16, and on the south by the Kancamagus Highway (NH 112). Section 3 includes the west and northwest portion of this central region, including the Franconia Range, Twin Range, and Willey Range. Most of the Pemigewasset Wilderness is also covered here. Note that in this guide the term *Pemigewasset Wilderness* is used strictly to refer to the officially designated wilderness area. Section 3 is divided from Section 4, which covers the eastern portion of the central region, by the Wilderness Trail (described in Section 3), and by a continuation of the line of the Wilderness Trail east from its terminus at Stillwater Junction, over the plateau between Mt. Bemis and Mt. Willey, to US 302 in Crawford Notch. There are only two points of contact between trails described in Section 3 and those described in Section 4: first, where the Cedar Brook Trail (Section 4) meets the Wilderness Trail, just east of the latter's crossing of the East Branch of the Pemigewasset River on a suspension bridge; and second, where the Carrigain Notch Trail (Section 4) meets the Wilderness Trail and Shoal Pond Trail at Stillwater Junction. The AMC Franconia map (map 5) covers all of Section 3.

In this section the Appalachian Trail follows the Liberty Spring Trail and the Franconia Ridge Trail over Little Haystack Mtn. and Mt. Lincoln to Mt. Lafayette. It then runs along the Garfield Ridge Trail, passing close to the summit of Mt. Garfield, to Galehead Hut. Following the Twinway over South Twin Mtn. and Mt. Guyot, and passing near the summit of Zealand Mtn., it reaches Zealand Falls Hut, then takes the Ethan Pond Trail to US 302 in Crawford Notch.

FRANCONIA NOTCH AND THE FLUME

Franconia Notch lies between the Franconia Range on the east, and the Kinsman Range and Cannon Mtn. on the west. The region includes many interesting and accessible natural features such as the Profile (Old Man of the Mountain); Indian Head; Profile, Echo, and Lonesome lakes; the Flume, and the Pool, and the Basin. The Flume and Pool are described below; the others, which are west of US 3, are discussed in Section 5. From the Flume area north to Echo Lake, the valley bottom and lower slopes on both sides lie within Franconia Notch State Park. The recently completed construction of the Franconia Notch Parkway, the link in I-93 through Franconia Notch, has compelled the relocation of the lower portions of many of the trails covered in this section; except for minor adjustments, all such relocations have been completed. Information regarding trails and other facilities is available at the Flume Visitor Center at the south end of the park, and also at Lafayette Place and the Cannon Mountain Tramway. Hiker parking is available at the Flume Visitor Center and the Basin, Lafayette Place, and Old Man parking lots. There is no parking at the Appalachian Trail crossing near the former Whitehouse Bridge site, which is now reached by the Whitehouse Trail from the hikers' parking lot on US 3 just north of the Flume Visitor Center. A paved bike path runs the entire length of the notch from the Flume to the Skookumchuck Trail and is available for pedestrian use, though those on foot should be careful not to unnecessarily impede bicycle traffic. The AMC, USFS, and the NHDP maintain an information booth during the summer and on fall weekends at the Lafayette Place parking area to provide information about weather, trail conditions, facilities, and regulations.

The Flume, one of the best-known features in the Franconia region, is a narrow gorge that can be reached from the Flume Visitor Center by graded trails or by an NHDP bus. There is a network of graded trails that connect points of interest, and a boardwalk through the Flume itself. It is open to visitors from about May 30 to October 15; an admission fee is charged for the Flume and the Pool. In the Flume, you can see broad ledges worn smooth by the action of the water and scoured by an avalanche that swept away a famous suspended boulder in June 1883. At the upper end, Avalanche Falls is worth visiting. The Pool is a pothole formation in the Pemigewasset River, over 100 ft. in diameter and 40 ft. deep; it can be reached by a path of about 0.5 mi. from the visitor center. In the winter this is an easy, popular, and beautiful area to walk in, and there is no admission fee; however, several of the boardwalks are removed for the season, restricting access to some parts of the Flume.

GEOGRAPHY

The Pemigewasset Wilderness is a vast, forested area surrounded by high mountains and drained by the East Branch of the Pemigewasset River. A bit more than a century ago, it was an untracked wilderness; then during the period between 1890 and 1940, lumber operations left it a virtual wasteland, logged and burned almost to total destruction (often referred to as the "so-called Pemigewasset Wilderness"). Though the birch forests that clothe its slopes in many areas still testify subtly to the devastation of the not-so-distant past, the beauty of the area is almost completely restored, and a recent act of Congress establishing the Pemigewasset Wilderness has once again officially entitled it to the name of Wilderness. The history of the logging, and of the railroads that made it possible, is recounted in C. Francis Belcher's *Logging Railroads of the White Mountains*, published by AMC Books. The long ridge of Mt. Bond divides the main part of the Pemigewasset Wilderness north of the East Branch into two lobes.

The Franconia Range and the Twin Range are two high ridges that form a great horseshoe enclosing the western lobe of the Pemigewasset Wilderness. This lobe is drained by Franconia and Lincoln brooks, which almost encircle the long wooded ridge called Owl's Head Mtn. Starting at the southwest end of the horseshoe and running almost due north, the main ridge rises over several lower mountains to the high peaks of the Franconia Range: Mts. Flume, Liberty, Little Haystack, Lincoln, and Lafayette, the high point on the ridge. Swinging around to the east, the ridge crosses Mt. Garfield, Galehead Mtn., and South Twin Mtn., passing its lowest point (other than the ends), about 3400 ft., between Garfield and Galehead. Rising again to South Twin, where a major spur ridge leads north to North Twin Mtn., the main ridge runs southeast to Mt. Guyot. Here another major spur, Zealand Ridge, runs east; before it comes to an end at Zealand Notch, another ridge runs north from it over the Little River Mtns., which consist of Mt. Hale and the Sugarloaves. From Mt. Guyot the main ridge runs south over Mt. Bond and Bondcliff before dropping to the East Branch. To the east of the great horseshoe lies the Willey Range, forming the west wall of Crawford Notch and the east wall of the broad, flat eastern lobe of the Pemigewasset Wilderness. The Rosebrook Range is a low northwest spur of the Willey Range. The broad plateau that connects the Willey Range to the Nancy Range and Mt. Carrigain runs south from the Willey Range. Slopes rise steeply to this plateau from Crawford Notch, bearing the highest waterfalls in the White Mtns., then incline gradually westward into the Pemigewasset Wilderness.

The Franconia Range ranks second among the ranges of the White Mtns. in elevation only. Its sharp, narrow ridge contrasts strikingly with the broad, massive Presidential Range. Mt. Lafayette (5260 ft.) was called "Great Haystack" on Carrigain's map of 1816, but was renamed in honor of the Marquis de Lafayette in gratitude for his assistance in the War of Independence. The highest part of the ridge, from Mt. Lafayette over Mt. Lincoln (5089 ft.) to Little Haystack Mtn. (4760 ft.), extends well above treeline. This part of the ridge is a Gothic masterpiece; especially when seen from the west (particularly from North Kinsman), it suggests the ruins of a gigantic medieval cathedral. The peaks along the high, serrated ridge are like towers supported by soaring buttresses that rise from the floor of the notch. Part of the ridge between Lincoln and Little Haystack is a knife-edge with interesting rock formations. To the south rise the sharp, ledgy peaks of Mt. Liberty (4459 ft.) and Mt. Flume (4328 ft.), which are connected to each other and to Little Haystack Mtn. by long, graceful parabolic ridges. Both of these peaks have very fine views in all directions, particularly to the east over Mt. Bond and the Pemigewasset Wilderness. Eagle Cliff (3420 ft.), a northwesterly spur of Mt. Lafayette, is remarkable for its sheer cliffs and for the "Eaglet," a detached finger of rock that can be seen best from the vicinity of the Tramway parking area. At the south end of the range, the ledges of Little Coolidge Mtn. (2421 ft.) overlook the town of Lincoln. There is no maintained trail to these ledges, but they can be reached by bushwhacking from Lincoln village.

The Twin Range is connected to the Franconia Range by the Garfield Ridge, which runs north from Lafayette, then swings to the east and culminates in the rocky peak of Mt. Garfield (4500 ft.). Garfield rises like a sphinx watching over the valleys of Franconia and Lincoln brooks to the south, providing one of the finest views in the White Mtns., including a spectacular panorama of the higher Franconias to the south. After passing Galehead Mtn. (4024 ft.), a wooded hump with a restricted but excellent view of the Franconias, the ridge reaches South Twin Mtn. (4902 ft.), where the views from the open summit are similar to Garfield's, but from a different perspective. The summit of North Twin (4761 ft.) is densely wooded, but a ledge almost at the summit on the west and another a short distance northeast provide magnificent views. Haystack Mtn. (2713 ft.), also sometimes called the Nubble, is a small but very prominent rocky peak that rises sharply from the lower end of North Twin's north ridge; it has no maintained trail.

The main ridge now swings southeast, then south, crossing the bare summits of Mts. Guyot (4580 ft.) and Bond (4698 ft.), and then Bondcliff (4265 ft.), the fine series of crags and ledges southwest of Mt. Bond. These three peaks, in addition to the spur of Bond called West Bond (4540 ft.), command views that are unequaled in the White Mtns. for their expansive views of forests and mountains, with virtually no sign of roads or buildings. For example, from the summit of Mt. Bond only the summit buildings on Mt. Washington and the Loon Mtn. ski slopes give visible evidence of human intrusion. Arnold Guyot was the geographer who made the first accurate map of the White Mtns., supplanting the previous best map, the work of Prof. G. P. Bond of Harvard; thus the most remote set of peaks in the White Mtns. bear the names of these two pioneer mapmakers. Guyot named several important peaks, including Mt. Tripyramid. Wherever there were mountains to be explored, Guyot could be found—there are also mountains named for him in several other ranges, including the Great Smoky Mtns., the Colorado Rockies, and the Sierra Nevada of California; a crater on the moon also bears his name.

The interior of the western lobe is a relatively narrow valley surrounded by steep slopes and occupied mainly by Owl's Head Mtn. (4025 ft.), one of the more remote major peaks in the White Mtns., named for the shape of its south end. The summit is wooded, but the great western slide provides some superb views up to the Franconia Ridge and the isolated valley of Lincoln Brook.

The high point of the Zealand Ridge, Zealand Mtn. (4260 ft.), is wooded and without views, but there is a magnificent outlook from Zeacliff, overlooking Zealand Notch and the eastern part of the Pemigewasset Wilderness from the east end of the ridge. Originally called the New Zealand Valley, presumably owing to its remoteness, the name was shortened to Zealand for the convenience of the railroad and post office. Much of Zealand Notch and the area to the north was reduced to a jumble of seared rock and sterile soil by a series of intensely hot fires around 1900. It has now made a reasonably complete recovery, a remarkable and outstanding testimony to the infinite healing powers of nature. Nowhere else in New England is there a better example of regeneration after disaster. At the height-of-land in Zealand Notch is Zealand Pond, which has beaver dams as well as outlets at both ends; its waters eventually flow to the sea by both the Merrimack and the Connecticut rivers.

The Little River Mtns., lying between the Zealand River and Little River, offer excellent and easily attained panoramas of the surrounding summits from Mt. Hale (4054 ft.), Middle Sugarloaf (2539 ft.), and North Sugarloaf (2310 ft.). Mt. Hale was named for the Rev. Edward Everett Hale, author of the patriotic tale, "The Man Without a Country."

The Willey Range is a high ridge that rises sharply out of Crawford Notch. The ridge is rather narrow, with steep sides, but its crest undulates for about 2.5 mi. with relatively broad summits and shallow cols. The main peaks (from south to north) are Mt. Willey (4302 ft.), named for the family that was killed by a landslide on its east face in 1826; Mt. Field (4326 ft.), named for Darby Field; and Mt. Tom (4047 ft.), named for Thomas Crawford. All are wooded to the top, but Willey has good outlooks to the east over Crawford Notch, and to the south into the eastern lobe of the Pemigewasset Wilderness. A westerly spur ends abruptly at Zealand Notch with the cliffs of Whitewall Mtn. (3410 ft.). Mt. Avalon (3450 ft.) and Mt. Willard (2850 ft.) are easterly spurs offering fine views for relatively little exertion; in fact probably no other spot in the White Mtns. afford so grand a view as Mt. Willard for as little effort. The Rosebrook Range continues northwest from Mt. Tom over Mt. Echo (3084 ft.), Mt. Stickney (3070 ft.), Mt. Rosebrook (3007 ft.), and Mt. Oscar (2746 ft.). There are no hiking trails on these peaks, but the summit ledges of Mt. Oscar, with magnificent views over the Zealand Valley, can be reached by following ski slopes of the Bretton Woods Ski Area close to the col between Mt. Oscar and Mt. Rosebrook. The ridge can then be followed northwest without a maintained trail about 0.3 mi. to the ledges.

Arethusa Falls and Ripley Falls are situated on brooks that flow down the steep west side of Crawford Notch; in times of high water, these waterfalls can be quite spectacular. Between them stands Frankenstein Cliff, named for George L. Frankenstein, an artist whose work in the White Mtns. was once well known. A network of trails connects these features and affords the opportunity for a variety of shorter day hikes.

The interior of the eastern lobe is broad and relatively flat, with no important mountains, but Thoreau Falls, Ethan Pond, and Shoal Pond are interesting features. This region was the site of the most extensive logging in the White Mtns.; in the wake of the devastation that resulted, part of the eastern lobe was commonly referred to as the Desolation Region.

HUTS, SHELTERS, AND CAMPING

HUTS

For information concerning AMC Huts or Crawford Notch Hostel, including opening and closing schedules, contact AMC Reservations, Pinkham Notch Visitor Center, Box 298, Gorham NH 03581 (603-466-2727).

Greenleaf Hut (AMC)

Greenleaf Hut is located at the junction of the Old Bridle Path and Greenleaf Trail on Mt. Lafayette, at about 4200 ft., overlooking Eagle Lake. It is reached from US 3 via the Greenleaf Trail (2.5 mi.) or Old Bridle Path (2.9 mi.), and is 1.1 mi. from the summit of Mt. Lafayette and 7.7 mi. from Galehead Hut. The hut accommodates thirty-four guests, and is open to the public from early May to mid-October (caretaker basis in May).

Galehead Hut (AMC)

Galehead Hut, built in 1932, is located at about 3800 ft. on a little hump on the Garfield Ridge, near the Twinway and the Garfield Ridge, Frost, and Twin Brook trails. Hikers can reach it in 4.6 mi. from the Gale River Loop Rd. (FR 25 and FR 92) via the Gale River and Garfield Ridge trails. The hut accommodates thirty-eight guests and is open to the public from mid-May to mid-October (caretaker basis in May).

Zealand Falls Hut (AMC)

This hut, built in 1932, is located at about 2700 ft. beside Zealand Falls on Whitewall Brook, at the north end of Zealand Notch, near the Twinway and the Zealand and Ethan Pond trails. Hikers can reach it from the Zealand Rd. via the Zealand Trail in 2.8 mi. The hut accommodates 36 guests and is open to the public from late May to mid-October, and on a caretaker basis from October to May. In winter Zealand Rd. is closed; adding 3.5 mi. to the trip.

Crawford Notch Hostel (AMC)

Low-cost, self-service lodging for those willing to provide their own meals is available in historic Crawford Notch. Guests must supply food and sleeping bags; cooking facilities and equipment are provided. The hostel is an excellent choice for families and small groups, and is a convenient base for a wide range of hiking trips and other outdoor activities. The main hostel building, the recently renovated Shapleigh studio, has accommodations for twenty-four people in two bunkrooms, along with toilet facilities, showers, and a complete kitchen with stove, refrigerator, and sinks. The hostel is heated in fall, winter, and spring. Two adjacent cabins, heated by wood stoves, accommodate eight persons each; cabin guests are welcome to use all hostel facilities. There is a caretaker in residence, and the hostel is open to the public; AMC members receive a discount. Overnight lodging is available May to October, and reservations are encouraged.

CAMPING

Pemigewasset Wilderness

In this area, camping and fires are prohibited above treeline, within 0.25 mi. of 13 Falls Campsite, Thoreau Falls, Galehead Hut, Garfield Ridge Campsite, Guyot Campsite, or within 0.25 mi. of the Wilderness Trail or the

East Branch of the Pemigewasset River from the Wilderness boundary near the Franconia Brook Trail junction to the Thoreau Falls Trail junction near the confluence with the North Fork, except at designated sites. No campsite may be used by more than ten persons at any one time, and hiking groups may not exceed ten persons.

Restricted Use Areas

The WMNF has established a number of Restricted Use Areas (RUAs) where camping and wood or charcoal fires are prohibited from May 1 to November 1. The specific areas are under continual review, and areas are added to or subtracted from the list in order to provide the greatest amount of protection to areas subject to damage by excessive camping, while imposing the lowest level of restrictions possible. Violation of regulations in RUAs is usually punished by fines. A general list of RUAs follows, but one should obtain a map of current RUAs from the WMNF.

(1) Camping is not permitted above treeline (where trees are less than 8 ft. tall) except in winter, and even then it is allowed only on sites that are covered with at least two feet of snow and never on frozen bodies of water. Small signs on most trails mark the point where the restricted area begins, but the absence of such signs should not be construed as proof of the legality of a site.

(2) No camping is permitted within 1/4 mi. of most facilities such as huts, cabins, shelters, or tentsites, except at the facility itself. No camping is permitted within 0.25 mi. of Garfield Pond.

(3) No camping is permitted within 200 ft. of certain trails, except at designated sites. In 1991, designated trails included those portions of the Old Bridle Path, Falling Waters Trail, and Liberty Spring Trail that are not in Franconia Notch State Park (where all camping is prohibited). No camping is permitted within 0.25 mi. of the Wilder-

ness Trail (Lincoln Woods Trail) or the East Branch of the Pemigewasset River from the Kancamagus Highway to the Wilderness boundary near the Franconia Brook Trail junction, except at Franconia Brook Campsite.

Franconia Notch State Park

Camping and fires are prohibited in Franconia Notch State Park, except at Lafayette Place Campground (fee charged).

Established Trailside Campsites

Camp 16 Campsite (WMNF), located at the junction of the Wilderness and Bondcliff trails, has been closed, and camping there is prohibited.

13 Falls Campsite (WMNF), located at the junction of the Franconia Brook, Lincoln Brook, and Twin Brook trails, has six tent platforms. The former shelter has been removed.

Franconia Brook Campsite (WMNF) is located on the Wilderness Trail 2.8 mi. from the Kancamagus Highway, and has sixteen tent platforms. The former shelter has been removed.

Guyot Campsite (AMC), located on a spur path from the Bondcliff Trail between the Twinway and the summit of Mt. Bond, has an open log shelter accommodating twelve, with six tent platforms in addition. There is a fine spring that is reliable in summer but may not flow in the cold seasons. A caretaker is in charge during the summer months, and a fee is charged.

Liberty Spring Campsite (AMC), located on the Liberty Spring Trail 0.3 mi. below its junction with the Franconia Ridge Trail, has twelve tent platforms. A caretaker is in charge during the summer months, and a fee is charged. The former shelter has been removed.

Garfield Ridge Campsite (AMC), located on a short spur path from the Garfield Ridge Trail 0.4 mi. east of Mt. Garfield, has seven four-person tent platforms and one twelve-person shelter. A caretaker is in charge during the summer months, and a fee is charged.

Ethan Pond Campsite (AMC) is located near the shore of Ethan Pond, about 2.8 mi. from the Willey House Station. There is a shelter (capacity eight) and tent platforms (capacity twenty). Water may be obtained where the side path crosses the inlet brook.

THE TRAILS

Franconia Ridge Trail (AMC)

This trail follows the backbone of the ridge that runs south from the summit of Mt. Lafayette over Mt. Lincoln, Little Haystack Mtn., Mt. Liberty, and Mt. Flume, ending at a junction with the Flume Slide Trail and the Osseo Trail. Much work has been done to define and stabilize the trail and to reduce erosion; hikers are urged to stay on the trail to save the thin alpine soils and fragile vegetation. From Mt. Lafayette to the Liberty Spring Trail, it is part of the Appalachian Trail.

Caution: The portion of the Franconia Ridge above treeline, from Lafayette to Little Haystack, is almost constantly exposed to the full force of any storms, and is dangerous in bad weather or high winds. In particular, due to the sharpness and narrowness of the ridge, the danger from lightning is unusually high, and hikers should avoid the ridge when electrical storms appear to be brewing.

This description of the path follows the southbound direction (away from Mt. Lafayette). See below for a description in the reverse direction.

Leaving the summit of Mt. Lafayette, the trail descends rather steeply and passes through a small scrub patch in the col that might provide some shelter in bad weather. It then climbs across a prominent hump, descends to another sag, then climbs again to the summit of Mt. Lincoln at 1.0 mi. It descends sharply, keeping mostly just to the east of the crest of the knife-edged ridge between Mt. Lincoln and Little Haystack Mtn., which is very narrow with steep slopes on both sides; then it follows the nearly level, broader ridge in the open to the junction with the Falling Waters Trail on the right at 1.7 mi., just under the summit rock of Little Haystack Mtn.

The Franconia Ridge Trail continues to the south end of the Little Haystack summit ridge, enters the scrub and descends steeply over ledges for a short distance, then moderates and follows the long, fairly gradual ridge to a junction right with the Liberty Spring Trail at 3.5 mi. There is water at Liberty Spring Campsite, 0.3 mi. down this trail. The Franconia Ridge Trail ascends to the rocky summit of Mt. Liberty at 3.8 mi., reaching the summit from the east, then makes a hairpin turn and descends to the east just a few yards south of its ascent route. The descent is steep at first, then moderates. The trail passes through two small sags and ascends to the open summit of Mt. Flume, then descends along the edge of the west-facing cliff (use extra caution in windy or slippery conditions) and enters the woods. It ends 0.1 mi. south of the summit in a little col, at the junction with the Osseo Trail straight ahead and the Flume Slide Trail on the right.

Franconia Ridge Trail (map 5:H5)
Distances from Mt. Lafayette summit
> *to* Mt. Lincoln summit: 1.0 mi., 40 min.
> *to* Falling Waters Trail: 1.7 mi., 1 hr.
> *to* Liberty Spring Trail: 3.5 mi., 2 hr. 5 min.
> *to* Mt. Liberty summit: 3.8 mi., 2 hr. 15 min.
> *to* Mt. Flume summit: 4.9 mi., 3 hr.
> *to* Flume Slide Trail/Osseo Trail junction: 5.0 mi.
>   (8.0 km.), 3 hr. 5 min.

Franconia Ridge Trail (AMC) [in reverse]
The trail begins 0.1 mi. south of the summit of Mt. Flume in a little col, at the junction with the Osseo Trail

and the Flume Slide Trail. It climbs out of the scrub and ascends along the edge of the west-facing cliff (use extra caution in windy or slippery conditions). From Mt. Flume it descends across a lesser knob, crosses two small sags, and climbs at a progressively steepening grade to the open summit of Mt. Liberty at 1.2 mi., reaching the summit from the east, then makes a hairpin turn and descends to the east just a few yards north of its ascent route. The trail then descends across ledges into the woods and passes a junction left with the Liberty Spring Trail at 1.5 mi. There is water available at Liberty Spring Campsite, 0.3 mi. down this trail. The trail continues down and then up the long, gradual ridge, becoming rather steep over ledges as it approaches the treeline on Little Haystack. At 3.4 mi. it reaches the junction with the Falling Waters Trail on the left, just under the summit rock of Little Haystack Mtn.

From Little Haystack the trail follows a nearly level ridge in the open to the foot of Mt. Lincoln, then ascends sharply, keeping mostly just to the east of the crest of the knife-edged ridge between Mt. Lincoln and Little Haystack Mtn., which is very narrow with steep slopes on both sides. After passing over the summit of Mt. Lincoln at 4.1 mi., it descends to a sag, climbs across a prominent hump, then descends to another sag, passing through a small scrub patch that might provide some shelter in bad weather. The trail then climbs steeply to the summit of Mt. Lafayette, where it meets the Greenleaf Trail on the left (west) and the Garfield Ridge Trail continuing straight ahead along the north ridge.

Franconia Ridge Trail (map 5:H5)

Distances from Flume Slide Trail/Osseo Trail junction

   to Mt. Flume summit: 0.1 mi., 5 min.

   to Mt. Liberty summit: 1.2 mi., 55 min.

   to Liberty Spring Trail: 1.5 mi., 1 hr. 5 min.

   to Falling Waters Trail: 3.4 mi., 2 hr. 20 min.

to Mt. Lincoln summit: 4.1 mi., 2 hr. 50 min.

to Mt. Lafayette summit: 5.0 mi. (8.0 km.), 3 hr. 35 min.

Flume Slide Trail (AMC)

This trail runs from the Liberty Spring Trail 0.6 mi. from its junction with the Cascade Brook and Whitehouse trails, to the Franconia Ridge Trail 0.1 mi. south of the summit of Mt. Flume. The Flume Slide Trail is extremely steep and rough, with polished rock slabs that are extremely slippery when wet (they are nearly always wet, due to the many seep springs on these steep slopes). The trail is not recommended for descent, and its use is discouraged in wet weather when the ledges are more than ordinarily dangerous. Views from the trail itself are very limited, as it ascends a part of the old slide that is almost completely overgrown. The route over the slide is marked by paint on the ledges.

The trail leaves the Liberty Spring Trail on an old logging road that contours to the right (south). Soon the trail swings left off the logging road in a more easterly direction and begins a gradual ascent on the southwest shoulder of Mt. Liberty, with occasional slight descents. At 0.3 mi. it crosses a small brook, and about 0.1 mi. farther crosses a large brook on stepping stones. After rising from the brook bed, the trail climbs gradually, crossing several more small brooks. At 1.5 mi. the trail crosses a small brook, bears right after 40 yd., then turns left in another 20 yd., avoiding a beaten path straight ahead. At 1.9 mi. it crosses Flume Brook for the first time and follows it closely, making several more crossings of the main brook and its branches. In this region follow the trail carefully; in general it keeps close to the brook. As the trail ascends, it leaves the remnants of the brook behind, and slide gravel becomes more prominent underfoot. At 2.6 mi. there is a restricted view up to the summit crags of Mt. Flume. Now the climbing begins in earnest, and the first ledges are soon reached. While on the slide be careful not to dislodge stones that might endanger climbers below, and beware of rockfall from above. After struggling up the smooth, wet ledges with occasional outlooks, the trail turns left at 3.1 mi. and continues on a steep, rocky, rooty path through the woods to the main ridgecrest, where the Franconia Ridge Trail leads left (north) and the Osseo Trail leads right (south). A few steps before this junction is reached, a beaten path leads 30 yd. right (south) to a small crag with an excellent view.

Flume Slide Trail (map 5:H4–H5)
Distances from Liberty Spring Trail
   to foot of slide: 2.6 mi., 1 hr. 50 min.
   to Franconia Ridge Trail: 3.3 mi. (5.3 km.), 2 hr. 55 min.

Liberty Spring Trail (AMC)
This trail climbs past Liberty Spring Campsite to the Franconia Ridge Trail 0.3 mi. north of Mt. Liberty, originating on the Franconia Notch bike path just north of the bridge over the Pemigewasset River, near the site of the former Whitehouse Bridge parking area (parking no longer available); the Cascade Brook Trail (Section 5) begins just south of this bridge. This trailhead is reached from the hikers' parking lot on US 3 just north of the Flume Visitor Center by the Whitehouse Trail or from the Basin parking areas by the paved bike path. The trail ascends steadily and steeply at times, but the footing, while not smooth, is always reasonably good. This trail is part of the Appalachian Trail.

From the bike path, the trail climbs moderately northeast through hardwood growth. At 0.4 mi. it turns sharp right, joining the old main logging road from the former Whitehouse mill, and soon levels off. At 0.6 mi. the Flume Slide Trail leaves right (south). The Liberty Spring Trail bears left, ascending gradually, and crosses a large brook at 1.1 mi. It then climbs moderately, turns sharp left off the logging road at 1.4 mi., then turns sharp right at 2.2 mi. and climbs more steeply by switchbacks. The footing is rough in some places. At 2.6 mi. the trail reaches Liberty Spring Campsite (3800 ft.) on the left and the spring (last reliable water source) on the right. The path then ascends fairly steeply through evergreens and ends in 0.3 mi. at the Franconia Ridge Trail; turn left (north) for Mt. Lafayette, right (south) for Mt. Liberty.

Liberty Spring Trail (map 5:H4–H5)
Distances from Whitehouse Trail
   to sharp left turn: 1.4 mi., 1 hr. 10 min.
   to Liberty Spring Campsite: 2.6 mi., 2 hr. 30 min.
   to Franconia Ridge Trail: 2.9 mi. (4.7 km.), 2 hr. 55 min.
   to Mt. Liberty summit (via Franconia Ridge Trail): 3.2 mi. (5.1 km.), 3 hr.

Whitehouse Trail (AMC)
This trail connects the hikers' parking lot off US 3 just north of the Flume Visitor Center with the Liberty Spring Trail and the Cascade Brook Trail (Section 5), near the former parking area site at Whitehouse Bridge (where parking is no longer available). Thus it is the usual route to these trails for hikers who arrive in the area by automobile.

   The trail leaves the parking lot and runs north parallel to the main highway, passing over a minor ridge. It descends to the bike path at 0.6 mi. and follows it to the junction with the Cascade Brook Trail, which diverges left just before (south of) the bridge over the Pemigewasset River. The Whitehouse Trail continues across the bridge and ends in another 50 yd. where the Liberty Spring Trail diverges right off the bike path.

Whitehouse Trail (map 5:H4)
Distance from Flume hikers' parking area
   to Liberty Spring Trail: 0.8 mi. (1.3 km.), 25 min.

Falling Waters Trail (AMC)

This trail begins at the Lafayette Place parking lots which are lcoated on each side of the Franconia Notch Parkway and climbs to the Franconia Ridge Trail at the summit of Little Haystack Mtn., passing numerous waterfalls in its lower part. It is steep and rough in parts, and better for ascent than descent, but not normally dangerous unless there is ice on the ledgy sections near the brook.

The trail leaves the parking lot on the east side of the parkway (reached from the west side by a paved path 0.1 mi. long) near the hiker information booth, travels in common with the Old Bridle Path, and passes through a clearing into the woods. In 0.2 mi. it turns sharp right from the Old Bridle Path and immediately crosses Walker Brook on a bridge, then leads away from the brook heading southeast and east. At 0.7 mi. it crosses Dry Brook (use care if the water is high), turns left and follows up the south bank to a beautiful cascade known as Stairs Falls. Above the falls the trail passes beneath Sawteeth Ledges and crosses the brook to the north bank just below Swiftwater Falls, which descend 60 ft. in a shady glen. Continuing on the north bank, the trail climbs on graded switchbacks for a short distance to an old logging road that rises gradually in the narrow gorge of Dry Brook. The trail leaves the old road at a steep embankment, ascends in graded sections to Cloudland Falls (80 ft.), and climbs steeply to a viewpoint overlooking the head of the falls and out over the valley toward Mt. Moosilauke on the skyline.

At the head of Cloudland Falls are two 25-ft. falls practically facing each other. The one to the south, which emerges from the woods, is on the branch of Dry Brook that runs down from Little Haystack, while the other is on the Mt. Lincoln branch. The trail continues steeply on the north bank of the Mt. Lincoln branch, soon crosses to the south bank, crosses back to the north side, climbs to and follows an old logging road, and recrosses to the south bank at 1.6 mi. Here it swings right away from the brook and angles uphill on an old logging road. After a view (cut) to the west, the trail takes the left fork of the old road, then leaves it on the left and ascends the ridge via a series of switchbacks.

At the south end of the last switchback, at 2.8 mi., a side trail leads south about 100 yd. to the northeast corner of Shining Rock, where there are good views north and west over Franconia Notch. This steep granite ledge, over 200 ft. high and nearly 800 ft. long, is usually covered with water from springs in the woods above and, seen from across the notch, shines like a mirror in the sunlight. *Caution:* Climbing Shining Rock without rock climbing equipment and training is extremely dangerous. The cliff is wet and slippery; several serious injuries have occurred here.

The main trail continues north for a short distance, turns right, and climbs in a nearly straight line to the summit of Little Haystack.

Falling Waters Trail (map 5:H4–H5)
Distances from Lafayette Place parking area

> to Dry Brook: 0.7 mi., 25 min.
>
> to highest crossing of Dry Brook: 1.6 mi., 1 hr. 20 min.
>
> to Shining Rock side path: 2.8 mi., 2 hr. 35 min.
>
> to Franconia Ridge Trail: 3.2 mi. (5.1 km.), 3 hr. 5 min.

Old Bridle Path (AMC)

This trail runs from the Lafayette Place parking lots, which are located on each side of the Franconia Notch Parkway, to Greenleaf Hut, where it joins the Greenleaf Trail. It affords fine views, particularly those into Walker Ravine, from many outlooks in the upper half of the trail. For much of its length, it follows the route of a former bridle path.

The trail leaves the parking lot on the east side of the parkway (reached from the west side by a paved path 0.1 mi long) near the hiker information booth, in common with the Falling Waters Trail, and passes through a clearing into the woods. In 0.2 mi. the Falling Waters Trail turns sharp right and immediately crosses Walker Brook on a bridge, while the Old Bridle Path continues along the brook for 50 yd., then swings left away from the brook and starts to climb at a moderate grade. At 1.2 mi. it comes to the edge of the bank high above Walker Brook, then swings away again. At 1.6 mi. the trail makes a sharp left turn with rock steps at the edge of the ravine, where there is a glimpse of Mt. Lincoln through the trees, then turns right and soon gains the ridge. At 1.9 mi. the first of the spectacular outlooks from the brink of the ravine is reached, and there are several more along the next 0.1 mi. The trail then ascends the steep part of the ridge, sometimes called Agony Ridge. At 2.4 mi. an unmarked side path diverges right, passes two fine outlooks, and rejoins the main trail 40 yd. above the lower junction. Still climbing, the trail passes a view to Cannon Mtn., Kinsman Mtn., and Mt. Moosilauke from a grassy spot, then crosses a small sag through a patch of dead trees and soon reaches Greenleaf Hut.

Old Bridle Path (map 5:H4–H5)

Distances from Lafayette Place parking area

    to sharp turn with rock steps: 1.6 mi., 1 hr. 25 min.

    to Greenleaf Hut: 2.9 mi. (4.7 km.), 2 hr. 40 min.

Greenleaf Trail (AMC)

This trail runs from the Cannon Mountain Tramway parking lot on the west side of the Franconia Notch Parkway to Greenleaf Hut, where the Old Bridle Path joins, and then to the summit of Mt. Lafayette, where it ends at the junction of the Franconia Ridge and Garfield Ridge trails. Until it reaches the hut, the trail is almost completely in the woods with few views, except when it traverses Eagle Pass, a wild, narrow cleft between Eagle Cliff and the west buttress of Mt. Lafayette that has many interesting cliff and rock formations.

From the parking lot, Greenleaf Trail follows a sidewalk through the parkway underpass, turns left and follows the northbound ramp for 50 yd., then turns right across a ditch into the woods (sign). It runs roughly parallel to the parkway, crosses the gravel outwash of a slide at 0.7 mi., then climbs moderately by numerous switchbacks to Eagle Pass at 1.5 mi. The path leads east nearly level through the pass, crosses a small overgrown gravel slide, then swings more south and rises by long switchbacks, angling up a northwest shoulder over loose stones that are slippery in wet weather. It finally reaches the top of the shoulder and continues a short distance to Greenleaf Hut at 2.7 mi.

At the hut, the Old Bridle Path enters on the right from Lafayette Place. The Greenleaf Trail heads toward Lafayette, enters the scrub, and dips slightly, passing south of the Eagle Lakes, two picturesque shallow tarns (the upper lake is rapidly becoming a bog). The trail rises, passing over several minor knobs, and at 3.2 mi. swings left after passing a sandy area on the right. It soon climbs above the scrub into the open and ascends at a moderate grade, sometimes on rock steps between stone walls. At 3.6 mi. the trail bears left around a ledge on the right side of the trail from which issues a remarkable spring, very small but fairly reliable. Now the trail turns right and soon reaches the summit of Mt. Lafayette. Here the Garfield Ridge Trail leads north and then northeast to Mt. Garfield, Garfield Ridge Campsite, Galehead Hut, and the Twin Range. To the south the Franconia Ridge Trail leads to Liberty Spring Campsite or to the Kancamagus Highway via the Osseo Trail.

Greenleaf Trail (map 5:G4–H5)

Distances from Tramway parking area

  to Eagle Pass: 1.5 mi., 1 hr. 15 min.

  to Greenleaf Hut: 2.7 mi., 2 hr. 25 min.

  to Mt. Lafayette summit: 3.8 mi. (6.1 km.), 3 hr. 35 min.

Skookumchuck Trail (WMNF)

This is an attractive and less frequently used route from
the Franconia Notch area to the north ridge of Mt.
Lafayette, 0.7 mi. below the summit. It begins on US 3 at
a parking lot that also serves the north end of the Franconia Notch bike path, located 0.3 mi. south of the junction
of US 3 and NH 141 and just north of where US 3
divides to enter I-93 and the Franconia Notch Parkway.

Leaving the parking lot, the trail runs south, leading
gradually away from the road, crossing a grassy logging
road three times. At 1.1 mi. it reaches the old route at the
edge of Skookumchuck Brook and follows the brook
upstream. At 1.8 mi. it crosses a small tributary on a rock
bridge, climbs steeply away from the brook on rock
steps, then continues up the valley well above the brook
at a moderate grade through a fine stand of birch. At 2.5
mi. it passes a small brook (unreliable water source) and
continues to a shoulder at 3.6 mi., where there is a
glimpse ahead to Lafayette's north peak. After a short,
gradual descent, the trail angles to the north at mostly
easy grades, then emerges above treeline just before
reaching its junction with the Garfield Ridge Trail.

Skookumchuck Trail (map 5:G4–G5)

Distances from US 3

  to Garfield Ridge Trail: 4.3 mi. (6.9 km.), 3 hr. 35 min.

  to Mt. Lafayette summit: 5.0 mi. (8.1 km.), 4 hr. 15 min.

Garfield Ridge Trail (AMC)

This trail runs from the junction with the Franconia
Ridge and Greenleaf trails at the summit of Mt.

Lafayette to the Twinway near Galehead Hut, traversing the high ridge that joins the Franconia Range to South Twin Mtn. and passing near the summit of Mt. Garfield on the way. The footway is rough, and there are numerous minor gains and losses of elevation, so the trail is more difficult than you might gather from a glance at the map. Allow extra travel time, particularly if you plan to carry a heavy pack.

This description of the path follows the northbound direction (away from Mt. Lafayette). See below for a description of the path in the reverse direction.

The trail leaves the summit of Mt. Lafayette and runs north along the ridge over the north peak to a junction on the left with the Skookumchuck Trail on a shoulder at 0.7 mi. Swinging northeast, the Garfield Ridge Trail drops steeply to timberline and then continues to descend at a moderate grade near the crest of the ridge to a sag at 1.7 mi. From here the trail passes over a series of knobs on a large, wooded hump and descends its rough end to a tangled col at 2.5 mi., then climbs gradually toward Mt. Garfield. At 3.0 mi., near the foot of Garfield's cone, it passes to the right (south) of Garfield Pond, then climbs steeply, with many rock steps, to its high point on Mt. Garfield at 3.5 mi.; the bare summit, with magnificent views, rises 60 yd. to the right (south) over open ledges. The trail then descends steeply, bearing right at 3.7 mi. at the junction where the Garfield Trail enters left from US 3. At 3.9 mi., where there is a small brook beside the trail, a side path runs left 200 yd. to the AMC Garfield Ridge Campsite, passing a good outlook over Franconia Brook Valley on the way. The main trail continues to descend, crosses a small brook, and reaches a major col at 4.4 mi., where the Franconia Brook Trail leaves right and descends to 13 Falls. From this junction the Garfield Ridge Trail runs along the bumpy ridge, sometimes north and sometimes south of the crest, with many ups and downs. After passing a good outlook to Owl's Head Mtn. and descending a steep pitch, it reaches the junction where the Gale River Trail enters from the left at 6.0 mi. The Garfield Ridge Trail now contours around the steep slope of Galehead Mtn., then turns right and climbs to a junction with the Twinway and the Frost Trail 40 yd. from Galehead Hut; turn right to reach the hut.

Garfield Ridge Trail (map 5:I17-G6)

Distances from Mt. Lafayette summit

> *to* high point on Mt. Garfield: 3.5 mi., 2 hr. 10 min.
>
> *to* Garfield Ridge Campsite spur path: 3.9 mi., 2 hr. 20 min.
>
> *to* Franconia Brook Trail: 4.4 mi., 2 hr. 40 min.
>
> *to* Gale River Trail junction: 6.0 mi., 3 hr. 40 min.
>
> *to* Galehead Hut: 6.6 mi. (10.7 km.), 4 hr. 10 min.

Garfield Ridge Trail (AMC) [in reverse]

From its junction with the Twinway and the Frost Trail 40 yd. from Galehead Hut, the Garfield Ridge Trail descends moderately, then swings left and contours around the steep slope of Galehead Mtn. to the junction where the Gale River Trail enters from the right at 0.6 mi. The Garfield Ridge Trail climbs a steep pitch to a good outlook to Owl's Head Mtn. It then runs along the humpy ridge, sometimes north and sometimes south of the crest, with many ups and downs, to a major col at 2.2 mi. where the Franconia Brook Trail leaves left and descends to 13 Falls. From this junction the Garfield Ridge Trail ascends moderately, crosses a small brook, and soon becomes much steeper. At 2.7 mi., where there is a small brook beside the trail, a side path runs right 200 yd. to the AMC Garfield Ridge Campsite, passing a fine outlook over the Franconia Brook valley on the way. The main trail continues to climb steeply past a junction at 2.9 mi. where the Garfield Trail enters left from US 3, and then reaches its high point on Mt. Garfield at 3.1 mi.;

the bare summit, with magnificent views, lies 60 yd. to the left (south) over open ledges. The trail then descends steeply, with many rock steps, and passes to the left (south) of Garfield Pond at 3.6 mi., near the foot of Garfield's cone. After descending gradually to a tangled col at 4.1 mi., it ascends the rough end of a large wooded hump and passes over a series of knobs to a sag at 4.9 mi. From here it ascends near the crest of the ridge at a moderate grade, then climbs steeply past the timberline to a junction on the right with the Skookumchuck Trail on a shoulder at 5.9 mi. The Garfield Ridge Trail then follows the crest of the ridge over the north peak of Mt. Lafayette to the main summit, where the Greenleaf Trail enters on the right and the Franconia Ridge Trail continues straight ahead.

Garfield Ridge Trail (map 5:H5–G6)

Distances from Galehead Hut

> *to* Gale River Trail junction: 0.6 mi., 20 min.
> *to* Franconia Brook Trail: 2.2 mi., 1 hr. 20 min.
> *to* Garfield Ridge Campsite spur path: 2.7 mi., 1 hr. 50 min.
> *to* high point on Mt. Garfield: 3.1 mi., 2 hr. 15 min.
> *to* Mt. Lafayette summit: 6.6 mi. (10.7 km.), 4 hr. 55 min.

Garfield Trail (WMNF)

This trail runs from the Gale River Loop Rd. (FR 92) to the Garfield Ridge Trail 0.2 mi. east of the summit of Mt. Garfield, which is bare rock with magnificent views. The trail follows an old road used for access to the former fire tower, and its grades are easy to moderate except for the short steep pitch just below the summit. You can reach the trailhead by leaving US 3 at a small picnic area 0.3 mi. south of its intersection with Trudeau Rd. (often called Five Corners, this intersection has signs for Trudeau Rd. and for the Ammonoosuc District Ranger Station). Avoiding a right fork, follow the Gale River Loop Rd. south for 1.2 mi., then swing left and cross a bridge to a parking lot on the right. (Straight ahead on this road it is 1.6 mi. to the trailhead for the Gale River Trail.) This trail lies within the watershed of a municipal water supply, and hikers and campers should exercise care not to pollute the streams.

The trail begins at the parking lot, climbing an embankment and following the top of the north bank of the South Branch of the Gale River through fine woods with many large hemlocks. At 0.7 mi. it descends and swings to the right toward the river, joins the old route of the trail, and turns left on it. The trail now climbs slowly away from the river heading generally south. It crosses Thompson and Spruce brooks and a snowmobile that has bridges across the two brooks, which flow close by on either side; then it recrosses Spruce Brook at 1.2 mi. At 2.8 mi. the trail crosses a ridge and descends slightly; there are many fine birches in this area, particularly below the trail. From here the Garfield Trail climbs by several sweeping switchbacks, enters the evergreens, and reaches a blowdown area at 4.1 mi. Here it turns sharp left and climbs easily through an area of large conifers around the east side of the cone of Mt. Garfield to a junction with the Garfield Ridge Trail, which enters from the left, ascending from Garfield Ridge Campsite. The summit of Garfield is reached in 0.2 mi. by turning right and following the steep, rocky section of the Garfield Ridge Trail to its high point, then scrambling over the ledges on the left for another 60 yd. to the foundation of the old fire tower.

Garfield Trail (map 5:G5)
Distances from Gale River Loop Road (FR 92)
   to Garfield Ridge Trail: 4.8 mi. (7.7 km.), 3 hr. 45 min.
   to Mt. Garfield summit (via Garfield Ridge Trail):
      5.0 mi. (8.0 km.), 4 hr.
   to Garfield Ridge Campsite (via Garfield Ridge
      Trail): 5.0 mi. (8.1 km.), 3 hr. 50 min.

Gale River Trail (WMNF)

This trail runs from the Gale River Loop Rd. (FR 92) to the Garfield Ridge Trail 0.6 mi. west of Galehead Hut. You can reach the trailhead by leaving US 3 at its intersection with Trudeau Rd. (often called Five Corners, this intersection has signs for Trudeau Rd. and for the Ammonoosuc District Ranger Station). Follow the Gale River Rd. (FR 25) southeast, bearing left at 0.6 mi., then turn sharp right at 1.3 mi. on the Gale River Loop Rd. and continue to the parking area on the left at 1.6 mi. (Straight ahead on the road it is 1.6 mi. from here to the Garfield Trail parking lot.) This trail lies within the watershed of a municipal water supply, and hikers and campers should exercise care not to pollute the streams.

The trail enters the woods, soon descends a bank and crosses a tributary brook, then turns right on an old logging road that climbs easily along the west side of the North Branch of the Gale River, some distance away from the stream. At 1.4 mi. it reaches the edge of the stream, crosses it on a bridge at 1.7 mi., and becomes somewhat rougher, with several bypasses of muddy sections and washouts. The trail passes through an old logging campsite, crosses a major tributary, and recrosses to the west side of the North Branch at 2.5 mi. on stepping stones (difficult only in very high water). After passing the gravel outwash of an overgrown slide, the trail emerges at 3.1 mi. on a gravel bank above the stream at the base of a slide, where there are fine views up the valley and toward the Twins. The trail now becomes much steeper and rougher, and ends with a fairly steep climb to the Garfield Ridge Trail.

Gale River Trail (map 5:G5–G6)

Distances from Gale River Loop Road (FR 92)

　to Garfield Ridge Trail: 4.0 mi. (6.4 km.), 2 hr. 50 min.
　to Galehead Hut (via Garfield Ridge Trail): 4.6 mi. (7.4 km.), 3 hr. 25 min.

Frost Trail (AMC)

This short trail leads from Galehead Hut to the summit of Galehead Mtn. Leaving the hut clearing, it descends into a sag, then turns sharp right at a junction where the Twin Brook Trail enters left. After a short distance, the Frost Trail ascends a steep pitch, at the top of which a side path leads left 30 yd. to an excellent outlook over the Twin Brook valley. The main trail continues at a moderate grade to the rather flat summit, where there is a good though somewhat restricted view of Mt. Garfield and the Franconia Ridge.

Frost Trail (map 5:G6)

Distance from Galehead Hut
  to Galehead Mtn. summit: 0.5 mi. (0.8 km.), 25 min.

Twinway (AMC)

This trail extends from Galehead Hut to the junction with the Zealand Trail and the Ethan Pond Trail 0.2 mi. beyond Zealand Falls Hut, forming a very important ridgecrest link along the north edge of the Pemigewasset Wilderness, connecting the mountains of the western part of the region—the Franconia Range, Garfield, and the Twins—to the Bonds, the Zealand-Hale region, the Willey Range, and the northern parts of the Pemigewasset Wilderness. It offers magnificent views from the summits of South Twin Mtn. and Mt. Guyot and from the outlook at Zeacliff, and connecting trails lead to a number of other superb outlooks. For its entire length the Twinway is part of the Appalachian Trail.

This description of the path follows the eastbound direction (from Galehead Hut to Zealand Falls Hut). See below for a description in the reverse direction.

From the junction of the Frost and Garfield Ridge trails 40 yd. from Galehead Hut, the Twinway passes over a ledgy hump with an outlook to the right, descends to a sag, then climbs steadily and steeply up the cone of

South Twin to the south knob of the summit at 0.8 mi. Here the North Twin Spur begins, running straight ahead 40 yd. to the north knob and then on to North Twin, while the Twinway turns right (south) and descends along the ridge toward Mt. Guyot, with easy to moderate grades after an initial steep pitch below the summit. At 1.8 mi. the trail crosses a ledgy hump with views ahead to Guyot and Carrigain and back to South Twin. It descends easily to the col, then climbs out of the scrub to open rocks on the side of Guyot and passes the junction with the Bondcliff Trail on the right at 2.8 mi. Guyot Campsite is 0.8 mi. from this junction via the Bondcliff Trail and a spur path.

The Twinway now turns left and ascends in the open to the flat summit of Guyot at 2.9 mi., and, re-entering the woods, descends at a moderate grade on the long ridge toward Zealand Mtn., reaching the col at 3.9 mi. It then climbs rather steeply, and, at 4.1 mi., a few yards before reaching the height-of-land, passes a small cairn marking a side path on the left that runs nearly level 0.1 mi. to the true summit of Zealand Mtn. The main trail continues down the ridge, passes a ledge overlooking Zeacliff Pond at 5.1 mi., then descends a steep pitch, and in a sag at 5.3 mi. passes a side path that leads right to the shore of Zeacliff Pond in 0.1 mi. The main trail follows a ridge over a number of ledgy humps, passing the junction right with the Zeacliff Trail at 5.7 mi. It soon reaches a loop side path that leads right over the magnificent Zeacliff outlook and rejoins the main trail 50 yd. east of its point of departure. Here the Twinway turns left and descends moderately through birch woods. At 6.9 mi. the trail crosses two branches of Whitewall Brook on ledges, and the Lend-a-Hand Trail immediately enters on the left. The Twinway passes Zealand Falls Hut at 7.0 mi., descends steeply on rock steps for a short distance, passing a side path right to a viewpoint for

Zealand Falls, then crosses the outlet of Zealand Pond and reaches the grade of the old logging railroad. Here the Zealand Trail turns left and the Ethan Pond Trail turns right, both on the railroad grade.

Twinway (map 5:G6–G7)

Distances from Galehead Hut

    to South Twin summit: 0.8 mi., 1 hr.

    to Bondcliff Trail: 2.8 mi., 2 hr. 5 min.

    to Zealand Mtn. summit spur: 4.1 mi., 2 hr. 50 min.

    to Zeacliff Trail: 5.7 mi., 3 hr. 40 min.

    to Zealand Falls Hut: 7.0 mi., 4 hr. 20 min.

    to Ethan Pond Trail/Zealand Trail junction: 7.2 mi. (11.6 km.), 4 hr. 30 min.

Twinway (AMC) [in reverse]

From the junction of the Zealand and Ethan Pond trails, the Twinway crosses the outlet of Zealand Pond, then climbs steeply on rock steps to Zealand Falls Hut, passing a side path left to a viewpoint for Zealand Falls. It ascends moderately, passing a junction on the right with the Lend-a-Hand Trail just before it crosses two branches of Whitewall Brook on ledges, and continues to climb through birch woods. At 1.4 mi., where the trail swings right, a loop side path continues straight ahead, passing over the magnificent Zeacliff outlook and rejoining the main trail 50 yd. west of its point of departure. The Twinway passes a junction with the Zeacliff Trail on the left, then follows the ridge over several ledgy humps and crosses a sag at 1.9 mi., where a side path leads left to the shore of Zeacliff Pond in 0.1 mi. The main trail ascends rather steeply to a ledge overlooking the pond, then continues along the crest of the ridge over several wooded knobs. At 3.1 mi., just after crossing the height-of-land on the last of these knobs, it reaches a small cairn marking a side path on the right that runs nearly level 0.1 mi. to the true summit of Zealand Mtn. The main trail descends sharply to a col, then climbs moderately up the long ridge to Mt. Guyot, breaking into the open just as it reaches that summit. It then descends a short distance over open rocks to the junction with the Bondcliff Trail on the left at 4.4 mi. Guyot Campsite is 0.8 mi. from this junction via the Bondcliff Trail and a spur path.

From this junction the Twinway swings right and descends into the scrub, passes through a col, and then begins the long, gradual climb toward South Twin. At 5.5 mi. the trail crosses a ledgy hump with views ahead to South Twin and back to Guyot and Carrigain. After ascending a short steep pitch up the cone of South Twin, it reaches the south knob of the summit at 6.4 mi. Here the North Twin Spur begins, turning right and running 40 yd. to the north knob and then on to North Twin, while the Twinway turns left (west) and begins a steady steep descent toward Galehead Hut. At the bottom of this descent it crosses a small sag, passes over a ledgy hump with an outlook left, and soon reaches a junction 40 yd. from the hut, where the Garfield Ridge Trail enters on the right and the Frost Trail continues straight to the hut.

Twinway (map 5:G6–G7)

Distances from Ethan Pond Trail/Zealand Trail junction

　　to Zealand Falls Hut: 0.2 mi., 15 min.
　　to Zeacliff Trail: 1.5 mi., 1 hr. 25 min.
　　to Zealand Mtn. summit spur: 3.1 mi., 2 hr. 35 min.
　　to Bondcliff Trail: 4.4 mi., 3 hr. 30 min.
　　to South Twin summit: 6.4 mi., 4 hr. 45 min.
　　to Galehead Hut: 7.2 mi. (11.6 km.), 5 hr. 10 min.

North Twin Spur (AMC)

North Twin Spur connects the Twinway on the summit of South Twin with the North Twin Trail on the summit of North Twin. It leaves the Twinway at the south knob of South Twin, crosses the north knob in 40 yd., and descends moderately to the fern-filled col at 0.8 mi. Then it ascends to the summit of North Twin, where the North Twin Trail continues straight ahead and a spur path leads left 60 yd. to a fine outlook.

North Twin Spur (map 5:G6)

Distance from the Twinway

    to North Twin summit: 1.3 mi. (2.0 km.), 45 min.

North Twin Trail (WMNF)

This trail ascends to the summit of North Twin from Haystack Rd. (FR 304). Haystack Rd. begins on US 3 about 2.3 mi. west of Twin Mountain village, just west of a large WMNF boundary sign, and runs south 2.5 mi. to a parking area just past its crossing of the Little River. *Caution:* The three crossings of the Little River on this trail are very difficult or impassable at high water; the third is the least difficult, and the first two may be avoided by staying on the east bank and bushwhacking along the river. This trail is in the watershed of a municipal water supply, and hikers and campers should take care not to pollute the streams.

    The trail leaves the parking area and crosses the river three times, ascending easily on an old railroad grade with occasional bypasses. After the third crossing, at 1.9 mi., the trail begins to climb away from the river and railroad grade, crossing and recrossing a tributary brook. The long, steady climb continues, and at 3.5 mi. the trail becomes quite steep, reaching the ledgy end of the ridge at 4.0 mi. The trail now climbs easily, passes a superb outlook ledge at 4.2 mi., and reaches the summit of North Twin at 4.3 mi. The North Twin Spur continues straight ahead to South Twin, and a side path leads right 60 yd. to an excellent outlook.

North Twin Trail (map 5:G6)

Distances from Haystack Road

    to third crossing of Little River: 1.9 mi., 1 hr. 15 min.

    to North Twin summit: 4.3 mi. (7.0 km.), 3 hr. 40 min.

Zeacliff Trail (AMC)

This trail runs from the Ethan Pond Trail 1.3 mi. south of its junction with Zeland Pond to the Twinway 0.1 mi. west of the Zeacliff outlook. It is an attractive trail, much less frequently used than most trails in this area, but extremely steep and rough in parts and not recommended for hikers with heavy packs. Practically all of it lies in the Pemigewasset Wilderness.

The trail leaves the Ethan Pond Trail and descends west over open talus, then drops very steeply to cross Whitewall Brook at 0.2 mi. It climbs very steeply, up an old slide at first, then the grade eases up at 0.6 mi. Soon the trail reaches the top of the ridge, where it ascends gradually through a beautiful birch forest, then swings left and angles up to a rock face at 1.1 mi. The main trail turns right here and ascends steeply to the right of the rock face, while a rough and somewhat obscure loop path runs under the rock face, then swings right, passes an outlook toward Carrigain Notch, and rejoins the main trail. Above this point the trail ascends steeply to the Twinway. Turn right for the Zeacliff outlook.

Zeacliff Trail (map 5:G7)

Distance from Ethan Pond Trail

to Twinway: 1.4 mi. (2.3 km.), 1 hr. 25 min.

Zeland Trail (WMNF)

The Zealand Trail runs from the end of Zealand Rd. to a junction with the Ethan Pond Trail and the Twinway just below Zealand Falls Hut. You can reach the trailhead by following Zealand Rd. (FR 16), which leaves US 302 at Zealand Campground about 2.3 mi. east of Twin Mountain village, to a parking area on the left 3.5 mi. from US 302, just before a gate. Zealand Rd. is closed to public vehicular use from mid-November to mid-May; there is a parking area across US 302 just east of Zealand Rd. The Zealand Trail is relatively easy, following an old railroad grade much of the way, and passing through an area of beaver swamps, meadows, and ponds. All major brook crossings have bridges, but the trip can be a very wet one in wet weather, and some of the bridges occasionally float away.

Leaving the parking area, the trail follows the railroad grade, then a somewhat rough bypass. It then returns to the grade and approaches Zealand River at 0.8 mi., near some ledges in the stream. Here it diverges right from the grade and continues on the west bank, then makes the first of several brook crossings at 1.5 mi. The trail now passes through an area of beaver activity, staying mostly on the railroad grade, and at 2.3 mi. the A–Z Trail enters from the left. The Zealand Trail crosses the outlet brook and skirts Zealand Pond, ending at 2.5 mi. where the Ethan Pond Trail continues straight ahead and the Twinway turns right to Zealand Falls Hut, 0.2 mi. away.

Zealand Trail (map 5:G7)
Distances from end of Zealand Road

    to A-Z Trail: 2.3 mi., 1 hr. 20 min.

    to Ethan Pond Trail/Twinway junction: 2.5 mi. (4.1 km.), 1 hr. 30 min.

    to Zealand Falls Hut (via Twinway): 2.8 mi., 1 hr. 40 min.

Lend-a-Hand Trail (AMC)

This trail connects Zealand Falls Hut with the summit of Mt. Hale. The grade is fairly easy but the footing is rather rough for a good part of its distance, particularly for those trying to balance heavy packs, since there are many log bridges across a very wet section. The trail takes its name from a journal for charitable organizations that was edited by Edward Everett Hale, the Boston pastor and author for whom Mt. Hale was named.

This trail diverges right (north) from the Twinway 0.1 mi. above Zealand Falls Hut and climbs steadily, crossing a small brook three times. After about 0.5 mi. the grade becomes easy in a long section with numerous log bridges, where small brooks flow in and through the trail. At 1.5 mi. the trail enters a scrubby, ledgy area and ascends moderately. In a rocky area at 1.9 mi. a ledge 15 yd. right of the trail offers a beautiful view. At 2.4 mi. the trail climbs another rocky pitch and continues in dense conifers to the summit, where the Hale Brook Trail leaves east (right). Many of the rocks on this bare summit are reputed to be strongly magnetic.

Lend-a-Hand Trail (map 5:G7–G6)
Distance from Twinway
to Mt. Hale summit: 2.7 mi. (4.3 km.), 2 hr.

Hale Brook Trail (WMNF)

This trail climbs from Zealand Rd. (FR 16), at a parking area 2.5 mi. from US 302, to the bare summit of Mt. Hale, where there are excellent views. The trail is relatively easy, with moderate grades and good footing, and passes through a scenic birch forest much of the way.

The trail leaves the parking area, crosses a cross-country ski trail, then ascends steadily to cross Hale Brook at 0.8 mi. It continues the steady climb, then swings left at 1.1 mi. and ascends gradually across the steep slope above Hale Brook, recrossing the brook in its rocky bed at 1.3 mi. Now the trail ascends by several switchbacks, crossing a small brook at 1.7 mi. Still ascending, and curving gradually to the right, it enters the conifers and attains the summit from the east.

Hale Brook Trail (map 5:G7–G6)
Distance from Zealand Road
to Mt. Hale summit: 2.2 mi. (3.5 km.), 2 hr. 15 min.

Sugarloaf Trail (WMNF)

This trail ascends both North Sugarloaf and Middle Sugarloaf from Zealand Rd. (FR 16), just south of the bridge over the Zealand River 1.0 mi. from US 302. Parking is available just north of the bridge. These two little peaks offer excellent views from their open ledgy summits for a relatively small effort.

Leaving the road, the Sugarloaf Trail follows the river for 0.2 mi., coinciding with the Trestle Trail, then swings left as the Trestle Trail continues along the river. After this junction the Sugarloaf Trail immediately crosses a snowmobile trail and a dirt road, and climbs gradually, passing a few large boulders, where it turns sharp right (arrow). At 0.7 mi. it makes an abrupt ascent toward the col between North and Middle Sugarloaf. In this col, at 0.9 mi., the trail divides. The left branch turns sharp right after about 0.2 mi. and climbs to the summit of Middle Sugarloaf at 0.5 mi. from the col, becoming very steep in the last ledgy section. The right branch descends slightly and then climbs to the summit of North Sugarloaf at 0.3 mi. from the col.

Sugarloaf Trail (map 5:F6)
Distances from Zealand Road
>   *to* Middle Sugarloaf: 1.4 mi. (2.3 km.), 1 hr. 10 min.
>   *to* North Sugarloaf: 1.2 mi. (1.9 km.), 1 hr.

Trestle Trail (WMNF)

This short loop trail begins and ends at the bridge over the Zealand River on Zealand Rd. (FR 16), 1.0 mi. from US 302. (Parking is located at the north end of the bridge.) An information leaflet is usually available at the trailhead. The Trestle Trail leaves the road at the south end of the bridge and follows the river, coinciding with the Sugarloaf Trail for 0.2 mi. After the Sugarloaf Trail diverges left, the Trestle Trail leads away from the river, crosses a snowmobile trail, then turns right at a large boulder and follows the snowmobile trail for a short distance. Then the trail turns sharp right on an old railroad grade, crosses Zealand River on a bridge at 0.6 mi., and soon enters Sugarloaf II Campground. After following the campground road for 0.1 mi., it re-enters the woods and returns to Zealand Rd. at the north end of the bridge.

Trestle Trail (map 5:F6)
Distance of loop
  from Zealand Rd.: 1.0 mi. (1.6 km.), 35 min.

Mount Willard Trail

This path runs from the AMC's Crawford Depot information center, on the west side of US 302 across from Saco Lake, to the ledges above the cliffs overlooking Crawford Notch. The upper part was formerly a carriage road, and the trail has easy grades, good footing, and magnificent views from the ledges, offering perhaps the finest views in the White Mtns. for the amount of effort required.

From Crawford Depot this trail coincides with the Avalon Trail for 0.1 mi., then turns left, runs level, and soon turns right to begin the ascent. In another 100 yd. the trail bears right, bypassing to the west a severely washed-out portion of the old carriage road. At 0.5 mi., the trail passes to the left of Centennial Pool. Beyond this point the trail bears left and at 0.7 mi. rejoins the old carriage road, which it follows the rest of the way. At 1.5 mi. a rough spur path 0.2 mi. long leads left to the head of Hitchcock Flume and an outlook, while the main trail continues to the ledges just east of the true summit.

Mount Willard Trail (map 5:G8)
Distance from Crawford Depot
  to Mt. Willard summit: 1.6 mi. (2.6 km.), 1 hr. 15 min.

Avalon Trail (AMC)

This trail runs from the AMC's Crawford Depot information center on the west side of US 302 to the Willey Range Trail 90 yd. north of the summit of Mt. Field, passing a short spur path to the fine outlook on Mt. Avalon along the way. Some parts are steep and rough, but these are not severe.

About 0.1 mi. from Crawford Depot, the Mount Willard Trail leaves left, and the Avalon Trail ascends gradually and soon crosses a brook. Just beyond this crossing a loop path diverges left, passes by Beecher and Pearl cascades, and shortly rejoins the main trail. The main trail continues at an easy grade, recrosses the brook at 0.8 mi., and begins a moderate ascent. At 1.3 mi. the A-Z Trail to Zealand Falls Hut diverges right. The Avalon Trail soon begins to climb rather steeply, and at 1.8 mi., in the small col just below Mt. Avalon's summit, a short side path diverges left and climbs steeply 100 yd. to this fine viewpoint. The main trail passes through a flat, ledgy area, then climbs steadily, with restricted views to the northeast, to the Willey Range Trail. To reach the summit of Mt. Field go left (south) 90 yd.

Avalon Trail (map 5:G8–G7)
Distances from Crawford Depot

　to A-Z Trail: 1.3 mi., 1 hr. 5 min.
　to Mount Avalon Spur Path: 1.8 mi., 1 hr. 40 min.
　to Willey Range Trail: 2.8 mi. (4.5 km.), 2 hr. 35 min.

A-Z Trail (AMC)

This trail runs from the Avalon Trail to the Zealand Trail, crossing the Willey Range at the Field-Tom Col, providing a route to Zealand Falls Hut from US 302 at the Crawford Depot.

It diverges right from the Avalon Trail 1.3 mi. from Crawford's, crosses a steep gully, then climbs steadily, angling up along the side of the valley. At 0.6 mi. it crosses the brook and soon begins to climb more steeply, reaching the height-of-land at 1.0 mi., where the Mount Tom Spur diverges right. The trail starts to descend gradually, and in 80 yd. the Willey Range Trail enters on the left. The trail descends more steeply until it crosses the Mt. Field Brook at 1.6 mi., then continues its descent at easy to moderate grades, passing through a logged area

and crossing several small brooks, and reaches the
Zealand Trail 2.3 mi. from the end of Zealand Rd.
Zealand Falls Hut is 0.5 mi. left via the Zealand Trail and
Twinway.

A-Z Trail (map 5:G7)
Distances from Avalon Trail
  to Willey Range Trail: 1.0 mi., 1 hr.
  to Zealand Trail: 3.7 mi. (6.0 km.), 2 hr. 25 min.
  to Zealand Falls Hut (via Zealand Trail and Twin-
    way): 4.2 mi., 2 hr. 40 min.

Ethan Pond Trail (AMC)
The Ethan Pond Trail begins at the Willey House Station,
reached by a paved road 0.3 mi. long that leaves the west
side of US 302 opposite the Webster Cliff Trail, about 1
mi. south of the Willey House site. It ends at the junction
of the Zealand Trail and the Twinway, 0.2 mi. below
Zealand Falls Hut, and is part of the Appalachian Trail.

The trail begins in a parking area just below the railroad tracks, crosses the tracks just north of the station,
and at 0.2 mi. the Arethusa–Ripley Falls Trail diverges
left. The Ethan Pond Trail climbs steadily, then becomes
more gradual, and at 1.3 mi. the Kedron Flume Trail
enters on the right. At 1.6 mi. the Willey Range Trail
leaves straight ahead, and the Ethan Pond Trail turns left
and climbs steadily to the height-of-land at 2.1 mi., passing from Crawford Notch State Park into the WMNF. It
enters and follows an old logging road down to a point
close to the southeast corner of Ethan Pond, which however is not visible from the trail. This pond is named for
its discoverer, Ethan Allen Crawford. Here, at 2.6 mi.
from Willey House Station, a side trail right leads in 250
yd. to Ethan Pond Campsite.

At 4.4 mi. the Ethan Pond Trail bears right, merging
into a spur of the old Zealand Valley railroad and following it to the main line at 4.6 mi., where the Shoal Pond

Trail enters left. At 4.9 mi. the Ethan Pond Trail crosses the North Fork on a wooden bridge, and at 5.1 mi. the Thoreau Falls Trail diverges left to continue down the North Fork. The Ethan Pond Trail follows the old railroad grade on a gradual curve into Zealand Notch, with its steep, fire-scarred walls. As the trail crosses the talus slopes of Whitewall Mtn. it comes into the open with fine views, and at 5.9 mi., in the middle of this section, the Zeacliff Trail diverges left. The Ethan Pond Trail soon re-enters the woods and continues on the remains of the railroad grade to the junction with the Zealand Trail and the Twinway. For Zealand Falls Hut turn sharp left onto the Twinway and follow it for 0.2 mi.

Ethan Pond Trail (map 5:H8–G7)

Distances from Willey House Station

   to Willey Range Trail: 1.6 mi., 1 hr. 25 min.

   to side trail to Ethan Pond Campsite: 2.6 mi., 2 hr. 5 min.

   to Shoal Pond Trail: 4.6 mi., 3 hr.

   to Thoreau Falls Trail: 5.1 mi., 3 hr. 20 min.

   to Zeacliff Trail: 5.9 mi., 3 hr. 40 min.

   to Zealand Trail/Twinway: 7.2 mi. (11.6 km.), 4 hr. 20 min.

   to Zealand Falls Hut (via Zealand Trail and Twinway): 7.4 mi., 4 hr. 30 min.

Kedron Flume Trail (AMC)

This trail runs from the Willey House site on US 302 to the Ethan Pond Trail 0.3 mi. south of its junction with the Willey Range Trail, passing Kedron Flume, an interesting cascade. The trail has easy to moderate grades with good footing as far as Kedron Flume. Past the flume it is very steep and rough.

Leaving US 302 south of the Willey House site, the trail passes through a picnic area and enters the woods. At 0.4 mi. it crosses the railroad tracks, where there is a good view of Mt. Willey. At 1.0 mi., after a short descent, it crosses Kedron Brook. Above is an interesting flume and below is a waterfall where there is an excellent outlook; use care on slippery rocks. Above here the trail makes a very steep and rough climb, following a small brook part of the way, then becomes easier as it approaches the Ethan Pond Trail.

Kedron Flume Trail (map 5:G8)

Distances from Willey House site

> *to* Kedron Flume: 1.0 mi., 50 min.
> *to* Ethan Pond Trail: 1.3 mi., 1 hr. 15 min.

Willey Range Trail (AMC)

This trail begins on the Ethan Pond Trail 1.6 mi. from the Willey House Station, then runs over the summits of Mt. Willey and Mt. Field to the A-Z Trail in the Field-Tom Col. Along with the Ethan Pond, A-Z, and Avalon trails, it makes possible various trips over the Willey Range to or from Willey House Station, the Crawford Depot, and Zealand Falls Hut. The section on the south slope of Mt. Willey is very steep and rough.

The trail continues straight ahead where the Ethan Pond Trail turns left, crosses Kedron Brook in 100 yd., and at 0.2 mi. turns sharp left and crosses a smaller brook. At 0.4 mi. it crosses another small brook, then climbs a very steep and rough slope with several ladders and offers occasional outlooks. The best view is from the east outlook, near the summit, reached by an unsigned path that leaves on the right 40 yd. below the summit cairn. The main trail reaches the summit at 1.1 mi., circles to the south outlook, then descends gradually, keeping mostly to the west side of the ridge. It loses only 300 ft. in altitude at its low point, then climbs to the summit of Mt. Field at 2.5 mi. About 90 yd. north of this summit the Avalon Trail diverges right, and the Willey Range Trail climbs over a small knob and descends gradually northwest to the A-Z Trail in the Field-Tom Col at 3.4

mi. Turn left to reach Zealand Falls Hut or right to reach
the Mount Tom Spur, Crawford Depot, and US 302.

Willey Range Trail (map 5:G8–G7)

Distances from Ethan Pond Trail
> *to* Mt. Willey summit: 1.1 mi., 1 hr. 20 min.
> *to* Mt. Field summit: 2.5 mi., 2 hr. 15 min.
> *to* A-Z Trail: 3.4 mi. (5.6 km.), 2 hr. 45 min.

Mount Tom Spur (AMC)

This short trail runs from the A-Z Trail to the summit of
Mt. Tom. It leaves the A-Z Trail at the height-of-land, 80
yd. east of the Willey Range Trail junction, and climbs at
a moderate grade. At 0.3 mi. there is a good view from a
blowdown patch, and the trail continues to a false summit, where it swings left and reaches the true summit in
another 60 yd.

Mount Tom Spur (map 5:G7)

Distance from A-Z Trail
> *to* Mt. Tom summit: 0.6 mi. (0.9 km.), 25 min.

Arethusa Falls Trail (NHDP)

This trail is the direct route to Arethusa Falls, which are
over 200 ft. high, the highest in New Hampshire. It
begins at the Arethusa Falls parking lot on the west side
of US 302, 3.4 mi. south of the Willey House site in
Crawford Notch State Park. The trail crosses the railroad
and leads left (south) for 50 yd., turns right into the
woods, and soon passes a spur path left to some cascades.
It follows old roads above the north bank of Bemis
Brook. The Bemis Brook Trail, which diverges left at 0.1
mi. and rejoins at 0.5 mi., provides an attractive alternative route closer to the brook. At 0.8 mi. another spur
leads left to cascades, and at 1.2 mi. it crosses Bemis
Brook on a bridge and reaches Arethusa Falls, where it
ends at the junction with the Arethusa–Ripley Falls Trail.

Arethusa Falls Trail (map 5:H8)

Distance from Arethusa Falls parking area
  to Arethusa Falls: 1.3 mi. (2.1 km.), 1 hr. 10 min.

Bemis Brook Trail (NHDP)

This is a slightly longer alternative route to the lower part of the Arethusa Falls Trail, running closer to Bemis Brook. It departs to the left from the Arethusa Falls Trail 0.1 mi. from its start at the railroad, angles toward the brook, and then follows close to the brook, passing spur paths leading left to Fawn Pool, Coliseum Falls, and Bemis Brook Falls. It then climbs steeply up the bank to rejoin the Arethusa Falls Trail.

Bemis Brook Trail (map 5:H8)

Distance from Arethusa Falls Trail
  to rejoining Arethusa Falls Trail: 0.5 mi. (0.7 km.),
     30 min.

Arethusa–Ripley Falls Trail (AMC/NHDP)

These two spectacular waterfalls in Crawford Notch are connected by a trail that starts at the upper end of the Arethusa Falls Trail, just below the falls. It immediately crosses the brook and angles up the side of the valley away from the falls on a graded path, then doubles back on the south side of a smaller brook, which it soon crosses. Becoming rougher, it leads northeast across several small watercourses to the plateau behind Frankenstein Cliff. Turning east, the trail passes a southeast outlook and then the junction on the right with the Frankenstein Cliff Trail at 1.3 mi., and again heads north across the plateau. With various views of Mt. Webster, Crawford Notch, and Mt. Willey, the trail drops gradually and then more steeply on switchbacks to a spur path left to the top of Ripley Falls, which are about 100 ft. high. In dry weather, the water flow is rather low. The rocks just off the path near the falls are slippery and should be avoided.

After crossing Avalanche Brook at the foot of the falls at 2.5 mi, the path rises slightly to the east to join the Ethan Pond Trail 0.2 mi. from the Willey House Station; continue straight ahead for that destination.

Arethusa–Ripley Falls Trail (map 5:H8)

Distances from Arethusa Falls

   to Frankenstein Cliff Trail: 1.9 mi., 45 min.
   to Ripley Falls: 2.5 mi., 1 hr. 20 min.
   to Ethan Pond Trail: 2.8 mi. (4.5 km.), 1 hr 30 min.
   to Willey House Station: 3.0 mi. (4.8 km.), 1 hr. 40 min.

Frankenstein Cliff Trail (NHDP)

This trail provides acces to Frankenstein Cliff, a prominent bluff that juts out from the tableland south of Mt. Willey and affords excellent views of the lower part of Crawford Notch. It begins at the Arethusa Falls parking lot on the west side of US 302, 3.4 mi. south of the Willey House site in Crawford Notch State Park.

Leaving the parking lot, the trail runs below and roughly parallel to the railroad grade, generally level with many minor ups and downs. At 0.6 mi. it reaches the junciton with the former route of the trail, where it turns shap left and passes under the Frankenstein railroad trestle near the south abutment. (Trespassing on the railroad, including the use of its bed as a footway, is extremely dangerous and is prohibited.) It ascends by swithbacks and over stone steplike formations through the woods beneath the cliffs and up to the ridge, climbing rather steeply in places. It then passes through open hardwood forest, crossing a streambed where there is usually water. It passes through a fine area of spruce and balsam to an outlook at 1.3 mi., similar to that from Mt. Willard, with a view south in the notch.

Leaving the outlook, the trail ascends gradually through a fine stand of spruce in a west-northwest direction, skirting the top of the cliffs, with views of the valley and Mt. Bemis, and passing just south of the summit of a small knob. At one point there is a view of Arethusa Falls far up at the head of the valley. Near the height-of-land the trail levels off, then descends the ridge for a short distance, and winds gradually downward to meet the Arethusa–Ripley Falls Trail.

Frankenstein Cliff Trail (map 5:H8)

Distances from the Arethusa Falls parking area

to Frankenstein Cliff outlook: 1.3 mi., 1 hr. 10 min.
to Arethusa–Ripley Falls Trail: 2.1 mi. (3.4 km.), 1 hr. 45 min.

Wilderness Trail (WMNF)

The Wilderness Trail stretches for 8.9 mi. along the East Branch of the Pemigewasset River, from the Kancamagus Highway (NH 112) to Stillwater Junction, forming the central artery from which numerous trails diverge and lead to various parts of the Pemigewasset Wilderness and to the adjoining mountains. For most of its length, the trail follows the bed of a logging railroad that last operated in 1948. It begins at a large parking area (Lincoln Woods) just east of the highway bridge over the East Branch, 4.1 mi. from the information center at the I-93 exit in Lincoln and about 0.3 mi. beyond the Hancock Campground. The USFS has renamed the segment of this trail between the Kancamagus Highway and the Pemigewasset Wilderness boundary near Franconia Brook as the Lincoln Woods Trail, in an attempt to emphasize which part of the trail lies within the designated Wilderness and which part lies outside. However, since it seems unlikely that popular usage will also change, in this guide the entire trail from the Kancamagus Highway to Stillwater Junction will continue to be referred to as the Wilderness Trail in the hope of minimizing confusion. This trail receives extremely heavy use, particularly in the few miles nearest the highway, and camping is strictly regulated. Obtain details concerning such restrictions at the Lincoln Woods Information Center, located next to the parking area, or from other USFS sources.

The trail runs across the porch of the information center, then descends slightly to cross the East Branch on a suspension bridge and turns right, following the railroad bed, climbing almost imperceptibly. At 1.4 mi. the Osseo Trail diverges left, and at 2.6 mi. the Black Pond Trail leaves left. The Franconia Brook Campsite is situated on the left at 2.8 mi. Just before the bridge across Franconia Brook, a side trail leads north up the west bank 0.4 mi. to Franconia Falls, where the brook falls over broad ledges with many fine cascades and pools.

The Wilderness Trail crosses Franconia Brook on a footbridge, and in about 50 yd. at 2.9 mi., the Franconia Brook Trail climbs the bank on the left (north). Here the Wilderness Trail enters the Pemigewasset Wilderness. From the junction the trail bears right and continues to swing to the east. It crosses a brook at 3 9 mi., and reach to the Camp 16 clearing (where camping is no longer permitted) at 4.7 mi. Here the Bondcliff Trail diverges left (north), and the Wilderness Trail crosses Black Brook on a bridge to the left of the old railroad bridge. This bridge, the last railroad trestle still standing, is the subject of a major administrative debate as to whether it is a nonconforming artificial structure in Wilderness that by law must be removed, or an important historical artifact that by law must be preserved. At 5.4 mi. the Wilderness Trail crosses to the south bank of the East Branch on a 180-ft. suspension bridge. On the far side, the Cedar Brook Trail (see Section 4) branches to the right (southwest).

Continuing upstream from the bridge, the Wilderness Trail now skirts the end of the long north ridge of Mt. Hancock, and just after crossing a small slide it reaches

North Fork Junction at 6.3 mi., where the Thoreau Falls Trail diverges left (north) and the Wilderness Trail continues straight ahead. At 7.2 mi. the trail diverges from the railroad grade (which crossed the river here), crosses Crystal Brook, and soon rejoins the railroad, which has crossed back to this bank. After passing through the clearing of Camp 18, the trail leaves the railroad for the last time at 8.0 mi. and follows a path along the bank that crosses a low, piney ridge then descends to cross the Carrigain Branch (which may be difficult at high water) at 8.7 mi. Soon it reaches Stillwater Junction, coming into the junction at a right angle to the stream. Here the Carrigain Notch Trail (Section 4) leads right (southeast) to Desolation Shelter and Sawyer River Rd., while the Shoal Pond Trail crosses the stream directly ahead at an old dam (no bridge). (Avoid the path angling left down to the stream, which is an abandoned section of the Wilderness Trail.)

Wilderness Trail (map 5:I5–H7)

Distances from Kancamagus Highway

> *to* Franconia Brook Trail: 2.9 mi., 1 hr. 35 min.
>
> *to* Bondcliff Trail: 4.7 mi., 2 hr. 35 min.
>
> *to* Cedar Brook Trail: 5.4 mi., 2 hr. 55 min.
>
> *to* Thoreau Falls Trail: 6.3 mi., 3 hr. 25 min.
>
> *to* Stillwater Junction: 8.9 mi. (14.3 km.), 4 hr. 55 min.
>
> *to* Desolation Shelter (via Carrigain Notch Trail): 9.5 mi., 5 hr. 15 min.

Osseo Trail (AMC)

This trail connects the lower end of the Wilderness Trail with the south end of the Franconia Ridge, near Mt. Flume. It begins on the west side of the Wilderness Trail, 1.4 mi. north of the parking area on the Kancamagus Highway. It heads west, following a brook in a flat area, then climbs the bank to the right and soon enters a section of an old incline logging railroad grade at one of its switchbacks. It continues up the valley on the grade and then on old logging roads not far above the brook. At 2.1 mi. the trail turns right and climbs by switchbacks to the top of the ridge above the valley to the north, then ascends the ridge—winding at first, then climbing by zigzags as the ridge steepens. At the top of this section are several wooden staircases, and at 3.2 mi. a side path (sign) leads right to a "dowilook" with a very fine view of Mt. Bond. Soon the trail reaches the top of the ridge, and its grade becomes easy until it reaches the crest of the Franconia Ridge in a flat area at 3.7 mi. The trail turns sharp right here and ascends near the crest of a narrow ridge to a junction with the Flume Slide Trail on the left and the Franconia Ridge Trail straight ahead.

Osseo Trail (map 5:H5)

Distance from Wilderness Trail

   to Flume Slide Trail/Franconia Ridge Trail junction:
      4.1 mi. (6.6 km.), 3 hr. 30 min.

Black Pond Trail (WMNF)

This short, easy spur trail leaves the Wilderness Trail 2.6 mi. from the Kancamagus Highway and ends at Black Pond, where there is an interesting view of the lower ridges of Mt. Bond from the western shore. Diverging left (west) from the Wilderness Trail, it first follows a former logging railroad spur, then leaves it on the left after 150 yd. and skirts the north shore of an old ice pond, which is in sight but not actually reached. Beyond the boggy pond it joins an old logging road, crosses the Camp 7 clearing (now overgrown by raspberries), and approaches Birch Island Brook, then bears slightly right away from it up a moderate incline. At 0.5 mi. it makes a short but sharp descent to cross the outlet brook from Black Pond, then recrosses it at a boggy spot. Soon it crosses the outlet brook for the third time and follows it to Black Pond, then skirts the southwest side of the pond and ends at the viewpoint.

Black Pond Trail (map 5:H6–H5)
Distance from Wilderness Trail
   to Black Pond: 0.8 mi. (1.4 km.), 30 min.

Franconia Brook Trail (WMNF)

This trail runs from the Wilderness Trail 2.9 mi. from the Kancamagus Highway to the Garfield Ridge Trail 0.9 mi. east of the summit of Mt. Garfield.

It diverges north from the Wilderness Trail at a point about 50 yd. east of the footbridge across Franconia Brook, at the boundary of the Pemigewasset Wilderness, and climbs up a steep bank to an old railroad grade, which it follows. It crosses Camp 9 Brook twice, and at 1.0 mi. swings right off the railroad grade to bypass a section flooded by an enthusiastic beaver colony. The trail crosses Camp 9 Brook again, turns sharp left back along the brook (avoid the beaten path ahead that leads into a swamp) and climbs its bank, and soon rejoins the railroad grade, turning sharp right on it and continuing to the junction with the Lincoln Brook Trail, which diverges left (west) at 1.7 mi.

The Franconia Brook Trail passes several small open swamps that lie to the right, with occasional short sections made wet by beaver activity, and continues to ascend gradually on the old railroad grade, crossing Hellgate and Redrock brooks and passing through clearings at the sites of Camps 10, 12, and 13. At 5.2 mi. it reaches 13 Falls, a beautiful waterfall and cascade, and turns right, leaving the old railroad grade on an old logging road. In 100 yd. the Lincoln Brook Trail re-enters from the left (west), and in quick succession a spur path leads right to 13 Falls Campsite and the Twin Brook Trail branches off to the right. The Franconia Brook Trail continues on an old logging road and crosses a branch of Franconia Brook at 6.2 mi., then climbs somewhat more steeply along old logging roads to the top of the ridge, where it ends at the

Garfield Ridge Trail. Garfield Ridge Campsite is 0.6 mi. left (west) by the Garfield Ridge Trail and spur path; Galehead Hut is located 2.2 mi. right.

Franconia Brook Trail (map 5:H6–G5)

Distances from Wilderness Trail

to Lincoln Brook Trail (from junction): 1.7 mi., 1 hr.

to 13 Falls Campsite: 5.2 mi., 3 hr.

to Garfield Ridge Trail: 7.4 mi. (11.9 km.), 4 hr. 40 min.

Lincoln Brook Trail (WMNF)

This trail begins and ends on the Franconia Brook Trail, and together these two trails make a complete circuit around the base of Owl's Head Mtn. The south junction is 1.7 mi. north of the Wilderness Trail, and the north junction is near 13 Falls Campsite. *Caution:* Several of the brook crossings on this trail may be very difficult at high water.

Turning left (west) off the Franconia Brook Trail, the Lincoln Brook Trail leads southwest through the woods to join an old railroad bed just before the crossing of Franconia Brook at 0.5 mi. In another 0.4 mi. it crosses Lincoln Brook from the north to the south side. (These crossings, which may be particularly difficult at high water, can be avoided by bushwhacking along the west banks of Franconia and Lincoln brooks from Franconia Brook Falls, following old logging roads part of the way. Another possible route involves bushwhacking due north from the end of the Black Pond Trail; this route rises easily through open woods, then descends a rather steep bank just before reaching the Lincoln Brook Trail, The Franconia Falls route is easier going toward the Wilderness Trail, and the Black Pond route is easier coming from it. The Black Pond route requires careful use of map and compass.) Beyond the Lincoln Brook crossing, the Lincoln Brook Trail follows the brook upstream on a long northward curve. It crosses a small brook at 2.2 mi.,

then the larger Liberty Brook at 2.8 mi. Soon it enters the
Camp 11 clearing, climbs left to avoid a mudhole, rejoins
the road, and crosses Lincoln Brook (sometimes difficult) to the east side at 3.0 mi. At 3.4 mi. it traverses the
base of an old slide from Owl's Head, then crosses Lincoln Brook again at 4.3 mi. and continues north, crossing
a divide into the Franconia Brook drainage with some
glimpses of the northern Franconia Range behind (west)
and Mt. Garfield to the north. Parts of the trail through
and north of the divide are rough, and there is an extensive boggy area at the height-of-land where the trail is
often very wet and muddy and may be somewhat difficult to follow. From the divide the trail descends to cross
a west fork of Franconia Brook at 6.6 mi., then turns
sharp right and follows a logging road down the left bank
of the brook past cascades and pools. It then swings right
off the old road, passes waterfalls, crosses the main
stream and rejoins the Franconia Brook Trail near 13
Falls Campsite.

Lincoln Brook Trail (map 5:H6–H5)
Distances from Franconia Brook Trail
> to Owl's Head slide: 3.4 mi., 2 hr. 10 min.
> to 13 Falls Campsite: 6.9 mi. (11.1 km.), 4 hr. 10 min.

Owl's Head Path
This unofficial, unmaintained path ascends the slide on
the west side of this remote mountain, starting from the
Lincoln Brook Trail at a small cairn 3.4 mi. from its south
junction with the Franconia Brook Trail and 0.4 mi.
beyond the second crossing of Lincoln Brook. (*Note:*
Hikers often mistake Liberty Brook for Lincoln Brook,
and thus think they have already passed the Owl's Head
path when they arrive at the Lincoln Brook crossing that
is about 0.2 mi. beyond Liberty Brook but still 0.4 mi.
before the Owl's Head Path. At the slide, the main brook
is nearby on the west and the steep mountainside rises

immediately to the east.) The slide is very steep and rough, and though considerably overgrown it is still potentially dangerous because of loose rock and smooth ledges, especially when wet. Great care should be taken both ascending and descending. Hikers who find the slide unappealing may be able to bushwhack up or down the steep slope to the north, parallel to the slide, through mostly open woods. Since Owl's Head signs are apparently highly prized souvenirs, both the junction with the Lincoln Brook Trail and the summit usually lack such identification.

There is no well-defined path on the slide, but several routes are usually marked by cairns of varying size and visibility. In general, it is easier to ascend on the south side, which is mostly ledge with good holds for hands and feet, and descend on the north side, which is mostly loose gravel. (In other words, it is usually better to keep to the right.) At the top of the slide, 0.3 mi. and 700 ft. above the Lincoln Brook Trail, just before the trail enters the woods there is a small spring spurting from the rock like a fountain, which unfortunately is not completely reliable. From here a well-trodden, unmaintained path climbs rather steeply up to the ridge, which is reached at 0.8 mi., then swings left and runs near the crest with minor ups and downs until it finally climbs a short pitch and abruptly reaches a tiny clearing at the wooded summit. Above the slide, the path is sometimes blocked for short distances by blowdowns; be careful to return to the path after passing these obstructions. Ambitious tree-climbers may obtain excellent views. If this summit had a view it would be one of the finest in the mountains, due to its strategic location in the center of the great horseshoe formed by the ridge running from the Franconias to the Bonds.

Owl's Head Path (map 5:H5)

Distance from Lincoln Brook Trail

to Owl's Head summit: 1.0 mi. (1.5 km.), 1 hr. 15 min.

Distance from Kancamagus Highway
> *to* Owl's Head (via Wilderness Trail, Franconia Brook
> Trail, Lincoln Brook Trail, and slide): 9.0 mi. (14.4
> km.), 6 hr.

Twin Brook Trail (AMC)

This trail connects 13 Falls Campsite to Galehead Hut.
At the start, take care to follow blazes at sharp bends,
avoiding several old logging roads. The Twin Brook
Trail diverges from the Franconia Brook Trail near the
campsite and rises gradually east-northeast, soon entering a beautiful birch forest. After 0.4 mi. the trail swings
to the northeast and heads up the valley of Twin Brook,
keeping to the left (west) of the brook, which is occasionally audible but not visible. After traversing four distinct minor ridges of Galehead Mtn. in the next mile, the
trail eventually climbs more steeply to its terminus on the
Frost Trail 0.1 mi. from Galehead Hut. Turn right to
reach the hut.

Twin Brook Trail (map 5:G5–G6)

Distances from 13 Falls Campsite
> to Frost Trail: 2.6 mi. (4.1 km.), 2 hr. 5 min.
> to Galehead Hut (via Frost Trail): 2.7 mi. (4.3 km.), 2
> hr. 10 min.

Bondcliff Trail (AMC)

This trail begins on the Wilderness Trail at Camp 16, 4.7
mi. from the Kancamagus Highway, ascends over Bondcliff and Mt. Bond, and ends at the Twinway just west of
the summit of Mt. Guyot. It connects the Pemigewasset
Wilderness with the high summits of the Twin Range.
The long section on Bondcliff and one shorter section on
Guyot are above treeline, with great exposure to the
weather. The views from this trail are unsurpassed in the
White Mtns.

Leaving the Wilderness Trail at Camp 16, the Bond-cliff Trail runs level for 100 yd., then turns sharp left at a phantom crossing of Black Brook and climbs a bank to an old logging road. Soon it enters a relocated section (this relocation has eliminated four crossings of Black Brook). At 1.1 mi. it rejoins the logging road along the brook and ascends easily, though parts of the road are severely eroded. It then crosses the brook four times; the second crossing, at 1.9 mi., provides the last sure water. At the third crossing, at 2.5 mi., the trail turns right across the brook bed, climbs a steep slope on rock steps, then swings left to another old logging road and crosses a gravel bank where one can look almost straight up to the summit of Bondcliff. In a short distance it makes the last brook crossing in a steep, south-facing ravine; if the brook is dry here, you can usually find water a short distance farther up in the streambed. The trail winds up a small "hanging" ridge that protrudes into the main ravine, then at 3.2 mi. swings left and begins a long side-hill ascent up the steep slope on a logging road, heading back to the southwest. At 4.1 mi. the trail reaches the crest of Bondcliff's south ridge, swings north, and ascends the ridge to a short, rather difficult scramble up a ledge. Soon it breaks out of the scrub and climbs along the edge of the cliffs, with spectacular views, reaching the summit of Bondcliff at 4.4 mi. *Caution:* The trail runs above treeline for about a mile and is dangerous in bad weather. When visibility is poor or weather bad, stay well to the east of the edge of the precipices.

The trail now descends the open ridge into a long, flat col, then ascends the steep slope of Mt. Bond, re-entering scrubby woods about halfway up. At 5.6 mi. the trail passes just west of the summit of Mt. Bond, which commands a magnificent unrestricted view of the surrounding wilderness and mountains. The trail descends north, crossing a minor knob, then drops down rather steeply past the spur path to West Bond at 6.1 mi., and leaves the Pemigewasset Wilderness. It reaches the Bond-Guyot Col at 6.3 mi., where a spur path descends right (east) 0.2 mi. and 250 ft. to Guyot Campsite and its spring. It then ascends to the bare south summit of Mt. Guyot, and continues in the open 0.2 mi. to its junction with the Twinway 0.1 mi. west of the higher, but less open, north summit of Guyot. Go straight ahead here for the Twins and Galehead Hut, or turn right for Zealand Mtn. and Zealand Falls Hut.

Bondcliff Trail (map 5:H6–G6)
Distances from Wilderness Trail

to Bondcliff summit: 4.4 mi., 3 hr. 30 min.

to Mt. Bond summit: 5.6 mi., 4 hr. 25 min.

to Guyot Campsite spur: 6.3 mi., 4 hr. 50 min.

to Twinway: 6.9 mi. (11.1 km.), 5 hr. 15 min.

West Bond Spur (AMC)

This short path leaves the Bondcliff Trail 0.6 mi. north of the summit of Mt. Bond and 0.2 mi. south of the spur to Guyot Campsite. It descends moderately for 0.3 mi. to the col, ascends moderately for a short distance, then climbs the steep cone to the summit, the most easterly of several small peaks on a ridge running east and west. Views are magnificent from this sharp rocky peak, perched high above the valleys of an extensive wilderness area.

West Bond Spur (map 5:H6)
Distance from Bondcliff Trail

to West Bond summit: 0.5 mi. (0.8 km.), 25 min.

Thoreau Falls Trail (WMNF)

This trail runs from the Wilderness Trail at North Fork Junction, 6.3 mi. from the Kancamagus Highway, past Thoreau Falls, to the Ethan Pond Trail roughly halfway between Ethan Pond Campsite and Zealand Falls Hut.

Much of it follows an old railroad grade, but there are a few rather steep and rough sections. Practically the entire trail lies within the Pemigewasset Wilderness.

The trail diverges left (north) from the Wilderness Trail on a railroad bed, which it leaves after 0.4 mi. to cross the East Branch of the Pemigewasset on a 60-ft. bridge, then returns to the railroad bed and follows it along the North Fork. At 2.1 mi. it leaves the grade for good and soon turns right on a bypass that avoids two former crossings of the North Fork. Rejoining the old route at 2.9 mi., it follows a logging road, then leaves it left at 3.6 mi. and soon becomes rougher and steeper, reaching a ledge next to the North Fork at 4.0 mi. The trail approaches Thoreau Falls and climbs steeply on a rough footpath to the right of the falls, which are beautiful when there is a good flow of water, then crosses the North Fork at the top of the falls at 5.0 mi. (In high water there may be a better brook crossing just upstream from the trail.) Leaving the stream, the trail soon ends at the Ethan Pond Trail, about 0.2 mi. north of the latter's bridge over the North Fork. Turn left to reach Zealand Falls Hut or right to reach Ethan Pond Shelter.

Thoreau Falls Trail (map 5:H6–G7)
Distance from Wilderness Trail
   to Ethan Pond Trail: 5.1 mi. (8.2 km.), 2 hr. 55 min.

Shoal Pond Trail (AMC)

This trail runs from its junction with the Wilderness Trail and the Carrigain Notch Trail (see Section 4) at Stillwater Junction to the Ethan Pond Trail between Zealand Falls Hut and Ethan Pond Campsite. At Stillwater Junction, the trail leads across the East Branch on the foundation of an old dam (no bridge), turns left on a railroad bed and almost immediately leaves it on the right, then soon bears right onto another railroad bed. Leaving the railroad temporarily, the trail crosses Shoal Pond Brook at 0.6 mi.; this crossing may be difficult if the water is high. The trail regains the railroad bed and passes a spur path on the right at 1.0 mi. that leads to a pleasant pool in the brook. At 1.2 mi. it bears left off the railroad bed and follows logging roads, crossing Shoal Pond Brook from west to east at 1.4 mi. and recrossing the brook at 2.4 mi. At 3.2 mi. the trail crosses the brook for the last time, from west to east, and soon reaches Shoal Pond. Because of bogginess caused by beaver activity, the trail keeps away from the pond, staying to the east. At 3.7 mi. the trail passes the junction with its abandoned east fork and continues to the Ethan Pond Trail.

Shoal Pond Trail (map 5:H7–G7)

Distances from Stillwater Junction

    to Shoal Pond: 3.2 mi., 1 hr. 55 min.

    to Ethan Pond Trail: 4.0 mi. (6.4 km.), 2 hr. 15 min.

SECTION 4
The Carrigain and Moat Regions

This section covers the eastern portion of the central region of the White Mtns. (that part not included in Section 3), consisting of the areas bounded on the north by US 302, on the east by NH 16, and on the south by the Kancamagus Highway (NH 112); at the western edge it includes all areas and trails south and east of the Wilderness Trail. For a more precise description of the western boundary of Section 4, see the first paragraph of Section 3. Section 4 includes Mt. Carrigain and Mt. Hancock, the lesser mountains that surround them, and the lower but interesting mountains that rise to the east between the Saco and Swift rivers, principally Mt. Tremont and the Moat Range. No single AMC map covers the entire area, roughly speaking, the area to the west of Bear Notch Rd. is covered by the Franconia map (map 5), the majority of the area to the east by the Chocorua-Waterville map (map 4), and the northern edge of the eastern section by the Mt. Washington Range map (map 6).

The Appalachian Trail does not pass through this section.

GEOGRAPHY

Mt. Carrigain (4680 ft.) is the central and highest point of a mass of jumbled ridges that divides the watershed of the East Branch of the Pemigewasset River from that of the Saco River and its tributary, the Swift River. It was named for Philip Carrigain, New Hampshire Secretary of State from 1805 to 1810, who made a map of the whole state in 1816, including an early attempt to portray the White Mtn. region. He was one of the party that named Mts. Adams, Jefferson, Madison, and Monroe in 1820. The view from the observation tower on the summit takes in a wide area and includes most of the important peaks of the White Mtns.; Carrigain has one of the finest viewpoints in the White Mtns. The view from Signal Ridge, Carrigain's southeasterly spur, is also magnificent. The northeasterly spur, Vose Spur (3870 ft.), forms the west wall of Carrigain Notch, facing Mt. Lowell on the east; Vose Spur has no trails and is fairly difficult to ascend.

Mt. Hancock rises to the west of Mt. Carrigain. It is a long ridge with several summits, of which the most important are the North Peak (4403 ft.), the highest, and the South Peak (4274 ft.). Both peaks are wooded to the top, but there is an excellent outlook ledge near the summit of the North Peak, and a good but restricted outlook from the South Peak. At one time this was one of the most inaccessible mountains in the White Mtns., but it is now easily climbed. The ridge between Mt. Carrigain and Mt. Hancock has no trail, and travel along it is extremely difficult; the line along this ridge on maps is part of the Lincoln-Livermore town boundary. Carrigain Pond, a beautiful and remote mountain pond that is one of the higher sources of the Pemigewasset River, is just north of the ridge. The Captain (3530 ft.), located only 0.3 mi. from Carrigain Pond, is a striking little peak with sheer cliffs overlooking the Sawyer River Valley; it is well hidden at the end of this isolated valley and can be seen from only a few viewpoints.

Mt. Lowell (3743 ft.), Mt. Anderson (3722 ft.), Mt. Nancy (3906 ft.), and Mt. Bemis (3706 ft.) are a group of peaks northeast of Carrigain Notch that lie on the watershed between the Saco and the East Branch of the Pemigewasset. The region is notable for its concentration of four ponds—Nancy, Norcross, Little Norcross, and Duck—at an altitude of about 3100 ft., and for a stand of virgin spruce just south of Nancy Pond on the north slopes of Duck Pond Mtn. This is said to be one of the two largest remaining areas of virgin forest in the state, though the hurricane of 1938 did great damage, felling many of the older trees. In October 1964, the USFS established in this region the 460-acre Nancy Brook Scenic Area, to be maintained as nearly as possible in an undisturbed condition.

Mt. Tremont (3384 ft.) is the highest of several lower peaks that rise in the region around Sawyer Pond, east of Bear Notch Rd. Tremont lies south of the big bend in the Saco River; it is a narrow ridge, running north and south, with three conspicuous summits, of which the south is the highest. Still farther south is a fourth summit, Owl's Cliff (2951 ft.). The main summit of Tremont has spectacular views to the south, west, and north; Owl's Cliff has a good outlook to the south. Southwest of both Mt. Tremont and Sawyer Pond is Green's Cliff (2915 ft.), with cliffs on its south and east faces; it is very prominent from the overlooks on the eastern half of the Kancamagus Highway. Ledges near its summit provide interesting views, but there is no trail. Bartlett Haystack (3010 ft.), an aptly named mountain that was sometimes called Mt. Silver Spring in the days when hazy elegance was preferred to plain and effective description, is another interesting peak with no trails, which lies east of Mt. Tremont. A ledge just a few feet west of the summit, shaped like the prow of a ship, affords a magnificent view to the south, west, and north. It is a relatively easy bushwhack from Haystacks Rd. (FR 44), and is one of the more rewarding objectives available to experienced hikers who wish to begin to acquire the skills of navigation by map and compass. The USGS Bartlett quad, now available in provisional format, is very useful for the ascent of this peak. Leave FR 44 at any convenient point less than 0.5 mi. from its junction with the Bear Notch Rd. near the height-of-land in Bear Notch, climb roughly northwest to the crest of the peak's east ridge, then follow the ridge to the summit. For the descent (which, as is often the case, may involve more sophisticated navigation than the ascent), this ridge or the brook valley just to the north of it can be followed east to FR 44. It is also possible to descend somewhat more to the southeast, more directly toward Bear Notch, but it is best to avoid the steep and rough slope below the summit on the south. The WMNF Bartlett Experimental Forest occupies a large area on the slopes of Bartlett Haystack and Bear Mtn.

Moat Mtn. is a long ridge that rises impressively to the west of the Saco River nearly opposite North Conway. The whole ridge was burned over many decades ago, and all the major summits are still bare, with magnificent views; there are also numerous scattered outlooks along the wooded parts of the ridge. There has been some uncertainty about the names of the summits in the range, but in this guide the peaks are called North Moat (3201 ft.), Middle Moat (2802 ft.), and South Moat (2772 ft.). The peak at the apex of the Red Ridge (2750 ft.) has sometimes also been called Middle Moat. From North Moat a ridge runs west to Big Attitash Mtn. (2936 ft.), sometimes called West Moat, then the ridge passes over lesser summits of Big Attitash and swings southwest to Table Mtn. (2710 ft.), which has fine views to the south from several open ledges just below the summit. Next the ridge swings west again to the trailless Bear Mtn. (3217 ft.), which forms the east side of Bear Notch. On the east side of the Moat Range are White Horse Ledge (1470 ft.) and Cathedral Ledge (1150 ft.), two detached bluffs that present impressive cliffs to the Saco Valley. An auto road ascends to the summit of Cathedral Ledge. Farther to the north, Little Attitash Mtn. (2518 ft.) is a trailless peak on a long, curving ridge that extends northeast from Big Attitash to end in Humphrey's Ledge (1470 ft.). Pitman's Arch, a shallow cave in the face of Humphrey's Ledge, was once reached by a toll path that is now completely overgrown.

CAMPING

Pemigewasset Wilderness

In this area, camping and fires are prohibited above treeline within 0.25 mi. of 13 Falls Campsite, Thoreau Falls, Galehead Hut, Garfield Ridge Campsite, Guyot Campsite, or within 0.25 mi. of the Wilderness Trail or the East Branch of the Pemigewasset River from the wilderness boundary near the Franconia Brook Trail junction to the Thoreau Falls Trail junction near the confluence with the North Fork, except at designated sites. No campsite may be used by more than ten persons at any one time, and hiking groups may not exceed ten persons.

Restricted Use Areas

The WMNF has established a number of Restricted Use Areas (RUAs) where camping and wood or charcoal fires are prohibited from May 1 to November 1. The specific areas are under continual review, and areas are added to or subtracted from the list in order to provide the greatest amount of protection to areas subject to damage by excessive camping, while imposing the lowest level of restrictions possible. A general list of RUAs follows, but one should obtain a map of current RUAs from the WMNF.

(1) Camping is not permitted above treeline (where trees are less than 8 ft. tall) except in winter, and even then only on sites covered with at least two feet of snow and never on frozen bodies of water. The point where the restricted area begins is marked on most trails with small signs, but the absence of such signs should not be construed as proof of the legality of a site.

(2) No camping is permitted within 1/4 mi. of most facilities such as huts, cabins, shelters, or tentsites, except at the facility itself. In this section, camping is also prohibited at Diana's Baths, on the Moat Mtn. Trail. Camping is permitted at Desolation Shelter.

(3) No camping is permitted within 200 ft. of certain trails. In 1991, designated trails included the Sawyer Pond Trail from Sawyer River Rd. to the end of the 0.25-mi. Restricted Use Area around Sawyer Pond itself. No camping is permitted within 200 ft. of the junction of the Cedar Brook and Hancock Notch trails.

Established Trailside Campsites

Desolation Shelter (AMC) is located on the Carrigain Notch Trail beside Carrigain Branch, 0.6 mi. southeast of Stillwater Junction and the Wilderness Trail. It accommodates eight, and tenting at the site is permitted.

Sawyer Pond Campsite (WMNF) is located on Sawyer Pond, reached by the Sawyer Pond Trail. There are five tent platforms on the northwest side of the pond, and a shelter that accommodates eight.

ACCESS ROADS

Important access roads in this area include the Kancamagus Highway (NH 112), connecting I-93 and US 3 in Lincoln to NH 16 in Conway. It is now a regular state highway that is paved and well maintained, and open in winter except during the worst storms. Bear Notch Rd. runs 9.3 mi. from US 302 at the crossroads in Bartlett village to the Kancamagus Highway about 13 mi. west of Conway. It is paved, but not usually plowed in winter. North of Bear Notch it closely follows the line of an old railroad, and excellent outlooks have been cleared. The gravel Sawyer River Rd. (FR 34) begins on US 302 0.1 mi. north of the major bridge over Sawyer River, 1.6 mi. north of the Sawyer Rock picnic area, or 7.9 mi. south of the Willey House site in Crawford Notch State Park. There is no road sign except for a brown post with "FR 34" on it, and it is usually barred by a gate during the snow season.

THE TRAILS

Signal Ridge Trail (WMNF)

This trail ascends to the summit of Mt. Carrigain by way of Signal Ridge, starting from Sawyer River Rd. (FR 34) 2.0 mi. from US 302. The trail begins on the right just before the bridge over Whiteface Brook; there is a parking lot on the left, just beyond the bridge. There is a crossing of Whiteface Brook less than 0.2 mi. from the road that may be difficult at high water; at such times it may be best to avoid the crossing by bushwhacking up the south bank of the brook from the parking lot. The trail climbs moderately for most of its distance, using old roads that once provided access to the firewarden's cabin. The views from the observation tower on the summit and from Signal Ridge are magnificent. The loop back to Sawyer River Rd. via the Desolation and Carrigain Notch trails is interesting, but much longer, rougher, and more strenuous.

Leaving the road, the Signal Ridge Trail soon reaches and follows an old logging road that crosses Whiteface Brook at 0.2 mi., then follows the south bank of the attractive brook, passing small cascades and pools. At 0.8 mi. it begins to climb steadily away from the brook, then levels and crosses a flat divide. At 1.4 mi. Carrigain Brook Rd. (FR 86), a grass-grown logging road, crosses the trail at a right angle. (This road is not passable by vehicles, but can be followed south 1.6 mi. to Sawyer River Rd. about 0.3 mi. before the gate at the end of that road. There is a difficult brook crossing just before Sawyer River Rd., and the road is becoming overgrown.) At 1.7 mi. the Carrigain Notch Trail diverges right toward Desolation Shelter and the Pemigewasset Wilderness, and the Signal Ridge Trail soon crosses Carrigain Brook, which may be difficult at high water. The trail passes an area of beaver activity, crosses a brook, and begins to ascend, gradually at first. At 2.4 mi. it turns sharp left where an old road continues straight up the valley. The trail angles up the end of a ridge, turns right to climb, then makes another sharp left turn (arrow) at the site of an old camp and angles up again.

At 2.8 mi. the Signal Ridge Trail turns sharp right into a birch-lined straight section 1.0 mi. long that rises steadily at an angle up the steep side of the valley, with occasional views to the cliffs of Mt. Lowell across Carrigain Notch. At the end of this section, the trail turns sharp left and zigzags up the nose of Signal Ridge through several areas that were damaged by the windstorm of December 1980, reaching the high point of the bare crest of the ridge at 4.5 mi. Views are excellent, particularly to the cliffs of Mt. Lowell across Carrigain Notch. The trail descends slightly, then angles left around to the south slope of the summit cone, climbing gradually to the site of the old firewarden's cabin, where there is a well (water unsafe to drink without treatment). Bearing left from the small clearing, the trail soon swings right and climbs steeply to the small sag between Carrigain's two summit knobs, then turns right and soon reaches the summit. Here the Desolation Trail enters from the Pemigewasset Wilderness.

Signal Ridge Trail (map 5:I8–H7)
Distances from Sawyer River Road
> *to* Carrigain Notch Trail junction: 1.7 mi., 1 hr. 10 min.
> *to* Signal Ridge: 4.5 mi., 3 hr. 50 min.
> *to* Mt. Carrigain summit: 5.0 mi. (8.1 km.), 4 hr. 15 min.

Carrigain Notch Trail (AMC)
This trail runs from the Signal Ridge Trail, 1.7 mi. from Sawyer River Rd., through Carrigain Notch and past Desolation Shelter to the Wilderness and Shoal Pond trails (see Section 3) at Stillwater Junction.

It diverges right (north) from the Signal Ridge Trail and crosses Carrigain Brook in 60 yd.; care is required to find the trail on the opposite bank at this crossing, going either way. Continuing on logging roads at easy grades, it passes through an area of beaver activity, then several stony areas, and at 1.6 mi. turns left off the road to bypass a muddy section. Here, just off to the right of the trail, there is a view of the ledges of Vose Spur, which form the west side of Carrigain Notch. Soon returning to the road, the trail climbs more steeply, and at 2.3 mi. reaches its height-of-land well up on the west wall of the notch. Very soon it strikes and follows an old logging road on the north side of the notch and descends moderately, and at 3.1 mi. turns left off the logging road and follows a path through the woods that avoids the wet sections of the old road while continuing to use some of the dry parts. At 4.1 mi. the trail enters an old railroad grade and turns sharp left on it; the Nancy Pond Trail follows the grade to the right from this point. At 4.9 mi. the trail bears left off the railroad grade, then soon turns sharp right where the Desolation Trail continues straight across the brook. At 5.1 mi. it passes Desolation Shelter, then bears right away from the Carrigain Branch and reaches Stillwater Junction, here the Wilderness Trail turns sharp left, and the Shoal Pond Trail turns right across the East Branch of the Pemigewasset.

Carrigain Notch Trail (map 5:I8–H7)
Distances from Signal Ridge Trail

    to Carrigain Notch: 2.3 mi., 1 hr. 30 min.

    to Nancy Pond Trail: 4.1 mi., 2 hr. 30 min.

    to Desolation Shelter: 5.1 mi., 3 hr.

    to Stillwater Junction: 5.7 mi. (9.2 km.), 3 hr. 20 min.

Desolation Trail (AMC)

This trail runs from the Carrigain Notch Trail about 0.2 mi. southwest of Desolation Shelter to the summit of Mt. Carrigain. The upper part of the trail is very steep and rough, and requires great care, particularly on the descent or with heavy packs. In either direction substantial extra time may be required. Practically all of the trail lies within the Pemigewasset Wilderness.

The trail leaves the Carrigain Notch Trail at a sharp turn at the edge of a tributary of the Carrigain Branch and crosses the brook. It follows a railroad grade for 60 yd., then diverges left and climbs moderately, at times on old logging roads. It climbs into a stand of birches and merges into an unusually straight old logging road on the west side of the ridgecrest. *Caution:* For a long section of this road there is an old telephone wire at the left edge of the trail that is easy to trip over. The old road crosses to the east side of the ridge, deteriorates, and ends at 1.3 mi. The trail crosses a short section of slippery rock blocks and continues through an area where many rock steps have been built, then swings directly up the slope into virgin woods and climbs a very steep and rough section. The grade gradually eases up and the footing slowly improves as the trail reaches the crest of the steep ridge. At 1.8 mi. the trail abruptly reaches the top of the steep section, swings left, and angles around the cone at an easy grade until it reaches the last short steep pitch to the summit.

Desolation Trail (map 5:H7)

Distances from Carrigain Notch Trail

> to upper end of old logging road: 1.3 mi., 1 hr. 20 min.
>
> to Mt. Carrigain summit: 1.9 mi. (3.1 km.), 2 hr. 10 min.

Nancy Pond Trail (Camp Pasquaney/WMNF)

This trail begins on the west side of US 302, 2.8 mi. north of the Sawyer Rock picnic area and 6.7 mi. south of the Willey House site in Crawford Notch State Park. It passes Nancy Cascades and Nancy and Norcross ponds, and ends on the Carrigain Notch Trail 1.0 mi. north of Desolation Shelter.

Leaving US 302 it follows an assortment of paths and old roads, but is well marked with yellow paint and signs.

It first follows a logging road for 250 yd., diverges left and crosses a small brook, then joins a logging road along Halfway Brook. Soon it turns right off the road and crosses Halfway Brook, then a woods road joins from the right (descending, bear right here). The trail continues to the WMNF boundary, marked by a large pile of red-painted stones, at 0.8 mi. Here it enters and follows an old logging road along Nancy Brook, crossing the brook on the rocks at 1.6 mi. (may be difficult at high water). It continues upstream on the road and passes the remains of the Lucy mill at 1.8 mi. Above here the road virtually disappears, and the trail ascends through a rough area of landslides, recrosses Nancy Brook, and soon reaches the foot of Nancy Cascades at 2.4 mi., where the stream falls over a high, steep ledge into a beautiful pool.

The trail turns sharp left at the pool and ascends the steep slope by switchbacks, providing another outlook at the middle of the cascades, and passes near the top of the cascades, which are several hundred feet high, at 2.8 mi. (Snow may remain in this shady ravine quite late in the spring.) From the top of the cascades, the trail winds through the moss-carpeted virgin spruce forest past a small overgrown tarn to the northeast shore of Nancy Pond (4 acres in area) at 3.4 mi. Continuing along the north shore, the trail crosses the swamp at the upper end, then crosses over the almost imperceptible height-of-land that divides Saco from Pemigewasset drainage and reaches Little Norcross Pond. Skirting the north shore, it then climbs over another small rise to Norcross Pond (7 acres in area). Again hugging the north shore, and crossing into the Pemigewasset Wilderness, it enters a logging road 25 yd. before reaching the ledgy natural dam at the west end of Norcross Pond at 4.3 mi. (In the reverse direction, turn right off the logging road 25 yd. from the ledgy dam and follow a path along the shore of the pond.) At the ledges there is a commanding outlook to Mt. Bond and the Twin Range, with the Franconias in the distance.

After crossing the stream at the outlet of Norcross Pond, the Nancy Pond Trail descends gradually west on a logging road, passing a spring (iron pipe) on the south side of the trail at 5.5 mi. At 6.0 mi. the trail veers right, crosses Norcross Brook (may be difficult in high water), shortly reaches an old railroad bed, and swings left onto it. At 6.4 mi. it crosses Anderson Brook (may be difficult in high water), then passes along the south side of the Camp 19 clearing. At 6.8 mi. it turns left off the railroad grade and recrosses Anderson Brook on a bridge. On the other side, it follows another railroad grade, bearing right at a fork. It crosses Notch Brook and ends 25 yd. beyond, where the Carrigain Notch Trail enters sharp left from Sawyer River Rd., and continues straight ahead on the railroad grade to Desolation Shelter and Stillwater Junction.

Nancy Pond Trail (map 5:H8–H7)

Distances from US 302

> *to* foot of Nancy Cascades: 2.4 mi., 1 hr. 55 min.
>
> *to* Nancy Pond: 3.5 mi., 2 hr. 50 min.
>
> *to* Norcross Pond outlet: 4.3 mi., 3 hr. 15 min.
>
> *to* Carrigain Notch Trail: 7.1 mi. (11.4 km.), 4 hr. 40 min.
>
> *to* Desolation Shelter (via Carrigain Notch Trail): 8.1 mi. (13.0 km.), 5 hr. 10 min.

Cedar Brook Trail (WMNF)

This trail runs from the Hancock Notch Trail, 1.7 mi. from the Kancamagus Highway, to the Wilderness Trail at the east end of the suspension bridge, 5.4 mi. from the Kancamagus Highway. With the Hancock Notch Trail, this trail affords the most direct route to Mt. Hancock. The five crossings of the North Fork of the Hancock Branch between the Hancock Notch Trail and the Hancock Loop Trail are difficult in high water, but the first two are easily bypassed, and the others can be avoided by bushwhacking along the east bank to the Hancock Loop Trail (which makes the sixth crossing soon after its divergence from the Cedar Brook Trail).

Leaving the Hancock Notch Trail, the Cedar Brook Trail immediately crosses a small brook and climbs moderately on an old logging road for about 0.2 mi., then crosses the North Fork of the Hancock Branch five times in 0.4 mi. The first two crossings are only 40 yd. apart and can be avoided by following a well-beaten path on the near bank. The beginning of the Hancock Loop Trail is reached on the right at 0.7 mi., 150 yd. beyond the fifth crossing.

The Cedar Brook Trail soon passes into the Pemige wasset Wilderness, climbing moderately on a rough footway that occasionally must be carefully distinguished from miscellaneous brooks and muddy abandoned routes of the trail. It reaches the height-of-land between Mt. Hancock and Mt. Hitchcock at 1.4 mi. and descends on logging roads, swinging out to the west then back to the northeast side of the valley, crossing several brooks. It reaches the site of Camp 24A (sign) at 2.9 mi., then continues to descend on old roads, and at 4.1 mi. it descends a bank to the old logging railroad at the edge of Cedar Brook and turns sharp right on the railroad grade. Soon it passes through the extensive clearings of Camp 24 and descends toward the East Branch of the Pemigewasset. At 5.5 mi. an old grass-grown road enters on the left; this road, known as the East Branch Truck Rd. (FR 87), follows the east and south banks of the East Branch to the Wilderness Trail parking lot, but it is no longer used by vehicles within the Wilderness, and is unsigned and somewhat overgrown near this junction, so it is rather hard to identify. The Cedar Brook Trail swings to the east, paralleling the East Branch, and joins the Wilderness Trail at the east end of the suspension bridge.

Cedar Brook Trail (map 5:I6–H6)

Distances from Hancock Notch Trail

    to Hancock Loop Trail: 0.7 mi., 30 min.

    to height-of-land: 1.4 mi., 1 hr.

    to Camp 24A: 2.9 mi., 1 hr. 45 min.

    to Camp 24: 4.3 mi., 2 hr. 25 min.

    to Wilderness Trail: 6.1 mi. (9.7 km.), 3 hr. 20 min.

Hancock Notch Trail (WMNF)

This trail begins at the Kancamagus Highway at the hairpin turn, passes through Hancock Notch between Mt. Hancock and Mt. Huntington, then descends along the Sawyer River to the Sawyer River Trail. At the Kancamagus Highway terminus, parking is available at the Hancock Overlook just above the trailhead. With the Cedar Brook and Hancock Loop trails, this trail provides the most popular route to Mt. Hancock. From the Kancamagus Highway to the Cedar Brook Trail, the Hancock Notch Trail is heavily used, wide, and easily followed; from the Cedar Brook Trail to the Sawyer River Trail, it is wet and rough, and in places requires care to follow.

Leaving the Kancamagus Highway, the trail follows an old railroad bed, crossing a brook at 0.6 mi. and gradually approaching the North Fork of the Hancock Branch. It stays on the same side of the North Fork, swinging right slightly uphill to enter a logging road; take care not to follow the remains of the old railroad grade across the river. The trail follows the logging road at an easy grade, then descends slightly, crosses two brooks in less than 0.1 mi., and soon reaches the junction with the Cedar Brook Trail at 1.7 mi. (For Mt. Hancock, turn left on this trail across a small brook.) The Hancock Notch Trail rises somewhat more steeply for about 0.8 mi. to the notch, which is flat and very wet. East of the notch it passes through a dense stand of spruce on a rougher footway, descending quite rapidly at times. Soon the grade moderates, and the trail crosses to the north side of Sawyer River at 3.4 mi., then back to the south side at 4.0 mi. Soon the trail diverges from the river, passes by a beaver pond, and follows logging roads across a south branch of the river. Continuing to descend easily, it crosses Sawyer River twice more, at 5.3 mi. and 5.8 mi. (both crossings may be difficult at high water), and follows newer logging roads to its end at the Sawyer River Trail in Hayshed Field, an overgrown clearing 1.2 mi. from Sawyer River Rd.

Hancock Notch Trail (map 5:I6–I7)

Distances from Kancamagus Highway

    to Cedar Brook Trail: 1.8 mi., 1 hr. 5 min.

    to Hancock Notch: 2.5 mi., 1 hr. 35 min.

    to Sawyer River Trail: 6.7 mi. (10.8 km.), 3 hr. 40 min.

Hancock Loop Trail (AMC)

This trail makes a loop over both the major summits of Mt. Hancock. It is steep and rough, but well trodden and easy to follow, though the part on the ridge between the peaks is subject to blowdowns. It is most easily reached from the hairpin turn on the Kancamagus Highway by following the Hancock Notch and Cedar Brook trails for 2.5 mi. There are five brook crossings on the Cedar Brook Trail that may be difficult at high water.

Leaving the Cedar Brook Trail on the right (east), 150 yd. north of the fifth crossing of the North Branch of the Hancock Branch, the trail follows an old logging road and soon recrosses the main brook, then passes over a steep, rocky brook bed and a wet area. Keeping south of the main brook, some distance away from it and considerably higher, the trail continues its gradual ascent and reaches the loop junction at 1.1 mi. from the start. From this point the circuit over the two main summits of Mt. Hancock can be made in either direction, so for convenience of description the trail is divided into three segments: North Link, Ridge Link, and South Link.

The North Link diverges left from the logging road at the loop junction and descends moderately at an angle. Soon it crosses a flat gravel area, usually dry but often with water flowing into it from the brook bed above and disappearing into the sand, where the foot of the Arrow Slide is visible about 50 yd. to the left. The trail then climbs roughly parallel to the slide, first at a moderate grade angling across the hillside, then straight up, very steep and rough. Near the top, the trail veers left and becomes less steep. At the wooded summit of North Hancock, a side path leads left 40 yd. to a fine view south to the Sandwich Range and Osceola, while the Ridge Link turns right.

The South Link continues along the logging road from the loop junction for another 0.1 mi., then swings right up the mountainside. The climb to South Hancock is unrelievedly steep, crossing numerous old logging roads. (These are some of the roads so prominent as light green lines across the dark slope when seen from other peaks.) At the summit, the Ridge Link enters on the left (north), and a short path descends straight ahead (east) to a viewpoint overlooking the Sawyer River Valley.

The Ridge Link connects the summits of North and South Hancock. From the summit of North Hancock, it starts almost due north and curves to the right (east, then south), traversing the generally broad, bumpy ridge with several minor ups and downs, then climbs the final narrow section of ridge to the south peak at 1.4 mi., where the South Link enters on the right (west).

Hancock Loop Trail (map 5:I6–I7)
Distances from Cedar Brook Trail
> *to* loop junction: 1.1 mi., 50 min.
>
> *to* North Hancock (via North Link): 1.8 mi., 1 hr. 50 min.
>
> *to* South Hancock (via South Link): 1.6 mi., 1 hr. 35 min.

Distances of loop
>   *from* Cedar Brook Trail (in either direction): 4.8 mi.
>   (7.7 km.), 3 hr. 25 min.
>   *from* Kancamagus Highway: 9.8 mi. (15.7 km.), 6 hr.
>   15 min.

Sawyer River Trail (WMNF)

This trail leads from Sawyer River Rd. (FR 34), at the
end of the section open to public vehicular use about 4.0
mi. from US 302, to the Kancamagus Highway 3.1 mi.
west of the Sabbaday Falls parking area and 0.6 mi. east
of Lily Pond. Almost all the way it follows the bed of an
old logging railroad at easy grades.

The trail follows the gravel road past the gate, and in
100 yd. the Sawyer Pond Trail turns left to cross Sawyer
River on a footbridge. The Sawyer River Trail continues,
taking the left of two gated gravel roads at a fork, crosses
Sawyer River on the logging road bridge, and diverges
right onto the old railroad grade 100 yd. beyond the
bridge. (The gravel road can be followed 1.1 mi. to the
junction of the Sawyer River Trail and Hancock Notch
Trail at Hayshed Field, where it enters the Sawyer River
Trail at a right angle; there are excellent views of Mt.
Tremont and Mt. Carrigain from this road.) The railroad
grade continues along the Sawyer River for 0.7 mi., then
swings to the south. It crosses a washed-out area and two
brooks, and reaches the overgrown clearing called
Hayshed Field at 1.2 mi., where the Hancock Notch Trail
turns sharp right and the gravel road described above
enters on the left. The Sawyer River Trail follows the old
railroad bed across an imperceptible divide in the flat
region west of Green's Cliff, passing several beaver
swamps, and crosses Meadow Brook on a bridge at 2.5
mi. It follows the west bank of this stream for some distance, passing a junction where the Nanamocomuck (X-
C) Ski Trail enters on the left at 3.2 mi., then swings

southwest. The ski trail diverges right before the Sawyer River Trail crosses the Swift River (which can be very difficult in high water) at 3.5 mi. The trail now ascends easily upstream along the river, then climbs up the bank, bearing left twice, to the Kancamagus Highway.

Sawyer River Trail (map 5:I8–I7)

Distances from Sawyer River Road

   to Hancock Notch Trail: 1.2 mi., 40 min.

   to Kancamagus Highway: 3.8 mi. (6.1 km.), 2 hr.

Church Pond Loop Trail (WMNF)

This loop trail provides an interesting, short, level hike to Church Pond, passing through very flat, poorly drained region, providing access to a kind of terrain and forest that trails in the White Mtns. seldom visit. It is a very wet trip at times; the brook crossings can be quite difficult at high water. The trail begins in Passaconaway Campground just off the Kancamagus Highway, at the far end of the west loop road near Site 19 (currently the campground host's site). Parking at the trailhead is limited, so it may be necessary to use the Downes Brook Trail parking lot on the south side of the highway.

The path descends slightly and crosses Downes Brook and the Swift River in rapid succession. Both of these crossings may be difficult, and will often require wading. The trail exits from the Swift River by a small rocky wash a bit upstream from where it enters the stream, then turns right and enters the woods. This part of the trail, with its dense, fast-growing stream-side vegetation, may require considerable care to follow. At 0.3 mi. the loop junction is reached; it is 0.8 mi. to the pond by the left-hand path, or 1.4 mi. by the right-hand path (which is somewhat drier). The Nanamocomuck (X-C) Ski Trail uses the first part of each branch.

From here the loop is described in the clockwise direction. Taking the left-hand branch, the trail follows

an old logging road for 0.4 mi. to the junction where the
ski trail diverges left, then soon bears left and becomes a
footpath, crosses a boggy area on log bridges, and at 1.1
mi. emerges on a knoll overlooking Church Pond, where
there are fine views. Here the trail turns sharp right and
runs above the shore of the pond for about 250 yd., then
turns right again and starts back to the loop junction, running mostly on relatively high ground, repeatedly bearing right. The ski trail enters on the left 0.2 mi. before
the loop junction.

Church Pond Loop Trail (map 4:J8–I8)
Distance of loop
> *from* Passaconaway Campground. 2.8 mi. (4.5 km.),
> 1 hr. 25 min.

Sawyer Pond Trail (WMNF)

This trail begins at the Kancamagus Highway 0.6 mi.
east of Passaconaway Campground and 1.4 mi. west of
Bear Notch Rd., passes Sawyer Pond and its campsite,
and ends at Sawyer River Rd. (FR 34), near the gate that
ends public vehicular access at 4.0 mi. *Caution:* The
crossing of the Swift River near the Kancamagus Highway often requires wading, and can be dangerous at high
water. Grades are easy.

From the Kancamagus Highway, the trail passes
through a clearing, angles right to the bank of Swift
River, and fords the stream to a sand bar. It soon enters
the woods, where the Nanamocomuck (X-C) Ski Trail
joins on the right, and runs through a fine pine grove. At
0.7 mi. the ski trail diverges on the left, and at 1.1 mi. the
Brunel Trail diverges right. At 1.7 mi. the trail crosses a
new gravel logging road, then skirts the west slope of
Birch Hill, descends gently, and crosses a grass-grown
logging road diagonally at 2.6 mi. It then comes close to a
small brook, bears left away from it, passes over a flat
divide, and descends to Sawyer Pond. As the pond is

approached, there are a number of conflicting side paths; use care to stay on the correct path. At a point 15 yd. from the pond (good views), the trail turns left, crosses the outlet brook at 4.5 mi., and passes near the tent platforms of the Sawyer Pond campsite. In another 0.1 mi. it passes a side path that leads right 0.2 mi. to the shelter. It then descends gradually on an old logging road, and at 5.7 mi. turns sharp left off the road and recrosses the Sawyer Pond outlet brook. It runs to the bank of Sawyer River, turns right across a footbridge, then turns right again on the gravel extension of Sawyer River Rd. and continues about 100 yd. to the gate.

Sawyer Pond Trail (map 4:J8–I8)

Distances from Kancamagus Highway

    to Brunel Trail: 1.1 mi., 35 min.

    to Sawyer Pond: 4.5 mi., 2 hr. 40 min.

    to Sawyer River Rd.: 6.0 mi. (9.7 km.), 3 hr. 30 min.

Rob Brook Trail (WMNF)

This nearly level trail follows old roads and a logging railroad grade through an area of attractive ponds and swamps, with much beaver activity and some good views. It begins on Rob Brook Rd. (FR 35), which leaves Bear Notch Rd. about 0.8 mi. north of the Kancamagus Highway. Most of the trail is dry, but some brook crossings (including several made on beaver dams) are difficult at high water and wet in normal conditions.

It leaves Rob Brook Rd. on the right 0.1 mi. from Bear Notch Rd., then crosses back over Rob Brook Rd. at 0.5 mi. and descends easily on an old road. It crosses an area of open bogs with a glimpse of Mt. Carrigain, then takes the right branch at a fork where the Nanamocomuck (X-C) ski trail joins left; both branches are marked with blue diamonds. At 1.1 mi. it reaches an old railroad grade and turns sharp right onto it, while cross-country ski trails follow the grade to the left. Soon it joins Rob Brook and crosses it five times. At the third crossing, which is made on a long beaver dam, there is a fine view of Mt. Tremont and Owl's Cliff. The Rob Brook Trail ends at a junction with the Brunel Trail, which enters sharp left and then continues straight ahead on the railroad grade.

Rob Brook Trail (map 4:I9–I8)
Distance from Rob Brook Road
   to Brunel Trail: 2.3 mi. (3.7 km.), 1 hr. 15 min.

Brunel Trail (WMNF)

This trail runs from the Sawyer Pond Trail 1.1 mi. north of the Kancamagus Highway to the summit of Mt. Tremont. However, the most-used approach to this trail is the WMNF Rob Brook Rd. (FR 35), which leaves Bear Notch Rd. about 0.8 mi. north of the Kancamagus Highway. Rob Brook Rd. is closed to public vehicular travel, but it provides the easiest route to the point where the Brunel Trail departs from it, 2.6 mi. from Bear Notch Rd., since the Brunel Trail south of this point may be rather confusing where it crosses and recrosses the extension of Rob Brook Rd., and the ford of the Swift River near the start of the Sawyer Pond Trail is frequently difficult. The Rob Brook Trail provides a much more attractive alternative to this road walk, but is apt to make a hiker's boots soggy. Parts of the Brunel Trail are very steep and rough; since the footway is obscure in some areas, the yellow blazes must be followed with care. The views to the west from Mt. Tremont, and to the south from Owl's Cliff, are excellent.

The trail diverges right (northeast) from the Sawyer Pond Trail, and in 0.2 mi. it approaches the extension of Rob Brook Rd. (Plans call for a possible relocation of the trail in this area, perhaps avoiding this part of the road; if in doubt, this road can be followed to the right until trail signs are seen.) At the present time the trail enters the road, turns right and follows it for 60 yd., diverges left, follows a path through the woods for 0.1 mi., then crosses the road diagonally; all junctions with the road may not be well marked. The trail runs through the woods, crosses a grass-grown logging road, and reaches the old logging railroad bed at 0.7 mi. Here the Rob Brook Trail follows the railroad bed to the right, while the Brunel Trail turns left and follows the railroad bed to Rob Brook Rd. at 1.0 mi. The trail turns right onto the road, follows it for 0.2 mi., leaves it right, and crosses two small brooks. It then returns to the road and follows it right for another 0.1 mi. to the Albany-Bartlett town line (sign) at 1.3 mi., where the trail (sign) turns left off the road for the final time. This point is 2.6 mi. from Bear Notch Rd. via Rob Brook Rd.

Leaving Rob Brook Rd., the Brunel Trail passes through a stand of large conifers, and at 2.1 mi. it reaches and follows the edge of a logged area (follow blazes carefully). At 2.5 mi. it crosses a small brook, and soon passes several large boulders that announce the approach to the east end of Owl's Cliff. At 2.8 mi. the trail swings left and climbs a very steep section, then turns sharp right (arrow), and the grade moderates and finally becomes easy as the height-of-land is reached. At 3.2 mi. (1.9 mi. from Rob Brook Rd.) a spur path (sign) diverges left and climbs to a point just below the summit of Owl's Cliff, then descends slightly to a fine outlook ledge (dangerous if wet or icy) 0.2 mi. from the main trail. From the junction, the Brunel Trail descends easily into a col, then passes through a section where the footway is obscure (watch for blazes) and ascends very steeply; sections running straight up the slope alternate with old logging roads angling to the left. At 3.9 mi. (2.6 mi. from Rob Brook Rd.), the trail reaches the summit ledges of Mt. Tremont, where the Mount Tremont Trail enters from the north.

Brunel Trail (map 5:I8)

Distances from Sawyer Pond Trail

> *to* junction with Rob Brook Rd. at Albany-Bartlett
> town line: 1.3 mi., 40 min.
>
> *to* Owl's Cliff spur: 3.2 mi., 2 hr. 20 min.
>
> *to* Mt. Tremont summit: 3.9 mi. (6.3 km.), 3 hr. 5 min.

Distances from Bear Notch Road

> *to* junction with Brunel Trail at Albany-Bartlett town
> line (via Rob Brook Rd.): 2.6 mi., 1 hr. 20 min.
>
> *to* Mt. Tremont summit: 5.2 mi. (8.4 km.), 3 hr. 40 min.

Mount Tremont Trail (PEAOC)

This trail leaves the south side of US 302 0.5 mi. west of
the Sawyer Rock picnic area and 0.1 mi. west of the
bridge over Stony Brook, and climbs to the summit of Mt.
Tremont, which has excellent views. The trail suffered
some damage by blowdowns in the windstorm of December 1980, and following it may require care due to undergrowth in the areas thus opened to full sunlight. It is covered by maps 5 and 6, but not by either one of them alone.

Leaving US 302, it soon reaches and follows the west
side of Stony Brook. At 0.7 mi. it swings right, climbs
steadily for 0.3 mi. to the top of the ridge, then levels off
and crosses a recent logging road. In the next 1/4 mi.
there was much blowdown; follow the trail carefully. (It
is relatively straight, so one should look for it to continue
in the original line after bypassing a bad spot.)

At 1.5 mi. the trail crosses a branch of Stony Brook
after a slight descent, then zigzags up the steep northeast
side of the mountain at a moderate grade, crossing a
rather sharp boundary between birch woods and virgin
conifers at 2.4 mi. Reaching the ridge top, it passes an
outlook on the right, and continues to the ledgy summit.

Mount Tremont Trail (maps 5/6:I8)

Distance from US 302

> *to* Mt. Tremont summit: 2.8 mi. (4.6 km.), 2 hr. 40 min.

Boulder Loop Trail (WMNF)

This is a loop trail to ledges on a southwest spur of the Moat Range, starting from the north side of Dugway Rd. just west of the entrance to the WMNF Covered Bridge Campground. It offers excellent views for a relatively modest effort, though it does involve about 1000 ft. of climbing. An interpretive leaflet, keyed to numbered stations along the trail, is usually available at the trailhead.

The trail leaves Dugway Rd. and reaches the loop junction at 0.2 mi. From here the loop is described in the clockwise direction. Taking the left-hand branch, the trail shortly passes a large boulder (left), where it turns right and climbs moderately past an outlook to Chocorua, then soon turns sharp left. At 1.3 mi., at the main trail's high point, a spur path leads right (south) 0.1 mi. to ledges that afford a fine view of Mt. Passaconaway, Mt. Chocorua, and Middle Sister. The main trail continues around the ledges and descends toward Big Brook, then turns right below the ledges, crosses a stream and passes an overhanging boulder (left) at 2.3 mi., and then returns to the loop junction at 2.6 mi., 0.2 mi. from Dugway Rd.

Boulder Loop Trail (map 4:I10)

Distances from Dugway Road
    to loop junction: 0.2 mi., 5 min.
    to spur path to ledges: 1.3 mi., 1 hr. 10 min.
    to Dugway Rd. (complete loop including spur to ledges): 3.1 mi. (5.0 km.), 2 hr.

Moat Mountain Trail (WMNF)

This trail traverses the main ridge of Moat Mtn., providing magnificent views from numerous outlooks. Parts of the ridge are very exposed to weather, particularly the section that crosses Middle Moat and South Moat. The trail is covered by map 4 and map 6, but not by either one alone.

The south terminus of the trail is located on Dugway Rd. At the lights in Conway village, turn north (directly opposite NH 153) onto Passaconaway Rd., which becomes West Side Rd. Go left at a fork, then left on Still Rd., which becomes Dugway Rd. The Moat Mountain Trail leaves Dugway Rd. about 3.5 mi. from Conway (sign). Dugway Rd. continues and joins the Kancamagus Highway near Blackberry Crossing Campground. The northeast terminus is reached from Conway village via Passaconaway Rd. and West Side Rd., or from North Conway by taking the road just north of the Eastern Slope Inn west across the Saco River to West Side Rd. Once on West Side Rd., drive north to a point 0.7 mi. north of the road to Cathedral Ledge (2.2 mi. from NH 16 in North Conway), then turn left onto a gravel road that runs between farm fields, and park there.

From the northeast terminus, continue on foot on the gravel road 0.5 mi. to the clearing just below Diana's Baths mill site. The main path leaves the upper end of the clearing, close to the Baths, by a logging road that follows the north bank of Lucy Brook to a fork (sign) at 1.1 mi. Here the Red Ridge Trail turns left across the brook, eventually rejoining the Moat Mountain Trail at the apex of Red Ridge. The Moat Mountain Trail crosses Lucy Brook at 1.3 mi. and follows the south bank, then at 2.3 mi. turns abruptly left uphill, away from the stream (last sure water), where the Attitash Trail continues straight ahead along the stream toward Big Attitash Mountain. The Moat Mtn. Trail ascends through the woods, and at 2.7 mi. begins to pass over ledgy areas, reaching the first good outlook at 3.5 mi. It reaches a shoulder at 3.9 mi. and runs nearly level through a patch of larger trees, then climbs fairly steeply through decreasing scrub and increasing bare ledge to the summit of North Moat at 4.2 mi., where there is an unobstructed view in all directions.

From the summit of North Moat the trail descends sharply to the base of the cone, then easily along a shoulder with occasional views. At the end of the shoulder it drops steeply, passing over ledges that require some scrambling, then moderates and continues to a col in a fine spruce forest. Ascending again, it passes the junction with the Red Ridge Trail left (east) at 5.3 mi., just below several large rocks that provide good views. The trail descends to the major col on the ridge, then climbs up to low scrub followed by open ledges with continuous views, and passes east of the summit of Middle Moat (which can be reached in 80 yd. over open ledges) at 6.3 mi. The trail descends to a minor col with a patch of woods that would provide some shelter in a storm, then ascends to the summit of South Moat at 6.9 mi.

The trail then descends into scrub and gradually increasing numbers of beautiful red pines, with views decreasing in frequency. At 7.5 mi. the trail passes an outlook to Mt. Chocorua (on the ascent from the south terminus, this is the first good outlook reached), and the trail becomes steep with rough footing. Below this section the grade eases considerably, and at 8.3 mi. the trail passes the red-painted WMNF boundary and immediately becomes a well-defined logging road, with easy grades and footing. At 8.9 mi. it goes straight at a crossroads, then another road enters from the left (in the reverse direction, bear left at an arrow 0.2 mi. from Dugway Rd.), and the trail passes through a farmyard to Dugway Rd.

Moat Mountain Trail (maps 4/6:I11–I10)
Distances from West Side Road

> *to* Red Ridge Trail (lower junction): 1.1 mi., 40 min.
> *to* Attitash Trail: 2.3 mi., 1 hr. 25 min.
> *to* North Moat summit: 4.2 mi., 3 hr. 30 min.
> *to* Red Ridge Trail (upper junction): 5.3 mi., 4 hr. 5 min.
> *to* Middle Moat summit area: 6.3 mi., 4 hr. 45 min.
> *to* South Moat summit: 6.9 mi., 5 hr. 5 min.
> *to* Dugway Rd.: 9.2 mi. (14.8 km.), 6 hr. 15 min.

Distances from Dugway Road

> *to* South Moat summit: 2.3 mi., 2 hr. 15 min.
> *to* Middle Moat summit area: 2.9 mi., 2 hr. 35 min.
> *to* Red Ridge Trail (upper junction): 3.8 mi., 3 hr. 10 min.
> *to* North Moat summit: 5.0 mi., 4 hr.
> *to* Attitash Trail: 6.8 mi., 5 hr.
> *to* Red Ridge Trail (lower junction): 8.1 mi., 5 hr. 40 min.
> *to* West Side Rd.: 9.2 mi. (14.8 km.), 6 hr. 10 min.

Red Ridge Trail (WMNF)

This trail ascends Red Ridge, with magnificent views, leaving the Moat Mountain Trail 1.1 mi. from West Side Rd. and rejoining it at the unnamed peak at the apex of Red Ridge, 1.1 mi. south of the North Moat summit. With the Moat Mountain Trail, it provides a very attractive loop over the open summit of North Moat. The trail is covered by maps 4 and 6, but not by either one alone.

This trail branches left (south) from the Moat Mountain Trail and immediately crosses Lucy Brook. It ascends generally south at a gentle grade, crossing an area of active logging where it must be followed with care. The Red Ridge Link leaves on the left for White Horse Ledge at 0.8 mi., and the Red Ridge Trail generally descends gradually until it crosses the gravel Red Ridge Rd. (FR 379) at 1.5 mi. The trail now approaches Moat Brook and follows it, then crosses it at 2.0 mi. and zigzags upward, climbing to a gravel bank where there are good views. Continuing upward rather steeply, it ascends a steep ledge by means of an eroded trap dike and soon attains the crest of Red Ridge, where the grade moderates. Passing alternately through scrub and over ledges with good views, it reaches the bottom of an extensive open ledge section with magnificent views at 3.0 mi. At 3.4 mi. it re-enters scrub and soon rejoins the Moat Mountain Trail at the foot of several little rock knobs, on the main ridgecrest between North Moat and Middle Moat.

Red Ridge Trail (maps 4/6:I10)

Distances from Moat Mountain Trail (lower junction)

   to Red Ridge Link: 0.8 mi., 30 min.

   to crossing of Moat Brook: 2.0 mi., 1 hr. 15 min.

   to Moat Mountain Trail (upper junction): 3.6 mi. (5.7
      km.), 2 hr. 50 min.

Red Ridge Link (NHDP)

This short path links the Red Ridge Trail with the White
Horse Ledge Trail, connecting the trails on Moat Mtn.
with those on White Horse and Cathedral ledges. It leaves
the Red Ridge Trail on the left (east) 0.8 mi. from the
Moat Mountain Trail, just past the top of a small rise; the
trail sign is a few yards up the trail and may escape notice.
It ascends through hemlock forest and then younger
growth at a moderate grade, turning sharp left, then right
60 yd. farther, at the tops of two wooded ledges. These
turns may be difficult to see, particularly descending, if
the trail blazes are faded. It ends at the White Horse Ledge
Trail 0.2 mi. below the summit ledges.

Red Ridge Link (map 4:I10)

Distance from Red Ridge Trail

   to White Horse Ledge Trail: 0.4 mi. (0.7 km.), 25 min.

Attitash Trail (WMNF)

This trail runs from Bear Notch Rd., 2.7 mi. south of its
junction with US 302 in Bartlett village, to the Moat
Mountain Trail 2.3 mi. west of West Side Rd. The trail is
fairly easy to follow from Bear Notch Rd. to the ledges
of Table Mtn., where there are good views from an area
burned by a small forest fire in October 1984. Except for
these ledges, the trail is in the woods all the way, and
some sections between Table Mtn. and Big Attitash Mtn.
are quite difficult to follow, so at present this part of the
trail should be attempted only by those with excellent

navigational skills. The trail is covered by maps 4 and 6, but not by either one alone.

Leaving the small parking area on Bear Notch Rd., follow a grass-grown gravel logging road that crosses a major branch of Louisville Brook in about 120 yd. At 0.3 mi. the trail bears right on an older road as the gravel road bears left into a clear-cut area. The trail comes to the edge of Louisville Brook at 0.6 mi., at a small, ledgy cascade, then follows near the brook. In less than 0.1 mi. it turns left (arrow) at a logging road fork and ascends moderately to the col between Bear Mtn. and Table Mtn. at 1.3 mi. Here it turns sharp left and climbs more steeply, soon reaching the edge of the burned area, and crosses two ledges with excellent views to the south and southwest. At 1.9 mi. it reaches its high point on Table Mtn., and passes somewhat south of the summit, with views available a short distance to the right from the edge of the south cliff.

From this point the trail appears to be used more by moose than by humans, and is difficult to follow in some sections. It descends into a col at 2.5 mi., where there is a brook (unreliable), passes a ledgy spot with a glimpse of Mt. Carrigain, and soon climbs a very steep pitch to the main ridge of Big Attitash. From here the trail runs on the ridge top or a bit to its north side until it passes very close to the summit of Big Attitash at 4.7 mi. Then it descends, rather steeply at times, into the valley of Lucy Brook, which is crossed seven times. The first crossing, at 5.9 mi., may be dry; some of the crossings may be difficult in high water. The trail follows an old logging road along the brook, and at some of the crossings (which are mostly marked with arrows) care must be used to pick up the trail on the opposite bank. At 7.2 mi. it reaches the junction with the Moat Mountain Trail, which can be followed right to North Moat or straight ahead to Diana's Baths and West Side Rd.

Attitash Trail (maps 4/6:I9–I10)

Distances from Bear Notch Road

> *to* high point on Table Mtn.: 1.9 mi., 1 hr. 40 min.
>
> *to* Big Attitash Mtn. summit: 4.7 mi., 3 hr. 30 min.
>
> *to* Moat Mountain Trail: 7.2 mi. (11.6 km.), 4 hr. 45 min.

Paths on White Horse Ledge and Cathedral Ledge (NHDP)

These two bluffs on an eastern spur of the Moat Range afford interesting views and are reached by trails from Echo Lake State Park. Cathedral Ledge is also ascended by an automobile road. The cliffs on both bluffs are very popular with rock climbers, but cannot be safely ascended without proper equipment and training. The two principal trails are the White Horse Ledge Trail and the Bryce Path. The Bryce Path is named for James Bryce (later Viscount Bryce), a British statesman and author who wrote *The American Commonwealth,* an important study of the US government from a British perspective. This trail, which originally consisted of the path up the slope between the two cliffs and the branches to both summits, was laid out by Bryce in 1907 when he was British ambassador to the US. Construction on private land between Echo Lake and the foot of White Horse Ledge has compelled a major relocation of the southern part of the White Horse Ledge Trail. For the sake of simplicity, and in order to describe the trails in the sequence in which they are usually followed, the two trails are described here as a single loop trail over White Horse Ledge, with a spur path to Cathedral Ledge. They are covered by maps 4 and 6, but not by either one alone.

There are two routes available from roads to the loop junction:

(1) Leave NH 16 in North Conway just north of the Eastern Slope Inn and take the road running west across the Saco River. Turn left at 1.0 mi., then right at 1.4 mi.,

following signs for Echo Lake State Park, and reach the park gate at 1.5 mi. If the park is closed, there is parking available on an old segment of road to the left, and the park road can be followed from the gate to the trailhead (signs). From here the path descends 60 yd. nearly to the edge of Echo Lake, then bears left and runs along the lake, some distance away but mostly in sight of it. At 0.4 mi. the trail to the ledges turns sharp left, while the Lake Circuit continues around the lake and returns to the trailhead at the parking area in another 0.5 mi.; it is poorly marked and its footway is not always well defined, particularly in the vicinity of the main beach, but its route along the lakeshore is fairly obvious, and there are good views of the cliffs from the east shore. The trail to the ledges runs almost perfectly straight through attractive woods, crossing two unsigned but fairly well-beaten paths, and reaches a crossroads, which is the loop junction, at 0.7 mi.

(2) This route is shorter (saving a bit less than 0.5 mi. and about 10 min. each way) and avoids park admission fees, but is less attractive. It has sometimes been called the Bryce Link. Continue straight at 1.0 mi. from NH 16 instead of turning left for Echo Lake State Park, then turn left onto Cathedral Ledge Rd. at 1.5 mi. from NH 16. Follow this road (which ends in 1.8 mi. just below the summit of Cathedral Ledge) for 0.3 mi., then turn left and follow a rough dirt road 0.1 mi. to a parking area. Continue on the dirt road on foot 0.2 mi. to the loop junction at the crossroads.

At the crossroads, one road leads into a clearing with a cabin near its high point, and there is a fine view of the impressive slabs of White Horse Ledge. Facing this road (approximately south), which is the beginning of the part of the loop that circles and ascends White Horse Ledge from the south, access route 1 is on your left, access route 2 is behind you, and on your right is the part of the loop that ascends to the col between the two summits, giving access to either. The south part of the loop, from the loop junction to the Red Ridge Link junction near the summit of White Horse Ledge, is much less heavily used than the north part, and the footway is much less apparent, particularly in the newly relocated section, so it is not well suited for inexperienced hikers. The loop is therefore described in the counter-clockwise direction.

From the loop junction, the path (following the historic route of the Bryce Path) passes near to the foundation of an old sugar house and to the cabin in the clearing, then reaches a wooded rock slab and climbs directly uphill fairly steeply with rough footing for about 0.1 mi. It then bears right and runs almost level to a junction at 0.3 mi. from the loop junction.

Here the path to Cathedral Ledge continues almost straight across a flat, wooded upland for 0.2 mi., then turns sharp right and climbs rather steeply to a T intersection, where it turns left and reaches the turnaround at the top of the Cathedral Ledge Rd. in another 40 yd. Right at the T leads to the south outlook in 80 yd. The summit area is interlaced with countless beaten paths. The true summit is a wooded ledge, but there are several fine viewpoints from the rim of the summit area, including the fenced east outlook at the top of the main cliff.

The path to White Horse Ledge turns left uphill from the junction with the path to Cathedral Ledge. It turns right at a group of large boulders and climbs steeply for a short distance, then swings left and climbs moderately, and at 0.5 mi. from the loop junction it reaches an open ledge that provides the best view from the loop over White Horse Ledge. It continues to climb, soon returning to the woods, and reaches the summit area, bearing left and then swinging right to reach the highest ledge, where there is a fine view of Moat Mtn., at 0.9 mi. Swinging to the right off the ledge back into the woods, it descends

northwest and then west, then turns sharp left where the
Red Ridge Link enters on the right at 1.0 mi. From here
the trail must be followed with care. It descends by
switchbacks, then swings around the south end of White
Horse Ledge, and at 1.7 mi. it turns sharp left with a gravel road visible straight ahead through the trees. For a
while it runs near a line of WMNF boundary blazes, turns
sharp right where a pile of red-painted rocks (a WMNF
boundary marker) lies ahead, and then follows a narrow
strip of woods between a golf course and the boulders at
the foot of White Horse Ledge. At 2.5 mi. the rock
climbers' path to the base of White Horse Ledge enters
on the left; the steep slab, whose base is 80 yd. from this
junction, is worth a visit, but its ascent is a technical
climb that must be left to properly trained and equipped
rock climbers. From here the trail continues to the cabin
clearing and the loop junction at the crossroads.

White Horse Ledge Trail and
Bryce Path (maps 4/6:I11–I10)

Distances from Echo Lake parking area

> *to* loop junction: 0.7 mi., 20 min.
> *to* White Horse Ledge/Cathedral Ledge fork: 1.0 mi.,
> 40 min.
> *to* White Horse Ledge: 1.6 mi., 1 hr. 15 min.
> *to* loop junction: 3.5 mi., 2 hr. 20 min.
> *to* Echo Lake parking area (complete loop): 4.2 mi.
> (6.7 km.), 2 hr. 40 min.

Distances from Echo Lake parking area

> *to* Cathedral Ledge (via Cathedral Ledge branch): 1.4
> mi., 1 hr.
> *to* Echo Lake parking area (complete loop including
> Cathedral Ledge): 5.0 mi. (8.0 km.), 3 hr. 15 min.

SECTION 5
Cannon and Kinsman

This section covers the trails on Kinsman Mtn., Cannon Mtn., and the lower peaks in the same range, principally Mt. Wolf, the Cannon Balls, and Mt. Pemigewasset. It also covers trails on several smaller mountains to the west and north, including Bald Mtn. and Artist's Bluff, Cooley Hill, and Mt. Agassiz. The area is bounded on the east by I-93, US 3, and the Franconia Notch Parkway, and on the south by NH 112 (Lost River Rd.). The entire section is covered by the AMC Franconia map (map 5).

Construction of the Franconia Notch Parkway is now complete and any further related changes that might affect trails in this section should be minor. A paved bike path runs the entire length of the notch from the Flume to the Skookumchuck Trail and is available for pedestrian use, though those on foot should be careful not to unnecessarily impede bicycle traffic. The AMC, USFS, and the NHDP maintain an information booth during the summer and on fall weekends at the Lafayette Place parking area to provide information about weather, trail conditions, facilities, and regulations. Information concerning attractions in Franconia Notch is available at the Flume Visitor Center at the south end of the notch, and at Lafayette Place and the Tramway.

In this section the Appalachian Trail follows the Kinsman Ridge Trail from Kinsman Notch to Kinsman Junction (near Kinsman Pond), the Fishin' Jimmy Trail from Kinsman Junction to Lonesome Lake Hut, and the Cascade Brook Trail from Lonesome Lake Hut to a trail junction near the former Whitehouse Bridge site, which is reached by the Whitehouse Trail from the Flume Visitor Center or by the bike path from the Basin parking lots.

GEOGRAPHY

The Cannon-Kinsman range is the heart of this region. The northern half of the range is a high, well-defined ridge, of which Cannon Mtn. and the two peaks of Kinsman Mtn. are the most important summits. The southern half of the range is broad, with only one significant summit, Mt. Wolf.

Cannon Mtn. (4100 ft.) rises at the north end of the range. This dome-shaped mountain is famous for its magnificent profile, the Old Man of the Mountain, and for its imposing east cliff. The mountain takes its name from a natural stone table resting on a boulder that resembles a cannon when seen from Profile Clearing. The Great Stone Face, immortalized by Nathaniel Hawthorne, is formed by three ledges at the north end of the east cliff that are not in a vertical line and only appear to be a profile when viewed from the vicinity of Profile Lake. For some years state park personnel have protected the Old Man from the otherwise inexorable forces of ice and gravity by filling cracks with cement and maintaining a system of cables and turnbuckles. Cannon Mtn. has a major ski area operated by the state, and an aerial tramway (the successor to the first such passenger tramway in North America) that extends from a valley station (1970 ft.) just off the parkway to a mountain station (4000 ft.) just below the main summit. The tramway is operated in the summer for tourists and in the winter for skiers. Hiking is not permitted on ski trails in the summer.

On the ridge southwest of Cannon Mtn. are three humps called the Cannon Balls (east to west: 3769 ft., 3660 ft., and 3693 ft.). All are wooded, but the highest, the northeast Cannon Ball, has several good outlooks. Bridal Veil Falls, one of the more attractive falls in the mountains, is located on Coppermine Brook in the ravine between Cannon Mtn. and the Cannon Balls on the north side of the ridge. Lonesome Lake (2740 ft.) is

located on the high plateau that forms the floor of the
ravine south of the ridge between Cannon Mtn. and the
Cannon Balls. Trails completely encircle the lake, which
has excellent views from its shores. The whole area
around the lake lies within Franconia Notch State Park,
and camping is not permitted.

Kinsman Mtn. is located south of the Cannon Balls,
and its two peaks are the highest points on the ridge.
North Kinsman (4293 ft.) is wooded, and its true summit is actually a pointed boulder in the woods beside the
trail, but ledges just to the east of the summit command
magnificent views. The view of Mt. Lafayette and Mt.
Lincoln across Franconia Notch is particularly impressive. South Kinsman (4358 ft.) has a broad, flat summit
with two knobs of nearly equal height. The USGS Lincoln quad puts the summit elevation on the north knob,
which is just off the main trail, but the south knob bears
the cairn and is preferred by most hikers. Views are
fine, but one must wander around the summit plateau to
obtain the best outlooks. Kinsman Mtn. shelters two
very beautiful ponds: Kinsman Pond under the east
cliffs of North Kinsman, and Harrington Pond under the
bluff at the end of South Kinsman's south ridge. Two
spurs of the Kinsman group are especially notable. On
the west, Bald Peak (2470 ft.) is a flat, ledgy knob with
good views, reached by a spur path from the Mount
Kinsman Trail. On the east, lying below the massive
southeast ridge of South Kinsman, is Mt. Pemigewasset
(2557 ft.), with its famous natural rock profile, the Indian Head; the ledgy summit commands excellent views
and its ascent requires only a modest effort.

South of Kinsman Mtn., only Mt. Wolf has much
claim to prominence. Its summit bears a ledge with an
excellent view to the east and northeast. Although lacking in peaks, the southern part of the range does have
several aquatic attractions, including Lost River, Gordon

Pond and Gordon Fall, and Georgiana and Harvard falls. The Lost River Reservation, property of the SPNHF, lies about 5 mi. west of North Woodstock on NH 112 (Lost River Rd.). Here Lost River, one of the tributaries of Moosilauke Brook, flows for nearly 0.5 mi. through a series of caves and large potholes, for the most part underground. At one place it falls 20 ft. within one of the caves, and at another, known as Paradise Falls, it falls 30 ft. in the open air. Trails, walks, and ladders make the caves accessible. In order to protect the forest and caves, the SPNHF began to acquire the surrounding land in 1911, and it now owns about 770 acres bordering the highway on both sides for nearly 2.5 mi. The SPNHF maintains a nature garden containing more than three hundred indigenous plants and an Ecology Trail that circles the inner parking lot area and provides information at numbered and marked sites described in a brochure provided by the SPNHF. The reservation is open from May through October; an admission fee is charged.

This section also includes several scattered peaks and trails. Just northeast of Cannon Mtn. are Bald Mtn. (2340 ft.) and Artist's Bluff (2340 ft.), two small but interesting peaks at the north end of Franconia Notch that offer excellent views for little exertion. Bald Mtn. is a striking miniature mountain with a bold, bare, rocky cone, while Artist's Bluff is a wooded dome that bears the fine cliff for which it is named on its southeast face. Mt. Agassiz (2369 ft.), between the villages of Franconia and Bethlehem, is reached by a paved road 0.8 mi. long (formerly an auto toll road) that leaves NH 142 1.0 mi. south of its junction with US 302 in Bethlehem village. There is an excellent and extensive view from the summit. The former restaurant and observation tower are now a private residence, so hikers, who are currently welcome to enjoy the views from the summit (on foot only), should exercise great care to respect the rights of the property owner by staying away from all buildings. Cooley Hill (2485 ft.) is a wooded, viewless peak, but a trail built to its former fire tower has survived the loss of its principal reason for existence.

HUTS, SHELTERS, AND CAMPING

HUTS

Lonesome Lake Hut (AMC)

Lonesome Lake Hut, at about 2760 ft., is located on the west shore of Lonesome Lake, with superb views of the Franconia Range. The hut was built in 1964, replacing cabins on the northeast shore. It accommodates forty-six and is open to the public from early May to mid-October (caretaker basis in May, Setpember, and October). The hut may be reached by the Lonesome Lake Trail or the Whitehouse and Cascade Brook trails from the Franconia Notch Parkway, the Fishin' Jimmy Trail from Kinsman Junction, or by the Dodge Cutoff from the Hi-Cannon Trail. Camping is not permitted around the hut, the lake, or anywhere else in Franconia State Park except Lafayette Place Campground. For schedules and information contact AMC Reservations, Pinkham Notch Visitor Center, Box 298, Gorham NH 03581 (603-466-2727).

CAMPING

Restricted Use Areas

As of 1991, there were no Restricted Use Areas in this section, but campers should still employ good camping practices. Tent camping is permitted at all three shelters.

Franconia Notch State Park

No camping is permitted in Franconia Notch State Park except at Lafayette Campground (fee charged). In this section, the areas included in the park consist mostly of the northeast slopes of Cannon Mtn. and the regions surrounding Lonesome Lake and extending east from the lake to the Franconia Notch Parkway.

Established Trailside Campsites

Eliza Brook Shelter (AMC) is located on the Kinsman Ridge Trail at its crossing of Eliza Brook.

Kinsman Pond Campsite (AMC), with a shelter and tent platforms, is located on Kinsman Pond near Kinsman Junction, where the Kinsman Ridge, Kinsman Pond, and Fishin' Jimmy trails meet. There is a caretaker in the summer and a fee is charged.

Coppermine Shelter (WMNF) is located on the Coppermine Trail west of Bridal Veil Falls.

THE TRAILS

Kinsman Ridge Trail (AMC)

This trail follows the crest of the main ridge from the height-of-land on NH 112 in Kinsman Notch to the Tramway parking lot (look for trail sign on post and park nearby) just off the Franconia Notch Parkway. From NH 112 to Kinsman Junction, it is part of the Appalachian Trail. For much of its length it is a more difficult route than you might infer from the map. Footing is often rough and there are many minor ups and downs. Hikers with heavy packs should allow considerable extra time for many parts of the trail. There is little water on or near several long sections of the trail, and none that a cautious hiker will drink without treatment.

The following description of the path is in the northbound direction (from Kinsman Notch to the Tramway parking lot). See below for a description of the path in the reverse direction.

The trail leaves NH 112 just to the north of the height-of-land, 0.5 mi. north of the Lost River entrance and almost directly opposite the north terminus of the Beaver Brook Trail. It climbs a steep sidehill bearing gradually away from the road for 0.1 mi., and then swings right and climbs very steeply northeast through a part of the SPNHF Lost River Reservation. At 0.4 mi. the grade relaxes, and the trail soon crosses a swampy sag on log bridges and reaches a junction on the right at 0.6 mi. with the Dilly Trail from Lost River. At 0.9 mi. it crosses the summit of a wooded knob and descends steeply by zigzags, soon passes a small stream (unreliable), and follows the ridge over several minor humps. At 2.4 mi. it passes the first of two good outlooks to the east, then crosses a larger wooded hump, and descends past a boulder to the right of the trail that offers a view of Mt. Wolf ahead. At 3.3 mi. it reaches its low point south of Mt. Wolf, crossing a stagnant brook in a ravine, then ascends 30 yd. to the junction where the Gordon Pond Trail enters on the right, 0.3 mi. from Gordon Pond.

The trail climbs by short, steep sections alternating with easy sections, crossing a small brook (reliable water) at 3.9 mi., and ascends to a point just below the summit of the west knob of Mt. Wolf. Then it descends slightly into a shallow sag and climbs to a point near the summit of the east knob of Mt. Wolf at 4.6 mi., where it makes a sharp left turn. Here a side path leads right 60 yd. to the summit of the east knob, where there is a fine view of the Franconias and the peaks to the east and southeast. The main trail now descends the east side of Wolf's north ridge at a moderate grade, but with a rough footway and numerous short ascents interspersed. At 6.0 mi. the trail turns left, runs almost level, and meets the Reel Brook Trail, which enters left at 6.5 mi., just south of the col between Mt. Wolf and Kinsman Mtn. (this was the original Kinsman Notch). The Kinsman Ridge Trail continues along the ridge top, crosses under power lines at 7.0 mi., and descends to the bank of Eliza Brook at 7.5 mi., where a side path runs left 55 yd. to Eliza Brook Shelter.

The Kinsman Ridge Trail crosses Eliza Brook and in 50 yd. intersects a grass-grown gravel logging road and follows it to the left. (Watch carefully for the points where the trail turns off this road, going in either direction.) The trail follows the road for 0.3 mi., then turns left off it and follows a scenic section of Eliza Brook, with several attractive cascades and pools. At 8.6 mi. the trail recrosses Eliza Brook and climbs rather steeply to cross the bog at the east end of Harrington Pond on log bridges. Here, at 8.9 mi., there is an interesting view of the shoulder of South Kinsman rising above the beautiful pond. (*Note*: The section of the trail between Harrington Pond and South Kinsman may require much extra time, particularly for hikers carrying heavy packs, and is also somewhat exposed to weather.) The trail continues at a moderate grade for 0.3 mi., then climbs a steep pitch, crosses a minor hump and a blowdown patch, then struggles up a steep and rough pitch to an outlook where the climbing becomes somewhat easier. It continues to the bare south knob of South Kinsman's summit, which is very exposed to the weather, at 9.9 mi.

From here the Kinsman Ridge Trail crosses a scrub-filled sag, passes 15 yd. to the west of the north knob of South Kinsman at 10.0 mi., and descends relatively easily to the col between South and North Kinsman at 10.5 mi. The trail then climbs steadily to a side path (sign) at 10.9 mi. that leads right 25 yd. to a good outlook to the Franconias and continues another 70 yd. to a ledge that looks directly down on Kinsman Pond. The true summit of North Kinsman is a pointed boulder on the right of the main trail, 30 yd. north of the outlook spur. The Kinsman Ridge Trail now descends steeply to the junction with the Mount Kinsman Trail on the left at 11.3 mi., and continues to Kinsman Junction at 11.5 mi. Here the Fishin' Jimmy Trail continues the Appalachian Trail to Lonesome Lake, and the Kinsman Pond Trail bears right, leading in 0.1 mi. to Kinsman Pond and Kinsman Pond Shelter.

The Kinsman Ridge Trail turns sharp left at Kinsman Junction, and soon rises abruptly 100 ft. to a hump (3812 ft.) on the ridge. It then continues over the Cannon Balls, the three humps that make up the ridge leading to Cannon Mtn. After passing near the top of the first (west) Cannon Ball at 12.5 mi., it descends sharply to a deep ravine, where water is usually available in a small brook. The trail circles to the north of the second (middle) Cannon Ball and enters the next col with very little descent. After passing several scattered viewpoints while climbing over the third (northeast) Cannon Ball at 13.7 mi., it descends to the junction at 13.9 mi. with the Lonesome Lake Trail, which leads southeast 1.0 mi. to Lonesome Lake Hut (water can be found 0.2 mi. down this trail). In a few yards it reaches the low point in Coppermine Col, at the base of Cannon Mtn., then climbs very steeply among huge boulders. At 14.3 mi. the Hi-Cannon Trail enters right, and the Kinsman Ridge Trail climbs gradually to the gravel Rim Trail at 14.7 mi., where it encounters the maze of trails in the summit area. The true summit, with its observation platform and lookout tower, is reached in 120 yd. by following the gravel path straight ahead from this junction; a path continues from the tower down to the Tramway summit station.

The Kinsman Ridge Trail bears right at the junction and coincides with the Rim Trail for about 0.2 mi. around the edge of the summit plateau, affording excellent views, then turns sharp right downhill (sign) as the Rim Trail continues on toward the tramway terminal. Descending the semi-open east flank of the main peak over rocks and ledges, then through scrub, it crosses a moist sag and ascends slightly to the east summit. At the point where it makes a right-angle turn left (north), a side trail turns sharp right out upon the ledges to the southeast, where there is a magnificent view across the notch to the Franconia Range. The main trail drops steeply on a rough and rocky footway that improves somewhat in the lower half, and ends at the Tramway parking lot.

Kinsman Ridge Trail (map 5:I3–G4)

Distances from NH 112 in Kinsman Notch

　　to Dilly Trail: 0.6 mi., 40 min.
　　to Gordon Pond Trail: 3.3 mi., 2 hr. 20 min.
　　to Reel Brook Trail: 6.5 mi., 4 hr. 25 min.
　　to Eliza Brook Shelter spur: 7.5 mi., 4 hr. 55 min.
　　to Harrington Pond: 8.9 mi., 6 hr. 10 min.
　　to South Kinsman summit: 10.0 mi., 7 hr. 15 min.
　　to North Kinsman summit: 10.9 mi., 7 hr. 50 min.
　　to Mount Kinsman Trail: 11.3 mi., 8 hr.
　　to Kinsman Junction: 11.5 mi., 8 hr. 5 min.
　　to Lonesome Lake Trail: 13.9 mi., 9 hr. 40 min.
　　to Hi-Cannon Trail: 14.3 mi., 10 hr. 5 min.
　　to Rim Trail junction near Cannon Mtn. summit: 14.7 mi., 10 hr. 25 min.
　　to side path to ledges: 15.4 mi., 10 hr. 45 min.
　　to Tramway parking area: 16.9 mi (27.1 km.), 11 hr. 30 min.

Kinsman Ridge Trail (AMC) [in reverse]

From the Tramway parking area near the main buildings, the trail turns left and follows a gravel road to a picnic area (sign) for 150 yd., then turns right and follows the left edge of a ski trail for 80 yd. to the bottom of a steep slope. Turning left (signs) into the woods, the trail climbs moderately and then steeply, becoming steeper and rockier as it ascends. In a level area at 1.5 mi., a side path goes straight ahead out upon the ledges to the southwest, where there is a magnificent view across the notch to the Franconia Range. Here the main trail turns sharp right (west) to cross over the east summit and pass through a moist sag, after which it climbs rather steeply up through rocks and scrub to the gravel Rim Trail at 2.0 mi. Turning left (right leads to the Tramway terminal) and coinciding with the Rim Trail for 0.2 mi., affording excellent views, the Kinsman Ridge Trail continues straight ahead where the gravel path turns sharp right to reach the summit observation platform and lookout tower in 120 yd. and then continue to the Tramway summit station.

The Kinsman Ridge Trail descends gradually to the junction with the Hi-Cannon Trail on the left at 2.5 mi., then drops very steeply among huge boulders to Coppermine Col. It then climbs for a few yards to the junction on the left at 3.0 mi. with the Lonesome Lake Trail, which leads southeast 1.0 mi. to Lonesome Lake Hut (water can be found 0.2 mi. down this trail). The Kinsman Ridge Trail now continues over the Cannon Balls, the three humps that make up the ridge leading to Kinsman Mtn. It ascends rather steeply from the Lonesome Lake Trail junction and passes several scattered viewpoints while climbing over the first (northeast) Cannon Ball at 3.2 mi., then descends to a col. The trail circles to the north of the second (middle) Cannon Ball and descends moderately to a deep ravine, where water is usually available in a small brook, then ascends sharply and passes near the top of the third (west) Cannon Ball at 4.4 mi. After crossing another hump (3812 ft.) and dropping to a flat region, it reaches Kinsman Junction at 5.4 mi. Here the Fishin' Jimmy Trail (the Appalachian Trail) enters on the left from Lonesome Lake, and the Kinsman Pond Trail runs straight ahead, leading in 0.1 mi. to Kinsman Pond and Kinsman Pond Shelter.

From Kinsman Junction the Kinsman Ridge Trail (now the Appalachian Trail for the rest of its length) turns right and climbs up ledges to the junction where the Mount Kinsman Trail enters on the right at 5.6 mi., then continues to climb steeply to the summit of North Kinsman. Here a side path (sign) at 6.0 mi. leads left 25 yd. to a fine outlook to the Franconias and continues another 70 yd. to a ledge that looks directly down on Kinsman Pond. The true summit of North Kinsman is a pointed boulder on the left of the main trail, 30 yd. north of the outlook spur. The main trail descends steadily to the col between South and North Kinsman at 6.4 mi., then ascends relatively easily and passes 15 yd. to the west of the north knob of South Kinsman's summit at 6.9 mi.

The Kinsman Ridge Trail then crosses a scrub-filled sag to the bare south knob of South Kinsman, which is very exposed to the weather, at 7.0 mi. (*Note:* The section of the trail between South Kinsman and Harrington Pond may require much extra time, particularly for those with heavy packs, and is also somewhat exposed to weather.) From South Kinsman the trail descends moderately, then drops down a very steep and rough pitch, crosses a blow-down patch and a minor hump, then descends another steep pitch. It continues to descend at a moderate grade for 0.3 mi., then crosses the bog at the east end of Harrington Pond on log bridges. Here, at 8.0 mi., there is an interesting view of the shoulder of South Kinsman rising above the beautiful pond. The trail resumes a rather steep descent, then crosses Eliza Brook at 8.3 mi. and follows a very scenic section of the brook with several attractive cascades and pools. At 9.1 mi. the trail intersects a grass-grown gravel logging road and follows it to the right. (Watch carefully for the points where the trail turns off this road, going in either direction.) The trail follows the road for 0.3 mi., then turns right off it and in 50 yd. recrosses Eliza Brook, reaching a junction at 9.4 mi. where a side path runs right 55 yd. to Eliza Brook Shelter.

From here the Kinsman Ridge Trail ascends to the crest of the north ridge of Mt. Wolf, crosses under power lines at 9.9 mi., and follows the ridge top to the Reel Brook Trail, which enters right at 10.4 mi., just south of the col between Mt. Wolf and Kinsman Mtn. (this was the original Kinsman Notch). The main trail now runs almost level, then swings right and ascends the east side of Wolf's north ridge at a moderate grade, but with a rough footway and numerous short descents interspersed, to a point near the summit of the east knob of Mt. Wolf at 12.3 mi., where it makes a sharp right turn. Here a side path leads left 60 yd. to the summit of the east knob, where there is a fine view of the Franconias and the peaks to the east and southeast. The main trail descends slightly into a shallow sag, then ascends slightly to a point just below the summit of the west knob of Mt. Wolf. Here it turns left, descending by short, steep sections alternating with easy sections across a small brook (reliable water source) at 13.0 mi. to the junction with the Gordon Pond Trail on the left at 13.6 mi., 0.3 mi. from Gordon Pond.

The Kinsman Ridge Trail descends another 30 yd. to its low point south of Mt. Wolf, crosses a stagnant brook in a ravine, then ascends moderately past a boulder to the left of the trail that offers a view back to Mt. Wolf. It soon runs to the left of the summit of a large wooded hump, passes two good outlooks to the east, and follows the ridgecrest over several minor humps, finally ascending steeply by zigzags to the summit of a wooded knob at 16.0 mi. The trail now descends moderately to a junction with the Dilly Trail from Lost River on the left at 16.2 mi. The Kinsman Ridge Trail soon crosses a swampy sag on log bridges and begins a very steep descent southwest through a part of the SPNHF Lost River Reservation toward Kinsman Notch, swinging to the left with NH 112 visible below on the right for the last part of the descent.

Kinsman Ridge Trail (map 5:I3–G4)

Distances from Tramway parking area

    to side path to ledges: 1.5 mi., 1 hr. 45 min.

    to Rim Trail junction near Tramway terminal: 2.0 mi., 2 hr. 10 min.

to Hi-Cannon Trail: 2.5 mi., 2 hr. 20 min.
to Lonesome Lake Trail: 3.0 mi., 2 hr. 35 min.
to Kinsman Junction: 5.4 mi., 4 hr. 20 min.
to Mount Kinsman Trail: 5.6 mi., 4 hr. 25 min.
to North Kinsman summit: 6.0 mi., 4 hr. 50 min.
to South Kinsman summit: 6.9 mi., 5 hr. 30 min.
to Harrington Pond: 8.0 mi., 6 hr. 5 min.
to Eliza Brook Shelter spur: 9.4 mi., 6 hr. 45 min.
to Reel Brook Trail: 10.4 mi., 7 hr. 25 min.
to Gordon Pond Trail: 13.6 mi., 9 hr. 30 min.
to Dilly Trail: 16.2 mi., 11 hr. 10 min.
to NH 112 in Kinsman Notch: 16.9 mi. (27.1 km.),
    11 hr. 30 min.

Bald Mountain–Artist's Bluff Path (NHDP)

Artist's Bluff and the summit of Bald Mtn. provide fine views for very little effort. The trail begins and ends on NH 18 just west of its junction with the Franconia Notch Parkway, north of Echo Lake. The west trailhead is located at the edge of the large parking lot for the Roland Peabody Memorial Slope section of the Cannon Mountain Ski Area, on the north side of NH 18 about 0.4 mi. from the parkway. The east trailhead is on NH 18 opposite Echo Lake beach.

Leaving the Peabody Slopes parking lot, the trail follows an old carriage road and reaches the ridge top in 0.2 mi. At this point a spur path diverges left and climbs the rocky cone of Bald Mtn., reaching the top in 0.1 mi. About 25 yd. beyond the junction with the trail to Bald Mtn., the main trail turns right from the old road and runs over the wooded hump that bears the Artist's Bluff cliff on its east end, then descends to the top of a steep, gravelly gully at 0.7 mi., where an unmarked path leads left 50 yd. to the top of Artist's Bluff. The main trail continues down the gully to NH 18.

Bald Mountain–Artist's Bluff Path (map 5:G4)

Distances from Peabody Slopes parking area

　to fork in trail: 0.2 mi., 10 min.

　to Bald Mtn. (via spur path): 0.3 mi., 20 min.

　to Echo Lake beach (direct via Artist's Bluff): 0.8 mi. (1.3 km.), 35 min.

　to Echo Lake Beach (via Bald Mtn. and Artist's Bluff): 1.1 mi. (1.8 km.), 50 min.

Lonesome Lake Trail (AMC)

This trail begins on the west side of the Franconia Notch Parkway, at the picnic area of the south parking lot at Lafayette Campground, and runs past Lonesome Lake to the Kinsman Ridge Trail at Coppermine Col. It follows the route of an old bridle path much of the way to Lonesome Lake, with excellent footing and easy to moderate grades; beyond the lake it is of average difficulty.

The trail leaves the parking lot at a large trail sign, crosses the Pemigewasset on a footbridge and then crosses the Pemi Trail, and follows a yellow-blazed path through the campground, climbing at a moderate grade. At 0.3 mi. a bridge crosses a small brook at a sharp left turn in the trail, and at 0.4 mi. the Hi-Cannon Trail leaves right. From this point the trail ascends by three long switchbacks, then descends slightly to a junction at 1.2 mi. near the shore of Lonesome Lake, where the old bridle path ends; here the Cascade Brook Trail enters left and the Dodge Cutoff diverges right. For the shortest route to Lonesome Lake Hut follow the Cascade Brook and Fishin' Jimmy trails. The Lonesome Lake Trail becomes a footpath that continues along the north shore, coinciding with the Around-Lonesome-Lake-Trail, which diverges left after 0.2 mi. and leads to Lonesome Lake Hut in another 0.3 mi. The Lonesome Lake Trail continues northwest, soon begins to rise more steeply, and ends at the Kinsman Ridge Trail in Coppermine Col, 0.8 mi. southwest of the summit of Cannon Mtn.

Lonesome Lake Trail (map 5:H4)

Distances from Lafayette Campground parking area (west side)

    to Hi-Cannon Trail: 0.4 mi., 15 min.

    to Cascade Brook Trail/Dodge Cutoff: 1.2 mi., 1 hr. 5 min.

    to Lonesome Lake Hut (via Cascade Brook Trail and Fishin' Jimmy Trail): 1.6 mi., 1 hr. 20 min.

    to Kinsman Ridge Trail: 2.3 mi. (3.6 km.), 2 hr.

Around-Lonesome-Lake Trail (AMC)

This trail, composed mostly of portions of other trails, encircles Lonesome Lake and affords fine views, especially of the Franconia Range. The part on the west shore of the lake is subject to flooding in wet seasons, though log bridges cross most of the boggy places.

Starting at the junction of the Lonesome Lake and Cascade Brook trails, this trail follows the latter south along the east shore, then turns west and follows the Fishin' Jimmy Trail, crosses the outlet of the lake, and continues across the beach area as the Fishin' Jimmy Trail bears left to ascend to the hut. The trail continues north through the bogs along the west side of the lake (the only section not shared with another trail), crosses several inlet brooks, and meets the Lonesome Lake Trail after entering the woods. Here it turns right on the Lonesome Lake Trail and continues to the junction with the Cascade Brook Trail, completing the circuit.

Around-Lonesome-Lake Trail (map 5:H4)

Distance for complete loop

    from any starting point: 0.8 mi. (1.2 km.), 25 min.

Hi-Cannon Trail (NHDP)

This trail begins at the Lonesome Lake Trail 0.4 mi. from the parking area at Lafayette Campground, and ends on the Kinsman Ridge Trail 0.4 mi. south of the summit of Cannon Mtn. It is steep near Cliff House, somewhat rough at times, and potentially dangerous if there is ice on the ledges above Cliff House. It passes several fine viewpoints, particularly the ledges overlooking Lonesome Lake.

The trail diverges right (west) from the Lonesome Lake Trail and begins to ascend gradually by switchbacks. Watch carefully for a sharp right switchback at 0.1 mi., where an old logging road continues straight and rejoins the Lonesome Lake Trail. At 0.8 mi. the Dodge Cutoff from Lonesome Lake enters left at the top of a ridge. At 1.2 mi. there is a good outlook to the area around Lafayette Campground and across Franconia Notch, and 100 yd. farther the trail passes Cliff House (right)—a natural rock shelter—and ascends a ladder. It then passes along a cliff edge with three outlooks over Lonesome Lake in the next 0.2 mi. (use caution on the ledges). Then the trail ascends moderately to the top of the ridge, turns right, and at 2.0 mi. ends at its junction with the Kinsman Ridge Trail. To reach the summit of Cannon Mtn., follow the Kinsman Ridge Trail right 0.4 mi.

Hi-Cannon Trail (map 5:H4)

Distances from Lonesome Lake Trail

  to Dodge Cutoff: 0.8 mi., 50 min.

  to Kinsman Ridge Trail: 2.0 mi. (3.2 km.), 1 hr. 55 min.

  to Cannon Mtn. summit (via Kinsman Ridge Trail):
      2.4 mi., 2 hr. 15 min.

Dodge Cutoff (NHDP)

This direct connection between the Lonesome Lake and Hi-Cannon trails provides a shortcut between Lonesome Lake and Cannon Mtn. It was named in honor of Joe Dodge, a former manager of the AMC hut system.

It begins at the junction of the Lonesome Lake and Cascade Brook trails on the east shore of the lake, 0.3 mi. from Lonesome Lake Hut. After climbing over a low ridge and crossing a moist sag, it ascends, rather steeply for a while, to the Hi-Cannon Trail 0.8 mi. above the junction of the Lonesome Lake and Hi-Cannon trails.

Dodge Cutoff (map 5:H4)
Distance from Hi-Cannon Trail
   to Lonesome Lake Trail: 0.3 mi. (0.5 km.), 15 min.

Pemi Trail (NHDP)
This trail extends from Profile Lake to the Basin, providing pedestrians a fairly easy though not always plainly marked footpath that is an alternative route to the bike path along the central part of Franconia Notch. It has incorporated almost all of the former Profile Lake Trail, a name that is now applied to a short paved tourist path.

   The Pemi Trail leaves the southwest corner of the Old Man parking area on the west side of the Franconia Notch Parkway and ascends granite steps into the woods. It skirts the west shore of Profile Lake, crossing numerous unmarked paths used by rock climbers. At 0.7 mi. it enters the bike path, follows it right for 50 yd., then turns left and re-enters the woods. It runs close to the parkway, then crosses the Pemigewasset on a bridge at 1.2 mi. and recrosses on another bridge at 1.9 mi. In another 100 yd. it crosses the bike path and bears right onto a gravel road that leads into Lafayette Campground just below the headquarters buildings. It continues south on the campground road that follows most closely along the west bank of the river, crosses the Lonesome Lake Trail, and continues to its southern terminus at the beginning of the Basin-Cascades Trail, close to the Basin.

Pemi Trail (map 5:H4)
Distances from Old Man parking area (west side of parkway)
   to Lafayette Campground: 2.0 mi., 1 hr.
   to the Basin-Cascades Trail: 3.9 mi. (6.3 km.), 1 hr. 55 min.

Basin-Cascades Trail (NHDP)

This trail starts at the Basin (parking areas on either side of Franconia Notch Parkway) and ascends along the beautiful lower half of Cascade Brook to the Cascade Brook Trail. The brook is extremely scenic and trail grades are mostly moderate, but the footing is often fairly rough. From the parking areas on either side of the parkway, follow the tourist paths past the Basin and on to the west bank of the Pemigewasset, about 0.2 mi. from either starting point, where you will find the trailhead at the western edge of the maze of paths that surrounds the Basin.

From the trailhead (sign) the path angles toward Cascade Brook, passing a branch of the Pemi Trail on the right in 20 yd., and climbs along the brook past cascades, small falls, and ledges with views of the Franconia Range across the notch, reached by numerous unmarked side paths. At 0.4 mi. the trail passes a rough side path (no sign) that leads down to a good view of Kinsman Falls, and 50 yd. farther up, as the main trail comes out on the bank of the brook, a ledge on the left provides a viewpoint at the top of these falls. In another 100 yd. the trail crosses Cascade Brook on a high, rather rickety bridge and continues along the brook with more cascades and pools. It passes Rocky Glen Falls at 0.9 mi., then swings left up through a small box canyon and soon ends at the Cascade Brook Trail on the south bank of the brook. For a good view of Rocky Glen Falls from above, return cautiously about 60 yd. down the brook bank.

Basin-Cascades Trail (map 5:H4)
Distance from trailhead near the Basin
   to Cascade Brook Trail: 1.0 mi. (1.5 km.), 45 min.

Cascade Brook Trail (AMC)

This trail, a link in the Appalachian Trail, leads to Lonesome Lake from the bike path at the former Whitehouse

Bridge site, just south of the bike path's bridge over the Pemigewasset (the Liberty Spring Trail begins just north of the bridge). There is no parking at the Whitehouse Bridge site, which is reached in 0.8 mi. from the Flume Visitor Center hiker parking area via the Whitehouse Trail (see Section 3) or in 0.7 mi. via the bike path from the Basin parking lot on the northbound side of the parkway. It is in general a relatively easy trail, but the crossing of Cascade Brook may be difficult at high water.

From the junction with the bike path, the trail crosses under the parkway, then turns right at the edge of the parkway clearing and enters the woods. The trail climbs at a moderate grade, crosses Whitehouse Brook at 0.4 mi., and continues generally northwest, reaching a junction at 1.5 mi. at the edge of Cascade Brook, where the Basin–Cascades Trail enters right. For a good view of Rocky Glen Falls from above, walk cautiously about 60 yd. down the brook bank. The Cascade Brook Trail immediately crosses Cascade Brook on the rocks (may be difficult), and continues to climb along the northeast bank. At 2.0 mi. the Kinsman Pond Trail diverges left and crosses the brook, and from this point the Cascade Brook Trail follows an old logging road, becoming rougher and rockier, to the junction with Fishin' Jimmy Trail at the outlet of Lonesome Lake at 2.8 mi. From here Lonesome Lake Hut is 150 yd. to the left. The Cascade Brook Trail continues along the east side of the lake and ends at the Lonesome Lake Trail at 3.1 mi.

Cascade Brook Trail (map 5:H4)

Distances from Whitehouse Trail/Liberty Spring Trail junction

  to Basin-Cascades Trail: 1.5 mi., 1 hr. 5 min.
  to Kinsman Pond Trail: 2.0 mi., 1 hr. 25 min.
  to Fishin' Jimmy Trail: 2.8 mi., 2 hr. 5 min.
  to Lonesome Lake Trail: 3.1 mi. (5.0 km.), 2 hr. 10 min.

Fishin' Jimmy Trail (AMC)

This trail, a link in the Appalachian Trail, leads from Lonesome Lake to the Kinsman Ridge Trail at Kinsman Junction, near Kinsman Pond. Parts of it are steep and rough, with wooden steps on ledges. It received its peculiar name from the chief character in a story by Annie Trumbull Slosson, once a well-known regional author, who set the story's scene in this area.

Diverging from the Cascade Brook Trail at the south end of Lonesome Lake, the Fishin' Jimmy Trail crosses the outlet brook, passes the junction with the Around-Lonesome-Lake Trail near the beach at the southwest corner of the lake, and reaches Lonesome Lake Hut at 0.1 mi. It runs around the lower end of a ridge coming down from the Middle Cannon Ball, making several ascents and descents and passing over a ledgy ridgecrest at 0.6 mi. It then crosses several small brooks, with the last reliable water in a mossy, ledgy brook at 1.1 mi., and soon begins to climb, at times steeply but with occasional minor descents as well. At 1.7 mi. it curls around a large boulder on the left and passes through a fairly flat area. At 1.9 mi. it reaches the top of the serious climbing and ascends gradually to Kinsman Junction and the Kinsman Ridge Trail at 2.0 mi., 0.1 mi. north of Kinsman Pond Shelter on the Kinsman Pond Trail.

Fishin' Jimmy Trail (map 5:H4)

Distances from Cascade Brook Trail

   to Lonesome Lake Hut: 0.1 mi., 5 min.

   to Kinsman Junction: 2.0 mi. (3.3 km.), 1 hr. 45 min.

Kinsman Pond Trail (AMC)

This trail leads to Kinsman Pond and Kinsman Junction from the Cascade Brook Trail, 2.0 mi. from its beginning on the bike path at the Whitehouse Bridge site, reached by following the Whitehouse Trail (Section 3) 0.8 mi. north from the hikers' parking lot near the Flume

Visitor Center. The upper part of this trail is wet, steep, rocky, and very rough, and at times it shares the footway with small brooks, making rocks slippery; it may also be difficult to follow for short stretches.

Leaving the Cascade Brook Trail, the Kinsman Pond Trail immediately crosses to the southwest side of the brook and proceeds west on old logging roads. Soon it crosses a small brook and begins to rise moderately, following a brook past several small but attractive cascades and passing into virgin forest. The trail is rough and eroded in parts, but the brook and the dense boreal forest are beautiful. At 1.3 mi. the trail crosses the brook and runs in its bed for 0.1 mi. At 1.6 mi. the grade becomes easy, and the trail crosses the outlet brook from the pond at 1.9 mi., passes a water source left (sign), and reaches the foot of the pond at 2.1 mi. It climbs up and down on the ledgy east shore of the pond, with the impressive bulk of North Kinsman rising from the opposite shore, and passes Kinsman Pond Shelter (which accommodates twelve) and a tentsite. (Be sure to treat any water you obtain in this area.) Kinsman Junction, where the Kinsman Pond Trail meets the Kinsman Ridge and Fishin' Jimmy trails, is 0.1 mi. beyond the shelter.

Kinsman Pond Trail (map 5:H4)
Distance from Cascade Brook Trail
    to Kinsman Junction: 2.5 mi. (4.0 km.), 1 hr. 55 min.

Mount Pemigewasset Trail (NHDP)
This trail runs from the Flume Visitor Center parking area to the summit of Mt. Pemigewasset (Indian Head), where excellent views can be obtained with modest effort. Grades and footing are mostly easy. The trail reaches the vertical summit cliffs very abruptly, so care should be exercised, particularly with small children or in slippery conditions.

The trail follows the bike path north from the parking lot for 150 yd., then turns left on a gravel path and passes under old US 3 in a tunnel, crosses a brook on a major bridge, and then passes under both lanes of the parkway. It enters the woods at 0.4 mi. and crosses several small brooks on log bridges, climbing moderately. At 1.3 mi. it squeezes around a large boulder and swings left uphill, climbing a bit more steeply to the ridgecrest, which it follows to the left (south). It passes the junction with the Indian Head Trail (no sign) on the right at 1.7 mi. and reaches the summit ledges at 1.8 mi. Here yellow blazes will be seen leading down the ledges to the east; this is a very steep, unmaintained trail, dangerous in slippery conditions, that currently ends abruptly at the edge of the parkway, requiring a bushwhack through the woods above the highway to one of the two regular trailheads.

Mount Pemigewasset Trail (map 5:H4)
Distance from Flume Visitor Center parking area
   to Mt. Pemigewasset summit: 1.8 mi. (2.9 km.), 1 hr. 30 min.

Indian Head Trail (AMC)

This trail runs to the summit of Mt. Pemigewasset (Indian Head), where open ledges afford excellent views. It begins on the west side of US 3 south of the Indian Head Resort at a small parking area, reached by a short gravel road marked with a "Trailhead Parking" sign. This trail is not nearly as heavily used or as well marked as the Mount Pemigewasset Trail.

The trail leaves the parking area, accompanies a small brook under the parkway, and ascends by easy grades through hardwoods on an old logging road along the brook. At 1.1 mi. it leaves the old road and climbs moderately, circling well around the cliffs on the south side that form the Indian Head, and at 1.8 mi., just below the summit ledges, it joins the Mount Pemigewasset Trail (no sign) and follows it, to the right, to the summit.

Indian Head Trail (map 5:H4)

Distance from US 3

 to Mt. Pemigewasset summit: 1.9 mi. (3.0 km.), 1 hr.
  40 min.

Georgiana Falls Path

Georgiana Falls are a series of cascades on Harvard
Brook that end in a pool. Above Georgiana Falls there are
more cascades terminating in Harvard Falls about 0.4 mi.
farther up the brook. The path lies on private land and is
not officially maintained. It begins about 2.5 mi. north of
North Woodstock on Hanson Farm Rd., which leaves the
west side of US 3 opposite the Longhorn Restaurant,
crosses Hanson Brook on a bridge, and reaches a parking
area at about 0.1 mi. at the end of the pavement. Follow a
dirt road through a tunnel under the northbound lanes of
I-93 and bear right, then leftunder the southbound lanes.
At 0.5 mi., where the road bears right, the trail (blazed
red) turns left into the woods and follows the north side
of Harvard Brook, reaching the base of Georgiana Falls at
0.7 mi. and continuing up the brook on sloping rocks
beside the falls. Above these falls the path is neither
maintained nor marked; it re-enters the woods and fol
lows a steep, sometimes slippery path to Harvard Falls
and views of the Pemigewasset Valley and Loon Mtn.

Georgiana Falls Path (map 5:I4)

Distances from Hanson Farm Road

 to Georgiana Falls: 0.7 mi., 45 min.

 to Harvard Falls: 1.2 mi. (1.9 km.), 1 hr.

Gordon Pond Trail (WMNF)

This trail runs from NH 112 1.7 mi. west of its junction
with US 3 in North Woodstock to the Kinsman Ridge
Trail south of Mt. Wolf, passing Gordon Fall and Gordon Pond. The trailhead on NH 112 is located opposite
Govoni's Restaurant and Agassiz Basin (see Section 6);
there are signs here for the restaurant and Agassiz Basin

in the summer but not at other times. Park just west of the buildings.

The Gordon Pond Trail (WMNF sign) follows the driveway between the buildings on the north side of NH 112 ("No Trespassing" signs do not apply to hikers who stay on the trail), and at 0.1 mi. it turns right at a cross-roads and follows an old railroad grade. At 0.6 mi. it reaches the power lines, turns left and follows the power line clearing, then turns right and crosses under the lines into the woods, rejoining the old railroad grade at 1.0 mi. and following it to the left. At 1.3 mi. another road enters on the right. (*In* the opposite direction, bear right here; there may be an arrow pointing to the wrong branch.) At 1.8 mi. the trail approaches Gordon Pond Brook and a logging road crosses the brook, but the trail remains on the southwest bank and swings to the northwest to recross the power lines at 2.0 mi. The trail finally crosses Gordon Pond Brook (may be difficult at high water) at 2.2 mi. and continues along the north bank, crossing a tributary at 2.8 mi., then swings left to recross the main brook on a snowmobile bridge at 3.5 mi. It continues on an old road, becoming somewhat steeper, and crosses a minor ridge to the southerly branch of Gordon Pond Brook where it passes Gordon Fall. Crossing the brook on a ledge at the top of the fall at 3.9 mi., it soon recrosses, passes a very wet section of trail, then crosses Gordon Pond Brook at 4.6 mi. Just before it recrosses the main brook at 4.7 mi., unsigned paths lead right to the shore of the pond, where there is an interesting view of the steep face of Mt. Wolf. The trail itself does not come within sight of the pond, but continues at a level grade, bears left where an unsigned path enters right, and climbs easily to the Kinsman Ridge Trail.

Gordon Pond Trail (map 5:I4–I3)

Distances from NH 112

    to Gordon Fall: 3.9 mi., 2 hr. 40 min.

to Kinsman Ridge Trail: 5.0 mi. (8.0 km.), 3 hr. 25 min.

Dilly Trail (SPNHF)

This short trail runs from Lost River Reservation to the Kinsman Ridge Trail 0.6 mi. from NH 112. It is extremely steep and rough, but offers an interesting outlook across the valley. Its trailhead, shared with the Ecology Trail, is on a parking area access road directly across from a gazebo. In 25 yd. from the road the Ecology Trail leaves on the left, and the Dilly Trail soon begins to ascend a very steep, badly eroded gully with very loose footing, requiring caution, particularly when descending. At 0.4 mi., where the trail reaches the top rim of the steep slope, a side path leads sharp right 40 yd. to a fine outlook from the rim. The main trail turns sharp left, and continues at moderate grades to the Kinsman Ridge Trail.

Dilly Trail (map 5:I3)

Distances from Lost River Reservation parking lot
to lookout over Lost River: 0.4 mi., 30 min.
to Kinsman Ridge Trail: 0.5 mi., 40 min.

Coppermine Trail (WMNF)

This trail to Bridal Veil Falls begins on Coppermine Rd., which leaves the east side of NH 116 3.4 mi. south of NH 18 in Franconia (and 1.0 mi. south of the Franconia Airport) or 7.7 mi. north of NH 112 at Bungay Corner. Park near NH 116 and follow the road. At 0.4 mi. the trail bears left on an older road (hiker logo sign and yellow blazes). At 1.0 mi. the trail joins Coppermine Brook and follows along the north side, then crosses to the south side on a bridge at 2.3 mi., passes the WMNF Coppermine Shelter, and ends at the base of Bridal Veil Falls.

Coppermine Trail (map 5:G3–H4)

Distance from NH 116
to Bridal Veil Falls: 2.5 mi. (4.0 km.), 1 hr. 45 min.

Mount Kinsman Trail (WMNF)

This trail climbs to the Kinsman Ridge Trail 0.4 mi. north of North Kinsman from the east side of NH 116 at the Franconia-Easton town line, about 4 mi. south of NH 18 in Franconia village and 2.0 mi. north of the Easton town hall. There is a sign for the town line a few yards north of the trail, but none for the trail itself, which follows a logging road at a prominent gate opposite a house. The trail climbs at moderate grades but is sparsely marked, and some care is frequently required to follow it.

From the gate it follows a logging road that soon swings right, then bears right at a fork (arrow). Ascending easily, at times level, it passes a sugar house left at 0.6 mi., and at 1.1 mi. enters the WMNF, where a short loop path left bypasses a wet section of road. The road, now distinctly older and steeper, crosses a substantial brook at 1.5 mi. at the site of the former Kinsman Cabin (which has been dismantled). At 1.8 mi. it crosses a small brook that falls over a mossy ledge to the left of the trail, then at 2.1 mi. crosses Flume Brook. Just over Flume Brook, a side path on the right descends close to the brook bank for 150 yd. to small, steep-walled Kinsman Flume, a classic eroded dike with an overhanging boulder at the top that presents a reasonable facsimile of a profile. The main trail continues on the road for another 70 yd., then turns sharp left, where a spur path 0.2 mi. long diverges sharp right and makes an easy ascent to Bald Peak, a bare ledgy dome with fine views that crowns a west spur of Kinsman Mtn.

The axe-blazed trail now joins and follows Flume Brook, winding up the mountainside at easy to moderate grades, with good footing except for short, scattered steep pitches with rough footing. It crosses several small brooks and at 3.2 mi. climbs a ledge by means of a short ladder. Soon it swings right and angles upward, then swings left and climbs straight up to the ridge top, where it meets the Kinsman Ridge Trail. For North and South Kinsman turn right; to reach Kinsman Pond and Kinsman Junction turn left.

Mount Kinsman Trail (map 5:G3–H4)
Distances from NH 116

    to Bald Peak spur trail: 2.1 mi., 1 hr. 45 min.

    to Kinsman Ridge Trail: 3.7 mi. (5.9 km.), 3 hr. 15 min.

Reel Brook Trail (WMNF)

This trail ascends to the Kinsman Ridge Trail in the col between Mt. Wolf and South Kinsman (the original Kinsman Notch), 1.0 mi. south of Eliza Brook Shelter, from a gravel road that leaves NH 116 3.7 mi. north of the junction with NH 112 at Bungay Corner and 1.1 mi. south of the Easton town hall. The road, which is not plowed in winter, is passable by car to a fork (hiker logo on post) at 0.6 mi. from NH 116, where the left branch leads to an open field (parking). The grades on this trail are moderate, but the footing is often very muddy.

The trail enters the woods (sign) and follows a logging road southeast, parallel to but some distance northwest of Reel Brook, crossing several small brooks. At 1.2 mi. the road bears right and descends, and very shortly the trail diverges left, crosses a small brook, and turns left onto a wide logging road at 1.3 mi. (*In the opposite direction, this turn is potentially obscure; turn sharp right (arrow) 100 yd. after leaving power line clearing.*) In 100 yd. the trail enters the power line clearing, crosses it on a diagonal (avoid path diverging left up along the lines), and re-enters the woods. The old road crosses a tributary, then Reel Brook itself twice, and enters a newer logging road that descends from the left just before the third and last crossing of Reel Brook at 1.9 mi. The trail now follows the logging road away from the brook; the road is very muddy, with numerous loose stones, and caution must be used, especially descending.

It climbs moderately to a fork at 2.4 mi., where the main road swings left to the power lines, while the trail, with improved footing, forks right on another old logging road. In another 100 yd. the trail diverges right off this road, which swings left. From here the trail climbs gradually to the Kinsman Ridge Trail.

Reel Brook Trail (map 5:H3)

Distance from road fork near field
   to Kinsman Ridge Trail: 2.9 mi. (4.7 km.), 2 hr. 5 min.

Jericho Road Trail (WMNF)

This trail ascends to the site of the Cooley Hill fire tower from a point just north of the height-of-land on the west side of NH 116, 1.9 mi. north of its junction with NH 112 at Bungay Corner, starting on a gated gravel logging road (FR 480). It was originally constructed as a horse trail, and mostly follows logging roads of varying ages. There are no views, but some sections, particularly in the upper half, are quite pleasant for walking.

The trail follows the gravel road uphill and continues straight on an older road at 0.3 mi., where a newer branch road (FR 480A) bears right. After passing through a log yard at 1.3 mi., the road crosses a ditch where the newer section suddenly ends. The trail swings around the west side of a hump and descends into a sag, where it comes to a WMNF boundary corner distinctively marked with a pile of red-painted stones at 2.3 mi. Here the trail turns right off the road and, marked by flagging and axe blazes, continues to descend gradually, and then climbs moderately. At 2.6 mi. it comes out on another old road that ascends from the right, and turns sharp left and follows it up the crest of the ridge to a small wooded ledge near the concrete piers of the old fire tower. The trailless true summit of Cooley Hill is about 100 yd. north; from the end of the official hiking trail an unofficial trail bike track continues down the northwest side of the mountain.

Jericho Road Trail (map 5:H3)

Distance from NH 116
   to Cooley Hill: 3.2 mi. (5.2 km.), 2 hr. 15 min.

Cobble Hill Trail (WMNF)

This trail begins on NH 112 at a point 0.1 mi. west of the Woodsville Reservoir, and follows a gated gravel road (FR 310) and older logging roads along the west side of Dearth Brook to the WMNF boundary at the height-of-land between Cobble Hill and Moody Ledge. There are no views. At 0.7 mi. from NH 112 the abandoned South Landaff Rd. leaves left, leading in about 2 mi. to an extensive area of old ruined farms where there are many interesting stone walls, cellar holes, and other remnants of the hill farming culture that declined severely in the second half of the nineteenth century and mostly died out during the first decades of the twentieth century; this dying culture is the subject of much of Robert Frost's poetry. North of the height-of-land the old road continues for another 1.4 mi. down across private land to Mill Brook Rd. south of Landaff Center village, passing through woods much disrupted by logging.

Cobble Hill Trail (map 5:H2)

Distance from NH 112
   to WMNF boundary: 2.1 mi. (5.6 km.), 2 hr

SECTION 6
The Moosilauke Region

This section covers Mt. Moosilauke and several lower ranges and peaks, including the Benton Range and the Stinson-Carr-Kineo area. The section is bounded on the north by NH 112, on the east by US 3 (and I-93), and on the south by NH 25 from Plymouth to Woodsville. This section is partly covered by the AMC Chocorua-Waterville map (map 4) and the AMC Franconia map (map 5). Moosilauke itself is covered on both maps. The Benton Range is partly on map 5, but better covered by the USGS East Haverhill quad. The Stinson-Carr-Kineo region is covered by map 4.

In this section the Appalachian Trail (AT), maintained by the Dartmouth Outing Club (DOC), leaves NH 25 on the Town Line Trail, runs along North and South Rd. and Sanatorium Rd. for short distances, then follows the Glencliff Trail and Moosilauke Carriage Road to the summit of Mt. Moosilauke and descends on the Beaver Brook Trail to Kinsman Notch.

GEOGRAPHY

Mt. Moosilauke (4802 ft.) is the farthest west of White Mtn. peaks over 4000 ft., and the dominating peak of the region between Franconia Notch and the Connecticut River. There is disagreement whether the name should be pronounced to rhyme with "rock" or with "rocky"; at one time Moosilauke was commonly corrupted to "Moose-hillock," but the name actually means "a bald place" and has no reference to large, antlered beasts. The bare summit, once the site of a stone lodge called the Tip-Top House, commands an excellent view over ridge after ridge of the White Mtns. to the east, and across the Connecticut Valley to the west. It has several minor summits, the most important being the South Peak (4523 ft.), an excellent viewpoint that provides fine views into Tunnel Ravine that are denied to the main summit. To the north rise two prominent wooded humps, the trailless Mt. Blue (4529 ft.), and Mt. Jim (4172 ft.), which form the ridge that encloses Jobildunk Ravine, a glacial cirque on the east side of the mountain, through which the headwaters of the Baker River flow from their source in a bog that was once Deer Lake. The summit of Moosilauke is very exposed to weather, and there is no longer any shelter near the summit. A trail guide to Mt. Moosilauke, containing much information on the human and natural history of the mountain, has been published by the Environmental Studies Division of the DOC.

The Benton Range is composed of Black Mtn. (2830 ft.), Sugarloaf Mtn. (2609 ft.), the Hogsback (2810 ft.), Jeffers Mtn. (2994 ft.), Blueberry Mtn. (2662 ft.), and Owls Head (1967 ft.). Of these peaks, all but Jeffers provide excellent views, though only Black, Sugarloaf, and Blueberry mountains have trails.

Stinson Mtn. (2900 ft.), Carr Mtn. (3453 ft.), Rattlesnake Mtn. (1594 ft.), and trailless Mt. Kineo (3313 ft.) lie in the angle formed by the Pemigewasset and Baker rivers. Stinson Mtn. and Carr Mtn. offer excellent views from summits that once bore fire towers. In the northern part of the area is the site of the village of Peeling, a hill community that was the original settlement in the town of Woodstock but was deserted about the time of the Civil War. Most of the area has grown up, and only traces of the village remain. Those interested in visiting this region should contact the Pemigewasset Ranger District Office in Plymouth for information.

Agassiz Basin is an interesting series of potholes on Moosilauke Brook next to NH 112, 1.6 mi. west of North Woodstock. The basin is next to Govoni's

Restaurant, and there are signs during the summer season. There are two bridges across the gorge, connected by a short path on the south bank; the upper one reaches NH 112 on the porch of the restaurant. The entire loop is about 250 yd. long.

SHELTERS AND CAMPING
Restricted Use Areas
There are no Restricted Use Areas in this section. Tent camping is permitted at all three shelters.

Dartmouth College Land
No camping or fires are permitted on Dartmouth College land, which lies east and south of the summit of Moosilauke, roughly bounded by a line starting just south of Hurricane Mtn. and following the ridge-line over South Peak, Mt. Moosilauke, Mt. Blue, Mt. Jim, and Mt. Waternomee, and then south from Waternomee to NH 118.

Established Trailside Campsites
Jeffers Brook Shelter (DOC) is located just off the Town Line Trail.

Beaver Brook Shelter (DOC) is located at the base of Beaver Brook Trail, 0.4 mi. from NH 112 in Kinsman Notch.

Three Ponds Shelter (WMNF) is located on a knoll above the middle pond on a side trail from the Three Ponds Trail.

ACCESS ROADS
Ravine Lodge Rd., which is the access road to the DOC's Ravine Lodge (the lodge is not open to the public), leads to a trailhead where most of the trails on the southeastern part of Mt. Moosilauke begin. The road leaves NH 118 on the north, 5.8 mi. east of its northerly

junction with NH 25 and 7.2 mi. west of its junction with NH 112. From NH 118 it is 1.6 mi. to the turnaround at the end of the road where the trails begin. Tunnel Brook Rd. (FR 147) can be reached from Noxon Rd., which leaves NH 116 just west of the Benton-Landaff town line, 1.4 mi. west of its western junction with NH 112 and 1.5 mi. east of Benton village. Tunnel Brook Rd. can also be reached by taking the road south from NH 112 0.5 mi. east of its eastern junction with NH 116 at Bungay Corner. These two roads join at an acute angle, just west of a bridge over Tunnel Brook, and Tunnel Brook Rd. continues south from this junction. Lime Kiln Rd. leaves NH 25 in East Haverhill, 5.2 mi. north of Glencliff and 0.4 mi. north of a power line crossing where there is an interesting view of the Benton Range to the north. Lime Kiln Rd. turns left at a junction at 1.4 mi. and continues to a junction with NH 116 at 4.8 mi., 7.4 mi. west of the western junction of NH 116 and NH 112. Hubbard Brook Rd. (FR 22) begins 1.1 mi. west of US 3 at West Campton and runs through the Hubbard Brook Experimental Forest.

THE TRAILS

Beaver Brook Trail (DOC)

This trail, which runs from NH 112 at the height-of-land in Kinsman Notch to the summit of Moosilauke, is a link in the Appalachian Trail. It passes the beautiful Beaver Brook Cascades, but the section along the cascades is extremely steep and rough, making this trail the most arduous route to Moosilauke in spite of its relatively short distance. *Caution:* In icy conditions it may be dangerous.

Leaving NH 112 almost directly opposite the Kinsman Ridge Trail, this trail crosses a bridge over Beaver Brook, swings to the left, recrosses the brook on a bridge, and at 0.3 mi. passes a side path that leads left in 100 yd. to Beaver Brook Shelter (DOC). The main trail ascends along Beaver Brook, soon rising very steeply past Beaver Brook Cascades, with many rock steps, wooden steps, and hand rungs. At 1.1 mi. the cascades end, and the trail bears left along a tributary and becomes progressively easier, eventually following old logging roads to a junction in a flat area at 1.9 mi. Here the Asquam-Ridge Trail turns sharp left, while the Beaver Brook Trail bears right and ascends easily to the edge of Jobildunk Ravine, then contours along the brink of the ravine, with rough footing, passing several outlooks over the ravine. It passes close to, but not within sight of, the bog that was once Deer Lake, crossing two small outlet brooks at 2.7 mi. The trail climbs moderately to the edge of treeline, then the Gorge Brook Trail joins on the left just below the summit rocks and the two trails coincide for the last 50 yd. to the summit.

On the descent, though the trails are fairly well signed, the maze of beaten paths in this area might prove confusing in poor visibility. From its junction with the Gorge Brook Trail (which runs southeast along a grassy shoulder), the Beaver Brook Trail angles north into the scrub.

Beaver Brook Trail (map 5:I3)
Distances from NH 112

> *to* Asquam-Ridge Trail: 1.9 mi., 2 hr.
> *to* Mt. Moosilauke summit: 3.4 mi. (5.5 km.), 3 hr. 10 min.

Tunnel Brook Trail (WMNF)

This trail runs between Tunnel Brook Rd. (FR 147) and North and South Rd. (FR 19) through the deep valley between Mt. Moosilauke and Mt. Clough. To reach the north trailhead, follow the road that leaves NH 112 at a point 0.5 mi. east of its eastern junction with NH 116, go straight (south) on Tunnel Brook Rd. at a hairpin turn at

1.4 mi., and continue to the trailhead at the end of the maintained section, 3.8 mi. from NH 112. The south trailhead is located on North and South Rd. 0.4 mi. north of Sanatorium Rd. The central portion is subject to disruption by beaver activity, and, though the trail is currently well-maintained and clear, short sections could become very wet or obscure. There are good views of beaver ponds and the slides on Mt. Clough, and grades are mostly easy.

Leaving the parking area at the end of Tunnel Brook Rd., the trail continues south on an old logging road, crosses Tunnel Brook at 0.8 mi., recrosses at 1.3 mi., and soon reaches an outlook to the slides on Mt. Clough. At 1.6 mi. it recrosses Tunnel Brook on a beaver dam, and at 1.9 mi. it reaches an open spot on the shore of Mud Pond, with a view up to the South Peak of Moosilauke. Soon it crosses the outwash from a slide and begins to descend on a logging road along Slide Brook, passing a reservoir at 3.3 mi., and crossing and recrossing the brook. At 4.2 mi. it crosses Jeffers Brook, passes a camp, and ends at North and South Rd. Care should be taken not to pollute Slide Brook, the water supply for the NH Home for the Elderly in Glencliff.

Tunnel Brook Trail (map 5:I2)
Distances from end of Tunnel Brook Road
>   *to* Mud Pond: 1.9 mi., 1 hr. 10 min.
>   *to* North and South Rd.: 4.4 mi. (7.1 km.), 2 hr. 25 min.

Benton Trail (WMNF)

This trail ascends to the summit of Mt. Moosilauke from Tunnel Brook Rd. (FR 147). To reach the trailhead, follow the road that leaves NH 112 at a point 0.5 mi. east of its eastern junction with NH 116, go straight (south) on Tunnel Brook Rd. at a hairpin turn at 1.4 mi., and continue to the trailhead at 3.0 mi. from NH 112. It follows the route of an old bridle path with moderate grades and good footing, and, unless the brook near the start is high, it is probably the easiest route to the summit of Moosilauke.

The trail descends slightly from the parking lot to an old logging road, follows the road along Tunnel Brook for 0.1 mi., then crosses the brook (may be difficult at high water) and bears right on an old logging road, ascending the wooded spur that forms the south wall of Little Tunnel Ravine. At 1.3 mi. there is a splendid view to the left into the ravine. The trail passes a spring (sign) on the right at 2.2 mi., then soon turns sharp right and climbs at moderate grades through a beautiful evergreen forest to treeline, ascending the bare north ridge, marked by cairns, the last 0.2 mi. to the summit.

Benton Trail (map 5:I2–I3)
Distance from Tunnel Brook Road
> *to* Little Tunnel Ravine outlook: 1.3 mi., 1 hr. 10 min.
> *to* Mt. Moosilauke summit: 3.6 mi. (5.7 km.), 3 hr. 20 min.

Glencliff Trail (DOC)
This trail runs from Sanatorium Rd., 1.2 mi. from its junction with NH 25 in Glencliff village, to the Moosilauke Carriage Road in a sag just north of Mt. Moosilauke's South Peak. It is part of the Appalachian Trail. There is only one steep section, and the footing is generally good.

The trail leaves the road, passes a gate and enters a pasture, and soon crosses a small brook on a bridge. It joins a farm road (descending, bear left), then crosses a brook, follows a cart track along the left edge of a field, and enters the woods at 0.4 mi., where the Hurricane Trail immediately diverges right (east). The Glencliff Trail ascends moderately on a logging road that gradually fades away, crosses several small brooks, and passes a restricted outlook from a blowdown patch at 2.0 mi. Soon the trail swings right, going straight up the slope, and at 2.5 mi. it becomes quite steep. At the top of the ridge it levels and reaches the junction with a spur path (sign) that leads right 0.2 mi. to the open summit of South Peak. In a few more steps it enters the Moosilauke Carriage Road; to reach the summit, turn left.

Glencliff Trail (map 5:I2)

Distances from Sanatorium Road

to Moosilauke Carriage Road: 3.0 mi. (4.8 km.), 3 hr.

to Mt. Moosilauke summit (via Moosilauke Carriage Road): 3.9 mi. (6.3 km.), 3 hr. 35 min.

Town Line Trail (DOC)

This trail, a short link in the Appalachian Trail, runs from the east side of NH 25, just south of the Warren-Benton town line (parking 100 yd. south on the west side of NH 25), to North and South Rd. 0.1 mi. north of its junction with Sanatorium Rd. In times of high water the crossing of Oliverian Brook is It crosses Oliverian Brook (fairly difficult in moderate water) and follows the bank of the brook downstream, then swings left away from the brook, climbs moderately over a narrow ridgecrest, and continues across low ridges and shallow sags. At 0.9 mi. the trail crosses a good-sized brook on a bridge, and in another 70 yd. a side path leaves left and runs north 0.1 mi. to Jeffers Brook Shelter. The main trail soon reaches the bank of Jeffers Brook and continues to North and South Rd.

Town Line Trail (map 5:J2)

Distance from NH 25

to North and South Rd.: 1.1 mi. (1.8 km.), 45 min.

Hurricane Trail (DOC)

This trail runs around the lower south end of Mt. Moosilauke, making possible a number of loop trips by linking the low end of the Glencliff Trail, the lower part of the Moosilauke Carriage Road, and the complex of trails that leave Ravine Lodge Road. East of the Moosilauke

Carriage Road, the Hurricane Trail is level and clear; some parts to the west are steep and rough.

The Hurricane Trail continues straight where the Gorge Brook Trail turns right, 0.2 mi. from Ravine Lodge Road. It crosses Gorge Brook on a log bridge and descends to the bank of Baker River, where it picks up a logging road and follows it on a long curve away from the river. At 1.0 mi. it reaches the Moosilauke Carriage Road, coincides with it to the left (downhill) for 0.3 mi., crossing Big Brook on a bridge, then turns right (west) off the Moosilauke Carriage Road and follows a logging road into a small, moist clearing. Here it turns sharp left, follows Little Brook for a while, and climbs to the height-of-land at 2.6 mi. It continues nearly level for 0.2 mi., passing north of the little hump called Hurricane Mtn., then descends, rather steeply at times, to the Glencliff Trail 0.4 mi. from Sanatorium Rd.

Hurricane Trail (map 5:I3–I2)

Distances from Gorge Brook Trail

to Moosilauke Carriage Road (upper junction): 1.0 mi., 30 min.

to Glencliff Trail: 4.3 mi. (6.9 km.), 2 hr. 35 min.

Moosilauke Carriage Road (WMNF/DOC)

This former carriage road runs to the summit of Mt. Moosilauke from Breezy Point, site of the Moosilauke Inn. The road to Breezy Point leaves NH 118 2.5 mi. north of its junction with NH 25 (which is 1.0 mi. north of Warren village). Follow the road for 1.6 mi., past the driveway to the inn, and park where the road descends slightly (sign). Grades are easy but the footing is poor for several long sections; marking is skimpy in the first part, after which the trail becomes unmistakable.

Continuing on the dirt road, the trail enters a clearing at 0.3 mi., where it bears right at an old sign ("MT TRAIL") and continues on a logging road with no markings. The Hurricane Trail enters left at 1.3 mi., and the two trails cross Big Brook together on a bridge. The Hurricane Trail diverges right to Ravine Lodge Road after another 0.2 mi., and the old carriage road begins to climb by a series of switchbacks through a beautiful mature hardwood forest, with easy to moderate grades and excellent footing. At 3.1 mi. the Snapper Trail enters right, and soon the footing deteriorates, as the old road is severely washed out, with much loose rock. At 4.2 mi. the Glencliff Trail enters from the left; a few steps along the Glencliff Trail, a spur trail leads left 0.2 mi. to South Peak, a fine viewpoint. The old road, now part of the Appalachian Trail, continues along the ridge, with a narrow fringe of trees on each side. At 4.9 mi. it reaches treeline and ascends the windswept ridge to the summit.

Moosilauke Carriage Road (map 5:J2–I2)

Distances from Breezy Point

   to Snapper Trail: 3.1 mi., 2 hr. 25 min.

   to Glencliff Trail: 4.2 mi., 3 hr. 30 min.

   to Mt. Moosilauke summit: 5.1 mi. (8.3 km.), 4 hr. 5 min.

Gorge Brook Trail (DOC)

This trail runs from the end of Ravine Lodge Road to the summit of Mt. Moosilauke. The upper part has been completely relocated, making the trail substantially longer but eliminating the steep grades and rough footing of the former route. It is now a relatively easy trail that affords some interesting views as it climbs.

Leaving the turnaround at the end of Ravine Lodge Road, it follows the logging road for 100 yd., then turns left, descends to Baker River and crosses it on a footbridge, and immediately turns left at 0.2 mi. where the Asquam-Ridge Trail diverges right. At 0.3 mi. it turns sharp right as the Hurricane Trail continues straight, and at 0.4 mi. the Snapper Trail diverges left. The Gorge Brook Trail follows Gorge Brook, crossing it at 0.6 mi.

and recrossing at 1.3 mi., both times on bridges. At 1.6 mi. it passes the memorial plaque for the Ross McKenney Forest; here the new route begins and swings to the right of the former route. At 2.1 mi. it turns left onto an old logging road, passes a cleared outlook to the south, then turns left off the road and winds uphill at moderate grades, passing more outlooks. At 3.3 mi. it reaches a shoulder covered with low scrub that affords a view to the summit ahead, and at 3.7 mi. it joins the Beaver Brook Trail at the base of the summit rocks and coincides with it for the last 50 yd. to the summit.

On the descent, though the trails are fairly well marked by signs, the maze of beaten paths in this area might prove confusing in poor visibility. From its junction with the Beaver Brook Trail (which angles north into the scrub), the Gorge Brook Trail runs southeast along a grassy shoulder.

Gorge Brook Trail (map 5:J3–I3)
Distance from Ravine Lodge Road
  to McKenney Forest plaque: 1.6 mi., 1 hr. 15 min.
  to Mt. Moosilauke summit: 3.7 mi. (6.0 km.), 3 hr. 5 min.

Snapper Trail (DOC)
This trail, originally cut as a downhill ski trail, runs from the Gorge Brook Trail 0.4 mi. from Ravine Lodge Road to the Mt. Moosilauke Carriage Road 2.0 mi. below the summit of Mt. Moosilauke. It makes possible a number of loop hikes from Ravine Lodge Road, and now affords the shortest (though not the easiest) route to the summit of Mt. Moosilauke. Leaving the Gorge Brook Trail, it soon crosses Gorge Brook and another small brook on bridges, then ascends steadily, becoming steeper as it approaches the Carriage Road.

Snapper Trail (map 5:J3–I3)
Distance from Gorge Brook Trail
  to Moosilauke Carriage Road: 1.0 mi. (1.6 km.), 1 hr.

Distance from Ravine Lodge Road
> *to* Mt. Moosilauke summit (via Gorge Brook Trail,
> Snapper Trail, and Moosilauke Carriage Road):
> 3.4 mi. (5.5 km.), 2 hr. 55 min.

Asquam-Ridge Trail (DOC)

This trail runs from the Gorge Brook Trail 0.2 mi. from
Ravine Lodge Road to the Beaver Brook Trail on top of
the Blue Ridge, providing a long but rather easy route to
the summit of Mt. Moosilauke.

It leaves the Gorge Brook Trail, turning sharp right
just across the Baker River footbridge, and follows the
west bank of the river. At 0.5 mi. it enters a logging
road that comes up from the end of Ravine Lodge Road
and continues along the river, then crosses it on a footbridge at 1.5 mi. and turns sharp right to ascend gradually away from the river. At 1.9 mi. the trail turns sharp
left where the Al Merrill Loop (primarily a ski trail)
from Ravine Lodge Road enters straight ahead, and then
follows another logging road very gradually upward.
Eventually it encounters some steeper pitches, passes a
few yards left of the wooded summit of Mt. Jim, then
descends easily to the Beaver Brook Trail.

Asquam-Ridge Trail (map 5:J3–I3)
Distances from Gorge Brook Trail
> *to* Beaver Brook Trail: 3.9 mi. (6.4 km.), 2 hr. 55 min.
> *to* Mt. Moosilauke summit (via Beaver Brook Trail):
> 5.5 mi. (8.8 km.), 4 hr.

Blueberry Mountain Trail (WMNF)

This trail crosses the ridge of Blueberry Mtn., affording
interesting views from scattered pine-covered ledges on
both sides of the crest. The east terminus is reached by
following Sanatorium Rd. for 1.0 mi. from NH 25 in
Glencliff, then turning left (north) on North and South
Rd. and following it for 0.8 mi. to a small parking area

on the left. The west terminus is reached by taking Lime Kiln Rd. from NH 25 in East Haverhill, keeping straight ahead at a junction at 1.4 mi. where Lime Kiln Rd. turns left, and continuing to the trail sign on a side road that leaves left at 2.4 mi. Parking is available in a field on the right 0.1 mi. up this road, just before a gate that you should not drive past even if it is open. The western section of the trail is not being maintained at the present time, but trail-bike traffic has kept the footway fairly easy to follow for experienced hikers.

Starting at North and South Rd., the trail follows a relatively new logging road for 0.2 mi., then turns sharp right up a short, steep bank and follows old logging roads, crossing a newer grassy road at 0.4 mi. It enters coniferous woods and begins to ascend ledges with restricted views, then turns sharp right at 1.2 mi. and continues to climb. Soon it reaches ledges that are more open, with outlooks to the east and south, including an unusual and interesting view into the slide-scarred ravine of Slide Brook on Mt. Moosilauke. At 1.7 mi. it reaches the crest of the main ridge 0.1 mi. south of the true summit (which offers good views but requires a rough, though short, bushwhack).

The trail (official maintenance temporarily suspended) then descends gradually through scrubby trees and ledges with limited views, passing to the left of a boggy depression and crossing a small moist glen, then turns sharp right at a cairn capped with a shark-fin rock and soon reaches a fine view of Black Mtn., Sugarloaf, and the Hogsback. Other views to Sugarloaf and to the Connecticut Valley are passed as the trail descends on ledges. The trail drops below the ledges, passes through a short area of moss-carpeted coniferous woods, and enters the upper end of a system of logging roads that it follows the rest of the way. It crosses many small brooks and one rather wet stretch. At 3.2 mi.; after leaving an extensive section of birch woods, it crosses a stone wall and enters a region of abandoned farms where many stone walls and cellars holes remain, and mint that escaped from a farm garden still grows among the corduroy logs in the old road. At 4.0 mi. it enters a fairly new gravel road and turns sharp left on it, crossing the WMNF boundary in 125 yd. (This junction is not well marked and hikers following this trail in the eastbound direction need to watch carefully for the sharp right turn.) The newer road leads past a sawmill and a gate, passes a field with a good view up to Sugarloaf, and ends on the branch road from Lime Kiln Rd. just after passing a small sugar house.

Blueberry Mountain Trail (map 5:I1–I2)

Distance from North and South Road

> *to* ridgecrest near Blueberry Mtn. summit: 1.7 mi., 1 hr. 25 min.
>
> *to* branch road from Lime Kiln Rd.: 4.5 mi. (7.3 km.), 2 hr. 45 min.

Black Mountain Trail (WMNF)

This trail ascends Black Mtn. from the north, using old logging roads and the old tractor road to the former fire tower. It is a fairly easy way to ascend this attractive small mountain, but is much less interesting and only slightly easier than the Chippewa Trail. From the four-way intersection on NH 116 in Benton village, 2.9 mi. west of the western junction of NH 112 and NH 116, follow the road that runs uphill approximately south. At 0.8 mi. the road swings west and becomes gravel, and is marked with a USFS signpost as FR 76. Depending on the condition of the road, it may be possible to drive to a small parking space 1.4 mi. from NH 116 (bear left where a snowmobile trail leaves to the right at 1.3 mi.).

The trail follows the road, bearing slightly left in a log yard, then takes the right branch at a fork and winds uphill, passing near several logged areas. At 1.7 mi. the

Chippewa Trail joins from the right, and the open ledgy ridgecrest at the old fire tower site is another 40 yd. ahead. There are good views from the ridgecrest both east and west of the tower site; Tipping Rock, where there are more good views, stands 50 yd. to the east.

Black Mountain Trail (map 5:H1–I1)
Distance from marked parking space on FR 76
  to Black Mtn. summit: 1.7 mi. (2.7 km.), 1 hr. 30 min.

Chippewa Trail (WMNF)
This very scenic trail ascends Black Mtn. from Lime Kiln Rd., which leaves NH 25 in East Haverhill, bears left at a major fork at 1.4 mi., and continues to the trailhead at a point 3.1 mi. from NH 25. The trail, well blazed with yellow paint, begins on the right at a small parking area, marked with a hiker logo sign and a sign reading "Haverhill Heritage Trail 13: Lime Kilns."

The trail descends a short, fairly steep pitch, crosses a small brook and then a somewhat larger one, then climbs the bank to a logging road and turns right on it; the Lime Kilns are located to the left on this road (sign). In another 60 yd. the trail diverges left from this road on a much older road and begins the ascent of the mountain. At 0.6 mi. it passes to the left of a cellar hole in an overgrown pasture and, after passing through a shallow sag, begins to climb more steeply. It passes a WMNF boundary sign and then turns sharp left just before a rock outcrop on the ridgecrest, continuing to climb among ledges in woods dominated by red pines. At 1.1 mi. the main trail turns sharp left where a side path leads right 25 yd. to a ledge that affords fine views south and west. Do not confuse the blue blazes of a property line with trail blazes in this area. After 1.3 mi. the trail climbs mostly on ledges past excellent outlooks scattered along the way until it reaches a knob with an interesting view of the summit rocks ahead, then crosses a shallow, moist sag and reaches the junction with the Black Mtn. Trail from Benton village. The open ridge-crest at the old fire tower site is 40 yd. to the right, with good outlook points on the ridgecrest both east and west of the tower site. Tipping Rock, on a ledge with good views, is 50 yd. east of the tower site.

Chippewa Trail (USGS East Haverhill quad)
Distance from parking area off Lime Kiln Road
  to Black Mtn. summit: 1.8 mi. (2.9 km.), 1 hr. 40 min.

Sugarloaf Trail

This trail ascends Sugarloaf Mtn., which is an interest-ing, small mountain that offers a number of good view-points. The trail is not officially maintained and may be dangerous on the ledges, particularly in wet or icy con-ditions. To reach the trail, follow Lime Kiln Rd. north from NH 25 in East Haverhill, then at the junction at 1.4 mi. go straight ahead and continue 0.8 mi. Turn left here, then turn right at a garage in another 0.1 mi. and follow a dirt road. It may be necessary to park at an automobile junkyard on the left 0.1 mi. from the garage, as the road ahead is rough and space to park or turn around is extremely limited. The trail is described from the junkyard, though it may be possible for some vehi-cles to continue another 0.5 mi. to the actual trailhead.

The trail leaves the road on the right (sign) 0.5 mi. from the junkyard, just beyond a small brook. It crosses an old apple orchard, now mostly overgrown, then pass-es through a shallow, moist sag and begins to climb at moderate to steep grades. At 1.4 mi. it reaches a very steep ledge that is climbed by two ladders (use great caution), then turns sharp right and ascends near the edge of the cliff, with good outlooks. It then zigzags up rocks with increasing views until it reaches a bare ledge where trail marking currently ends, about 60 yd. below the true summit. There are a number of other good outlooks that can be reached by exploring scattered ledges separated by thick woods.

Sugarloaf Trail (USGS East Haverhill quad)
Distance from automobile junkyard
   to beginning of trail: 0.5 mi., 20 min.
   to Sugarloaf Mtn. summit: 1.7 mi. (2.7 km.), 1 hr. 35 min.

Stinson Mountain Trail (WMNF)
Reach the Stinson Mountain Trail by following Stinson Lake Rd. north from NH 25 in Rumney. At the foot of the lake, 5.0 mi. from NH 25 and 0.1 mi. south of the Stinson Lake General Store and Post Office, turn right uphill for 0.8 mi., then turn right again on the old Doe Town Rd. to a parking lot at 0.3 mi. on the left. The fire tower has been dismantled but fine views are still available in every direction except southwest. Metamorphosed strata make the summit ledge geologically interesting.

The trail leaves the parking lot and soon enters and follows an old farm road between stone walls. After passing a cellar hole to the left of the trail, it becomes steeper, and at 0.9 mi. it bears left, joining a logging road that comes up from the right. At 1.1 mi., the trail takes the right fork at a junction; left is the old tractor road to the summit, longer and less pleasant. The trail climbs by switchbacks and rejoins the old tractor road just below the summit (note the left turn here for the descent.) From the summit a spur path leads southwest about 80 yd. to a view over Stinson Lake.

Stinson Mountain Trail (map 4:K3)
Distance from parking lot
   to Stinson Mtn. summit: 1.8 mi. (2.9 km.), 1 hr. 35 min.

Rattlesnake Mountain Trail (WMNF)
Rattlesnake Mountain Trail has been radically changed by the elimination of its eastern half and the construction of a new loop trail over the ledges of Rattlesnake Mtn.,

which afford fine views over the Baker River Valley, so that it now provides excellent views for a very modest effort. It begins on Buffalo Rd., the road along the north bank of Baker River, 2.5 mi. west of Rumney village; or, from NH 25 6.4 mi. west of the West Plymouth traffic circle, follow Sand Hill Rd. across Baker River, then turn right after 0.3 mi. and follow Buffalo Rd. 1.2 mi. to a small parking area just before the Nathan Clifford birthplace historical marker.

The trail follows a logging road that soon becomes rather steep, then levels out on the ridgecrest and passes the west end of the summit loop on the right at 0.8 mi. In another 80 yd. the east end of the summit loop turns right off the old road and ascends over ledges with many fine views, reaching the summit at 1.3 mi., then turns sharp right at the base of the summit ledge and returns over a rocky knob to the old road at 1.7 mi. Turn left to return to the parking area.

Rattlesnake Mountain Trail (map 4:L2–L3)
Distance from Buffalo Road

to Rattlesnake Mtn. summit: 1.3 mi., 1 hr. 10 min.
for complete loop: 2.5 mi. (4.0 km.), 1 hr. 45 min.

Carr Mountain Trail (WMNF)

This trail provides access to the summit of Carr Mtn., where several rounded rock knobs provide excellent views. It begins on the Three Ponds Trail 0.5 mi. from the new parking area on Stinson Lake Rd., ascends to a short spur trail to the summit of Carr Mtn., and descends to the old Warren-Wentworth highway 0.1 mi. south of the former state fish hatchery. Maintenance has been suspended on the western half of the trail, and this section can be recommended only for hikers with extensive experience in following obscure trails (although it is easier to follow on the descent than ascent).

The trail diverges sharp left (south) from the Three Ponds Trail and descends to cross Sucker Brook at 0.2 mi. on flat ledges that are submerged when water flow is above average, then crosses an old road on the south bank of the brook. (The Sucker Brook crossing is difficult at high water, and the trail section between Three Ponds Trail and the brook receives little use and may be overgrown and obscure. Most use on the Carr Mountain Trail is by local residents who enter the trail from Stinson Lake Rd. by this route along the south bank of Sucker Brook. This is private land, and the landowner objects strongly to hikers' cars being parked in this area. The brook crossing can also be avoided by following the Three Ponds Trail to its bridge over Sucker Brook, then returning back southeast along the brook on the old logging road to the Carr Mountain Trail. This route is about 0.8 mi. longer than the direct trail route.)

The trail then climbs easily to meet its former route (an old wood road) and continues a moderate ascent, swinging sharp right at 1.4 mi. and then left at 1.7 mi. It winds upward near the crest of a ridge close to a small brook, and higher up it approaches and then crosses a very small, mossy brook, then zigzags upward and soon comes close to the crest of the main ridge. The ascent becomes gradual through dense, moist coniferous woods, and at 2.9 mi. a side path turns left to the summit area. The best view is probably from the top of the first knob encountered on the left side of this spur, which ends in about 70 yd. at the remnants of the former fire tower.

The main trail (no longer maintained and often difficult to follow) descends, reaching a small brook that it crosses several times, then enters logging roads that gradually become more and more discernible. At 4.8 mi. it turns sharp left on a much newer wood road (a very obscure spot in the ascent); right from this junction (straight ahead ascending) is an obscure footpath leading

0.2 mi. to Waternomee Falls. At 5.6 mi. the road passes a house and becomes a clear gravel road that continues to the old Warren-Wentworth highway opposite a small cemetery, near the old fish hatchery.

Carr Mountain Trail (map 4:K3–K2)

Distance from Three Ponds Trail

    to Carr Mtn. summit side path: 2.9 mi., 2 hr. 30 min.

    to old Warren-Wentworth highway: 6.5 mi. (10.5 km.), 4 hr. 20 min.

Three Ponds Trail (WMNF)

Three Ponds Trail starts on Stinson Lake Rd. at a new parking lot 6.9 mi. north of NH 25 and 1.8 mi. north of the Stinson Lake General Store and Post Office, passes the attractive ponds, crosses a low ridge, and descends to the gravel road used by the Hubbard Brook Trail 0.2 mi. from NH 118. This gravel road leaves NH 118 4.4 mi. northeast of the junction of NH 118 and NH 25, which is about 1 mi. north of Warren village.

Leaving the parking lot, it passes junctions with the Mount Kineo Trail right at 0.1 mi. and the Carr Moun tain Trail left at 0.5 mi. At 1.0 mi. it crosses Sucker Brook on a bridge and continues upstream along the brook, crossing it three more times without bridges. At 2.2 mi., a side path diverges right on the shore of the middle pond, passes Three Ponds Shelter on a knoll overlooking the pond, and rejoins the main trail. At 2.5 mi. the Donkey Hill Cutoff continues straight, while the Three Ponds Trail turns left across a brook on a beaver dam, picks up a logging road, and follows it to a point 80 yd. from the upper pond. Here the road continues to the edge of the pond, but the trail turns sharp left and starts to ascend. From here on it is much less heavily used and must be followed with some care. The trail enters a logging road, leaves it on a bypass around the swamp at Foxglove Pond, and crosses Brown Brook for the first of three times at 3.8 mi. The trail now climbs to the height-of-land at 5.1 mi., then descends, makes a hairpin turn right, and enters a system of logging roads, following them to the Hubbard Brook Trail 0.2 mi. east of NH 118.

Three Ponds Trail (map 4:K3–J3)

Distances from Stinson Lake Road

  to Three Ponds Shelter: 2.3 mi., 1 hr. 20 min.

  to height-of-land: 5.1 mi., 3 hr. 5 min.

  to Hubbard Brook Trail: 7.2 mi. (11.7 km.), 4 hr. 10 min.

Donkey Hill Cutoff (WMNF)

This trail links the Three Ponds Trail 2.5 mi. from the Stinson Lake Rd. parking area to the Mount Kineo Trail 1.7 mi. from the parking area, making a loop hike. It crosses several small ridges and follows the edge of an extensive beaver swamp for much of its distance.

Donkey Hill Cutoff (map 4:K3)

Distance from Three Ponds Trail

  to Mount Kineo Trail: 1.1 mi. (1.8 km.), 40 min.

Mount Kineo Trail (WMNF)

This trail begins on the Three Ponds Trail 0.1 mi. from the new parking lot on Stinson Lake Rd., crosses the ridge of Mt. Kineo almost 1.0 mi. east of the true summit, and descends to a spur road off Hubbard Brook Rd. (FR 22) 6.3 mi. from US 3 in West Thornton. The part of this trail south of the ridgecrest is an attractive woods walk.

Leaving the Three Ponds Trail, it proceeds north over several minor ups and downs and enters the old route of the trail (a logging road along Brown Brook) at 1.0 mi. The trail climbs along the attractive brook, and at 1.6 mi., where the Donkey Hill Cutoff diverges left, the Mount Kineo Trail crosses the brook on ledges. It runs northwest along the edge of a large swamp, then at 2.3 mi. it swings right, away from the swamp, crosses several small brooks, and eventually climbs east, alternately angling up on old logging roads and climbing straight up on steep, rough sections. At 3.9 mi. it crosses the ridge in a small col, then descends to an old logging road, which it follows through several extremely muddy stretches to a gravel spur road passable by cars, about 0.5 mi. from its junction with Hubbard Brook Rd. (sign).

Mount Kineo Trail (map 4:K3–J3)

Distances from Three Ponds Trail
   to Donkey Hill Cutoff: 1.6 mi., 1 hr.
   to height-of-land: 3.9 mi., 2 hr. 45 min.
   to Hubbard Brook Rd. spur: 5.1 mi. (8.2 km.), 3 hr. 20 min.

Hubbard Brook Trail (WMNF)

This trail leaves Hubbard Brook Rd. (FR 22) at a hairpin turn across Hubbard Brook, 7.6 mi. from US 3 in West Thornton, and runs to NH 118 4.4 mi. northeast of the junction with NH 25, which is 1.0 mi. north of Warren village. Its only significant attractions are several beaver ponds.

Leaving the road, it soon passes a beaver pond where the trail might be subject to disruption, but by following the north bank the trail will be found where it enters the woods just above the north end of the pond. It crosses a low height-of-land at 0.9 mi. and descends on an assortment of logging roads and paths, crosses a beaver dam between two ponds, and enters a gravel logging road at 2.0 mi. ("HB" blazed into tree at junction) that passes the Three Ponds Trail on the left at 2.3 mi. and continues to NH 118.

Hubbard Brook Trail (map 4:J3)

Distance from Hubbard Brook Road
   to NH 118: 2.5 mi. (4.1 km.), 1 hr. 20 min.

Peaked Hill Pond Trail (WMNF)

This trail follows a logging road to Peaked Hill Pond from US 3, north of exit 29 of I-93, at the 93 Motel. The trail is easy, and there are pleasant views from the shore of the pond, which is partly on private property. From US 3, follow the road west under I-93, then turn right at 0.4 mi. and park just before a steel gate at 0.6 mi. The road ascends gradually, and at 0.5 mi. from the gate a woods road bears right off the road to bypass an old pasture, and returns to the road and follows it to the right. It bears left at 0.9 mi., and at 1.5 mi. it leaves the road on the right, crosses the outlet brook, and continues to the shore of the pond, where blazes end.

Peaked Hill Pond Trail (map 4:K4)

Distance from gate

 to Peaked Hill Pond: 1.7 mi. (2.8 km.), 1 hr. 5 min.

SECTION 7
The Waterville Valley Region

This section covers the mountains that surround the valley of the Mad River, commonly called Waterville Valley, including Mt. Tecumseh, Mt. Osceola, Mt. Tripyramid, Sandwich Mtn., and their subordinate peaks. This region is bounded on the north by the Kancamagus Highway; on the east by a line between the Sleeper Ridge and Mt. Whiteface; on the south by NH 113, Sandwich Notch Rd., and NH 49; and on the west by US 3. At the boundary between Section 7 and Section 8 (Chocorua and the Eastern Sandwich Range), the only points of contact between trails are at the junction of the Sleeper Trail (Section 7) with the Downes Brook Trail (Section 8), and at the junction of the Flat Mountain Pond Trail (Section 7) with the McCrillis Trail (Section 8). The entire section is covered by the AMC Chocorua-Waterville map (map 4).

ROAD ACCESS

Waterville Valley. From I-93 near Campton, NH 49 (Mad River Rd.), runs northeast beside the Mad River for more than 11 mi. into the center of Waterville Valley, passing a group of lodges and condominiums and ending near the Waterville Valley library, Golf and Tennis Club, and the Snows Mountain Ski Area and ski-touring center. At 10.6 mi. from I-93, Tripoli Rd. turns sharp left, passing the road to the Mt. Tecumseh Ski Area at 1.3 mi., and soon after that it begins to follow the West Branch of the Mad River northwest to the height-of-land west of Waterville Valley (Thornton Gap, 2300 ft., the pass between Mts. Osceola and Tecumseh), then continues westward to its end at NH

175 (East Side Rd.) and I-93 near Woodstock. The road is gravel except for paved sections on each end, and much of it is narrow and winding. Drive slowly and with caution. This road has not been plowed during the winter. A road runs from Waterville Valley at the town library about 0.8 mi. west to Tripoli Rd. (FR 30) north of the ski area. Livermore Rd. (FR 53) branches right from this road just before it crosses the bridge over the west bank; coming from Tripoli Rd., the road to Waterville Valley village turns right just after crossing the bridge while Livermore Rd. bears left.

Sandwich Notch Rd., a rough dirt road, passes through a former farming region that has almost completely reverted to forest and has recently been added to the WMNF. It runs northwest from Center Sandwich to NH 49 between Campton and Waterville Valley. The road is sound, but narrow, steep and rough, and very slow going; it is maintained this way to protect it from becoming an attractive route for through traffic. Beede Falls (Cow Cave), in the Sandwich town park 3.4 mi. from Center Sandwich, is worth a visit. From NH 113 in Center Sandwich, take the road northwest from the village and keep left at 2.6 mi. where the righthand road leads to Mead Base (Explorer Scout camp), trailhead for the Wentworth Trail to Mt. Israel. The road continues past trailheads for the Crawford-Ridgepole Trail at 3.9 mi., the Guinea Pond Trail at 5.7 mi., and the Algonquin Trail at 7.3 mi., and ends at NH 49 at 11.0 mi.

In the Sandwich area, confusion sometimes results from the rather erratic behavior of NH 113 and NH 113A, the alternate routes between North Sandwich and Tamworth. Both roads change direction frequently, and NH 113 unites with and diverges from NH 25 between its two junctions with NH 113A. It is therefore necessary to study very carefully access directions for trailheads on the southeast slopes of the Sandwich Range.

Whiteface Intervale Rd. leaves NH 113A about 3 mi. north of the western junction of NH 113 and NH 113A, where NH 113A bends from north-south to east-west. Bennett Street turns left from Whiteface Intervale Rd. 0.1 mi. from NH 113A, continues straight past a junction at 1.7 mi., where it becomes rougher, and ends at 2.4 mi. at Jose's (rhymes with *doses*) bridge.

GEOGRAPHY

Mt. Tecumseh (4003 ft.), named for the Shawnee leader, is the highest and northernmost summit of the ridges that form the west wall of the valley. Thornton Gap separates Mt. Tecumseh from Mt. Osceola to the northeast; to the west and southwest, long ridges run out toward Woodstock and Thornton. On the end of the south ridge, the fine, rocky peak of Welch Mtn. (2605 ft.) overlooks the Campton meadows, and forms the west wall of the narrow south gateway to Waterville Valley through which the Mad River flows. The views from the open summit are excellent. Dickey Mtn. (2734 ft.) is close at hand to the northwest, with the best views from an open ledge 0.2 mi. north of its summit.

Mt. Osceola (4340 ft.), the highest peak in the region, lies north of the valley. It was named for the great chief of the Seminole people. It is a narrow, steep-sided ridge, with a number of slides in its valleys, and is particularly impressive when seen from the outlooks along the western half of the Kancamagus Highway. Although there is no longer a fire tower on its summit, is still commands magnificent views. Osceola has two subordinate peaks, the East Peak (4156 ft.) and the trailless West Peak (4114 ft.). West of Mt. Osceola is trailless Scar Ridge (3774 ft.), which runs northwest parallel to the Hancock Branch and ends at the lower peaks above Lincoln, of which the most important is Loon

Mtn. (3065 ft.), which can be ascended via the major ski area on its north slope. At the far west end is Russell Crag (1926 ft.), with interesting ledges but no trails; north of the crag is Russell Pond, with a WMNF campground that is reached by a paved road. To the east of Mt. Osceola is Mad River Notch, in which the Greeley Ponds are located, and across the notch is Mt. Kancamagus (3728 ft.), a trailless mass of rounded, wooded ridges, named for a Penacook sachem.

Mt. Tripyramid is the rugged and very picturesque mountain that forms the east wall of Waterville Valley, and overlooks Albany Intervale, which lies to the north and east. It was named by the illustrious cartographer Arnold Guyot for the three pyramidal peaks that cap the narrow, steep-sided ridge. North Peak (4140 ft.) affords a sweeping view to the north that is gradually becoming overgrown. Middle Peak (4110 ft.), the most nearly symmetrical pyramid of the three, provides a view toward Mts. Passaconaway and Chocorua from the summit; two fine outlooks over the Waterville Valley toward Tecumseh and Osceola lie to the west of the trail near the summit. South Peak (4090 ft.) is viewless. From South Peak, the high, rolling Sleeper Ridge (West Peak, 3870 ft.; East Peak, 3850 ft.) connects Mt. Tripyramid with Mt. Whiteface. Though this ridge could have been named quite aptly for the sleepy appearance of its two rounded, rather gently sloping domes, it is actually named for Katherine Sleeper Walden, a civic-minded local innkeeper whose efforts in trail-building (she founded the WODC), conservation, and public improvements were so energetic and pervasive that she earned the sobriquet of "matriarch of Wonalancet and the WODC" and is memorialized by two natural features (Sleeper Ridge and Mt. Katherine) and two trails (the Sleeper and Walden trails). A major east spur is called the Fool Killer (3570 ft.) because it blends into the main mass so well when viewed from a distance that incautious parties attempting to climb Mt. Tripyramid from the east, before the construction of the trails, often found themselves on top of the Fool Killer instead, separated from their goal by a long, scrubby ridge with deep valleys on either side.

Mt. Tripyramid is best known for its slides, great scars that are visible from long distances. The North Slide, which occurred during heavy rains in August 1885, is located on the northwest slope of North Peak. The slide exposed a great deal of bedrock that is geologically interesting, and is ascended mainly on steep ledges. The South Slide, which is located on the southwest face of the South Peak, fell in 1869 and is mostly gravel. Two smaller slides descend into the valley of Sabbaday Brook from the east face of Middle Peak. Tripyramid is steep and rugged, and all routes to its summits have at least one rough section. Consequently the mountain is more difficult to climb than a casual assessment of the altitude, distance, and elevation gain might suggest.

Sabbaday Falls, a picturesque, small waterfall and pool formed by an eroded trap-rock dike, is reached from Sabbaday Falls Picnic Area on the Kancamagus Highway by a gravel section of the Sabbaday Brook Trail.

Sandwich Mtn. (3993 ft.), sometimes called Sandwich Dome, is the westernmost major summit of the Sandwich Range and forms the south wall of the Waterville Valley. It looks over the lower Mad River to the west, and Sandwich Notch separates it from the Campton and Holderness mountains on the south and southwest. Sandwich Mtn. was once called Black Mtn., a name that has also been applied to its southwest spur (3500 ft.), which is ledgy with many fine outlooks, and to a nubble (2732 ft.) at the end of this spur. According to the USGS, the nubble is entitled to the name of Black

Mtn. To the northeast, a high pass separates Sandwich Mtn. from the long ridge of Flat Mtn. (3310 ft.) in Waterville; Pond Brook has cut a deep ravine between its east shoulder and the rounded Flat Mtn. (2950 ft.) in Sandwich. The Flat Mountain Ponds (2310 ft.) lie east of Sandwich Mtn. and west of Mt. Whiteface, between the two Flat Mtns.; originally two separate ponds, they have been united by the dam at their south end, making one larger pond. The area is still recovering from lumbering begun in 1920 and an extensive fire in 1923. In the flat region south of Sandwich Mtn. lie a number of attractive ponds, including Guinea Pond and Black Mountain Pond. South of these ponds is Mt. Israel (2630 ft.), which provides a splendid panorama of the Sandwich Range from its north ledge, and offers great rewards for the modest effort required to reach it.

Jennings Peak (3460 ft.) and Noon Peak (2976 ft.) form a ridge running north toward Waterville Valley. Sandwich Mtn. has fine views north over the valley, but those from Jennings Peak are even better. Acteon Ridge runs from Jennings Peak to the west over sharp, bare Sachem Peak (2860 ft.) and ends in the open rocky humps of Bald Knob (2300 ft.), which faces Welch Mtn. across the Mad River Valley; this ridge is occasionally traversed, although there is no path.

CAMPING
Sandwich Range Wilderness
In this area, camping and fires are prohibited above tree-line, and no campsite may be used by more than ten persons at one time.

Restricted Use Areas
The WMNF has established a number of Restricted Use Areas (RUAs) where camping and wood or charcoal

fires are prohibited from May 1 to November 1. The specific areas are under continual review, and areas are added to or subtracted from the list in order to provide the greatest amount of protection to areas subject to damage by excessive camping, while imposing the lowest level of restrictions possible. A general list of RUAs follows, but one should obtain a map of current RUAs from the WMNF.

(1) No camping is permitted above treeline (where trees are less than 8 ft. tall) except in winter, and even then it is allowed only on sites that are covered with at least two feet of snow and not located on frozen bodies of water. The point where the restricted area begins is marked on most trails with small signs, but the absence of such signs should not be construed as proof of the legality of a site.

(2) No camping is permitted within 1/4 mi. of most facilities such as huts, cabins, shelters, or tentsites, except at the facility itself.

(3) No camping is permitted, at any time of the year, within the Greeley Ponds Scenic Area or within 1/4 mi. of the Greeley Ponds Trail from the north boundary of the scenic area to the Kancamagus Highway. No camping is permitted within 1/4 mi. of the Sabbaday Falls Trail from the Kancamagus Highway to the Sandwich Range Wilderness boundary.

Established Trailside Campsites

Flat Mountain Pond Shelter (WMNF) is located on the shore of Flat Mountain Pond on the Flat Mountain Pond Trail. Tent camping is permitted in the area.

Black Mountain Pond Shelter (WMNF) is located on the shore of Black Mountain Pond on the Black Mountain Pond Trail. Tent camping is permitted in the area.

THE TRAILS

Mount Tecumseh Trail (WMNF)

This trail starts at the Waterville Valley Ski Area well to the right of the main lodge (as you face it), climbs the east slope of Mt. Tecumseh, then descends the northwest ridge to Tripoli Rd. (FR 30) 1.3 mi. west of the Mount Osceola Trail parking lot. The western part of the trail was relocated in 1991 to eliminate the former sections that used ski slopes.

Starting at the ski area parking lot, the trail follows the south side of Tecumseh Brook for 0.3 mi., then crosses the brook and follows a new section along a small ridge on the north side. At 0.8 mi. it drops down and recrosses the brook, then climbs to intersect the former route, an old logging road, about 20 yd. from the edge of the ski slope; good views can be obtained by following the old trail left to the open slope. The main trail turns right and follows the old road, angling upward along the south side of the Tecumseh Brook valley, then climbs to a flat area where it turns right. Here, at 1.9 mi., the Sosman Trail from the top of the ski area enters from the left. In another 120 yd. the Sosman Trail forks left to ascend the summit from the west. The Mount Tecumseh Trail swings right, descends slightly, circling the steep cone, and finally climbs steeply to the summit from the north. The summit has good views, particularly to Mt. Osceola and Mt. Tripyramid. The trail junctions at the summit have not usually been well signed; the Mount Tecumseh Trail leaves north (about 15° magnetic) for the ski area and west-northwest (about 310° magnetic) for Tripoli Rd., while the Sosman Trail runs almost due south (about 190° magnetic) along the ridgecrest, then turns sharp right (west) off the ridge and descends.

From the summit of Mt. Tecumseh, the trail descends west, then swings northwest past an excellent outlook, passes through a shallow col and ascends to the summit of the west ridge at 2.9 mi. It passes over numerous knobs, then descends to a col at 3.9 mi., where it turns right and angles down the north slope of the ridge on an old logging road. Near the bottom it turns right, crosses Eastman Brook, and ends at Tripoli Rd.

Mount Tecumseh Trail (map 4:J6)

Distances from Waterville Valley Ski Area parking lot
   to Mt. Tecumseh summit: 2.2 mi. (3.6 km.), 2 hr. 10 min.
   to Tripoli Rd.: 5.3 mi. (8.6 km.), 3 hr. 50 min.

Sosman Trail (WVAIA)

The Sosman Trail connects the summit of Mt. Tecumseh with the top of the ski area. It leaves the summit of Mt. Tecumseh along the ridge to the south, then turns to the west and switchbacks down the slope. It joins the Mount Tecumseh Trail at 0.2 mi., then after 120 yd. it diverges right and follows the ridge south, passing over a rocky hump with an interesting view of Tecumseh's summit cone, and comes out on a ledge at the top of the ski area. From here it is about 1.8 mi. to the base lodge via ski trails. To find the trail at the top of the ski area, ascend in a rocky area where the ledge has been fractured into flat plates, marked by a large cairn, and follow a beaten path that turns sharp left beneath two large black pipes; beyond this point the trail is easy to follow.

Sosman Trail (map 4:J6)

Distance from summit of Mt. Tecumseh
   to top of ski area: 0.8 mi. (1.3 km.), 30 min.

Welch-Dickey Loop Trail (WVAIA)

This loop trail affords fine views for a modest effort. The section that ascends Welch Mtn. is one of the first trails in this area to be clear of snow in the spring. Some of the ledges may be slippery when wet. From NH 49, about 4.5 mi. from its junction with NH 175, Upper Mad River Rd. goes northwest across the Mad River, and in 0.7 mi. Orris Rd. diverges right ("Welch Mtn." sign). Follow this road for 0.6 mi. and take a short fork right to a parking area, where the trail begins. In 15 yd. the trail forks. The right branch, leading to Welch Mtn., crosses a brook and follows its east side for about 0.5 mi., then turns sharp right and angles up southward to reach the ledges on the south ridge of Welch Mtn. at 0.9 mi. from the start. Then the trail climbs over open ledges interspersed with jack pines and dwarf birches to the ledgy summit of Welch Mtn. at 1.9 mi.

From here the loop drops steeply to a wooded col, then rises, working to the left around a high rock slab. Just above this a branch trail leads right 0.2 mi. to the north outlook from an open ledge. The main loop continues over the summit of Dickey Mtn. at 2.4 mi. and descends another prominent ridge to the southwest, with many outlook ledges, entering the woods to stay at the base of a fine ledge at 3.2 mi. It continues to descend, then turns left onto a logging road with a cellar hole on the right, and reaches the loop junction and the parking lot.

Welch-Dickey Loop Trail (map 4:K5)
Distances from Orris Road parking area

> *to* Welch Mtn. summit: 1.9 mi., 1 hr. 45 min.
> *to* Dickey Mtn. summit: 2.4 mi., 2 hr. 10 min.
> *to* Orris Rd. parking area (complete loop): 4.4 mi. (7.0 km.), 3 hr. 10 min.

Short Walks (WVAIA)

A system of local trails is maintained in the valley. Trail information and a map, "Hiking Trails of the Waterville Valley," may be obtained at the service station on Tripoli Rd. opposite the Waterville Campground or at the "Jugtown" store. These trails often intersect or coincide with ski-touring trails (marked in black and yellow) that may have the same name as a hiking trail but follow a somewhat different route. A separate map of these is available locally. Comments on some of the most interesting paths follow.

The Fletcher's Cascade Path (1.2 mi.), to the beautiful Fletcher's Cascades, leaves the Drake's Brook Trail 0.4 mi. from NH 49.

The Cascade Path (2.3 mi.) runs from the Finish Line Restaurant parking lot to a series of beautiful waterfalls on Cascade Brook at about 1.7 mi., then joins and follows a gravel logging road to the Livermore Trail at 2.1 mi. from the Livermore Rd. parking area. The Norway Rapids Trail (0.5 mi.) runs from the Cascade Path at 1.2 mi. to the Livermore Trail at 1.8 mi.; its crossing of Avalanche Brook is difficult in moderate water. The Boulder Path (1.0 mi.) begins on the Livermore Trail at 0.5 mi., leads past the Big Boulder in Slide Brook that is visible from the trail, and runs to the Snow's Mountain Ski Area parking lot. The Big Pines Path (0.2 mi.) leaves the Livermore Trail at 0.6 mi.

The Greeley Ledge Trail (0.2 mi.) leaves the top of the Snows Mountain Ski Area, passes Greeley Ledges, and ends on the Snows Mountain Trail at 0.7 mi. Elephant Rock Trail (0.3 mi.) begins on the Cascade Path at 0.5 mi. and runs past Elephant Rock to the top of the Snows Mountain Ski Area and the Greeley Ledge Trail.

The Scaur, a rock outlook between Mad River and Slide Brook with views north, south, and west, may be reached by the Scaur Trail (0.6 mi.) from the Greeley Ponds Trail 0.7 mi. from the Livermore Trail, or by the easier Kettles Path (0.9 mi.), which leaves the Livermore Trail at 0.9 mi. and joins the Scaur Trail at the foot of the final 0.2-mi. climb to the outlook.

On a shoulder of the East Peak of Mt. Osceola are the large Davis Boulders and Goodrich Rock (one of the largest glacial erratics in New Hampshire), reached by the Goodrich Rock Trail (0.8 mi.) from the Greeley Ponds Trail 0.9 mi. from the Livermore Trail.

The Flume, an attractive small gorge in the headwaters of Flume Brook (not to be confused with the Franconia Notch Flume), is reached by the Flume Path (1.3 mi.), which leaves the Greeley Ponds Trail 1.2 mi. from the Livermore Trail.

Snows Mountain Trail (WVAIA)

This trail follows the former Woodbury Trail to the shoulder of Snows Mtn., follows the ridge south and east to the summit, and descends the west slope of the mountain back to Waterville. (*Note:* Due to blowdown from recent storms, compounded by uncertainty concerning projected residential and ski-trail construction, this trail has not received full maintenance and some sections, particularly on the south loop beyond the summit outlook spur path, may be difficult to follow.)

The trail leaves the Finish Line Restaurant parking lot, crosses under the chair lift, and crosses the brown bridge at the north end of the tennis courts. It turns left on a paved road, then right onto a ski slope and ascends under the chair lift, then turns right into the woods (arrow) at 0.3 mi. and climbs for another 0.3 mi., then levels off. At 0.7 mi. the Greeley Ledge Trail leaves left to Greeley Ledges and the top of the ski slopes. At 1.2 mi. the Snows Mountain Trail reaches the end of the old Woodbury Trail section and turns right, climbing gradually to Snows Mountain Outlook, which offers a good view to the west. The ascent continues, passing a large boulder with a northeast view. The trail levels out, then climbs to a high point of the ridge. At 2.0 mi. a side trail leads left 0.1 mi. to a ledge at the summit. The Snows Moutanin Trail turns sharp right and descends, passing additional viewpoints to the south and west, and continues gradually down the west slope of the mountain to Upper Greeley Hill Rd., then runs past the swimming pool back to the starting point.

Snows Mountain Trail (map 4:J6)

Distances from Finish Line Restaurant

to Snows Mtn. summit spur: 2.0 mi., 1 hr. 35 min.

to Finish Line Restaurant (complete loop): 3.9 mi.
(6.3 km.), 2 hr. 35 min.

Mount Osceola Trail (WMNF)

This trail begins at a parking area on Tripoli Rd. (FR 30), just west of the height-of-land in Thornton Gap 7.0 mi. from I-93, climbs over Mt. Osceola and East Osceola, and descends to the Greeley Ponds Trail at the height-of-land in Mad River Notch. The trail from Thornton Gap to the summit of Mt. Osceola is relatively easy, with moderate grades and good footing, but the section between East Osceola and Greeley Ponds Trail is extremely steep and rough.

The trail leaves Tripoli Rd. and climbs moderately, going east across the south slope of Breadtray Ridge. At 1.3 mi. it begins to climb by switchbacks toward the ridge top, and at 2.3 mi. crosses a small brook (unreliable water source) on a log bridge. The trail resumes its switchbacks, gains the summit ridge and turns right, and soon reaches the summit ledge at 3.2 mi., with excellent views. The trail turns left and descends, alternating flat stretches with steep, rocky descents. Just before reaching the main col it descends a steep chimney, which can be avoided by a detour to the left (north). The trail passes the col at 3.8 mi. and climbs past a nice outlook on the left to the summit of East Osceola at 4.2 mi. The trail then crosses a lower knob, and descends steeply, then moderately, to a shoulder. At the top of a gully is an outlook 25 yd. to the left, and the main trail descends the steep, loose gully, goes diagonally across a small, rocky slide with good views, and continues to descend very steeply past a sloping rock face, where it turns left. At 4.9 mi. it turns sharp

left and descends moderately under the impressive cliffs
of the north spur to the Greeley Ponds Trail.

Mount Osceola Trail (map 4:J6–I6)
Distances from Tripoli Road

    to Mt. Osceola summit: 3.2 mi., 2 hr. 35 min.

    to Mt. Osceola, East Peak: 4.2 mi., 3 hr. 20 min.

    to Greeley Ponds Trail: 5.7 mi. (9.2 km.), 4 hr. 5 min.

Greeley Ponds Trail (WMNF)

This trail diverges from the Livermore Trail about 0.3
mi. from the parking area on Livermore Rd. (FR 53),
leads past the Greeley Ponds and through Mad River
Notch, and ends at the Kancamagus Highway 4.5 mi.
east of the Wilderness Trail parking lot. A ski-touring
trail marked with blue diamonds crosses the Greeley
Ponds Trail numerous times. Grades are easy, and the
ponds are beautiful.

    The trail leaves the Livermore Trail sharp left just
after the first bridge beyond the Depot Camp clearing,
and follows an old truck road past the Scaur Trail right at
0.7 mi. and the Goodrich Rock Trail left at 0.9 mi. The
truck road ends at 1.1 mi., where the trail crosses Mad
River on Knight's Bridge. At 1.2 mi. the Flume Path
diverges right, and the trail soon crosses Flume Brook
and passes the site of an old logging camp. It continues
across several small brooks and enters the Greeley Ponds
Scenic Area at 2.6 mi. The trail soon crosses Mad River
and reaches the lower Greeley Pond at 2.9 mi., then the
upper pond at 3.4 mi. Here an unmarked path crosses the
upper pond outlet to a fine view on a small beach. The
main trail ascends easily to Mad River Notch, passing
the Mount Osceola Trail left at the height-of-land at 3.8
mi., and descends over numerous brooks (all the difficult
crossings are bridged) to the Kancamagus Highway.

Greeley Ponds Trail (map 4:J6–I6)

Distances from Livermore Trail

   to lower Greeley Pond: 2.9 mi., 1 hr. 45 min.

   to Mount Osceola Trail: 3.8 mi., 2 hr. 15 min.

   to Kancamagus Highway: 5.1 mi. (8.2 km.), 2 hr. 55 min.

East Pond Trail (WMNF)

This trail runs north from Tripoli Rd. (FR 30), 5.4 mi. east of its intersection with I-93, to the Kancamagus Highway 3.7 mi. east of the Wilderness Trail parking lot. It passes scenic East Pond and crosses the pass between Mt. Osceola and Scar Ridge.

Leaving Tripoli Rd., the East Pond Trail follows a gated gravel road and continues straight on an older road where the gravel road swings right. At 0.4 mi., near the site of the old Tripoli Mill, the Little East Pond Trail turns left on an old railroad grade, while the East Pond Trail continues ahead on a logging road. At 0.8 mi. it crosses East Pond Brook, and at 1.4 mi., near the point where the East Pond Loop leaves left for Little East Pond, a side path leads right 40 yd. to the south shore of East Pond.

The trail swings left away from the pond and climbs on old logging roads to the height-of-land at 2.2 mi., then descends steadily on logging roads, crossing Cheney Brook at 3.1 mi. and Pine Brook at 4.3 mi. Just after the latter crossing (which may be difficult at high water) the trail reaches an old logging railroad spur and follows it almost all the way to the Kancamagus Highway.

East Pond Trail (map 4:J5–I6)

Distances from Tripoli Road

   to East Pond: 1.4 mi., 1 hr. 5 min.

   to Kancamagus Highway: 5.1 mi. (8.2 km.), 3 hr. 15 min.

Little East Pond Trail (WMNF)

This trail leaves the East Pond Trail left (northwest) 0.4 mi. from Tripoli Rd. and follows an old railroad grade slightly uphill, crossing Clear Brook at 0.7 mi., then soon bears sharp right from the end of the railroad grade. It climbs at a moderate grade to Little East Pond, where the East Pond Loop enters on the right.

Little East Pond Trail (map 4:I6–I5)

Distance from East Pond Trail
   to Little East Pond: 1.7 mi. (2.8 km.), 1 hr. 10 min.

East Pond Loop (WMNF)

This trail runs up and down over minor ridges at easy grades between East Pond and Little East Pond, making possible a loop trip that visits both ponds.

East Pond Loop (map 4:I6–I5)

Distance from East Pond
   to Little East Pond: 1.5 mi. (2.5 km.), 55 min.

Distance of complete loop to both ponds
   from Tripoli Rd.: 5.0 mi. (8.1 km.), 3 hr. 10 min.

Livermore Trail (WMNF)

This trail runs from a parking area at the beginning of Livermore Rd. near Waterville Valley to the Kancamagus Highway across from Lily Pond. It once connected Waterville Valley to the Sawyer River logging railroad, which led to the now deserted village of Livermore on Sawyer River. The Livermore Trail consists of logging roads of various ages and conditions; the gravel southern section, from Tripoli Rd. to Flume Brook Camp, is also called Livermore Rd. (FR 53).

From the parking area on Livermore Rd., the trail follows the gated gravel road across a bridge over a branch of Mad River. The Greeley Ponds Trail, another gravel road, diverges sharp left 40 yd. past the bridge, and soon the trail crosses Mad River itself on another bridge. In the next 2.0 mi. several of the WVAIA local paths intersect the trail: The Boulder Path diverges right at 0.5 mi. from the parking area; the Big Pines Path diverges left at 0.7 mi., and the

Kettles Path diverges left at 0.9 mi.; at 1.8 mi. the Norway Rapids Trail diverges right, and the Cascade Path diverges right across a major logging bridge at 2.1 mi.

At 2.6 mi. the south end of the Mount Tripyramid Trail diverges right over Avalanche Brook to the South Slide and the Tripyramid peaks. After passing the site of Avalanche Camp to the left of the trail at 3.1 mi., where the road becomes more grass-grown, the trail reaches a hairpin turn to the left at 3.6 mi., where the north end of the Mount Tripyramid Trail diverges right for the difficult North Slide and the summits. At 3.8 mi. the Scaur Ridge Trail diverges right, offering a longer but safer and easier route to the summit of North Tripyramid. After climbing steadily for some distance, the trail crosses Flume Brook at 4.8 mi. and soon passes the clearing of Flume Brook Camp on the right of the trail, becoming wet and muddy at times.

At 5.0 mi. the gravel road ends in a clearing. The Livermore Trail bears slightly right on an older road (sign), and climbs gradually into the very flat Livermore Pass (2864 ft.) at 5.6 mi. It descends slowly at first, runs in a dry brook bed for a while, then descends rather steeply, angling down the wall of a deep, wooded gorge. At 5.9 mi. it crosses the brook bed at the bottom of the gorge. The trail descends moderately, crossing several brooks, then bears left off the logging road at 6.7 mi. and crosses a moist area to a clearing at 7.1 mi. Here it turns right at an arrow on a post and follows a grassy, gravel logging road, passing several restricted but interesting views, and reaches the Kancamagus Highway east of Kancamagus Pass across from Lily Pond.

Livermore Trail (map 4:J6–I7)
Distances from Livermore Road parking area

　　to south end, Mount Tripyramid Trail: 2.6 mi., 1 hr. 30 min.

to north end, Mount Tripyramid Trail: 3.6 mi., 2 hr. 10 min.

to crossing of Flume Brook: 4.8 mi., 3 hr.

to Kancamagus Highway: 7.7 mi. (12.4 km.), 4 hr. 35 min.

Mount Tripyramid Trail (WVAIA)

This trail makes a loop over the three summits of Tripyramid from the Livermore Trail, and is usually done from north to south, in order to ascend the steep slabs of the North Slide and descend the loose gravel of the South Slide. The trail is almost entirely within the Sandwich Range Wilderness. (*Caution:* The steep slabs of the North Slide are difficult, and dangerous in wet or icy conditions. The loose footing on the South Slide may also be hazardous when wet or icy. Ice may form on the North Slide early in the fall and remain well into the spring. In poor conditions the Scaur Ridge Trail is a safer alternative. Allow plenty of time for this steep, rough trip.)

The north end of the loop leaves the Livermore Trail at a hairpin turn 3.6 mi. from the Livermore Rd. parking area (0.5 mi. beyond the Avalanche Camp clearing). The trail descends sharply for 50 yd. to cross Avalanche Brook (last reliable water), then ascends at a moderate grade, occasionally requiring some care to follow, and reaches the gravel outwash of the North Slide at about 0.5 mi. from the Livermore Trail. It now becomes extremely steep, climbing about 1200 ft. in 0.5 mi. Follow the paint blazes on the rocks. Soon the trail reaches the first slabs and views become steadily more extensive. At the top of the slide the trail turns left into the woods, and in 0.1 mi. the Pine Bend Brook Trail enters from the left 20 yd. below the summit of North Peak.

The Mount Tripyramid Trail and the Pine Bend Brook Trail now coincide. They cross over the summit of North Peak and descend at a moderate grade toward Middle Peak. Just north of the col between North and Middle peaks, the Sabbaday Brook Trail enters left from

the Kancamagus Highway, and the Pine Bend Brook
Trail ends. The Mount Tripyramid Trail crosses the col
and makes a steep ascent of the cone of Middle Peak.
There are two outlooks to the right of the trail near the
true summit, which is a few yards left at the high point of
the trail. The trail descends into the col between Middle
and South peaks, then climbs moderately to the wooded
summit of South Peak. From this summit the trail starts
to descend steeply, and soon reaches the top of the South
Slide. In another 60 yd. the Sleeper Trail to Mt. Whiteface diverges left at a sign. The descent to the foot of the
slide at 3.0 mi. is steep, with loose gravel footing. From
the bottom of the slide, in a small clearing, the trail follows logging roads, crossing several small brooks; Cold
Brook, the first sure water, is crossed at 4.1 mi. Continuing on old roads, the trail eventually crosses Avalanche
Brook and ends 25 yd. farther on the Livermore Trail,
2.6 mi. from the Livermore Rd. parking area.

Mount Tripyramid Trail (map 4:J7)

Distances from Livermore Trail
> *to* summit of North Peak: 1.2 mi., 1 hr. 30 min.
> *to* Sabbaday Brook Trail: 1.7 mi., 1 hr. 45 min.
> *to* summit of Middle Peak: 2.0 mi., 2 hr.
> *to* summit of South Peak: 2.4 mi., 2 hr. 15 min.
> *to* Sleeper Trail: 2.6 mi., 2 hr. 20 min.
> *to* Livermore Trail: 4.9 mi. (7.9 km.), 3 hr. 30 min.

Distance of complete loop
> *from* Livermore Rd. parking area: 11.0 mi. (17.7
> km.), 7 hr.

Scaur Ridge Trail (WMNF)

This trail runs from the Livermore Trail to the Pine Bend
Brook Trail, affording an easier, safer alternative route to
the North Slide. It is almost entirely within the Sandwich
Range Wilderness. It diverges right (east) from Livermore Trail 3.8 mi. from the Livermore Rd. parking area.

Following an old logging road at a moderate grade, it crosses a small brook at 0.9 mi., and soon bears left off the road. Climbing somewhat more steeply, it turns right at 1.1 mi. and enters the Pine Bend Brook Trail at the top of a narrow ridge at 1.2 mi. The summit of North Tripyramid is 0.8 mi. to the right via the Pine Bend Brook Trail.

Scaur Ridge Trail (map 4:J7)

Distance from Livermore Trail
   to Pine Bend Brook Trail: 1.2 mi. (1.9 km.), 1 hr. 5 min.

Distance of complete loop over Mt. Tripyramid
   from Livermore Rd. parking area (via Scaur Ridge
      Trail and South Slide): 12.1 mi., 7 hr. 20 min.

Pine Bend Brook Trail (WMNF)

This trail ascends North Tripyramid from the Kancamagus Highway 1.0 mi. west of the Sabbaday Falls Picnic Area. Parts of it are steep and rough.

The trail leaves the highway and very soon turns sharp right onto the grade of the old Swift River logging railroad. After 0.1 mi., it turns sharp left off the railroad grade and follows Pine Bend Brook southwest on an old logging road, making three crossings of the brook. After the third crossing, at 1.3 mi., the trail begins to swing more to the west, enters the Sandwich Range Wilderness, and crosses several small tributaries. It then passes over a minor divide to a westerly branch of Pine Bend Brook, which it crosses and recrosses (last sure water). After crossing the brook bed again in a rocky section at 2.2 mi., the trail becomes rough and steep as it ascends along the north bank of the brook valley, then recrosses the brook bed and angles steeply up an even steeper slope with very poor footing. Soon it reaches and ascends a minor easterly ridge, with much less difficult climbing. Shortly after reaching this ridge, there is a good view of Mt. Washington and the cliffs of Mt. Lowell.

Eventually the trail reaches the ridge running from Tripyramid north to Scaur Peak, crosses it and descends slightly to the west side, then turns left and continues almost level to the junction on the right at 3.2 mi. with the Scaur Ridge Trail. Rising gradually on the very narrow wooded ridge, the trail provides glimpses of the North Slide, then descends slightly. Soon it attacks the final steep, rough, and rocky climb to North Peak. The Mount Tripyramid Trail enters from the North Slide on the right 20 yd. below this summit. (There are good views from the top of the slide, 0.1 mi. from this junction via the Mount Tripyramid Trail.) The two trails coincide, passing the summit of North Peak and descending at a moderate grade to the junction with the Sabbaday Brook Trail just north of the col between North and Middle peaks.

Pine Bend Brook Trail (map 4:I7–J7)

Distances from Kancamagus Highway

   to Scaur Ridge Trail: 3.2 mi., 2 hr. 40 min.
   to summit of North Peak: 4.0 mi., 3 hr. 25 min.
   to Sabbaday Brook Trail: 4.5 mi. (7.2 km.), 3 hr. 40 min.

Sabbaday Brook Trail (WMNF)

This trail begins at the Sabbaday Falls Picnic Area and ascends to the col between North Tripyramid and Middle Tripyramid. There are numerous brook crossings, some of which may be difficult at high water. Except for the very steep, rough section just below the main ridge-crest, grades are easy to moderate and the footing is mostly good.

From the parking area follow a well-graded gravel path along the brook. A side path bears left and passes several viewpoints over Sabbaday Falls, rejoining at 0.3 mi., where the gravel path ends, and the trail continues on an old logging road with easy grades. At 0.7 mi. the trail makes the first of three crossings of Sabbaday Brook in 0.2 mi. (All three may be difficult in high water, but you can avoid the first two by bushwhacking along the west bank, since they are only 0.1 mi. apart.) The trail enters the Sandwich Range Wilderness, and for nearly 2.0 mi. follows the old logging road on the east bank of Sabbaday Brook, then turns sharp right, descends briefly, and makes a fourth crossing of the brook at 2.8 mi. Above this the brook and trail swing to the west, then northwest, up the narrow valley between Tripyramid and the Fool Killer, climbing more steadily and crossing the brook twice more. The trail passes the base of a small slide on the Fool Killer at 3.7 mi., crosses the brook for the seventh and last time (last water source) at the head of the ravine at 4.1 mi., then swings back to the south and soon re-enters the old route of the trail above the slide. From here it turns sharp right and climbs steeply up slabs and broken rock, then becomes less steep but remains rough, with many rocks and roots. Finally it levels off and meets the Pine Bend Brook Trail and the Mount Tripyramid Trail just north of the col between North and Middle Tripyramid; turn right to reach North Peak (0.5 mi.) or left to reach Middle Peak (0.3 mi.).

Sabbaday Brook Trail (map 4:J8–J7)

Distances from Sabbaday Falls Picnic Area

> to fourth crossing of Sabbaday Brook: 2.8 mi., 1 hr. 50 min.
>
> to Pine Bend Brook Trail/Mount Tripyramid Trail: 4.9 mi. (7.9 km.), 3 hr. 45 min.

Sleeper Trail (SSOC)

This trail connects Mt. Tripyramid with Mt. Whiteface and the eastern peaks of the Sandwich Range. It runs from the Downes Brook Trail (see Section 8) in the col between Mt. Whiteface and the Sleeper Ridge, over the high, double-domed Sleeper Ridge, to the Mount Tripyramid Trail high on the South Slide. It lies entirely within the Sandwich Range Wilderness.

The trail leaves the Downes Brook Trail 0.9 mi. below the summit of Mt. Whiteface and skirts north of a swampy area. The only reliable water source is just north of the junction on the Downes Brook Trail. It soon begins to ascend the East Sleeper, and there are occasional views to the east and north through the trees. Passing left (southwest) of the top of East Sleeper at 0.8 mi., where a side path (sign) leads right 0.1 mi. to this viewless summit, the trail descends into the col between the Sleepers and passes 30 yd. south of the summit of West Sleeper at 1.8 mi. After descending to the Tripyramid col the trail bears west and contours along South Tripyramid until it enters the South Slide on the smaller eastern slide. Small cairns and yellow blazes mark the winding route on the slide, as the trail climbs very steeply on loose gravel about 100 yd., then re-enters the woods on the opposite side. After running another 50 yd. through a brushy area the trail enters the larger western slide, where it meets the Mount Tripyramid Trail. To locate the beginning of the trail on the Tripyramid slide, look for a small sign at the extreme eastern edge of the western slide, 60 yd. below its top.

Sleeper Trail (map 4:J7)

Distance from Downes Brook Trail

to Mount Tripyramid Trail: 2.5 mi. (4.1 km.), 1 hr. 45 min.

Sandwich Mountain Trail (WMNF)

This trail runs to the summit of Sandwich Mtn. from a parking lot just off NH 49, 0.4 mi. southwest of its junction with Tripoli Rd. There are fine views from the trail at several different elevation levels.

The trail leaves the southwest corner of the parking lot, skirts left around a power station, and crosses Drakes Brook. If the brook is very high and the crossing difficult, it is possible to reach the trail on the other side of the brook by bushwhacking up the west bank from where Drakes Brook crosses NH 49 just north of the parking lot. The trail turns east soon after the crossing and climbs steeply to Noon Peak at 1.7 mi. It then follows a curving, gradual ridge that is covered with beautiful mosses, and passes several outlooks. There is a spring (unreliable water source) on the west side of the trail, which soon skirts the east slope of Jennings Peak. The Drakes Brook Trail enters left at 2.7 mi., and at 2.8 mi. a spur path leads right 0.2 mi. to the ledgy summit of Jennings Peak, which commands magnificent views. The trail enters the Sandwich Range Wilderness. The Smarts Brook Trail enters on the right at 3.3 mi., and the Sandwich Mountain Trail ascends moderately toward the summit of Sandwich Mtn. About 90 yd. below the summit the Algonquin Trail enters on the right, and 15 yd. below the summit the Bennett Street Trail enters on the right.

Sandwich Mountain Trail (map 4:J6–K7)

Distances from parking area off NH 49

   to Drakes Brook Trail: 2.7 mi., 2 hr. 15 min.

   to Sandwich Mtn. summit: 3.9 mi. (6.3 km.), 3 hr. 20 min.

Drakes Brook Trail (WMNF)

This trail leaves the same parking lot off NH 49 as the Sandwich Mountain Trail and rejoins that trail near Jennings Peak. The trail leaves east from the north side of the parking lot and follows a logging road for 0.4 mi. At this point the trail to Fletcher's Cascades continues up the road, and the Drakes Brook Trail diverges right and crosses Drakes Brook. The trail follows an old logging road, climbing away from the brook and returning to its bank several times. At 2.6 mi. it climbs by switchbacks up the west side of the ravine and joins the Sandwich Mountain Trail north of Jennings Peak, about 1.2 mi. from the summit of Sandwich Mtn.

Drakes Brook Trail (map 4:J6–K6)

Distances from parking area off NH 49

    to Sandwich Mountain Trail: 3.2 mi. (5.2 km.), 2 hr. 35 min.

    to Sandwich Mtn. summit (via Sandwich Mountain Trail): 4.4 mi. (7.1 km.), 3 hr.

Smarts Brook Trail (WMNF)

This trail follows the valley of Smarts Brook from NH 49 to the Sandwich Mountain Trail in the sag south of Jennings Peak. The valley is wild and pleasant, and the trail is relatively easy.

The trail leaves the east side of NH 49 from the south end of a parking area just northeast of the Smarts Brook bridge, crosses the brook on the highway bridge and immediately turns left and climbs a short distance to a logging road, which it follows left, joining a better road and passing a swimming hole in the brook on the left. At 1.3 mi. the Tri-Town (cross-country ski) Trail enters from the right, and an interesting but faintly marked loop side path turns sharp left and crosses the brook on a bridge, then turns right, follows the brook, recrosses it, and rejoins the main trail at 1.6 mi. The main trail continues straight ahead from its junction with the loop and the Tri-Town Trail, following older roads after the newer road diverges right shortly before the loop path rejoins. The trail enters the Sandwich Range Wilderness, crosses a tributary at 2.6 mi., and at 3.7 mi. passes several large boulders. It then crosses the brook, and passes several more very large boulders in the next 0.4 mi. Soon it turns left and climbs by a long switchback to the ridge top, where it meets the Sandwich Mountain Trail.

Smarts Brook Trail (map 4:K6)

Distances from parking area on NH 49

    to pools in Smarts Brook: 1.1 mi., 40 min.

    to Sandwich Mountain Trail: 5.1 mi. (8.2 km.), 3 hr. 45 min.

    to Sandwich Mtn. summit (via Sandwich Mountain Trail): 5.7 mi. (9.2 km.), 4 hr. 25 min.

Bennett Street Trail (WODC)

This trail runs to the summit of Sandwich Mtn. from the Flat Mountain Pond Trail 0.3 mi. from Bennett St. at Jose's bridge. Follow its blue blazes with care.

From Jose's bridge, go west on the Flat Mountain Pond Trail past a gate to a small clearing, where the Bennett Street Trail turns right. It follows a logging road along the southwest bank of Pond Brook, crossing several small streams, and at 0.6 mi. the Gleason Trail diverges left. The Bennett Street Trail soon passes a waterfall with a swimming hole, then bears away from Pond Brook and follows a tributary. At 1.6 mi. it crosses the Flat Mountain Pond Trail, which at this point is an old railroad grade. The Bennett Street Trail ascends the bank above the grade and climbs steadily, entering the Sandwich Range Wilderness, and at 2.3 mi. turns right on a logging road. At 2.9 mi. it turns left off the logging road and at 3.5 mi. the Gleason Trail rejoins on the left. The trail soon turns left onto another old road at a point where there is an unreliable spring on a side path right, and shortly passes a spur path left (sign) to another unreliable spring, then climbs to a junction with the Sandwich Mountain Trail; the summit lies 15 yd. to the right.

Bennett Street Trail (map 4:K7)

Distance from Flat Mountain Pond Trail

    to Sandwich Mtn. summit: 4.0 mi. (6.4 km.), 3 hr. 25 min.

Gleason Trail (AMC)

This trail begins and ends on the Bennett Street Trail, providing an alternative route to the summit of Sandwich Mtn. that is about 0.6 mi. shorter, but consequently steep-

er. The yellow blazes must be followed with care; the
trail is rather steep, and footing may be poor when the
trail is wet.

It diverges left from the Bennett Street Trail at 0.6
mi. (0.9 mi. from Jose's bridge) and ascends across a
ledgy brook to cross the Flat Mountain Pond Trail (old
railroad grade) at 0.5 mi. The trail soon turns left, entering the Sandwich Range Wilderness, and climbs through
a beautiful hardwood forest, then approaches a brook and
turns right without crossing it at 1.0 mi. Soon it turns left
onto a logging road, follows it for 40 yd., then turns right
off the road. It continues rather steeply to the ridge top at
1.5 mi., and then levels off. It then ascends moderately to
its upper junction with the Bennett Street Trail, 0.5 mi.
below the summit of Sandwich Mtn.

Gleason Trail (map 4:K7)

Distance from lower junction with Bennett Street Trail
   to upper junction with Bennett Street Trail: 2.2 mi.
      (3.6 km.), 2 hr. 15 min.

Flat Mountain Pond Trail (WMNF)

This trail runs to the ponds from Whiteface Intervale
Rd. about 0.3 mi. north of its intersection with Bennett
Street, then descends to Bennett Street at Jose's bridge.
It is an easy trail for most of its distance.

The trail leaves Whiteface Intervale Rd. just before
the bridge over Whiteface River on a gated logging
road, crosses a beaver pond outlet with good views,
bears left at a fork, and turns sharp right off the road at
0.6 mi. Soon it reaches an older, grassy logging road
and follows it left for 60 yd., then leaves this road right
and descends gradually to Whiteface River. It crosses
the river on a bridge at 1.6 mi., entering the Sandwich
Range Wilderness, and immediately picks up the older
route of the trail, a logging road that it follows to the left
upstream along the east bank. At 1.7 mi. the McCrillis

Trail turns sharp right up the bank, and the Flat Mountain Pond Trail continues to ascend along the river at comfortable grades, then crosses a major branch at 3.1 mi. Continuing the ascent, it passes over a small hump and descends to the edge of Flat Mountain Pond at 4.2 mi., where it enters the old railroad grade. It follows the grade to a fork at the edge of the major inlet brook; the trail follows the left fork across the stream, while the right fork runs to the edge of a swampy area. Continuing along the pond, the main trail soon diverges right to circle around an area in which the grade has been flooded, passes a boulder with a view of Mt. Whiteface, and returns to the grade at 5.3 mi., leaving the Sandwich Range Wilderness. Here, 70 yd. straight ahead on a spur path, is the Flat Mountain Pond Shelter, worth visiting just for the view across the pond. The main trail turns right on the railroad grade and descends gradually into the valley of Pond Brook.

At 6.3 mi. the grade makes a hairpin turn left at an old beaver pond, soon crosses a small brook, passes a logging camp site, and crosses the brook twice more. At 7.6 mi. the trail crosses a major tributary, swings left, and at 7.7 mi. the Bennett Street Trail crosses. After a wet section where the railroad ties remain, the Gleason Trail crosses at 8.2 mi. (junction has a sign for Gleason Trail only). Both the Bennett Street and Gleason trails can be used as attractive shortcuts to Jose's bridge. At 9.2 mi. the Guinea Pond Trail continues ahead on the railroad grade, while the Flat Mountain Pond Trail turns left on a logging road, passes a gate, goes through a small clearing where the Bennett Street Trail enters on the left, and passes a second gate just before reaching the parking area at Jose's bridge.

Flat Mountain Pond Trail (map 4:K8–K7)

Distances from Whiteface Intervale Road

  to McCrillis Trail: 1.7 mi., 1 hr.

to Flat Mountain Pond Shelter spur path: 5.3 mi., 3 hr. 20 min.

to Guinea Pond Trail: 9.2 mi., 5 hr. 20 min.

to Jose's bridge: 10.1 mi. (16.3 km.), 5 hr. 45 min.

Algonquin Trail (SLA)

This trail ascends Sandwich Dome from Sandwich Notch Rd., and has many extensive views from open ledges on the southwest shoulder, sometimes called Black Mtn. The trail is steep and rough, with a few rock scrambles that can be avoided via side paths.

The trail leaves the north side of Sandwich Notch Rd. 1.5 mi. north of the power line along the Beebe River and 3.7 mi. south of NH 49. It follows an old logging road across a brook and past a small meadow, and at 0.9 mi., in a small clearing, turns left off the road (watch carefully for yellow blazes). Soon it begins to climb steeply, then moderates and passes through a ledgy area with two small brooks, then climbs steeply again to a col at 2.1 mi., where it enters the Sandwich Range Wilderness. Here it turns right, descends slightly, then attacks the west end of the ridge, climbing steeply with two rock pitches, both of which can be avoided via paths to the right, former bypasses that have now become the established route of the trail; at the second, you'll miss the good views unless you walk back to the ledges. The grade moderates, and at 2.8 mi. (elevation 3300 ft.) the Black Mountain Pond Trail enters on the right. The Algonquin Trail continues to ascend moderately, then descends steeply into a small col at 3.5 mi., and ascends moderately again to the Sandwich Mountain Trail 90 yd. below the summit.

Algonquin Trail (map 4:K6)

Distance from Sandwich Notch Road

to Sandwich Mountain Trail: 4.5 mi. (7.3 km.), 3 hr. 30 min.

Black Mountain Pond Trail (SLA)

This trail runs from the Guinea Pond Trail 1.6 mi. from Sandwich Notch Rd., past Black Mountain Pond and its shelter, to the Algonquin Trail 1.8 mi. below the summit of Sandwich Mtn. Sections of the trail below Black Mountain Pond are wet, and the part from the pond to the ridge is very steep and rough.

This trail leaves the north side of the Guinea Pond Trail almost opposite the Mead Trail, crosses Beebe River (may be difficult at high water) and continues generally north to the west bank of Beebe River (which has turned north), which it recrosses at a large beaver dam. At 0.8 mi. it crosses an overgrown gravel road that crosses the brook on the left side of the trail, and enters the Sandwich Range Wilderness. It continues to ascend easily, and at 2.4 mi. reaches the west edge of Black Mountain Pond at the shelter. (The shelter and the area to the west are not within the Sandwich Range Wilderness.) It winds around in the woods near the pond, passing through a small stand of virgin spruce, then turns right and crosses a beaver dam with a small pond on the left, and begins the steep climb. About halfway up it reaches the first of several outlook ledges with good views south; views to the west increase as the trail works around toward the west end of the shoulder. At 3.3 mi. it passes a boulder cave, turns sharp right, and continues to meet the Algonquin Trail at an elevation of 3300 ft.

Black Mountain Pond Trail (map 4:K7–K6)

Distances from Guinea Pond Trail

> *to* Black Mountain Pond Shelter: 2.4 mi., 1 hr. 35 min.
>
> *to* Algonquin Trail: 3.5 mi. (5.6 km.), 2 hr. 45 min.

Guinea Pond Trail (WMNF)

The Guinea Pond Trail runs east from Sandwich Notch Rd. 5.7 mi. from Center Sandwich, just south of the bridge over Beebe River, to the Flat Mountain Pond Trail 0.9 mi. from Bennett Street at Jose's bridge. It follows a gated road to the old railroad grade in a power line clearing, and follows the grade along Beebe River past numerous ponds and swamps. At 1.2 mi. it passes a second gate, and soon the trail turns right, then left on a road, to bypass a flooded section of the grade. Soon the trail runs through the woods to bypass a flooded section of the road, then rejoins the railroad grade and reaches the junctions with the Mead Trail right at 1.6 mi. and the Black Mountain Pond Trail left 10 yd. farther. Continuing east, the trail crosses a brook twice; in high water, follow a path along the south bank. The trail crosses another brook, and at 1.8 mi. a side path runs left 0.2 mi. to the shore of Guinea Pond. At 2.8 mi. the trail crosses a branch of Cold River (may be difficult at high water) and continues on the grade to the junction with the Flat Mountain Pond Trail, which enters right from Jose's bridge and follows the grade ahead to Flat Mountain Pond.

Guinea Pond Trail (map 4:K6–K7)

Distances from Sandwich Notch Road

to Mead Trail/Black Mountain Pond Trail: 1.6 mi., 50 min.

to Flat Mountain Pond Trail: 4.0 mi. (6.4 km.), 2 hr. 5 min.

Mead Trail (SLA)

The Mead Trail ascends to the summit of Mt. Israel from the Guinea Pond Trail 1.6 mi. from Sandwich Notch Rd. It crosses a small ridge and a sag, then the power lines, and ascends along the ravine of a small brook, crossing it at 0.9 mi. It continues to ascend past a small spring (unreliable) to the Wentworth Trail; the summit ledge, with fine views, is 70 yd. left.

Mead Trail (map 4:K7)

Distance from Guinea Pond Trail
   to Wentworth Trail: 1.7 mi. (2.8 km.), 1 hr. 25 min.

Wentworth Trail (SLA)

This trail ascends Mt. Israel from Mead Base (Explorer Scout camp), located on a side road off Sandwich Notch Rd. 2.6 mi. from Center Sandwich, and affords splendid views of the Lakes Region and the Sandwich Range.

Park in the field below the camp buildings, and enter the woods at the left rear of the main camp building (sign). The trail, blazed in yellow, leads directly uphill, following an old cart path through an opening in a stone wall 0.3 mi. above the camp. It turns right and angles up the hillside above the wall, turns left, then turns right at a brook bed at 0.8 mi. Soon it begins to switchback up the slope, and at 1.5 mi. it passes a rock face right and a fine outlook 10 yd. left across Squam Lake and Lake Winnipesaukee. The trail reaches the ridge 100 yd. farther up, and climbing becomes easier, soon becoming almost level in a dense coniferous forest. Then the trail turns right at a ledge (good view north) near the summit of the west knob, and continues along the ridge to the junction on the left with the Mead Trail; the summit is a ledge 70 yd. past the junction.

Wentworth Trail (map 4:L7–K7)

Distance from Mead Base
   to Mt. Israel summit: 2.1 mi. (3.5 km.), 1 hr. 55 min.

SECTION 8
Mt. Chocorua and the
Eastern Sandwich Range

This section covers trails on Mts. Chocorua, Paugus, Passaconaway, and Whiteface, and their subsidiary peaks and ridges. The region is bounded on the north by the Kancamagus Highway (NH 112), on the east by NH 16, on the south by NH 25, and on the west by a line between the Sleeper Ridge and Mt. Whiteface. At the boundary between Section 7 (the Waterville Valley Region) and Section 8, the only points of contact between trails lie at the junction of the Sleeper Trail (Section 7) with the Downes Brook Trail (Section 8), and at the junction of the Flat Mountain Pond Trail (Section 7) and the McCrillis Trail (Section 8). The AMC Chocorua-Waterville map (map 4) covers the entire section. The Chocorua Mountain Club (CMC), Wonalancet Outdoor Club (WODC), and the WMNF maintain most of the trails in this area. The CMC marks its trails with yellow paint and signs, while the WODC trails have blue paint and signs. A newly-published (1991) contour map of the Sandwich Range Wilderness and the surrounding region, with short trail descriptions on the back, covers most of this section except for the east slopes of Mt. Chocorua; it can be obtained from the Wonalancet Outdoor Club, Wonalancet NH 03897. A contour map (9th ed., 1978) of the Chocorua-Paugus region, with a peak-identifying panorama of the view from Mt. Chocorua, is available from the Chocorua Mountain Club, Chocorua NH 03817.

GEOGRAPHY

The Sandwich Range extends about 30 mi. from Conway on the Saco River to Campton on the Pemigewasset, with summits of just over 4000 ft. rising abruptly about 3000 ft. from the lake country to the south. Although the range is not outstanding for its elevation—the North Peak of Mt. Tripyramid, at 4140 ft., is its highest point—the mountains are nevertheless quite rugged, and their viewpoints offer interesting combinations of mountain, forest, and lake scenery.

Mt. Chocorua (3475 ft.), the picturesque rocky cone at the east end of the range, is reputedly one of the most frequently photographed mountains in the world. It has a substantial network of trails; several trails are very heavily used, but it is usually possible to avoid crowds (until the summit is reached) by taking less popular trails. The Piper Trail, Champney Falls Trail, and Liberty Trail are probably the most popular. Confusion sometimes occurs from the fact that several trails are considered to extend all the way to the summit, although they converge below the summit, which is reached by only one path. Thus a given segment of trail may bear several names at once—at least according to trail signs—although in this guide one trail is usually considered to end where two merge, and only two trails (the Piper Trail and the Brook Trail) are described as reaching the summit. When descending from the summit, go 50 yd. southwest on the only marked path, down a small gully to the first junction. The trails on the open rocks are marked with paint, and junctions are signed with WMNF signs or paint, or both.

Caution: The extensive areas of open ledge that make Chocorua so attractive also pose a very real danger. Many of the trails have ledges that are dangerous when wet or icy, and the summit and upper ledges are severely exposed to lightning during electrical storms. The safety of any untreated water source in this heavily used are is very doubtful. Although Chocorua is relatively low compared to other major White Mtn. peaks, its trailheads are located at lower elevations, resulting in a substantial amount of elevation gain that makes Chocorua a strenuous trip.

Three Sisters, which forms the northern ridge of Mt. Chocorua, is nearly as high and also has bare summits. Middle Sister (3330 ft.), the highest of the three ledgy knobs, bears the remains of an old stone fire tower. White Ledge (2010 ft.) is a bluff just east of the Three Sisters, with a ledgy top from which there is a good view east. The ledgy south shoulder of Chocorua is called Bald Mtn. (2110 ft.). On the northwest side of the mountain is Champney Falls, named for Benjamin Champney (1817-1907), pioneer White Mtn. artist. The falls are beautiful when there is a good flow of water, but meager in dry seasons.

Mt. Paugus (3210 ft.), a low but rugged and shaggy mountain once aptly called "Old Shag," was named by Lucy Larcom for the Pequawket chief who led the Abenaki forces at the battle of Lovewell's Pond. All trails end at an overgrown ledge 0.3 mi. south of the wooded true summit, which is not reached by any trail. Paugus Pass (2210 ft.) is a pass on the ridge that connects Mt. Paugus with Mt. Passaconaway and the Wonalancet Range on the west.

Mt. Passaconaway (4060 ft.) is a graceful peak named for the legendary sachem of the Penacooks (his name means "Child of the Bear") who ruled at the time the first Europeans settled in New England. The mountain is densely wooded, but there is a good view into the Bowl from the true summit, and a fine outlook to the east and north from a ledge a short distance from the summit on the Walden Trail. A side path descends from the Walden Trail between the summit and the east outlook to the splendid, secluded north outlook. A major ridge extends southeast to Paugus Pass over the two subpeaks that give the mountain its characteristic steplike profile when viewed from the lake country to the south. Square Ledge (2690 ft.) is a bold, rocky promontory that is a northeast spur of the first subpeak. From the farther subpeak, which is sometimes called Mt. Hedgehog (3150 ft.), the Wonalancet Range runs south, consisting of Hibbard Mtn. (2910 ft.) and Mt. Wonalancet (2800 ft.); both peaks are wooded but have good outlook ledges. Wonalancet is named for a Penacook Sachem who was a son of Passaconaway. Another Hedgehog Mtn. (2530 ft.) is north of Passaconaway. This small but rugged mountain rises between Downes and Oliverian brooks and commands superb views over the Swift River Valley and up to Passaconaway; the best views are from ledges near the summit and on the east shoulder. Mt. Potash (2670 ft.) lies to the west of Hedgehog, between Downes and Sabbaday brooks. The summit is open and ledgy and affords excellent views of the surrounding mountains and valleys in all directions.

Mt. Whiteface (4010 ft.) doubtless received its name from the precipitous ledges of its south summit. The true summit of the mountain is wooded, but the slightly lower summit, 0.3 mi. south of the true summit, affords magnificent views from the bare ledge at the top of the precipices. Two lesser ridges run south on either side of the cliffs, while the backbone of the mountain runs north, then northeast, connecting it with Mt. Passaconaway. Sleeper Ridge on the northwest connects Whiteface to Mt. Tripyramid. East of Mt. Whiteface lies the Bowl, a secluded valley encircled by the main ridge of Mt. Whiteface and the south ridge of Mt. Passaconaway. This area has been reserved as a natural area, and is now included within the Sandwich Range Wilderness.

West of Mt. Whiteface the range sprawls; one major ridge continues northwest over the Sleeper Ridge to Tripyramid, then ends at Livermore Pass. West of this high pass lies the mountain mass composed of peaks such as Kancamagus, Osceola, Scar Ridge, and Tecumseh; these have not been traditionally regarded as part of the Sandwich Range, although connected with it. Another major ridge runs southwest over Sandwich Dome and soon loses its definition as it descends to the Campton mountains and toward the Squam Range. Everything west of the White-face–Sleeper Ridge Col is covered in Section 7.

CAMPING
Sandwich Range Wilderness
In this area camping and fires are prohibited above tree-line, and below treeline, no campsite may be used by more than ten persons at one time.

Restricted Use Areas
The WMNF has established a number of Restricted Use Areas (RUAs) where camping and wood or charcoal fires are prohibited from May 1 to November 1. The specific areas are under continual review, and areas are added to or subtracted from the list in order to provide the greatest amount of protection to areas subject to damage by excessive camping, while imposing the lowest level of restrictions possible. A general list of RUAs follows, but you should obtain a map of current RUAs from the WMNF.

(1) Camping is not permitted above treeline (where trees are less than 8 ft. tall) except in winter, and even then it is allowed only on sites that are covered with at least two feet of snow and not located on frozen bodies of water. Small signs mark the point where the restricted area begins, but the absence of such signs should not be construed as proof of the legality of a site.

(2) No camping is permitted within 1/4 mile of most facilities such as huts, cabins, shelters, or tentsites, except at the facility itself.

(3) No camping is permitted within 200 ft. of certain trails. In 1986, designated trails included the Champney Falls Trail up to the boundary of the Mt. Chocorua RUA.

(4) No camping is permitted at any time of the year on the upper part of Mt. Chocorua, except at Camp Penacook and Jim Liberty Cabin. Campfires are prohibited even at these sites.

Established Trailside Campsites

Camp Penacook (WMNF), located on a spur path off the Piper Trail on Mt. Chocorua, is an open shelter that accommodates six to eight, with a tent platform that accommodates the same number. There is water available nearby.

Jim Liberty Cabin (WMNF) is located on a ledgy hump 0.5 mi. below the summit of Mt. Chocorua. The water source is scanty in dry weather.

Old Shag Camp (CMC), on Mt. Paugus, has been removed.

Camp Rich (WODC) is located on the southwest side of Mt. Passaconaway on the Dicey's Mill Trail at about 3500 ft. elevation. It is an open log shelter for eight people. Wilderness policies will probably require its eventual removal.

Camp Shehadi (WODC) is an open shelter for six at the junction of the Rollins and Downes Brook trails, 0.1 mi. north of the south summit of Mt. Whiteface. The nearest reliable water is 0.9 mi. down the Downes Brook Trail. Wilderness policies will probably require its eventual removal.

Camp Heermance (WODC) is an open shelter accommodating six in a partially sheltered spot near the summit of Mt. Whiteface, about 20 yd. north of an unreliable spring near the top of the Blueberry Ledge Trail. The original shelter at this site was built in 1912. The nearest reliable water is 1.0 mi. down the Downes Brook Trail. Wilderness policies will probably require its eventual removal.

ROAD ACCESS

Confusion sometimes results from the rather erratic behavior of NH 113 and its alternate route between North Sandwich and Tamworth, NH 113A. Both roads change direction frequently, and NH 113 unites with and diverges from NH 25 between its two junctions with NH 113A. It is therefore necessary to study very carefully directions to trailheads on the southeast slopes of the Sandwich Range.

Whiteface Intervale Rd. leaves NH 113A about 3.0 mi. north of the western junction of NH 113 and NH 113A, where NH 113A bends from north-south to east-west. Bennett St. turns left from Whiteface Intervale Rd. 0.1 mi. from NH 113A, continues straight past a junction at 1.7 mi., where it becomes rougher, and ends at 2.4 mi. at Jose's (rhymes with *doses*) bridge.

Ferncroft Rd. leaves NH 113A at Wonalancet village, at a right angle turn in the main highway. It shortly passes the Wonalancet post office, and at 0.5 mi. a gravel road (FR 337) turns right 0.1 mi. to a parking area. No parking is permitted further up Ferncroft Rd.

Fowler's Mill Rd. runs between NH 16 (at the bridge that crosses the south end of Chocorua Lake, about 1.5 mi. north of Chocorua village), and NH 113A (3.3 mi. north of the eastern junction of NH 113 and NH 113A in Tamworth, and just north of the bridge over Paugus Brook). Paugus Mill Rd. (FR 68) branches north (sign) from Fowler's Mill Rd. 1.3 mi. east of NH 113A, and runs to a parking area at 0.7 mi., beyond which the road is closed to vehicles.

THE TRAILS
Champney Falls Trail (WMNF)
This heavily used trail runs from the Kancamagus Highway, 11.5 mi. from NH 16 in Conway, to the Piper Trail

in the flat saddle between Chocorua and the Three Sisters. Champney Falls are attractive, and the trail has moderate grades all the way.

Leaving the parking area, the trail soon crosses Twin Brook on a footbridge, turns right, and proceeds south with easy grades, mostly on an old logging road, to Champney Brook. At 1.4 mi. a loop path 0.4 mi. long diverges left to Pitcher Falls and Champney Falls. The main trail passes an outlook north, the loop path rejoins at 1.7 mi., and the steady ascent continues. At 2.4 mi. the trail reaches the first of several switchbacks, and at 3.0 mi. the Middle Sister Cutoff diverges left toward Middle Sister. Soon the Champney Falls Trail reaches the ledgy saddle with an outlook on a side path to the right—then it passes the junction left with the Middle Sister Trail, and in 80 yd. ends at its junction with the Piper Trail, 0.6 mi. from the summit of Chocorua.

Champney Falls Trail (map 4:J9)
Distances from Kancamagus Highway
  to Champney Falls loop: 1.4 mi., 1 hr.
  to Piper Trail: 3.2 mi., 2 hr. 35 min.
  to Mt. Chocorua summit (via Piper Trail): 3.8 mi. (6.1 km.), 3 hr. 5 min.

Middle Sister Cutoff

This short trail leads from the Champney Falls Trail, 3.0 mi. from the Kancamagus Highway, to the col between Middle Sister and First Sister, giving access to the fine views from the old tower site on Middle Sister. Leaving the Champney Falls Trail, it follows an old road past an outlook ledge, then swings right and soon reaches the Middle Sister Trail.

Middle Sister Cutoff (map 4:J9)
Distance from Champney Falls Trail
  to Middle Sister Trail: 0.3 mi. (0.5 km.), 15 min.

White Ledge Loop Trail (WMNF)

This loop trail to White Ledge has two entrance routes. The main one is located at White Ledge Campground; the alternative one leaves NH 16 opposite Pine Knoll Camp, about 0.5 mi. northeast of White Ledge Campground, and follows an old town road 0.5 mi. to the east branch of the trail, 0.6 mi. from the campground.

The main trail diverges right from the main campground road and forks at 0.3 mi. The east branch goes to the right across a small brook, runs to the junction with the alternative route at 0.6 mi., bears left in an open area and climbs to the height-of-land east of the main bluff of White Ledge at 1.3 mi. The trail now descends, and at 2.0 mi. it turns sharp left in an overgrown pasture and climbs moderately up the east end of White Ledge to the summit at 2.7 mi., where there is a good view east. The trail descends past an outlook to Mt. Chocorua, then turns sharp left at 3.7 mi. and reaches the loop junction at 4.1 mi.

White Ledge Loop Trail (map 4:J10)

Distances from White Ledge Campground

    to loop junction: 0.3 mi., 10 min.

    to White Ledge summit (via east branch): 2.7 mi., 2 hr. 5 min.

    to White Ledge summit (via west branch): 1.7 mi., 1 hr. 30 min.

    to White Ledge Campground (complete loop): 4.4 mi. (7.1 km.), 2 hr. 55 min.

Carter Ledge Trail (WMNF)

This trail provides an attractive route to Middle Sister from White Ledge Campground, or (via Nickerson Ledge Trail) from the Piper Trail. Carter Ledge, an interesting objective in its own right, is a nice, open ledge with views of Mt. Chocorua and one of three colonies of jack pine (*Pinus banksiana*) in the White Mtns.

The trailhead is located on the left branch of the campground road. Park in the parking lot at the campground picnic area. The trail diverges west from the left branch road 0.1 mi. south of the junction and climbs moderately to the long southeast ridge of Carter Ledge, passing the junction at 1.0 mi. where the Middle Sister Trail diverges right, then meeting the Nickerson Ledge Trail, which enters left at 2.0 mi. Soon the trail ascends a steep, gravelly slope, turns right at an outlook to Mt. Chocorua, passes through the jack pine stand and reaches the summit of the ledge at 2.8 mi. It passes through a sag, then works its way up the ledgy slope of Third Sister, steeply at times, and reaches the Middle Sister Trail 0.3 mi. northeast of Middle Sister.

Carter Ledge Trail (map 4:J10–J9)
Distances from White Ledge Campground
> *to* Nickerson Ledge Trail: 2.0 mi., 1 hr. 30 min.
> *to* Middle Sister Trail: 3.7 mi. (6.0 km.), 3 hr. 5 min.

Middle Sister Trail (WMNF)
This trail begins on the Carter Ledge Trail 1.0 mi. from the WMNF White Ledge Campground, climbs over the Three Sisters, and ends at the Champney Falls Trail in the saddle between the Sisters and Mt. Chocorua. It provides good views.

Leaving the Carter Ledge Trail, the Middle Sister Trail ascends through mixed hardwoods and softwoods and crosses Hobbs Brook at 1.3 mi., then skirts an area damaged by a December 1980 windstorm. At 1.8 mi. it joins the former route of the trail and climbs more steeply to the col between the Three Sisters ridge and Blue Mtn. at 2.4 mi., where the trail turns sharp left and ascends the northeast spur of the Third Sister, with several good outlooks. At 3.3 mi. the Carter Ledge Trail enters on the left, and the Middle Sister Trail crosses the ledgy summit of Third Sister and a small dip beyond, then reaches the summit of the Middle Sister at 3.6 mi. The trail continues across ledges marked by paint, passes the Middle Sister Cutoff right, and continues ahead over First Sister to its terminus on the Champney Falls Trail. From here it is 80 yd. (left) to the Piper Trail, then 0.6 mi. to the summit of Mt. Chocorua.

Middle Sister Trail (map 4:J10–J9)
Distances from Carter Ledge Trail
   to Middle Sister summit: 3.6 mi., 3 hr.
   to Champney Falls Trail: 4.1 mi. (6.6 km.), 3 hr. 20 min.

Piper Trail (WMNF)
This heavily used trail to Mt. Chocorua from NH 16, first blazed by Joshua Piper, begins behind the Piper Trail Cabins and Restaurant (sign, fee for parking). It leads across an open field, enters the woods, and follows a logging road across the WMNF boundary at 0.6 mi. The Weetamoo Trail diverges left at 0.8 mi., and the Nickerson Ledge Trail diverges right at 1.4 mi. After crossing the Chocorua River (a small brook at this point) at 2.0 mi., the trail then ascends moderately past a cleared out look to Carter Ledge, and goes up a series of switchbacks, stone steps, and paving. At 3.1 mi. a spur path diverges left 0.2 mi. to Camp Penacook (open shelter, tent platform, water available). The main trail turns sharp right and ascends, with more stone steps and paving, soon reaching open ledges with spectacular views to the north, east, and south. The Champney Falls Trail enters right at 3.9 mi., and in another 0.2 mi. the West Side Trail (sometimes considered, and signed as, a part of the Liberty Trail) enters on the right. The Piper Trail, marked with yellow paint, continues over open ledges to the summit. In bad weather it may be safer to use the West Side and Brook trails to reach the summit, since the Piper Trail crosses a ledge at the foot of a minor northern crag that may be dangerous in wet or windy conditions.

Piper Trail (map 4:J10–J9)

Distances from NH 16
> *to* Nickerson Ledge Trail: 1.4 mi., 1 hr.
> *to* Chocorua River crossing: 2.0 mi., 1 hr. 25 min.
> *to* Camp Penacook spur trail: 3.1 mi., 2 hr. 25 min.
> *to* Champney Falls Trail: 3.9 mi., 3 hr. 10 min.
> *to* Mt. Chocorua summit: 4.5 mi. (7.2 km.), 3 hr. 35 min.

Nickerson Ledge Trail (WMNF)

This trail connects the Piper Trail with the Carter Ledge Trail and Middle Sister, making possible loop hikes that include the attractive ledges on the northeast part of the mountain. It leaves the Piper Trail 1.4 mi. from NH 16 and climbs rather steeply 0.2 mi. to Nickerson Ledge, which has a restricted view of the summit of Mt. Chocorua, then continues with a gradual ascent to the Carter Ledge Trail 2.0 mi. above White Ledge Campground.

Nickerson Ledge Trail (map 4:J10)

Distance from Piper Trail
> *to* Carter Ledge Trail: 0.8 mi. (1.3 km.), 35 min.

Weetamoo Trail (CMC)

This trail connects the lower part of the Piper Trail, 0.8 mi. from NH 16, with the Hammond Trail well up on Bald Mtn., and gives access to the ledges of the south ridge of Mt. Chocorua from the Piper Trail.

The trail diverges left from the Piper Trail and crosses Chocorua River at 0.4 mi., then leaves the river and runs through a logged area, crosses a small brook (last sure water source) at 1.0 mi., then passes an outlook to Mt. Chocorua and reaches Weetamoo Rock, an immense boulder, at 1.7 mi. The trail ends at the Hammond Trail, 2.7 mi. from the summit of Mt. Chocorua.

Weetamoo Trail (map 4:J10–J9)

Distance from Piper Trail
> *to* Hammond Trail: 1.9 mi., 1 hr. 35 min.

Hammond Trail (CMC)

The Hammond Trail provides a route up Bald Mtn., the ledgy south ridge of Mt. Chocorua. The trailhead is on a dirt road that leaves NH 16 on the left (west) 3.0 mi. north of the junction with NH 113 in Chocorua village, directly opposite a large boulder; parking is on the right 0.4 mi. from NH 16.

The trail leaves the parking area, crosses Stony Brook, passes the WMNF boundary, then recrosses Stony Brook. At 0.8 mi. the trail crosses a logging road, then climbs steadily to the crest of Bald Mtn. at 1.9 mi. It crosses a sag, then ascends along the ridge. At 2.1 mi. the Weetamoo Trail enters on the right, and the Hammond Trail passes over several humps to its end at the junction with the Liberty Trail, 1.1 mi. from the summit of Mt. Chocorua.

Hammond Trail (map 4:J10–J9)

Distances from parking area off NH 16

   to Bald Mtn.: 1.9 mi., 1 hr. 45 min.

   to Liberty Trail: 3.0 mi., 2 hr. 40 min.

Liberty Trail (WMNF)

This is the easiest route to Mt. Chocorua from the southwest. It begins at the parking area just before the gate on Paugus Mill Rd. (FR 68). This is a very old path that was improved somewhat by James Liberty in 1887, and further developed as a toll bridle path by David Knowles and Newell Forrest in 1892. Knowles built the two-story Peak House in 1892, which was blown down in September 1915. The stone stable was rebuilt by the CMC in 1924 and named the Jim Liberty Shelter. This lasted till 1932, when the spring winds blew off the roof, and in 1934 the WMNF replaced it with an enclosed cabin with bunks.

The Liberty Trail follows a gated side road that branches right just before the gate on the main road (which continues to the Bolles and Brook trails), and ascends at a steady, moderate grade, mostly along the route of the former bridle path. It crosses Durrell Brook at 1.1 mi. and at 2.7 mi. it reaches the ridge top, where the Hammond Trail enters right. The Liberty Trail crosses a hump, descends into the sag beyond, then climbs to Jim Liberty Cabin at 3.3 mi., where a red-blazed side path leads right 0.1 mi. to a mediocre water source. The Liberty Trail swings to the left (west) at the foot of a ledge and follows the old bridle path, which was often blasted out of the rock. It circles around the southwest side of the cone, ascending moderately, and meets the Brook Trail on a ledge at 3.6 mi., 10 yd. before the Bee Line Trail enters the Brook Trail. The summit of Mt. Chocorua is 0.2 mi. farther via the Brook Trail. The summit can be avoided during bad weather by following the West Side Trail, which enters 25 yd. beyond the Bee Line Trail and runs north around the west side of the summit cone to the Piper Trail.

Liberty Trail (map 4:J9)

Distances from Paugus Mill Road parking area

   to Hammond Trail: 2.7 mi., 2 hr. 10 min.

   to Jim Liberty Cabin: 3.3 mi., 2 hr. 40 min.

   to Brook Trail: 3.6 mi., 3 hr. 5 min.

   to Mt. Chocorua summit (via Brook Trail): 3.9 mi. (6.2 km.), 3 hr. 20 min.

West Side Trail (WMNF)

The West Side Trail runs from the Piper Trail 0.4 mi. north of the summit of Mt. Chocorua to the ledge where the Liberty, Brook, and Bee Line trails join. Its grades are easy and it is well sheltered; it affords a route for avoiding the summit rocks in bad weather. It leaves the Piper Trail in a flat area north of the summit and circles the west side of the cone to the Brook Trail, 25 yd. above its junction with the Bee Line Trail.

West Side Trail (map 4:J9)

Distance from Piper Trail
   to Brook Trail: 0.5 mi. (0.7 km.), 20 min.

Brook Trail (CMC)

This trail runs from the parking area at the end of Paugus Mill Rd. (FR 68) to the summit of Mt. Chocorua. It was cut by the country people to avoid paying a toll on the Liberty Trail. High up, it ascends steep ledges with excellent views; it is much more scenic but also more difficult than the Liberty Trail, and potentially dangerous in wet or icy conditions. You can make an excellent loop trip by ascending the Brook Trail and descending the Liberty Trail.

From the parking area on Paugus Mill Rd., continue past the gate north on the gravel road. After 0.1 mi. the Bolles Trail diverges left, and at 0.4 mi., just before the bridge over Claybank Brook, the Brook Trail turns right off the gravel road. It follows the south bank of the brook, passes a junction left with the Bickford Path, and climbs well above the brook. At 1.8 mi. the trail returns to the brook at a tiny waterfall, and finally crosses it at 2.5 mi. The trail steepens, and the first ledge is reached at 3.0 mi. Now the trail climbs the steep, open ledges of Farlow Ridge, where it is marked with cairns and yellow paint. At 3.4 mi. the Liberty Trail comes in on the right, and the Bee Line Trail comes in 10 yd. beyond on the left on the same ledge. In about 25 yd. the West Side Trail, a bad weather summit bypass, turns left (north), and the Brook Trail climbs steeply east over the ledges, then swings left (northeast) to the junction where the Piper Trail enters from the left (sign). The two trails climb east to the summit through a small gully.

Brook Trail (map 4:J9)

Distances from Paugus Mill Road parking area
   to Claybank Brook crossing: 2.5 mi., 1 hr. 45 min.

to Liberty Trail: 3.4 mi., 2 hr. 50 min.
to Mt. Chocorua summit: 3.6 mi. (5.9 km.), 3 hr. 5 min.

Bee Line Trail (CMC)

This trail runs from the Old Paugus Trail on the south ridge of Mt. Paugus to the Brook Trail on the upper west ledges of Mt. Chocorua, linking the two summits almost by a bee line. On the upper part of Chocorua the trail is very rough with poor footing, and it crosses steep ledges that may be difficult or dangerous when wet or icy.

The trail leaves the Brook Trail on a ledge below the summit of Mt. Chocorua, 10 yd. north of the junction of the Brook and Liberty trails. In 100 yd. it makes a sharp right turn on a ledge (follow with care), and descends very steeply, partly in the track of a slide. At 0.9 mi. the trail crosses a brook in a steep ravine, becomes somewhat less steep, recrosses the brook and follows it on an old logging road, and reaches the Bolles Trail at 1.9 mi. This point is 2.0 mi. from the Paugus Mill Rd. parking area via the Bolles Trail.

The Bee Line Trail now crosses Paugus Brook, enters the Sandwich Range Wilderness, and runs over a narrow ridge. At 2.2 mi. the Bee Line Cutoff departs left (southeast), and the Bee Line Trail crosses a small brook and climbs steeply up the side of the mountain, making some use of old lumber roads, to the Old Paugus Trail near the top of the ridge.

Bee Line Trail (map 4:J9)

Distances from Brook Trail/Liberty Trail junction
to Bolles Trail: 1.9 mi., 1 hr.
to Old Paugus Trail: 3.0 mi. (4.8 km.), 2 hr. 5 min.

Bee Line Cutoff (CMC)

This trail provides a shortcut to the Bee Line Trail to Mt. Paugus from the Paugus Mill Rd. parking area. It is almost entirely within the Sandwich Range Wilderness.

It diverges northwest from the Bolles Trail 1.2 mi. from the parking area and follows an old lumber road. At 0.2 mi. it bears right, crosses a brook, and continues to the Bee Line Trail, 0.2 mi. west of the junction of the Bee Line and Bolles trails.

Bee Line Cutoff (map 4:J9)
Distance from Bolles Trail
    to Bee Line Trail: 0.6 mi. (1.0 km.), 20 min.

Bolles Trail (WMNF)

This trail connects the Paugus Mill Rd. (FR 68) parking lot with the Champney Falls Trail parking lot on the Kancamagus Highway, passing between Mt. Chocorua and Mt. Paugus, using old logging roads most of the way. It is named for Frank Bolles, who reopened a very old road in 1892 and called it the Lost Trail. South of the height-of-land, the majority of the trail lies in or near the Sandwich Range Wilderness.

The Bolles Trail diverges from the Brook Trail (which here is a gravel logging road) 0.1 mi. north of the Paugus Mill Rd. parking lot. At 0.2 mi. it crosses Paugus Brook (may be difficult at high water) and at 0.5 mi. the Old Paugus Trail and Bickford Path enter left. In 90 yd. the Bickford Path diverges right. Soon the Bolles Trail passes the huge Paugus Mill sawdust pile (left), and at 1.1 mi. the Bee Line Cutoff diverges left. The Bolles Trail now crosses two branches of Paugus Brook. (Avoid the herd path on the west bank at the second brook, where the bridge has been washed out of position.) At 1.9 mi. the Bee Line Trail crosses, and at 2.6 mi. the Bolles Trail recrosses Paugus Brook, turns right in an old logging camp (the trail here may be somewhat obscured by berry bush growth) and soon begins to climb more steeply through a sandy area to the height-of-land at 3.7 mi. The trail then descends steeply to Twin Brook, crosses it twelve times, and reaches the Kancamagus Highway just past the west end of the Champney Falls Trail parking lot.

Bolles Trail (map 4:J9)

Distances from Brook Trail

to Bickford Path/Old Paugus Trail: 0.5 mi., 20 min.

to Bee Line Trail: 1.9 mi., 1 hr. 10 min.

to Kancamagus Highway: 5.7 mi. (9.2 km.), 3 hr. 30 min.

Bickford Path (WODC)

This trail runs from NH 113A 1.1 mi. east of Wonalancet to the lower part of the Brook Trail, offering a walking route from Wonalancet to the Old Paugus, Bolles, and Brook trails to Mt. Chocorua and Mt. Paugus. Follow the trail's blue blazes carefully; there is no obvious footway.

The trail leaves NH 113A and ascends easily on an old logging road, passes behind two camps, and descends easily to a field with a private home at 0.7 mi. Turning left at the horse corral, it re-enters the woods at the east edge of the field, enters the WMNF, climbs moderately to a ridge top, and descends on the other side. The Old Paugus Trail enters left 20 yd. west of Whitin Brook, and the two trails cross the brook and meet the Bolles Trail at 2.0 mi. The Bickford Path turns left (north) on the Bolles Trail for 90 yd., then turns right (east), crosses Paugus Brook (may be difficult), and soon reaches a logging road (which leads to the right to the Paugus Mill Rd. parking area). The path turns left and follows the road for about 0.1 mi., then turns right (turns poorly marked), descends easily, and crosses Claybank Brook to the Brook Trail, where the Bickford Path ends.

Bickford Path (map 4:K9–J9)

Distances from NH 113A

to Bolles Trail: 2.0 mi., 1 hr. 15 min.

to Brook Trail: 2.7 mi. (4.3 km.), 1 hr. 35 min.

Old Paugus Trail (CMC)

This trail runs to the south knob of Mt. Paugus from the Bolles Trail 0.7 mi. from the Paugus Mill Rd. parking area. It is almost entirely within the Sandwich Range Wilderness. Portions of the trail are very steep and rough with poor footing, and may be dangerous in wet or icy conditions.

The trail leaves the Bolles Trail with the Bickford Path, crosses Whitin Brook, then the Bickford Path diverges left 20 yd. beyond the brook. The Old Paugus Trail continues along Whitin Brook, crosses it at 0.7 mi., then turns right at 1.0 mi. as the Whitin Brook Trail continues straight along the brook. The trail now climbs steeply, passes a junction left with the Big Rock Cave Trail at 1.3 mi., climbs a steep gully, then swings right along the base of a rock face, and climbs steadily through a spruce forest to the junction right with the Bee Line Trail at 2.1 mi. It then ascends sharply, passes an outlook on the right (sign), then eases up, passes the site of the former Old Shag Camp (now removed), crosses a small brook, and climbs to the south knob. Here the Old Paugus Trail ends and the Lawrence Trail continues ahead.

Old Paugus Trail (map 4:J9)

Distances from Bolles Trail

  to Bee Line Trail: 2.1 mi., 1 hr. 50 min.
  to Lawrence Trail: 2.8 mi. (4.5 km.), 2 hr. 30 min.

Whitin Brook Trail (CMC)

This trail runs from the Old Paugus Trail to the Cabin Trail and provides access to points in the vicinity of Paugus Pass from the Paugus Mill Rd. parking area. Follow it with care, particularly at the crossings of Whitin Brook; some of the old bridges over this brook are unsafe and should be avoided. The trail lies almost entirely within the Sandwich Range Wilderness.

The Whitin Brook Trail continues along Whitin Brook where the Old Paugus Trail turns right upslope, 1.0 mi. above the junction of the Old Paugus and Bolles trails. In 0.2 mi. the Big Rock Cave Trail crosses, then the Whitin Brook Trail crosses the brook three times. After the last crossing at 0.7 mi., the trail swings left away from the brook and climbs through spruce woods to the Cabin Trail, 0.4 mi. south of its junction with the Lawrence Trail.

Whitin Brook Trail (map 4:J9–J8)

Distance from Old Paugus Trail
    to Cabin Trail: 1.6 mi. (2.5 km.), 1 hr. 15 min.

Big Rock Cave Trail (WODC)

This trail runs from the Cabin Trail 0.3 mi. from NH 113A over the flat ridge of Mt. Mexico to the Whitin Brook and Old Paugus trails. It provides easy access to Big Rock Cave, an interesting boulder cave that invites exploration.

Diverging right from the Cabin Trail, it ascends moderately on an old logging road that fades away to a trail, reaching the very flat summit of Mt. Mexico at 1.1 mi. and entering the Sandwich Range Wilderness. From here it descends moderately, then steeply, and passes Big Rock Cave (right) at 1.6 mi. It then crosses Whitin Brook (may be difficult at high water) and the Whitin Brook Trail at 1.7 mi., and climbs to its end at the Old Paugus Trail.

Big Rock Cave Trail (map 4:K8–J9)

Distances from Cabin Trail
    to Big Rock Cave: 1.6 mi., 1 hr. 10 min.
    to Old Paugus Trail: 2.1 mi. (3.4 km.), 1 hr. 35 min.

Cabin Trail (WODC)

The Cabin Trail runs from NH 113A 0.5 mi. east of Wonalancet to the Lawrence Trail 0.3 mi. east of Paugus Pass. It starts on a driveway and passes a house, and at 0.3 mi. the Big Rock Cave Trail diverges right. The Cabin Trail ascends easily on a logging road over several small brooks to the height-of-land at 2.2 mi., where the Whitin Brook Trail enters from the right. The Cabin Trail stays to the east side of Whitin Ridge, passes two outlooks to Mt. Paugus, and ends at the Lawrence Trail just inside the Sandwich Range Wilderness.

Cabin Trail (map 4:K8–J8)

Distances from NH 113A

   to Whitin Brook Trail: 2.2 mi., 1 hr. 40 min.

   to Lawrence Trail: 2.7 mi. (4.3 km.), 2 hr.

Lawrence Trail (WODC)

This trail runs from the junction of the Old Mast Rd. and the Walden and Square Ledge trails, 2.0 mi. from the Ferncroft Rd. parking area (via the Old Mast Rd.), to the junction with the Old Paugus Trail on the south knob of Mt. Paugus. Sections of it are extremely steep and rough, with poor footing. The trail lies entirely within the Sandwich Range Wilderness.

The trail leaves the multiple junction at the north end of the Old Mast Rd., and descends slightly into Paugus Pass at 0.3 mi., where it is joined on the left (north) by the Oliverian Brook Trail from the Kancamagus Highway and on the right (south) by the Kelley Trail from Ferncroft. The Lawrence Trail climbs to a knob at 0.6 mi. where the Cabin Trail enters from the right. It then descends to the southeast side of the ridge at the base of the Overhang, passes along the face of high, wooded cliffs, and ascends a very steep and rough slope to an outlook to Mt. Paugus at 0.9 mi. The trail then descends steeply into a hollow and crosses two small brooks. It climbs steeply again, crosses another brook, and continues at a moderate grade to the south knob of Mt. Paugus, where the Old Paugus Trail continues ahead.

Lawrence Trail (map 4:J8–J9)

Distance from Old Mast Road
  to Old Paugus Trail: 2.1 mi. (3.4 km.), 1 hr. 40 min.

Kelley Trail (WODC)

This trail runs from the Ferncroft Rd. parking area to the Lawrence and Oliverian Brook trails at Paugus Pass, through an interesting ravine. The upper part of the trail is rough, with poor footing and numerous slippery rocks.

It leaves the Ferncroft Rd. parking area and follows a gated gravel logging road (FR 337), bearing right where the Old Mast Rd. bears left. In 0.2 mi. the Gordon Path leaves right (sign), and at 0.5 mi. the Kelley Trail diverges left from the gravel road, crosses a branch of the road at a brook crossing, and follows the brook. In about 0.5 mi. the trail begins to climb above the brook, then returns to the brook at the top of a small cascade. It now crosses the brook (or its dry bed) five times, then climbs steeply out of a small box ravine and soon reaches Paugus Pass, just inside the Sandwich Range Wilderness.

Kelley Trail (map 4:K8–J8)

Distance from Ferncroft Road parking area
  to Lawrence Trail: 2.2 mi. (3.6 km.), 1 hr. 40 min.

Oliverian Brook Trail (WMNF)

This trail runs from the Kancamagus Highway to the Lawrence and Kelley trails at Paugus Pass. It begins at a new parking lot 0.1 mi. in from the Kancamagus Highway on a gravel road that begins 1.0 mi. west of the Bear Notch Rd. intersection. Much of the trail, particularly south of the Passaconaway Cutoff, is very wet.

The trail follows the gravel road beyond the gate for 0.1 mi., then turns sharp left on a cross-country ski trail that it follows for another 0.1 mi., then turns sharp right on the old route of the trail. It crosses an old railroad bed and a recent logging road, then joins an old railroad grade along the west side of Oliverian Brook and follows it for nearly 0.5 mi. At 1.1 mi. it turns left off the railroad grade, and at 1.9 mi. the Passaconaway Cutoff diverges right (southwest). The Oliverian Brook Trail continues south and crosses a major tributary at 2.2 mi., then the main brook at 2.7 mi. Soon it crosses a side channel of the main brook to an island, then crosses the main channel, and reaches the junction right with the Square Ledge Branch Trail at 3.3 mi., shortly after the crossing of Square Ledge Brook. The trail then enters the Sandwich Range Wilderness, crosses Oliverian Brook, climbs up on the bank above the brook, then recrosses on a bridge and continues to climb along the brook to Paugus Pass.

Oliverian Brook Trail (map 4:J8)
Distances from Kancamagus Highway
   to Passaconaway Cutoff: 1.9 mi., 1 hr. 5 min.
   to Square Ledge Branch Trail: 3.3 mi., 2 hr.
   to Paugus Pass: 4.4 mi. (7.1 km.), 2 hr. 40 min.

Old Mast Road (WODC)
This trail runs from the Ferncroft Rd. parking area to the junction with the Walden, Square Ledge, and Lawrence trails 0.3 mi. west of Paugus Pass. The original road was reputedly built for hauling out the tallest timbers as masts for the British navy.

   Leaving the parking area, the trail takes the left hand road (the right is the Kelley Trail). At 0.1 mi. the Wonalancet Range Trail diverges left, just before the bridge over Spring Brook. Soon the trail crosses the WMNF boundary, and at 0.9 mi. it crosses an overgrown logging road, then soon enters another old road and follows it for 0.1 mi. The trail continues to climb, then levels, passes a small brook left, and ends at the multiple junction, just inside the Sandwich Range Wilderness.

Old Mast Road (map 4:K8–J8)

Distance from Ferncroft parking area
> *to* Lawrence Trail/Walden Trail/Square Ledge Trail:
> 2.0 mi. (3.2 km.), 1 hr. 35 min.

Dicey's Mill Trail (WODC)

This trail ascends Mt. Passaconaway from the Ferncroft Rd. parking area, with moderate grades and good footing. It was the earliest trail to be laid on the mountain.

From the parking area, return to Ferncroft Rd. and turn right, following the gravel road past Squirrel Bridge, where the Blueberry Ledge Trail turns left. Pass a gate (not intended to keep out hikers) and a house, and continue on the road, which becomes a logging road. About 40 yd. before the trail enters the WMNF and Sandwich Range Wilderness at 0.8 mi., a marked path left crosses Wonalancet River to the Blueberry Ledge Cutoff on the opposite bank. Soon the trail swings right and steepens, then the grade becomes easy again and continues to the junction left with the Wiggin Trail at 1.9 mi. At 2.3 mi. the Dicey's Mill Trail crosses the river, passes a large boulder, and begins a long ascent angling up the side of a ridge, following an old logging road at a moderate grade through hardwoods, with occasional views of the Wonalancet Range. At the ridge top, at 3.7 mi., the Rollins Trail from Mt. Whiteface enters on the left. The Dicey's Mill Trail then climbs through a rough, wet section, crosses a small brook, and reaches the junction at 3.9 mi. where the East Loop continues straight. Here the Dicey's Mill Trail turns left, passes Camp Rich (25 yd. left on a side trail), and climbs, steeply at times, to join the Walden Trail. The summit and south outlook are 40 yd. right on a spur path, while the Walden Trail leads 90 yd. to the east outlook.

Dicey's Mill Trail (map 4:K8–J8)

Distances from Ferncroft Road parking area
> *to* Wiggin Trail: 1.9 mi., 1 hr. 20 min.

to Rollins Trail: 3.7 mi., 2 hr. 55 min.

to Mt. Passaconaway summit: 4.6 mi. (7.3 km.), 3 hr. 45 min.

East Loop (WODC)

This very short trail begins on the Dicey's Mill Trail, at the right angle turn near the small brook just below Camp Rich, and descends slightly to the base of the final ascent of Mt. Passaconaway on the Walden Trail. It lies entirely within the Sandwich Range Wilderness. Signs are often missing, and its junction with the Walden Trail escapes notice particularly easily.

East Loop (map 4:J8)

Distance from Dicey's Mill Trail

to Walden Trail: 0.2 mi. (0.4 km.), 10 min.

Walden Trail (WODC)

This trail ascends Mt. Passaconaway from the junction of the Old Mast Road and the Square Ledge and Lawrence trails via the southeast ridge. It is a more interesting but longer and rougher route to Passaconaway from Ferncroft Rd. (via the Old Mast Road) than the direct Dicey's Mill Trail. It lies almost entirely within the Sandwich Range Wilderness.

The trail runs northwest from the Old Mast Road up a very steep slope with poor footing. At the top of the shoulder the grade eases and the trail crosses a minor knob and a sag, then climbs again and passes a side path that leads right 20 yd. to a view of Mt. Washington. At 0.7 mi. it passes the large boulder that is the true summit of Mt. Hedgehog, and at 0.9 mi. the Wonalancet Range Trail enters left. The Walden Trail now descends steeply to a col, follows along a brook bed (possible water) for 50 yd., then climbs very steeply again over the next sub-peak, descends easily to a col, and climbs gradually to the junction right with the Square Ledge Trail at 2.1 mi. The trail now starts to angle upward around the south face of the mountain, and at 2.2 mi. the East Loop continues straight where the Walden Trail swings right and climbs steeply to the east outlook. The junction with the Dicey's Mill Trail is 90 yd. beyond the outlook, and the summit is 40 yd. left from that junction. Between the east outlook and the Dicey's Mill Trail a side path descends right 0.3 mi. to a fine north outlook.

Walden Trail (map 4:J8)

Distances from Old Mast Road

> *to* Square Ledge Trail: 2.1 mi., 1 hr. 40 min.
>
> *to* Mt. Passaconaway summit: 2.8 mi. (4.5 km.), 2 hr. 30 min.

Wonalancet Range Trail (WODC)

This trail ascends from the Old Mast Road, 0.1 mi. from the Ferncroft Rd. parking area, over the Wonalancet Range to the Walden Trail west of Mt. Hedgehog. There are good views from ledges on the way, and the trail offers an alternative, but longer and rougher, route to Mt. Passaconaway from Ferncroft.

The trail diverges left from the Old Mast Road just before the bridge over Spring Brook, and crosses a logging road on a steep bank, entering the Sandwich Range Wilderness. It runs through a flat area, then passes a logged area, crossing an old logging road at 0.7 mi. At 1.3 mi. it starts to climb steeply, crosses a fine outlook ledge, then swings around to the south edge of Mt. Wonalancet and turns north to cross the summit at 1.8 mi. The trail descends to a col and then climbs to the summit of Mt. Hibbard, where there is an outlook west at 2.7 mi. It continues to ascend moderately, then descends slightly to the junction with the Walden Trail.

Wonalancet Range Trail (map 4:K8–J8)

Distances from Old Mast Road

> *to* Mt. Wonalancet summit: 1.8 mi., 1 hr. 40 min.
>
> *to* Walden Trail: 3.2 mi. (5.1 km.), 2 hr. 40 min.

Passaconaway Cutoff (WMNF)

This trail provides the shortest route to Mt. Passaconaway from the north, running from the Oliverian Brook Trail, 1.9 mi. from its parking lot off the Kancamagus Highway, to the Square Ledge Trail (and thence to the summit via the Walden Trail). Leaving the Oliverian Brook Trail, the cutoff follows an old logging road, crosses a brook at 0.5 mi., then runs above the brook to the junction with the Square Ledge Trail.

Passaconaway Cutoff (map 4:J8)

Distance from Oliverian Brook Trail
    to Square Ledge Trail: 1.7 mi. (2.8 km.), 1 hr. 25 min.

Distance from Kancamagus Highway
    to Mt. Passaconaway summit (via Oliverian Brook, Square Ledge, and Walden trails): 5.1 mi. (8.2 km.), 4 hr.

Square Ledge Trail (WODC)

This trail runs from the junction of the Old Mast Road and the Walden and Lawrence trails, over Square Ledge, to the Walden Trail just below the summit cone of Mt. Passaconaway. It lies within the Sandwich Range Wilderness from its southern terminus to the Passaconaway Cutoff.

From the junction at its southern end, it descends from the height-of-land, crossing two small brooks, and at 1.1 mi., just before the second brook, the Square Ledge Branch Trail diverges right (east) to join the Oliverian Brook Trail. A short distance farther, the main trail makes a sharp turn left (west) to ascend the ledge. It bears east for a short distance, then climbs very steeply to the shoulder. At 1.5 mi., at a sharp left turn, a spur leads right 20 yd. to Square Ledge outlook, where there is a fine view across the valley. Leaving the ledge, the trail ascends to the wooded summit of the knob above the ledge, and then descends to the junction right with the Passaconaway Cutoff at 2.1 mi. The Square Ledge Trail turns sharp left, crosses a dip, passes through an old logging camp site, and crosses a small slide, then becomes steep as it climbs to the Walden Trail.

Square Ledge Trail (map 4:J8)
Distances from Old Mast Road/Lawrence Trail/Walden Trail

  to Passaconaway Cutoff: 2.1 mi., 1 hr. 20 min.
  to Walden Trail: 2.8 mi. (4.2 km.), 2 hr.

Square Ledge Branch Trail (WMNF)
This short trail begins on the Oliverian Brook Trail 3.4 mi. from the Kancamagus Highway, and runs to the Square Ledge Trail below the steep section that ascends the ledge. It is used to make a loop over Square Ledge from the Kancamagus Highway.

Square Ledge Branch Trail (map 4:J8)
Distance from Oliverian Brook Trail

  to Square Ledge Trail: 0.5 mi. (0.8 km.), 25 min.

UNH Trail (WMNF)
This loop trail to the ledges of Hedgehog Mtn. begins at the new Downes Brook Trail parking lot, at the end of a gravel road that leaves the south side of the Kancamagus Highway opposite the WMNF Passaconaway Campground. It offers fine views for a modest effort. It was named for the University of New Hampshire Forestry Camp that was formerly located nearby.

The trail leaves the Downes Brook Trail on the left 60 yd. from the edge of the parking lot and follows an old railroad grade 0.2 mi. to the loop junction; here the west branch of the loop turns right uphill, while the east branch continues straight on the old railroad grade. From this point the loop will be described in the clockwise direction (east branch to summit, then west branch back) although the loop is equally good in the opposite direction.

From the loop junction, the east branch continues on the railroad grade, then bears right off it at 0.4 mi. and follows a logging road, climbing moderately. It crosses a small brook at 1.6 mi. from the parking lot, shortly swings left to a view north and east, then bears right to reach the east ledges at 2.0 mi., with fine views south and east. The trail then runs along the top of the cliffs on the south face, enters the woods under the steep, ledgy south side of the main peak, and bears gradually toward the north onto the west slope of the peak, which it climbs in a short series of switchbacks to the summit of Hedgehog Mtn. at 2.9 mi. The trail then descends steadily, and makes a left turn at 3.7 mi., where a side path leads 60 yd. right to Allen's Ledge and its restricted view. The main trail descends to a logging road, turns right on it, and follows it to the loop junction.

UNH Trail (map 4:J8)

Distances from parking lot off Kancamagus Highway

 to east ledges: 2.0 mi., 1 hr. 40 min.

 to Hedgehog Mtn. summit: 2.9 mi., 2 hr. 15 min.

 to Kancamagus Highway (complete loop): 4.8 mi. (7.7 km.), 3 hr. 15 min.

Mount Potash Trail (WMNF)

This trail ascends to the open ledges of Mt. Potash, providing excellent views for relatively little effort, from the Downes Brook Trail, 0.3 mi. from the new parking lot on the road that leaves the Kancamagus Highway almost directly opposite the entrance to the Passaconaway Campground.

The trail turns sharp right off the Downes Brook Trail, heads generally southwest, and crosses Downes Brook (may be difficult) at 0.1 mi. After crossing the brook, the trail turns sharp left and soon crosses a logging road. At 0.9 mi. it turns sharp left and climbs, swinging left off the old route of the trail at 1.2 mi., then swinging right to rejoin the old route, which it follows to the left. It crosses a southeast outlook and ascends moderately on scattered ledges, then at 1.6 mi. leaves the old route again and angles up the east side of the mountain, circling clockwise around the cone to avoid the steepest ledges, and finally gains the summit from the south.

Mount Potash Trail (map 4:J8)

Distance from Downes Brook Trail
   to Mt. Potash summit: 1.9 mi. (3.1 km.), 1 hr. 40 min.

Rollins Trail (WODC)

The Rollins Trail runs along the high ridge that connects Mt. Whiteface to Mt. Passaconaway. It begins on the Downes Brook Trail at Camp Shehadi, in the col between the true summit and the open south summit of Mt. Whiteface, and ends on the Dicey's Mill Trail 0.2 mi. below Camp Rich. On the ridge of Mt. Whiteface some sections are steep and rough. It lies entirely within the Sandwich Range Wilderness.

From the Downes Brook Trail in the col, the Rollins Trail climbs north rather steeply, then runs along the ridgecrest to the true summit (no marking) of Mt. Whiteface at 0.2 mi. It continues along the narrow ridge, with outlooks to the east across the Bowl, descending gradually with occasional steep pitches to the Whiteface-Passaconaway col. The trail then angles slightly upward around the south face of Passaconaway and meets the Dicey's Mill Trail.

Rollins Trail (map 4:J8)

Distance from Downes Brook Trail
   to Dicey's Mill Trail: 2.3 mi. (3.7 km.), 1 hr. 15 min.

Blueberry Ledge Trail (WODC)

This trail, which was opened in 1899, ascends Mt. Whiteface (ending on the lower south summit) from the Ferncroft Rd. parking area. The trail is very scenic, but the upper part is steep; and though wooden steps have been placed and rock steps blasted, it is still difficult, particularly on the descent, and is dangerous in icy conditions.

From the parking area, return to Ferncroft Rd. and follow it to Squirrel Bridge at 0.3 mi., where the Dicey's Mill Trail continues straight ahead. The Blueberry Ledge Trail turns left across the bridge and follows a private gravel road, avoiding driveways, then diverges left into the woods where the road curves right to a house. Here, at 0.5 mi., the Pasture Path to Mt. Katherine leaves left. In 0.1 mi. the trail joins an old road, and the Blueberry Ledge Cutoff diverges right to follow the Wonalancet River. The trail crosses into the WMNF and Sandwich Range Wilderness, and at 0.9 mi. it continues straight where the McCrillis Path to Whiteface Intervale Rd.—not to be confused with the McCrillis Trail to Mt. Whiteface follows the old road sharp left. The Blueberry Ledge Trail passes through a flat area, ascends moderately, and at 1.6 mi. reaches the bottom of the ledges (views are very limited) and climbs to the top of the ledges, where there is a view of the Ossipee Range. It re-enters the woods, and the Blueberry Ledge Cutoff immediately rejoins right at 2.0 mi. The trail climbs gently through open hardwoods and then rises steeply past Wonalancet Outlook to the top of the ridge, drops slightly into a hollow, then ascends to a junction with the Wiggin Trail on the right at 3.2 mi. Now the trail climbs moderately, then swings sharp right at an outlook (may be dangerous if icy) at 3.6 mi., climbs a ledge by wooden steps, and continues along the steep, rough, rocky ridge, with several excellent viewpoints. At the top of the ridge it passes a spur path to Camp Heermance, then joins the Downes Brook and McCrillis trails just north of the ledges of the lower south summit. The true summit is 0.3 mi. farther north via the Downes Brook and Rollins trails.

Blueberry Ledge Trail (map 4:K8–J8)

Distances from Ferncroft Road parking area

>   *to* Blueberry Ledge Cutoff, upper junction: 2.0 mi., 1 hr. 30 min.

>   *to* McCrillis Trail/Downes Brook Trail: 3.9 mi. (6.2 km.), 3 hr. 25 min.

Blueberry Ledge Cutoff (WODC)

This trail begins and ends on the Blueberry Ledge Trail, and provides a walk along the Wonalancet River as an alternative to the viewless ledges. It is equal in distance, but somewhat rougher than the parallel section of the Blueberry Ledge Trail.

It leaves the Blueberry Ledge Trail 0.6 mi. from the Ferncroft Rd. parking area, and descends slightly to the river bank. At 0.3 mi. the Dicey's Mill Trail lies just across the river; an old logging road crosses the river at this point and the Blueberry Ledge Cutoff follows it upstream into the Sandwich Range Wilderness. The trail soon climbs a small ridge and returns to the bank high above the brook, then swings away from the brook, meets and follows a small tributary, then swings right and climbs steeply to the bottom of the upper ledge. Marked by cairns and paint it climbs parallel to the Blueberry Ledge Trail, enters the woods at the top of the ledge, then swings left to meet the Blueberry Ledge Trail.

Blueberry Ledge Cutoff (map 4:K8)

Distance from Blueberry Ledge Trail, lower junction

>   *to* Blueberry Ledge Trail, upper junction: 1.4 mi. (2.3 km.), 1 hr. 10 min.

Wiggin Trail (WODC)

This trail, cut in 1895 and nicknamed "The Fire Escape," connects the Dicey's Mill Trail 1.9 mi. from the Ferncroft Rd. parking area with the Blueberry Ledge Trail just below the upper ledges. It is steep and rough, and lies entirely within the Sandwich Range Wilderness.

Leaving the Dicey's Mill Trail, it crosses Wonalancet River (may be difficult at high water), bears left and ascends a little knoll, crosses a small brook, and bears right. It tends to angle to the right as it climbs. Eventually it reaches the Blueberry Ledge Trail just north of a small hollow.

Wiggin Trail (map 4:J8)

Distance from Dicey's Mill Trail
  to Blueberry Ledge Trail: 1.1 mi. (1.8 km.), 1 hr. 15 min.

McCrillis Trail (WMNF)

This trail ascends Mt. Whiteface—ending at the lower south summit—from the Flat Mountain Pond Trail (see Section 7), 1.7 mi. from Whiteface Intervale Rd. It is steep and rough, but sheltered, and lies entirely within the Sandwich Range Wilderness. Do not confuse this trail with the McCrillis Path, which runs from Whiteface Intervale Rd. to the Blueberry Ledge Trail.

Leaving the Flat Mountain Pond Trail on the east bank of Whiteface River, the McCrillis Trail ascends a bank, then runs east nearly level to intersect the former route, an old logging road, at 0.4 mi. Turning left on this road, it climbs moderately, passing through a wet area, and at 2.0 mi. begins to climb steeply. At 2.6 mi. it passes the first of several outlooks, some of which provide good views onto the "white face." The trail re-enters the woods, climbs steeply again, and finally climbs along the edge of the southwest ledges (use caution) to the Downes Brook and Blueberry Ledge trails just north of the ledges of the lower south summit. The true summit is 0.3 mi. farther north via the Downes Brook and Rollins trails. (Descending, walk from the highest rock southwest along the edge of the ledges.)

McCrillis Trail (map 4:K8–J8)

Distances from Flat Mountain Pond Trail
  to base of steep climb: 2.0 mi., 1 hr. 35 min.

> *to* Downes Brook Trail/Blueberry Ledge Trail: 3.2
> mi. (5.1 km.), 3 hr.

McCrillis Path (WODC)

This trail follows old roads with mostly easy grades
from the Blueberry Ledge Trail, 0.9 mi. from the Ferncroft Rd. parking area, to Whiteface Intervale Rd. Do
not confuse it with the McCrillis Trail to Mt. Whiteface.
Use of the part west of the height-of-land is not recommended, since it lies mostly on private property and is
not officially maintained, and may be serverely overgrown and obscure.

It leaves the Blueberry Ledge Trail left, following
the old road, and climbs to the height-of-land. Tilton
Spring Path leaves left at 0.2 mi., there is a small cellar
hole on the right at 0.8 mi., and the trail enters recent
logging at 1.1 mi. A branch road enters on the right at
1.3 mi., just across Tewksberry Brook (eastbound, bear
right across brook), and at 2.1 mi. the road reaches the
edge of a very wet, open meadow (markings end at a
faded old sign 30 yd. back). Turn right on a gravel road
and follow it to a gravel pit, bear left, turn left on another gravel road at an intersection, and reach the Whiteface Intervale Rd. just east of Whiteface Auto Body.
The trailhead for the Flat Mountain Pond Trail is 0.6 mi.
to the right (west, then south).

McCrillis Path (map 4:K8)
Distance from Blueberry Ledge Trail
> *to* Whiteface Intervale Rd.: 2.3 mi. (3:8 km.), 1 hr. 15 min.

Downes Brook Trail (WMNF)

This trail ascends Mt. Whiteface—ending at the lower
south summit—from a new parking area, 0.1 mi. from
the Kancamagus Highway by a gravel road that leaves
on the south side almost directly opposite Passaconaway
Campground. The trail crosses Downes Brook ten times,
and several crossings may be difficult at high water.

Leaving the parking area, the trail follows the edge of a sandpit, and the UNH Trail diverges left on an old railroad grade in 60 yd. The Downes Brook Trail enters the woods and follows an old logging road that runs along Downes Brook, at first some distance away and later mostly along the bank. At 0.3 mi. the Mount Potash Trail diverges right, and at 0.7 mi. the Downes Brook Trail makes the first of four crossings of Downes Brook in a span of 0.6 mi. At 2.3 mi. it crosses an extensive gravel outwash, crosses the main brook twice more, and passes through an old logging camp at 3.0 mi. After three more crossings, there are views of the slides on the steep slope of Mt. Whiteface across the valley, and the trail crosses the brook for the last time in the flat col between Sleeper Ridge and Mt. Whiteface. Here, at 5.2 mi., just before a swampy area, the Sleeper Trail (see Section 7) leaves right, and the Downes Brook Trail turns left and climbs moderately to the col between the true summit and the bare south summit of Mt. Whiteface at 6.0 mi. Here, at Camp Shehadi, the Rollins Trail leaves left (north), passing over the true summit of Whiteface at 0.2 mi., and continuing toward Mt. Passaconaway. The Downes Brook Trail turns right, climbs a short, steep pitch, and soon ends at the junction with the Blueberry Ledge and McCrillis trails just north of the bare ledges of the south summit.

Downes Brook Trail (map 4:J8)
Distances from Kancamagus Highway
> *to* Sleeper Trail junction: 5.2 mi., 3 hr. 40 min.
> *to* McCrillis Trail/Blueberry Ledge Trail: 6.1 mi. (9.8 km.), 4 hr. 25 min.

Shorter Paths in the Ferncroft Area (WODC)
These trails are not as well-beaten as the more important paths, and signs and other markings are frequently sparse or absent, so they must be followed with great

care. They also frequently cross private property, and landowner rights and privacy must be respected.

The Brook Path (2.1 mi.) leaves NH 113A opposite the Cabin Trail trailhead and follows the north bank of Wonalancet River for 0.9 mi., then crosses on a bridge and follows the south bank for another 0.9 mi. to Old Lock Rd., which it follows to NH 113A just south of the bridge across Wonalancet River. The Gordon Path (1.0 mi.) runs from the Kelley Trail, 0.2 mi. from the Ferncroft Rd. parking area, to NH 113A, 0.3 mi. west of the trailhead for the Cabin and Big Rock Cave trails. The Pasture Path (1.1 mi.) leads from the Blueberry Ledge Trail, 0.5 mi. from the Ferncroft Rd. parking area, passes Tilton Spring at 0.6 mi., and continues to the summit of Mt. Katherine, a broad ledge with restricted views. The Red Path (0.7 mi.) runs from the Wonalancet post office to Tilton Spring. The Tilton Spring Path (0.9 mi.) runs from Tilton Spring to the McCrillis Path 0.2 mi. from the Blueberry Ledge Trail.

SECTION 9
The Carter and Baldface Ranges

This section covers the Carter-Moriah Range and the Baldface Range, the valley of the Wild River that lies between them, and the lower mountains on the long ridges that extend south from the two major ranges. The major peaks in the Carter-Moriah Range are: Wildcat Mtn., Carter Dome, Mt. Hight, South Carter Mtn., Middle Carter Mtn., Mt. Moriah, and Shelburne Moriah Mtn. The major peaks in the Baldface Range are: North Baldface, South Baldface, West Royce Mtn., and East Royce Mtn. The major peaks in the southern part of this region are: Black Mtn., North and South Doublehead, Kearsarge North, and Black Cap. The area is bounded on the west by NH 16, on the north by US 2, and on the east and south by ME 113/NH 113 (which crosses the state line several times). Many trails in this section coincide with or intersect cross-country ski trails; use care in distinguishing one from the other. Almost the entire area is covered by the AMC Carter–Mahoosuc map (map 7); the exception is the Green Hills of Conway range at the far south end of the region, which is covered by the USGS North Conway quad.

In this section the Appalachian Trail begins at NH 16 opposite Pinkham Notch Visitor Center and follows the Lost Pond, Wildcat Ridge, Nineteen-Mile Brook, Carter-Moriah, Kenduskeag, and Rattle River trails to US 2 east of Gorham. It crosses the summits of Wildcat Mtn., Carter Dome, Mt. Hight, South Carter Mtn., and Middle Carter Mtn., and near the summit of Mt. Moriah.

GEOGRAPHY

The Carter–Moriah Range would be much more prominent among White Mtn. ranges were it not for those
neighbors that rise 1500 ft. higher across Pinkham Notch.
On a ridge about 10 mi. long are eight significant peaks
over 4000 ft. and the wild, spectacular Carter Notch. Mt.
Hight and Shelburne Moriah Mtn. command the finest
views in the range, while those from Carter Dome and
Mt. Moriah are also excellent. To the east the range overlooks the broad, forested valley of the Wild River and the
rocky peaks of the Baldface group, and far beyond lies
the Atlantic, which reflects the sun on the southeast hori-
zon behind Sebago Lake on clear mornings.

Wildcat Mtn. rises at the south end of the range. Of
its numerous summits, the highest is the one nearest to
Carter Notch; its five most prominent summits are designated, from east to west, A Peak (4422 ft.), B Peak
(4330 ft.), C Peak (4298 ft.), D Peak (4010 ft.), and E
Peak (4041 ft.). The mountain is heavily wooded, but
there are magnificent outlook ledges on the Wildcat
Ridge Trail west of E Peak, a lookout tower with extensive views on D Peak near the top of the Wildcat Ski
Area, a good view east to the Baldface area from C
Peak, and fine views straight down into Carter Notch
from A Peak.

Carter Notch, the deep cleft between Carter Dome
and Wildcat Mtn., includes some of the finest scenery in
this region. The two small, beautiful Carter Lakes lie in
the notch. The actual notch (3388 ft.) is located north of
the lakes, but the Rampart, a barrier of rocks, rises on the
south side, so that the lakes are totally enclosed and their
outlet is forced to run underground. Above the lakes the
impressive cliffs of Wildcat Mtn. rise vertically nearly
1000 ft. to the west, and to the east Carter Dome rises
steeply, with the immense boulder called Pulpit Rock
jutting out above the notch. Large sections of the cliffs

on each side have fallen into the notch to form caves where ice sometimes remains through the summer. A rough trail over the Rampart leaves the Wildcat River Trail about 100 yd. south of Carter Notch Hut and runs east over the huge rocks, where there is a good view toward Jackson and many boulder caves that invite exploration (use caution).

Carter Dome (4832 ft.) once bore a fire tower on its flat, scrub-fringed summit. There are excellent views in most directions from open areas in the vicinity of the summit. Mt. Hight (4675 ft.) is a bare rock peak with some of the best views in the range. South Carter Mtn. (4430 ft.) is wooded with no views. Middle Carter Mtn. (4610 ft.) is wooded, but there are good outlooks from various points along its ridgecrest, including an excellent view of the Presidentials 70 yd. north of the summit. North Carter Mtn. (4530 ft.) has views from its summit and from ledges along the ridge north and south of the summit; the best views are east to the Baldface Range. Imp Mtn. (3730 ft.) is a trailless north spur of North Carter. Imp Profile (3165 ft.) is an interesting cliff on a west spur of North Carter. The profile is best seen from the Pinkham B (Dolly Copp) Rd. at the monument marking the site of the Dolly Copp house.

Mt. Moriah (4049 ft.) has fine views in all directions from its ledgy summit block. Mt. Surprise (2194 ft.) is a northwest spur of Moriah that offers restricted views. Mt. Evans (1443 ft.) is a low north spur of the Moriah group that affords fine views for comparatively little effort of Mt. Washington and the Northern Peaks and good views up and down the Androscoggin River and across to the Mahoosuc Range. Shelburne Moriah Mtn. (3735 ft.) offers magnificent views—surpassed in this range only by Mt. Hight—from acres of flat ledges at the summit and outlooks on its southwest ridge.

The Baldface-Royce Range extends southwest from Evans Notch, between the Wild River and the Cold River. The summits are relatively low, but so are the valleys; thus the mountains rise impressively high above their bases. North Baldface (3591 ft.) and South Baldface (3569 ft.) are the highest peaks in the range. A fire swept their upper slopes in 1903 and the resulting great expanses of open ledge make the circuit over these peaks one of the finest trips in the White Mountains. With Eagle Crag (3030 ft.), a northeast buttress, these peaks enclose a cirquelike valley on their east. To the southwest are Sable Mtn. (3490 ft.) and Chandler Mtn. (3329 ft.), wooded and trailless, and to the southeast is Eastman Mtn. (2936 ft.), which affords fine views from its ledgy summit.

A ridge descends northeast from Eagle Crag over Mt. Meader (2782 ft.), which has ledgy outlooks, to the Basin Rim, where there are fine views from the brink of a cliff, then ascends to the Royces. West Royce Mtn. (3210 ft.), with good views to the east and southeast from a ledge near the summit, is located in New Hampshire, and East Royce Mtn. (3114 ft.), with good views in nearly all directions, lies in Maine; the state line crosses slightly to the east of the col between them.

A number of lower mountains rise from the ridges that extend south from the main ranges. Spruce Mtn. (2272 ft.), which is trailless, and Eagle Mtn. (1615 ft.) are small peaks on a south ridge of Wildcat Mtn. Eagle Mtn. has a path and views from the summit. Black Mtn. (3303 ft.), which lies across Perkins Notch from Carter Dome, is a long ridge with seven summits (more or less). Only the southernmost summit, the Knoll (1910 ft.), and a knob (2758 ft.) in the middle of the ridge offer good views. North Doublehead (3050 ft.), with a cabin on the summit and good outlooks east and west near the summit, and South Doublehead (2938 ft.), with good views from several ledges, form a small, sharp ridge southeast of

Black Mtn. Southwest of Doublehead is the low range composed of Thorn Mtn. (2287 ft.) and Tin Mtn. (2030 ft.); the former trail on Thorn Mtn. has been closed. East of Doublehead lie the valleys of Slippery Brook and the East Branch of the Saco. Mountain Pond—a crescent-shaped body of water about 0.75 mi. long by 0.5 mi. wide, entirely surrounded by woods and overlooked by Baldface, Mt. Shaw, and Doublehead—is located in Slippery Brook Valley.

Kearsarge North (3268 ft.), sometimes called Mt. Pequawket, rises above Intervale. The summit bears an abandoned fire tower, and the views are magnificent in all directions; this is one of the finest view points in the White Mtns. Bartlett Mtn. (2661 ft.) is a shoulder extending westward toward Intervale; it has no trails, but has a number of ledges that invite exploration. Running south from Kearsarge North are the Green Hills of Conway: Hurricane Mtn. (2101 ft.), Black Cap (2370 ft.), Peaked Mtn. (1734 ft.), Middle Mtn. (1850 ft.), Cranmore Mtn. (1690 ft.), and Rattlesnake Mtn. (1590 ft.). Only Hurricane Mtn., Black Cap, Peaked Mtn., and Cranmore Mtn. have trails; all four, especially Black Cap and Peaked Mtn., have fine views. There is a range of trailless hills extending northeast from Kearsarge North, of which the most prominent is Mt. Shaw (2566 ft.).

HUTS, SHELTERS, AND CAMPING
Carter Notch Hut (AMC)
The AMC constructed this stone hut in 1914. It is located at an elevation of 3288 ft., about 60 yd. south of the smaller lake, at the southern terminus of the Nineteen-Mile Brook Trail and the northern terminus of the Wildcat River Trail. The hut, with two bunkhouses, accommodates forty guests. It is open from early-June to early-September, and September through May on a caretaker basis.

For current information and schedule, contact AMC Reservations, Pinkham Notch Visitor Center, Box 298, Gorham NH 03581 (603-466-2727).

Restricted Use Areas

The WMNF has established a number of Restricted Use Areas (RUAs) where camping and wood or charcoal fires are prohibited from May 1 to November 1. The specific areas are under continual review, and areas are added to or subtracted from the list to provide the greatest protection to areas subject to damage by excessive camping, while imposing the lowest level of restrictions possible. A general list of RUAs follows, but you should obtain a map of current RUAs from the WMNF.

(1) Camping is not permitted above treeline (where trees are less than 8 ft. tall) except in winter, and even then it is allowed only on sites that are covered with at least two feet of snow and not located on frozen bodies of water. The point where the restricted area begins is marked on most trails with small signs, but the absence of such signs should not be construed as proof of the legality of a site. The area around the summit of Carter Dome is under this restriction.

(2) No camping is permitted within 1/4 mi. of most facilities such as huts, cabins, shelters, or tentsites, except at the facility itself. In this section, only Carter Notch Hut and Imp Campsite, plus the area around Zeta Pass, have this restriction. Tent camping is permitted at other shelters and cabins.

(3) No camping is permitted within 200 ft. of certain trails. In 1991, these included the Lost Pond Trail.

Established Trailside Campsites

Imp Campsite (AMC) is located on a spur path from the Carter-Moriah Trail between Moriah and North Carter. There is a shelter and tentsites. In summer there is a caretaker, and a fee is charged. Water is available in a nearby brook.

Rattle River Shelter (WMNF) is located on the Rattle River Trail 1.7 mi. from US 2.

Spruce Brook Shelter (WMNF) is located on the Wild River Trail about 3.2 mi. from Wild River Campground.

Perkins Notch Shelter (WMNF) is located on the southeast side of Wild River, just south of the No-Ketchum Pond, with bunk space for six.

Blue Brook Shelter (WMNF) is located on the Black Angel Trail (and a branch trail connecting to the Basin Trail) 0.3 mi. west of Rim Junction.

Baldface Shelter (WMNF) is located on the Baldface Circle Trail, just below the ledges on South Baldface. The water source near the shelter is not reliable.

Province Pond Shelter (WMNF) is located on the Province Brook Trail at Province Pond.

Mountain Pond Shelter (WMNF) is located on the Mountain Pond Loop Trail at Mountain Pond.

Doublehead Cabin (WMNF) is located at the summit of North Doublehead, with bunks for eight. There is no water nearby.

Black Mountain Cabin (WMNF) is located on the Black Mountain Ski Trail. It has bunks for eight guests. There is no water near the cabin or on the trail.

THE TRAILS
Wildcat Ridge Trail (AMC)

This trail runs from the Glen Ellis Falls parking lot on NH 16, over the numerous summits of Wildcat Mtn., to the Nineteen-Mile Brook Trail 0.3 mi. north of Carter Notch Hut. It is more commonly entered by the Lost Pond Trail from Pinkham Notch Visitor Center, which avoids the often difficult crossing of the Ellis River;

from the Lost Pond Trail to Carter Notch it is a part of the Appalachian Trail. The sections from the Lost Pond Trail to E Peak and from A Peak to Carter Notch are very steep and rough, and there are several ups and downs along the trail that make it somewhat more difficult than you might infer from a casual glance at the map or the distance summary. Hikers with heavy packs should allow substantial extra time. *Caution:* The section between NH 16 and E Peak may be dangerous when wet or icy.

The trail starts on the east side of NH 16 opposite the parking area for Glen Ellis Falls, and leads east across the stream (may be very difficult) to a target. At 0.1 mi. the Lost Pond Trail enters on the left, and the trail shortly begins the very steep climb up the end of the ridge (use care on all ledge areas), crossing two open ledges, both with fine views of Mt. Washington across Pinkham Notch. At 0.9 mi. it passes a level, open ledge with fine views south, dips slightly, then resumes the climb. At 1.2 mi. a side path (sign) leads left to a spring, and at 1.5 mi. the main trail climbs to the top of a steep ledge with a superb view of the southeast face of Mt. Washington. The trail continues to climb over several knobs and passes 3 yd. left of the summit of E Peak at 1.9 mi., then descends to the summit station of the Wildcat Ski Area in the col at 2.1 mi. From here the easiest ski trails (those farthest to the north) descend to the base lodge in 2.6 mi.

The trail climbs to the summit of D Peak, where there is an observation tower; an easier trail maintained by the ski area parallels this segment to the west. The Wildcat Ridge Trail next descends into Wildcat Col, the deepest col on the main ridge, at 2.5 mi. It passes over a small hogback and through a second sag, then begins the climb to C Peak over several "steps"—fairly steep climbs interspersed with level sections. There is a good outlook east from C Peak, at 3.3 mi., followed by a significant descent into a col and a climb to B Peak, then a shallower col and an easy climb to A Peak at 4.2 mi. As the trail turns left near this summit there is a spur path that leads right 20 yd. to a spectacular view into Carter Notch. The trail now descends rather steeply to the Nineteen-Mile Brook Trail at the height-of-land in Carter Notch. For Carter Notch Hut, turn right (south).

Wildcat Ridge Trail (map 7:G9–F10)

Distances from NH 16

to summit of E Peak: 1.9 mi., 2 hr. 15 min.
to Wildcat Col: 2.5 mi., 2 hr. 45 min.
to summit of C Peak: 3.3 mi., 3 hr. 30 min.
to summit of A Peak: 4.2 mi., 4 hr. 35 min.
to Nineteen-Mile Brook Trail: 4.9 mi. (7.9 km.), 5 hr.

Lost Pond Trail (AMC)

This trail runs from Pinkham Notch Visitor Center to the lower end of the Wildcat Ridge Trail, and is part of the Appalachian Trail. It avoids the difficult and some-times dangerous crossing of the Ellis River at the begin-ning of the Wildcat Ridge Trail. It leaves NH 16 oppo-site Pinkham Notch Visitor Center, crosses the Ellis River, and turns south at the end of the bridge, where the Square Ledge Trail leaves on the left. The Lost Pond Trail follows the Ellis River, which is soon joined by the larger Cutler River. The trail follows the east bank, then leaves it and climbs moderately to Lost Pond at 0.5 mi. It follows the east shore with good views, descends slightly, and joins the Wildcat Ridge Trail.

Lost Pond Trail (map 7:F9–G9)

Distance from NH 16

to Wildcat Ridge Trail: 0.9 mi. (1.5 km.), 30 min.

Square Ledge Trail (AMC)

This trail (with blue blazes) diverges left where the Lost Pond Trail turns south 20 yd. beyond the east end of the bridge across Ellis River. It climbs moderately, and after 80 yd. a spur path leads left 50 yd. to a ledge which, though overgrown, offers a fine view of Pinkham Notch Visitor Center. The trail bears right, swinging to the east, and crosses the Square Ledge Loop Ski Trail, then rises moderately, passing Hangover Rock. It then ascends to the base of Square Ledge, swings around to the east side, and climbs steeply via a V-slot 50 yd. to an outlook that has excellent views of Pinkham Notch and Mt. Washington.

Square Ledge Trail (map 7:F9–F10)
Distance from Lost Pond Trail
   to Square Ledge: 0.5 mi. (0.8 km.), 30 min.

Thompson Falls Trail (WMNF)

This trail runs from the Wildcat Ski Area to Thompson Falls, a series of high falls on a brook flowing from Wildcat Mtn. Except in wet seasons, the brook is apt to be rather low, but the falls are well worth visiting for the excellent views of Mt. Washington and its ravines from the large sloping ledges over which the brook flows.

From the Wildcat Ski Area parking area, cross the bridge to the east side, turn left and follow the Nature Trail north; continue ahead where a branch leaves left at 0.1 mi. and also where a loop leaves right and returns. Leaving the Nature Trail, the trail to the falls crosses a small stream and a maintenance road. It then leads up the south side of the brook to the foot of the first fall at 0.6 mi., crosses to the north side above the fall, bears right, and continues up the brook for another 0.1 mi.

Thompson Falls Trail (map 7:F10)
Distance from Wildcat Ski Area
   to end of trail: 0.7 mi. (1.1 km.), 30 min.

Carter-Moriah Trail (AMC)

This trail runs 13.8 mi. from Gorham to Carter Notch, following the crest of the Carter Range. To reach the trailhead at Gorham, follow US 2 east from Gorham about 0.5 mi.; then take a sharp right on Bangor Rd. just past the bridge and railroad track crossing, and follow this paved road about 0.5 mi. to the turnaround at its end. (On foot from Gorham, follow the road that leaves the east side of NH 16 just south of the railroad tracks. Bear right in 0.1 mi. on Mill Street, and in 0.1 mi. more a path left leads across the Peabody River on a footbridge. Turn right here and follow the road to its end where the trail enters the woods left.) From the Kenduskeag Trail near the summit of Mt. Moriah to Carter Notch, this trail is part of the Appalachian Trail. Water is very scarce on the trail.

The following description of the path is in the southbound direction (from Gorham to Carter Notch). See below for a description of the path in the reverse direction.

Part I. Gorham to Mt. Moriah

The trail follows a logging road up a steep bank, then climbs moderately through second-growth woods past a clear-cut. It bears right, then left along the edge of another clear-cut, and ascends through open hardwoods above the more recently logged area. At 2.0 mi. a ledge to the right affords good views, and the trail soon passes to the right of the insignificant summit of Mt. Surprise and its tiny box canyon. It soon becomes steeper and climbs over ledges that have excellent views. The trail stays near the ridge top, but winds from side to side, occasionally dipping below the crest. At 4.2 mi. there is a glimpse of Moriah's summit ahead, and at 4.5 mi. a spur path leads right 50 yd. to the ledgy summit of Mt. Moriah, which affords excellent views.

Part II. Mt. Moriah to North Carter

From the junction with the Mt. Moriah summit spur path, two routes descend the ledges of the Moriah summit block. The right-hand one is probably easier, but both are rock scrambles, and are dangerous when icy (in which case it may be better to bushwhack through the woods). By either route, it is less than 100 yd. to the junction where the Kenduskeag Trail turns left, then right, toward Shelburne Moriah Mtn. Here the Carter-Moriah Trail turns right (southwest). From this junction south it is part of the Appalachian Trail and has white blazes. It follows the ridgecrest south through woods and over an open knob, then descends moderately to excellent outlooks from the south cliffs, and reaches the col at 5.9 mi. Here the Moriah Brook Trail enters left and the Carter-Moriah Trail turns right and follows a boardwalk. In 40 yd. the Stony Brook Trail enters straight ahead, and the Carter-Moriah Trail turns left. It continues with several minor ups and downs and crosses some ledges. At 6.6 mi. a spur trail descends right 0.2 mi. to Imp Campsite, which has a shelter, tent platforms, and water. The main trail crosses a small brook and passes through a wet area, ascending on the plateau south of Imp Mtn., and at 7.7 mi. begins a rather steep and rough climb to North Carter Mtn., which is reached at 8.2 mi.

Part III. North Carter to Zeta Pass

The path continues south, passes a fine outlook, and winds along the crest of the ridge. At 8.5 mi. the North Carter Trail enters right, and the trail continues over numerous ledgy humps and boggy depressions. The best views in this area are from the ledgy hump called Mt. Lethe, a few steps to the left of the trail. A good outlook to the Presidentials is passed 70 yd. before the trail reaches the wooded summit of Middle Carter Mtn. (sign) at 9.1 mi. The trail then descends easily, passes an open area with a view west, ascends a short, steep ledge, and descends to the col between Middle and South Carter at 10.0 mi. It then ascends to a point 10 yd. left (east) of the summit of South Carter (sign) at 10.4 mi., and descends gradually, with occasional steeper sections, to Zeta Pass, where it makes a short ascent to the junction right with the Carter Dome Trail at 11.2 mi. There may occasionally be water on a side path from the Carter Dome Trail 80 yd. below this junction.

Part IV. Zeta Pass to Carter Notch

The two trails climb easily to the south for 0.2 mi., then the Carter Dome Trail continues ahead, and the Carter-Moriah Trail turns left and climbs rather steeply up to the summit of Mt. Hight at 11.8 mi. At this bare summit, which commands the best views in the range, the trail makes a very sharp right turn; great care must be exercised to stay on the trail if visibility is poor, particularly northbound, since a beaten path continues north from the summit. (Compass bearings from the summit are: southbound, 240° magnetic; northbound, 290° magnetic.) The trail passes through a shallow sag and the Carter Dome Trail re-enters right at 12.2 mi. In another 25 yd. the Black Angel Trail enters left, and the Carter-Moriah Trail climbs steadily to the summit of Carter Dome at 12.6 mi., where the Rainbow Trail enters left. The trail then descends moderately, passing a side path at 13.1 mi. that leads right 60 yd. to a fine spring. At 13.5 mi. a side path leads 30 yd. left to an excellent outlook over Carter Notch. Soon the trail begins to descend very steeply to Carter Notch, ending on the Nineteen-Mile Brook Trail at the shore of the larger Carter Lake. Carter Notch Hut is 0.1 mi. left.

Carter-Moriah Trail (map 7:E10–F10)

Distances from Bangor Road

to Mt. Moriah summit: 4.5 mi., 3 hr. 50 min.

to Moriah Brook and Stony Brook trails: 5.9 mi., 4 hr. 35 min.

to Imp Shelter spur trail: 6.6 mi., 5 hr. 5 min.

Carter-Moriah Trail (AMC) [in reverse]
Part I. Carter Notch to Zeta Pass

The trail begins on the Nineteen-Mile Brook Trail at the shore of the larger Carter Lake, 0.1 mi. north of Carter Notch Hut. It climbs very steeply at first, then moderates, and at 0.3 mi. a side path leads 30 yd. right to an excellent outlook over Carter Notch. The trail continues to climb at a moderate grade, passing a side path at 0.7 mi. that leads left 60 yd. to a fine spring, and at 1.2 mi. it reaches the summit of Carter Dome, where the Rainbow Trail enters right. The Carter-Moriah Trail descends steadily, and at 1.6 mi. the Black Angel Trail enters on the right. In another 25 yd., as the Carter Dome Trail continues straight ahead, the Carter-Moriah Trail turns right, passes through a shallow sag, and ascends moderately to the summit of Mt. Hight at 2.0 mi. At this bare summit, which commands excellent views, the trail makes a very sharp left turn; great care must be exercised to stay on the trail if visibility is poor, particularly northbound, since a beaten path continues north from the summit. (Compass bearings from the summit are: northbound, 290° magnetic; southbound, 240° magnetic.) The trail descends rather steeply and rejoins the Carter Dome Trail at 2.4 mi., and the two trails continue to Zeta Pass at 2.6 mi., where the Carter Dome Trail turns left and descends toward NH 16. There may occasionally be water on a side path from the Carter Dome Trail 80 yd. below this junction.

Part II. Zeta Pass to North Carter

From the junction with the Carter Dome Trail in Zeta Pass, the trail descends slightly to the actual low point of the pass, then ascends gradually, with occasional steeper sections, to a point 10 yd. right (east) of the summit of South Carter (sign) at 3.4 mi. It descends to the col between Middle and South Carter at 3.8 mi., then ascends easily, descending a short, steep ledge and passing an open area with a view west, and reaches the wooded summit of Middle Carter Mtn. (sign) at 4.7 mi. There is a good outlook to the Presidentials 70 yd. farther along the trail. The trail now descends over numerous ledgy humps and boggy depressions. The best views in this area are from the ledgy hump called Mt. Lethe, a few steps to the right of the trail. At 5.3 mi. the North Carter Trail enters on the left, and the Carter-Moriah Trail winds along the crest of the ridge past a fine outlook to the summit of North Carter at 5.6 mi.

Part III. North Carter to Mt. Moriah

The Carter-Moriah Trail makes a rather steep and rough descent from North Carter, and at 6.1 mi. the grade becomes easy to moderate as the trail descends on the plateau south of Imp Mtn., passing through a wet area and crossing a small brook. At 7.2 mi. a spur trail descends left 0.2 mi. to Imp Campsite, which has a shelter, tent platforms, and water. The main trail crosses some ledges and continues with several minor ups and downs to the col south of Mt. Moriah at 7.9 mi. Here the Stony Brook Trail enters left, and the Carter-Moriah Trail turns sharp right on a boardwalk, and in 40 yd. the Moriah Brook Trail enters on the right. Here the Carter-Moriah Trail turns left and starts up the ledgy ridge of Mt. Mori-

ah, soon reaching excellent outlooks from the south cliffs.
It continues to climb moderately up ledges to a shoulder,
then follows the ridgecrest north through woods and over
an open knob to a junction at 9.3 mi., where the
Kenduskeag Trail (continuing the Appalachian Trail
north) goes straight and then turns right toward Shelburne
Moriah Mtn. At this junction the Carter-Moriah Trail
turns left, and two routes ascend the ledges of the Moriah
summit block. The left-hand one is probably easier, but
both are rock scrambles, and are dangerous when icy (in
which case it may be better to bushwhack through the
woods). By either route, it is less than 100 yd. to the junction with the spur path that leads left 50 yd. to the ledgy
summit of Mt. Moriah, which affords excellent views.

Part IV. Mt. Moriah to Gorham

The trail descends moderately, staying near the ridge top
but winding from side to side, occasionally dipping
below the crest. It then becomes steeper and climbs
down over ledges that have excellent views. After a fairly level section below the ledges, it passes to the left of
the insignificant summit of Mt. Surprise and its tiny box
canyon at 11.8 mi. and descends again, passing the last
open ledge, which is just to the left of the trail. Soon it
enters second-growth woods in a fairly recently logged
area and descends on logging roads. It follows the right
edge of a clear-cut and then bears right, and continues
on logging roads until it finally descends a steep bank to
the end of Bangor Rd.

Carter-Moriah Trail (map 7:E10–F10)

Distances from Nineteen-Mile Brook Trail
    to Carter Dome summit: 1.2 mi., 1 hr. 25 min.
    to Black Angel Trail: 1.6 mi., 1 hr. 35 min.
    to Mt. Hight summit: 2.0 mi., 1 hr. 50 min.
    to Zeta Pass: 2.6 mi., 2 hr. 10 min.
    to South Carter summit: 3.4 mi., 2 hr. 50 min.

to Middle Carter summit: 4.7 mi., 3 hr. 40 min.

to North Carter Trail: 5.3 mi., 4 hr. 5 min.

to Imp Shelter spur trail: 7.2 mi., 5 hr. 5 min.

to Moriah Brook and Stony Brook trails: 7.9 mi., 5 hr. 25 min.

to Mt. Moriah summit: 9.3 mi., 6 hr. 40 min.

to Bangor Rd.: 13.8 mi. (22.2 km.), 8 hr. 55 min.

Nineteen-Mile Brook Trail (WMNF)

This trail runs from NH 16 about 1 mi. north of the Mt. Washington Auto Rd. to Carter Notch Hut, and is the easiest route to the hut. *Caution:* Sections of the trail close to the brook bank sometimes become dangerously icy in the cold seasons.

Leaving NH 16, the trail follows the northeast bank of Nineteen-Mile Brook on the remains of an old road, and the Nineteen-Mile Brook Link Trail (primarily a ski trail for winter access from the Great Gulf parking area) enters on the left. At 1.2 mi. the main trail passes a dam in the brook, and at 1.9 mi. the Carter Dome Trail diverges left for Zeta Pass. Here the Nineteen-Mile Brook Trail crosses a tributary on a footbridge, and at 2.2 mi. crosses another brook at a small cascade, also on a footbridge. At 3.1 mi. the trail crosses a small brook and begins to ascend more steeply to the height-of-land at 3.6 mi., where the Wildcat Ridge Trail diverges right (west), and a side path leads left to a view of the Rampart. The Nineteen-Mile Brook Trail drops steeply to the larger Carter Lake, passes the Carter-Moriah Trail left at 3.8 mi., crosses between the lakes, and reaches Carter Notch Hut and the junction with the Wildcat River Trail.

Nineteen-Mile Brook Trail (map 7:F10)

Distances from NH 16

to Carter Dome Trail: 1.9 mi., 1 hr. 25 min.

to Wildcat Ridge Trail: 3.6 mi., 2 hr. 45 min.

to Carter Notch Hut: 3.8 mi. (6.2 km.), 2 hr. 55 min.

Carter Dome Trail (WMNF)

This trail runs from the Nineteen-Mile Brook Trail 1.9 mi. from NH 16 to Zeta Pass and the summit of Carter Dome, following the route of an old road that served the long-dismantled fire tower that once stood on Carter Dome. Grades are steady and moderate all the way.

Leaving the Nineteen-Mile Brook Trail, the Carter Dome Trail follows a tributary brook, crossing it at 0.5 mi. and recrossing at 0.8 mi. At the latter crossing it swings left, then in 50 yd. turns sharp right and ascends by a series of seven switchbacks, passing a good spring left at 1.1 mi., and passing questionable water right (sign) 80 yd. below the junction with the Carter-Moriah Trail at Zeta Pass at 1.9 mi. The Carter Dome Trail coincides with the Carter-Moriah Trail to the right (south), then at 2.1 mi. the Carter–Moriah Trail turns left to Mt. Hight—good views, but steep and exposed to weather— while the sheltered Carter Dome Trail continues its steady ascent. At 2.7 mi. the Carter-Moriah Trail re-enters from the left, the Black Angel Trail enters from the left in 25 yd. more, and the Carter Dome and Carter-Moriah trails coincide to the junction with the Rainbow Trail at the summit of Carter Dome.

Carter Dome Trail (map 7:F10)

Distances from Nineteen-Mile Brook Trail

to Zeta Pass: 1.9 mi., 1 hr. 45 min.

to Carter Dome summit: 3.1 mi. (5.0 km.), 2 hr. 50 min.

Imp Trail (WMNF)

The Imp Trail makes a loop over the cliff that bears the Imp Profile, providing fine views. The ends of the loop are about 0.3 mi. apart on NH 16, with the north end about 2.6 mi. north of the Mt. Washington Auto Rd. and 5.4 mi. south of Gorham.

The north branch of the trail heads east up the south side of the Imp Brook Valley, through a pleasant stand of hemlocks, then crosses the brook at 0.8 mi. It angles north up to a ridge, and follows its crest, nearly level for some distance. The trail angles more steeply up the north side of the ridge and continues nearly to the bottom of a ravine northeast of the cliff, then turns right and circles steeply to the viewpoint at 2.2 mi.

From the cliff, the trail skirts the edge of the Imp Brook ravine and crosses a large brook in about 0.3 mi. Becoming somewhat rough, it continues generally south to the junction with the North Carter Trail left at 3.1 mi., then passes the site of an old logging camp. Here the Imp Trail turns right and descends a logging road generally southwest; then, just before reaching Cowboy Brook, turns northwest. After crossing another brook, in about 0.8 mi., it follows an old logging road north down to cross a small brook; it then immediately crosses a larger brook, turns sharp left, runs about level for 75 yd., and ends at NH 16.

Imp Trail (map 7:F10)
Distances from northern terminus on NH 16
 to viewpoint: 2.2 mi., 1 hr. 55 min.
 to North Carter Trail: 3.1 mi., 2 hr. 35 min.
 to southern terminus on NH 16: 6.3 mi. (10.1 km.), 4 hr. 15 min.

North Carter Trail (WMNF)

This trail leaves the south branch of Imp Trail 2.9 mi. from NH 16, just above an old logging camp site. It follows an old logging road, and at 0.3 mi. turns right on another old road. At 0.5 mi. it leaves the road sharp left and climbs more steeply to the Carter-Moriah Trail 0.3 mi. south of the summit of North Carter.

North Carter Trail (map 7:F10)
Distance from Imp Trail
 to Carter-Moriah Trail: 1.2 mi. (1.9 km.), 1 hr. 15 min.

Stony Brook Trail (WMNF)

This trail begins at a new parking area just off NH 16 on a gravel road just south of the bridge over the Peabody River, about 2 mi. south of Gorham. It ends in the col between North Carter and Moriah and provides the best access to the beautiful south ledges of Mt. Moriah. The lower part of the trail has been relocated onto WMNF land to avoid an area of private home construction on the former route.

From NH 16 the trail crosses Stony Brook on a footbridge and follows the brook upstream for 0.8 mi., then recrosses the brook and rejoins the old route, a logging road that becomes less and less obvious. It ascends moderately, and at 2.3 mi. the trail crosses Stony Brook at a pleasant small cascade and pool and begins to climb more steeply. At 3.1 mi. it crosses a small brook on a mossy ledge and climbs steadily to the ridge and the Carter-Moriah Trail.

Stony Brook Trail (map 7:E10–F11)
Distance from NH 16
   to Carter-Moriah Trail: 3.6 mi. (5.8 km.), 2 hr. 55 min.

Kenduskeag Trail (WMNF)

This trail runs from the Carter-Moriah Trail near the summit of Mt. Moriah to the Shelburne Trail in the col between Shelburne Moriah Mtn. and Howe Peak, 4.5 mi. south of US 2. Its name is an Abenaki word meaning "a pleasant walk." The ledges of Shelburne Moriah afford excellent views. From Mt. Moriah to the Rattle River Trail it is part of the Appalachian Trail.

From the trail junction below the summit ledges of Mt. Moriah, the trail turns sharp right in 15 yd. and runs over a lesser summit, then descends steeply past an outlook, moderates, and continues the descent to the junction with the Rattle River Trail at 1.4 mi. The trail now climbs over a section of knobs and ledges, with fine views, to the

flat, ledgy summit of Shelburne Moriah Mtn. at 2.7 mi.
The upper part of this section of trail is very exposed to
weather—in fact, more so than any other part of the
Carter-Moriah Range. The trail descends steadily to a
sharp, narrow col at 3.3 mi., then climbs over two knolls
with views, and ends at the Shelburne Trail.

Kenduskeag Trail (map 7:E11–E12)

Distances from Carter-Moriah Trail

to Rattle River Trail: 1.4 mi., 45 min.

to Shelburne Moriah Mtn. summit: 2.7 mi., 1 hr. 35 min.

to Shelburne Trail: 4.1 mi. (6.5 km.), 2 hr. 25 min.

Rattle River Trail (WMNF)

This trail runs to the Kenduskeag Trail in the
Moriah–Shelburne Moriah col from US 2 near the east
end of the bridge over Rattle River, about 300 yd. east
of the North Rd. intersection and 3.5 mi. east of the
eastern junction of US 2 and NH 16 in Gorham. It is
part of the Appalachian Trail.

From US 2 the trail leads generally south, following
a logging road on the east side of the stream. A snowmobile trail enters right at 0.3 mi., the trails cross a tributary at 0.6 mi., and soon the snowmobile trail leaves
left. At 1.7 mi. the Rattle River Trail passes the WMNF
Rattle River Shelter (left), and soon crosses Rattle River
(may be difficult at high water), then crosses back over
its westerly branch. At 3.2 mi. it again crosses the river,
and starts to climb steadily. It passes a small cascade left
at 3.7 mi., and soon bears away from the brook and
climbs steeply to the ridge top, where it meets the
Kenduskeag Trail.

Rattle River Trail (map 7:E11)

Distances from US 2

to Rattle River Shelter: 1.7 mi., 1 hr. 5 min.

to Kenduskeag Trail: 4.3 mi. (6.9 km.), 3 hr. 25 min.

Mount Evans Trail (AMC)

This short path ascends little Mt. Evans, beginning on US 2 0.1 mi. west of the sign for Shadow Pool and 0.8 mi. west of the Rattle River Trail parking area. For a modest effort, its ledges afford fine views of Mt. Washington and the Northern Peaks, and good views up and down the Androscoggin River and across to the Mahoosuc Range. It begins on private property, on a road that is posted against vehicular entry.

Follow a dirt road marked by a trail sign. In 0.1 mi., beyond the power line clearing, there is a yarding area for lumbering operations; enter the woods at a sign and ascend an old logging road. In 100 yd. the road crosses a small brook, and the trail takes the left branch (sign) at a fork, following another old logging road. In another 100 yd. from the fork, the trail turns left (sign) and becomes a footpath, climbing to the crest of a narrow ridge in about 50 yd. and following the ridgecrest south, ascending by switchbacks when the ridgecrest broadens. As the trail approaches the summit, just after passing an overhanging rock outcrop, a faint unsigned path leads left to a narrow viewpoint to the Mahoosuc Range and the valley below. In a few more steps, the trail crosses a large ledge with views of the Presidentials, and the blazes end shortly beyond at a trail sign in a flat area. Here a beaten path leads left to a ledge with views of the Mahoosucs and a large boulder that is, perhaps, the actual summit.

Mount Evans Trail (map 7:E11)

Distance from US 2

   to Mt. Evans summit: 0.7 mi. (1.1 km.), 35 min.

Shelburne Trail (WMNF)

This trail begins on FR 95 1.0 mi. from US 2 near the Maine–New Hampshire border, passes through the col between Shelburne Moriah Mtn. and Howe Peak, and descends to Wild River Rd. For the north terminus, leave US 2 about 9 mi. east of Gorham, at the west end of an abandoned wayside area just west of the Maine–New Hampshire border; go about 0.1 mi. into this area, and take FR 95 (a good gravel road) right for 0.9 mi. to a gate. At the Wild River end the trail leaves Wild River Rd. (FR 12) 0.6 mi. north of Wild River Campground and fords the river, which can be difficult even at moderate water levels. For this reason the Wild River end of the trail is often approached via the Wild River Trail, the Moriah Brook Trail bridge, and the Highwater Trail.

The trail follows the continuation of FR 95 past the gate (follow with care in this area of active logging). At 2.1 mi., shortly after the first bridge, it turns left off the main road (sign) onto an older logging road and begins to climb. At 3.9 mi. the trail crosses a very small stream twice, and shortly reaches the height-of-land, where it meets the eastern terminus of the Kenduskeag Trail at 4.0 mi. (To reach Shelburne Moriah Mtn., follow this trail right.) The Shelburne Trail continues over the height of land and descends steadily, crossing a brook and entering an old logging road. It then turns sharp left at 6.3 mi. onto another logging road, which it follows east down the valley of Bull Brook, soon crossing a branch of the brook. At 7.0 mi. the Highwater Trail enters from the right (south) and leaves on the left (north) 10 yd. farther on. This junction may be poorly signed. To avoid the Wild River crossing, follow the Highwater Trail south to the Moriah Brook Trail bridge. The main trail continues straight across a dry channel and fords Wild River to Wild River Rd.

Shelburne Trail (map 7:E12–F12)
Distances from gate on FR 95

　　to Kenduskeag Trail: 4.0 mi., 3 hr.

　　to Wild River Rd.: 7.2 mi. (11.6 km.), 4 hr. 35 min.

Wild River Trail (WMNF)

This trail begins at the end of Wild River Rd. (FR 12) at Wild River Campground, runs along the Wild River Valley to Perkins Notch, and descends to the Wildcat River Trail between Carter Notch Rd. and Carter Notch. Wild River Rd. leaves ME 113 just south of the bridge over Evans Brook at Hastings and runs 5.7 mi. to the campground, where there is a fork. Follow the right branch to a parking area.

The trail follows an old logging railroad bed that continues Wild River Rd. generally southwest on the southeast bank of Wild River. At 0.3 mi. the Moriah Brook Trail leaves right to cross the river on a bridge, and at 1.0 mi. the trail narrows. At 2.6 mi. the Black Angel Trail enters left and coincides with the Wild River Trail as both turn west and cross to the northwest side of Wild River on Spider Bridge. Just across the bridge, the Highwater Trail from Hastings enters right and ends, and the Wild River and Black Angel trails turn left onto an old railroad grade. In 0.1 mi. the Black Angel Trail diverges right for Carter Dome. The Wild River Trail continues generally southwest, passes Spruce Brook Shelter (right), then crosses Spruce Brook at 3.5 mi. on a snowmobile bridge. At 4.4 mi. it crosses Red Brook (may be difficult at high water, but it is possible to continue on snowmobile trail and cross on bridge just upstream), then leaves the old railroad bed and bears right. At 4.8 mi. the Eagle Link leaves left for Eagle Crag, and at 5.7 mi. the trail crosses to the south bank of Wild River on a snowmobile bridge. At 6.3 mi. the East Branch Trail leaves left, and the Wild River Trail crosses the Wild River to the north bank, then recrosses for the last time at 6.7 mi.

Soon the trail skirts the south side of No-Ketchum Pond, passes the WMNF Perkins Notch Shelter at 7.0 mi., heads more west, and begins a gradual climb into Perkins

Notch. At 7.8 mi. the Rainbow Trail leaves right for
Carter Dome, and at 8.5 mi. the Bog Brook Trail leaves
left for Carter Notch Rd. From this junction the trail
descends gradually and ends at the Wildcat River Trail.

Wild River Trail (map 7:F12–G10)

Distances from Wild River Campground parking area

    to Moriah Brook Trail: 0.3 mi., 10 min.

    to Spider Bridge: 2.7 mi., 1 hr. 30 min.

    to Eagle Link: 4.8 mi., 3 hr. 5 min.

    to East Branch Trail: 6.3 mi., 3 hr. 50 min.

    to Perkins Notch Shelter: 7.0 mi., 4 hr. 10 min.

    to Rainbow Trail: 7.8 mi., 4 hr. 40 min

    to Bog Brook Trail: 8.5 mi., 5 hr.

    to Wildcat River Trail: 9.6 mi. (15.5 km.), 5 hr. 35
    min.

Hastings Trail (WMNF)

The Hasting Trail starts at a parking lot at the junction
of ME 113 and Wild River Rd. (FR 12) about 100 yd.
south of Evans Brook bridge, at the deserted logging
village of Hastings. It follows logging roads to its termi
nus on US 2, 60 yd. inside the east end of an abandoned
wayside area immediately west of the Maine–New
Hampshire border, about 9.2 mi. east of Gorham and 2.0
mi. west of Gilead ME.

From Wild River Rd. the trail crosses Wild River on
the 180-ft. suspension footbridge. On the west bank the
Highwater Trail leaves left, heading up the northwest
side of the river. The Hastings Trail enters the woods on
a logging road running generally north. After passing
the remains of an old telephone line, it follows an old,
narrow logging road, then at 2.0 mi. descends (right)
onto an old, broad logging road marked as a snowmobile trail, then turns right again at 2.3 mi. onto a private
dirt road that it follows to the old wayside area.

Hastings Trail (map 7:E13–E12)

Distance from Hastings

   to abandoned wayside area: 2.8 mi. (4.5 km.), 1 hr.
   25 min.

Highwater Trail (WMNF)

This trail runs along the northwest side of Wild River
from Hastings on ME 113 to the Wild River Trail at the
west end of Spider Bridge, providing a means of avoiding unbridged crossings of the Wild River, which are
frequently very difficult. Most of the way it follows old
logging roads with easy grades, close to the river, but
often it is not blazed or signed clearly at intersections.

   It leaves the Hastings Trail left (south) at the west
end of the suspension bridge, across from the parking lot
at Hastings. At 0.7 mi. it bears right on an old logging
road that angles somewhat away from the river. The trail
crosses into NH and continues up the river, then enters
FR 52 and follows it for a while, passing a logging
bridge across Wild River at 2.3 mi. Heading generally
southwest, it crosses Martins Brook at 4.0 mi. At 5.3
mi., the Highwater Trail enters the Shelburne Trail,
turns right and follows it for 10 yd., then turns left off it
(no signs) and soon crosses Bull Brook on a bridge. At
6.7 mi. it reaches the footbridge where the Moriah
Brook Trail crosses Wild River, 0.3 mi. above Wild
River Campground. It joins the Moriah Brook Trail,
then the trails turn sharp right after 0.1 mi., and at 7.0
mi. the Highwater Trail turns left off the Moriah Brook
Trail and crosses Moriah Brook (difficult in high water).
The trail continues on top of a steep bank, then crosses
and follows logging roads, each for a short distance. It
crosses Cypress Brook at 9.5 mi. and soon ends near
Spider Bridge at its junction with the coinciding Black
Angel and Wild River trails.

Highwater Trail (map 7:E13–F11)

Distances from Hastings Trail

   to FR 52 bridge: 2.3 mi., 1 hr. 15 min.

   to Shelburne Trail: 5.3 mi., 2 hr. 40 min.

   to Moriah Brook Trail: 6.7 mi., 3 hr. 30 min.

   to Wild River Trail/Black Angel Trail: 9.6 mi. (15.4 km.), 5 hr. 5 min.

Burnt Mill Brook Trail (WMNF)

This trail ascends from Wild River Rd. (FR 12), 2.7 mi. south of ME 113, to the Royce Trail in the col between East Royce Mtn. and West Royce Mtn. From Wild River Rd. the trail ascends logging roads south, passing a cascade at 0.6 mi. At 1.4 mi. it begins to climb more steeply, crosses Burnt Mill Brook at 1.7 mi., and ascends to the col between the Royces, where it meets the Royce Trail.

Burnt Mill Brook Trail (map 7:F12)

Distance from Wild River Road

   to Royce Trail: 2.0 mi. (3.2 km.), 1 hr. 50 min.

Moriah Brook Trail (WMNF)

This trail ascends to the col between Mt. Moriah and North Carter from the Wild River Trail 0.3 mi. south of Wild River Campground. It is an attractive trail, passing Moriah Gorge, traversing fine birch woods that have grown up after fires, and providing good views up to the impressive south cliffs of Moriah.

The trail leaves right from the Wild River Trail and in 75 yd. crosses the Wild River on a footbridge, where the Highwater Trail joins right. The trail turns left and follows the river bank about 0.1 mi., then turns sharp right and generally follows the course of the former lumber railroad up Moriah Brook, and at 0.4 mi. the Highwater Trail leaves left. At 1.4 mi. the Moriah Brook Trail crosses Moriah Brook (may be difficult at high water); the gorge downstream from this crossing merits exploration. The trail follows the south bank of the brook, then recrosses at 2.8 mi., and in another 0.4 mi. passes some attractive cascades and pools, crosses a ledge, then crosses a branch of Moriah Brook just above the confluence with the main brook. The trail continues through birch woods and crosses the main brook four more times, the last crossing in a boulder area below a small cascade at 4.7 mi. The trail becomes rather wet, and winds through almost pure stands of white birch below the impressive south cliffs of Mt. Moriah, then climbs to the col and the Carter-Moriah Trail.

Moriah Brook Trail (map 7:F12–F11)
Distances from Wild River Trail
   to Carter-Moriah Trail: 5.5 mi. (8.8 km.), 3 hr. 45 min.

Black Angel Trail (WMNF)

This trail begins at Rim Junction—where the Basin and Basin Rim trails cross—and descends to cross the Wild River on Spider Bridge along with the Wild River Trail, then climbs to the Carter-Moriah Trail 0.4 mi. north of Carter Dome.

   Leaving Rim Junction, it descends gradually southwest 0.5 mi. to Blue Brook Shelter, where a branch trail runs right (north) for 0.3 mi. to connect with the Basin Trail 0.3 mi. west of Rim Junction. From Blue Brook Shelter the Black Angel Trail ascends moderately west and passes through a col, then descends to an old logging road and follows it generally west for 1.4 mi. down the Cedar Brook Valley, remaining on the north side of the stream and making several obvious shortcuts at curves. The trail then leaves the logging road, turns more north, and joins the Wild River Trail to cross Wild River on Spider Bridge at 2.8 mi. Just across the bridge the Highwater Trail leaves right for Hastings, and the Black Angel and Wild River trails continue ahead.

The Black Angel Trail diverges right in 0.1 mi., and rises slowly through open woods. About 1.5 mi. up from the Wild River the grade steepens; at 5.2 mi. the trail crosses a north branch of Spruce Brook, and about 0.5 mi. beyond enters virgin timber. The grade lessens as the trail angles up the east slope of Mt. Hight, passes lookout points on its south-southeast slope, swings southwest, and ends at the Carter-Moriah Trail.

Black Angel Trail (map 7:F12–F10)

Distances from Rim Junction

    to Blue Brook Shelter: 0.5 mi., 15 min.

    to Spider Bridge: 2.8 mi., 1 hr. 40 min.

    to Carter-Moriah Trail: 7.7 mi. (12.5 km.), 5 hr. 40 min.

Basin Trail (WMNF)

The Basin Trail runs from Wild River Campground to Basin Pond (0.7 mi. from NH 113, near Cold River Campground), crossing the ridge connecting Mt. Meader to West Royce somewhat north of its lowest point, giving easy access to the magnificent views along the brink of the cliffs.

Leaving the parking area at Wild River Campground, it follows an old lumber road. At 0.4 mi., where the road swings right, the trail continues straight ahead and soon approaches the southwest bank of Blue Brook, which it follows for about 0.8 mi. At 1.3 mi. it crosses the brook at the foot of a pretty cascade and then follows the northeast bank, passing opposite a very striking cliff to the south of the brook. The trail leaves Blue Brook, crosses another small brook, then climbs somewhat more steeply. At 2.0 mi. a side trail branches right 0.3 mi. to Blue Brook Shelter and the Black Angel Trail, and at 2.2 mi. the Basin Trail crosses the Basin Rim Trail and meets the Black Angel Trail at Rim Junction. Follow the

Basin Rim Trail 0.1 mi. north to reach a fine viewpoint at the top of the cliff that overhangs the Basin.

The trail now descends very steeply along the south side and foot of a great cliff, and crosses a wide, stony brook. At 3.0 mi. it passes the upper end of a loop path, slightly longer than the main trail, that leads right 0.1 mi. to Hermit Falls and then returns to the main trail 0.2 mi. below its point of departure. The Basin Trail descends to an old logging road and turns right on it, and runs across numerous small brooks, using segments of old roads, to the parking area.

Basin Trail (map 7:F12)

Distances from Wild River Campground

to Rim Junction: 2.2 mi., 1 hr. 30 min.

to Hermit Falls loop path, lower junction: 3.2 mi., 2 hr.

to Basin Pond parking area: 4.5 mi. (7.2 km.), 2 hr. 40 min.

Eagle Link (AMC)

This trail runs from the Wild River Trail 4.8 mi. southwest of Wild River Campground to the junction with the Baldface Circle and Meader Ridge trails 0.2 mi. south of Eagle Crag. It leaves the Wild River Trail and soon crosses Wild River (may be difficult at high water), then bears sharp right and ascends generally east at a moderate grade. It crosses a small brook at 1.2 mi., angles up the north slope of North Baldface, and ends at the junction of the Baldface Circle and Meader Ridge trails.

Eagle Link (map 7:F11–F12)

Distances from Wild River Trail

to Baldface Circle Trail/Meader Ridge Trail: 2.7 mi. (4.4 km.), 1 hr. 45 min.

Royce Trail (AMC)

The Royce Trail runs to the summit of West Royce Mtn. from the west side of ME 113, about 0.3 mi. north of the access road to the WMNF Cold River Campground.

Leaving ME 113, it follows a narrow road about 0.3 mi., then crosses the Cold River, and bears right off the road onto a blue-blazed footpath. The trail recrosses the river at 0.7 mi. and again at 1.4 mi., then, after crossing the south branch of Mad River, it rises more steeply and soon passes Mad River Falls, where a side path leads left 25 yd. to a viewpoint. The trail becomes rather rough, with large boulders, and rises steeply under the imposing ledges for which East Royce is famous. At 2.7 mi. the Laughing Lion Trail enters right, and at a height-of-land at 2.9 mi., after a very steep ascent, the Royce Connector Trail to East Royce branches right. The Royce Trail bears left at this junction and descends somewhat, then climbs to the height-of-land between the Royces at 3.6 mi., where the Burnt Mill Brook Trail to Wild River Rd. bears right, while the Royce Trail turns abruptly left (west) and ascends the steep wall of the pass. It then continues by easy grades over ledges and through stunted spruce to the summit of West Royce, where it meets the Basin Rim Trail.

Royce Trail (map 7:F12)
Distances from ME 113
- *to* Mad River Falls: 1.6 mi., 1 hr.
- *to* Laughing Lion Trail: 2.7 mi., 2 hr.
- *to* Royce Connector Trail: 2.9 mi., 2 hr. 25 min.
- *to* West Royce Mtn. summit: 4.3 mi. (7.0 km.), 3 hr. 20 min.

Royce Connector Trail (AMC)
This short trail connects Royce Trail and East Royce Trail, permitting the ascent of either Royce from either trail, and provides good views from ledges along the way.

Royce Connector Trail (map 7:F12)
Distance from Royce Trail
- *to* East Royce Trail: 0.2 mi. (0.3 km.), 5 min.

East Royce Trail (AMC)

This trail climbs rather steeply to East Royce Mtn. from the west side of ME 113 just north of the height-of-land. Leaving the highway, it immediately crosses Evans Brook and ascends steeply, crossing several other brooks in the first 0.5 mi. At the final brook crossing at 1.0 mi., the Royce Connector Trail to the Royce Trail for West Royce leaves on the left. The East Royce Trail emerges on ledges at about 1.1 mi., reaches a subsidiary summit with views to the south at 1.4 mi., and turns right and climbs to the true summit. Here a spur trail can be followed right (north) over several more ledges to a large open ledge with a beautiful outlook to the north and west.

East Royce Trail (map 7:F13–F12)
Distance from ME 113
> *to* East Royce Mtn. summit: 1.5 mi. (2.4 km.), 1 hr. 30 min.

Laughing Lion Trail (CTA)

This trail begins on the west side of ME 113, just north of a roadside picnic area and about 2.3 mi. north of the road to Cold River Campground, and ends on the Royce Trail. It descends to Cold River and ascends west to a ridgecrest, which it follows north, alternating moderate and steep sections and providing occasional good views down the valley, then swings west and levels off just before it ends at the Royce Trail.

Laughing Lion Trail (map 7:F12)
Distances from ME 113
> *to* Royce Trail: 1.1 mi. (1.8 km.), 1 hr.

Basin Rim Trail (AMC)

This trail follows the ridge that runs from Mt. Meader, starting from the east knob, at the junction with the Mount Meader and Meader Ridge trails, and ending at the summit of West Royce Mtn., where it meets the

Royce Trail. It has fine views, particularly at the top of the cliff that forms the wall of the Basin.

The trail leaves the east knob of Mt. Meader and descends north over the ledges. Just after crossing a small brook, it reaches a col, then ascends slightly along the east side of a prominent hump called Ragged Jacket. The trail soon descends steeply from ledge to ledge down the north slope to the lowest point of the ridge (1870 ft.), then rises gradually over ledges to Rim Junction at 1.4 mi., where the Basin Trail crosses and the Black Angel Trail also enters. At 1.5 mi. a short spur leads right to Basin Outlook, a magnificent viewpoint at the edge of the cliffs on the east. In the next 0.3 mi. there are more excellent views east over the great cliff of the Basin Rim. Passing west of the prominent southeast knee of West Royce, the trail climbs, with only short intervening descents. At 2.6 mi. it climbs a very steep pitch to an outlook to the Carter-Moriah Range, then passes a small brook (unreliable water source), and ends at the summit of West Royce Mtn.

Basin Rim Trail (map 7:F12)

Distances from Mount Meader Trail/Meader Ridge Trail

to Rim Junction: 1.4 mi., 45 min.

to West Royce Mtn. summit: 3.9 mi. (6.3 km.), 2 hr. 45 min.

Mount Meader Trail (AMC)

This trail runs from the west side of NH 113, about 0.5 mi. north of the entrance to the Baldface Circle Trail, to a junction with the Meader Ridge and Basin Rim trails on the ridgecrest at an easterly knob of Mt. Meader.

From NH 113 it follows a logging road (do not block entrance) that stays on the north side of Mill Brook, and at 1.0 mi. passes a side path left that runs 0.1 mi. to Brickett Falls. The trail turns left uphill off the logging road (sign), and at 2.1 mi. it begins a steep climb up the ridge heel, turning sharp left at the top of the heel at 2.5 mi. Coming out on open ledges with fine views at 2.9 mi., it soon reaches the east knob of Mt. Meader.

Mount Meader Trail (map 7:G12–F12)

Distance from NH 113

to Meader Ridge Trail: 3.0 mi. (4.8 km.), 2 hr. 25 min.

Meader Ridge Trail (AMC)

This trail runs along the ridgecrest from the junction with the Mount Meader and Basin Rim trails on the east knob of Mt. Meader to the junction with the Baldface Circle Trail and Eagle Link, 0.2 mi. south of Eagle Crag.

From the east knob of Mt. Meader, the trail descends slightly in a southwest direction and in 0.2 mi. reaches the true summit of Mt. Meader. Descending again, with a small intervening ascent, it passes several good viewpoints to the east. At 0.4 mi. a short side path (sign) leads west 100 yd. up to a large open ledge with fine views to the west. The Meader Ridge Trail passes the deepest col of the ridge at 0.6 mi., where it crosses an unreliable small brook; sometimes there is also water upstream a short distance in a swampy place called the Bear Traps. The trail then climbs to an intermediate peak at 1.2 mi. and descends to another col at 1.4 mi. Climbing again, it emerges from timberline at 1.9 mi., passes over the summit of Eagle Crag, and then descends slightly to meet the Baldface Circle Trail and Eagle Link.

Meader Ridge Trail (map 7:F12)

Distances from Mount Meader Trail/Basin Rim Trail

to Baldface Circle Trail/Eagle Link: 2.0 mi. (3.2 km.), 1 hr. 15 min.

Baldface Circle Trail (AMC)

This trail makes a loop over North and South Baldface from NH 113 at a new parking area, 0.1 mi. north of the driveway to the AMC Cold River Camp. It is one of the most attractive trips in the White Mountains, with about 4 mi. of open and semi-open ledge providing long stretches of unobstructed views and great exposure to storms. This strenuous trip should not be underestimated.

Leaving NH 113 about 60 yd. north of the parking area, the trail reaches Circle Junction at 0.7 mi., where a side path leads right (north) 0.1 mi. to Emerald Pool. From here, the trail is described in a clockwise direction—up South Baldface, over to North Baldface, and down from Eagle Crag—but the circuit in the reverse direction is equally fine.

From Circle Junction, the south branch follows an old road, then turns left (south), crosses a brook bed, and climbs past the junction with the Slippery Brook Trail on the left at 0.9 mi. to an old logging road that it follows for almost a mile. At 1.2 mi. a loop path 0.5 mi. long leads left to Chandler Gorge (a small flume with several pools and lesser cascades in a rocky bed), and rejoins the main trail 0.1 mi. above its departure point. The trail swings around the south side of Spruce Knoll and, at 2.5 mi., it leaves the old road in a rocky area and soon reaches Last Chance Spring (unreliable water source) and South Baldface Shelter. In a short distance the trail comes out on the ledges and climbs very steeply in the open on rocks that are dangerous if wet or icy. At 3.0 mi. the trail reaches the crest of a rounded ridge and swings left, ascending near the crest toward a knob, becoming much less steep. On that knob, at 3.2 mi., the Baldface Knob Trail enters on the left (south). The Baldface Circle Trail then ascends to the summit of South Baldface at 3.7 mi.

Bearing right at the summit of South Baldface, it follows the broad ridge, descending into the shelter of mature conifers at 4.0 mi., then coming out on a semi-open knob at 4.2 mi. From here to North Baldface the trail runs mostly in the open, though there are several small cols where some shelter could be obtained in a storm. At 4.9 mi. it mounts the last steep pitch to the summit of North Baldface, then descends steeply to the broad, lumpy, ledgy ridge that runs toward Eagle Crag. At 5.8 mi. the Bicknell Ridge Trail leaves right, providing a scenic alternative route to NH 113.

At 6.1 mi. the trail reaches a multiple junction where the Eagle Link leaves left (west) for the Wild River Valley, the Meader Ridge Trail continues straight ahead (north) for Eagle Crag and Mt. Meader, and the Baldface Circle Trail turns sharp right and descends steeply on ledges for 0.2 mi. At the base of the ledges the trail swings left and, after a gradual section, descends moderately. At 6.9 mi. it crosses a very small brook (unreliable water source) with a ledgy, mossy bed and becomes less steep; at 7.3 mi. it enters an old logging road and follows it to the right. At 7.7 mi. the Eagle Cascade Link, 0.7 mi. long, leaves on the right, crosses the brook (use caution) above Eagle Cascade in 0.4 mi., and climbs to the Bicknell Ridge Trail. At 8.4 mi. the Bicknell Ridge Trail enters right just after crossing a branch of Charles Brook on flat ledges. The Baldface Circle Trail now angles left away from the brook and then returns to it, and crosses it (may be difficult in high water) at 9.0 mi., just before reaching Circle Junction.

Baldface Circle Trail (map 7:G12)

Distances from NH 113

 to Circle Junction: 0.7 mi., 25 min.

 to Slippery Brook Trail junction: 0.9 mi., 30 min.

 to South Baldface Shelter: 2.5 mi., 2 hr.

 to Baldface Knob Trail: 3.2 mi., 2 hr. 50 min.

 to South Baldface summit: 3.7 mi., 3 hr. 20 min.

 to North Baldface summit: 4.9 mi., 4 hr.

 to Eagle Link/Meader Ridge Trail: 6.1 mi., 4 hr. 40 min.

 io Bicknell Ridge Trail, lower junction: 8.4 mi., 5 hr. 30 min.

to Circle Junction (loop): 9.1 mi., 6 hr. 10 min.
to NH 113: 9.8 mi. (15.8 km.), 6 hr. 30 min.

Bicknell Ridge Trail (CTA)

This trail begins on the north branch of the Baldface Circle Trail 1.4 mi. from NH 113 and ends on the same trail 0.9 mi. north of North Baldface. Diverging from the Baldface Circle Trail, it immediately crosses a branch of Charles Brook, and ascends gradually through second-growth hardwood. After about 1.0 mi., it turns more west, rises more rapidly along the south side of Bicknell Ridge, and, just before the first ledges, crosses a brook bed where there is usually water among the boulders. Soon the trail emerges on the open ledges, and the Eagle Cascade Link enters right from Eagle Cascade and the Baldface Circle Trail. Above this junction the trail mostly travels over broad, open ledges with excellent views, then reaches the ridge top, where it rejoins the Baldface Circle Trail.

Bicknell Ridge Trail (map 7:G12)

Distances from Baldface Circle Trail (lower junction)
  to Eagle Cascade Link: 1.4 mi., 1 hr. 20 min.
  to Baldface Circle Trail, upper junction: 2.5 mi. (4.0 km.), 2 hr. 30 min.

Baldface Knob Trail (WMNF)

This trail, in combination with the Slippery Brook Trail, provides an alternative route to South Baldface that avoids the steep ledges on the Baldface Circle Trail. It begins at the Slippery Brook Trail in the col between Eastman Mtn. and South Baldface, opposite the beginning of the Eastman Mountain Trail, then climbs to Baldface Knob and continues along the open ridge to the Baldface Circle Trail on the shoulder below the summit of South Baldface.

Baldface Knob Trail (map 7:G12)
Distance from Slippery Brook Trail
    to Baldface Circle Trail: 0.7 mi. (1.1 km.), 35 min.

Eastman Mountain Trail (CTA)
This trail ascends Eastman Mtn. from the Slippery
Brook Trail at the height-of-land in the col between
Eastman Mtn. and South Baldface, opposite the lower
terminus of the Baldface Knob Trail. The trail descends
slightly then rises steeply onto the north ridge, where
outlooks provide fine views of South Baldface and
Sable Mtn. It continues generally southeast to the summit, which has a rewarding view in all directions.

Eastman Mountain Trail (map 7:G12)
Distance from Slippery Brook Trail
    to Eastman Mtn. summit: 0.8 mi. (1.3 km.), 40 min.

Slippery Brook Trail (WMNF)
This trail runs from the south branch of the Baldface
Circle Trail 0.9 mi. from NH 113 through the col
between South Baldface and Eastman Mtn. to Slippery
Brook Rd. (FR 17, called Town Hall Rd. at its southern
end), 7.0 mi. from NH 16A.

Leaving the Baldface Circle Trail, it soon crosses a
branch of Chandler Brook, ascends generally southwest
through woods, crosses another branch brook, and
reaches the col between South Baldface and Eastman
Mtn. at 2.4 mi., where the Baldface Knob Trail leaves
right (north) for South Baldface and the Eastman Mountain Trail leaves left (south). The Slippery Brook Trail
soon descends to Slippery Brook, which it crosses six
times. Shortly after the last crossing, at a clearing, it
passes the junction left with the abandoned Bradley
Brook Trail. The trail stays on the east bank, crosses a
logging road, and ends at Slippery Brook Rd., 200 yd.
north of the gate. (In the reverse direction, it diverges
left from the road north of the gate.)

Slippery Brook Trail (map 7:G12–G11)

Distances from Baldface Circle Trail

   to Baldface Knob Trail/Eastman Mountain Trail: 2.4
       mi., 2 hr. 20 min.

   to last crossing of Slippery Brook: 4.0 mi., 3 hr. 10 min.

   to Slippery Brook Rd.: 6.4 mi. (10.3 km.), 4 hr. 20 min.

Mountain Pond Loop Trail (WMNF)

This trail begins on Slippery Brook Rd. (FR 17, called
Town Hall Rd. at its southern end), 6.3 mi. from NH
16A. East of Mountain Pond the former route of the trail
has been officially closed by the WMNF, and the cabin
formerly at the pond has been removed. At 0.3 mi. from
the road, there is a fork; bearing left, the trail reaches the
Mountain Pond Shelter at 1.0 mi., then continues around
the pond and returns to the fork, crossing the outlet
brook, which may be difficult in high water.

Mountain Pond Loop Trail (map 7:G11)

Distance from Slippery Brook Road

   of complete loop: 2.7 mi. (4.3 km.), 1 hr. 25 min.

East Branch Trail (WMNF)

This trail begins on Slippery Brook Rd. (FR 17, called
Town Hall Rd. at its southern end), 4.8 mi. from NH
16A and just south of the junction with East Branch Rd.
(FR 38). It follows the East Branch of the Saco River,
recrosses the road (which is passable for cars), then
crosses at height-of-land and ends on the Wild River
Trail at the foot of the hill east of Perkins Notch, 0.3 mi.
east of Perkins Notch Shelter. It is very muddy south of
the height-of-land, at times difficult to follow, and the
three crossings of the East Branch are hard at normal
water levels and would be hazardous at high water (but
can be avoided by starting at the upper road crossing).

   Leaving Slippery Brook Rd., the trail descends to
cross Slippery Brook, then enters and follows an old railroad bed on the east side of the East Branch. At 2.3 mi. it

crosses East Branch Rd., then crosses the East Branch three times (may be difficult); the last crossing is at a stretch of still water, and 0.1 mi. beyond East Branch Rd. enters from the left and ends. Here also a road leads left to connect with the Bald Land Trail (sign). The East Branch Trail then crosses Gulf Brook, leaves the railroad bed within 0.1 mi., and follows old logging roads. At 4.9 mi. the trail crosses Black Brook and shortly bears northwest away from the river, then climbs by easy grades to a divide between Black Mtn. and a prominent southwest spur of North Baldface at 7.2 mi. The logging road dwindles to a trail, passes through a patch of spruce, and descends to its junction with the Wild River Trail on the south bank of Wild River.

East Branch Trail (map 7:H11–G11)

Distances from Slippery Brook Road

    to crossing of East Branch Rd.: 2.3 mi., 1 hr. 20 min.

    to end of East Branch Rd.: 3.5 mi., 1 hr. 55 min.

    to height-of-land: 7.2 mi., 4 hr. 20 min.

    to Wild River Trail: 7.6 mi. (12.2 km.), 4 hr. 35 min.

Bald Land Trail (WMNF)

This trail follows an old roadway from Black Mtn. Rd. to the East Branch through the divide between Black Mtn. and North Doublehead. It is marked in parts as a cross-country ski trail and crosses several other ski trails, and is somewhat hard to follow because it is not well marked or signed as a hiking trail. The west trailhead is reached in 3.0 mi. from NH 16 in Jackson by following NH 16B to Dundee Rd., taking the latter past Black Mountain Ski Area, then bearing left uphill on Black Mountain Rd. to a small parking area on the right. The east trailhead is at the end of East Branch Rd. (FR 38), a branch of Slippery Brook Rd. (FR 17).

The trail passes a gate and follows the East Pasture (ski) Trail for 0.4 mi., then diverges right (sign), crosses

Great Brook and follows an old road with a stone wall on the right. At 0.8 mi. turn right on the main ski trail, which leads into an overgrown pasture with fine views of Doublehead Mtn., then bear left away from the pasture and soon rejoin the old ski trail that continued straight at the 0.8-mi. junction. At 1.2 mi. bear left onto an old logging road (marked by orange tape) and ascend through an overgrown pasture. Bear left at an old ski trail (arrow) just before crossing the Bald Land Ski Trail at a double blue diamond marker. (If you miss the unsigned turn at 1.2 mi., you can continue up the Bald Land Ski Trail to the Scenic Vista Spur, then turn sharp left and follow the main ski trail just past the height-of-land to its intersection with the hiking trail at the double blue diamonds; turn right there.) Descend along the hiking trail, crossing a logging road (Woodland Ski Trail) at 2.0 mi., and continue to the East Branch Rd.

Bald Land Trail (map 7:G11)
Distance from Black Mountain Rd.
> *to* East Branch Rd.: 2.1 mi. (3.4 km.), 1 hr. 15 min.

Rainbow Trail (WMNF)

This trail climbs to the summit of Carter Dome from the Wild River Trail in Perkins Notch about 0.8 mi. west of the Perkins Notch Shelter near No-Ketchum Pond. After leaving the Wild River Trail, it passes through a sag, then ascends steadily on the southeast slope of Carter Dome. At 1.5 mi. it passes just east of the summit of a southerly knob and runs in the open with fine views, returns into the woods at a sag, then climbs moderately to the Carter-Moriah Trail at the summit of Carter Dome.

Rainbow Trail (map 7:G11--F10)
Distances from Wild River Trail
> *to* south knob: 1.5 mi., 1 hr. 40 min.
> *to* Carter Dome summit: 2.5 mi. (4.0 km.), 2 hr. 25 min.

Bog Brook Trail (WMNF)

This trail begins at a small parking area on Carter Notch Rd., about 3.0 mi. from NH 16B just west of its sharp turn at the crossing of Wildcat Brook. It ends on the Wild River Trail 1.5 mi. west of Perkins Notch Shelter. Some brook crossings may be difficult at high water.

The trail follows a dirt road (sign) past a camp and bears right off the road into the woods (marked by blue diamonds) at a turnaround at the WMNF boundary. Running nearly level, it crosses Wildcat Brook, another brook, and then the Wildcat River, a tributary of Wildcat Brook. In 60 yd. the Wildcat River Trail continues straight ahead, while the Bog Brook Trail diverges right. The trail ascends moderately, crossing a gravel logging road (FR 233) that leads (left) back to Carter Notch Rd. The trail then follows Bog Brook through a wet area, crossing and recrossing the brook, to the Wild River Trail.

Bog Brook Trail (map 7:G10)

Distances from Carter Notch Rd.

   to Wildcat River Trail: 0.7 mi., 25 min.
   to Wild River Trail: 2.8 mi. (4.5 km.), 1 hr. 45 min.

Wildcat River Trail (AMC)

This trail runs to Carter Notch Hut from the Bog Brook Trail just east of the Wildcat River crossing 0.7 mi. from Carter Notch Rd. Brook crossings may be difficult at high water.

From the Bog Brook Trail junction, the trail follows the east bank of Wildcat River, crossing a gravel logging road (FR 233) that leads back (left) to Carter Notch Rd. At 1.0 mi. the trail crosses Bog Brook, and the Wild River Trail enters right at 1.9 mi. Soon the trail crosses Wildcat River, turns sharp right in 100 yd., and continues to ascend at a moderate grade. It climbs toward Carter Notch, passes a side trail right that leads to the Rampart, and in 100 yd. reaches Carter Notch Hut and the junction with the Nineteen-Mile Brook Trail.

Wildcat River Trail (map 7:G10–F10)

Distances from Bog Brook Trail

to Bog Brook crossing: 1.0 mi., 40 min.

to Wild River Trail: 1.9 mi., 1 hr. 15 min.

to Carter Notch Hut: 3.6 mi. (5.8 km.), 2 hr. 40 min.

Hutmen's Trail (HA)

This trail crosses the flat ridge between Spruce Mtn. on the south and Wildcat Mtn. on the north, running from NH 16 to NH 16B. This trail's future is uncertain; it will probably be relocated, and at present it can be followed with reasonable ease from the NH 16 terminus—4.2 mi. north of Jackson and 5.6 mi. south of Pinkham Notch Visitor Center—only as far as Marsh Brook, just east of the ridgecrest. The old description of the trail to this point is reprinted here. It may be possible for experienced route-finders to follow the entire trail to NH 16B, but inexperienced hikers should not attempt it at all. Hikers wishing to use this trail should inquire at Pinkham Notch Visitor Center for recent information.

The trail crosses a small field, begins to ascend the moderately steep west slope of Spruce Mtn., and shortly approaches a small brook (right). After about 0.4 mi. it begins to level, bears away (left) from the brook, turns more north, and shortly crosses another brook on a bridge. The trail then goes through an old spruce and softwood area, nearly level, bears right (east) as it reaches the height-of-land, and passes along the south edge of an old pasture (left). It continues on a level grade for another 0.3 mi. through the woods, then begins to descend at a moderate grade to Marsh Brook. From there it continues down to NH 16B.

Hutmen's Trail (map 7:G10)

Distances from NH 16

to Marsh Brook: 1.8 mi., 1 hr. 15 min.

to NH 16B (via former route): 2.3 mi. (3.5 km.), 1 hr. 30 min.

Hall's Ledge Trail (HA)

This trail starts on the east side of NH 16, just south of the bridge over the Ellis River, 5.2 mi. north of the covered bridge in Jackson. Use the Rocky Branch Trail parking lot, 0.1 mi. north of the NH 16 bridge. The trail ends on the Carter Notch Rd. 0.1 mi. north of the Bog Brook Trail parking area.

From NH 16, follow the river a short distance, then veer right uphill toward an overgrown field. Turn right, following cairns, then turn left uphill into woods and ascend to a high bank overlooking a brook. To this point the trail is marked with yellow blazes. It bears away from the brook and in about 0.1 mi. begins a short, steep ascent. From the top of this rise it runs generally north and northeast through fine woods with intervals of level stretches and slight rises, then ascends moderately through a section of spruce a short distance below the ledge. The ledge, on the left, is small and overgrown; at 1.7 mi., at the end of a straight, almost level stretch of about 100 yd., Mt. Washington, Boott Spur, and the Gulf of Slides may be seen through the trees. From here the trail coincides with the Hall's Ledge Ski Trail and the Wildcat Valley Ski Trail to Carter Notch Rd.

Hall's Ledge Trail (map 7:G10)

Distances from NH 16

to Hall's Ledge: 1.6 mi., 1 hr. 40 min.

to Carter Notch Rd.: 3.3 mi. (5.3 km.), 2 hr. 30 min.

Black Mountain Ski Trail (WMNF)

This trail to Black Mountain Cabin and a knob (2758 ft.) on the ridge of Black Mtn. that provides fine views, begins at a sign on Carter Notch Rd. 3.7 mi. from Wentworth Hall in Jackson. It follows a dirt road (Melloon Rd.) east past the Jackson Town Dump and the Wildcat Valley Ski Trail, then enters the woods behind a brown house and ascends steadily to the cabin. Continuing to the left of the cabin, the trail reaches a fork in 0.3 mi. A short distance to the left is the summit of the knob, with fine views to Mt. Washington, Wildcat Mtn., and Carter Notch. Straight ahead is the East Pasture (ski) Trail; a short distance down this trail, an unmarked trail turns right and returns to the cabin.

Black Mountain Ski Trail (map 7:G10)
Distances from Carter Notch Road
 to cabin: 1.6 mi., 1 hr. 30 min.
 to summit of knob: 1.9 mi. (3.1 km.), 1 hr. 45 min.

Eagle Mountain Path
Eagle Mtn. is a small peak that can be climbed from NH 16B, 0.8 mi. from Wentworth Hall in Jackson, by a path that starts in the parking lot behind the Eagle Mountain House. The path has fallen into disrepair in recent years, but there is interest in keeping it open. Interested parties should inquire at the Eagle Mountain House. Start uphill on a dirt road, and soon turn right and pass a large pump house on the right. The road becomes older, then becomes a path, and ascends to an open swampy area. Cairns mark the way along the right side of the swamp and into the woods, where the climbing becomes steeper. After passing a large boulder on the right, turn left uphill by switchbacks. At the summit there is a large cairn, and a splendid view a few steps south.

Eagle Mountain Path (map 7:H10)
Distance from NH 16B
 to summit of Eagle Mtn.: 0.9 mi. (1.4 km.), 50 min.

Doublehead Ski Trail (WMNF)
This trail ascends North Doublehead from the east (left) side of Dundee Rd. 2.9 mi. from NH 16 at the Jackson covered bridge. Take NH 16B, turn right on Dundee Rd., bear right over the bridge and continue to the parking area. The trail enters the woods, swings left, and

becomes steeper. At 0.6 mi. it bears slightly left where the Old Path leaves right. The ski trail ascends by a zigzag route on the west slope of North Doublehead, terminating at the WMNF Doublehead Cabin on the summit. The nearest water is alongside the trail about halfway down. Beyond the cabin, a path leads in 30 yd. to a good view east, overlooking Mountain Pond.

Doublehead Ski Trail (map 7:H11–G11)
Distance from Dundee Rd.
>   *to* North Doublehead summit: 1.8 mi. (2.9 km.), 1 hr. 40 min.

Old Path (JCC)

This trail ascends to North Doublehead from the Doublehead Ski Trail, 0.6 mi. from Dundee Rd. It diverges right and passes a brook left in 50 yd., rises at a moderate grade for about 0.1 mi., then steepens somewhat until it reaches the height-of-land in the col between the peaks at 0.6 mi. Here the New Path enters right, and the Old Path turns left and ascends moderately, then more steeply, passing a side path left to a splendid view west. In a short distance it reaches the summit of North Doublehead, the cabin, and the Doublehead Ski Trail.

Old Path (map 7:H11–G11)
Distance from Doublehead Ski Trail
>   *to* North Doublehead summit: 0.9 mi. (1.4 km.), 1 hr.

New Path (JCC)

This trail ascends South Doublehead and continues to the col between South and North Doublehead, where it meets the Old Path. It starts on Dundee Rd., 3.4 mi. from NH 16 at the Jackson covered bridge and 0.5 mi. beyond the parking area for the Doublehead Ski Trail. It is marked with cairns, and is steep in its upper half.

The trail descends slightly as it leaves the road and in 60 yd. bears right, then left, and follows a logging road at a slight upgrade. At 0.3 mi. from Dundee Rd. bear left and in about 100 yd. descend slightly and cross a small brook. Proceed uphill for 100 yd. and bear right at a cairn. About 0.2 mi. from this point the trail crosses a small, almost flat, ledge, and crosses a smaller ledge a short distance beyond. From here the trail begins the steep climb to South Doublehead, approaching it from the southeast slope. It meets the ridge crest at a point between two open ledges. The summit of South Doublehead, with a view, is right; the New Path turns left, crosses a fine outlook ledge, and descends slightly to meet the Old Path in the col to the north.

New Path (map 7:H11)
Distances from Dundee Rd.
>   *to* South Doublehead: 1.2 mi., 1 hr. 25 min.
>   *to* Old Path: 1.4 mi. (2.3 km.), 1 hr. 30 min.

Mount Kearsarge North Trail (WMNF)
This trail ascends Kearsarge North from the north side of Hurricane Mountain Rd., 1.5 mi. east of NH 16 near the state highway rest area at Intervale. It is a relatively easy trail to the magnificent views of Kearsarge North, but the total climb of 2700 ft. should not be underestimated.

Leaving the road, the trail runs level for a short distance, then climbs rather easily past a summer residence on an old road well up on the bank above a brook. At 1.1 mi. it passes several boulders and the old road starts to become rougher. It climbs steadily into a ledgy area, where there are views to Mt. Chocorua and Moat Mtn., crosses the crest of the ridge connecting Kearsarge North to Bartlett Mtn. at 2.4 mi., then swings right and ascends mostly along the north side of the ridge. At 2.9 mi. the trail makes a sharp right turn at a steep spot, then angles upward, circling around to the west edge of the summit ledges, and climbs to the tower.

Mount Kearsarge North Trail (map 7:I11–H11)

Distances from Hurricane Mountain Rd.

   to boulders: 1.1 mi., 55 min.

   to crest of ridge: 2.4 mi., 2 hr. 15 min.

   to Kearsarge North summit: 3.1 mi. (5.0 km.), 2 hr.
      50 min.

Weeks Brook Trail (WMNF)

This trail ascends Kearsarge North from South Chatham
Rd., 5.2 mi. from ME 113 in North Fryeburg ME and 0.1
mi. north of the east terminus of Hurricane Mountain Rd.
Following the trail requires some care, particularly in the
part near the road and in the upper part.

   The trail leaves the main road on a private driveway
near a house on the south side of a branch of Weeks
Brook. It crosses the brook (arrow) at 0.1 mi. to a clearing, where it follows the north side of the brook on
another logging road. (In high water use a bridge about
50 yd. upstream from the marked crossing.) At 0.4 mi.
the trail crosses into the WMNF and reaches a clearing at
1.2 mi., where it bears right, then re-enters the woods.
The road quickly becomes older and rougher, and begins
to climb gradually, then moderately, to Shingle Pond. At
2.8 mi. the trail makes its closest approach to the pond,
which has been visible for some time. At 3.2 mi. the trail
reaches Weeks Brook, then crosses on a ledge and follows the north bank of the attractive brook, crossing and
recrossing a branch several times. It enters an open
boggy area at 4.0 mi., where the trail turns sharp left at a
sign. The trail makes a winding ascent (watch for
arrows), first moderately, then steeply, enters low scrub
and blueberries, passes a fine view east as it turns sharp
right, then reaches a ledge with views south, from which
the fire tower is visible. From here to the summit the trail
may be somewhat obscure but the direction is obvious
(however, follow trail with extreme care when descend-

ing). On the summit it meets the Mount Kearsarge North Trail from Hurricane Mountain Rd.

Weeks Brook Trail (map 7:I12–H11)

Distance from South Chatham Rd.

to Kearsarge North summit: 4.9 mi. (7.8 km.), 3 hr. 50 min.

Province Brook Trail (WMNF)

This trail provides an easy hike to Province Pond, where there is a WMNF shelter. North of the shelter the former route of the trail has been officially closed by the WMNF. The trail begins at the end of Peaked Hill Rd. (FR 450) 2.6 mi. from South Chatham Rd. Peaked Hill Rd. leaves South Chatham Rd. 4.4 mi. from ME 113 in North Fryeburg ME and 0.9 mi. north of the east end of Hurricane Mountain Rd.

The trail leaves the north end of Peaked Hill Rd. and heads northwest up Province Brook on a logging road. After descending slightly and swinging north, it crosses Province Brook on a bridge shortly before reaching the south end of Province Pond on a grassy bank. Turn sharp right here (no sign), and follow a yellow-blazed path along the east shore of the pond to Province Pond Shelter on the north shore.

Province Brook Trail (map 7:H12)

Distances from north end of Peaked Hill Rd.

to Province Pond Shelter: 1.6 mi. (2.6 km.), 1 hr.

Hurricane Mountain Path

The trail to the summit of Hurricane Mtn. leaves the north side of Hurricane Mountain Rd. (no sign) 3.7 mi. east of NH 16 and 0.1 mi. west of the height-of-land, diagonally opposite the Black Cap Path. Follow an old road for about 0.3 mi., then bear right onto the trail and follow cairns that lead to open ledges and the north end of the wooded summit.

Hurricane Mountain Path (map 7:I12)

Distance from Hurricane Mountain Rd.

   to Hurricane Mtn. summit: 0.5 mi. (0.8 km.), 25 min.

Black Cap Path

The orange-blazed path to the bare summit of Black Cap, which affords the best views in the Green Hills range, leaves the south side of Hurricane Mountain Rd. 3.7 mi. from NH 16 and 0.1 mi. west of the height-of-land, at a sign. It passes through spruce, then beech forest. At 0.7 mi. a branch trail leaves right and runs 1.2 mi. to Cranmore Mtn., and the Black Cap Path soon reaches the summit ledges.

Black Cap Path (USGS North Conway quad)

Distance from Hurricane Mountain Rd.

   to Black Cap summit: 1.1 mi. (1.8 km.), 55 min.

   to Cranmore Mtn. (via branch trail): 1.9 mi. (3.1 km.), 1 hr. 20 min.

Peaked Mountain Path

This sharp, rocky knoll, bare except for a few small pines, affords good views. From NH 16 in North Conway, take Artist's Falls Rd. (across from the Millbrook House) for 0.5 mi., then turn right on Woodland Rd. for 0.9 mi. to its end at a small reservoir (parking). The start of the trail is marked by a cairn below the fence on the downhill side of the reservoir. In 25 yd. it crosses the brook at a small flume, continues straight ahead for a few yards, then bears sharp left and continues straight ahead again, ascending fairly steeply to the top of the first ledges. Here, at a large cairn and a 6-ft. rectangular boulder, a loop trail to the ledges diverges sharp right, marked by ribbons and cairns, while the main trail continues straight ahead.

   The ledge loop is by far the more attractive way to ascend. It follows along the top of the ledges for about

0.3 mi., then ascends left through a narrow belt of woods, climbing steeply to the top of a shoulder of the mountain. Continue right along an almost level grassy shelf, turning abruptly left through a wooded hollow, where the loop intersects the main trail—which enters at a right angle, marked by a double set of ribbons. Continue straight ahead to climb steeply to the "Peak," where there are views south and west. On returning down the main trail from the loop junction, in 0.2 mi. look for a conical "smashed" boulder 6 ft. high, where another loop trail, marked by ribbons and cairns, can be taken to the right. This trail is less steep than the ascent route, connecting with an old logging road in about 0.3 mi. Bear left here, then go straight at the first junction, before crossing Artist's Falls Brook. After crossing the brook, bear left at a logging road junction to return to the starting point.

Peaked Mountain Path (USGS North Conway quad)

Distance from Woodland Rd.

   to Peaked Mtn. summit (by either route): 1.3 mi. (2.0 km), 1 hr. 15 min.

SECTION 10
Speckled Mountain Region

This section covers the mountains and trails east of Evans Notch and the valleys of Evans Brook and Cold River, almost all contained within the WMNF. The section is bounded on the west by ME 113/NH 113, the highway that runs through Evans Notch from Chatham NH to Gilead ME, and on the north by US 2. Except for a sliver of land near North Chatham NH, the entire section lies in Maine. The newest designated Wilderness in the WMNF, the Caribou–Speckled Mountain Wilderness, occupies most of the central portion of this region. The area suffered a destructive windstorm in December 1980; all trails have now been reopened, but some may pose route-finding problems for several more years due to undergrowth in areas where the forest canopy is gone. The AMC Carter-Mahoosuc map (map 7) covers the entire area, except for the trails on and near Albany Mtn., which are covered by the USGS East Stoneham quad.

The Appalachian Trail does not pass through this section.

GEOGRAPHY

The major part of this region is occupied by a jumbled mass of ridges with numerous ledges; although the peaks are not high, they offer a variety of fine walks. With the exception of a few trails off ME 113, this area probably receives less hiking traffic than any comparable section of the WMNF, allowing visitors to enjoy trails that are scenic though not spectacular in relative solitude.

Speckled Mtn. (2906 ft.) is the highest peak of the region, and is one of at least three mountains in Maine that have been known by this name. The summit's open ledges have excellent views in all directions. Mt. Caribou (2828 ft.)—called Calabo in the Walling map of Oxford County (1853)—is the second-highest peak in the area. It has a bare, ledgy summit that affords excellent views. Albany Mtn. (1910 ft.) has open ledges near its summit with excellent views. Blueberry Mtn. (1781 ft.) is a long, flat spur running southwest from Speckled Mtn. The top is mostly one big ledge, with sparse and stunted trees. Numerous open spaces afford excellent views, especially from the southwest ledges on the summit. In the valley between Blueberry Mtn. and the west ridge of Speckled Mtn., Bickford Brook passes two sets of flumes, falls, and boulders of unusual beauty.

Deer Hill (1367 ft.), often called Big Deer, is located south of Speckled Mtn. and east of Cold River. The views from the east and south ledges are excellent. Little Deer Hill (1090 ft.), a lower hill west of Deer Hill that rises only about 600 ft. above the valley, gives fine views of the valley and the Baldfaces from its summit ledges. Pine Hill (1250 ft.) and Lord Hill (1257 ft.) rise southeast of Deer Hill, with scattered open ledges that afford interesting views.

The Roost (1374 ft.) is a small hill near Hastings, with open ledges that afford fine views of the Wild River Valley, the Evans Brook Valley, and many mountains.

CAMPING
Restricted Use Areas
There were no RUAs in this region as of 1991.

Caribou–Speckled Mountain Wilderness
In this recently established area, including most of the central part of the region covered by this section, camping and fires are prohibited above treeline. No campsite may be used by more than ten persons at one time.

Established Trailside Campsites

Caribou Shelter (WMNF) is located on the Caribou Trail northeast of the summit of Mt. Caribou. The spring nearby is not a reliable water source. Wilderness policies will probably require its eventual removal.

THE TRAILS

Roost Trail (WMNF)

This trail ascends to the Roost, a small mountain with good views, from two trailheads about 0.7 mi. apart on the east side of ME 113. The north trailhead is located just north of a bridge over Evans Brook, 0.1 mi. north of the junction of ME 113 with Wild River Rd. at Hastings ME; the south trailhead is located just south of another bridge over Evans Brook.

Leaving the south trailhead, the trail ascends a steep bank for 30 yd., then bears right (east) and ascends gradually along a wooded ridge, crosses a small brook at 0.3 mi., then rises somewhat more steeply and emerges on a small rock ledge at the summit at 0.5 mi. Here a side trail descends 0.1 mi. west through woods to spacious open ledges, where the views are excellent. The main trail descends generally southeast at a moderate grade and crosses a small brook, then turns right (west) on an old road (no sign) and follows it past a cellar hole and an old clearing back to ME 113.

Roost Trail (map 7:E13)

Distances from ME 113, north trailhead

   to the Roost: 0.5 mi., 30 min.

   to ME 113, south trailhead: 1.2 mi. (2.0 km.), 50 min.

Wheeler Brook Trail (WMNF)

The trailheads for this trail are located on the south side of US 2, 2.3 mi. east of the junction of US 2 and ME 113, and on Little Lary Brook Rd. (FR 8) 1.6 mi. from its junction with ME 113, which is 9.2 mi. north of the road to Cold River Campground and 3.7 mi. south of the junction of US 2 and ME 113.

From US 2, the Wheeler Brook Trail follows the west side of Wheeler Brook, crosses the brook four times, and rises about 1400 ft., generally following an old logging road, to its highest point on the northwest slope of Peabody Mtn. at 2.1 mi. (There is no trail to the wooded summit of Peabody Mtn.) The trail then descends generally southwest, swings left onto an old logging road, and reaches Little Lary Brook Rd. Turn left on Little Lary Brook Rd., then left at the junction with FR 185, and continue to a locked gate near the bridge over Little Lary Brook, 1.6 mi. from ME 113.

In the reverse direction, proceed along Little Lary Brook Rd. about 100 yd. from the locked gate, then turn right at the junction where FR 185 continues straight ahead. The trail leaves the road on the right in another 0.3 mi. It is very sparsely marked at this end, so exercise care in following it.

Wheeler Brook Trail (map 7:E13)

Distance from US 2

    to gate on Little Lary Brook Rd.: 3.5 mi. (5.6 km.), 2 hr. 30 min.

Caribou Trail (WMNF)

This trail gives access to the attractive ledges of Caribou Mtn. Its west trailhead, which it now shares with the Mud Brook Trail, lies on the east side of ME 113 about 6 mi. north of the road to WMNF Cold River Campground. The east trailhead is on Bog Rd. (FR 6), which leaves the south side of US 2 1.3 mi. west of the West Bethel Post Office (there is currently a sign for Pooh Corner Farm at this junction, but no road sign) and leads 2.8 mi. to the trailhead where a gate ends public travel on the road.

From ME 113, the trail runs north, crosses Morrison Brook on a footbridge at 0.3 mi. and follows the brook, crossing it several more times. The third crossing, at 1.9 mi., is located at the head of Kees Falls, a 25-ft. waterfall. The trail levels off at the height-of-land as it crosses the col between Gammon Mtn. and Mt. Caribou at 2.9 mi. Soon the Mud Brook Trail leaves right to return to ME 113 via the summit of Mt. Caribou, passing Caribou Shelter and Caribou Spring (unreliable) in 0.3 mi. The Caribou Trail continues ahead at the junction, descends more rapidly, turns northeast toward the valley of Bog Brook, which lies east of Peabody Mtn., and follows a succession of logging roads. At 4.8 mi. it bears left in a clearing, then bears left again on the extension of Bog Rd. (FR 6) and continues to the gate.

Caribou Trail (map 7:E13–E14)

Distances from ME 113

> *to* Mud Brook Trail: 2.9 mi., 2 hr. 10 min.
>
> *to* Caribou Mtn. summit (via Mud Brook Trail): 3.5 mi., 2 hr. 40 min.
>
> *to* Bog Rd.: 5.4 mi. (8.7 km.), 3 hr. 25 min.

Mud Brook Trail (WMNF)

This trail begins on ME 113 at the same point as the Caribou Trail, about 6 mi. north of the road to WMNF Cold River Campground, then passes over the summit of Mt. Caribou and ends at the Caribou Trail in the pass between Caribou Mtn. and Gammon Mtn. Despite its ominous name, the footing on the trail is good.

From ME 113, it trail runs generally south, then turns east along the north side of Mud Brook, rising gradually, then crosses the headwaters of Mud Brook at 2.4 mi. and swings left (north) uphill, climbing more steeply. The trail crosses several smaller brooks and at 3.3 mi. comes out on a small, bare knob with excellent views east. It turns left into the woods and makes a short descent into a small ravine, then emerges above timberline and crosses ledges to the summit of Mt. Caribou at 3.8 mi. It then descends north, passes Caribou Spring (unreliable water source) left at 4.1 mi. and Caribou Shelter right 70 yd. farther, and meets the Caribou Trail in the pass.*

Mud Brook Trail (map 7:F13–E13)

Distances from ME 113

to Mt. Caribou summit: 3.8 mi., 2 hr. 55 min.

to Caribou Trail: 4.4 mi. (7.1 km.), 3 hr. 10 min.

Haystack Notch Trail (WMNF)

This trail, with good footing and easy grades but some potentially difficult brook crossings, runs through Haystack Notch. Its west trailhead lies on the east side of ME 113, 4.8 mi. north of the road to WMNF Cold River Campground. The east trailhead is located on the Miles Notch Trail 0.2 mi. from that trail's north terminus, which is reached by following the road that leads south from US 2 opposite the West Bethel Post Office to a crossroads at 3.1 mi., then taking the road that runs right (west), continuing straight ahead at a junction just beyond a small cemetery. The road becomes rather rough after about 1 mi. from the crossroads, and it may not be possible for some cars to drive all the way to the trailhead, which is about 2.5 mi. from the crossroads.

Leaving ME 113, the trail runs generally east along the east branch of Evans Brook, crossing it several times. The first crossing in particular may be difficult at high water. At 2.1 mi. it crosses through Haystack Notch and descends down the valley of the West Branch of the Pleasant River, making several crossings of that brook, some of which may be difficult at high water. Eventually it merges into an old logging road and meets the Miles Notch Trail, where it ends.

Haystack Notch Trail (map 7:F13–E14)

Distances from ME 113

    to Haystack Notch: 2.1 mi., 1 hr. 30 min.

    to Miles Notch Trail: 5.4 mi. (8.7 km.), 3 hr. 5 min.

Albany Notch Trail (WMNF)

This trail passes through the notch west of Albany Mtn. Parts of its northern section still suffer from invasion by berry bushes as a result of the loss of mature forest in the windstorm of 1980, and the southern section, which is located mostly on old, overgrown logging roads, is poorly marked and requires much care to follow. Most hikers use the north section, which makes possible a loop hike over Albany Mtn. in combination with the Albany Mountain Trail and the branch trail that runs from the height-of-land in Albany Notch to the base of the ledges on the Albany Mountain Trail. To reach the north trailhead, follow the road that leads south from US 2 opposite the West Bethel Post Office, which becomes FR 7 when it enters the WMNF at 4.5 mi. At 5.8 mi., turn right on FR 18, following signs for Crocker Pond Campground. The trailhead is located on the right in another 0.6 mi., just past the end of an extensive beaver swamp; the sign is hard to see from the road because it is located at the back of a small clearing and is blocked by a large tree. To reach the south trailhead, leave ME 5 at the west end of Keewaydin Lake, 2.4 mi. west of the East Stoneham Post Office and 0.7 mi. east of the Lovell-Stoneham town line, and follow Bartlettboro Rd. north. Bear right on Birch Ave. at 0.4 mi. from ME 5, and continue to the trailhead, which is 1.0 mi. from ME 5. Park carefully to avoid blocking any roads; the road that the trail follows is passable for at least another 0.2 mi., but parking is extremely limited.

    Leaving the clearing on FR 18, the trail follows an old logging road that becomes well defined after the first few yards. At 0.6 mi. the Albany Notch Trail bears right at the junction where the Albany Mountain Trail diverges left (south). At 1.2 mi. it enters the region damaged by blow-down, where berry bushes are a nuisance, though the trail becomes markedly drier underfoot. Returning to mature woods at 1.4 mi., it climbs at a moderate grade to the left of a small brook, and at 1.7 mi. it reaches the junction where the branch trail leads left (east) 0.4 mi. to the Albany Mountain Trail at the base of the ledges.

The trail now descends moderately with a few steeper pitches just below the pass, and crosses a small brook several times. It then runs mostly on a very old road until it reaches a much newer logging road at 2.4 mi. and turns left on this road (when ascending, turn sharp right). The road, which is fairly easy to follow but rather wet and overgrown, with little evident footway, passes junctions with a snowmobile trail on the left at 2.8 mi. and 3.1 mi.; at the second junction the road bears right and improves greatly, then crosses Meadow Brook on a snowmobile bridge at 3.6 mi. and continues to the trailhead.

Albany Notch Trail (USGS East Stoneham quad)
Distances from FR 18

 to Albany Mountain Trail: 0.6 mi., 25 min.

 to branch trail junction in Albany Notch: 1.7 mi., 1 hr. 15 min.

 to trailhead on Birch Ave.: 4.2 mi. (6.7 km.), 2 hr. 30 min.

Albany Mountain Trail (WMNF)

This trail ascends the north slope of Albany Mtn. to an open ledge near its summit that affords a good view east and north. It begins on the Albany Notch Trail 0.6 mi. from FR 18.

Leaving the Albany Notch Trail, it soon turns left onto a skidder road that it follows for 20 yd., then bears right off it and continues to ascend moderately through woods where there has been some light to moderate wind damage. At 0.6 mi. the trail turns right at the foot of a small mossy rock face, and climbs to the junction at 0.9 mi. where the branch trail leads right (west) 0.4 mi. to the Albany Notch Trail at the height-of-land in Albany Notch. Soon the trail passes a ledge with a good view of the Baldfaces and Mt. Washington and continues to the northeast outlook, where regular marking ends. The true summit, wooded and not reached by any well-defined trail, is located about 100 yd. south. The summit area has other viewpoints not reached by the trail that repay efforts devoted to cautious exploration by experienced hikers. The best viewpoint on the mountain lies about 0.1 mi. southwest of the true summit; a sketchy and incomplete line of cairns leads to it.

Albany Mountain Trail (USGS East Stoneham quad)
Distance from Albany Notch Trail
  to Albany Mtn. upper outlook: 1.3 mi. (2.1 km.), 1
    hr. 5 min.

Albany Brook Trail (WMNF)

This short, easy trail follows the shore of Crocker Pond and then leads to attractive, secluded Round Pond. It begins at the turnaround at the end of the main road at Crocker Pond Campground (do not enter the actual camping area), reached by following the road that runs south from US 2 opposite the West Bethel Post Office, which becomes FR 7 when it enters the WMNF at 4.5 mi. At 5.8 mi., turn right on FR 18, following signs 1.5 mi. to the campground entrance.

Leaving the turnaround, the trail descends to a small brook and follows the west shore of Crocker Pond for 0.2 mi., then joins and follows Albany Brook with gentle ups and downs. At 0.9 mi. it goes straight through a logging-road intersection with a clearing visible on the right, and soon reaches the north end of Round Pond.

Albany Brook Trail (USGS East Stoneham quad)
Distance from Crocker Pond Campground
   to Round Pond: 1.0 mi. (1.6 km.), 30 min.

Miles Notch Trail (WMNF)

This trail runs through Miles Notch, giving access to the east end of the ledgy ridge that culminates in Speckled Mtn. To reach its south terminus, near which the Great Brook Trail also begins, leave ME 5 in North Lovell ME on a road with signs for Evergreen Valley Ski Area; follow that road northwest for 1.8 mi., then turn right onto Hut Rd. just before the bridge over Great Brook and continue 1.5 mi. to the trailhead. To reach the north terminus, follow the road that leads south from US 2 opposite the West Bethel Post Office to a crossroads at 3.1 mi., then take the road that runs right (west), continuing straight ahead at a junction just beyond a small cemetery. The road becomes rather rough after about 1 mi. from the crossroads, and it may not be possible for some cars to drive all the way to the trailhead, which is about 2.5 mi. from the crossroads.

From the south terminus, the trail follows an old logging road generally north and at 0.3 mi. bears left off the road (arrow). It climbs over a small ridge and at 1.2 mi. enters another old logging road and follows it to the left for 0.2 mi., after which it leaves the old road on the right and soon crosses a branch of Beaver Brook. At 2.3 mi. it crosses Beaver Brook, passes over a steeper section, runs in the gully of a small brook, then turns left away from the brook and reaches Miles Notch at 2.9 mi. The trail now descends gradually, and at 3.2 mi. the Red Rock Trail leaves on the left for the summit of Speckled Mtn. The Miles Notch Trail then descends moderately, crossing Miles Brook repeatedly. At 5.4 mi. the Haystack Notch Trail enters on the left and the Miles Notch Trail soon reaches its northern end.

Miles Notch Trail (map 7:F14–E14)

Distances from south terminus

to Red Rock Trail: 3.2 mi., 2 hr. 15 min.

to north terminus: 5.6 mi. (9.0 km.), 3 hr. 30 min.

Bickford Brook Trail (WMNF)

This trail ascends Speckled Mtn. from the Brickett Place on ME 113, 0.2 mi. north of the road to WMNF Cold River Campground. The trail enters the woods near the garage, then turns right onto an old WMNF service road to Speckled Mtn. at 0.3 mi., and the two coincide for the next 2.5 mi. At 0.7 mi. the Blueberry Ridge Trail leaves right (east) for the lower end of the Bickford Slides and Blueberry Mtn.; it rejoins the Bickford Brook Trail 0.5 mi. below the summit of Speckled Mtn., affording the opportunity for a loop hike. At 0.9 mi. the Bickford Slides Loop enters on the right from the lower end of the Upper Slides, and at 1.1 mi. the spur path along the Upper Slides enters on the right. The Bickford Brook Trail soon swings away from the brook and winds up a southwest spur to the crest of the main west ridge of the Speckled Mtn. range, where the Spruce Hill Trail enters left at 3.1 mi. The Bickford Brook Trail then passes west and north of the summit of Ames Mtn. into the col between Ames Mtn. and Speckled Mtn., where the Blueberry Ridge Trail rejoins right at 3.8 mi. The Bickford Brook Trail then continues upward to the summit.

Bickford Brook Trail (map 7:F12–F13)

Distances from ME 113

to Blueberry Ridge Trail, lower junction: 0.7 mi., 35 min.

to Spruce Hill Trail: 3.1 mi., 2 hr. 30 min.

to Blueberry Ridge Trail, upper junction: 3.8 mi., 2 hr. 55 min.

to Speckled Mtn. summit: 4.3 mi. (6.9 km.), 3 hr. 20 min.

Blueberry Ridge Trail (CTA)

This trail begins and ends on the Bickford Brook Trail, leaving at a sign 0.6 mi. from its trailhead at the Brickett Place on ME 113, and rejoining 0.5 mi. below the summit of Speckled Mtn. (The upper part of the Blueberry Ridge Trail may also be reached from Shell Pond Rd. via the Stone House or White Cairn trails.) It descends toward Bickford Brook, and at 0.1 mi., just before the main trail crosses Bickford Brook, it crosses the Bickford Slides Loop.

Bickford Slides Loop. This loop path, 0.5 mi. long, leaves the Blueberry Ridge Trail 0.1 mi. from its lower junction with the Bickford Brook Trail. At this junction, a spur path descends along Bickford Brook 50 yd. to the Lower Slides, while the main path crosses Bickford Brook and climbs along it 0.3 mi. to another junction near the base of the Upper Slides. Here the main path recrosses the brook at the base of the Upper Slides and joins the Bickford Brook Trail 0.9 mi. from NH 113, while a spur path 0.3 mi. long continues up along the brook and the Upper Slides, then crosses the brook above the slides and joins the Bickford Brook Trail 1.1 mi. from ME 113.

From the junction with the Bickford Slides Loop, the Blueberry Ridge Trail crosses the brook (may be difficult at high water) and ascends southeast to an open area just over the crest of Blueberry Ridge, where the White Cairn Trail enters right at 0.7 mi. An overlook loop 0.5 mi. long, with excellent views to the south, leaves the Blueberry Ridge Trail shortly after this junction and rejoins it shortly before the Stone House Trail enters on the right at 0.9 mi., a few steps past the high point of the trail on Blueberry Mtn. From the junction with the Stone House Trail, marked by signs and a large cairn, the Blueberry Ridge Trail bears left and descends to a spring (unreliable water source) a short distance from the trail on the left (north). Here it turns sharp right and continues over ledges marked by cairns, through occasional patches of woods, passing over several humps. The trail ends at the Bickford Brook Trail in the shallow pass at the head of the Rattlesnake Brook ravine, about 0.5 mi. below the summit of Speckled Mtn.

Blueberry Ridge Trail (map 7:F13)

Distances from Bickford Brook Trail, lower junction

   to Stone House Trail: 0.9 mi., 55 min.

   to Bickford Brook Trail, upper junction: 3.1 mi., 2 hr. 25 min.

Spruce Hill Trail (WMNF)

This trail begins on the east side of ME 113 3.0 mi. north of the road to WMNF Cold River Campground, opposite the start of the East Royce Trail, and ascends to the Bickford Brook Trail, with which it forms the shortest route (though not a particularly scenic one) to the summit of Speckled Mtn. It ascends moderately through woods, with restricted views of Evans Notch, to the summit of Spruce Hill at 1.5 mi. It then descends into a sag and climbs to meet the Bickford Brook Trail on the ridgecrest west of Ames Mtn.

Spruce Hill Trail (map 7:F13)

Distances from ME 113

   to Bickford Brook Trail: 1.9 mi. (3.0 km.), 1 hr. 30 min.

   to Speckled Mtn. summit (via Bickford Brook Trail): 3.1 mi., 2 hr. 20 min.

Cold Brook Trail (WMNF)

This trail ascends Speckled Mtn. from a trailhead reached from ME 5 in North Lovell ME. Follow the road with signs for Evergreen Valley Ski Area for 1.9 mi. and take the first right (with an Evergreen Valley sign) just after the bridge over Great Brook, then continue to a gravel road on the right 2.2 mi. from ME 5. The WMNF sign is on the paved road, but it may be possible to drive 0.5 mi. on the rough gravel road to a parking area.

Beyond here the road becomes rougher, and in 0.7 mi. from the paved road it bears left past a gate. The next 1.0 mi. is on a muddy road that circles on contour to a cabin, the Duncan McIntosh House. Continuing ahead on the road, take the left fork, then the right. The trail descends to Cold Brook and crosses it at 1.9 mi., just above a fork. It then climbs and circles along the farther branch, passes west of Sugarloaf Mtn., and ascends the south side of Speckled Mtn., passing a junction left at 2.7 mi. with the Link Trail (not described in this guide) from the Evergreen Valley Ski Area. It emerges on semi-open ledges at 3.5 mi., passes two excellent south outlooks, and bears right to re-enter the woods at 4.4 mi. At 4.9 mi. it emerges on semi-open ledges again and soon reaches the junction with the Red Rock Trail right and the Bickford Brook Trail left, where it follows the latter trail left 30 yd. to the summit of Speckled Mtn.

Cold Brook Trail (map 7:F14–F13)

Distance from paved road
    to Speckled Mtn. summit: 4.9 mi. (7.9 km.), 3 hr. 45 min.

Red Rock Trail (WMNF)

This trail ascends Speckled Mtn. from the Miles Notch Trail 0.3 mi. north of Miles Notch, 3.2 mi. from its southern trailhead and 2.4 mi. from its northern trailhead. It traverses the long eastern ridge of the Speckled Mtn. range, affording fine views of the surrounding mountains.

It leaves the Miles Notch Trail, descends to cross Miles Brook in its ravine, then angles up the north slope of Miles Knob and gains the ridgecrest northwest of that summit. It descends to a col, then ascends to the summit of Red Rock Mtn. at 1.2 mi. and follows the ridge, with several ups and downs, over Butters Mtn. at 2.5 mi. and then on to the next col to the west. Here, at 3.4 mi., the

Great Brook Trail diverges left (east) and descends southeast to its trailhead, very close to the southern trailhead of the Miles Notch Trail. The Red Rock Trail swings south, crosses the summit of Durgin Mtn. at 4.4 mi., then runs generally southwest to the junction with the Cold Brook Trail and Bickford Brook Trail 30 yd. east of the summit of Speckled Mtn. There is a spring near the trail about 0.1 mi. east of the summit.

Red Rock Trail (map 7:F14–F13)

Distances from Miles Notch Trail

to Great Brook Trail: 3.4 mi., 2 hr. 15 min.

to Speckled Mtn. summit: 5.6 mi. (9.0 km.), 3 hr. 50 min.

Great Brook Trail (WMNF)

This trail ascends to the Red Rock Trail east of Speckled Mtn. To reach its trailhead, leave ME 5 in North Lovell, Maine on a road with signs for Evergreen Valley Ski Area; follow that road northwest for 1.8 mi., then turn right onto Hut Rd. just before the bridge over Great Brook and continue 1.5 mi. to the trailhead, which is located about 100 yd. past the southern trailhead for the Miles Notch Trail.

The trail continues up the gravel road and bears right onto FR 4 at 0.8 mi., just after crossing Great Brook on a bridge with a gate. At 1.8 mi. it turns left onto a grassy older road and follows Great Brook. At 3.0 mi. it crosses a branch of Great Brook, then bears left (arrow), becomes steeper, and continues along Great Brook to the ridge crest, where it joins the Red Rock Trail in the col between Butters Mtn. and Durgin Mtn.

Great Brook Trail (map 7:F14–F13)

Distances from trailhead

to Red Rock Trail: 3.7 mi. (5.9 km.), 2 hr. 35 min.

to Speckled Mtn. summit (via Red Rock Trail) 5.8 mi., 4 hr. 20 min.

Stone House Trail (CTA)

This trail ascends to the scenic ledges of Blueberry Mtn. from Shell Pond Rd. To reach the trailhead, leave NH 113 on the east side 0.7 mi. north of AMC Cold River Camp and follow Shell Pond Rd. 1.1 mi. to a padlocked steel gate that makes it necessary to park cars at that point.

The trail leaves left (north) 0.5 mi. beyond the gate, east of an open shed. It follows a logging road, and approaches Rattlesnake Brook. At 0.2 mi. it merges with a private road (descending, bear right at arrow) and immediately reaches the junction with a spur path that leads right 30 yd. to a bridge overlooking Rattlesnake Flume, a small, attractive gorge. The main trail soon swings right (arrow) and at 0.5 mi. another spur leads right 0.1 mi. to Rattlesnake Pool, which lies at the foot of a small cascade. The main trail soon enters the WMNF and at 1.2 mi. begins to climb rather steeply straight up the slope, running generally northwest to the top of the ridge, where it ends at the Blueberry Ridge Trail only a few steps from the top of Blueberry Mtn. To reach Speckled Mtn., turn right on the Blueberry Ridge Trail.

Stone House Trail (map 7:F13)

Distance from Shell Pond Rd.

to Blueberry Mtn. summit: 1.5 mi. (2.4 km.), 1 hr. 20 min.

White Cairn Trail (CTA)

This trail provides access to the open ledges on Blueberry Mtn. and, with the Stone House Trail, makes an easy half-day circuit. It begins on Shell Pond Rd., which leaves NH 113 on the east side 0.7 mi. north of AMC Cold River Camp and runs 1.1 mi. to a padlocked steel gate that makes it necessary to park cars at that point. The trail leaves Shell Pond Rd. at a clearing 0.3 mi. beyond the gate. It follows old logging roads north and west to an upland meadow, passing into the WMNF at 0.3 mi., then at 0.8 mi. begins to climb steeply up the right (east) margin of the cliffs visible from the road, then turns sharp left and begins to climb on ledges. The grade moderates as the trail runs northwest along the crest of the cliffs to the west, with views to the south. At 1.2 mi. it passes a spring, then swings right (north) and passes another spring before ending at the junction with the Blueberry Ledge Trail, 0.2 mi. west of the upper terminus of the Stone House Trail. A loop trail that leaves the Blueberry Ledge Trail near its junction with this trail provides a scenic alternate route to the Stone House Trail.

White Cairn Trail (map 7:F13)
Distance from Shell Pond Road
>   *to* Blueberry Ridge Trail: 1.4 mi. (2.3 km.), 1 hr. 20 min.

Shell Pond Trail (WMNF)
This trail runs between Shell Pond Rd., at the locked gate 1.1 mi. from NH 113, and Deer Hill Rd. (FR 9), 3.5 mi. from NH 113. Shell Pond Rd. leaves NH 113 on the east side 0.7 mi. north of AMC Cold River Camp. From the gate on Shell Pond Rd., continue east on the road. The White Cairn Trail leaves left at 0.3 mi. and the Stone House Trail leaves left at 0.5 mi. At 0.6 mi. the Shell Pond Trail passes the Stone House (left). Just beyond here the trail proper begins, following an old road. The trail crosses Rattlesnake Brook on a bridge at 1.1 mi., passes through a wet area, and turns left off the road at 1.3 mi., where the old road leads straight to circle Shell Pond. (The trail itself does not come within sight of the pond.) This turn is marked by a sign for the Stone House Farm and a cairn (but no sign or arrow) for the trail. From here the trail ascends gradually to Deer Hill Rd.

Shell Pond Trail (map 7:F13–G13)
Distance from gate on Shell Pond Rd.
>   *to* Deer Hill Rd.: 1.8 mi. (2.9 km.), 1 hr.

Horseshoe Pond Trail (CTA)

This trail, blazed with bright yellow paint, starts from Deer Hill Rd. (FR 9), 4.7 mi. from NH 113, at a parking area at a curve in the road, where the pond is visible; it ends on the Conant Trail. It descends moderately past the Styles grave, enclosed by a stone wall, then enters a recent logging road and turns right on it. In a few steps, the Horseshoe Pond Loop, 0.4 mi. long, leaves left for the northwest shore of Horseshoe Pond. The main trail continues on the logging road, then bears right on another logging road at 0.3 mi., and the Horseshoe Pond Loop rejoins on the left at an incipient apple orchard in 100 yd. The trail ascends through the clear-cut resulting from timber salvage operations after the 1980 windstorm, following cairns and overgrown skid roads back into the woods to the old trail, which continues to the Conant Trail between Lord Hill and Harndon Hill.

Horseshoe Pond Trail (map 7:G13)
Distance from Deer Hill Rd.
  to Conant Trail: 1.1 mi. (1.8 km.), 50 min

Conant Trail (CTA)

This loop path to Pine Hill and Lord Hill is frequently referred to (and may be signed as) the Pine-Lord-Harndon Trail, though it does not go particularly close to the summit of Harndon Hill, it should not be confused with the Conant Path, a short trail near AMC Cold River Camp. It is an interesting and fairly easy walk with a number of good outlooks, but since it passes through areas where the windstorm of 1980 destroyed the forest canopy, following parts of it may require care. It is reached by following Deer Hill Rd. (FR 9) and making a right turn 1.5 mi. from NH 113, then turning left almost immediately and parking near a dike.

The trail runs straight ahead along the dike across Colton Brook—Colton Dam is located several hundred yards to the right from here—and continues to the loop junction at 0.4 mi., where the path divides. From here the path is described in a counter-clockwise direction. The south branch turns right and follows a logging road (Hemp Hill Rd.) to a level spot at 1.0 mi. near the old Johnson cellar hole, then turns left on a logging road, then left again in a few steps. The trail turns left again at 1.2 mi. and ascends Pine Hill, rather steeply at times, passing a ledge with a fine view to the west at 1.4 mi. It reaches the west end of the summit ridge and continues to the most easterly knob, which has a good view north, at 2.0 mi. The trail zigzags down past logged areas, crosses Bradley Brook at 2.3 mi. and then climbs, crossing the logging road that provides access to the mine on Lord Hill and passing an outlook over Horseshoe Pond. It reaches ledges near the summit of Lord Hill at 3.0 mi., where the Mine Loop leaves on the left.

Mine Loop. This path is 1.0 mi. long, 0.1 mi. shorter than the section of Conant Trail it bypasses. Except for one critical turn mentioned below, it is fairly easy to follow. From the junction with the Conant Trail near the summit of Lord Hill, it climbs briefly to the ledge at the top of the old mica mine and then descends on a woods road, and at 0.1 mi. it passes a spur path that leads right 30 yd. to the mine. At 0.3 mi. it turns sharp left on a logging road, then at 0.5 mi. it reaches a fork and turns sharp right back on the other branch of the road, which shows less evidence of use. This turn is easily missed because it is difficult to mark adequately and the correct road is less obvious than the main road. (The main road, continuing straight at this fork, crosses the Conant Trail between Pine Hill and Lord Hill and continues south toward Kezar Lake.) At a clearing the Mine Loop leaves the road on the right and descends 50 yd. to rejoin the Conant Trail 1.1 mi. from its trailhead.

From Lord Hill the Conant Trail descends to the junction with the Horseshoe Pond Trail on the right at 3.2 mi., where it turns left, then soon turns left again and runs at a fairly level grade along the south side of Harndon Hill. It passes a cellar hole, and the Mine Loop rejoins on the left at 4.1 mi. At 4.5 mi. the road passes a gate, becomes wider, reaches the loop junction, and continues straight ahead across the dike to the trailhead.

Conant Trail (map 7:G13)
Distance from trailhead off Deer Hill Rd.
  for complete loop: 5.2 mi. (8.3 km.), 3 hr. 10 min.

Little Deer–Big Deer Trail (CTA)

This trail ascends Little Deer Hill and Big Deer Hill, running from the AMC Cold River Camp to Deer Hill Rd. (FR 9). It leaves Cold River Camp on a gravel road that runs east, passing the Conant Path on the right, the Tea House Path on the left, and then a spur left to the Leach Link Trail just after crossing Cold River on the dam. It crosses the Leach Link Trail at 0.3 mi., and climbs moderately past an outlook west, then bears left onto ledges and reaches the summit of Little Deer Hill at 0.9 mi. Here the Ledges Trail enters on the right. The main trail descends into a sag, then climbs to the summit of Big Deer Hill at 1.6 mi. It then descends the south ridge with several fine outlooks, turning left at 2.1 mi. where a connecting path to the Ledges Trail and Little Deer Hill leaves on the right. (This connecting path descends to a spur path at 0.6 mi., which leads right 0.2 mi. to the summit of Deer Hill, and then continues from the spur junction to end at the Ledges Trail at 0.8 mi.) Soon the main trail turns left again, then turns right onto an old logging road at 2.3 mi. Here a spur path follows the logging road left for a few steps, then descends in 0.2 mi. to Deer Hill Spring (Bubbling Spring), an interesting shallow pool with air bubbles rising through a small area of light-colored sand. The main trail descends from the junction to Deer Hill Rd.

Little Deer–Big Deer Trail (map 7:G12–G13)
Distances from Cold River Camp

> *to* Little Deer Hill summit: 0.9 mi., 45 min.
> *to* Big Deer Hill summit: 1.6 mi., 1 hr. 20 min.
> *to* Deer Hill Rd.: 2.9 mi. (4.7 km.), 2 hr.

Ledges Trail (CTA)

The Ledges Trail passes interesting ledges and a cave, but is very steep and rough, dangerous in icy conditions, and not recommended for descent. It leaves the south end of the Leach Link Trail and climbs steeply with numerous outlooks. At 0.2 mi. the connecting path that leads in 0.8 mi. to the Little Deer–Big Deer Trail south of Big Deer diverges right, affording an alternate route to the summit of Little Deer via the spur path (0.2 mi. long) that leaves it 0.2 mi. from the Ledges Trail. At 0.4 mi. the Ledges Trail divides; the right branch, which is slightly longer, rejoins in about 100 yd. Just above the point where these branches rejoin, the spur path from the connecting path mentioned above enters on the right, and soon the trail reaches the summit of Little Deer Hill.

Ledges Trail (map 7:G12)
Distance from Leach Link Trail

> *to* Little Deer Hill summit: 0.5 mi. (0.8 km.), 35 min.

Leach Link Trail (CTA)

This trail gives access to Little Deer Hill and Big Deer Hill from Shell Pond Rd., which leaves NH 113 on the east side 0.7 mi. north of AMC Cold River Camp. The trail leaves Shell Pond Rd. just east of the bridge over Cold River and at 0.4 mi. crosses Shell Pond Brook (may be difficult at high water). On the far bank the Shell Pond Brook Trail enters on the left; this is an alternate route from Shell Pond Rd., 0.5 mi. long, that makes the Shell

Pond Brook crossing on a snowmobile bridge (useful at high water). At 1.1 mi. a spur path leads right to the Little Deer–Big Deer Trail, which is crossed in another 50 yd.; to the left the Little Deer–Big Deer Trail ascends Little Deer Hill, and to the right it leads to the dam at the AMC Cold River Camp. From here the Leach Link Trail continues along the river, ending at the Ledges Trail.

Leach Link Trail (map 7:G12)

Distance from Shell Pond Rd.

   to Ledges Trail: 1.5 mi. (2.4 km.), 45 min.

SECTION 11
Mahoosuc Range Area

This section includes the region along the Maine/New Hampshire border that lies east and north of the Androscoggin River, which runs south from Lake Umbagog near Errol to Gorham then swings east from Gorham to Bethel ME. It is bounded by NH 16 on the west, by US 2 on the south, and by NH 26/ME 26 on the northeast. The backbone of the region is the Mahoosuc Range, which rises from the east bank of the river above Berlin and Gorham, runs east, then gradually swings toward the north to its far end at Grafton Notch. This section covers the main Mahoosuc Range and all the trails on it, but does not cover some of the routes on eastern spurs of the range that lie wholly within Maine. Those mountains and routes are covered by the *AMC Maine Mountain Guide*. The most important peaks in the Mahoosuc Range are Old Speck Mtn., Mahoosuc Arm, Goose Eye Mtn., Mt. Carlo, Mt. Success, Cascade Mtn., and Mt. Hayes. The region is completely covered by the AMC Carter-Mahoosuc map (map 7).

In this section the Appalachian Trail begins at the trailhead of the Rattle River Trail (Section 9) on US 2, follows the highway west 0.2 mi. to North Rd., then follows North Rd. for 0.5 mi., crossing the Androscoggin, and turns left on Hogan Rd. for 0.2 mi. to the Centennial Trail. It then follows the Centennial Trail, the Mahoosuc Trail, and the Old Speck Trail to Grafton Notch, the eastern boundary of the area covered in this guide; the Baldpate Mountain Trail continues the Appalachian Trail on the opposite side of the notch. In its course through the Mahoosucs, the Appalachian Trail crosses the summits of Cascade Mtn., Mt. Success, and Mt. Carlo, and passes near the summits of Mt. Hayes, Goose Eye Mtn., Mahoosuc Arm, and Old Speck Mtn.

GEOGRAPHY

The southern part of the Mahoosuc Range is a broad, ledgy, lumpy ridge, with numerous spurs extending south toward the Androscoggin Valley. The main peaks, from west to east, are Mt. Hayes (2555 ft.), Cascade Mtn. (2631 ft.), Bald Cap (3065 ft.) and its two subsidiary peaks, Bald Cap Peak (2795 ft.) and North Bald Cap (2893 ft.); all three Bald Cap peaks are trailless. The northern part of the range is higher and narrower, with a well-defined ridgecrest and two long subsidiary ridges running southeast toward the Androscoggin and Bear rivers; the Sunday River flows between these subsidiary ridges. The main peaks, from southwest to northeast, are Mt. Success (3565 ft.), Mt. Carlo (3565 ft.), the three peaks of Goose Eye Mtn. (West Peak, the highest, 3870 ft.; East Peak, 3794 ft.; North Peak, 3690 ft.), Fulling Mill Mtn. (North Peak, 3450 ft.), Mahoosuc Mtn. (3490 ft.), Mahoosuc Arm (3790 ft.), and Old Speck Mtn. (4180 ft.). Old Speck is the third-highest mountain in Maine; its name distinguishes it from the several other Speckled mountains (so called for their scattered open ledges) in the area. Mt. Success is named for the unincorporated township in which it is located, Mt. Carlo for a dog. The origin of Goose Eye Mtn.'s peculiar name is in doubt; the most plausible explanation maintains that geese in their flights south from the Rangeley Lakes appear almost to graze its summit, and it is, therefore, "goose high."

The views from Goose Eye, a striking rock peak, are among the best in the White Mtns., and most of the other peaks have fine views, either from the summits or from the numerous open ledges scattered throughout the range. There are several fine mountain ponds, including Speck Pond (one of the highest ponds in Maine), Gentian Pond, Dream Lake, and Page Pond. The most remarkable feature of the range is Mahoosuc Notch, where the trail winds around and under huge fragments of rock that have fallen from the cliffs of Mahoosuc Mtn. to the northwest; Fulling Mill Mtn. forms the southeast wall.

The Alpine Cascades on Cascade Brook, which flows from the northwest slope of Cascade Mtn., are an attractive sight except in dry seasons. They can be approached from the gravel road along the railroad tracks on the east side of the Androscoggin, probably best reached from NH 16 by crossing the river at the highway bridge just south of Berlin and following the road south along the railroad. Nearly opposite the Cascade Mill of the James River Co., a footpath diverges left across the tracks, then divides into three paths; the right branch leads about 100 yd. to the foot of Cascade Falls.

From the major peaks of the southern part of the range, ridges run toward the Androscoggin, bearing interesting smaller peaks. Among these mountains are Middle Mtn. (2010 ft.), Mt. Crag (1412 ft.), Mt. Ingalls (2242 ft.), Mt. Cabot (1512 ft.), and Crow's Nest (1287 ft.). There are also two interesting waterfalls on the south side of the range. Dryad Fall is reached via the Dryad Fall Trail. Lary Flume is a wild chasm that resembles the Ice Gulch and Devil's Hopyard, with many boulder caves and one fissure cave. There is no trail, but experienced climbers have visited it by ascending along the brook that may be reached by bushwhacking east where the Austin Brook Trail begins its last 0.5 mi. of ascent to Gentian Pond.

ACCESS ROADS

Success Pond Rd. runs from the east side of the Androscoggin River in Berlin to Success Pond in about 14 mi., and continues to ME 26 north of Grafton Notch. Over the years this has been perhaps the most difficult road in the White Mtns. for a person unfamiliar with the area to find; important landmarks disappeared or changed

and the first part of the road itself was moved with
astounding but unpredictable regularity. However, it now
appears that the situation may have become somewhat
stable. Leave NH 16 just south of Berlin, 4.5 mi. north of
the eastern junction of US 2 and NH 16 in Gorham, and
cross the Androscoggin on the Cleveland Bridge. At the
east end of the bridge, the road (Unity St.) swings left
and passes straight through traffic lights in 0.7 mi. from
NH 16. At 0.8 mi. the road bears right across railroad
tracks and becomes Hutchins St. It turns sharp left at 1.6
mi., at Frank's Village Store, and continues past the
James River millyard At 1.9 mi. from NH 16, where
there has usually been a large sign reading "OHRV
PARKING 1 MILE," the Success Pond Rd. begins on
the right (east). It no longer winds among the huge wood
piles of the millyard, but you should still watch for large
trucks, especially those entering from the right. The first
part of the road has been difficult to distinguish from
branch roads, but once past this area it is well defined.
The road is not generally open to public vehicular use in
winter. Trailheads are marked only with small AMC
standard trail signs, often at old diverging logging roads
with no well-defined parking area, so you must look for
them carefully. The lower parts of the trails originating
on this road have been disrupted frequently in the past by
construction of new logging roads; great care is necessary to follow the proper roads, ascending or descending

North Rd. provides access to the trails on the south
side of the Mahoosuc Range. This road leaves US 2 about
2.8 mi. east of its easterly junction with NH 16 in
Gorham, and crosses the Androscoggin River on the Lead
Mine Bridge; the Appalachian Trail follows this part of
the road. North Rd. then swings east and runs along the
north side of the river to rejoin US 2 just north of Bethel
ME. Bridges connect North Rd. with US 2 at the villages
of Shelburne NH and Gilead ME.

CAMPING

Land in this section is owned by the state of Maine and by the James River Co. along with other private interests. Hiking is permitted through their courtesy. No part of this section is included in the WMNF. Camping and wood fires are prohibited by state laws except at authorized campsites (shelters and Trident Col).

Trident Col Campsite (AMC) is located on a side path from the Mahoosuc Trail in Trident Col. There are sites for four tents. Water is available about 50 yd. below (west of) the site.

Gentian Pond Campsite (AMC) on Gentian Pond has a large shelter and tentsites.

Carlo Col Shelter (AMC) is located on the Carlo Col Trail, 0.3 mi. below the Mahoosuc Trail at Carlo Col.

Full Goose Shelter (AMC) is located on the Mahoosuc Trail between Fulling Mill Mtn. and Goose Eye Mtn. There is a spring 30 yd. east of the shelter.

Speck Pond Campsite (AMC), located at Speck Pond on the Mahoosuc Trail, includes a shelter and tent platforms. There is a caretaker present in the summer, and a fee is charged.

THE TRAILS

Mahoosuc Trail (AMC)

This trail extends along the entire length of the Mahoosuc Range from Gorham NH to the summit of Old Speck. Beyond its junction with the Centennial Trail, the Mahoosuc Trail is a link in the Appalachian Trail. Camping is limited to the tentsites at Trident Col and to the four shelters: Gentian Pond (with tentsites), Carlo Col, Full Goose, and Speck Pond (which also has tent platforms). The sites may have a caretaker, in which case a fee is charged. Water is scarce, particularly in dry weather, and its purity is always in question. This is a rugged trail—

particularly for those with heavy packs—with numerous minor humps and cols, and many ledges, some of them quite steep, that are likely to be slippery when wet. *Caution:* Mahoosuc Notch is regarded by many who have hiked the entire length of the Appalachian Trail as the most difficult mile; it can be hazardous in wet or icy conditions and can remain impassable due to unmelted snowdrifts through the end of May and perhaps even longer. Do not be deceived by the relatively low elevations; this trail is among the most rugged of its kind in the White Mtns.

Part I. Gorham to Centennial Trail

To reach the trail, cross the Androscoggin River by the footbridge under the Boston & Maine Railroad bridge, 1.3 mi. north of the Gorham Post Office on NH 16. On the east bank, follow the road to the right (southeast) along the river for 0.4 mi., then cross the canal through the open upper level of the powerhouse (left of entrance). Beyond, keep straight ahead about 100 yd. to the woods at the east end of the dam, where the trail sign will be found. The trail is sparsely blazed in blue. Turn left and follow an old road north along the side of the canal for 0.1 mi., then turn right uphill on an old logging road. At 0.8 mi. from NH 16 the trail crosses a power-line clearing, then bears right and reaches but does not cross a brook, and follows it closely for 100 yd. It ascends at only a slight grade to a side path at 1.1 mi. that leads right 0.2 mi. to Mascot Pond, just below the cliffs seen prominently from Gorham. The Mahoosuc Trail crosses a woods road then ascends a brook valley, which it crosses several times. At 2.5 mi. it passes a short spur (sign) that leads left to Popsy Spring, climbs steeply, and emerges on the southwest side of the flat, ledgy summit of Mt. Hayes. An unmarked footway leads a few yards right to the best viewpoint south over the valley. A cairn marks the true summit of Mt. Hayes at 3.1 mi. The trail descends on open ledges with good views north to the junction on the right with the Centennial Trail at 3.2 mi.

Part II. Centennial Trail to Gentian Pond

From here north the Mahoosuc Trail is part of the Appalachian Trail, marked with white blazes. It descends north to the col between Mt. Hayes and Cascade Mtn. at 4.1 mi., where there is sometimes water. The trail then ascends Cascade Mtn. by a southwest ridge, over ledges and large fallen rocks, emerging on the bare summit ledge at 5.1 mi. It turns back sharply into the woods, descending gradually with occasional upgrades to the east end of the mountain, then enters a fine forest and descends rapidly beside cliffs and ledges to Trident Col at 6.3 mi., where a side path leads left 0.2 mi. to Trident Col Tentsite, which has space for four tents. Water is available about 50 yd. below (west of) the site. The bare ledges of the rocky cone to the east of Trident Col repay the effort required to scramble to its top; a route ascends between two large cairns near the tentsite side path.

The trail descends rather steeply to the southeast, and runs along the side of the ridge at the base of the Trident, which is made up of the previously mentioned cone, the ledgy peak just west of Page Pond, and a somewhat less prominent peak between them. The trail crosses several small brooks, at least one of which usually has water. It follows a logging road for 0.1 mi., then turns left off the road at a sign and ascends to Page Pond at 7.3 mi. The trail passes the south end of the pond, crosses a beaver dam, and climbs gradually, then more steeply, to a short spur path at 7.9 mi. that leads left to a fine outlook from ledges near the summit of Wocket Ledge, a shoulder of Bald Cap. The main trail crosses the height-of-land and descends east, crosses the upper (west) branch of Peabody Brook, then climbs around the nose of a small ridge and descends gradually to the head of Dream Lake. The trail bears left here, then right around the north end of the lake and crosses the inlet brook at 9.0 mi. Just beyond, the Peabody Brook Trail leaves on the right.

From this junction, the Mahoosuc Trail follows a lumber road left for 100 yd. It soon recrosses the inlet brook, passes over a slight divide into the watershed of Austin Brook, ascends through some swampy places, and descends to Moss Pond at 10.5 mi. It continues past the north shore of the pond and follows an old logging road down the outlet brook, then crosses the brook, turns abruptly right downhill from the logging road, and descends to Gentian Pond. It skirts the southwest shore of the pond, then drops to cross the outlet brook. A few yards beyond, at 11.2 mi., is Gentian Pond Campsite (shelter and tentsites), and here the Austin Brook Trail diverges right for North Rd. in Shelburne.

Part III. Gentian Pond to Carlo Col

From Gentian Pond Shelter the trail climbs to the top of the steep-sided hump whose ledges overlook the pond from the east, then descends moderately to a sag. It then starts up the west end of Mt. Success, climbing steeply at first to the lumpy ridge, and passes a small stream at 12.6 mi. in the col that lies under the main mass of Mt. Success. The trail now climbs rather steeply and roughly for about 0.5 mi. to the relatively flat upper part of the mountain, then ascends over open ledges with an outlook to the southwest, passes through a belt of high scrub, crosses an alpine meadow, and finally comes out on the summit of Mt. Success at 14.0 mi.

The trail turns sharp left here and descends through scrub, then forest, to the sag between Mt. Success and a northern subpeak, where the Success Trail enters left at 14.6 mi. The main trail climbs slightly, then descends moderately to the main col between Mt. Success and Mt. Carlo at 15.3 mi. The trail then rises over a low hump and descends to a lesser col, where it turns right, then left, passes the Maine–New Hampshire border signs, and ascends moderately again. At 16.4 mi. it drops sharply past a fine outlook ledge into the little box ravine called Carlo Col. The Carlo Col Trail from Success Pond Rd. enters left here; Carlo Col Shelter is located 0.3 mi. down the Carlo Col Trail, at the head of a small brook.

Part IV. Carlo Col to Mahoosuc Notch

From Carlo Col the trail climbs steadily to the bare southwest summit of Mt. Carlo at 16.8 mi., where there is an excellent view. It then passes a lower knob to the northeast, and descends through a mountain meadow, where there is a fine view of Goose Eye ahead, to the col at 17.4 mi. The trail turns more north and climbs steeply to a ledgy knoll below Goose Eye, then passes through a sag and climbs steeply again to the narrow ridge of the main peak of Goose Eye Mtn. at 18.2 mi. Use care on the ledges. Here, at the ridge top, the Goose Eye Trail branches sharp left, reaching the open summit and its spectacular views in 0.1 mi. and continuing to Success Pond Rd. From the ridge top junction the Mahoosuc Trail turns sharp right (east) and follows the ridgecrest through mixed ledge and scrub to a col, then climbs steeply through woods and open areas to the bare summit of the East Peak of Goose Eye Mtn. Here it turns sharp left (north) down the open ledges of the ridge, and enters the scrub at the east side of the open part. Beyond the col the trail runs in the open nearly to the foot of the North Peak, except for two interesting box ravines, where there is often water. At the summit of the North Peak, at 19.8 mi., the trail turns sharp right (east) along the ridgecrest, then swings northeast down the steep slope, winding through several patches of scrub. At the foot of the steep slope it enters the woods and angles down the west face of the ridge to the col at 20.8 mi. Full Goose Shelter is located on a ledgy shelf near here; there is a spring 80 yd. to the right (east of the shelter). The trail then turns sharp left and ascends, coming into the open about 0.3 mi. below the summit of the South Peak of Fulling Mill Mtn., which is reached at 21.3 mi. Here the trail turns sharp left, runs through a meadow, and descends northwest through woods, first gradually then steeply, to the head of Mahoosuc Notch at 22.3 mi. Here the Notch Trail to Success Pond Rd. diverges sharp left (southwest).

Part V. Mahoosuc Notch to Old Speck

From the head of Mahoosuc Notch the trail turns sharp right (northeast) and descends the length of the narrow notch along a rough footway, passing through a number of boulder caverns, some with narrow openings where progress will be slow and where ice remains into the summer. The trail is blazed on the rocks with white paint. *Caution:* Use great care when traveling through the notch due to slippery rocks and dangerous holes; the notch may be impassable through early June because of snow, even with snowshoes. Heavy backpacks will impede progress considerably.

At the lower end of the notch, at 23.4 mi., the trail bears left and ascends moderately but roughly under the east end of Mahoosuc Mtn. along the valley that leads to Notch 2, then crosses to the north side of the brook at 23.9 mi. The trail then winds upward among rocks and ledges on the very steep wooded slope of Mahoosuc Arm with a steep, rough footway. A little more than halfway up it passes the head of a little flume, in which there is sometimes water. At 25.0 mi., a few yards past the top of the flat ledges near the summit of Mahoosuc Arm, the May Cutoff diverges left and leads 0.3 mi. over the true summit to the Speck Pond Trail. The Mahoosuc Trail swings right and wanders across the semi-open summit plateau for about 0.5 mi., then drops steeply to Speck Pond (3430 ft.), one of the highest ponds in Maine, bordered with thick woods. The trail crosses the outlet brook and continues around the east side of the pond to Speck Pond Campsite at 25.9 mi. (in summer, there is a caretaker and a fee for overnight camping). Here the Speck Pond Trail to Success Pond Rd. leaves on the left.

The trail then climbs to the southeast end of the next hump on the ridge, passes over it, and runs across the east face of a second small hump. In the gully beyond, a few yards east of the trail, there is an unreliable spring. The trail climbs on the west shoulder of Old Speck, reaching an open area where the footway is well defined on the crest. Near the top of the shoulder the trail bears right, re-enters the woods, and follows the wooded crest with blue blazes that mark the boundary of Grafton Notch State Park. The Old Speck Trail, which continues the Appalachian Trail north, diverges left to Grafton Notch at 27.0 mi., and the Mahoosuc Trail runs straight ahead to the summit of Old Speck and its observation tower, where the rather poorly marked East Spur Trail enters.

Mahoosuc Trail (map 7:E10–C13)

Distances from NH 16 in Gorham

  to Mt. Hayes summit: 3.1 mi., 2 hr. 20 min.
  to Centennial Trail: 3.3 mi., 2 hr. 25 min.
  to Cascade Mtn. summit: 5.1 mi., 3 hr. 35 min.
  to Trident Col: 6.3 mi., 4 hr. 20 min.
  to Page Pond: 7.3 mi., 5 hr.
  to Wocket Ledge: 7.9 mi., 5 hr. 50 min.
  to Dream Lake, inlet brook crossing: 9.0 mi., 6 hr. 20 min.
  to Gentian Pond Shelter: 11.2 mi., 8 hr.
  to Mt. Success summit: 14.0 mi., 10 hr. 50 min.
  to Success Trail: 14.6 mi., 11 hr. 20 min.
  to Carlo Col Trail: 16.4 mi., 13 hr. 20 min.
  to Mt. Carlo: 16.8 mi., 13 hr. 50 min.

   to Goose Eye Trail: 18.2 mi., 15 hr. 20 min.
   to Goose Eye Mtn., East Peak: 18.6 mi., 15 hr. 45 min.
   to Goose Eye Mtn., North Peak: 19.8 mi., 16 hr. 5 min.
   to Full Goose Shelter: 20.8 mi., 16 hr. 35 min.
   to Notch Trail: 22.3 mi., 17 hr. 30 min.
   to foot of Mahoosuc Notch: 23.4 mi., 19 hr. 20 min.
   to Mahoosuc Arm summit: 25.0 mi., 21 hr.
   to Speck Pond Shelter: 25.9 mi., 21 hr. 40 min.
   to Old Speck Trail junction: 27.0 mi., 22 hr. 45 min.
   to Old Speck Mtn. summit: 27.3 mi. (43.9 km.), 23 hr.

Success Trail (AMC)

This trail ascends to the Mahoosuc Trail 0.6 mi. north of
Mt. Success from Success Pond Rd. 5.4 mi. from
Hutchins St. Note that the trail sign is easy to miss. The
trail follows a logging road, bears right at a fork at 0.1
mi., and passes straight through a clearing, entering the
woods at a sign in 0.4 mi. Soon the trail starts to climb
steadily on the road, and at 1.4 mi. reaches the upper edge
of an area of small second-growth trees, swings right, and
ascends more steeply. At 1.6 mi. a loop path 0.3 mi. long
diverges right to a spectacular ledge outlook with fine
views of the Presidentials and the mountains of the North
Country. In a little over 100 yd. the upper end of the loop
path rejoins, and the main trail ascends to a ridgecrest,
from which it descends very gradually to a brook (unreliable water source) at an old logging campsite. The trail
now makes an easy climb up a shallow ravine, part of the
way in the bed of a small, unreliable brook (follow paint
blazes carefully), and soon reaches the Mahoosuc Trail at
the main ridgecrest.

Success Trail (map 7:D12)

Distances from Success Pond Road
   to Mahoosuc Trail: 2.4 mi. (3.8 km.), 2 hr.
   to Mt. Success summit (via Mahoosuc Trail): 3.0 mi.,
     2 hr. 30 min.

Carlo Col Trail (AMC)

This trail ascends to the Mahoosuc Trail at the small box ravine called Carlo Col; it leaves Success Pond Rd. in common with the Goose Eye Trail 8.1 mi. from Hutchins St. From the road the two trails follow a broad logging road, and in 100 yd. the Goose Eye Trail diverges sharp left down an embankment, while the Carlo Col Trail continues straight ahead on the road, which it follows east for 0.8 mi. with little gain in elevation. Turning left off the road at a log yard, the trail immediately crosses the main brook (may be difficult at high water), continues near it for about 0.3 mi., then turns left away from the brook and follows a branch road with a steeper grade. It swings back to the south, crossing over the north and south branches of the main brook, and bends east up the rather steep south bank of the south branch. Avoiding several false crossings of this brook, it climbs to Carlo Col Shelter at 2.4 mi. (last water, perhaps for several miles). The trail continues up the dry ravine and ends at the Mahoosuc Trail at Carlo Col. There is a fine outlook ledge a short distance to the right (west) on the Mahoosuc Trail.

Carlo Col Trail (map 7:C12–C13)

Distance from Success Pond Road
  to Mahoosuc Trail: 2.6 mi. (4.1 km.), 2 hr. 5 min.

Goose Eye Trail (AMC)

This trail ascends Goose Eye Mtn. from Success Pond Rd., starting with the Carlo Col Trail 8.1 mi. from Hutchins St., and reaches the Mahoosuc Trail 0.1 mi. beyond the summit. This is a generally easy trail to a very scenic summit, but there is one fairly difficult scramble up a ledge just below the summit. From the road the two trails follow a broad logging road, and in 100 yd. the Goose Eye Trail diverges sharp left down an embankment, then turns sharp right onto another logging road, while the Carlo Col Trail continues straight ahead on the first road. The Goose Eye Trail follows the logging road, crosses two brooks, and enters a more recent gravel road that comes in from the right (descending, bear right). In 100 yd. it diverges right (watch carefully for sign) from the gravel road, passes through a clear-cut area, crosses a wet section, and at 1.4 mi. it reaches the yellow-blazed Maine–New Hampshire state line. The trail angles up the south side of a ridge at a moderate grade through hardwoods, climbs more steeply uphill, then becomes gradual at the crest of the ridge; at 2.6 mi. there is a glimpse of the peak of Goose Eye ahead. The trail ascends moderately along the north side of the ridge, then steeply, scrambling up a difficult ledge that may be dangerous if wet or icy, then comes out on the open ledges below the summit. From the summit, which has magnificent views, the trail continues 0.1 mi. to the Mahoosuc Trail, which turns right (southbound) and runs straight ahead (northbound).

Goose Eye Trail (map 7:C12–C13)

Distances from Success Pond Road

 to Goose Eye Mtn. summit: 3.1 mi., 2 hr. 40 min.

 to Mahoosuc Trail: 3.2 mi. (5.2 km.), 2 hr. 45 min.

Notch Trail (AMC)

This trail ascends to the southwest end of Mahoosuc Notch, providing the easiest access to this wild and beautiful place. It begins on a spur road that leaves Success Pond Rd. 10.9 mi. from Hutchins St. and runs 0.3 mi. to a small parking area. The trail continues on the spur road across two bridges, then turns left (sign) onto an old logging road at 0.3 mi. It ascends easily along a slow-running brook with many signs of beaver activity, following logging roads much of the way with bypasses at some of the wetter spots. At the height-of-land it meets the Mahoosuc Trail. Turn left for the notch; very soon after entering the Mahoosuc Trail, the valley, which has been an ordinary one, changes sharply to a chamber formation, and the high cliffs of the notch, which have not been visible at all on the Notch Trail, come into sight.

Notch Trail (map 7:C12–C13)
Distance from spur road off Success Pond Rd.
   to Mahoosuc Trail: 2.2 mi. (3.5 km.), 1 hr. 30 min.

Speck Pond Trail (AMC)
This trail ascends to Speck Pond from Success Pond Rd.; take the right fork of the road 11.4 mi. from Hutchins St., and continue 0.8 mi. to the trailhead. The trail leaves the road, enters the woods, and follows the north side of a small brook for 1.4 mi. It then swings left away from the brook, climbs rather steeply at times, passes a relatively level section, then climbs rather steeply to the junction at 3.1 mi. with the May Cutoff, which diverges right and leads over the true summit of Mahoosuc Arm to the Mahoosuc Trail. The Speck Pond Trail passes an excellent outlook over the pond and up to Old Speck, then descends steeply to the pond and reaches the campsite and the Mahoosuc Trail.

Speck Pond Trail (map 7:C13)
Distance from branch of Success Pond Rd.
   to Speck Pond Campsite: 3.6 mi. (5.8 km.), 3 hr.

May Cutoff (AMC)
This short trail runs from the Speck Pond Trail to the Mahoosuc Trail, across the true summit of Mahoosuc Arm, with only minor ups and downs.

May Cutoff (map 7:C13)
Distance from Speck Pond Trail
   to Mahoosuc Trail: 0.3 mi. (0.5 km.), 10 min.

Old Speck Trail (AMC)
This trail, part of the Appalachian Trail, ascends Old Speck Mtn. from a well-signed parking area on ME 26 at

the height-of-land in Grafton Notch. From the north side of the parking lot follow the left trail; the right trail goes to Baldpate Mtn. In 0.1 mi., the Eyebrow Trail leaves right to circle over the top of an 800-ft. cliff shaped like an eyebrow. The Old Speck Trail crosses a brook and soon begins to climb, following a series of switchbacks to approach the falls on Cascade Brook. Above the falls the trail, now heading more north, crosses the brook for the last time (last available water), and at 1.1 mi. passes the upper terminus of the Eyebrow Trail on the right. The main trail bears left, ascends gradually to the north ridge, where it bears more left and follows the ridge, which has occasional views southwest. High up the trail turns southeast toward the summit, and at 3.1 mi. the Link Trail (no sign) diverges left. The Old Speck Trail turns more south and ascends to the Mahoosuc Trail, where it ends. The flat, wooded summit of Old Speck, where an observation tower affords fine views, is 0.3 mi. left (east); Speck Pond Shelter is located 1.1 mi. to the right.

Old Speck Trail (map 7:B13–C13)

Distances from ME 26

> *to* Eyebrow Trail, upper junction: 1.1 mi., 1 hr. 5 min.
>
> *to* Link Trail: 3.1 mi., 2 hr. 40 min.
>
> *to* Mahoosuc Trail: 3.5 mi. (5.6 km.), 3 hr. 10 min.
>
> *to* Old Speck Mtn. summit (via Mahoosuc Trail): 3.8 mi., 3 hr. 20 min.

Link Trail

The Link Trail descends very steeply from the Old Speck Trail, 3.1 mi. from ME 26, to the site of the former firewarden's cabin, giving access to the East Spur Trail, which provides an attractive but much more difficult loop to the summit. It is blazed in blue and fairly well beaten, but may not have signs at either end.

Link Trail (map 7:C13)

Distance from Old Speck Trail
    to East Spur Trail: 0.3 mi. (0.5 km.), 15 min.

East Spur Trail

This trail ascends the east spur of Old Speck; it is much steeper and rougher than the Old Speck Trail, and can be fairly hard to follow, but it has much better views. *Caution:* This trail is not recommended for inexperienced hikers or in bad weather. It begins at the site of the old firewarden's cabin, reached from the Old Speck Trail via the Link Trail. Both trails are marked here only by blue blazes on rocks, and you must avoid the abandoned firewarden's trail, which was once the Appalachian Trail and can still be seen quite clearly running up and down the ravine. The East Spur Trail crosses the brook and ascends steeply, then angles upward around the nose of the ridge, passing through an extensive area of open ledge with good views. Returning to the woods, it passes to the left of a large pointed boulder and climbs up on ledges, some of which are quite steep and would be dangerous if wet or icy, with very fine views. It then swings left and climbs through scrub that still permits views, and ends at the north terminus of the Mahoosuc Trail in a small clearing 30 yd. north of the summit of Old Speck Mtn.

East Spur Trail (map 7:C13)

Distance from Link Trail
    to Old Speck summit: 1.0 mi. (1.6 km.), 1 hr.

Eyebrow Trail

The Eyebrow Trail provides an alternative route to the lower part of the Old Speck Trail, passing along the edge of the cliff called the Eyebrow that overlooks Grafton Notch. The trail leaves the Old Speck Trail on the right 0.1 mi. from the parking area off ME 26. It turns right at the base of a rock face, crosses a rock slide (potentially dangerous if icy), then turns sharp left and ascends steadily, bearing right where a side path leaves straight ahead for an outlook. Soon the trail runs at a moderate grade along the top of the cliff, with good views, then descends to an outlook and runs mostly level until it ends at the Old Speck Trail.

Eyebrow Trail (map 7:B13)
Distance from Old Speck Trail, lower junction
   to Old Speck Trail, upper junction: 1.2 mi. (1.9 km.),
      1 hr. 10 min.

Centennial Trail (AMC)

This trail, a part of the Appalachian Trail, begins on Hogan Rd.; this dirt road turns west from North Rd. north of where it crosses the Androscoggin River, just before it swings abruptly to the east. There is a small parking area 0.2 mi. from North Rd., and parking is also permitted at the junction of North Rd. and Hogan Rd.; in any case, do not block the road. The Centennial Trail was constructed by the AMC in 1976, its centennial year.

From the parking area on Hogan Rd., the trail runs generally northwest. After 50 yd. on an old road, it bears left up a steep bank into the woods, levels off, and reaches the first of many stone steps in 0.1 mi. The trail ascends rather steeply, then more gradually, with a limited view of the Androscoggin River. It turns left onto a woods road and crosses a brook at 0.7 mi. (last available water). The trail then crosses a logging road and climbs past several restricted viewpoints, then descends to a sag in a birch grove at 1.6 mi. Climbing again, it soon turns sharp left and continues upward past ledges that provide increasingly open views. At 2.8 mi. the trail reaches an easterly summit of Mt. Hayes, where there is an excellent view of the Carter-Moriah Range and Northern Presidentials from open ledges. The trail descends slightly, then ascends across a series of open ledges to end at the Mahoosuc Trail at 3.1 mi. The summit of Mt. Hayes, with fine views, is 0.2 mi. left; the Appalachian Trail turns right (north) on the Mahoosuc Trail.

Centennial Trail (map 7:E11–D11)
Distance from Hogan Rd.

   to Mahoosuc Trail: 3.1 mi. (5.0 km.), 2 hr. 30 min.

Peabody Brook Trail (AMC)

This trail ascends to the Mahoosuc Trail at Dream Lake from North Rd., 1.3 mi. east of US 2. Overnight parking is not permitted at the base of this trail.

   The trail follows a logging road between two houses and turns right onto an old logging road at 0.5 mi. It continues north along the brook and bears right at a fork at 0.8 mi., soon becomes a trail, and begins to ascend moderately. At 1.2 mi. a path leaves left and leads in 0.3 mi. to Giant Falls. The main trail rises more steeply, and at 1.5 mi. there is a glimpse of Mt. Washington and Mt. Adams through open trees. The trail climbs a short ladder just beyond here. At 2.1 mi. it crosses the east branch of the brook, then recrosses it at 2.4 mi. From here the trail climbs easily to Dream Lake and the junction on the right with the Dryad Fall Trail at 3.0 mi., and continues to the Mahoosuc Trail.

Peabody Brook Trail (map 7:E11–D11)
Distance from North Rd.

   to Mahoosuc Trail: 3.1 mi. (5.0 km.), 2 hr. 20 min.

Austin Brook Trail (AMC)

This trail ascends to the Mahoosuc Trail at Gentian Pond from North Rd., 0.6 mi. west of Meadow Rd. (which crosses the Androscoggin at Shelburne village). There is limited parking on the south side of the road. The trail passes through a turnstile on private land and follows the west side of Austin Brook, crossing the Yellow Trail at 0.4 mi. The trail follows logging roads along the brook, then crosses it and reaches the gravel Mill Brook Rd., which is normally gated at North Rd., at 1.1 mi. (Austin Brook and Mill Brook are different names for the same stream.) Turn left on the logging road, and continue past a brook crossing to the junction left with the Dryad Fall Trail at 1.9 mi. At 2.1 mi. the trail turns left onto an old logging road. At 3.1 mi. the trail crosses the brook that drains Gentian Pond and climbs steeply to the Mahoosuc Trail at Gentian Pond Shelter.

Austin Brook Trail (map 7:E12–D12)
Distance from North Rd.

to Gentian Pond: 3.5 mi. (5.7 km.), 2 hr. 30 min.

Dryad Fall Trail (AMC)

This trail runs from the Austin Brook Trail to the Peabody Brook Trail near Dream Lake, passing Dryad Fall, one of the highest cascades in the mountains—particularly interesting for a few days after a rainstorm, since its several cascades fall at least 300 ft. over steep ledges. The trail is blazed in yellow.

The trail leaves the Austin Brook Trail on the left 1.9 mi. from North Rd., just past the third brook crossing. It gradually ascends old logging roads then drops down (right) to Dryad Brook, which it follows nearly to the base of the falls at 0.5 mi. *Caution:* Rocks in the vicinity of the falls are very slippery and hazardous. From here the trail climbs steeply northeast of the falls. At 0.6 mi. it turns right away from the falls, then turns left on an old road and comes back to the top of the falls. It then turns left on another road and crosses Dryad Brook at 0.9 mi., then climbs at mostly moderate grades to the Peabody Brook Trail near Dream Lake 0.1 mi. east of the Mahoosuc Trail. (Descending, watch carefully for the junction where the trail turns down steeply to the right off the logging road above the falls.)

Dryad Fall Trail (map 7:D12–D11)

Distances from Austin Brook Trail
> *to* Dryad Fall: 0.5 mi., 30 min.
> *to* Peabody Brook Trail: 1.8 mi. (2.9 km.), 1 hr. 40 min.

Scudder Trail

This trail, blazed red and white, provides access to the ledges and summit of Mt. Ingalls. It begins on Mill Brook Rd., a gated logging road that leaves North Rd. about 50 yd. west of Meadow Rd. (the road that crosses the Androscoggin on a bridge from Shelburne village). It diverges (orange blazes, no sign) from Mill Brook Rd. on the second road right, 0.5 mi. from North Rd., crosses the Yellow Trail and shortly enters an open area. Bearing left, the trail continues as a woods road to a sign on the right, where it follows another road that climbs to the Ingalls-Cabot col at 1.3 mi., where the Judson Pond Trail leads right to the summit of Mt. Cabot via the Red Trail. The Scudder Trail turns sharp left at the col and soon comes out on a ledge on the west side of the ridge, with views over the Androscoggin Valley. The trail climbs back eastward, passing the blue blazes of a Boise-Cascade Co. boundary in a ravine beneath a high cliff. The trail wanders back and forth, emerging on open ledges on both sides of the ridge, and finally circles an extensive ledge with views southwest. It then climbs 150 yd. to the wooded summit of Mt. Ingalls. A beaten path, axe-blazed with some white paint markings, leads down 0.1 mi. to Roy's Pond, a scenic mountain tarn.

Scudder Trail (map 7:E12–D12)

Distances from Mill Brook Rd.
> *to* Ingalls-Cabot col: 1.3 mi., 55 min.
> *to* Mt. Ingails summit: 2.7 mi. (4.4 km.), 2 hr. 10 min.

Middle Mountain Path

This trail ascends Middle Mtn., an interesting peak with good views, but at present it is severely overgrown and can be recommended only for hikers who are experienced in following obscure trails and routes. Follow Gates Brook Rd., a woods road that leaves North Rd. on the north just east of Gates Brook, 2.4 mi. from the west junction of North Rd. and US 2. Continue on this road for about 0.9 mi., past a trail on the right at 0.4 mi. that leads to Mt. Crag, then take a left branch that leads up the ravine between First Mtn. and Middle Mtn., at one point making a sharp left turn up a blowdown-strewn gully. The trail, blazed yellow, should not be confused with large yellow boundary markings on the woods road and on the summit trail. Just before the height of land, the trail turns off the road right and climbs, at first steeply, along the ridge to the bare summit of Middle Mtn., where there are fine views.

Middle Mountain Path (map 7:E12–D11)
Distance from North Rd.

   to Middle Mtn. summit: 1.7 mi. (2.7 km.), 1 hr. 30 min.

Mt. Crag

This small mountain is easily climbed and offers an excellent view up and down the Androscoggin Valley. It has two trails.

(1) The Yellow Trail. This attractive trail gives convenient access to the Austin Brook Trail and Mt. Crag from the Philbrook Farm Inn on North Rd. (For the shortest route to Mt. Crag via the Yellow Trail, follow the Austin Brook Trail 0.4 mi. in from North Rd., then go left on the Yellow Trail to Mt. Crag.) The Yellow Trail leads west from the north end of the access road behind the inn's cottages. It coincides with the Red Trail to Mt. Cabot for 50 yd., then branches left and leads west on a practically level grade. It crosses in sequence several woods roads, the Scudder Trail, Mill Brook Rd., Austin Brook, and the Austin Brook Trail. After the Austin Brook Trail junction, at 1.0 mi., it heads generally northwest to the sum-

mit of Mt. Crag at 1.8 mi., going through an extensive lumbered area (but it is easy to follow).

(2) Take Gates Brook Rd., a woods road that leaves North Rd. on the north just east of Gates Brook, 2.4 mi. from the west junction of North Rd. and US 2. A trail leaves this road 0.4 mi. from North Rd., on the right, and climbs steeply 0.3 mi. to the Yellow Trail a few steps below the summit.

Mt. Cabot and Crow's Nest

This range runs south and southeast from Mt. Ingalls. Several trails, distinguished by color, start from the access road at the Philbrook Farm Inn on North Rd. The path farthest to the east is the White Trail, which leads to Crow's Nest. The Blue and Red trails both lead to the summit of Mt. Cabot, making a loop trip possible. The Yellow Trail, described above, runs west to Mt. Crag and also provides access to Mt. Ingalls via the Scudder Trail.

The White Trail is best reached from the dirt road that starts immediately west of the fire pond east of the Philbrook Farm Inn. Follow this road to the first cottage, where the White Trail turns right by a large rock. Shortly the Wiggin Rock Trail (Orange Trail) leaves left, while the White Trail climbs east along an old logging road through a recently logged area (follow blazes carefully). Leaving the logging road right at 1.2 mi., it makes a short, steep ascent to the wooded summit of Crow's Nest at 1.3 mi. The trail ends a few yards farther at a limited viewpoint to the northeast.

The Wiggin Rock Trail (Orange Trail) climbs from its junction with the White Trail for 0.2 mi. to Wiggin Rock, a small ledge with a view southeast across the Androscoggin Valley. Beyond the viewpoint, the trail drops steeply for another 0.2 mi. to the Blue Trail.

The Blue Trail starts from the gravel road immediately to the west of the Philbrook Farm Inn, follows a good wood road, and passes the Orange (Wiggin Rock) Trail on the right in 80 yd. Shortly before this road reaches an old reservoir, the Blue Trail turns right on a badly eroded road. The Blue Trail continues much of the way on logging roads at an easy grade to a boundary marker, beyond which the trail climbs more steeply for about 0.3 mi. to the summit of Mt. Cabot and the Red Trail at 1.3 mi. The summit is wooded, but a ledge on the right shortly before the summit gives a view east, and an orange-blazed trail from the summit leads left to an open ledge with views southwest.

The Red Trail bears left from the Blue Trail on the access road west of the Philbrook Farm Inn, coinciding for 50 yd. with the Yellow Trail, which then diverges left. The Red Trail continues on a series of logging roads, passes an orange-blazed trail to a viewpoint (Mary's Aerie) on the right, crosses a small brook, circles around, and finally climbs steeply to approach Mt. Cabot from the north. The Judson Pond Trail leads left (downhill) shortly before the Red Trail reaches the summit and the junction with the Blue Trail at 1.4 mi. (See Blue Trail for views.)

The Judson Pond Trail (which no longer reaches Judson Pond, due to logging activity in that region) is an orange-blazed connecting trail that diverges from the Red Trail 0.1 mi. northwest of the summit of Mt. Cabot, and in 0.2 mi. reaches the Ingalls-Cabot Col and the junction with the Scudder Trail. Beyond this point the trail has been abandoned.

Update: The Wright Trail

Since the first printing of the *White Mountain Guide 25th edition* a new trail, the Wright Trail, has been created that climbs the east side of Goose Eye Mountain from the Sunday River Road in Ketcham, ME. See map 7:c13 of this guide. A full description may be found in the *AMC Maine Mountain Guide 7th edition.*

SECTION 12
The North Country

This section covers all of New Hampshire west of NH 16 and north of US 2. The Cherry-Dartmouth Range, which rises south of US 2 between Jefferson and Twin Mtn., is also included here. From the hiker's point of view, the heart of this section is the three principal ranges in the triangle formed by US 2, US 3, and NH 110; the corners of this triangle are located roughly at the towns of Lancaster, Groveton, and Gorham. This region is composed of the Pliny, Pilot, and Crescent ranges; the very similar Cherry-Dartmouth Range to the south should also be considered with this group. These are relatively compact mountain ranges, with officially maintained trail networks, on or adjacent to lands of the WMNF. North of NH 110 lies the North Country proper, a sparsely populated region with extensive woodlands owned mostly by large corporations that manage the land for lumber and pulpwood production. This region, similar to the small, adjacent corner of Vermont and the much vaster woodlands of northern Maine to the east, is on the southern edge of the great band of boreal forest that covers much of Ontario and Quebec. There are only a few trails to widely scattered natural features, and the region is far better known for hunting, fishing, and snowmobiling than for hiking. Even the southern part of the area has a higher level of logging activity than the main ranges of the White Mtns. to the south and east, along with hiking trails that frequently have much less use and less intensive maintenance. This area can perhaps best be understood as a transitional zone between the main ranges, with their heavily used, intensively maintained trail systems visiting almost every significant feature, and the vast commercial woodlands of the north, where logging roads are the principal routes of travel both by wheel and on foot, and logging activity is visible almost everywhere.

This section covers four relatively distinct ranges and trail networks, treated in separate subsections: (A) The Cherry-Dartmouth Range, which includes the main peak of Cherry Mtn. and its fine northern crag, Owl's Head; (B) the Crescent Range, including Mt. Randolph, Mt. Crescent, Lookout Ledge, the Ice Gulch, and the rest of the Randolph Mountain Club (RMC) trail system north of US 2; (C) the Pilot-Pliny Range, including Mt. Waumbek, Mt. Starr King, Mt. Weeks, Terrace Mtn., Mt. Cabot, the Bulge, the Horn, and the region of the headwaters of the Upper Ammonoosuc River to the east of Unknown Pond, whose most prominent features are Rogers Ledge and the Devil's Hopyard; and (D) the North Country proper, whose principal points of interest are the Percy Peaks and Sugarloaf, Dixville Notch and Table Rock, the Diamond Peaks, and Magalloway Mtn. Subsections A, B, and C are completely covered by map 8, the Pilot map; subsection D requires USGS maps as indicated for each objective.

A. THE CHERRY-DARTMOUTH RANGE

Though technically speaking this range is the western extension of the Presidential Range, in terrain, type and amount of use, as well as nature of the trail system—in sum, its general flavor for hiking visitors—it is far more similar to its neighbors to the north than to the great mountains connected to it in the east. Cherry Mtn. is a prominent mountain located in the town of Carroll, west of the Presidential Range. The highest peak is Mt. Martha (3573 ft.), which has good outlooks from the summit area, although the former fire tower has been dismantled. A northern spur, Owl's Head (3258 ft.), has a spectacular view from a fine ledge just south of the wooded summit. The Dartmouth Range is a ridge with numerous humps running southwest to northeast, lying between Cherry Mtn. and the Presidentials. The range is completely trailless; Mt. Dartmouth (3727 ft.) and Mt. Deception (3671 ft.) are the most important summits. Cherry Mountain Rd. (FR 14), 6.9 mi. long, runs from US 302 about 0.8 mi. west of the Fabyan Motel to the junction of NH 115 and NH 115A, passing through the high notch that separates the two mountain masses. Refer to map 8, Pilot.

The Pondicherry Wildlife Refuge, a 300-acre wild tract of pond and bog located mostly in Jefferson with a few acres in Whitefield, is a National Natural Landmark. It consists of Big Cherry Pond (about 90 acres) and Little Cherry Pond (about 25 acres). As "Great Ponds," these are in the custody of the state. Surrounding each are bands of open bog and bog-swamp forest belonging to the Audubon Society of New Hampshire. "Pondicherry" is the old name for Cherry Pond and nearby Cherry Mtn. The NH Fish and Game Department, and the Audubon Society, manage the refuge jointly. Fishing is allowed, but not hunting or trapping. At least fifty kinds of water birds and an unusual variety of mammals have been recorded in the refuge, and several uncommon species of both water and land birds nest there. Pondicherry is also interesting for its vegetation and its spectacular views of the Presidential Range. Best access is east from White-field Airport by following either the old B&M Railroad right-of-way, which is passable by car, and then the tracks beyond, or the old Maine Central right-of-way off the road from the airport to NH 115.

THE TRAILS
Cherry Mountain Trail (WMNF)

This trail runs across the ridge of Cherry Mtn. just south of the summit (which is reached by a spur path). The west trailhead lies at a newly constructed parking lot opposite Lennon Road on NH 115, 1.9 mi. from its junction with US 3; the east trailhead, which is far less frequently used, is located on Cherry Mountain Rd. (FR 14) (which is narrow—use care) just north of its height-of-land, 3.2 mi. from US 302 and 3.7 mi. from NH 115.

Leaving NH 115 on a recently built logging road, the trail passes straight through a log yard at 0.3 mi., and continues straight ahead at 0.5 mi. where another road diverges right. In 0.7 mi. it becomes a footpath on an old roadbed, climbing higher above the brook that it parallels, and passes a spring left at 1.3 mi. At 1.7 mi. the trail reaches the ridgecrest, and a spur path turns left and climbs 0.2 mi. to the summit of Mt. Martha, where it meets Martha's Mile.

From the junction with the summit spur, the Cherry Mountain Trail turns right and descends on an old road with excellent footing, and at 3.3 mi. it passes the junction on the right with the abandoned Black Brook Trail. The Cherry Mountain Trail continues down the slope on the road and ends at Cherry Mountain Rd.

Cherry Mountain Trail (map 8:F6–F7)
Distances from NH 115

> *to* Mt. Martha summit spur trail: 1.7 mi., 1 hr. 45 min.
> *to* Mt. Martha summit (via spur trail): 1.9 mi., 1 hr. 55 min.
> *to* Cherry Mountain Rd.: 5.2 mi. (8.4 km.), 3 hr. 30 min.

Owl's Head Trail (RMC)

This trail ascends to the beautiful outlook on Owl's Head. It begins on NH 115 at a parking lot with the Stanley Slide historical marker, 5.9 mi. from the junction with US 3 and 0.7 mi. from the junction with NH 115A. The trail runs through the woods, dropping into the trench left by an 1885 landslide at 0.7 mi. It soon enters the older route of the trail, and crosses a gravel logging road into a region that has been recently logged. Following the trail along skid roads and through second growth requires some care. At the top of the logged area the trail turns sharp right into the overgrown track of the slide, where footing is slippery and poor. The trail reaches the ridge above the slide and continues steeply to the summit, where Martha's Mile continues across the magnificent outlook ledge and on to Mt. Martha.

Owl's Head Trail (map 8:E7)

Distance from NH 115
   to Owl's Head summit: 1.9 mi. (3.1 km.), 2 hr.

Martha's Mile

Martha's Mile is a link trail between the summits of Mt. Martha and Owl's Head. It leaves the ledge at the summit of Owl's Head, swings north, then sharp left, and descends a very short, steep pitch. It then descends easily to a col and climbs moderately, with excellent footing, to the summit of Mt. Martha.

Martha's Mile (map 8:E7–F6)

Distance from Owl's Head
   to Mt. Martha summit: 0.8 mi. (1.3 km.), 40 min.

B. CRESCENT RANGE

The Crescent Range lies north of US 2 and west of NH 16 in the towns of Jefferson, Randolph, and Berlin. The chief summits, west to east, are Mt. Randolph, Mt. Crescent, Black Crescent Mtn., Mt. Jericho, and Mt. Forist. Mt. Crescent (3251 ft.) derives its name from the shape of the ridge on which it is the highest summit. It is ascended by the Mount Crescent and Crescent Ridge trails. Mt. Randolph (3081 ft.) is the heavily wooded peak at the southern end of the Crescent Ridge, reached by the Crescent Ridge Trail. Black Crescent Mtn. (3264 ft.) lies to the north across the deep notch called Hunter's Pass. It is the highest peak in the range but has no trails; hikers with sufficient map and compass skills can ascend it fairly easily from the Bog Dam Rd. on the west, or by a much more difficult but more interesting route from the head of the Ice Gulch, climbing up a slide that affords excellent views. Lookout Ledge (2240 ft.) is a granite cliff on a knob of the southeast ridge of Mt. Randolph that affords one of the best views of the floor of King Ravine and its rock glacier, with moderate effort. It is reached by the Pasture Path, Ledge Trail, Sargent Path, Vyron D. Lowe Trail, and Crescent Ridge Trail. The ledge is on private property and no fires are permitted. Boy (Bois) Mtn. (2220 ft.) is a small peak at the west edge of the Crescent Range that offers an interesting view.

Mt. Jericho (2487 ft.) lies at the east end of the Crescent Range, just west of Berlin NH. Like many northern mountains, its summit was bared by the forest fires of the early 1900s. Now partially overgrown, it still offers a fine view east to the Mahoosucs and an obstructed view of the Carter Range, the northern Presidentials, and the Tinker Brook Valley. Mt. Forist (2068 ft.) has an impressive east cliff that rises abruptly from the edge of the city of Berlin. Locally known as Elephant Mtn. because of its shape as seen from Berlin, it was named for Merrill C. Forist, an early settler. The summit is on the elephant's "head," and there is an outlook on its "rear end." (Note that the name of this mountain is spelled incorrectly on the USGS Berlin quadrangle.) There is no maintained hiking trail to the summit of either Mt. Jericho or Mt. Forist, but experienced hikers with map and compass skills may be able to make some use of old paths and more recent snowmobile trails while bushwhacking up these mountains; there is a snowmobile trail network generally north of the ridge line that may help to provide access to these two mountains.

The Ice Gulch, one of the wildest and most beautiful places in the White Mtns., is a deep cut on the southeast slope of the Crescent Range, between Mt. Crescent and Black Crescent Mtn. The bed of the gulch is strewn with great boulders that lie in picturesque confusion, similar to those scattered over the floor of King Ravine. Among the boulders are many caves, some with perpetual ice. Springs and the melting ice form the headwaters of Moose Brook. Two paths lead to the gulch: the Cook Path to the head, and the Ice Gulch Path to the foot and from there up through the gulch. A short trail, the Peboamauk Loop, follows Moose Brook below the Ice Gulch, past Peboamauk Fall and several fine springs back to the Ice Gulch Path. The walk along the gulch is very strenuous with constant scrambling over wet, slippery rocks, requiring great care.

Most of the paths in this region are part of the Randolph Mountain Club (RMC) trail system. The town of Randolph consists of two sections: the lower section lies along Durand Rd. (the former US 2), in the Moose River Valley, and the upper section is situated on Randolph Hill, a plateau extending southeast from the foot of Mt. Crescent, reached by Mt. Crescent Rd. Lowe's Store and the Ravine House site are in the lower section, and the Mt. Crescent House site is in the upper section. On the south slope of the hill, connecting the two sections of the town and providing access from various points to major mountain trails, is a well-developed network of paths maintained by the RMC. These short and less important trails are omitted from this guide, but they are described in detail, along with the other RMC trails that are covered in this guide, in the RMC guidebook *Randolph Paths*. Several of these paths are merely connecting links for local residents, but some afford pleasant, easy walks or visit attractive spots such as Mossy Glen. They also are shown on the RMC map of the Randolph Valley and the Northern Peaks, which is more useful for the Crescent Range area than the AMC Pilot map (map 8) (which covers the entire area) or the USGS Pliny Range quad (which covers most of it).

Active lumbering and residential developments on the south slopes may intrude on some of the following trails, many of which are partly or wholly on private land. Watch carefully for markers and signs, and inquire locally for further information.

THE TRAILS

Boy Mountain Path

This path ascends Boy (Bois) Mtn., a small mountain located east of Jefferson Highlands, with an open ledge near the summit that provides a fine and easily accessible view of the northern Presidential Range. It is maintained by the Carter-Bridgman family. There is no trail sign where it leaves US 2, 1.3 mi. east of the junction of US 2 and NH 115. Park on the terrace south of the highway, west of the branch road to Jefferson Notch, and not in the driveway to the Carter estate. Go up the dirt drive between the garden and the raspberry patch and pass between the house and barn. From this point signs and arrows mark the path to the summit.

Boy Mountain (map 8:E8)

Distance from US 2

    to Boy Mtn. summit: 0.7 mi. (1.1 km.), 40 min.

Vyron D. Lowe Trail (RMC)

This path ascends to Lookout Ledge from the vicinity of Lowe's Store and Cabins, near the west end of Durand Rd. Entering the woods north of Durand Rd. just east of

Lowe's Cabins (sign), the trail parallels the road, then ascends, crossing a number of logging roads and logged areas. At 1.8 mi. it joins the Crescent Ridge Trail. Turn right (east) for Lookout Ledge.

Vyron D. Lowe Trail (map 8:E9)
Distance from Durand Rd.

   to Lookout Ledge: 1.9 mi. (3.0 km.), 1 hr. 25 min.

Sargent Path

This is the most direct route to Lookout Ledge, as well as the steepest. The trail is little used but well blazed, and with care it can be readily followed. The Cutter family maintains it. Leave Durand Rd. opposite a dark red cottage 0.8 mi. west of the Ravine House site and 0.9 mi. east of Randolph Spring. The path immediately bears left and rises steadily to the ledge, where it meets the Ledge and Crescent Ridge trails.

Sargent Path (map 8:E9)
Distance from Durand Rd.

   to Lookout Ledge: 0.8 mi. (1.3 km.), 50 min.

Ledge Trail (RMC)

Leading from the Ravine House site to Lookout Ledge, this trail forms a steep but direct route to the outlook. At the west end of the hotel site, look for a trail sign on the driveway. Follow blazes across a rocky slope above which the Eusden house is visible. The trail soon leaves the yard and, rising steadily northwest, climbs through deep and beautiful woods to the notch at 0.6 mi., where the Notchway diverges right for Randolph Hill. The Ledge Trail turns sharp left, steepens, and leaves the woods to follow an overgrown lumber road through second growth, then bears right off the road and shortly intersects the Pasture Path on the right at 1.2 mi. The trail re-enters the woods and climbs steeply over some rocks, then descends slightly, passing the Eyrie (a small

outlook), and continues a few yards more to its end at
the Crescent Ridge Trail. Just below is Lookout Ledge.

Ledge Trail (map 8:E9)

Distance from Ravine House site
> *to* Lookout Ledge: 1.3 mi. (2.1 km.), 1 hr. 10 min.

Pasture Path (RMC)

This trail leads from Randolph Hill Rd. to the Ledge
Trail. The Pasture Path begins at Randolph Hill Rd.
about 0.1 mi. above Stearns Rd. and runs west through
old pastures and woods, using parts of Stearns Rd.,
Glover Spring Rd., and High Acres Rd., passing the
Diagonal, Wood Path, EZ Way, and Bee Line. At 1.2
mi., the path leaves High Acres Rd. below High Acres,
passes through ancient forest and then light woods.
Grassy Lane diverges right, and the Pasture Path enters
young second growth and turns sharp left onto a logging
road at 1.9 mi. Soon it turns sharp right off the road
where the Notchway continues straight ahead, and runs
across several tributaries of Carlton Brook, then ascends
to meet the Ledge Trail 0.2 mi. below Lookout Ledge.

Pasture Path (map 8:E9)

Distances from Randolph Hill Rd.
> *to* Ledge Trail: 2.7 mi. (4.4 km.), 1 hr. 35 min.
> *to* Lookout Ledge (via Ledge Trail): 2.9 mi., 1 hr. 40 min.

Notchway (RMC)

This is a connecting path from the Ledge Trail 0.6 mi.
from Durand Rd. to the Pasture Path about 2.0 mi. west
of the Mt. Crescent House site. The Notchway leaves
the Ledge Trail at the notch, ascends slightly, passes
through a lumbered area, an old forest, and a swamp,
crosses three tributaries of Carlton Brook, and then
rises. Follow arrows left to a logging road and from
there to the Pasture Path.

Notchway (map 8:E9)

Distance from Ledge Trail

 to Pasture Path: 0.5 mi. (0.8 km.), 20 min.

Mount Crescent Trail (RMC)

This trail begins at Randolph Hill Rd. about 0.3 mi. west of the Mt. Crescent House site, opposite the head of Grassy Lane. Do not park here; leave cars at the Mt. Crescent House site. The trail coincides for 0.1 mi. with Cook Path, which then branches right. The Mount Crescent Trail continues on the logging road for another 0.1 mi. to the junction with the Carlton Notch Trail, where it turns right and begins to ascend the mountain.

At 0.3 mi. from Randolph Hill Rd., the Boothman Spring Cutoff enters from the Mt. Crescent House site, and the main trail steepens. At 0.7 mi. it passes Castleview Loop, which leads left 80 yd. to Castleview Rock. At 1.1 mi. the Crescent Ridge Trail, an alternate route that rejoins at the north summit of Mt. Crescent, branches right. The Mount Crescent Trail ascends northwest to the south viewpoint and then to the south summit of Mt. Crescent, where there is a glimpse of the Northern Peaks. It then continues for 0.2 mi. to the north summit, also wooded, from which the Pliny and Pilot ranges can be seen across the broad valley of the Upper Ammonoosuc. The trail ends here, at the second junction with the Crescent Ridge Trail.

Mount Crescent Trail (map 8:E9)

Distance from Randolph Hill Rd.

 to Mt. Crescent, north summit: 1.7 mi. (2.7 km.), 1 hr. 40 min.

Crescent Ridge Trail (RMC)

This trail branches right from the Mount Crescent Trail 1.1 mi. from Randolph Hill Rd. and crosses the east flank of the mountain. From there it turns west and climbs to the north outlook, where it again meets the Mount Crescent Trail at 0.6 mi. Continuing southwest, it descends gradually, crossing Carlton Brook, to Carlton Notch, where it crosses the Carlton Notch Trail at 1.3 mi. The Crescent Ridge Trail then ascends the ridge that rises west from Carlton Notch and passes Lafayette View, an outlook with an excellent view of King Ravine and Mts. Madison, Adams, and Jefferson. The trail then descends into the col between Mt. Randolph and the higher, unnamed peak north of it, crosses the headwaters of a branch of Carlton Brook, and climbs to the summit of Mt. Randolph. From here the trail descends steeply on an old lumber road past the Vyron D. Lowe Trail to the Ledge Trail just above Lookout Ledge.

Crescent Ridge Trail (map 8:E9)
Distances from Mount Crescent Trail
>   *to* Mt. Crescent, north outlook: 0.6 mi., 30 min.
>   *to* Carlton Notch Trail: 1.3 mi., 50 min.
>   *to* Lafayette View: 2.3 mi., 1 hr. 30 min.
>   *to* Mt. Randolph summit: 2.9 mi., 1 hr. 55 min.
>   *to* Lookout Ledge: 3.8 mi. (6.1 km.), 2 hr. 25 min.

Castleview Loop (RMC)
The Castleview Loop diverges left from the Mount Crescent Trail 0.7 mi. from Randolph Hill Rd. In a few feet a side trail leads left to Castleview Rock, an interesting boulder. The main trail descends gently through light woods, passing Castleview Ledge, which is named for its unique view of the Castellated Ridge of Mt. Jefferson. Entering thick forest, the loop then descends steeply and ends at the Carlton Notch Trail near the Mt. Crescent Water Co. Reservoir.

Castleview Loop (map 8:E9)
Distance from Mount Crescent Trail
>   *to* Carlton Notch Trail: 0.4 mi. (0.6 km.), 15 min.

Carlton Notch Trail (RMC)

The Carlton Notch Trail leads from the Mount Crescent Trail to the Crescent Ridge Trail in Carlton Notch, the pass between Mt. Randolph and Mt. Crescent. The section of trail that formerly continued from the notch to the Pond of Safety has been abandoned.

The trail starts on the Mount Crescent Trail 0.2 mi. from Randolph Hill Rd. and 0.1 mi. above its junction with the Cook Path. The Mount Crescent Trail turns right at this point, and the Carlton Notch Trail continues straight ahead. The trail rises gently on an old logging road, passing the Mt. Crescent Water Co. Reservoir and the Castleview Loop (right) at 0.7 mi. from Randolph Hill Rd. It then ascends moderately to Carlton Notch, where it ends at the Crescent Ridge Trail.

Carlton Notch Trail (map 8:E9–E8)
Distance from Randolph Hill Rd.
    to Carlton Notch: 1.7 mi. (2.5 km.), 1 hr. 20 min.

Boothman Spring Cutoff (RMC)

This short path circumvents the road walk and saves a bit of distance on the way to the Cook Path and Mount Crescent Trail from the Mt. Crescent House site on Randolph Hill Rd., a good starting point with parking space. The trail is level throughout, leading from the old hotel driveway (sign), through a field, then into the woods. At 0.3 mi. it passes Boothman Spring, then at 0.5 mi. it crosses the Cook Path to the Ice Gulch, then a lumber road, and ends at the Mount Crescent Trail.

Boothman Spring Cutoff (map 8:E9)
Distance from Mt. Crescent House site
    to Mount Crescent Trail: 0.6 mi. (0.9 km.), 20 min.

Cook Path (RMC)

This trail begins on Randolph Hill Rd. opposite Grassy Lane, about 0.3 mi. west of the Mt. Crescent House site.

Do not leave cars here; park at the Mt. Crescent House site. The trail coincides with the Mount Crescent Trail for about 0.1 mi., then branches right, passing an old trail, and at 0.3 mi. crosses the Boothman Spring Cutoff, a shortcut from the Mt. Crescent House site. It ascends over a low ridge and then descends easily to the head of Ice Gulch, where it ends. The Ice Gulch Path begins here and descends through the Ice Gulch.

Cook Path (map 8:E9–D9)

Distance from Randolph Hill Rd.
    to Ice Gulch Path: 2.5 mi. (4.0 km.), 1 hr. 40 min.

Ice Gulch Path (RMC)

This path gives access to the wild, beautiful Ice Gulch from Randolph Hill Rd., running to the bottom of the Ice Gulch and then up through it. The following description assumes that the trip will be made in the traditional direction; that is, by following the Cook Path to the head of the gulch, then descending through it and returning to Randolph Hill Rd. via the Ice Gulch Path. *Caution:* The trip through the gulch itself is one of the most difficult and strenuous trail segments in the White Mtns., involving nearly constant scrambling over wet, slippery rocks, and it may take much more time than the standard formula allows. There is no way to exit from the ravine in the mile between the Vestibule and Fairy Spring; hikers must either continue down or retrace their steps back up to the Cook Path, and should take this fact into account when considering the suitability of this trip for their party or estimating the amount of time they should allow for it.

From the Cook Path at the head of the Ice Gulch, the descent is very steep for 0.1 mi. to the Vestibule, where there is an excellent spring. The steep descent continues generally southeast, with views toward Gorham and down the gulch. At the foot of the gulch the trail passes Fairy Spring on the right (west). Just below this spring, at

0.9 mi., the Peboamauk Loop leaves on the left to follow the brook down to Peboamauk Fall. The Ice Gulch Path turns right here and climbs steeply up the west bank of the ravine, then heads south across several wet areas to the Marked Birch, where it bears right as the Peboamauk Loop rejoins on the left. The Ice Gulch Path runs southwest for about 2.0 mi., crossing three major brooks and a woods road, and ends at Sky Meadows on Randolph Hill Rd., about 0.4 mi. east of the Mt. Crescent House site.

Ice Gulch Path (map 8:E9–D9)

Distances from head of Ice Gulch
> *to* site of Marked Birch: 1.4 mi., 45 min.
> *to* Randolph Hill Rd.: 3.4 mi. (5.5 km.), 1 hr. 45 min.

Peboamauk Loop (RMC)

This loop path (Peboamauk means "winter's home") is an alternate route to the main Ice Gulch Path. It passes Peboamauk Fall, a fine cascade, and travels beside a pleasant stream. On the descent, the path leaves the Ice Gulch Path on the left at the foot of the Ice Gulch just below Fairy Spring, and descends steeply along Moose Brook for 0.4 mi. to Peboamauk Fall, then rises steeply to rejoin the Ice Gulch Path at the Marked Birch.

Peboamauk Loop (map 8:E9)

Distance from Ice Gulch Path, upper junction
> *to* Ice Gulch Path, lower junction: 0.5 mi. (0.8 km.), 20 min.

C. PLINY AND PILOT RANGES

These two ranges are essentially one mountain mass, extending north and south between the Israel and Upper Ammonoosuc rivers, east of Lancaster. The Pliny Range forms the semicircular southern end of this mass; its chief summits are Mt. Starr King, Mt. Waumbek, and the three peaks of Mt. Weeks. Across Willard Notch from Mt. Weeks, the Pilot Range begins, including Terrace Mtn., Mt. Cabot, Mt. Mary, and Hutchins Mtn., which is often known as Mt. Pilot. A spur that extends northeast from Mt. Cabot carries the Bulge and the Horn. Mt. Cabot is the highest peak in the entire North Country. Two fire towers that are accessible by auto provide excellent views that may be helpful to hikers planning trips in this region. Mt. Prospect (2306 ft.) is located in Weeks State Park, the former estate of John W. Weeks (see Mt. Weeks below), reached by a paved road (small fee charged) that leaves US 3 at its high point between Whitefield and Lancaster. Milan Hill (1737 ft.) is located in Milan Hill State Park (campground) on NH 110B west of Milan village; it offers a panoramic view that includes the Mahoosucs and the mountains north of NH 110 as well as the region covered in this subsection. This entire subsection is covered by the AMC Pilot map (map 8); the USGS Pliny Range and Percy quadrangles may also be useful.

Mt. Starr King (3907 ft.) was named for Thomas Starr King, a minister in Boston and San Francisco who was the author of *The White Hills*, one of the most important and influential books ever written about the White Mtns.; King Ravine on Mt. Adams and a peak in the Sierra Nevada of California are also named for him. New Hampshire's Mt. Starr King is located northeast of Jefferson village, from which it is reached by the Starr King Trail. The summit is wooded, but there is a fine, cleared vista toward the Presidentials. Mt. Waumbek (4006 ft.) lies immediately east of Mt. Starr King and is also reached by the Starr King Trail, as well as being the southern terminus of the Kilkenny Ridge Trail. Formerly called Pliny Major, Mt. Waumbek is the highest point of the Pliny Range. It has only a very restricted view east. Mt. Weeks is located northeast of Mt. Waumbek and has three distinct peaks—the North Peak (3901 ft.), the Middle Peak (3684 ft.), and the South Peak (3885 ft.)—all of which are traversed by the new section of the Kilkenny Ridge Trail. All three summits are wooded with no significant views. Formerly known as Round Mtn., it was renamed to honor John W. Weeks, who was the sponsor and chief proponent of the Weeks Act (1911), the piece of federal legislation that authorized the purchase of lands for national forests and thereby made possible the establishment of the WMNF.

The Pilot Range begins on the north side of Willard Notch with Terrace Mtn. (3655 ft.), a narrow ridge with several summits, named for its appearance when seen from the west. It is traversed by the Kilkenny Ridge Trail, and its principal summit affords an interesting if somewhat restricted view. Mt. Cabot (4170 ft.), the highest peak of the North Country, is located north of Terrace Mtn. and Bunnell Notch. Its true summit is wooded with no views, but good outlooks east and west have been cleared at the site of the former fire tower, 0.3 mi. southeast of the true summit, and there is an excellent vista from the ledges above Bunnell Notch. The Bulge (3920 ft.) and the Horn (3905 ft.) lie just north of Mt. Cabot. They are reached via the Kilkenny Ridge Trail, which follows the ridge that joins them to Mt. Cabot over the Bulge and then circles around the northwest side of the Horn, which is ascended by a spur path. The Bulge is a wooded hump with no views. The Horn is a fine, sharp peak composed of a jumble of bare rocks that afford views in all directions; it is unquestionably one of the finest summits in the region.

Hutchins Mtn. (3710 ft.), sometimes also called Mt. Pilot, was named after Alpheus Hutchins, an early settler. It lies at the northwest end of the Pilot Range, separated from Mt. Cabot by Mt. Mary and several unnamed peaks. It has no regular trail but can be ascended by experienced bushwhackers by following a private logging road that leaves the road from Grange to Groveton via Lost Nation at a sharp turn near an old schoolhouse at the foot of the mountain (use care not to block any roads). The most frequently used route follows the logging road that runs up the southeast side of Cummings Brook into the basin below the summit, then ascends to the southwest ridge of Hutchins Mtn. and follows it to the summit. See the USGS Percy quadrangle.

The wide valley east of the Pilot Range and north of the Crescent Range, drained by the headwaters of the Upper Ammonoosuc River, has been traditionally known to local residents as the Kilkenny, from the uninhabited township in which many of the peaks of the Pilot and Pliny ranges, including Mt. Waumbek and Mt. Cabot, are located. Ironically, most of the region usually called by the name of Kilkenny lies in the towns of Berlin, Randolph, Milan, and Stark, with very little in Kilkenny itself, though if the Pilot and Pliny ranges are included in the region (as is sometimes the case) the name of Kilkenny is then amply justified. It is a rather flat, densely forested region known well by loggers and those who love to hunt and fish, but not to nearly the same extent by hikers. Historically this region has been a major timber harvest area, and many of the features of interest reflect past and present logging activity both on private inholdings and on the National Forest lands, which are managed for multiple use. The trails in this region generally follow an extensive network of old, older, and ancient logging roads or railroad grades. Primary trails are usually blazed with yellow paint. The visual environment on the maintained trails has generally been screened from logging activity, but the longer view often includes vegetational diversity resulting from timber harvest and reforestation, and access roads may be in evidence. As a result of the variety of vegetation types, chances are excellent that one will see many kinds of native wildlife. The Kilkenny Ridge Trail links some of the main attractions of this area, including the Devil's Hopyard and Rogers Ledge. There are primitive campsites at Rogers Ledge and Unknown Pond. This is a backcountry area in which trails are normally maintained only once annually. It may be useful to check with the Androscoggin District Office in Gorham (603-466-2713) for the current status of particular trails.

The center of this area is accessible by York Pond Rd. (FR 13) to the Berlin Fish Hatchery at York Pond, and by Bog Dam Rd. (FR 15), which makes a 15.5 mi. loop south of York Pond. Bog Dam Road follows in part the earlier Upper Ammonoosuc Trail and logging road network, passing the sites of several former logging camps. With the present Upper Ammonoosuc Trail and the Landing Camp Trail, it provides access to Bog Dam, built to provide a "head" of water for the spring logging drives and later used as a town water supply. York Pond Rd. leaves NH 110 7.4 mi. northwest of its beginning at NH 16 in Berlin. There is a gate at the Berlin Fish Hatchery that is locked from 4 P.M. to 8 A.M. Hikers who plan to leave cars at the trailheads west of this gate should make prior arrangements in person at the gate-house, or by phone with the hatchery (603-449-3412). Foot travel through the gate is not restricted.

The South Pond Recreation Area is a picnic and swimming area operated by the WMNF at South Pond, south of NH 110 in Stark. No camping is allowed here. This is the northern terminus of the Kilkenny Ridge Trail and the Devil's Hopyard Trail. The access road to South Pond Recreation Area has a gate 1.1 mi. from the trailhead in the picnic area; this gate is kept locked from 8 P.M. to 9 A.M. during the season when the beach and picnic area are open. At other times it is usually locked, but it is normally left open from Labor Day to the end of hunting season. Foot travel is always permitted. Check with the Androscoggin District Office of the WMNF (603-466-2713) for details.

The Devil's Hopyard is a picturesque gorge on a brook that empties into South Pond. It resembles the Ice Gulch in Randolph, but is shorter and narrower. Rogers Ledge (2945 ft.), one of the most interesting little-known mountains in the White Mtns., lies about 3.5 mi. northwest of York Pond. It was named in honor of Major Robert Rogers, leader of Rogers's Rangers in the French and Indian Wars. The entire southwest face of the mountain is a cliff, and the view from the top includes the Kilkenny area, the Pilot Range, the Mahoosucs, and the Presidential Range. It may be reached from South Pond by the Kilkenny Ridge Trail, or from the York Pond Fish Hatchery by the Mill Brook Trail and the Kilkenny Ridge Trail. Unknown Pond, which is reached by the Kilkenny Ridge Trail or the Unknown Pond Trail, is one of the jewels of the White Mtns.; a beautiful mountain tarn in a birch forest carpeted with dense ferns, offering a spectacular view up to the rugged and picturesque Horn from its shore. Pond of Safety is a small but attractive pond that lies just north of the Crescent Range and east of the Pliny Range in the town of Randolph. It derived its name from an incident that occurred during the American Revolution. Several local men who had joined the Continental Army differed with the authorities as to the terms of their enlistment. They retired to this isolated region to hunt and fish, and remained out of reach until there was no further danger that they might be apprehended as deserters. The pond has continued to be a place of refuge from the woes of civilization for fishermen, hunters, cross-country skiers, and snowmobilers, but unfortunately there is no longer a purely pedestrian trail to the pond. It may be reached from Bog Dam Rd.by the WMNF Pond of Safety Trail, a series of logging roads heavily used by snowmobiles in winter, and from

Jefferson by Stag Hollow Rd., which is passable by four-wheel-drive vehicle.

THE TRAILS
Kilkenny Ridge Trail (WMNF)

The Kilkenny Ridge Trail is a ridge-top trail that runs from South Pond Recreation Area off NH 110 to the summit of Mt. Waumbek. From South Pond, it climbs over Rogers Ledge, descends to Unknown Pond, then circles to the northwest side of the Horn to gain the crest of the Pilot-Pliny ridge at the col between the Bulge and the Horn (the Horn is reached by a spur path), and then follows the backbone of the main ridge over the Bulge, Mt. Cabot, Terrace Mtn., and the three peaks of Weeks to its southern end on Mt. Waumbek. This trail was designed primarily to provide an extended route for backpackers interested in avoiding crowds of day-hikers, since, except for the section that coincides with the Mount Cabot Trail, use of those sections and features that are accessible to day-hikers is very light. The trail has generally easy to moderate grades, and reaches several fine viewpoints—notably the Horn and Rogers Ledge—but has long stretches of woods-walking that are pleasant but lacking in significant views.

From the parking lot at South Pond, go right (south) toward the shore to the sign for the Devil's Hopyard. At 0.7 mi. the Devil's Hopyard Trail diverges right (west) and the Kilkenny Ridge Trail continues straight ahead. It crosses two brooks on bridges, and runs southeast and south following old logging roads. At 2.5 mi. the trail bears sharp right (west), crossing from one logging road to another, then resumes its generally southerly course, crossing the town boundary between Stark and Kilkenny at 3.2 mi. At 3.4 mi. the grade steepens along the crest of a narrowing ridge, and the trail ascends to a sharp left turn at 4.1 mi. with the summit of Rogers Ledge a few steps ahead. The best view is at the edge of the cliff, reached by a short spur on the right just before this turn. From the south-facing ledge the view includes the Presidential Range, the Androscoggin River Valley, the Mahoosuc Range, the entire Kilkenny basin, and the northern shoulder of Mt. Cabot.

Descending from Rogers Ledge, the trail curves east around the foot of the ledge and passes a side path to a backcountry campsite at 4.6 mi., then continues to its junction with Mill Brook Trail at 4.7 mi. from South Pond. The trail continues west, passing a beaver pond at 5.3 mi., and at 6.0 mi. begins the steady ascent to the ridge east of Unknown Pond. It reaches the crest of the ridge at 6.4 mi. and descends to the pond at 6.8 mi., where it meets the Unknown Pond Trail.

The Kilkenny Ridge Trail follows the Unknown Pond Trail to the right for 100 yd., then turns sharp left off it and runs around the north shore of the pond. Crossing two small brooks, it swings north around the end of the ridge and begins the climb up the north slope of the Horn to the sag between the Bulge and the Horn at 8.5 mi. Here a side trail leads left (east) 0.3 mi. to the open rocks of the Horn, from which there are magnificent views. The Kilkenny Ridge Trail turns right (west) and ascends to the wooded summit of the Bulge, drops to the saddle, and climbs to the true summit of Mt. Cabot at 9.6 mi., where it joins the Mount Cabot Trail.

The two trails descend together past the lower but more open summit of Cabot and the cabin just below it, and continue to descend easily past the fine outlook from Bunnell Rock on the left as the trail makes a great curving change of direction. At 11.0 mi., where the Mount Cabot Trail turns sharp right and continues its descent to East Lancaster, the Kilkenny Ridge Trail bears slightly left and runs southeast with gentle ups and

downs. At 11.3 mi. it meets the Bunnell Notch Trail, follows it to the left for 0.1 mi., and then leaves it on the
right to begin the ascent of Terrace Mtn., climbing moderately to the partly overgrown helispot at the summit of
the northern knob. It then continues along the ridge with
many ups and downs over small peaks, passing an older
and almost unrecognizable overgrown helispot on the
way. At 13.3 mi., where a spur path continues straight
0.1 mi. to the interesting but restricted outlook at the
summit of Terrace Mtn., the main trail turns sharp left
and drops off the ridge, then begins a long circling
descent to the York Pond Trail.

Crossing a small brook at its low point in Willard
Notch, the trail ascends slightly to the York Pond Trail
at 14.4 mi., follows it left (east) for 100 yd., then leaves
it on the right and begins a rather long and winding
ascent of North Weeks, reaching the summit at 15.7 mi.,
where there is a canister maintained by the Four Thousand Footer Club. The trail descends at easy to moderate
grades past a small spring (unreliable water source) at
16.0 mi. to a potential campsite in the main col at 16.5
mi. Ascending again, it passes over Middle Weeks at
17.1 mi. and crosses through a much shallower col to
South Weeks at 18.1 mi. Here a short spur continues
straight to another canister at the blowdown-infested
summit, while the main trail turns left and descends to
the col between Weeks and Waumbek at 18.7 mi. From
here it swings to the west and ascends along the crest of
the ridge, slowly gaining elevation in spite of occasional
losses, then crosses the interesting, rather steep-sided
east knob of Waumbek, and continues another 0.2 mi. to
the true summit, where it meets the Starr King Trail.

Kilkenny Ridge Trail (map 8:B8–C8)
Distances from South Pond Recreation Area
    to Rogers Ledge: 4.1 mi., 2 hr. 55 min.
    to Mill Brook Trail: 4.7 mi., 3 hr. 15 min.

to Unknown Pond: 6.8 mi., 4 hr. 45 min.

to the side trail to the Horn: 8.5 mi., 5 hr. 55 min.

to Mt. Cabot summit: 9.6 mi., 6 hr. 35 min.

to departure from Mount Cabot Trail: 11.0 mi., 7 hr. 15 min.

to Terrace Mtn. summit spur: 13.3 mi., 8 hr. 50 min.

to York Pond Trail (west junction): 14.4 mi., 9 hr. 25 min.

to North Weeks summit: 15.7 mi., 10 hr. 40 min.

to South Weeks summit: 18.1 mi., 12 hr. 20 min.

to Mt. Waumbek summit: 20.6 mi. (33.1 km.), 13 hr. 50 min.

Devil's Hopyard Trail (WMNF)

This trail begins at the South Pond Recreation Area off NH 110 and provides access to the wild and beautiful Devil's Hopyard, a small gorge with cliffy walls and a boulder-strewn floor. At the start it coincides with the Kilkenny Ridge Trail, which leads south from the picnic area, skirting the west side of the pond, and crosses a brook in 0.6 mi. After 60 yd., the Devil's Hopyard Trail diverges right (west) from the Kilkenny Ridge Trail (sign). At 0.8 mi. it recrosses the brook to the north side and enters the Hopyard. The small stream that drains the gorge is for the most part completely out of sight beneath moss-covered boulders, while ledges overhang the path. (Use caution where rocks are wet or covered with moss.) At 1.2 mi. the path rises steeply on the rocks at the west end of the Hopyard, and ends at a cascade.

Devil's Hopyard Trail (map 8:B8)

Distance from South Pond

to end of trail: 1.3 mi. (2.0 km.), 50 min.

Starr King Trail (RMC/WMNF)

This trail begins on a gravel road to several homes that leaves the north side of US 2 (trail sign) 0.2 mi. east of its junction with NH 115A. Go up the road, bearing left to avoid driveways on the right, then bear right at 0.2 mi. where the road straight ahead (former route of trail, used by pedestrians) is much rougher, and continue to a small parking lot on the left. If the parking lot cannot be reached by car (as when unplowed in winter), park in the lot for the Jefferson village swimming pool, just east of the junction of US 2 and NH 115A, and walk up the road; do not interfere with the roads by parking cars on them. The trail is generally easy all the way up, with moderate grades and good footing.

From the parking area, ascend gradually on a grassy logging road for 100 yd., then turn left (arrow) and ascend another 100 yd. to meet the old route of the trail, a logging road on which the trail turns right uphill and soon passes the stone foundations of a springhouse (right). At 0.4 mi. the trail bears right at a fork (where the left branch will soon cease to be discernible) and ascends the broad southwest ridge of the mountain. At 1.4 mi. it angles left and runs north on a long traverse of the west flank of the mountain, passing a spring on the left (downhill side) of the trail at 2.1 mi. Swinging right and leaving the traverse at 2.5 mi., the trail climbs to the summit at 2.6 mi., then continues another 60 yd. to an excellent cleared vista south and west at the site of a former shelter. From the remains of the old cabin's fireplace, the trail enters the woods again, angling left, then swings right (east) and follows close to the crest of the ridge or slightly below it on one side of the other, dipping just below the col on the south and then rising to the summit of Mt. Waumbek, where it meets the south end of the Kilkenny Ridge Trail.

Starr King Trail (map 8:D7)

Distances from US 2

> *to* beginning of traverse: 1.4 mi., 1 hr. 30 min.
>
> *to* Mt. Starr King summit: 2.6 mi., 2 hr. 35 min.
>
> *to* Mt. Waumbek summit: 3.6 mi. (5.8 km.), 3 hr. 10 min.

Mount Cabot Trail (WMNF)

In addition to ascending Mt. Cabot, this trail provides access to the York Pond Trail and to the Kilkenny Ridge Trail. From the junction of US 2 and NH 116 just west of the village of Jefferson, go west 0.2 mi., then turn right (north) on North Rd. for 2.3 mi., then turn right again on Gore Rd. (which becomes Garland Rd. at a sharp left turn). At 4.0 mi. from US 2, turn right again on Pleasant Valley Rd., and at 4.8 mi. turn right on Arthur White Rd. and continue 0.4 mi. to the parking area (sign) about 50 yd. before the end of the road at Heath's Gate; do not block the road or the driveway. Any or all of the road signs at intersections may be missing, so the directions given above should be followed with care. The trail follows logging roads and the old tractor road to the former fire tower almost all the way, with steady moderate grades; footing is fair to good on the upper part, but the lower part has a severely eroded stretch of logging road.

From Heath's Gate, the Mount Cabot Trail follows a logging road through a cut-over area 0.4 mi. to the old Kilkenny logging railroad bed. Here the York Pond Trail to York Pond and the Berlin Fish Hatchery by way of Willard Notch goes right (southeast) along the railroad bed. The Mount Cabot Trail continues ahead on a recent road for another 0.4 mi., then the newer road ends and the trail becomes a footway on older roads to the Bunnell Brook crossing at 2.2 mi. After zigzagging up from the brook, and passing the Kilkenny Ridge Trail on the right at 2.5 mi., the trail swings right (southeast) past a limited southwest outlook. In another 100 yd., after swinging to the left, the trail passes a spur path right (sign) at 2.9 mi. that leads to Bunnell Rock, a ledge at the cliff-top that offers an excellent vista to the south—probably the best view on the trail. From here the trail turns northeast again and climbs through evergreens, with two switchbacks, to the old firewarden's cabin, maintained by the Jefferson Boy Scouts and the Pinkerton Academy Outing Club. From the cabin the trail climbs a few steps to the rocky area where the fire tower was located (views), then passes through a shallow sag and climbs gradually to the true summit (sign). The Kilkenny Ridge Trail begins here, leading over the Bulge to Unknown Pond, Rogers Ledge, and South Pond.

Mount Cabot Trail (map 8:D7–C8)

Distances from Heath's Gate

> *to* York Pond Trail: 0.4 mi., 15 min.
> *to* Bunnell Brook crossing: 2.2 mi., 1 hr. 35 min.
> *to* outlook (Bunnell Rock): 2.9 mi., 2 hr. 20 min.
> *to* cabin: 3.5 mi., 2 hr. 55 min.
> *to* Mt. Cabot summit: 3.9 mi. (6.2 km.), 3 hr. 5 min.

York Pond Trail (WMNF)

This trail leaves York Pond Rd. (FR 13) near its west end, and follows old logging roads through Willard Notch to the old Kilkenny logging railroad bed, on which it continues to East Lancaster at Heath's Gate (see Mount Cabot Trail). It is blazed with yellow paint. The eastern and western ends are in generally excellent condition with good footing (see the warning above concerning the locked gate at the fish hatchery), but much of the central part of the trail from the Kilkenny Ridge Trail to the logging railroad bed is wet and muddy.

From the fish hatchery gate at York Pond, continue west 2.1 mi. on York Pond Rd. to a fenced raceway. The trailhead (sign) is on the road to the left. The entrance to the trail is gated, but foot travel is not restricted. The York Pond Trail follows a gravel road for 0.2 mi., then bears left (arrow) where the Bunnell Notch Trail diverges right. In 100 yd. it crosses a small dam, then continues up the south side of the brook, crossing two branches. At 0.9 mi. it begins to swing up a hardwood ridge, following a well-defined old logging road in excellent condition. At 2.4 mi. it reaches its highest point just east of Willard Notch on a minor ridge from North Weeks. Descending slightly, it passes two junctions with the Kilkenny Ridge Trail 100 yd. apart; at the first, the Kilkenny Ridge Trail leads left (south) to Mt. Weeks and Mt. Waumbek, and at the second it leads right (north) to Terrace Mtn., Mt. Cabot, and South Pond. The York Pond Trail contours along the south side of the notch, rising and falling and remaining somewhat above the floor of the notch. It then descends gradually through several swampy areas and crosses a number of small streams, becoming very muddy at times, then crosses a fairly substantial branch of Garland Brook at 4.6 mi. and joins the old logging railroad grade, where the footing improves greatly. At 5.6 mi. it crosses the WMNF boundary and at 6.6 mi., just after crossing a stream on a culvert bridge, it bears right at a fork (the more obvious left branch is the Tekwood Rd., which continues down Garland Brook to Pleasant Valley Rd.). The trail continues on the old railroad grade in a northwesterly direction and joins the Mount Cabot Trail at 7.0 mi. Turn right (east) for Mt. Cabot or left (west) to reach the parking area at Heath's Gate (the former White's farm) in East Lancaster at 7.4 mi.

York Pond Trail (map 8:D8–D7)

Distances from York Pond trailhead

    to high point of trail: 2.4 mi., 1 hr. 45 min.

    to WMNF boundary: 5.6 mi., 3 hr. 20 min.

    to Mount Cabot Trail: 7.0 mi., 4 hr.

    to Heath's Gate: 7.4 mi. (11.9 km.), 4 hr. 15 min.

Bunnell Notch Trail (WMNF)

This trail connects the York Pond Rd. with the Kilkenny Ridge Trail in Bunnell Notch and the Mount Cabot Trail just above the crossing of Bunnell Brook. It has been reopened recently after having been abandoned around

1980, and although it can be followed fairly readily by experienced hikers, it is rough and somewhat wet, and not yet marked or signed in accordance with usual standards. Its future may perhaps still be in doubt, so hikers not skilled in following poorly marked trails might be well advised to check on its condition with the Androscoggin Ranger District Office before attempting to use it. Its principal importance is that it makes possible a rather long but very attractive loop trip to Unknown Pond, the Horn, and Mt. Cabot.

Leaving the York Pond Trail 0.2 mi. from York Pond Rd., it follows logging roads, climbing at a moderate grade up the valley of Bunnell Brook to the height-of-land in Bunnell Notch. Here the Kilkenny Ridge Trail leaves on the left (south) for Terrace Mtn. and Mt. Waumbek, and in another 0.1 mi. it leaves on the right (north) for Mt. Cabot and South Pond. The Bunnell Notch Trail then descends moderately to the Mount Cabot Trail a few yards above the Bunnell Brook crossing.

Bunnell Notch Trail (map 8:D8–D7)
Distances from York Pond Trail
   to Kilkenny Ridge Trail (east junction): 2.6 mi., 2 hr.
   to Mount Cabot Trail: 3.1 mi. (5.1 km.), 2 hr. 15 min.

Unknown Pond Trail (WMNF)

This trail connects York Pond Rd. with Mill Brook Road near the village of Stark, passing beautiful Unknown Pond and crossing the Kilkenny Ridge Trail. The south terminus is on York Pond Rd. 2.0 mi. west of the fish hatchery gate (sign) between a small pond and a beaver swamp (see warning above concerning the locked gate at the fish hatchery). The north terminus is at a gate on Mill Brook Rd. (FR 11) 3.7 mi. south of NH 110. There is a sign (hiker symbol) on NH 110 at the beginning of Mill Brook Rd., and a sign ("Trail" with arrow) at the gate.

There is a WMNF sign where the trail leaves the forest road, just east of a bridge across Mill Brook.

Leaving York Pond Rd., the trail reaches an old railroad grade at 0.2 mi. and, turning left on it, continues northwest, crossing Unknown Pond Brook at 1.9 mi. After recrossing the main stream at 2.2 mi., the trail soon begins the ascent to Unknown Pond, which it reaches at 3.3 mi. Nearby there is a backcountry campsite with a pit toilet.

The Kilkenny Ridge Trail enters right (east) at the southeast corner of the pond, and coincides with it for 100 yd. as the trail swings east around the pond through birch woods carpeted with ferns, passing a beautiful view up to the picturesque Horn rising over the pond. At the northeast corner of the pond, the Kilkenny Ridge Trail leaves left (west) toward Mt. Cabot and the Unknown Pond Trail goes north toward Mill Brook Rd. in Stark, crossing a moist area and descending moderately in beautiful birch woods for a mile. It then becomes more gradual, soon crossing the Kilkenny-Stark town line. It traverses the slope east of Mill Brook and ends at Mill Brook Rd. (FR 11) in 2.2 mi. Turn right (northeast) and continue on the road to the gate.

Unknown Pond Trail (map 8:D8–C8)
Distances from York Pond Rd.

    to Unknown Pond: 3.3 mi., 2 hr. 20 min.
    to Mill Brook Rd.: 5.5 mi., 3 hr. 30 min.
    to WMNF gate: 6.3 mi. (10.2 km.), 3 hr. 55 min.

Mill Brook Trail (WMNF)

Formerly a through route from Stark village to York Pond, the north section of this trail, from the junction with the Kilkenny Range Trail at the height-of-land to Stark, has been abandoned by the WMNF, and beaver activity and logging have obliterated the old footway. The remaining part is important mostly because it is the most convenient route from the south to the spectacular views from Rogers Ledge. It now begins near the main building of the Berlin Fish Hatchery on York Pond Rd. (FR 9). (The lower part of the trail may be difficult to locate; if so, ask at the hatchery for directions.)

From the trail sign on York Pond Rd., ascend gradually on a paved road for 0.2 mi., then follow a dirt road (sign) to the left of a fish hatchery building. After 100 yd., bear right off the dirt road (no sign) and go behind an old brown pumphouse on a concrete dam by a small pond, then turn left onto an old grassy woods road. The trail joins Cold Brook and ascends along it for about 1.3 mi. then diverges right (east) up a side stream. It crosses the Berlin-Milan town boundary at 1.7 mi. and the Milan-Kilkenny boundary at 2.7 mi. Just north of the height-of-land, the trail ends at the Kilkenny Ridge Trail. To the right (east) it is 0.6 mi. to Rogers Ledge; to the left (west) it is 2.1 mi. to Unknown Pond.

Mill Brook Trail (map 8:C8)
Distance from York Pond Rd.

   to Kilkenny Ridge Trail: 3.8 mi. (6.1 km.), 2 hr. 25 min.

Pond of Safety Trail (WMNF)

This trail, which follows logging roads that are also used as snowmobile trails, leaves Bog Dam Rd. (FR 15) 7.9 mi. south of its eastern junction with York Pond Rd. (FR 13). From Bog Dam Rd., the trail follows a gated logging road (FR 236), crossing a branch of the Upper Ammonoosuc River at 0.1 mi. At 0.5 mi. it turns right onto the state snowmobile trail and follows it west toward Pond of Safety. There may be signs at this turn.

Rising gradually, the trail bears west and southwest on a logging road to a junction at 1.7 mi., where the Pond of Safety Trail turns left (southeast). There are snowmobile trail signs and an obscure Forest Service arrow at this junction. From here the trail, on an increasingly good logging road, crosses the ridge it has been climbing and descends through several clearings to a large wooden shed at 2.5 mi. The road goes left (east) at this point, passes the obscure intersection with the abandoned part of the Carlton Notch Trail at 2.9 mi., crosses a brook, and meets Stag Hollow Rd., which leads 3.8 mi. to Ingerson Rd. near Jefferson. Here a road leads right (west) 0.2 mi. to a clearing from which a path right (north) descends to the boggy shore of the Pond of Safety.

Pond of Safety Trail (map 8:D9–E8)

Distance from Bog Dam Rd.

   to Pond of Safety: 3.2 mi. (5.1 km.), 1 hr. 45 min.

Upper Ammonoosuc Trail (WMNF)

This trail, a remnant of a former 19-mi. through route from Jefferson to West Milan, crosses between the two sides of Bog Dam Rd. (FR 15); the east trailhead is 4.1 mi. south of its eastern junction with York Pond Rd., and the west trailhead is 5.3 mi. south of its western junction with York Pond Rd.

From the east trailhead, the trail leads generally southwest, crossing Bend Brook at 0.5 mi., and reaches the site of Bog Dam at 0.9 mi. There is a clearing here, and a pool in the river, but the dam that formerly provided a "head" of water for river driving each spring is gone. At 1.7 mi. the Landing Camp Trail diverges left (east). At 1.9 mi. the trail fords the Upper Ammonoosuc River (wading often required) and at 2.3 mi. crosses Keenan Brook on a potentially unsound bridge. It then rises to the west trailhead on Bog Dam Rd.

Upper Ammonoosuc Trail (map 8:D9–D8)

Distances from Bog Dam Rd. (east side)

   to Landing Camp Trail: 1.7 mi., 50 min.

   to Bog Dam Rd. (west side): 2.8 mi. (4.4 km.), 1 hr. 20 min.

Landing Camp Trail (WMNF)

This trail links the Upper Ammonoosuc Trail with the southern part of Bog Dam Rd.; it is the remnant of an old trail that connected Bog Dam with Randolph through Hunter's Pass. It leaves the east side of Bog Dam Rd. 6.2 mi. south of its eastern junction with York Pond Rd. (The site of the former logging Camp 19 is located in this vicinity.) Descending gradually, the trail passes a clearing at the site of the former Camp 18 at 1.2 mi., crosses three small streams, rises over a knoll, and descends to run nearly level to its end on the Upper Ammonoosuc Trail.

Landing Camp Trail (map 8:D9)

Distance from Bog Dam Rd.

 to Upper Ammonoosuc Trail: 1.9 mi. (3.0 km.), 55 min.

West Milan Trail (WMNF)

This trail runs between York Pond Rd. (FR 13), just west of the bridge over the Upper Ammonoosuc River 1.8 mi. from NH 110, and Spruceville Rd. (FR 460), at a gate 1.5 mi. south of its beginning on NH 110 just west of the junction of NH 110 and NH 110A in West Milan. Much of the first 0.8 mi. passes through private land logged in 1986; close attention to trail signs and paint blazes is advised. The trail follows a snowmobile trail most of the way.

 From York Pond Rd. (sign), the trail follows a gravel road for 100 yd., then bears right at a clearing onto an old railroad grade. It soon crosses the Berlin-Milan town line, then crosses Fogg Brook on a snowmobile bridge at 0.8 mi., after leaving the logged area. It continues to cross Fifield Brook on a snowmobile bridge at 1.7 mi., and Higgins Brook on a similar bridge at 3.8 mi. In 50 yd. after this crossing the snowmobile trail bears left uphill, but the West Milan Trail continues straight (no sign) on the railroad grade. The snowmobile trail rejoins on the left at 4.2

mi., and just beyond the point where an old logging road enters left (west) at 4.3 mi., the trail turns right onto another logging road (FR 460) and continues 100 yd. to a gate and another 50 yd. to the Spruceville Rd. trailhead.

West Milan Trail (map 8:C9)

Distance from York Pond Road
    to Spruceville Road: 4.5 mi. (7.2 km.), 2 hr. 15 min.

D. THE NORTH COUNTRY

As C. F. Belcher comments (*Appalachia* XXXIII:37), referring to the Kilkenny region that lies to the south, "this area has built up a legend of isolation and mystery... even though for years it has been the intimate hunting and fishing preserve of those living nearby and a knowing few"—and, one might add, a source of income for the wood products industries and their employees and suppliers. These remarks apply, with emphasis, to the true North Country, the region north of NH 110 and NH 110A between Groveton and Milan. The appearance of wilderness masks the active presence of logging operations, and the lack of marked and signed trails disguises the extensive network of paths known very well to many local residents and others who enjoy the sense of being far from the crowds. To the south of this region, the mountain backcountry is mostly within the WMNF and has a well-developed trail system. In the great tracts of the North Country there are only a few hiking trails, even on mountains over 3000 ft., and most of these are not regularly maintained by any organization. Many experienced hikers will find pleasure in the area's remoteness, but those who expect to find their trails groomed and manicured are doomed to disappointment, and possibly to the inconvenience of getting lost. The scarcity of settlements and the confusing river drainages make the usual advice about following a stream when lost inappropriate; you must have a map and compass, know how to use them, and be prepared to traverse considerable distances on a compass course to the nearest road, possibly obstructed by swamps or logged areas with slash piles and dense second growth of blackberry, raspberry, and cherry. In general, camping and fires are prohibited throughout the region; due to the large amounts of drying slash in the extensive logged-over areas, the risk of a large forest fire is far greater than in the selectively logged areas to the south, and most landowners are intensely concerned about the possibility of a hiker or camper carelessly starting a major fire.

From the Presidential Range this vast wooded region extends over 30 mi. north to the Canadian border. It varies in width from 20 mi. at the southern end to less than 15 mi. at Pittsburg. Its natural boundaries are the Upper Ammonoosuc, Androscoggin, and Magalloway rivers on the south and east, and the Connecticut River on the west. To the south, below the line made by NH 110 and NH 110A between the towns of Groveton and Milan, the mountains are still relatively high—two just over 4000 ft.—and grouped compactly into ranges, like those farther south. Above this line lies the true North Country, a region similar to the adjacent section of Maine. The mountains are lower—only about ten exceed 3500 ft.—and most have wooded summits. The noteworthy mountains, for example the Percy Peaks, Mt. Magalloway, and Rump Mtn., are scattered, separated by long stretches of less interesting terrain. Although the main backbone of the White Mtns.—the divide between the Connecticut River and the streams and lakes to the east—continues north through this country to the Canadian border, it crosses for the most part a broad upland jumbled with medium-sized, rounded mountains, with no outstanding summits directly on the divide. Except for Dixville Notch, there is little rugged mountain scenery, although there are several large lakes.

South of NH 110, good public roads are always within a reasonable distance, but there are only three main highways in this northern section. US 3 follows the Connecticut Valley to its uppermost headwaters on the Canadian border beyond the Connecticut Lakes; NH 145 is an alternate road between Colebrook and Pittsburg. On the east side of the state, NH 16, which continues as ME 16, accompanies the Androscoggin and Magalloway rivers north to the outlet of Lake Aziscohos, then swings east to the Rangeley Lakes. NH 26, the only east-west paved road north of NH 110, crosses from Errol to Colebrook through Dixville Notch. Even public secondary roads are few and short, although the paper companies have constructed an intricate system of good main-haul gravel roads. Many of these have gates or are restricted, and heavy log trucks have the right of way on all of them. These roads are not signed, and the lack of striking landmarks makes travel on them confusing for the inexperienced. Because this northern section is managed for the continuous production of timber, roads and trails may change radically from one year to the next. Visitors may find it helpful to obtain specific information about current conditions in advance. Among official sources that may be of help are the NH Fish and Game District Chief and Rangers; information on how to contact them can be obtained from NH Fish and Game in Concord. The chief landowners are: International Paper, in Stratford NH and Augusta ME; Champion International, in West Stewartstown NH; Boise Cascade, Woods Department, in Rumford ME; James River, in Groveton NH and Berlin NH; Diamond International, in Groveton, New Hampshire. For the Dartmouth College Grant, ask at the Second College Grant gatehouse near Wentworth Location NH, or contact the Director of Outdoor Programs, Dartmouth College, PO Box 9, Hanover NH 03755.

Only a few trails in this region are suitable for this guide. Many natural features, particularly ponds, are reached by woods roads passable to four-wheel-drive vehicles or snowmobile trails, with limited appeal to pedestrian users; but many others, including most mountain summits, are simply pathless. Many trails, including several to fire towers that used to be operated in the North Country, have fallen into disuse or been abandoned, and can no longer be followed except by hikers with fairly sophisticated navigational skills. Whatever the reasons, over the past decade or so there has been a definite decline in the number of trails in this region suitable for and open to use by the general hiking public.

The one exception to this trend is in the valley of Nash Stream north of NH 110 between Groveton and Stark, where a large tract of land has been purchased to be managed cooperatively by the WMNF and the state of New Hampshire. While major benefits to hikers have yet to develop, there are certainly many enticing possibilities within this tract. Included in this recent purchase are the Percy Peaks and their trail, and most of the trail to Sugarloaf, but not its summit. The Percy Peaks, located northeast of Groveton, are the most conspicuous mountains in the northern view from Mt. Washington. The summit of the North Peak (3418 ft.) is bare, except for low scrub; that of the South Peak (3220 ft.) is wooded, but there are several good viewpoints. The trail described in this guide is on North Percy; there is no maintained trail to South Percy. Sugarloaf Mtn. (3701 ft.) rises east of North Stratford at the head of Nash Stream, and its bare rocky peak commands an extensive view, particularly of the Percy Peaks. Blue Mtn. (3723 ft.), a trailless peak in the same mountain mass, is the highest peak in New Hampshire outside the WMNF. Devil's Slide (1700 ft.) is a small mountain with a sheer cliff that rises 700 ft. on the north edge of Stark village. There is no trail, but a very steep and rough ascent may be made up the west slope by cautious bushwhackers.

North of Berlin and east of the main divide lies a region of rivers and lakes of special interest to those who love fishing and canoeing. Among these waterways, which include Lake Umbagog and the Androscoggin, Magalloway, and Diamond rivers, there are a few hills from which the view is worth the visit. Much of this land is in private hands, with gates on the access roads. Dartmouth College and Boise Cascade Corporation are the chief landowners. Both are hospitable to hikers, but do not usually permit vehicular traffic over their roads, which limits access to the region due to the considerable distances that are frequently involved. The Thirteen Mile Woods, along the Androscoggin River between Milan and Errol, is managed by a consortium of landowners and state agencies. This provides a scenic drive along the river, access to fishing and canoeing, and a public campground at Mollidgewock. The former firewarden's trail to Signal Mtn., a small mountain west of Errol with an abandoned and unsafe fire tower that overlooks this region, has been devastated by logging and can no longer be recommended to the general hiker.

Far north of Hanover, above the headwaters of the Androscoggin River, lies the Second College Grant, given to Dartmouth College by the state in 1807 "for the assistance of indigent students." On this grant, between Errol NH and Wilsons Mills ME; the Swift Diamond and the Dead Diamond come together to form the Diamond River, which then enters the Magalloway River from the west. This in turn joins the Androscoggin River at Umbagog Lake. Branches of the Dead Diamond extend well up into the Connecticut Lakes region. (Refer to the USGS Errol quadrangle.) Immediately below the confluence of its two branches, the Diamond has carved a wild and beautiful gorge between the Diamond Peaks on the north and Mt. Dustan on the south.

This valley is served by Dartmouth's private logging road, open to pedestrians but not to vehicles without a permit. At 9.0 mi. north of Errol, or 0.5 mi. west of the Maine–New Hampshire state line, this gravel road leaves NH 16 on the west near a small cemetery. The College Grant gatehouse is reached in 1.0 mi. Hikers may leave their cars here, cross the Diamond on a logging bridge, and proceed up through the gorge. Good viewpoints are reached in about 0.5 mi., the Dartmouth Peaks Camp at 1.1 mi., and the Management Center at 1.5 mi. Hellgate, another scenic gorge, named because of the trouble river drivers had getting their logs through its narrow channel without jamming, is 12.5 mi. from the gatehouse. For hikers, the principal feature of interest is the path that runs from the Management Center to the fine ledges on the Diamond Peaks (2071 ft.). Other short paths to points of interest have also been opened. For further information, call the gatekeeper (603-482-3225), or write to the Director of Outdoor Programs, Dartmouth College, PO Box 9, Hanover NH 03755.

Dixville Notch, the most spectacular spot in the North Country, lies between Sanguinary Mtn. (north) and Mt. Gloriette (south). With the Mohawk River flowing west and Clear Stream east, the notch itself is less than 2 mi. in length with a steep grade on each side, and is only wide enough to admit the highway. The cliff formations, composed of vertical strata, are impressively jagged. Just west of the notch is the Balsams, a hotel and resort complex that includes most of the land west of the notch on both sides of NH 26. The management maintains a number of summer and winter trails, including both cross-country ski and snowmobile trails and some paths that are suitable for horse travel. Part of their operation is the Wilderness Ski Area on the west slopes of Dixville Peak. The Balsams has a guide to paths in the notch, available in summer from the information booth on NH 26 just across from the hotel entrance road.

The mountains in the vicinity of Dixville Notch are relatively low and have no open summits. Mt. Gloriette (2780 ft.) forms the south side of the notch, and bears the rock formations Table Rock, Old King, Third Cliff, and Profile Cliff. There were once paths to all of them, but only that to Table Rock is now maintained and signed, and hiking to the others is not encouraged. Table Rock (2540 ft.) is a cliff that juts out from the north side of Mt. Gloriette, south of the highway. Formed of vertical slabs, it is less than 10 ft. wide at its narrowest point and extends over 100 ft. from the shoulder of the mountain. The view is spectacular and extensive. It can be climbed by a trail that begins and ends at points 0.5 mi. apart on NH 26 in the heart of the notch. The rock formation known as the Profile can be seen high up on the cliffs by looking south from the high point in the notch. On the north side of the road just west of the high point, is Lake Gloriette (1871 ft.), an artificial lake on the grounds of the Balsams, formed from the headwaters of the Mohawk River.

Dixville Peak (3482 ft.) is the highest mountain in the vicinity of Dixville Notch, but it is wooded, except for the cleared summit. It is accessible by snowmobile trails; inquire at the Balsams information booth. Sanguinary Mtn. (2748 ft.) forms the north wall of Dixville Notch and is named for the color of its cliffs at sunset. The Sanguinary Ridge Trail, which does not go to the summit, traverses the cliffs north of the notch, running between one trailhead at the hotel entrance road and another at a picnic area north of the highway 1 mi. east of the Balsams. A very short trail (sign) from the same picnic area leads to a small but attractive flume. A little farther east on the south side of the highway is a second picnic area from which a slightly longer trail leads to Huntingdon

Cascades. There are no maintained trails to Cave Mtn. (3185 ft.) or Mt. Abeniki (2780 ft.).

Some 10 mi. above Colebrook, the Connecticut River Valley bends northeast and, just beyond the village of Beecher Falls VT, comes wholly within New Hampshire. Between its source near the Canadian border and the village of Pittsburg, the river passes through a chain of lakes of increasing size, numbered first to fourth in upstream order from the south. A high dam at Pittsburg created Lake Francis—the lowest lake in the series, below First Lake—and dams are responsible for the present size of both First and Second lakes. First Lake (5.5 mi. long and 2.5 mi. wide at its broadest) and Lake Francis are the largest bodies of water in New Hampshire north of the Presidential Range. US 3, the only major highway in the region, passes close to all of the lakes except Fourth, crossing the river from west to east between Second and Third lakes, and eventually entering Canada. Refer to USGS Second Lake, Indian Stream, and Moose Bog quadrangles. Much of the land in the Connecticut Lakes Region is privately owned. While the owners do not discourage the use of their lands for hiking, they do request that these activities be limited to the daylight hours. Overnight camping and open fires are prohibited. Use of registered vehicles is limited to those roads that are not gated and not posted for road closure. Use of ATVs is prohibited at all times.

The town of Pittsburg is a notable historical curiosity, since it was once—in the minds of its residents, at least— an independent republic. Lying in a region that was claimed by both the United States and Canada until the Webster-Ashburton treaty of 1842 awarded it to the United States, the township was proclaimed by its residents as the "Republic of Indian Stream" in 1832; this tiny republic, which had its own written constitution, managed its own affairs for three years until trouble with the large, quarrelsome neighbor to the north led to its occupation by the large, quarrelsome neighbor to the south.

Mt. Magalloway (3360 ft.), located east of First Connecticut Lake, overlooks the Middle Branch of the Dead Diamond River; it has the only existing mountain trail of any consequence in the Connecticut Lakes region. A fire tower (no longer operated most of the time) affords excellent views; there are also good views from a ledge near the summit. Deer Mtn. (3005 ft.) is located west of the Connecticut River, between Second and Third lakes. The former fire tower has been removed, eliminating the unique view, particularly over the wilderness lying north toward the Canadian border, that was once available from its summit. The upper part of the former firewarden's trail can probably still be followed, but it can only be reached by a rough bushwhack through second growth and slash, since the lower part of the trail has been obliterated by logging. Fourth Connecticut Lake (2605 ft.), a little pond northwest of Third Lake and just south of the Canadian border, is the ultimate source of the Connecticut River. Once considered as remote a spot as the mountains had to offer, it is located in a 78-acre reservation given by Champion International to the Nature Conservancy in 1990, and is now accessible from US 3 by a maintained trail. Rump Mtn. (3647 ft.) is located in Maine just east of the New Hampshire border, 7 mi. south of the Canadian line. Rump Mtn. was formerly known as Mt. Carmel, or Camel's Rump, from its appearance from the southwest; it can best be viewed from the far side of the dam on Second Connecticut Lake a few yards from US 3. This attractive but remote mountain has views of three states and Quebec province, and an unusual view of Bigelow Mtn. near Stratton ME; the dubious claim is sometimes made that in clear weather Katahdin may be visible. Rump Mtn. is on land now owned by the Boise Cascade Corporation. Although the company does not object to hikers crossing their lands, there may be restrictions on vehicle travel and camping is not permitted. It would probably be useful to contact the corporation Woods Department, Rumford ME or its district forester in West Milan NH. The most convenient access is probably from the East Inlet Rd., ascending to the narrow east-west ridge near the state line and following this ridge to the summit ledge on the far eastern knob; but only hikers thoroughly experienced in wilderness navigation should consider this trip, since the route-finding is not easy and it is possible to wind up a very long way from the starting point.

THE TRAILS
Percy Peaks Trail

This trail ascends North Percy Peak from Nash Stream Rd. Leaving NH 110 2.6 mi. east of Groveton, go north on Emerson Rd. 2.2 mi. until the paved road makes a prominent curve to the right (east); here the gravel Nash Stream Rd. turns left (north). Formerly owned and maintained by Diamond International, this road has usually been closed from spring thaw through Memorial Day weekend in the past. Follow the road for 2.7 mi. to a small parking area (sign) on the east side; the trail (sign) begins 50 yd. farther up, also on the east side of the road. Refer to the AMC Pilot map (map 8); the USGS Percy quadrangle may be useful, but shows only the long-defunct trail from Christine Lake.

   The current trail is a combination of the lower part of the former West Side Trail and the Notch Trail. The upper part of the former West Side Trail has been officially closed. This section of trail, one of the most spectacular and challenging in New England, was laid out by Robert and Miriam Underhill, noted rock climbers, who delighted in finding short but challenging routes to good viewpoints. Though it crossed rock slabs that are steep and exposed where use of hands is required, it was not a rock climb in the technical sense, nor was it more difficult than some other officially maintained trails, such as the North Slide of Tripyramid or the Huntington Ravine Trail or the Holt Trail on Cardigan, although like those trails it was hazardous in wet or icy weather. (The only recorded hiking fatality on this mountain occurred on the slippery slabs below the former trail junction, along which the trail still passes.) The route can probably still be followed by those interested in undertaking a rewarding challenge at their own risk; particular caution should be exercised on wet spots, and the steeper slabs to the south (right side) of the route should be avoided.

South Percy, which offers interesting views from a number of ledges near the summit, has no maintained trail, but an obscure footway with some flags leads to it from the col between the peaks. It is also a very steep but fairly short and relatively easy bushwhack within the capacity of many cautious though inexperienced bushwhackers; the route-finding is quite straightforward—as a matter of fact, the route seems to be nearly straight up—but be careful to stay away from some low cliffs and excessively steep ledges, particularly on the descent. If you are interested in making this ascent, it might be best to climb North Percy first, then study South Percy carefully while descending back to the notch.

Leaving Nash Stream Rd., the trail ascends moderately for 0.3 mi., then bears right and crosses a small stream, and follows logging roads at easy to moderate grades, generally parallel to and north of Slide Brook. At 1.0 mi. the trail turns left at a large boulder and becomes steeper and soon reaches the base of the lower slabs. The slabs in this area are mossy and extremely slippery when wet; stay to the right (south) of the slabs, ignoring any remaining blazes painted on the rocks to the left (such blazes were placed in an unusually dry year). At 1.2 mi.

the trail reaches the former trail junction, where the old trail continued straight up the ledges, and the current trail now turns right on the former Notch Trail.

The trail now traverses several ledges, staying north of the low point in the notch. Toward the east side of the notch a flagged route to South Percy leads right (south). Leaving the notch at 1.7 mi., the trail swings left (north) and ascends along a rocky outcrop with increasingly wide views. It comes out on open ledges with scattered scrub and follows blazes and cairns to the summit, from which there are good views in all directions.

Percy Peaks Trail (map 8:B7)
Distances from Nash Stream Rd.

to former Notch Trail junction: 1.2 mi., 1 hr. 10 min.

to North Percy summit: 2.2 mi. (3.5 km.), 2 hr. 10 min.

Sugarloaf Trail

The Sugarloaf Trail, now in good shape after a period of neglect, provides access to the bare rock summit of Sugarloaf Mtn., which commands sweeping views of the Nash Stream Valley and surrounding areas. The trail ascends the east side of the mountain by a direct route, following a logging road that was the firewarden's trail to the former fire tower. From NH 110 2.6 mi. east of Groton, take Emerson Rd. north until it swings right (east) at 2.2 mi., then follow the gravel Nash Stream Rd. left (north) for 8.3 mi. to a point 60 yd. beyond its crossing of Nash Stream. Park off the road in a grassy area. Refer to the USGS Percy and Guildhall quadrangles.

The trail (sign) passes to the left of a camp, crosses a small brook, and continues through an open field. It enters the woods and swings northwest, ascending at a steady grade to the firewarden's cabins (abandoned) at 1.6 mi. Above the cabins, near a spring, the trail bears right at a fork (the left branch is an overgrown alternate route to the summit). It climbs to the ridge north of the summit, turns left (south), and reaches the summit ledges.

Sugarloaf Trail (USGS Percy quad)

Distances from Nash Stream Rd.

>*to* the warden's cabins: 1.6 mi., 1 hr. 35 min.

>*to* Sugarloaf Mtn. summit: 2.1 mi. (3.4 km.), 2 hr. 10 min.

Diamond Peaks Trail

The Diamond Peaks (2071 ft.) are a nearly semicircular ridge that rises between the Dead Diamond and Magalloway rivers. Refer to the USGS Errol quad (which does not show the trail). Their most attractive feature is a high cliff on the concave side of the ridge, facing south, with a number of viewpoints.

The trail begins 1.5 mi. from the gatehouse, on the north side of the clearing across the road from the Dartmouth Management Center. It crosses a cutover area, then enters the woods and begins to ascend. At 0.3 mi. a side trail leads left 80 yd. to Alice Ledge, with a view of the Management Center area. The main trail turns gradually more to the south and climbs over the relatively flat west peak with several good outlooks, descends slightly, and climbs to the slightly higher and much sharper east summit, where there is another viewpoint.

Diamond Peaks Trail (USGS Errol quad)

Distance from the Management Center

>*to* Diamond Peaks, east summit: 1.1 mi. (1.8 km.), 55 min.

Table Rock Trail

This short, rough loop path begins and ends on NH 26 and gives access to Table Rock, which is perhaps the most spectacular viewpoint in the White Mtns., consisting of a narrow ledge rising several hundred feet over a cliff face. There may be better scenery in the White Mtns., but few trails reach airier spots from which to view it. The east trailhead (no sign), which gives access to the much steeper section of the loop, is in a parking lot 0.1 mi. east of the main entrance to the Balsams. The west trailhead, with a sign, is 0.4 mi. west of the Balsams main entrance near a Pedestrian Crossing sign.

Beginning at the west trailhead, the trail follows a cross-country ski trail (signed as #5) for 25 yd., then diverges left and climbs to the height-of-land. It then descends gradually 50 yd., turns left on the Diamond D Trail, and follows this trail 25 yd. to the junction with the spur path that leads 50 yd. left out onto Table Rock. From the spur junction, continuing to the east trailhead, the trail turns right and virtually plunges down to NH 26. There are several intersecting paths in this area; use caution, particularly in descending, as the signs are placed for ascent only. In descending by the easier western route, enter the woods above Table Rock, avoid a path west, and take the next right (west) fork.

Table Rock Trail (USGS Dixville quad)
Distances to Table Rock
   from west trailhead: 0.7 mi. (1.2 km.), 40 min.
   from parking area: 0.2 mi. (0.4 km.), 30 min.

Sanguinary Ridge Trail
This trail provides access to the spectacular views from the open rocks of Sanguinary Ridge, beginning and ending on NH 26. It is marked with directional signs and long pale yellow paint blazes. The western trailhead is at the main entrance to The Balsams. The eastern trailhead is 1.0 mi. to the east at the Flume Brook picnic area of the Dixville Notch State Wayside, a rest area on the north side of NH 26 east of the notch, where there is also a short trail to the small flume on Clear Stream.

Leaving the picnic area, it climbs a scenic ridge, following an old 1920s trail in places as well as the blue-blazed state park boundary, through balsam and spruce forests with some hardwoods. Along the ridgecrest and overlooking the notch are outlook points with views of Table Rock and Old King cliffs, and toward Errol and the Mahoosuc Range. At 1.0 mi. it crosses the height-of-land and switchbacks down to the most spectacular viewpoint, a rocky pinnacle overlooking Lake Gloriette and the Balsams Hotel. The trail continues to descend by graded switchbacks past Index Rock to the entrance road at the Balsams Hotel.

Sanguinary Ridge Trail (USGS Dixville quad)

Distances from the Flume Brook picnic area

    to the height-of-land: 1.0 mi., 1 hr. 10 min.

    to the Balsams Hotel entrance road: 1.5 mi. (2.4 km.), 1 hr. 30 min.

Mount Magalloway Trail

To reach the trail to the fire tower on this peak, take the gravel road that turns southeast from US 3 4.7 mi. north of the First Connecticut dam. This is a main-haul logging road on which trucks have the right of way. At 1.2 mi. cross the Connecticut River on a bridge and continue straight. Bear left at 2.3 mi. and again at 2.9 mi. Turn right at 5.3 mi. and again at 6.3 mi. At 8.3 mi. from US 3 the good road ends in a grassy clearing (no sign), and the trail continues on the firewarden's jeep road to the summit. The Bobcat Trail, an alternate route to the summit, has not been maintained and is severely overgrown.

    The trail continues on the rough, eroded jeep road, passing a cabin and a spring in 0.1 mi. Beyond the cabin, the trail ascends moderately on the old road with a few relatively steep grades to the summit, reaching the fire tower at 0.8 mi. There are excellent views southeast toward Aziscohos Lake and northeast to Rump Mtn. A short trail behind the warden's cabin leads to the top of the ledges, from which there is also a good view.

Mount Magalloway Trail
(USGS Second Connecticut Lake quad)

Distance from gravel road
>   *to* fire tower and Mt. Magalloway summit: 0.8 mi.
>   (1.2 km.), 50 min.

Fourth Connecticut Lake Trail

This path begins at the US Customs station at the Canadian border on US 3. Hikers are asked to register at the customs office. Parking is available nearby. From the boundary marker just north of the customs building, follow the international boundary uphill to the left (west). The boundary is a wide swath cut through the forest and marked at irregular intervals by brass discs set in concrete. At 0.6 mi. leave the boundary on the left (south) on a well-defined path (sign) and descend gradually 200 yd. to Fourth Lake.

Fourth Connecticut Lake Trail
(USGS Second Connecticut Lake quad)

Distance from US Customs station
>   *to* Fourth Lake: 0.7 mi. (1.2 km.), 40 min.

SECTION 13
Middle Connecticut River Mountains

This section covers the chain of medium-sized mountains that rises east of and roughly parallel to the Connecticut River between Hanover and Glencliff. This range, which includes Moose Mtn., Holts Ledge, Smarts Mtn., Mt. Cube, Mt. Mist, and Webster Slide Mtn., is traversed by the Appalachian Trail and the network of side trails maintained by the Dartmouth Outing Club (DOC). A substantial portion of this network, both Appalachian Trail and side trails, has been relocated in the last decade, and a considerable amount of completely new trail has been constructed. The boundaries of this region are NH 10 on the west, US 4 on the south, NH 118 on the east, and NH 25 on the east and north. The extreme northeastern end of this section is shown on both the AMC Chocorua-Waterville map (map 4) and the AMC Franconia map (map 5). The whole region is also covered by USGS quads, but the most useful map for this section is published by the DOC, and shows the DOC trail network, which consists of the Appalachian Trail and its side trails from Pomfret VT to Kinsman Notch in New Hampshire. This map, which may be obtained from the Director of Trails and Shelters, Box 9, Robinson Hall, Dartmouth College, Hanover NH 03755, includes all trails described in this section. Unless otherwise noted, all sections of the Appalachian Trail are described from south to north.

After reaching the New Hampshire boundary at the bridge over the Connecticut River close to the western edge of both the town of Hanover and the campus of Dartmouth College, the Appalachian Trail passes through Hanover and proceeds eastward out of town to a region of

517

low hills, then finally reaches Moose Mtn., the southern-most mountain of consequence in the chain. From here northward the AT is never far from the divide between the Connecticut and Pemigewasset drainages, but the mountains that it passes near to or over do not really form a range, since they are mostly clearly separate peaks rising from a hilly upland with no significant connecting ridges between them. Moose Mtn. (North Peak, 2300 ft.; South Peak, 2290 ft.), is located in Hanover; the Moose Mountain Trail (new AT) now crosses the South Peak and passes near the summit of the North Peak. Passing through the notch between the two peaks is the old Province Rd., laid out in 1772 to connect Governor Wentworth's residence in Wolfeboro with the Connecticut Valley towns, where the residents were disaffected and rebellious toward the royal government in New Hampshire. Holts Ledge (2110 ft.) has good views to the east and southeast. Smarts Mtn. (3238 ft.), located in Lyme, affords interesting views of a less-known area from its abandoned fire tower. Mt. Cube (2909 ft.), located in Orford, has several fine viewpoints, and is one of the more rewarding small mountains in the region. Webster Slide Mtn. (2184 ft.) rises steeply above Wachipauka Pond, with excellent views, while nearby wooded Mt. Mist (2230 ft.) has a fine outlook.

CAMPING

Most of this area is private land, where camping and fires are permitted only at official campsites. The northern part, north of NH 25C, is in the WMNF; here camping is permitted in accordance with the usual restrictions. There are no RUAs in this section in 1991.

Established Trailside Campsites

Velvet Rocks Shelter (DOC) is located on a spur path 0.2 mi. from the Velvet Rocks Trail (AT) and 1.8 mi. north of the center of Hanover.

Moose Mountain Shelter (DOC) is located on the Clark Pond Loop on the east side of Moose Mtn., 0.3 mi. east of the Appalachian Trail.

Trapper John Shelter (DOC) is near Holts Ledge, 1.0 mi. from Cummins Pond Rd. via the Holts Ledge Trail (AT) and a spur path.

Smarts Campsite (DOC), with tent platforms, is near the summit of Smarts Mtn.

Hexacuba Shelter (DOC) is an innovative hexagonal shelter for ten people on a spur path 0.2 mi. off the Kodak Trail (AT) 1.6 mi. south of the south peak of Mt. Cube. The former Mt. Cube Shelter, 0.2 mi. from Quinttown Rd. via the South Cube Trail, still exists.

THE TRAILS
Velvet Rocks Trail (DOC)
This section of the Appalachian Trail passes through the town of Hanover and continues through the more rural outskirts of the town to the foot of Moose Mtn., passing Velvet Rocks Shelter. Strictly speaking, only a 3.7-mi. segment in the middle of this trail is officially known as the Velvet Rocks Trail, but for convenience the remaining sections of the AT between the Connecticut River and Three Mile Rd. at the base of Moose Mtn. are included here. As this is generally a moderately populated area, a great deal of the trail is necessarily on roads of various kinds, and though there are interesting segments, the main purpose of this part of the AT is to cross the Connecticut Valley and connect the mountains of Vermont with the mountains of New Hampshire.

Beginning at the state line on the Connecticut River bridge between Hanover NH and Norwich VT, the AT follows West Wheelock St. to the square at the town common in Hanover. Turning right on North Main St., it soon turns left onto Lebanon St., and merges into NH 120 at 1.2 mi. In 100 yd. it turns left (sign) toward Chase

Field and traverses the south end of the field on a gravel road, passes a gate, and enters the woods at 1.4 mi. At this point the segment that is officially known as the Velvet Rocks Trail begins. The trail swings left and ascends past a limited north outlook, and at 2.1 mi. a spur path leads left 0.2 mi. to Velvet Rocks Shelter, where the Old Velvet Rocks Trail continues another 0.5 mi. to East Wheelock St.. just west of Balch Hill Rd. At 2.6 mi., a spur path leads left 0.1 mi. to the Old Velvet Rocks Trail 0.3 mi. above East Wheelock St, and another spur path descends left 0.2 mi. to a spring. At 3.1 mi. the Trescott Road Spur descends 0.4 mi. to Trescott Rd. (the continuation of East Wheelock St.). The main trail passes a campsite, crosses the height-of-land, and descends with some ups and downs to Trescott Rd. at 5.1 mi., where the official Velvet Rocks Trail ends.

The trail now ascends through a pine plantation, then turns left on an old logging road at 5.8 mi. and follows it for 100 yd., then bears left off the road and ascends, turning sharp right at a stone wall, then sharp right again onto Paine Rd. (dirt). At 6.5 mi. it turns right onto Dogford Rd. (paved), and at 7.0 mi. it turns right onto the Etna–Hanover Center Rd. (paved). It passes a cemetery and then turns left into the woods and ascends gradually through a region of old fields with stone walls. At 9.2 mi. it turns right onto an old trail segment, then bears right off it at 9.6 mi. and soon reaches Three Mile Rd., at a spot that can also be reached by following dirt roads east, then south from Hanover Center.

Velvet Rocks Trail (DOC map)

Distance from Connecticut River bridge

to Velvet Rocks Trail (official west end): 1.4 mi., 45 min.

to Velvet Rocks Shelter spur: 2.1 mi., 1 hr. 15 min.

to Velvet Rocks Trail (official east end): 5.1 mi., 2 hr. 50 min.

to Three Mile Rd.: 9.7 mi. (15.6 km.), 5 hr. 30 min.

Moose Mountain Trail (DOC)

This is the Appalachian Trail from Three Mile Rd. to Goose Pond Rd. Leaving Three Mile Rd., the trail descends across Mink Brook and then ascends to a junction at 0.4 mi. Here the Fred Harris Trail leaves left for Goose Pond Rd. The Moose Mountain Trail climbs moderately past a clearing with views to the southeast, and reaches the summit of the South Peak of Moose Mtn. at 1.9 mi., then descends to the notch between the two peaks of Moose Mtn., where it crosses the Clark Pond Loop at 2.4 mi. The Clark Pond Loop leads left (west) 0.6 mi. to the Fred Harris Trail and right (east) 0.3 mi. to Moose Mountain Shelter. This short path, the remnant of a much longer trail that is no longer maintained, now consists entirely of a segment of the historic old Province Rd.

Ascending from the notch, the trail ascends at easy to moderate grades with a few minor descents to its high point on the North Peak of Moose Mtn. at 3.9 mi., where there is a view to the southwest. It then descends past a northeast outlook, crosses Hewes Brook at 5.2 mi., and continues to Goose Pond Rd., which it reaches at a point 3.5 mi. east of NH 10.

Moose Mountain Trail (DOC map)

Distances from Three Mile Rd.

 to Clark Pond Loop: 2.4 mi., 1 hr. 40 min.

 to Goose Pond Rd.: 5.6 mi. (8.9 km.), 3 hr. 25 min.

Fred Harris Trail (DOC)

This trail begins on Goose Pond Rd., 3.1 mi. east of NH 10 and 0.4 mi. west of the Appalachian Trail crossing, and runs west of Moose Mtn. to the Moose Mountain Trail (AT) 0.4 mi. east of Three Mile Rd., making possible a loop hike over Moose Mtn. It makes use of a variety of logging roads and country dirt roads. At 3.1 mi. the Clark Pond Trail diverges left (east) to cross the AT

between the two peaks of Moose Mtn. and continue to
Moose Mountain Shelter. The Fred Harris Trail passes
Harris Junction at 3.7 mi., where a side trail leads left to
Harris Cabin (private), and then continues to the Moose
Mountain Trail (AT).

Fred Harris Trail (DOC map)

Distance from Goose Pond Rd.

  to Moose Mountain Trail: 4.0 mi. (6.4 km.), 2 hr. 15 min.

Holts Ledge Trail (DOC)

This is the segment of the Appalachian Trail that crosses
between Goose Pond Rd. and Cummins Pond Rd., passing over Holts Ledge. The endangered peregrine falcon
has nested there in recent years, and portions of the ledge
may be closed during the nesting season to prevent dis-
turbance to the birds. The northern terminus is located on
Cummins Pond Rd., just west of the Dartmouth Skiway,
and the south terminus is located on Goose Pond Rd., 3.5
mi. east of NH 10. Because Holts Ledge is more frequently ascended from the north, this trail is described in
the north to south direction.

  Leaving Cummins Pond Rd., the trail ascends, much
of the time parallel to a ski trail (do not hike on ski trail).
At 0.8 mi. it passes a side path that leads in 0.3 mi. to
Trapper John Shelter, and continues to ascend, turning
sharp right onto the Papoose Ski Trail and following it
for 0.2 mi., then leaving it on the right. The trail turns
sharp right where a fence 50 yd. to the left protects the
falcon nesting area, and climbs past an excellent northeast outlook to the crest of Holts Ledge at 1.7 mi. The
trail descends, turning sharp right at 1.9 mi., then follows
a wood road, swinging east then south past a beaver
flowage before ascending gradually to Goose Pond Rd.

Holts Ledge Trail (DOC map)

Distances from Cummins Pond Rd.

  to crest of Holts Ledge: 1.7 mi., 1 hr. 55 min.

to Goose Pond Rd.: 3.7 mi. (5.9 km.), 2 hr. 35 min.

Lambert Ridge Trail (DOC)

This is the segment of the Appalachian Trail between Cummins Pond Rd. 2.9 mi. east of Lyme Center and the summit of Smarts Mtn. Ascending from the road moderately by switchbacks, it reaches a ledge with a view east at 0.8 mi. and continues along the ridge with occasional views. At 1.8 mi. there is a fine view of the summit ahead, and the trail descends into a sag with a small stream at 2.3 mi. It then swings right (east) and ascends again to join the Ranger Trail at 3.3 mi. At 3.7 mi. a spur leads right 50 yd. to a tent platform with a fine view, and at 3.9 mi. the J Trail diverges right and carries the Appalachian Trail northward. The Ranger Trail continues another 50 yd. to the fire tower, passing a spur 30 yd. right to the warden's cabin (locked). Potable water is often available in a spring 0.2 mi. north of the summit on a blue-blazed portion of the former AT north, which is abandoned beyond the spring.

Lambert Ridge Trail (DOC map)

Distance from Cummins Pond Rd.
  to Ranger Trail: 3.3 mi., 2 hr. 30 min.
  to J Trail: 3.9 mi. (6.2 km.), 3 hr.

Ranger Trail (DOC)

This trail, the old firewarden's route to the fire tower on Smarts Mtn., ascends to the summit from Cummins Pond Rd. 2.9 mi. east of Lyme Center (where the Lambert Ridge Trail begins). The upper 0.6 mi. coincides with the Lambert Ridge Trail and is part of the Appalachian Trail. The lower section, which may not be maintained, is not signed or blazed but is easy to follow.

The trail starts up a woods road, with a brook on the right (east). The road ends at a garage at 1.9 mi., and the trail turns right across the brook. The brook is recrossed at 2.3 mi. (last reliable water source), and the grade steepens as the trail becomes rough, eroded, and slippery in places. At 3.0 mi. the Lambert Ridge Trail enters on the left, and the two trails running together become the Appalachian Trail. At 3.5 mi. a spur leads right 50 yd. to a tent platform with a fine view, and at 3.6 mi. the J Trail diverges right and carries the Appalachian Trail northward. The Ranger Trail continues another 50 yd. to the fire tower, passing a spur 30 yd. right to the warden's cabin (locked).

Ranger Trail (DOC map)
Distance from Cummins Pond Rd.
 to Lambert Ridge Trail: 3.0 mi., 2 hr. 15 min.
 to Smarts Mtn. summit: 3.6 mi. (5.8 km.), 2 hr. 45 min.

J Trail (DOC)
This is the segment of the Appalachian Trail from the summit of Smarts Mtn. to Jacobs Brook Rd. 2.4 mi. from NH 25A. Jacobs Brook Rd. leaves NH 25A (no sign) 3.9 mi. east of its junction with NH 10, crosses Quinttown Rd. at 1.2 mi., and reaches a locked gate at 1.9 mi. The trailhead is 0.5 mi. past the gate; in winter or mud season, it may be necessary to walk the 1.2 mi. from Quinttown Rd. This trail is described here from north to south.

 The trail descends gradually and crosses a suspension bridge over the South Branch of Jacobs Brook and ascends through long-overgrown pastures, then reaches evergreen woods as the grade becomes easier on the J-shaped ridge at 1.8 mi. At 3.5 mi. the trail swings right (west) and descends slightly, passes a spring on the left, then continues to the coinciding Lambert Ridge and Ranger trails at 3.8 mi. The Ranger Trail continues another 50 yd. to the fire tower, passing a spur leading right 30 yd. to the warden's cabin (locked). Potable water is often available in a spring 0.2 mi. north of the summit on a blue-blazed portion of the former AT north, which is abandoned beyond the spring.

J Trail (DOC map)

Distance from Jacobs Brook Rd.
    to Lambert Ridge Trail: 3.8 mi. (6.1 km.), 2 hr. 50 min.

Kodak Trail (DOC)

This is the segment of the AT from Jacobs Brook Rd. 2.4 mi. from NH 25A to the main (south) peak of Mt. Cube. Jacobs Brook Rd. leaves NH 25A (no sign) 3.9 mi. east of its junction with NH 10, crosses Quinttown Rd. at 1.2 mi., and reaches a locked gate at 1.9 mi. The trailhead is 0.5 mi. past the gate; in winter or mud season, it may be necessary to walk the 1.2 mi. from Quinttown Rd.

The trail ascends moderately from the road, swinging right as it climbs to the top of Eastman Ledges at 0.6 mi., where there is a fine view of Smarts Mtn. The trail descends and swings to the north, passing over a low ridge and descending to cross the North Branch of Jacobs Brook at 1.1 mi. At 1.5 mi. a spur path leads right uphill 0.2 mi. to hexagonal Hexacuba Shelter; shelter users should obtain water from the brook at the spur path junction. The main trail soon ascends roughly by switchbacks to the southwest ridge and reaches ledges with southwest views. It descends into a sag at 2.6 mi. and then climbs on scattered ledges to the bare summit, where the South Cube Trail and the Mount Cube Trail enter.

Kodak Trail (DOC)

Distance from Jacobs Brook Rd.
    to Mt. Cube summit: 3.0 mi. (4.9 mi.), 2 hr. 20 min.

Mount Cube Trail (DOC)

This is the segment of Appalachian Trail from the main (south) summit of Mt. Cube to NH 25A, 4.6 mi. west of NH 25 and 1.9 mi. east of its high point near Mt. Cube Farm. It is described here from north to south.

Leaving NH 25A, the trail ascends gradually on an old woods road past stone walls and a cellar hole, then crosses a gravel road at 0.5 mi. and swings right and narrows. At 1.5 mi. it turns left onto an old logging road, follows it for 50 yd., then turns right off it and soon crosses Brackett Brook on a log bridge. At 2.5 mi. there is a stone chair on the right. At 3.3 mi. the trail reaches the old route of the AT along the ridge between the two peaks of Mt. Cube; the Mount Cube Trail turns left and follows the old route to the summit of the bare south peak, where it meets the Kodak Trail and the South Cube Trail, while a spur path follows a segment of the old AT to the right 0.3 mi. from the junction, past the fine northeast outlook, to the north peak, which has a view to the east.

Mount Cube Trail (DOC map)
Distance from NH 25A

to Mt. Cube summit: 3.4 mi. (5.4 km.), 2 hr. 40 min.

South Cube Trail (DOC)

This is the blue-blazed former route of the Appalachian Trail to the main (south) summit of Mt. Cube from Quinttown Rd., which runs south from NH 25A 1.7 mi. west of the height-of-land near Mt. Cube Farm, and reaches the trailhead in about 1 mi. This is by far the shortest route to the summit of Mt. Cube. The trail leaves Quinttown Rd. on an old logging road and ascends past a short spur left to the old Cube Shelter at 0.2 mi. It continues to ascend steadily, reaching ledges 100 yd. below the bare summit. From the summit, the Kodak Trail runs south and the Mount Cube Trail north; the fine northeast outlook and the east outlook from the north peak can be reached by following the Mount Cube Trail and a spur path (part of the former AT) north for 0.4 mi.

South Cube Trail (DOC map)
Distance from Quinttown Rd.

to Mt. Cube summit: 1.5 mi. (2.5 km.), 1 hr. 30 min.

Atwell Hill Trail (DOC)

This is the segment of Appalachian Trail from NH 25A to Atwell Hill Rd. opposite the Ore Hill Trail, 3.3 mi. south of NH 25C and 2.1 mi. north of NH 25A. The trailhead on NH 25A is 4.5 mi. west of NH 25 and 0.1 mi. east of the Mount Cube Trail. The trail ascends gradually from NH 25A and bears left onto an old woods road at 0.2 mi. At 1.2 mi. it bears right (east) off the woods road and continues to Atwell Hill Rd.

Atwell Hill Trail (DOC map)

Distance from NH 25A

   to Atwell Hill Rd.: 1.7 mi., 1 hr. 10 min.

Ore Hill Trail (DOC)

This is the segment of Appalachian Trail from Atwell Hill Rd, opposite the Atwell Hill Trail, 3.3 mi. south of NH 25C and 2.1 mi. north of NH 25A, to NH 25C at a point 3.5 mi. west of NH 25 and 0.1 mi. west of the Wachipauka Pond Trail. It ascends across power lines and through a part of Sentinel State Forest to the height-of-land on Sentinel Mtn. at 0.8 mi., then descends. At 2.0 mi. it crosses a small stream on a log bridge and swings right (east) on an old woods road for 0.1 mi., then leaves it left (north) and ascends to its high point on Ore Hill at 2.8 mi., where it bears right and descends to NH 25C.

Ore Hill Trail (DOC map)

Distance from Atwell Hill Rd.

   to NH 25C: 3.4 mi. (5.4 km.), 2 hr. 15 min.

Wachipauka Pond Trail (DOC)

This segment of the Appalachian Trail, which runs from NH 25C to NH 25, leaves NH 25C at a point 3.4 mi. west of NH 25 and 0.1 mi. east of the Ore Hill Trail. Its trailhead on NH 25, 1.4 mi. west of the junction of NH 25 and NH 112, 0.6 mi. west of the Glencliff Post Office and 150 yd. south of the Town Line Trail. It is described here from north to south. Leaving NH 25, it begins as a woods road but soon becomes a foot trail and climbs moderately to its high point on Wyatt Hill at 1.2 mi., then descends west gradually to the north end of Wachipauka Pond. The trail contours around the base of Webster Slide Mtn. above the west shore of the pond, and at 2.3 mi. the Webster Slide Trail leaves right for the spectacular summit ledges of Webster Slide Mtn. The main trail passes Hairy Root Spring, then climbs gradually, passing a short spur path left to an excellent east outlook, and crosses the wooded summit of Mt. Mist at 3.1 mi. It descends gradually, then rises slightly as it passes around a low hill, and continues across Ore Hill Brook to NH 25C.

Wachipauka Pond Trail (map 5:J2/DOC map)
Distances from NH 25
> *to* Webster Slide Trail: 2.3 mi., 1 hr. 30 min.
> *to* NH 25C: 4.9 mi. (7.9 km.), 3 hr. 10 min.

Webster Slide Trail (DOC)
The spectacular outlook from this mountain's east ledges, which look straight down onto Wachipauka Pond, is reached by a spur trail that leaves the Wachipauka Pond Trail (AT) right (west) 2.3 mi. from NH 25. It follows an old woods road (former route of Appalachian Trail) for 0.2 mi., then turns sharp right and climbs rather steeply to the summit at 0.6 mi. and continues down past the ruins of the former shelter to the ledgy viewpoint.

Webster Slide Trail (map 5:J1/DOC map)
Distance from Wachipauka Pond Trail
> *to* Webster Slide Mtn. ledge outlook: 0.7 mi. (1.2 km.), 45 min.

SECTION 14
Cardigan and Kearsarge

This section includes Mt. Cardigan and its subsidiary peaks, as well as Plymouth Mtn. and Mt. Kearsarge. It is bounded on the north by US 4, NH 118, and NH 25; on the east by I-93; and on the southwest by I-89. The AMC Cardigan map (map 2) covers the Cardigan area; Plymouth Mtn. is on the USGS Holderness quad, and Mt. Kearsarge is on the USGS Mt. Kearsarge quad.

MT. CARDIGAN

The outstanding peak of west central New Hampshire, Mt. Cardigan is located in Orange (near Canaan) and Alexandria (near Bristol). Excellent views are available from the steep-sided rock dome of "Old Baldy" itself, as well as from the South Peak—also noted for its blueberries in season—and from Firescrew, the north peak, named for a spiral of fire and smoke that rose from it during the conflagration in 1855 that denuded the upper slopes of the mountain. Though relatively low, Cardigan provides a great variety of terrain, from low hardwood forests to the wind-swept summit. Its trails vary from gentle woods walks, to the West Ridge Trail (a traditional first "big mountain climb" for children), to the Holt Trail, with upper ledges that constitute one of the more difficult scrambles among the regular hiking trails in New England. From the east, you can make a fine circuit by ascending Cardigan by the Holt, Cathedral Forest, and Clark trails—or by taking the much more challenging Holt Trail all the way—and returning over Firescrew via the Mowglis and Manning trails.

Most of the mountain is within a state reservation of over 5000 acres. Adjacent to the park is the AMC's 1000-

529

acre Cardigan Reservation, which occupies much of Shem Valley and portions of the east slopes of the mountain. The AMC Cardigan Lodge, which has a main lodge, a cottage, a campground, and Hi-Cabin, provides meals and lodging to the public during the summer season. A trail map, showing hiking and ski trails, is available at the lodge. Nearby Newfound Lake, with Wellington State Park, offers swimming, boating, and fishing. For reservations contact the Manager, AMC Cardigan Lodge, RFD, Bristol NH 03222 (603-744-8011). The usual approach is from Bristol, easily accessible from I-93. Turn left (west) from NH 3A at the stone church at the foot of Newfound Lake, continue straight ahead through the crossroad at 1.9 mi., bear right at 3.1 mi., and turn left at 6.3 mi. At 7.4 mi. from the church, turn right on a gravel road, then bear right at 7.5 mi. at the Red Schoolhouse, and continue to the lodge at 8.9 mi. This road is plowed in winter, but must be driven with great care.

While many of the trails on Mt. Cardigan are heavily used and well beaten, others, noted in the individual descriptions, are lightly used, sparsely marked, and receive little maintenance. Such trails may be difficult to follow if not recently maintained, in the early part of the season when a footway is not clearly established, or in the fall when covered by leaves. Although these trails are not recommended for the inexperienced, they may be followed fairly readily by experienced hikers, although you should carry map and compass, keep track of your location on the map, and carefully follow whatever markings do exist.

THE TRAILS
West Ridge Trail (NHDP)
This is the main trail to Mt. Cardigan from the west, as well as the shortest and easiest route to the summit. From

NH 118, 0.5 mi. north of Canaan, turn right at a large
Cardigan State Park sign. Bear right 2.7 mi. from NH
118, shortly after crossing Orange Brook. At 3.4 mi. bear
left to a parking area at 4.1 mi., where there are picnic
tables and restrooms.

The well-beaten trail starts at a sign in the parking
area. At 0.4 mi. it turns left onto a snowmobile trail, and
at 0.5 mi. the South Ridge Trail diverges right at a sharp
turn in the West Ridge Trail. The trail turns left off the
snowmobile trail, crosses a small brook on a bridge, and
climbs to a junction with the Skyland Trail right. It then
crosses a rustic bridge and reaches the site of the Hermitage (shelter removed in 1991) at 1.1 mi. Here the
Hurricane Gap Trail diverges right (no sign) for Hi-
Cabin and the Clark Trail, but it passes through a fragile
area and is closed between this junction and the South
Ridge Trail except when there is deep snow cover.
Shortly beyond the Hermitage site, an unsigned branch
of the South Ridge Trail leads right to the warden's
cabin. The West Ridge Trail ascends marked ledges to
join the Clark Trail just below the summit.

West Ridge Trail (map 2)
Distance from Cardigan State Park parking area
   to Mt. Cardigan summit: 1.5 mi. (2.5 km.), 1 hr. 15 min.

South Ridge Trail

This trail provides access to Mt. Cardigan, South Peak,
and Rimrock, and also makes possible a scenic loop in
combination with the West Ridge Trail. It diverges right
from the West Ridge Trail 0.5 mi. from the State Park
parking area, crosses a brook and climbs, rather steeply
at times, to Rimrock, where it crosses the Skyland Trail
at 0.7 mi. (Descending, follow the left of two lines of
cairns on the ledge below Rimrock.) The trail continues
across marked ledges and passes the summit of South
Peak at 1.0 mi., where a poorly marked spur descends on

the right to. the Hurricane Gap Trail. The South Ridge Trail turns left and descends to cross the Hurricane Gap Trail (the portion of the Hurricane Gap Trail west of the South Ridge Trail is closed except in deep snow cover), then turns sharp right at a junction (left is the branch trail that leads 0.2 mi. to the West Ridge Trail near the Hermitage site), and continues to the warden's cabin, where it ends at the Clark Trail.

South Ridge Trail (map 2)

Distance from West Ridge Trail
    to Clark Trail: 1.3 mi. (2.1 km.), 1 hr.

Distance from Cardigan State Park parking area
    for complete loop (via West Ridge, Clark, and South Ridge trails): 3.6 mi. (5.8 km.), 2 hr. 30 min.

Orange Cove Trail

This trail, which is really an unsigned dirt road used as an access trail, provides a direct approach from the west to Mowglis Trail, Cilley's Cave, Hanging Rocks, and Crag Shelter. Follow directions above for West Ridge Trail, but bear left 2.7 mi. from NH 118 immediately after crossing Orange Brook. Follow this road 1.2 mi. to the end of the pavement. The trail (no sign) is the old Groton-Orange Road and is easy to follow. It passes the State Park boundary, bears left at a fork, and climbs easily past a large beaver pond at 1.0 mi. to end at the Mowglis Trail in the col between Cilley's Cave and Cataloochee Mtn. The Mowglis Trail continues straight ahead on the old road to Groton, or turns sharp right on a foot path to Cilley's Cave and Mt. Cardigan.

Orange Cove Trail (map 2)

Distance from end of paved road
    to Mowglis Trail: 1.6 mi. (2.5 km.), 1 hr.

Mowglis Trail

This trail has been maintained by Camp Mowglis on Newfound Lake since 1921. From Hebron village on the north end of the lake, follow signs to Sculptured Rocks State Geological Site on the Cockermouth River, an interesting glacial gorge with potholes that is a popular picnic spot with a good swimming hole. Continue 1.0 mi. farther on Sculptured Rocks Rd. to a point just beyond the green bridge over Atwell Brook. The trail (no sign) follows the old Groton-Orange Road, which forks left and follows Atwell Brook, ascending at a moderate grade. It may be possible to drive 1.4 mi. to a logging road fork, where the trail keeps right on the old road. The trail ascends past the State Park boundary at 2.4 mi., to a junction with the Orange Cove Trail at 3.5 mi. in the col between Cilley's Cave and Cataloochee Mtn. Here the Orange Cove Trail continues ahead on the old road, while the Mowglis Trail turns left and climbs briefly to a junction with the Elwell Trail at 3.7 mi. Soon after this junction a spur trail (sign) leads left 80 yd. to Cilley's Cave, a lonely, rocky retreat, where it is said a hermit once lived, and about 0.3 mi. farther another spur leads left to Hanging Rocks.

Hanging Rocks is an interesting glacial formation that forms a natural shelter. About 100 yd. from the Mowglis Trail the spur forks. The right fork leads 0.1 mi. across the top of the ledge, with a fine view east, and the left fork descends 0.1 mi. among the rocks at the foot of the ledge. There is a steep connecting link at the far end of these two paths.

The Mowglis Trail then ascends more steeply, and at 4.6 mi. passes Crag Shelter—an open shelter accommodating fifteen, maintained by Camp Mowglis—and continues to a north outlook, where the trail turns sharp right and climbs to the summit of Firescrew at 5.1 mi., where it meets the Manning Trail. It descends across wide ledges deeply marked by glacial action, and passes a side trail left, marked by a sign painted on the rocks, that descends 0.2 mi. and 200 ft. to Grotto Cave and a smaller boulder cave. The main trail then ascends steeply to the summit of Mt. Cardigan.

Mowglis Trail (map 2)

Distance from Sculptured Rocks Rd.
   to Mt. Cardigan summit: 5.7 mi. (9.2 km.), 4 hr.

Elwell Trail

The Elwell Trail extends over 10 mi. from Newfound Lake to the Mowglis Trail 2.0 mi. north of Mt. Cardigan. It is named in honor of Col. Alcott Farrar Elwell, who directed Camp Mowglis for fifty years and helped develop many of the trails in this region. The trail begins on West Shore Rd. directly opposite the entrance to Wellington State Park. At 0.5 mi. it passes a spur trail that leads left 0.2 mi. to Goose Pond, crosses the open summit of Little Sugarloaf at 0.8 mi., continues along the ridge, and finally climbs steeply to the summit of Sugarloaf at 1.7 mi. About 100 yd. past this summit the trail turns sharp left, descends steeply, then runs fairly level across the old Hebron-Alexandria Turnpike.

It then climbs by steep switchbacks, with rough footing, to the summit ridge of Bear Mtn., where there are several good outlooks across Newfound Lake. The Elwell Trail continues along the ridge, passes under power lines, and crosses the Welton Falls Trail at 4.6 mi. It ascends gradually with occasional steep pitches past several scenic outlooks to the summit of Oregon Mtn. The trail descends sharply to a junction with the Carter Gibbs Trail (right) and the Old Dicey Rd. (left) at 7.7 mi., then crosses a brook and climbs gradually to the summit of Mowglis Mtn. at 8.7 mi., where a tablet on the right honors Camp Mowglis. It descends again to the next col at 9.8 mi., where the Back 80 Trail diverges left for Cardigan Lodge, then climbs fairly steeply to a spur trail leading left 130 yd.

to Cilley's Cave (sign), and descends slightly to end at the Mowglis Trail. Between Mowglis Mtn. and the Back 80 Trail junction the trail must be followed with care.

Elwell Trail (map 2)
Distance from West Shore Rd.
   to Mowglis Trail: 10.4 mi. (16.7 km.), 7 hr. 15 min.

Carter Gibbs Trail

This trail leaves Sculptured Rocks Rd. at a small gravel turnout on the south side, 0.2 mi. east of the Sculptured Rocks parking area. Due to logging activity it is currently very difficult to follow, and cannot be recommended except to experienced route-finders, but it is being retained in this guide in the hope that it will be restored. It may be possible to drive the first 1.2 mi. Leaving Sculptured Rocks Rd., it follows a gravel road for about 0.5 mi., then turns left where a right fork crosses Dane Brook on a snowmobile bridge. In another 0.3 mi. it bears right at a fork and follows an old logging road that gradually peters out. The trail then climbs more steeply to the height-of-land between Oregon Mtn. and Mowglis Mtn., where a side path (sign) leads right 0.2 mi. to an outlook on Carter's Knob. The main trail then descends sharply 0.3 mi. to the Elwell Trail opposite the upper terminus of the Old Dicey Rd.

Carter Gibbs Trail (map 2)
Distance from Sculptured Rocks Rd.
   to Elwell Trail: 3.0 mi. (4.8 km.), 2 hr. 15 min.

Welton Falls Trail

This trail provides a route from Hebron to the Elwell Trail. The section continuing south of the ridgecrest to Welton Falls Rd. is currently almost impossible to follow, but a new route has been located and should be open in the near future, which will make possible a number of attractive loop trips involving sections of the Elwell Trail. The trail diverges left from Hobart Hill Rd. 0.8 mi. from the village square in Hebron. The only sign at the trailhead is a small Mowglis trail marker. The trail follows an old road across a brook through a ruined farm, makes a sharp right turn in a log yard, then angles up the hillside to another old road. It turns left and ascends this road, passing under power lines, and crosses the Elwell Trail at the top of the ridge at 1.5 mi. Beyond this point it is not currently maintained.

Welton Falls Trail (map 2)
Distance from Hobart Hill Rd.
  to Welton Falls Rd.: 1.5 mi. (2.3 km.), 1 hr. 10 min.

Old Dicey Rd.
Follow the route described above for Cardigan Lodge but bear right 6.3 mi. from the stone church and follow the road for another 1.2 mi. Where the good road turns sharp right uphill, continue straight ahead another 0.1 mi. to a parking area at a washed-out bridge. Follow the road, which is the Old Dicey Rd., across the brook. At 0.2 mi. the Manning Trail diverges left on a cart track, while the Old Dicey Rd. continues to a clearing at 1.1 mi. Here the Back 80 Loop continues straight ahead, and the Old Dicey Rd. turns right and climbs past an old cellar hole, along a small brook, to end at the Elwell Trail opposite the south terminus of the Carter Gibbs Trail.

Old Dicey Rd. (map 2)
Distance from parking area
  to Elwell Trail: 2.0 mi. (3.3 km.), 1 hr. 30 min.

Back 80 Loop
This short trail connects the Old Dicey Rd. with the Back 80 Trail and makes possible a circuit to Welton Falls from Cardigan Lodge. It follows an old road straight ahead from the clearing where the Old Dicey Rd. turns right, then bears left to cross two brooks within a short

distance, and ascends across another brook and the 93Z Ski Trail to meet the Back 80 Trail at a cellar hole.

Back 80 Loop (map 2)
Distance from Old Dicey Rd.
   to Back 80 Trail: 0.8 mi. (1.2 km.), 35 min.

Back 80 Trail
This trail diverges right from the Holt Trail about 100 yd. west of Cardigan Lodge and follows an old logging road. At 0.3 mi. the Short Circuit Ski Trail diverges right, at 0.4 mi. the Whitney Way Ski Trail diverges left, and at 0.8 mi. the trail turns sharp right where the Alleeway Ski Trail turns left and reaches a cellar hole. The trail to the right is the Back 80 Loop to Welton Falls; the Back 80 Trail turns left (follow the trail with care from here on). It crosses the 93Z Ski Trail, then a brook at a scenic little waterfall. It turns sharp left at 1.2 mi. at the east corner of Back 80 Lot and runs along the northern border of the lot. The trail goes around a flowage from a beaver dam, which may force a detour through the woods, passes a junction at 1.8 mi. with the Duke's Link Ski Trail, then turns sharp right, crosses a brook, turns left, and follows the brook and the edge of another beaver pond to the back corner post (marked Draper-NHFS-AMC). The trail then ascends gradually across a brook to end at the Elwell Trail in the col between Mowglis Mtn. and Cilley's Cave.

Back 80 Trail (map 2)
Distance from Holt Trail
   to Elwell Trail: 2.4 mi. (3.9 km.), 1 hr. 30 min.

Manning Trail
This trail was constructed by the AMC as a memorial to the three Manning brothers, Robert, Charles, and Francis, who were killed by a train during a blizzard in 1924 while hiking on a section of track near Glencliff often used as a

shortcut between DOC trails. The trail diverges left from the Old Dicey Rd. 0.2 mi. from the parking area near the washed-out bridge on Welton Falls Rd., follows a cart path to the Fowler River, crosses on stones, and enters the Welton Falls Reservation (NHDP). It continues up-river to a deep, mossy ravine and the main falls. There are many attractive falls and rapids, as well as spectacular potholes, above and below the main falls. From Welton Falls the trail climbs and descends many small ridges, usually in sight of the river, then at 1.1 mi. it turns right, crosses the river without a bridge (difficult at high water), and ascends to a plateau, where it passes through a grove of spruces. It crosses the 93Z Ski Trail, then descends through a picnic area to Cardigan Lodge. (To reach the Manning Trail to Welton Falls from the lodge, ascend through a picnic area to the road at the right of the fireplace.)

The Manning Trail continues past the lodge, coincides with the Holt Trail for 0.3 mi., then diverges right and passes the old Holt cellar hole. The Duke's Ski Trail leaves to the right, then the Manning Trail turns right at an arrow, crosses back over the Duke's Ski Trail, and climbs through the woods to the first ledges. It passes a small brook, then climbs again to a great open ledge with fine views. At the top of this ledge it turns left through scrubby woods, ascending steeply at times, then follows cairns and paint markings across flat ledges to the cairn where it ends at the Mowglis Trail, just below the summit of Firescrew. The summit of Mt. Cardigan is reached by turning left on the Mowglis Trail.

Manning Trail (map 2)

Distances from Old Dicey Rd.

    to Cardigan Lodge: 1.6 mi., 1 hr.

    to Mowglis Trail: 4.0 mi. (6.4 km.), 3 hr.

Distance from Cardigan Lodge

    to Mt. Cardigan summit (via Manning Trail and Mowglis Trail): 3.0 mi. (4.8 km.), 2 hr. 30 min.

Holt Trail

This is the shortest route, but far from the easiest, from Cardigan Lodge to the summit of Mt. Cardigan. The upper ledges are very steep, and the scramble up these ledges is more difficult than any other trail in this section, and may be dangerous in wet or icy conditions. The trail is maintained by Camp Mowglis and named for the camp's founder, Elizabeth Ford Holt.

From Cardigan Lodge the Holt Trail follows a gravel road to a junction with the Manning Trail, then a lumber road almost to the Bailey Brook bridge. There it diverges right, and the Alexandria Ski Trail continues straight. The Holt Trail stays on the north bank of the brook, then crosses at the head of Elizabeth Falls to rejoin the Alexandria Ski Trail near Grand Junction. The Cathedral Forest Trail diverges left, providing an easier ascent of Mt. Cardigan via Cathedral Forest and the Clark Trail. The Alexandria Ski Trail also diverges left here, and shortly beyond the Alleeway Ski Trail diverges right. The Holt Trail continues along Bailey Brook to a point directly under the summit, climbs steeply on a rocky path through woods, then emerges on open ledges and makes a rapid, very steep ascent over marked ledges to the summit.

Holt Trail (map 2)

Distances from Cardigan Lodge

to Grand Junction: 1.1 mi., 35 min.

to Mt. Cardigan summit: 2.2 mi. (3.6 km.), 2 hr.

Cathedral Forest Trail

This trail diverges left from the Holt Trail at Grand Junction and ascends to the Clark Trail in the Cathedral Forest, providing the easiest route to the summit of Cardigan from the east. About 100 yd. above the junction the Vistamont Trail branches left to Orange Mtn. Ascending in graded switchbacks past the huge but rapidly decaying dead trunk of the Giant of the Forest, the trail joins the Clark Trail at a large cairn.

Cathedral Forest Trail (map 2)

Distances from Holt Trail, Grand Junction

to Clark Trail: 0.6 mi., 30 min.

to Mt. Cardigan summit (via Holt, Cathedral Forest, and Clark trails): 2.6 mi. (4.2 km.), 2 hr. 10 min.

Clark Trail

This trail begins on the Woodland Trail 1.2 mi. from Cardigan Lodge, continuing straight ahead on an older road at a point where the Woodland Trail turns sharp left on the logging road it has been following. It passes an old cellar hole, enters the state reservation at a level grade in a beautiful forest, then climbs steeply to cross the Vistamont Trail at 0.8 mi. The grade becomes easier, and the Clark Trail reaches the Cathedral Forest, where the Cathedral Forest Trail enters from the right at 1.1 mi. As the trail continues a moderate ascent, the Alexandria Ski Trail enters right near P. J. Ledge, and 30 yd. farther the Hurricane Gap Trail leaves left for Hi-Cabin and the Hermitage site. The Clark Trail continues past a side trail left that leads to a spring and Hi-Cabin, then climbs on ledges and through scrub to the warden's cabin at 1.8 mi., where it meets the South Ridge Trail. Turning right, it follows marked ledges steeply to the summit.

Clark Trail (map 2)

Distance from the Woodland Trail

to Mt. Cardigan summit: 2.0 mi. (3.2 km.), 1 hr. 50 min.

Hurricane Gap Trail

This trail connects the east and west sides of the mountain through the col between Cardigan and South Peak. The western half passes through a fragile area and has been closed to all use except when there is deep snow cover. The trail leaves the Clark Trail just above P. J. Ledge, passes an unsigned spur right to a spring, then reaches the AMC Hi-Cabin, where another spur trail leads right 60 yd. to the spring and 40 yd. farther to the Clark Trail. It climbs past a spur that leads 0.1 mi. left to South Peak, then crosses the South Ridge Trail at 0.4 mi. at the height-of-land, and descends on the winter-only section to the West Ridge Trail at the Hermitage site.

Hurricane Gap Trail (map 2)
Distance from Clark Trail
    to South Ridge Trail: 0.4 mi., 20 min.
    to West Ridge Trail: 0.5 mi. (0.9 km.), 25 min.

Vistamont Trail

The Vistamont Trail connects the Holt Trail with the Skyland Trail at Orange Mtn. (sometimes also called Gilman Mtn.). It leaves the Cathedral Forest Trail left about 100 yd. above Grand Junction and rises over a low ridge, where it crosses the Clark Trail at 0.6 mi. It then drops to cross a branch of Clark Brook, and ascends by switchbacks up the east spur of Orange Mtn., climbing moderately on open ledges to the Skyland Trail 80 yd. southeast of the rocky summit, where there are fine views.

Vistamont Trail (map 2)
Distance from Cathedral Forest Trail
    to Skyland Trail: 1.6 mi. (2.6 km.), 1 hr. 20 min.

Woodland Trail

This trail runs from Cardigan Lodge to the Skyland Trail near the summit of Church Mtn. It leaves the parking lot to the left of the pond, crosses the outlet brook on a bridge, and passes the east entrance of the Kimball Ski Trail. It continues through woods past the Brock Farm cellar hole and field, then turns right on a rough dirt logging road at 0.7 mi. At 1.2 mi., where the Clark Trail continues straight ahead on an older road, the Woodland Trail follows the more recent logging road as it turns sharp left and descends across a brook, then climbs to a large beaver pond at 2.1 mi. From here on the trail is harder to follow and great care must be used. It ascends along the inlet brook, crosses it, and doubles back along the edge of the pond, then climbs moderately past a corner post marked "Draper" in a boggy area near a large boulder. Finally it rises more steeply to end at the Skyland Trail at the northwest shoulder of Church Mtn.

Woodland Trail (map 2)
Distance from Cardigan Lodge
   to Skyland Trail: 3.3 mi. (5.2 km.), 2 hr. 15 min.

Skyland Trail

This trail runs from Alexandria Four Corners to the West Ridge Trail just below the Hermitage. It follows the western and southern boundaries of Shem Valley, and in 4.5 mi. crosses five of the six peaks that extend south and southeast from Cardigan summit. It is lightly marked for much of its distance and, particularly between Brown Mtn. and Orange Mtn., must be followed with great care. It is, however, a very scenic route.

The trail starts at Alexandria Four Corners, reached by following signs from the stone church at the foot of Newfound Lake to Alexandria village. Continue through the village on the main road, which turns sharp right, then left, pass under the power lines and then, as the main road turns sharp left for Danbury, continue straight ahead for about 4.0 mi. to the crossroads (sign: "Rosie's Rd."). Best parking is here; do not block roads above.

The trail follows the road right (north) from the corner and soon bears left at a fork. At 0.3 mi. it turns sharp left (arrow) on a short road to a clearing, and ascends moderately to the edge of a logged area and a house. It climbs to an outlook near the wooded summit of Brown Mtn., then turns left and crosses the col to the east knob of Church Mtn. (2290 ft.) at 1.1 mi., where there is an outlook. It continues past a junction (right) at 1.3 mi. with the Woodland Trail coming up from Cardigan Lodge, then follows the ridge top over Grafton Knob (2210 ft.) to Crane Mtn. (2430 ft.) at 2.1 mi., with good views from several ledges near the summit. The Skyland Trail continues to Orange Mtn. (2630 ft.) at 3.3 mi., where the Vistamont Trail enters 80 yd. before the summit. There are excellent views from the summit ledges. The trail descends to a col, then climbs fairly steeply to Rimrock at 4.3 mi., where it crosses the South Ridge Trail. It descends along a ledge (follow the right of two lines of cairns) and soon enters the West Ridge Trail just below the Hermitage site.

Skyland Trail (map 2)
Distance from Alexandria Four Corners
  to West Ridge Trail: 4.6 mi. (7.3 km.), 3 hr. 15 min.

Ski Trails at Cardigan Lodge

The AMC maintains a number of ski trails in the woods around Cardigan Lodge, in addition to the hiking trails, many of which are also skiable. A map available at the lodge shows most of these trails and their ratings, which range from novice cross-country to expert alpine terrain on the ledges of Cardigan and Firescrew. Some of these trails were cut as alpine trails in the days before modern tows became common. Ski trails are not maintained for summer use, and hikers are requested not to use them.

PLYMOUTH MOUNTAIN

Plymouth Mtn. (2187 ft.) lies in Plymouth, northeast of Newfound Lake. The true summit is wooded, but nearby open ledges afford excellent views. Refer to the USGS Holderness quadrangle.

Plymouth Mountain Trail

At the crossroads on NH 3A near the head of Newfound Lake, where the lake shore road to Hebron village runs

west, go east on Pike Hill Rd. and bear left at the first
fork. Since the road has frequently been impassable
beyond, this may be the best spot to park. In another 1.1
mi., after the second bridge over a brook and 0.2 mi. past
a snowmobile trail on the right, the trail leaves right on an
old logging road (sign). It is marked by stenciled Camp
Mowglis signs. It crosses a brook (follow trail with care),
follows another old road upward, and turns sharp left
where a branch trail enters right. (Descending, turn sharp
right here where the branch trail, marked by a Mowglis
sign, goes almost straight ahead.) The trail ascends to an
outlook over Newfound Lake, becomes less steep, crosses
a false summit, and climbs to the true summit (sign).
From here an open ledge 30 yd. straight ahead (east) provides fine views of Franconia Notch and the White Mtns.,
while a line of cairns leads right (southwest) to an outlook
over Newfound Lake to Mt. Cardigan.

Plymouth Mountain Trail (USGS Holderness quad)
Distances from US 3A

to start of foot trail: 1.4 mi., 1 hr.

to Plymouth Mtn. summit: 2.9 mi. (4.6 km.), 2 hr. 15 min.

MT. KEARSARGE

Mt. Kearsarge (2937 ft.) is located in Warner, Wilmot,
Andover, and Salisbury. It has a bare summit with lovely views in all directions. Mt. Kearsarge probably was
discovered shortly after the Pilgrims landed. On a sev-
enteenth-century map (Gardner's) it appears as Carasar-
ga, but since Carrigain's map of 1816 Kearsarge has
remained the accepted spelling. On the summit there is
a fire tower and an airways beacon, on separate prominent ledges about 30 yd. apart, and a firewarden's cabin
near the tower. Refer to the USGS Mt. Kearsarge quadrangle.

Wilmot (Northside) Trail

From NH 11 between Wilmot Flat and Elkins, take Kearsarge Valley Rd. south, then follow signs to Winslow State Park and the site of the old Winslow House (caretaker's cabin, picnic area, water, and parking space; nominal admission fee). The trail starts from the parking area to the left of a service garage. It is well beaten and marked with red paint. It crosses under power lines and climbs moderately to a fork. (The left branch rejoins above and is slightly shorter but rougher.) The right branch climbs more steeply past Halfway Rock, angles upward to an outlook north, then turns south and ascends over bare ledges, marked with orange paint, to the summit.

Wilmot Trail (USGS Mt. Kearsarge quad)
Distance from parking area, Winslow State Park
    to Mt. Kearsarge summit: 1.1 mi. (1.8 km.), 1 hr. 5 min.

Warner (Southside) Trail

Leave NH 103 in Warner and follow signs to the gate at Rollins State Park. A small fee is charged, and the gate is often closed weekdays before Memorial Day and after Labor Day. There is a picnic area with tables, fireplaces, and water. The road then mainly follows the route of the old carriage road along the crest of Mission Ridge and ends at a parking area 3.7 mi. above the toll gate. There are more picnic tables and fireplaces here, but no water.

The trail follows the old carriage road, now badly eroded, to a ledge with a fine view. (An unsigned, red-blazed trail, 0.1 mi. longer and rough, bypasses the worst section of the old road to the right and rejoins at the outlook.) The trail then swings left and rises to the foot of the summit ledges, where there are toilets. An orange-blazed trail diverges sharp right, a direct route to the warden's cabin. The main trail, blazed in silver, continues across the ledges to the beacon and tower.

From the west end of the parking area, an unsigned trail starts as a cart track to the foot of the ledges and, marked with red paint on the rocks, climbs steeply to the top. Faded paint blazes lead along sparsely wooded ledges toward the tower, then to the main trail below the beacon.

Warner Trail (USGS Mt. Kearsarge quad)
Distance from parking area, Rollins State Park
   to Mt. Kearsarge summit: 0.6 mi. (1.0 km.), 25 min.

SECTION 15
Monadnock and Southwestern New Hampshire

This section covers the area west of the Merrimack River and south of I-89. Mt. Monadnock is by far the best-known and most popular peak in the area. Other peaks include the Pack Monadnocks, Temple Mtn., and Barrett Mtn. on the Wapack Trail. Monadnock itself is covered by the AMC Grand Monadnock map (map 1), and the Wapack Trail is covered by USGS maps and by a map of the Wapack Trail published by the Friends of the Wapack and available from the AMC. Other mountains are covered by USGS quadrangles as indicated in their descriptions. In addition to the areas for which trails are described in this section, mention should be made of Pisgah State Park in Chesterfield, Hinsdale, and Winchester. This undeveloped park contains 13,000 acres within which there are a number of hiking and multi-use trails and a great opportunity for exploration.

The Metacomet-Monadnock Trail, 160 mi. long, begins in the Hanging Hills of Meriden CT, and runs north along the trap rock ridge that borders the Connecticut River. It traverses Mt. Tom and the Holyoke Range, and passes over the Northfield Hills and Mt. Grace. The New Hamsphire section includes Little Monadnock Mtn. and Gap Mtn., and terminates at Grand Monadnock. The trail is clearly marked by white rectangular paint blazes. Space constraints prevent its coverage by this guide. The 1990 edition of the *Metacomet-Monadnock Trail Guide*, published by the Berkshire Chapter of the AMC, is available from the AMC.

The Monadnock-Sunapee Greenway, 48 mi. long, continues north from Mt. Monadnock. The SPNHF and

AMC cooperatively maintain this trail, which runs mostly over hills and along ridges between these two major
peaks in southwest New Hampshire. Because a large part
of this trail is located on private property, users should be
particularly aware of their status as guests and avoid
thoughtless behavior that could jeopardize this privilege.
The 1991 edition of the *Monadnock-Sunapee Greenway
Guide*, which includes several side trails in the Mt.
Sunapee area, is available from the AMC or the SPNHF.

Sunapee Mtn. (2730 ft.), the northern terminus of the
Greenway, is an irregular, massive, heavily wooded
mountain located in Newbury at the south end of Lake
Sunapee. The mountain is heavily wooded, but Lake
Solitude near its summit is unique for its high elevation,
remoteness, and beauty of setting. Nearby are cliffs that
rise 300 ft. to White Ledge, where there is a fine view
southeast over the wild country of the Merrimack-Con-
necticut watershed. Refer to the USGS Sunapee quadrangle. Mt. Sunapee State Park is on NH 103, 7 mi. east of
Newport. There is a state-owned ski area on the north
slope of the mountain; a hikers' map is available at the
lodge. The mountain is easily climbed via the ski slopes
(about 1.5 mi.). A trail, part of the Greenway, leads from
the summit 1.6 mi. to Lake Solitude and connects to the
Andrews Brook Trail from the east and to the Five Sum-
mers Trail from Pillsbury State Park in Washington.
Consult the Greenway guide for details.

MT. MONADNOCK

Mt. Monadnock (3165 ft.), also called Grand Monadnock,
rises in the towns of Jaffrey and Dublin, about 10 mi.
north of the New Hampshire–Massachusetts border. It is
an isolated mountain that towers 1500 to 2000 ft. above
the surrounding country, visible from most of the prominent viewpoints in central New England. Its summit com-

mands exceptionally extensive and distant views; Mt. Washington is sometimes visible when it has snow cover. Two prominent southern crags are worthy of note: Monte Rosa (2510 ft.) on the southwest ridge, and Bald Rock (2628 ft.), signed as Kiasticuticus (literally Skinhead) Peak, on the south ridge. Combining extremely rugged mountain scenery with a relatively short and easy ascent and convenient access from the population centers of southern New England, Monadnock is reputedly (after Fujiyama) the second most frequently climbed mountain in the world; on one Columbus Day in the late 1970s, it was ascended by throngs estimated at nearly 10,000 people. It would be wise to regard *any* water source on this mountain with extreme suspicion.

There are several major trails to the summit and a network of connecting and secondary trails on the east, south, and west sides of the main peak. This network had deteriorated badly after a fire in 1954 destroyed the old hotel called the Halfway House, where many amateur trail builders had their base of operations, but most of these trails have been restored by the dedicated efforts of state park personnel. It is possible to ascend Monadnock in relative solitude on these attractive trails, particularly if you avoid weekends. The White Arrow Trail—the most direct route to the summit on this side—and many other trails begin near the Halfway House site, a starting point for many attractive circuit trips that is located on the west flank of Monadnock's south ridge at about 2100 ft. It is reached by a former toll road, now closed to public vehicular use but open for hikers. This road leaves a parking area on NH 124 near the height-of-land, 5.0 mi. west of Jaffrey and about 4 mi. east of Troy, and climbs 1.2 mi. to the old hotel site.

The upper 500 ft. of the mountain is open ledge, bared by a series of forest fires. Farmers frequently set fires to clear the lower slopes for pasture, and about 1800 a major fire of unknown origin burned for about two weeks, greatly damaging the forests on the upper part of the mountain. Subsequent fires and windstorms completed the devastation, creating an impenetrable maze of blown-down trees that was a natural lair for wolves who preyed on the sheep on the pastures. (During the first half of the nineteenth century, sheep were probably the most important agricultural product in the western NH hill country.) Sometime between 1810 and 1820, a fire set by farmers attempting to oust the wolves got out of control, and burned with an intensity that consumed even the soil and reduced the upper part of the mountain to bare, sterile rock. Since then small plants, shrubs, and trees have lodged themselves in various cracks and crannies, creating small pockets of soil and beginning the process that, if left undisturbed, will restore the mountain forest in a few millennia.

Visitors from outside the immediate vicinity of the mountain began to arrive at about the same time as the last of the great fires, and by 1850 Monadnock was established as a major attraction for New Englanders. Due to the proximity of the mountain to Concord MA, where the Transcendentalist literary movement with its deep interest in nature developed around the figures of Ralph Waldo Emerson and Henry David Thoreau, Mt. Monadnock attained the status of something like a sacred mountain and was immortalized in the works of these notable writers and others. Monadnock's slopes probably bear more historic trails and former trails and ruins than any other mountain in New England, including Mt. Washington. The *Monadnock Guide*, published by the SPNHF, provides details of much of this history, as well as extensive information about the natural history of the mountain.

The public reservation on the mountain now comprises about 5000 contiguous acres cooperatively administered by the state, the town of Jaffrey, the Association to

Protect Mt. Monadnock, and the SPNHF. At Monadnock State Park, just off Memorial Rd., the state maintains picnic grounds, a parking lot, and a public campground (fees charged for each). Camping is not permitted anywhere on the mountain, except at the state park campground. Dogs are not allowed anywhere in the state park.

THE TRAILS
White Arrow Trail

One of the oldest routes to the summit, this trail continues along the north end of the toll road from the site of the Halfway House. It is marked by painted white arrows. It follows the road, which soon ends, and immediately begins to climb rather steeply through the woods on a broad, rocky way past Quarter-Way Spring. At 0.6 mi. the Sidefoot Trail enters from the right, coinciding with the Amphitheater Trail, which continues across the White Arrow Trail (no sign) toward the Smith Summit Trail. The White Arrow Trail soon reaches the treeline, where it bears left and starts to ascend the ledges in the open. Just below the summit a side path on the right makes an interesting scramble up a narrow gully. The main trail soon gains the summit plateau where it meets the Dublin and Marlboro trails, and turns right in company with these trails to reach the summit in another 75 yd.

White Arrow Trail (map 1)
Distance from Halfway House site
   to Mt. Monadnock summit: 1.1 mi. (1.7 km.), 1 hr. 5 min.

Distance from NH 124
   to Mt. Monadnock summit (via old toll road): 2.3 mi. (3.7 km.), 2 hr.

Dublin Path (SPNHF)

This trail ascends Monadnock from the north; it is a link in the Monadnock-Sunapee Greenway. From the flagpole in Dublin village, go west on NH 101 (Main St.). At 0.4 mi. bear left on East Lake Rd., which becomes Old Marlboro Rd. At 2.5 mi. go left downhill on Old Troy Rd., pass through a crossroads, and continue to a small clearing on the right at 4.0 mi., where there is parking space. (Beyond the houses at 3.4 mi. the road becomes narrow and poor; it may be impassable when muddy.) The trail, marked with white Ds, starts opposite the clearing and climbs to the tip of the ridge, passing an unreliable spring at 1.0 mi. It follows the ledgy ridge with occasional good views, passes another unreliable spring at the foot of a rock at 1.8 mi., and emerges above timberline. The Marlboro Trail joins on the right at 2.0 mi., just beyond a prominent cap of rock, a false summit. The Dublin Path continues upward to meet the White Arrow Trail 75 yd. below the true summit.

Dublin Path (map 1)

Distance from Old Troy Rd.

to Mt. Monadnock summit: 2.2 mi. (3.5 km.), 2 hr.

Pumpelly Trail (SPNHF and AMC)

This is the longest, most strenuous, and most scenic direct route to the summit of Monadnock. Follow NH 101 (Main St.) west from the flagpole in Dublin village for 0.4 mi., then turn left on East Lake Rd. (sign). The trail (no sign) leaves the road left at 0.4 mi., opposite a log cabin on the pond, 75 yd. east of where the road reaches the shore.

The trail follows a woods road for 120 yd., then turns right into a narrow path through a stone wall (small cairn and sign), then turns left onto a woods road again at 0.2 mi. It crosses Oak Hill and continues with gradual ups and downs, becoming a foot path, then at 1.8 mi. it turns sharp left and begins the rather steep and rough ascent of the north end of Dublin Ridge. The trail zigzags up and emerges on the first semi-open ledges on the shoulder of the mountain at 2.2 mi., almost exactly halfway to the summit. From here the trail is rough and rocky, running near the ridgecrest with many minor ups and downs, but offers many excellent views from bare ledges. At 3.0 mi. the Cascade Link enters on the left, ascending from the Monadnock State Park trail network on the eastern slopes, and at 3.7 mi. the Spellman Trail also enters on the left just below the Sarcophagus, a huge rectangular boulder in plain view. From here onward the trail, marked by large cairns, runs mostly on open ledge where many glacial striations are plainly visible. It soon passes a small alpine meadow, and at 4.0 mi. the Red Spot Trail enters left. In another 100 yd., the Old Link Trail, marked with yellow spots and cairns, leaves left for the Smith Connecting Trail, which continues over the White Dot and White Cross trails to Bald Rock, linking the Pumpelly Trail with the complex of trails that radiate from the Halfway House site. The Pumpelly Trail soon passes through a little col with steep, ledgy walls, comes completely into the open in another 80 yd., and continues over the ledges to the summit.

Descending, the trail runs nearly due east; look for a large white arrow on summit rock marked Pumpelly Trail. There are few cairns for the first 200 yd. and care must be taken to locate the first one. In several cases the cairns are rather small.

Pumpelly Trail (map 1)
Distance from Old Marlboro Rd.
   to Mt. Monadnock summit: 4.4 mi. (7.1 km.), 3 hr. 30 min.

White Dot and White Cross Trails
These two trails have a common origin, coincide for their first 0.7 mi., then separate, but rejoin for the last 0.3 mi. to the summit. Both trails start on a broad jeep road near the Visitors Center at the west end of Poole Memorial Rd. in

Monadnock State Park. They descend slightly and cross a small brook. At 0.5 mi. the Spruce Link, a cutoff 0.3 mi. long that rejoins the White Cross Trail above Falcon Spring, leaves left. The White Dot and White Cross trails then climb gradually through woods to a junction with the Cascade Link at Falcon Spring at 0.7 mi. The White Dot Trail is steeper, but not much shorter than the White Cross, while views from the White Cross are more interesting.

The White Dot Trail goes straight at the junction just above Falcon Spring, ascends the steep ridge, and emerges at 1.1 mi. on the semi-open plateau near treeline. It passes the Old Ski Path, which runs right (north) 0.2 mi. to the Red Spot Trail, then climbs on ledges through meager evergreens. At 1.6 mi. the White Dot Trail crosses the Smith Connecting Trail, which circles the east side of the summit cone from Bald Rock to the Red Spot Trail, connecting the Halfway House site to the Pumpelly Trail. The White Dot rejoins the White Cross Trail at 1.7 mi. and continues up slanting ledges to the summit.

The White Cross Trail leaves left at the junction just above Falcon Spring, and angles gradually uphill. At 0.9 mi. the Spruce Link re-enters on the left, and the White Cross Trail turns sharp right and starts to climb at moderate grades over boulders left by an old slide. It passes through an old burn (good views back to the east and south across a ravine called Dingle Dell) and finally reaches the flat southeast shoulder. It soon emerges from sparse evergreens on the ledges. The Smith Connecting Trail crosses at 1.8 mi., and the White Cross rejoins the White Dot Trail at 1.9 mi. and continues to the summit. Above where the White Dot Trail rejoins, the trail is most frequently marked with white dots rather than white crosses.

White Dot Trail (map 1)

Distance from Poole Memorial Rd.

> *to* Mt. Monadnock summit: 2.0 mi. (3.2 km.), 1 hr. 45 min.

White Cross Trail (map 1)

Distance from Poole Memorial Rd.

    to Mt. Monadnock summit: 2.2 mi. (3.5 km.), 1 hr. 45 min.

Harling Trail (SPNHF)

The Harling Trail is reached from Poole Memorial Rd. 0.2 mi. east of the entrance to Monadnock State Park; follow the Hinkley Trail, a connecting trail 0.6 mi. long, to its end, then take Cross-country Ski Trail #18, which is the Harling Trail but has no specific trail sign. The trail runs west on an old woods road and reaches the Cascade Link a short distance north of the Falcon Spring junction. From here, follow the Cascade Link right for the Red Spot, Spellman, and Pumpelly trails.

Harling Trail (map 1)

Distance from Poole Memorial Rd.

    to Cascade Link (via Hinkley Trail): 1.3 mi. (2.1 km.), 55 min.

Cascade Link (AMC)

This trail runs between Falcon Spring junction and the Pumpelly Trail, angling upward, south to north. With the Pumpelly Trail, it is an interesting descent route from the summit to the state park. With either the Spellman Trail or the Red Spot Trail it offers the most varied ascents from the east side of the mountain.

    The Cascade Link starts at the Falcon Spring junction, reached via the White Dot and White Cross trails. It runs northeast, descends slightly, passes the Harling Trail on the right, and continues through spruce woods to a brook and the little cascades for which this trail is named. At 0.3 mi. it crosses the brook and climbs gradually along its east side, rising about 300 ft. before it leaves the brook and winds over ledges in thick woods. The Birchtoft Trail enters on the right at 0.5 mi., and the Red Spot Trail leaves to the left for Dublin Ridge and the Pumpelly Trail in another 30 yd., just before an old east-west stone wall. At 0.7 mi. the Spellman Trail leaves left, and the Cascade Link climbs close to the east bank of a small brook to where the brook rises, close to the boundary between Dublin and Jaffrey. From there, prominent cairns mark the Cascade Link over open ledges to a saddle on the Dublin Ridge (2700 ft.), where it ends at the Pumpelly Trail. (The Pumpelly Trail is a picturesque descent route with many outlooks, marked with yellow paint blazes.)

Cascade Link (map 1)

Distance from Falcon Spring
   to Pumpelly Trail: 1.4 mi. (2.3 km.), 1 hr. 30 min.

Spellman Trail

This trail leaves the Cascade Link 0.7 mi. from Falcon Spring and makes the steepest climb (700 ft. in about 0.6 mi.) on the mountain, up to the Pumpelly Trail just north of the Sarcophagus. The Spellman Trail is a good scramble in its middle section, with excellent views back to the east. This trail is difficult to follow when snow covers the white dots that mark the route on the rocks, because in winding about to avoid the worst ledges, the trail does not always follow a clear line.

Spellman Trail (map 1)

Distance from Cascade Link
   to Pumpelly Trail: 0.6 mi. (0.9 km.), 40 min.

Red Spot Trail

This trail, much less challenging than the Spellman Trail, provides a scenic alternative to the more heavily used trails on the east side of the mountain. It leaves the Cascade Link 0.5 mi. from Falcon Spring, 30 yd. beyond the Birchtoft Trail, and ascends somewhat roughly via long switchbacks. At 0.4 mi. the Old Ski Path leaves left for the White Dot Trail. At 0.7 mi. the Red Spot Trail emerges on ledges with good views, then passes the northern end of the Smith Connecting Trail at 0.9 mi. and soon ends at the Pumpelly Trail 0.4 mi. below the summit.

Red Spot Trail (map 1)
Distance from Cascade Link
    to Pumpelly Trail: 1.0 mi. (1.7 km.), 55 min.

Birchtoft Trail

This trail leaves the Monadnock Recreation Area located on Dublin Rd. 1 mi. north of Poole Memorial Rd. The Monadnock Recreation Area campground is privately owned; there is a parking fee, and hikers are requested to register at the lodge office. Follow the recreation area entrance road a short distance. Turn left on the first driveway and follow it 100 yd. to the shore of Gilson Pond (parking). The trail (sign) skirts the east and south shores of the pond and ascends by easy grades to end at the Cascade Link 0.5 mi. from Falcon Spring.

Birchtoft Trail (map 1)
Distance from Gilson Pond
    to Cascade Link: 2.1 mi. (3.3 km.), 1 hr. 25 min.

Marlboro Trail (SPNHF)

This is one of the oldest trails to the summit, dating to 1850 or earlier. Follow NH 124 west from Jaffrey, past roads to Monadnock State Park and the Halfway House site. Take Shaker Farm Rd., the first dirt road on the right north of the Troy-Marlboro town line, 0.6 mi. north of Perkins Pond. Follow this road 0.7 mi. to a clearing on the left and an old cellar hole (parking). The trail follows a woods road for 0.9 mi. to a wall running east-west, then climbs up the nose of the ridge to the open ledges, marked with cairns and white Ms. At 1.3 mi. the Marian Trail leaves the Marlboro Trail on the right at the ledges known as the Stone House (about 2450 ft.). The Marl-boro Trail climbs to a shoulder 0.2 mi. below the summit, where it joins the Dublin Path (which comes up from the left) and continues to the summit.

Marlboro Trail (map 1)

Distances from parking area, road west of Perkins Pond
  to Dublin Path: 1.9 mi., 1 hr. 45 min.
  to Mt. Monadnock summit: 2.2 mi. (3.5 km.), 2 hr.

Halfway House Site Region

There are good, varied walks here. A particularly rewarding round trip to the summit combines an ascent over Bald Rock via the Cliff Walk and the Smith Connecting, Red Spot, and Pumpelly trails with a descent on the Smith Summit Trail and one of the trails over Monte Rosa.

One of the finest scenic trails on Mt. Monadnock is the Cliff Walk, marked with white Cs, which begins on the Parker Trail 0.4 mi. from the old toll road and runs 1.5 mi. along the south and east edge of the south ridge, from Hello Rock to Bald Rock, past splendid viewpoints—notably Thoreau's Seat, Emerson's Seat, and What Cheer Point—and historical points such as the Graphite Mine (left), which was operated around 1850. Several paths lead up to the Cliff Walk from the Halfway House site. Three such trails are the Hello Rock, Point Surprise, and Thoreau trails, which leave the Halfway House clearing at the southeast corner between the road and Moses Spring. The Hello Rock Trail ascends gradually 0.4 mi. through a fine forest to the Cliff Walk at Hello Rock. At 80 yd. above the Halfway House site, the Point Surprise Trail diverges left and ascends 0.3 mi. to the Cliff Walk, and the Thoreau Trail diverges farther left and climbs 0.4 mi. to the Cliff Walk at Thoreau's Seat.

Bald Rock is the bare peak on the south ridge of Monadnock; its highest point is a pointed boulder inscribed Kiasticuticus Peak. From Bald Rock, the Smith Connecting Trail, marked with yellow Ss, descends a short distance, soon passes Coffee Pot Corner, and shortly reaches the Four Spots, a trail junction. The Smith Connecting Trail goes right at this junction, eventually crosses the White Cross Trail, then the White Dot Trail, and ends at the Red Spot Trail just below the Pumpelly Trail, a total of 0.7 mi. The trail that forks left at the Four Spots junction, is the eastern end of the Amphitheater Trail; it climbs with little grade to join the Sidefoot Trail, which soon reaches the White Arrow Trail, after which the Amphitheater Trail continues west (no sign) to the Smith Summit Trail.

The Sidefoot Trail is an excellent alternative to the lower part of the White Arrow Trail and avoids much of the very heavy traffic on that trail. To reach the Sidefoot Trail, climb the bank at the left of the Halfway House clearing and follow a path a few yards into the woods to a trail junction. The Sidefoot Trail leaves left and climbs 0.7 mi. to join the White Arrow Trail at Halfway Spring. Three trails in close succession—the Do Drop Trail (0.2 mi.), the Noble Trail (0.3 mi.), and the unsigned Hedgehog Trail (0.3 mi.)—leave to the right of the Sidefoot Trail and climb steeply to the Cliff Walk.

The Monte Rosa Trail leaves the tiny clearing of the former picnic grounds just past the north end of the Halfway House clearing, crosses the Royce (Metacomet-Monadnock) Trail, and climbs to a junction at 0.3 mi. where the Fairy Spring Trail, an alternate path that runs 0.3 mi. from the picnic grounds past the foundation of Fassett's Mountain House and Fairy Spring, enters on the right. In a few steps above this junction, the Monte Rosa Trail bears left (right is the Smith Bypass, leading directly to the Tooth), and ascends to the summit of Monte Rosa at 0.4 mi. The Great Pasture Trail leaves the junction of the Marian and Mossy Brook trails, ascends to the summit of Monte Rosa and the Monte Rosa Trail at 0.3 mi., then descends steeply to the Tooth, a large pointed boulder, and continues to the Smith Summit Trail at 0.4 mi.

The Smith Summit Trail (marked by white dots) circles gradually up the west side of the mountain 0.6 mi. to the White Arrow, Dublin, and Marlboro trails just below the summit; a short side trail to the top of the Black Precipice (sign) leaves to the right just above the lower end of the Smith Summit Trail, providing a view of the Amphitheater, and the Amphitheater Trail leaves right a short distance farther up and runs 0.4 mi. across the White Arrow and Sidefoot trails to the Smith Connecting Trail. The Cart Path leads west from the toll road about 0.3 mi. below the Halfway House site, crosses the Royce (Metacomet-Monadnock) Trail, and ends abruptly at 0.5 mi. at the junction with the Mossy Brook Trail. The Mossy Brook Trail continues 0.3 mi. to the junction with the Marian and Great Pasture trails. The Marian Trail leaves this junction, then turns sharp right near the Bear Pit, a depression to the west so named because a bear was once reputedly trapped in the quagmire, and continues 0.6 mi. to the Marlboro Trail at the Stone House.

Parker Trail (SPNHF)

The Parkter Trail begins at the picnic area at Monadnock State Park, on the west side of the outlet brook from the reservoir, and heads west across the south slope of the mountain to the old toll road. It maintains a gentle grade and provides easy walking through mature woods. This trail has signs at both ends and is blazed with yellow paint. At 0.6 mi. the Lost Farm Trail diverges right for the upper part of the Cliff Walk, and at 1.1 mi. the lower end of the Cliff Walk is on the right. The Parker Trail joins the toll road 0.6 mi. above NH 124 and 0.6 mi. below the Halfway House site.

Parker Trail (map 1)
Distance from west side of reservoir outlet brook
    to toll road: 1.5 mi. (2.4 km.), 50 min.

Lost Farm Trail

This trail branches right from the Parker Trail 0.6 mi. from the state park and leads in 1.1 mi. to Emerson's Seat on the Cliff Walk. A fine circuit walk from the park headquarters combines this trail with the Cliff Walk, the Smith Connecting Trail, and either the White Cross or the White Dot trails.

Lost Farm Trail (map 1)

Distance from Parker Trail
    to Cliff Walk: 1.1 mi. (1.7 km.), 45 min.

WAPACK TRAIL

This is for the most part, a skyline trail that follows the ridge of the Wapack Range for approximately 21 mi. It runs from Watatic Mtn. in Ashburnham MA over Barrett and Temple mountains and across the Pack Monadnocks in New Hampshire. There are many open ledges with fine views, and the spruce forest found in several places is similar to that of a more northern region. The trail is blazed with yellow triangles and marked by cairns on open ledges. An organization named Friends of the Wapack has been established to protect and maintain the trail (PO Box 106, Greenville NH 03048).

Section I. Watatic Mountain

The southern end of the Wapack Trail has been relocated recently. The trail now begins in a small parking area off MA 119, about 1.5 mi. east of the Massachusetts–New Hampshire border and 1.5 mi. west of its junction with MA 101 northeast of Ashburnham. It passes a small pond and ascends to a junction where it turns right; here the Mid-State Trail continues straight for 1.0 mi. and rejoins the Wapack Trail at the state line. The Wapack Trail climbs past two viewpoints to a shelter (Camp Gardner) in poor condition, then swings left and reaches the fire tower on Mt. Watatic at 1.2 mi., where there is a sweeping view. Here the old route of the Wapack Trail leaves on the right and makes a steep descent on a heavily used eroded path along the power and telephone lines to MA 119, 0.7 mi. west of its junction with MA 101 northeast of Ashburnham. The Wapack Trail turns left and descends northwest across old ski trails and through spruce woods that are a state bird sanctuary, then crosses overgrown pastures on Nutting Hill, passing the summit, a ledgy area in a clearing, at 2.0 mi. It then descends to a junction near cellar holes (obscured by bushes) that mark the Nutting Place, settled by James Spaulding just before the American Revolution and continued by his son-in-law, Jonas Nutting, until about 1840.

From the Nutting Place junction the trail continues north on a long-abandoned road into beech woods and at 2.4 mi. crosse a wall that runs east-west on the Massachusetts–New Hampshire border, where the Mid-State Trail re-enters on the left. A few yards west of the trail, close to the wall, are two stone survey monuments, one erected in 1834. The trail continues north past the old woods roads and cellar holes of long-deserted farms, and reaches Binney Hill Rd. at 3.5 mi. This part of Binney Hill Rd. is no longer maintained, and it is possible to drive in from NH 119 for only about 0.3 mi. to an area where parking is limited because of private residences. The trail turns left (west) on this road and follows it for 0.2 mi. to the point where the Barrett Mtn. section of the Wapack Trail turns to the right off the road.

Section II. Barrett Mountain

The Barrett Mtn. section of the Wapack Trail runs from Binney Hill Rd. to Wapack Lodge on NH 123/124. Shortly after leaving Binney Hill Rd. (signed Pond Trail) at 3.7 mi., the trail crosses a small brook, then skirts the Binney Ponds near their west shores. (Flooding from beaver dams may require a detour here.) The trail traverses the ridge of Barrett Mtn., nearly 3 mi. long and partly wooded, with four summits (the highest is 1881 ft.) and numerous outlooks. Two private trails intersect the Wapack Trail along this ridge, so hikers should be especially careful to identify the Wapack Trail at any junctions. In the saddle between the third and fourth summits, the trail crosses the location of one of the oldest roads from Massachusetts to the hill towns, the Boston Road, built in 1753. After descending from the northern end of Barrett Mtn., the trail enters an area where it encounters several ski trails, ascends an outlying knoll, then descends to Wapack Lodge, a private residence (no longer identified by a sign) located on NH 123/124 on the site of a house built in 1776 by Deacon John Brown of Concord MA.

Section III. Kidder Mountain

The Wapack Trail next crosses the lower western slopes of Kidder Mtn. From Wapack Lodge it crosses the highway at 9.1 mi. and enters a dirt road opposite the lodge driveway, and soon enters the woods. At 9.7 mi. the trail turns left on an old grassy road with bordering stone walls and crosses under a power line 150 yd. beyond. (A blue-blazed side trail leads right from here along the power lines, then left into the woods to the summit of Kidder Mtn. with good views at 0.9 mi.) The Wapack Trail descends to a junction with a gravel road from the left at a pond on the right. Here it turns right onto a woods road, crosses the pond outlet, and ascends gradually to the Wildcat Hill–Conant Hill saddle, where there is an old homestead site to the right. The trail descends gradually, still on the old roadway, crosses the outlet of a beaver pond on the right, then bears left onto Todd Rd. at 11.0 mi. and continues to Nashua Rd. (the road from Temple to Jaffrey) at 11.4 mi.

Section IV. Temple Mountain

The trail crosses Nashua Rd. and continues straight ahead along Sharon Rd. for 0.4 mi., bears right at a fork, then turns right 30 yd. beyond to follow a dirt road for a short distance before entering the woods. (From Sharon Rd. north, the trail passes through private land known as Avelinda Forest. Please observe the No fires–No smoking rules posted in the forest.) The trail then ascends the south end of Temple Mtn., which has several bare summits—but the highest, Holt Peak (2084 ft.), is broad, wooded, and viewless. A short distance south of Holt Peak, the trail crosses a stone wall, then turns sharp left and parallels the wall a short distance before climbing to the summit at 14.3 mi. (An alternate route, used mostly as a ski bypass and marked by old red blazes, continues straight ahead beyond the wall, swings to the east of the summit, and rejoins the main trail 0.3 mi. north of the summit.) The trail follows the ridge, which has wide views, especially toward Grand Monadnock. Stone monuments mark the Sharon-Temple town line, which also follows this ridge. From the north summit the trail descends through the Temple Mountain Ski Area to NH 101 in Peterborough Gap at 16.2 mi., a few yards east of the road up South Pack Monadnock, which leaves NH 101 at the height-of-land.

Section V. Pack Monadnock

This extended ridge culminates in two open peaks, Pack Monadnock (2310 ft.), usually called South Pack Monadnock, and North Pack Monadnock (2278 ft.); *pack* is an Indian word meaning "little." It lies between Peterborough and Temple NH, and is a well-known landmark in southern New Hampshire and eastern Massachusetts. On the summit of South Pack is a small state reservation, General James Miller Park. (To reach the park, drive up the road that starts at the parking lot located just off NH 101, about 100 yd. west of the Temple Mtn. parking lot.)

The Wapack Trail crosses NH 101 just east of the state park sign, enters the woods, and reaches a trail junction 25 yd. east of the parking area (sign "Foot Trails" at the east end of the parking area). The blue-blazed trail right is the former route of the Wapack Trail, now the Marion Davis Trail. (This trail angles up the east side of the mountain, then climbs moderately past two radio towers to the automobile road just below the summit at a small sign reading Parking Lot.) The official Wapack Trail is somewhat more difficult than the former route, particularly for descent. It continues north from the trail junction near the parking area, crosses the automobile road and immediately scrambles up a steep ledge. Turning northwest, it skirts the crest of ledges with views southwest and passes two crevice caves. The trail turns east through woods and over ledges, crosses a hollow, then runs north, angling upward parallel to the automobile road through a beautiful hemlock forest. It then turns sharp right and ascends to the fire tower on the summit of South Pack at 17.6 mi. Continuing north from north end of the summit road to the left of a stone lean-to (sign, Wapack) it descends gradually over ledges. (In this area you will encounter a trail marked with yellow Cs several times.)

The Wapack Trail leads down the wooded north slope past a spring, ascends over the knoll sometimes called the Middle Peak, passes the Cliff Trail right, then ascends directly to the summit of North Pack at 20.0 mi. This ledgy peak provides fine views of central New Hampshire, the Contoocook River Valley, and, on a clear day, of Mt. Washington and other White Mtn. peaks. The trail descends north, northwest, then north again through overgrown pastures (take care to distinguish the trail from other paths), and ends at Old Mountain Rd., 2.6 mi. west of NH 31 (via Old Mtn. Rd. to Russell Station Rd.).

Wapack Trail

Distances from MA 119

    to Watatic Mtn. summit: 1.2 mi., 50 min.

    to Binney Hill Rd. near Binney Ponds: 3.7 mi., 2 hr. 30 min.

    to Barrett Mtn., south summit: 5.1 mi., 3 hr. 35 min.

    to Barrett Mtn., north summit: 7.5 mi., 5 hr. 15 min.

    to NH 123/124: 9.1 mi., 6 hr. 15 min.

    to Nashua Rd.: 11.4 mi., 7 hr. 15 min.

    to Temple Mtn., main summit (Holt Peak): 14.3 mi., 9 hr. 20 min.

    to NH 101: 16.2 mi., 10 hr. 35 min.

    to South Pack Monadnock summit: 17.6 mi., 11 hr. 50 min.

    to North Pack Monadnock summit: 20.0 mi., 13 hr.

    to Old Mountain Rd.: 21.6 mi. (34.8 km.), 13 hr. 45 min.

SECTION 16
The Lakes Region and Southeastern New Hampshire

This section covers trails on the Squam Range, the Rattlesnakes, and Red Hill, all of which lie near Squam Lake; on the Belknap and Ossipee ranges near Lake Winnipesaukee; on the Pawtuckaway Mtns. to the south of the big lakes; on Green Mtn. in Effingham; and on Blue Job Mtn. in the Blue Hills Range in Farmington. Most of the Squam Range, the Rattlesnakes, and part of Red Hill are covered by the AMC Chocorua-Waterville map (map 4); the remaining mountains are covered by USGS maps as indicated in the descriptions. In addition to areas with trails described in this section, Bear Brook State Park (9300 acres) in Allenstown should be mentioned as an area with hiking opportunities.

SQUAM LAKE AREA

In the vicinity of Squam Lake, the low peaks of the Squam Range and the Rattlesnakes to the north, and Red Hill to the east, have excellent views, combining lakes and mountains. Most of the trails are maintained by the Squam Lakes Association and are blazed with yellow paint. Refer to map 4, Chocorua-Waterville, the USGS Squam Mtns. quadrangle, and, for Red Hill, the USGS Winnipesaukee and Chocorua quadrangles. The SLA Trails Guide (1973) and a detailed map of the area by Bradford Washburn are available from the Squam Lakes Association, Main St., Holderness NH 03245.

The Squam Range is a long ridge that stretches from Sandwich Notch Rd. to Holderness, lying northwest of NH 113 and roughly parallel to it. The most frequently climbed peaks are Mt. Morgan (2220 ft.) and Mt. Percival (2212 ft.). You can make a scenic circuit by ascending the Mount Percival Trail, following the Crawford-Ridgepole Trail along the ridge, and descending on the Mount Morgan Trail. West Rattlesnake (1260 ft.) and East Rattlesnake (1289 ft.) are two low mountains near the north end of Squam Lake. The summits are very easily climbed and the views are rewarding for the small effort involved. West Rattlesnake has fine views to the south and west from its southwest cliff. East Rattlesnake has a more limited but still excellent view over Squam Lake. Red Hill (2029 ft.), located north of Center Harbor, provides fine views of lakes and mountains, especially of Squam Lake, from a fire tower. Eagle Cliff is a precipitous ledge on the west side of Red Hill that also offers a fine if less extensive view from its top. The Science Center of New Hampshire, located on NH 113 near its intersection with US 3, maintains trails to good outlooks on Mt. Fayal (1050 ft.); hikers are required to pay an admission fee.

THE TRAILS
Rattlesnake Paths (SLA)

The Old Bridle Path is the easiest route to the West Rattlesnake outlooks. A very short and easy route to an excellent viewpoint, it receives very heavy use. The path leaves NH 113 between Center Sandwich and Holderness, 0.5 mi. northeast of the road to Rockywold and Deephaven camps and opposite the entrance to the Mount Morgan Trail (small parking area), and follows an old cart road 0.9 mi. to the summit. Descending, this trail begins slightly northwest of the summit cliffs.

The Ramsey Trail is a much steeper route to West Rattlesnake. It leaves the road to Rockywold and Deephaven camps, 0.7 mi. from NH 113 and 90 yd. east of the entrance to the camps, along with the Undercut Trail (sign), which has another entrance almost opposite the camp entrance. In 0.1 mi. there is a crossroads, where the Ramsey Trail takes a sharp right and climbs steeply 0.4 mi. to a point just north of the summit cliffs, joining the Old Bridle Path (no sign at top). Left at the crossroads is the alternate route 0.1 mi. to the road; the Undercut Trail continues straight ahead from the crossroads and runs 0.9 mi. (follow markings very carefully) to NH 113 0.1 mi. west of the Old Bridle Path parking area.

The Pasture Trail leads to West Rattlesnake from the road to Rockywold and Deephaven camps 0.9 mi. from NH 113. Park in the small area to the right before the first gate. The trailhead is 100 yd. east of the gate. Start on a road to the left, then turn right past Pinehurst Farm buildings. At 0.2 mi. the East Rattlesnake and Five Finger Point trails diverge right, and in 15 yd. the Pasture Trail bears left where the Col Trail continues straight ahead. The trail reaches the cliffs at 0.6 mi. from the gate after a moderate ascent.

The Col Trail continues straight where the Pasture Trail bears left 0.2 mi. from the gate on the road to Rockywold and Deephaven camps. In 0.3 mi. it joins the Ridge Trail, follows it right for 30 yd., then turns left (sign, Saddle), passes over the height-of-land and descends (follow with care) to the edge of a beaver swamp. It enters an old road and turns left, then bears right and reaches a gravel road 0.7 mi. from the Ridge Trail junction. This trailhead is reached in 0.2 mi. from NH 113 at a point 0.3 mi. east of the Holderness-Sandwich town line.

The Ridge Trail connects West and East Rattlesnake. It begins just northeast of the cliffs of West Rattlesnake and descends gradually. At 0.4 mi. the Col Trail comes in from the right, and just beyond leaves again to the left. The Ridge Trail ascends, and the East Rattlesnake Trail enters from the right at 0.8 mi. The Ridge Trail reaches the outlook ledge at 0.9 mi., and continues to the summit and the Butterworth Trail at 1.0 mi.

The East Rattlesnake Trail branches right from the Pasture Trail 0.2 mi. from the gate. In 25 yd. the Five Finger Point Trail continues straight ahead. The East Rattlesnake Trail turns left and ascends steadily 0.4 mi. to the Ridge Trail, 0.1 mi. west of the outlook. The Five Finger Point Trail runs on a slight downgrade for 0.7 mi., to a loop path 1.3 mi. long that circles around the edge of Five Finger Point, with several interesting viewpoints.

The Butterworth Trail leads to East Rattlesnake from Metcalf Rd., which leaves NH 113 0.7 mi. east of the Holderness-Sandwich town line. The trail leaves Metcalf Rd. on the right 0.5 mi. from NH 113, and climbs moderately 0.7 mi. to the summit. The viewpoint is 0.1 mi. farther via the Ridge Trail.

Old Highway (SLA)

This trail, used to reach the lower ends of the Prescott Trail and Old Mountain Rd., continues straight where NH 113 turns right 1.3 mi. northeast of Holderness and 0.2 mi. beyond a gravel pit where parking is available on the shoulder of NH 113. A century ago, the old road followed by this trail was part of the main highway between Holderness and Center Sandwich. It leaves NH 113 at the same point as a paved driveway. The Prescott Trail diverges left (north) at the height-of-land at 0.9 mi., 100 yd. beyond the Prescott Cemetery, and the Old Mountain Rd. diverges left at an acute angle at 1.1 mi. and runs near the edge of a large field. The Old Highway continues past a sugar house to a locked gate at the edge of a paved road that runs to NH 113 (no parking here).

Old Highway (map 4: L6)

Distances from NH 113

    to Prescott Trail: 0.9 mi., 30 min.
    to paved road: 1.4 mi. (2.2 km.), 45 min.

Prescott Trail (SLA)

This trail to Mt. Livermore (1500 ft.) turns left off the Old Highway at the height-of-land 0.9 mi. from NH 113, 100 yd. beyond the Prescott cemetery. It follows a logging road for 0.2 mi., then turns sharp left off it and ascends gradually, then turns right uphill at 0.3 mi. The main trail climbs by switchbacks over a low ridge and descends gradually to the Crawford-Ridgepole Trail, which enters left at 1.0 mi. From this point the two trails ascend together via switchbacks. Just below the summit they turn sharp right and ascend steeply to the summit, which has a view over Squam Lake.

Descending, the Crawford-Ridgepole Trail heading south and the Prescott Trail leave the summit together, turn sharp right (west) and descend along an old stone wall, then turn left onto an old bridle trail. After 0.4 mi. the Crawford–Ridgepole Trail leaves on the right.

Prescott Trail (map 4:L6)

Distances from Old Highway Trail

    to Crawford-Ridgepole Trail: 1.0 mi., 45 min.

    to summit of Mt. Livermore: 1.4 mi. (2.2 km.), 1 hr. 10 min.

Old Mountain Road (SLA-Webster)

This trail leaves the Old Highway Trail, 1.1 mi. from its western end at NH 113, and ascends on an old road to the Crawford–Ridgepole Trail at the low point between Mt. Livermore and Mt. Webster. The old road continues from here descending to the north, no longer an official trail.

Old Mountain Rd.(map 4:L6)

Distance from Old Highway

    to Crawford-Ridgepole Trail: 0.7 mi. (1.1 km.), 30 min.

Mount Morgan Trail (SLA)

This trail leaves the west side of NH 113, 0.5 mi. northeast of the road that leads to Rockywold and Deephaven camps. From a small clearing (parking), the trail follows a logging road, turning left off it almost immediately. The trail bears right at a fork and soon begins the steeper ascent of the southeast slope of the mountain. At 1.7 mi. the Crawford-Ridgepole Trail enters left from Mt. Webster, and the two trails coincide to a junction where the Crawford-Ridgepole Trail diverges right for Mt. Percival. Here the Mount Morgan Trail leads left to the clifftop viewpoint; part way along a short spur leaves it on the right and runs to the true summit.

Mount Morgan Trail (map 4:L6)
Distance from NH 113

    to Mt. Morgan summit: 2.1 mi. (3.4 km.), 1 hr. 30 min.

Mount Percival Trail (SLA)

This trail leaves the north side of NH 113, 0.3 mi. northeast of the Mount Morgan Trail parking area (best place to park). It follows a logging road past a gate to an old clearing, then bears left into the woods. The trail becomes steep at 1.6 mi., climbing past a fine view of Squam Lake to the summit, where it joins the Crawford-Ridgepole Trail. Just below the summit a path diverges left and ascends roughly through a cave, then rejoins the main path just below the summit.

Mount Percival Trail (map 4:L6)
Distance from NH 113

    to Mt. Percival summit: 1.9 mi. (3.1 km.), 1 hr. 30 min.

Doublehead Trail (SLA)

The Doublehead Trail provides access to a ledge high on Doublehead Mtn. that provides one of the finest views in the Squam Range. It begins on NH 113 at a point 3.5 mi. southwest of Center Sandwich, following a gravel road (part of the old Holderness–Center Sandwich highway) that diverges right (west) at an angle past an old cemetery and a residence. Vehicles should park near NH 113.

The trail proper leaves the old highway on the right 1.0 mi. from NH 113 and follows a logging road through a clearing. At 1.5 mi. the trail turns left onto a skidder road and enters an overgrown logged area where the footway is poorly defined and blazes must be followed with care. In another 100 yd. the trail turns sharp right (arrow) across a small brook, follows another skidder road, and joins a small brook. At the top of a steep pitch it turns sharp left and soon crosses a stone wall, where it re-enters mature woods. It ascends steeply up the valley of a small brook, then swings right and climbs to a ledge at 2.3 mi. with excellent views to the south, then turns left off the ledge and climbs to the Crawford-Ridgepole Trail 80 yd. west of the summit of East Doublehead.

Doublehead Trail (map 4:L6)
Distance from NH 113

> *to* Crawford-Ridgepole Trail: 2.4 mi. (3.9 km.), 1 hr. 50 min.

Crawford-Ridgepole Trail (SLA)

This trail follows the backbone of the Squam Range, from Sandwich Notch Rd. to the south knob of Cotton Mtn. Except for the segment between Mt. Percival and Mt. Morgan, the trail is used infrequently, despite fine views in the Squam-Doublehead section.

The trail starts on the Sandwich Notch Rd. 0.5 mi. beyond Beede Falls (Cow Cave) and 2.0 mi. from the power line along the Beebe River. From the road (sign) it ascends steeply, crosses an unnamed wooded peak (2218 ft.), and continues along the ridge to Doublehead Mtn. (2158 ft.), where there is a good view north just before the summit of East Doublehead. At 1.9 mi., 100 yd. beyond the summit of East Doublehead, the trail bears right and descends where the Doublehead Trail diverges left to NH 113. There is a beautiful viewpoint, well worth the side trip, on the Doublehead Trail 0.1 mi. from this junction. Continuing much of the way over ledges (slippery when wet), the Crawford-Ridgepole Trail crosses the east summit of Mt. Squam (2223 ft.), where there is a fine view, at 3.0 mi. The trail continues to the Mount Percival Trail and Mt. Percival's excellent views at 4.4 mi., passes just west of the actual high point of the range (sometimes called the Sawtooth, it can be reached by a short but thick bushwhack and has a good view), and continues to a junction with the Mount Morgan Trail at 5.2 mi. Here the Mount Morgan Trail leads right to a cliff-top viewpoint; part way along a side path leaves it on the right for the true summit of Mt. Morgan.

From this junction the Crawford-Ridgepole Trail and the Mount Morgan Trail coincide, descending to a junction at 5.6 mi. where the Mount Morgan Trail continues its descent to NH 113, and the Crawford-Ridgepole Trail turns right for Mt. Webster. At 7.2 mi. a spur path leads left 50 yd. to the summit of Mt. Webster, and at 7.5 mi. an unmarked spur leads left a few steps to the beautiful east outlook.

The trail continues past the junction with the Old Mountain Rd. at 9.6 mi., and continues to the summit of Mt. Livermore (view) at 10.0 mi. Coinciding with the Prescott Trail, it descends west from Mt. Livermore along a stone wall then turns left on an old carriage road and descends by switchbacks. At 10.3 mi. the Prescott Trail branches left, and the Crawford-Ridgepole Trail crosses two tiny streams near a low col, then climbs through a rocky area in a beautiful hemlock grove to a south spur of Cotton Mtn. Here the Crawford-Ridgepole Trail ends, as the former connector to the trails of the Science Center of New Hampshire has been closed by the SCNH, which requires an admission fee for use of its trails. From the spur of Cotton Mtn., you can descend by following the yellow blazes of the former Cotton Mountain Trail down to the edge of the large gravel pit and thence to NH 113 near the

Old Highway trailhead. This old trail has been somewhat disrupted by logging but can be followed downhill fairly readily, though ascent by this route is not recommended.

Crawford-Ridgepole Trail (map 4:L6)

Distances from Sandwich Notch Rd.

> *to* East Doublehead summit: 1.9 mi., 1 hr. 40 min.
>
> *to* Mt. Squam, east summit: 3.0 mi., 2 hr. 15 min.
>
> *to* Mt. Percival summit: 4.4 mi., 3 hr. 15 min.
>
> *to* Mt. Morgan summit: 5.2 mi., 4 hr.
>
> *to* Mt. Livermore summit: 10.0 mi., 6 hr. 30 min.
>
> *to* spur of Cotton Mtn.: 11.3 mi. (18.1 km.), 7 hr. 15 min.

Red Hill Trail

In Center Harbor at the junction of NH 25 and NH 25B, go northwest on Bean Rd. for 1.4 mi., then turn right (east) and follow Sibley Rd. (sign for fire lookout) for 1.1 mi., then turn left and continue 0.1 mi. and park on the side of the road. The trail, an old jeep road, soon makes a sharp right turn uphill and crosses a brook. At 0.4 mi. it swings left around a cellar hole. At 1.0 mi. there is a piped spring left. The Eagle Cliff Trail enters left just before the fire tower and firewarden's cabin on the summit of Red Hill.

Red Hill Trail (map 4:L7)

Distance from parking area

> *to* Red Hill summit: 1.7 mi. (2.7 km.), 1 hr. 15 min.

Eagle Cliff Trail (SLA)

This trail ascends Red Hill via Eagle Cliff, which has fine views but may be hazardous in wet or icy conditions. From the junction of NH 25 and NH 25B in Center Harbor, follow Bean Rd. for 5.2 mi. to a turnout at the edge of Squam Lake. The trail is well marked but there is no trail sign at the trailhead, which is difficult to see from the road: it is a path through a ditch in a thicket, 200 yd. south of the lakeside turnout, 50 yd. north of a high hedge, and directly opposite a sign reading Traffic Turning and Entering.

The trail climbs through an overgrown field, and enters the woods. It ascends on a well-beaten path, becoming steep and rough as it gets well up on the ledge, and reaches the main viewpoint on Eagle Cliff at 0.6 mi. From the upper ledge, the trail enters the woods and continues along the ridge toward the fire tower on Red Hill. It crosses a knoll and descends very steeply to a col at 1.0 mi., where the Teedie Trail enters on the right; the Teedie Trail, which leads in 0.6 mi. to a private residence on Bean Rd. south of the beginning of the Eagle Cliff Trail, should be considered as a way of avoiding the descent over the Eagle Cliff ledges in adverse conditions. The Eagle Cliff Trail crosses another knoll and ascends steadily through mixed logged areas and mature woods. It levels out and meets the Red Hill Trail just below the summit of Red Hill. Descending, it diverges right from the Red Hill Trail (jeep road) just below the firewarden's cabin (sign).

Eagle Cliff Trail (map 4:L7)
Distance from Bean Rd.

to Red Hill fire tower: 2.6 mi. (4.1 km.), 2 hr.

OSSIPEE MOUNTAINS

These mountains, located northeast of Lake Winnipesaukee, occupy a nearly circular tract about 9 mi. in diameter. Mt. Shaw (2990 ft.), the highest of the Ossipees, can be ascended by an unmaintained trail from NH 171. Refer to màp 4, Chocorua-Waterville. Also see the USGS Chocorua, Ossipee Lake, Winnipesaukee, and Wolfeboro quadrangles, which corner near the center of the Ossipee Mtns. The Chocorua and Winnipesaukee quadrangles show (inaccurately in some cases) the locations of many of the old carriage roads of the Plant Estate, now operated as a commercial tourist attraction called

Castle in the Clouds. These old roads are used for horse-back riding in summer and snowmobiling in winter. There are no regularly maintained hiking trails on the range, but the two trails described below can be followed fairly well by experienced, observant hikers. Other paths have been cut from time to time and may be encountered, but these are not usually marked and cleared well enough to be followed by hikers who are not familiar with them.

THE TRAILS

Mount Shaw Trail

This trail (no sign) begins at a dirt road on the north side of NH 171, 3.9 mi. east of the junction of NH 109 and NH 171, 3.8 mi. west of Tuftonboro, 9.7 mi. west of the junction of NH 171 and NH 28 in Ossipee, and just east of a road from Melvin Village and a bridge over Fields Brook. The trail is not easy to follow and not recommended for inexperienced hikers, and must be followed very carefully; it is blazed irregularly in dark red, which is sometimes difficult to see. In addition, it is overgrown in places and has suffered much blowdown recently.

The trail follows the dirt road north 0.3 mi. to a hemlock grove (left), where there is a cascade on the left. The trail detours above the stream around a washout, then bears left and follows the stream. It reaches a fork at 0.7 mi., where it bears right then keeps right after passing through an old logging camp clearing. At 0.9 mi. it bears left on an old road and goes through a deep cut, then bears right. The trail again bears left at 1.1 mi. and then leaves the road on the right at 1.4 mi., follows the east bank of Fields Brook and then crosses it, and bears right at a cairn. It recrosses to the east bank at 1.8 mi. and climbs steeply out of the ravine to join an old carriage road at 2.5 mi., where it turns right and passes a side trail at 2.7 mi. that leads right 0.3 mi. to an open knob with a good view over

Lake Winnipesaukee (this knob is often referred to as Black Snout, but it is not the peak labeled Black Snout Mtn. on maps). The Mount Shaw Trail continues on the carriage road and reaches the summit at 3.5 mi.

Mount Shaw Trail (USGS Winnipesaukee quad)
Distance from NH 171
   to Mt. Shaw summit: 3.5 mi. (5.6 km.), 2 hr. 45 min.

Bald Knob Trail

This trail (no sign) begins on NH 171, at the Moulton-borough-Tuftonboro town line, about 0.5 mi. west of the Mt. Shaw trailhead at the Fields Brook bridge. Follow the dirt road into the gravel pit. In 100 yd. bear right on the road and descend through the pit. In another 100 yd. bear right at some burned ruins, then in another 50 yd. turn sharp left onto a dirt road. This road crosses a wet area and bears right as it enters the woods. The trail, scantily blazed in yellow, ascends steeply over rough and eroded terrain, reaching the first ledge at 0.7 mi. It passes more ledges with excellent vistas and then goes into the woods again, runs through an area with a number of boulders, and heads generally north, ascending at a less steep grade. The trail then turns south, scrambles up through a wide V in the rock, and meets an old carriage road turnaround before reaching Bald Knob with its fine views of Lake Winnipesaukee.

Bald Knob Trail (USGS Winnipesaukee quad)
Distance from NH 171
   to Bald Knob: 1.0 mi. (1.6 km.), 1 hr.

THE BELKNAP RANGE AND MT. MAJOR

The Belknap Mtns. are an isolated range west of Lake Winnipesaukee in Gilford. The principal peaks, from north to south, are Mt. Rowe (1670 ft.), Gunstock Mtn. (2250 ft.), Belknap Mtn. (2384 ft.), and Piper Mtn. (2030 ft.). A fire tower on Belknap and an observation tower on

Gunstock, as well as numerous scattered ledges on all the peaks, provide fine views of Lake Winnipesaukee, the Ossipee and Sandwich ranges, and Mt. Washington. Principal trailheads are located at the Gunstock Recreation Area (east side) and Belknap Carriage Rd. (west side). The East Gilford Trail also ascends from the east. Paths along the ridge connect all four summits. Mt. Major (1784 ft.), which has excellent views over Lake Winnipesaukee, is located in Alton, east of the Belknap Mtns. Refer to the USGS Winnipesaukee quadrangle.

The Gunstock Recreation Area is a four-season recreation area off NH 11A, operated by Belknap County. It includes a major downhill ski area located on Mt. Rowe and Gunstock Mtn., and a 420-site campground. Ellacoya State Beach on Lake Winnipesaukee is nearby. The chairlift on Gunstock Mtn. operates on weekends and holidays in summer. The ski trails can be used to ascend Gunstock Mtn. and Mt. Rowe; several routes that run mostly on ski trails have been designated as hiking trails, and a map of these is available at the base lodge.

The Belknap Carriage Rd., which provides access to all the trails on the west side of the Belknap Range, is reached by leaving NH 11A at Gilford village and following Belknap Mountain Rd. south, bearing left at 0.8 mi. and right at 1.4 mi. At 2.4 mi. the Belknap Carriage Rd. forks left and leads in 1.5 mi. to a parking area. Various relatively easy loop hikes may be made from this trailhead. For the Green, Red, and Blue Dot trails, follow the road up to the firewarden's garage (signs on wall). The White Trail is a short distance down the road.

THE TRAILS
Mount Major Trail

This trail begins at a parking area (large sign) on NH 11, 4.2 mi. north of Alton Bay and 1.7 mi. north of the junction of NH 11 with NH 11D. The trail follows a lumber road west for 0.7 mi., then diverges sharp left on a path marked with dark-blue paint. It climbs steeply through second growth and over ledges to the ruins of a stone hut at the top. At several points there are one or more alternate paths, all of which lead to the summit.

Mount Major Trail (USGS Winnipesaukee quad)
Distance from NH 11
    to Mt. Major summit: 1.5 mi. (2.4 km.), 1 hr. 20 min.

East Gilford Trail

This trail, perhaps the most attractive on the Belknap Range, is also sometimes referred to as the Yellow Trail. To reach it, turn right off NH 11A on Bickford Rd., 1.7 mi. south of the Gunstock Recreation Area road, then turn left on Wood Rd. and park near the junction, not near the house. The trail (sign) follows a cart track at the left of the white house at the end of the road, circles around to the right, and bears right at a fork. Halfway up, near a brook on the right, the trail turns sharp left and climbs more steeply to the first outlook, where the unmaintained Round Pond Trail enters left. It then continues at a moderate grade, mostly on ledges, and joins the Piper Trail; the two trails coincide for the final 0.2 mi. to the Belknap Mtn. summit.

East Gilford Trail (USGS Winnipesaukee quad)
Distance from Wood Rd.
    to Belknap Mtn. summit: 2.1 mi. (3.4 km.), 1 hr. 40 min.

Saddle Trail

This blue-blazed trail runs along the crest of the Belknap Ridge between Gunstock Mtn. and Belknap Mtn. From the summit of Gunstock Mtn., the trail runs south along the right edge of the ski trails, then turns right into woods (watch carefully for arrow) and descends to the col, where the Blue Dot Trail enters right at 0.4 mi. It then ascends Belknap Mtn. and ends at the Red Trail just before the summit.

Saddle Trail (USGS Winnipesaukee quad)

Distance from Gunstock Mtn. summit
   to Belknap Mtn. summit: 0.9 mi. (1.4 km.), 45 min.

Blue Dot Trail

This trail runs from Belknap Carriage Rd. to the Belknap-Gunstock col, from which either peak may be ascended via the Saddle Trail. It follows the road past the Red and Green trails, descends slightly to cross a brook, then diverges right and climbs to the Saddle Trail.

Blue Dot Trail (USGS Winnipesaukee quad)

Distance from Belknap Carriage Rd. parking area
   to Saddle Trail: 0.6 mi. (1.0 km.), 25 min.

Green Trail

The Green Trail from Belknap Carriage Rd. is the shortest route to Belknap Mtn., but is rather rough. It leaves the road behind the garage and crosses a service road and telephone line. There are several alternate paths (including the road), any of which may be followed to the warden's cabin, where there is a well, and to the tower at the summit.

Green Trail (USGS Winnipesaukee quad)

Distance from Belknap Carriage Rd. parking area
   to Belknap Mtn. summit: 0.7 mi. (1.1 km.), 40 min.

Red Trail

This less steep, more scenic route from Belknap Carriage Rd. to the summit of Belknap Mtn. leaves the road just beyond the Green Trail and climbs past a good outlook (west) to the summit.

Red Trail (USGS Winnipesaukee quad)

Distance from Belknap Carriage Rd. parking area
   to Belknap Mtn. summit: 0.8 mi. (1.3 km.), 45 min.

White Trail

This white-blazed trail ascends to the summit of Belknap Mtn. via the Belknap-Piper col. It begins on Belknap Carriage Rd. 0.2 mi. below the parking area, just below a small bridge. It ascends to the col at 0.4 mi., where the Old Piper Trail goes right to Piper Mtn., then turns left and climbs to the junction with the East Gilford Trail, which enters from the right on the ledges. The two trails coincide to the summit and its fire tower.

White Trail (USGS Winnipesaukee quad)
Distance from Belknap Carriage Rd. parking area
to Belknap Mtn. summit: 1.2 mi. (1.9 km.), 1 hr.

Old Piper Trail

This blue-blazed trail leaves the White Trail in the Belknap-Piper col and climbs to a large cairn in the Piper Mtn. blueberry fields, where the well-defined trail ends. The true summit of Piper Mtn. is 0.2 mi. farther south and may be reached by random paths made by blueberry pickers.

Old Piper Trail (USGS Winnipesaukee quad)
Distance from Belknap Carriage Rd. parking area
to Piper Trail: 0.7 mi. (1.1·km.), 30 min.

GREEN MOUNTAIN

Green Mountain Trail

Green Mtn. (1907 ft.) is an isolated hill in the town of Effingham. The state owns 15 acres on the summit, which has a 50-ft. fire tower with an extended view. Refer to the USGS Ossipee Lake quadrangle.

From the junction of NH 25 and NH 153 northbound in Effingham Falls, follow NH 25 west for 0.2 mi., then turn left at a church (fire lookout sign). Follow this road south for 1.0 mi., then turn left again on High Watch Rd., then left again in 0.2 mi. at a T-junction. The trail (a road closed by a chain) is 1.2 mi. farther on the right, just past High Watch Learning Center. The trail ascends moderately on this road to a fenced utility building, then climbs more steeply to the Green Mtn. summit.

Green Mountain Trail (USGS Ossipee Lake quad)
Distance from High Watch Rd.

    to Green Mtn. summit: 1.4 mi. (2.2 km.), 1 hr. 15 min.

BLUE JOB MOUNTAIN
Blue Job Mountain Trail

Blue Job Mtn. (1356 ft.) is part of the Blue Hill Range, located in Strafford and Farmington. There are excellent views from a fire tower on the summit. Refer to the USGS Alton quadrangle.

    The trail begins on Crown Point Rd., 5.6 mi. from NH 202A, just past the end of the blacktop. Crown Point Rd. leaves NH 202A at Glenn's Garage, 5.4 mi. east from its junction with NH 126 in Center Strafford, or 2.8 mi. west of its junction with NH 202 near Rochester. There is both a shaded foot trail and a cart track through blueberry fields to the summit.

Blue Job Mountain Trail (USGS Alton quad)
Distance from parking area

    to Blue Job Mtn. summit: 0.5 mi. (0.8 km.), 25 min.

PAWTUCKAWAY MOUNTAINS

The Pawtuckaways in Nottingham are a series of three parallel ridges—North Mtn. (995 ft.), Middle Mtn. (845 ft.), and South Mtn. (885 ft.)—all contained within Pawtuckaway State Park (5535 acres), the finest natural area in southeastern New Hampshire. The valley east of North Mtn. contains an extraordinary collection of huge boulders and several other unusual and interesting rock formations, designated as the Boulder Natural Area. Refer to the USGS Mt. Pawtuckaway quadrangle.

The mountains may be reached from NH 107 between Deerfield and Raymond, 3.2 mi. north of NH 101 Business Loop, where there is a fire lookout sign. The road leads east, becoming gravel after 0.9 mi. Bear right at 1.2 mi., and reach the south junction of a loop road (Reservation Rd.) at 2.3 mi. This road is rough and eroded at times, but walking distances from it are relatively short. The east branch of the loop is the normal driving route, since part of the west branch is often under more than a foot of water from a beaver flowage near its midpoint, which makes it a problem to pass through either in a car or on foot.

For the South Mtn. and Middle Mtn. continue straight from the south junction of the loop road for another 0.2 mi., then bear left (sign, Lookout Tower) 0.8 mi. to the former location of the ranger's camp, where there is a tiny old graveyard. The Mountain Trail from the main part of the state park enters just beyond here at a small parking area on the right, and the path to the South Mtn. tower (described below as part of the Mountain Trail) leaves the parking area on the right. The main trail to the Boulder Natural Area and North Mtn. begins 1.3 mi. farther along the road.

The easiest road access to the mountains is from the state park off NH 156, but walking distances are much longer. Reach the trails by following the road toward the swimming beach, passing a toll booth (fee charged in summer), and then passing a pond left. Trail maps are usually available at the State Park Visitors Center. The trails in the eastern part of the park are maintained for multiple use, and are particularly favored by trail bikers in summer and snowmobilers in winter. These trails are sometimes muddy in places and offer few long-range views, but frequently traverse interesting woodlands and pass near extensive swamps. They will probably appeal most to hikers looking for pleasant but not spectacular walks fairly close to home. In addition to the Mountain Trail, which is described in detail below, the following trails may be of interest. The Round Pond Trail leaves the Mountain Trail 0.5 mi. from the road to the beach and runs 1.9 mi. to Reservation Rd. opposite the south loop junction. The Fundy Trail leaves the road to the beach 1.4 mi. from the parking area and runs 1.8 mi. along the edge of Burnhams Marsh and then the lake itself to the Fundy Bay boat launch area. The Shaw Trail leaves the Fundy Trail 1.0 mi. from the road to the beach and runs 3.1 mi. to Reservation Rd. at location #5, north of the trailhead for South Mtn.

Mountain Trail (NHDP)

This trail, the easiest route to South Mtn. from the main part of Pawtuckaway State Park, leaves the park road just past the toll booth and pond at the location signed #2 (keyed to park trail map) It passes a chain gate and runs along the edge of the pond. At 0.5 mi. it bears right where the Round Pond Trail continues ahead. Bear right again at a junction at 1.9 mi. (left goes to Reservation Rd.), and reach Reservation Rd. at the parking area near the site of the firewarden's camp at 2.5 mi. From here the path climbs steeply to the open summit ledges. At a small service building just below the summit, where the trail turns sharp right, a side trail turns left to an old well and continues to the Devil's Staircase (or Indian Steps) and open ledges north-northwest of the tower.

Mountain Trail (USGS Mt. Pawtuckaway quad)
Distance from state park road
    to summit tower, South Mtn.: 2.9 mi. (4.7 km.), 2 hr.

Distance from Reservation Rd.
    to summit tower, South Mtn.: 0.4 mi. (0.7 km.), 20 min.

Middle Mountain Trail (NHDP)

The trail to Middle Mtn. begins on an old road just south of the site of the old firewarden's camp. The trail rises on the old road at a moderate grade along a stone wall, then

turns sharp left and climbs a steep, badly eroded section
to the upper shoulder of the mountain. From there the trail
ascends with gentle grades over the almost imperceptible
summit and descends to a ledge overlooking ponds and
swamps and affording distant views to the southwest.

Middle Mountain Trail (USGS Mt. Pawtuckaway quad)
Distance from Reservation Rd.

to Middle Mtn. summit: 1.0 mi. (1.6 km.), 50 min.

North Mountain Trail (NHDP)

From the site of the former firewarden's camp, continue
0.8 mi. to the north loop junction, then bear right (at location signed #6) for another 0.5 mi. As the road bears
upward to the right, there are two obscure trailheads on the
left. The trail to the boulders and North Mtn. runs under a
large fallen tree with BOULDERS carved into it by a chain
saw. The trail, blazed in white, descends gradually 0.2 mi.
to the boulders. Just beyond the boulders the trail turns
sharp left at a junction (sign on tree, Dead Pond). Straight
ahead from this junction (sign, Lower Slab) a blazed trail
leads around a beaver pond and past some rock formations
to the road; turn right on the road to loop back to the starting point. The main trail runs to Dead Pond at 0.6 mi., then
turns left and climbs steeply to the Devil's Den (a crevice
in the rocks to the left of the trail) and an outlook right.
From here the trail angles steeply up the north side of the
ridge and, marked with cairns, continues roughly along the
top to a small col below boulder cliffs. It climbs by a
switchback in beautiful hemlock woods to an outlook
where there is a Public Service Company reflector, then
continues along the ridge to the overgrown summit.

Several other trails are being developed on North Mtn.
A white-blazed trail continues from the summit down the
southwest end of the mountain, passing several interesting
viewpoints and ending on a dirt road. Following white
blazes to the right on this road, Reservation Rd. is reached

at a large cellar hole west of the south loop junction; following white blazes to the left on this road, then bearing left on an older road, a bluff overlooking a swampy area is reached, where there is a good view of the ledges on North Mtn. From this bluff a faintly blazed trail climbs gradually, then very steeply, to the North Mountain Trail at the Public Service Company reflector. A road continues from the bluff to a former picnic area, where the main road bears right to the west branch of the loop road just south of the north loop junction, and a lesser road turns left to descend to the north spur road about 0.2 mi. above the trailhead for the North Mtn. Trail.

North Mountain Trail (USGS Mt. Pawtuckaway quad)
Distance from trailhead
    to North Mtn. summit: 1.5 mi. (2.5 km.), 1 hr. 15 min.

APPENDIX A
Four Thousand Footers

The Four Thousand Footer Club was formed in 1957 to bring together hikers who had traveled to some of the less frequently visited sections of the White Mtns. At that time, such peaks as Hancock, Owl's Head, and West Bond had no trails and were practically never climbed, while other peaks on the list that had trails were seldom climbed, and the problem of over-use was unknown, except in the Presidentials and Franconias. Today the Four Thousand Footer Club is composed of active hikers whose travels in the mountains have made them familiar with many different sections of the White Mtn. back-country, and with the problems that threaten to degrade the mountain experience that we have all been privileged to enjoy. The Four Thousand Footer Committee hopes that this broadened experience of the varied beauties of our beloved peaks and forests will encourage our members to work for the preservation and wise use of wild country, so that it may be enjoyed and passed on to future generations undiminished.

The Four Thousand Footer Committee recognizes three lists of peaks: the White Mountain Four Thousand Footers, the New England Four Thousand Footers, and the New England Hundred Highest. Separate awards are given to those who climb all peaks on a list in winter; to qualify as a winter ascent, the hike must not begin before the hour and minute of the beginning of winter or end after the hour and minute of the end of winter. As of April 1991, these clubs had the following number of officially registered members: White Mountain Four Thousand Footers 4531 (winter 154), New England Four Thousand Footers 1098 (winter 54), New England Hundred Highest 260 (winter 30). To qualify for membership, a hiker must climb on foot to and from each summit on the list. The official lists of the Four Thousand Footers in New Hampshire, Maine, and Vermont are included at the end of this appendix. Applicants for the White Mountain Four Thousand Footer Club must climb all forty-eight peaks in New Hampshire, while applicants for the New England Four Thousand Footer Club must also climb the twelve peaks in Maine and the five in Vermont.

The New England Hundred Highest Club list differs substantially from the other two because it includes a considerable number of peaks without trails; several of these peaks require advanced wilderness navigation skills of the group leader, and two are on private land where written permission to enter may be required. Peaks on this list for which routes are described in this guide include: Sandwich Mtn. (3993 ft.), with several trails in Section 7; the Horn (3905 ft.), on a spur path from the Kilkenny Ridge Trail; the East Sleeper (3850 ft.), just off the Sleeper Trail; and the Northeast Cannon Ball (3769 ft.), on the Kinsman Ridge Trail. A copy of the full list and related information is available on request from the Committee.

If you are seriously interested in becoming a member of one or more of the clubs sponsored by the Four Thousand Footer Committee, please send a self-addressed, stamped envelope to the Four Thousand Footer Committee, Appalachian Mountain Club, 5 Joy St., Boston MA 02108, and an information packet including application forms will be sent to you. If you are interested in the New England Four Thousand Footer Club and/or the New England Hundred Highest Club, please specify this, since these lists are not routinely included in the basic information packet. After climbing each peak, please record the date of the ascent, companions, if any, and other remarks.

Applicants for any of the clubs need not be AMC members, although the Committee strongly urges all hikers who make considerable use of the trails to contribute to their maintenance in some manner. Membership in the AMC is one of the most effective means of assisting these efforts.

Criteria for mountains on the official list are: (1) each peak must be 4000 ft. high, and (2) must rise 200 ft. above the low point of its connecting ridge with a higher neighbor. The latter qualification eliminates such peaks as Clay, Franklin, North Carter, Guyot, Little Haystack, South Tripyramid, Lethe, Blue, and Jim. All sixty-five Four Thousand Footers are reached by well-defined trails, although the path to Owl's Head and some short spur trails to other summits are not officially maintained.

On the following lists, elevations have been obtained from the latest USGS maps, some of which are now metric, requiring conversion from meters to feet. Where no exact elevation is given on the map, the elevation has been estimated by adding half the contour interval to the highest contour shown on the map; elevations so obtained are marked on the list with an asterisk (*).

FOUR THOUSAND FOOTERS IN NH

Mountain	Elevation (feet)	(meters)	Date Climbed
1. Washington	6288	1917	_____
2. Adams	5774	1760	_____
3. Jefferson	5712	1741	_____
4. Monroe	5384*	1641*	_____
5. Madison	5367	1636	_____
6. Lafayette	5260*	1603*	_____
7. Lincoln	5089	1551	_____
8. South Twin	4902	1494	_____
9. Carter Dome	4832	1473	_____
10. Moosilauke	4802	1464	_____
11. Eisenhower	4761	1451	_____
12. North Twin	4761	1451	_____
13. Bond	4698	1432	_____

14. Carrigain	4680	1426	_____
15. Middle Carter	4610*	1405*	_____
16. West Bond	4540*	1384*	_____
17. Garfield	4500*	1372*	_____
18. Liberty	4459	1359	_____
19. South Carter	4430*	1350*	_____
20. Wildcat	4422	1348	_____
21. Hancock	4403	1342	_____
22. South Kinsman	4358	1328	_____
23. Osceola	4340*	1323*	_____
24. Flume	4328	1319	_____
25. Field	4326	1319	_____
26. Pierce (Clinton)	4310	1314	_____
27. Willey	4302	1311	_____
28. North Kinsman	4293	1309	_____
29. South Hancock	4274	1303	_____
30. Bondcliff	4265	1300	_____
31. Zealand	4260*	1298*	_____
32. Cabot	4170*	1271*	_____
33. East Osceola	4156	1267	_____
34. North Tripyramid	4140	1262	_____
35. Middle Tripyramid	4110	1253	_____
36. Cannon	4100*	1250*	_____
37. Passaconaway	4060	1237	_____
38. Hale	4054	1236	_____
39. Jackson	4052	1235	_____
40. Moriah	4049	1234	_____
41. Tom	4047	1234	_____
42. Wildcat E	4041	1232	_____
43. Owl's Head	4025	1227	_____
44. Galehead	4024	1227	_____
45. Whiteface	4010*	1222*	_____
46. Waumbek	4006	1221	_____
47. Isolation	4005	1221	_____
48. Tecumseh	4003	1220	_____

FOUR THOUSAND FOOTERS IN MAINE

Mountain	Elevation (feet)	(meters)	Date Climbed
1. Katahdin, Baxter Peak	5267	1605	_____
2. Katahdin, Hamlin Peak	4751	1448	_____
3. Sugarloaf	4250*	1295*	_____
4. Old Speck	4180	1274	_____
5. Crocker	4168	1270	_____
6. Bigelow, West Peak	4150	1265	_____
7. North Brother	4143	1263	_____
8. Saddleback	4116	1255	_____
9. Bigelow, Avery Peak	4088	1246	_____
10. Abraham	4049	1234	_____
11. Saddleback, the Horn	4023	1226	_____
12. South Crocker	4010*	1222*	_____

FOUR THOUSAND FOOTERS IN VERMONT

Mountain	Elevation (feet)	(meters)	Date Climbed
1. Mansfield	4393	1339	_____
2. Killington	4235	1291	_____
3. Camel's Hump	4083	1244	_____
4. Ellen	4083	1244	_____
5. Abraham	4006	1221	_____

APPENDIX B
About the Appalachian Mountain Club

The Appalachian Mountain Club pursues a vigorous conservation agenda while encouraging responsible recreation, based on the philosophy that succcessful, longterm conservation depends upon firsthand experience of the natural environment. Fifty thousand members have joined the AMC to pursue their interests in hiking, canoeing, skiing, walking, rock climbing, bicycling, camping, kayaking, and backpacking, and—at the same time—to help safeguard the environment in which these activities are possible.

Since it was founded in 1876, the Club has been at the forefront of the environmental protection movement. By cofounding several of New England's leading environmental organizations, and working in coalition with these and many more groups, the AMC has positively influenced legislation and public opinion.

Volunteers in each chapter lead hundreds of outdoor activities and excursions and offer introductory instruction in backcountry sports. The AMC education department offers members and the public a wide range of workshops, from introductory camping to the intensive Mountain Leadership School taught on the trails of the White Mountains.

The most recent efforts in the AMC conservation program include river protection, Northern Forest Lands policy, support for the American Heritage Trust, Sterling Forest (NY) preservation, and support for the Clean Air Act.

The AMC's research department focuses on the forces affecting the ecosystem, including ozone levels, acid rain and fog, climate change, rare flora and habitat protection, and air quality and visibility.

The Club operates eight alpine huts in the White Mountains that provide shelter, bunks and blankets, and hearty meals for hikers. Pinkham Notch Visitor Center, at the foot of Mt. Washington, is base camp to the adventurous and the ideal location for individuals and families new to outdoor recreation. Comfortable bunkrooms, mountain hospitality, and home-cooked, family-style meals make Pinkham Notch Visitor Center a fun and affordable choice for lodging.

At the AMC headquarters in Boston and at Pinkham Notch Visitor Center in New Hampshire, the bookstore and information center stock the entire line of AMC publications, as well as other trail and river guides, maps, reference materials, and the latest articles on conservation issues. Guidebooks and other AMC gifts are available by mail order (AMC, P.O. Box 298, Gorham NH 03581) or call toll-free 800-262-4455. Also available from the bookstore or by subscription is *Appalachia,* the country's oldest mountaineering and conservation journal.

We invite you to join the Appalachian Mountain Club and share the benefits of membership. Every member receives *Appalachia Bulletin,* the membership magazine that, ten times a year, brings you news about environmental issues and AMC projects, plus listings of outdoor activities, workshops, excursions, and volunteer opportunities. Members also enjoy discounts on AMC books, maps, educational workshops, and guided hikes, as well as reduced fees at all AMC huts and lodges in Massachusetts and New Hampshire. To join, call 617-523-0636; or write to: AMC, 5 Joy Street, Boston MA.

AMC Trails

The AMC Volunteer Trails Program is active throughout the AMC's chapters and maintains over 1,200 miles of trails, including 350 miles of the Appalachian Trail. Under the supervision of experienced leaders, hundreds of volunteers spend from one afternoon to two weeks working on trail projects.

As a well known and respected authority on hiking trails, the AMC works cooperatively with many federal, state, and local agencies, corporate and private landowners, and numerous other trail clubs and outdoor organizations.

AMC trails are maintained through the coordinated efforts of many people who volunteer their labor or contribute financial support, and the trails program staff and seasonal crew. Most of the difficult major construction projects are handled by the AMC trail crew, based in the White Mtns., which began operations in 1917 and is probably the oldest professional crew in the nation. Hikers who have benefited from the trails can help maintain them by donating their time for various projects and regularly scheduled volunteer trips with the AMC chapters. For hikers who are willing to assume responsibility for regular light maintenance of a trail, there is an Adopt-a-Trail Program.

For more information on any aspect of the Club's trail and shelter efforts, contact AMC Trails Program, Pinkham Notch Visitor Center, Box 298, Gorham NH 03581, or AMC Trails Program, 5 Joy St., Boston MA 02108. Comments on the AMC's trail work and information on problems you encounter when hiking or camping are always welcome.

APPENDIX C
Easy-to-Moderate Hikes

This section is intended to supply readers with a certain number of suggestions for easy and moderate hikes in the areas covered by this guide. Since we expect that in many cases readers will be looking for trips within a reasonable driving distance of their present or planned base of operations, this section has been organized into regions by road access to trailheads rather than following the pattern of the body of this book, which is organized by mountain ranges. These regions have been created for convenience and have not been strictly defined. The numbers in brackets indicate distance, elevation gain, and time calculated by the normal formula; "ow," "rt," and "lp" mean "one way," "round trip," and "loop," respectively. It should be repeated that the time allowances are merely a very rough estimate—many parties will require more time, and many will require less—and they do not include time for extensive stops for scenery appreciation or rest.

Whoever compiles a list such as this one faces certain problems that should be understood by the user. Many of the obvious candidates for inclusion on such a list naturally attract large numbers of people, and many hikers who visit one of them are likely to find a beautiful spot that is simply too crowded for them to enjoy. One of the most important criteria used in choosing these suggested hikes has been whether the places, and the trails that lead to them, can withstand any likely increase in use. All of us should be thoroughly aware of our role in protecting the beauty of the lands we pass through—the capacity of the land increases when we walk through it lightly and quietly. Any comments from users who try these trips are greatly appreciated. Please address them to: Editor, *White Mountain Guide,* Appalachian Mountain Club, 5 Joy St., Boston MA 02108.

GORHAM–PINKHAM NOTCH REGION

Easy Trips

Because mountains rise quickly on all sides of this region, there are relatively few short, easy hikes available. In the vicinity of **Pinkham Notch,** Lost Pond is a pleasant spot with excellent views across to the east face of Mt. Washington, reached by the Lost Pond Trail, which is part of the Appalachian Trail [rt: 1.0 mi., 100 ft., 0:35]. The Thompson Falls Trail, which begins at Wildcat Ski Area, visits cascades flowing over flat ledges that offer good views [rt: 1.4 mi., 200 ft., 0:50]. Square Ledge, a rocky lookout on the east side of Pinkham Notch, is a fairly rugged but short trip [rt: 1.2 mi., 400 ft., 0:50]. The Devil's Hopyard, which lies well to the north of the Presidentials and is reached from NH 110 via the access road to South Pond [rt: 2.6 mi., 500 ft., 1:35], provides an easily visited miniature version of the more spectacular but much more difficult similar gorges, the Ice Gulch and Mahoosuc Notch.

On the **north side of the range** the RMC trail system provides access to a number of falls and cascades. All these falls are essentially small cascades on rocks and ledges or in small gorges formed by the steep mountain brooks, and are not spectacular in any sense. However, they do provide pleasant walks along the banks of sparkling, splashing brooks. Triple Falls on Evans Brook can be visited in a very short trip, though the trail to these cascades is fairly steep [rt: 0.4 mi., 200 ft., 0:20]. One of the best possibilities for an easy hike is the loop via the Fallsway and Brookbank, which passes Gordon, Salroc, and Tama falls [lp: 1.5 mi., 400 ft., 0:55]. Another possibility is the lower end of the Howker Ridge Trail, which passes Coosauk and Hitchcock falls, as well as some smaller falls and the interesting little gorge called the Devil's Kitchen [rt: 2.0 mi., 400 ft., 1:10].

A good trip involving many **waterfalls** can be made by taking the Amphibrach past Cold Brook Fall, and then making the side trips to the pleasant, broad Coldspur Ledges via the short eastern extension of the Monaway and to Spur Brook Falls via the Cliffway. You can return by the same route [rt: 4.8 mi., 1300 ft., 3:05] or lengthen the trip by continuing to the end of the Amphibrach at the junction called the Pentadoi, then following the Randolph Path down to the Valley Way and soon diverging on either the Fallsway or the Brookbank [lp: 5.3 mi., 1700 ft., 3:30]. Another good trip follows the Maple Walk and Sylvan Way to the Howker Ridge Trail near Coosauk Fall, then ascends the Kelton Trail and descends past the fine views of the Inlook Trail, then follows the Brookside, Valley Way, and either the Fallsway or the Brookbank out to the parking area [lp: 4.0 mi., 1500 ft., 2:45]. The Kelton Trail and Inlook Trail both have fairly steep sections with rough footing.

Pine Mtn., at the northeast end of the Presidential Range, probably offers the best views in this region for the effort required. The main trail is a good gravel road, closed to public vehicular use but open to hiking [rt: 4.0 mi., 800 ft., 2:25]. This may be an asset for people who may lack the agility to enjoy the rough footing on most mountain trails (such as the very young and the old), but many hikers will find this route boring in spite of the rewards to be gained at the summit; for such people a shorter and more sporty ascent on the branch trail over the south ledges is available [lp: 3.5 mi., 800 ft., 2:10]. In the Nash Stream valley northeast of Groveton, **Percy Peak** [rt: 4.4 mi., 2200 ft., 3:20] and **Sugarloaf** [rt: 4.2 mi., 2200 ft., 3:10] offer fine views.

Moderate Trips

King Ravine is usually regarded as a route to the summit of Mt. Adams, and in that role its three trails each make up a part of three of the most strenuous and beautiful routes to Mt. Adams. But this wild ravine, with its rugged scenery and its fascinating boulders and boulder caves, is a completely worthy objective in its own right. The shortest, easiest route to the ravine floor is via the Air Line, Short Line, and King Ravine Trail [rt: 6.2 mi., 2400 ft., 4:20]. It is also feasible to visit King Ravine as an extension of a trip mentioned in the Easy section, following the Amphibrach to the Pentadoi and the King Ravine Trail from there to the floor of the ravine, then descending on the Short Line to the Randolph Path, Valley Way, and Fallsway or Brookbank [lp: 7.0 mi., 2400 ft., 4:40].

The Imp Face, a cliffy outlook on the northern part of the Carter Range, is a worthwhile objective reached by a loop path [lp: 6.3 mi., 2300 ft., 4:10] of which the northern half is both shorter and more interesting [rt: 4.4 mi., 1700 ft., 3:05]. Several peaks that are somewhat distant from Gorham but are readily reached by NH 110 also offer very rewarding moderate trips. **Rogers Ledge,** a spectacular remote and seldom-visited viewpoint, can be reached from South Pond via the Kilkenny Ridge Trail [rt: 8.2 mi., 1900 ft., 5:05] or from York Pond via the Mill Brook and Kilkenny Ridge trails [rt: 8.8 mi., 1500 ft., 4:40]. An excellent hike to **Unknown Pond and the Horn** can also be made from NH 110 via the Unknown Pond and Kilkenny Ridge trails [rt: 9.8 mi., 2400 ft., 6:05]; Mt. Cabot, the northernmost four thousand footer that virtually everyone climbs from East Lancaster, can be added to this trip [rt: 12.0 mi., 3400 ft., 7:40].

On the larger mountains in the area, there are a number of trips that seem particularly worthy of mention. A very good loop can be made by following the Nineteen Mile Brook Trail to the **Carter Lakes,** then taking the Carter-Moriah Trail over Carter Dome and Mt. Hight (the best viewpoint on the Carter Range) and descending via the relatively easy Carter Dome Trail [lp: 10.2 mi., 3400 ft., 6:50]. The ascent of **Mt. Moriah** via the Stony Brook and Carter-Moriah trails is very scenic, affording excellent views from ledges along the way as well as at the summit [rt: 10.0 mi., 3100 ft., 6:35]. **Shelburne Moriah** via the

Rattle River and Kenduskeag trails also offers exceptional views from ledges at the summit and on the upper part of the ridge [rt: 11.2 mi., 2900 ft., 7:05].

In the **Mahoosuc Range area,** a particularly rewarding loop trip can be made by the Goose Eye, Mahoosuc, and Carlo Col trails [lp: 7.6 mi., 2700 ft., 5:10]. Mahoosuc Notch is also a very attractive feature, but while the normal loop route via the Notch, Mahoosuc, and Speck Pond trails is extremely scenic, it is also very strenuous and requires a spotting a car or walking back to the road at the end [lp: 9.4 mi., 2500 ft., 5:55 (but probably much longer)]. The alternative route is to come back through the notch from the far side, thus going through it twice, something that most hikers find daunting to contemplate [rt: 6.6 mi., 1200 ft., 3:55 (but could easily take as much as twice that long)].

CONWAY–CRAWFORD NOTCH REGION
Easy Trips
Arethusa Falls and **Ripley Falls** are the two highest waterfalls in New Hampshire. Arethusa Falls [rt: 2.6 mi., 1000 ft., 1:50] is somewhat more demanding than Ripley Falls [rt: 1.0 mi., 500 ft., 0:45]; on a visit to Arethusa Falls, the Bemis Brook Trail can be used either ascending or descending to obtain additional views of other falls in Bemis Brook. By spotting a car, you can visit both of the big falls in one trip via the Arethusa–Ripley Falls Trail [lp: 4.3 mi., 1100 ft., 2:40]. It is also possible to use the Frankenstein Cliff Trail to make a loop that includes Arethusa Falls and Frankenstein Cliff [lp: 4.7 mi., 1400 ft., 3:05].

Sawyer Pond, reached by the Sawyer Pond Trail, is an attractive and popular mountain pond situated at the base of Mt. Tremont [rt: 3.0 mi., 500 ft., 1:45]. **Church Pond** is another attractive but far less popular pond reached by a loop path from the Kancamagus Highway [lp: 2.8 mi., 100 ft., 1:25]; it lies in a flat region of swamps and poorly drained woodlands, very different from the terrain usually crossed by hiking trails—visitors should expect wet feet. **The Rob Brook Trail** is a somewhat similar trail that follows an old railroad grade through an area of swamps and beaver ponds [rt: 4.6 mi., 100 ft., 2:20]. The **Boulder Loop Trail** is an interpretive nature trail that ascends a small mountain, a spur of the Moat group, that has good views from a ledge [lp: 3.1 mi., 900 ft., 2:00]. **Big Rock Cave,** an interesting boulder cave on a southern spur of Mt. Paugus reached by the Big Rock Cave Trail, is an interesting objective for young children [rt: 3.2 mi., 1100 ft., 2:10].

Iron Mtn., reached by the Iron Mountain Trail, has a broad ledge with an excellent view on its south end [rt: 3.2 mi., 1000 ft, 2:05]. **Mt. Stanton** and **Mt. Pickering** are two small mountains that offer beautiful red pine woods with scattered ledges, each with a different interesting view [rt: 4.2 mi., 1800 ft., 3:00]. They are on the Mount Stanton Trail, which continues over several small ledgy peaks called the Crippies; the trail is not recommended beyond the last Crippie [rt: 6.6 mi., 2400 ft., 4.30]. **Mt. Crawford,** reached by the Davis Path, is a beautiful rock peak with extensive views [rt: 5.0 mi., 2100 ft., 3:35]; it is also part of an excellent longer trip that includes Stairs [rt: 9.8 mi., 3000 ft., 6:25] or Resolution [rt; 9.2 mi , 2800 ft., 6:00] or both [rt: 11.0 mi., 3400 ft., 7:10]. **Mt. Willard** has long been celebrated for the view of Crawford Notch from the brink of its impressive cliffs [rt: 3.2 mi., 900 ft., 2:05]. The best view available from the Willey Range is found on the little crag called **Mt. Avalon,** reached by the Avalon Trail [rt: 3.6 mi., 1600 ft., 2:35]; visitors should make the short side trip on the loop to Beecher and Pearl cascades on the way. **Sugarloaf Mtn.** near **Twin Mountain** NH offers excellent views for modest effort from its two open summits [rt: 3.4 mi., 1100 ft., 2:15].

South Moat is a bare summit with excellent views in all directions [rt: 4.6 mi., 2200 ft., 3:25]. **Hedgehog Mtn.,** reached by the UNH Trail, which is a loop [lp: 4.8 mi., 1700 ft., 3:15], and **Mt. Potash,** reached by the Mount Potash Trail [rt: 4.4 mi., 1500 ft., 1:55], are two small peaks on the north side of the Sandwich Range that offer excellent views from their ledges.

A number of the higher peaks in the Crawford Notch area can be reached with relatively moderate effort. **Mt. Jackson** is reached by the Jackson branch of the Webster-Jackson Trail [rt: 5.2 mi., 2200 ft., 3:35]; **Mt. Webster** by the Webster branch of the Webster-Jackson Trail [rt: 5.0 mi., 2000 ft, 3:30; a loop can be made over both summits [lp: 6.5 mi., 2500 ft, 4:30]. If a car spot is available, one can ascend Mt. Webster by the Webster-Jackson Trail and then make a leisurely descent of the magnificent Webster Cliff Trail down to the notch [lp: 5.8 mi., 2000 ft., 3:55]. **Mt. Hale** can be climbed by the Hale Brook Trail [rt: 4.4 mi., 2300 ft., 3:20]; an interesting longer loop can be made by following the Lend-a-Hand Trail from the summit to Zealand Falls Hut, then following the Zealand Trail back out to Zealand Rd. [lp: 8.7 mi., 2400 ft., 5:35].

Moderate Trips

Mt. Chocorua is one of the most popular peaks in the White Mtns., and the easier trails usually have heavy traffic, but the crowds can often be avoided except at the summit. One of the better routes available is to ascend via the Piper, Nickerson Ledge, Carter Ledge, Middle Sister, and Piper trails, and descend by the Liberty, Hammond, Weetamoo, and Piper trails [lp: 10.7 mi., 3300 ft., 7:00]. The trip over **North Moat** via the Red Ridge and Moat Mountain trails is one of the most beautiful trips in this region, traversing large amounts of open ledge [lp: 10.0 mi., 2800 ft., 6:10]. **Kearsarge North,** reached by the Mount Kearsarge North Trail, offers one of the finest views in the White Mtns. [rt: 6.2 mi., 2600 ft., 4:10]. **Mt. Tremont** offers excellent views but is far less frequently climbed; the Mount Tremont Trail must therefore be followed with considerable care [rt: 5.6 mi., 2600 ft., 4:05]. **Mt. Carrigain,** which many people believe has the best view of all in the Whites, is reached by the Signal Ridge Trail [rt: 10.0 mi., 3200 ft., 6:35]. The trip on the **Nancy Pond Trail** to Nancy Cascades [rt: 4.8 mi., 1200 ft., 3:00] is attractive in itself, but it is worth the effort to continue to the unusual ledge that dams Norcross Pond and affords a fine view into the Pemigewasset Wilderness [rt: 8.6 mi., 2100 ft., 5:20].

Mt. Whiteface, located at the southern edge of the high mountain region, offers an excellent view over the lake country to the south from the broad ledges south of the summit; it can be ascended by the moderately challenging Blueberry Ledge Trail [rt: 7.8 mi., 3000 ft., 5:25] or by a longer but more routine route via the Flat Mountain Pond and McCrillis trails [rt: 9.8 mi., 3200 ft., 6:30]. **Zeacliff** is a perch at the northern end of the Pemigewasset Wilderness that commands one of the finest outlooks in the Whites; it can be reached by the Zealand Trail and Twinway [rt: 7.8 mi., 2100 ft., 4:55].

The **Evans Notch** region is one of the less frequently visited corners of the White Mtns., but the **Baldface Circle** trip is one of the finest ridge traverses in the Whites. You can either do the trip on the Baldface Circle Trail all the way [lp: 9.8 mi., 3200 ft., 6:30], or avoid the steep ledges on South Baldface by using the Slippery Brook and Baldface Knob trails [lp: 10.6 mi., 3300 ft., 6:55].

LINCOLN–FRANCONIA NOTCH REGION
Easy Trips
Bald Mtn. is a scale model mountain; very impressive in appearance, it can be climbed very easily [rt: 0.6 mi., 300 ft., 0:25]. Unfortunately, the view from its once highly admired neighbor, Artists Bluff [lp: 1.3 mi., 400 ft.,

0:50], has been severely marred by the extensive inter-
changes of the Franconia Notch Parkway at its foot. The
Basin-Cascades Trail follows **Cascade Brook** from the
Basin area to the Cascade Brook Trail; there are many
broad ledges and small cascades, and one can stop, enjoy,
and turn back at any point or continue all the way to
Rocky Glen Falls [rt: 2.0 mi., 600 ft., 1:20].

Eagle Pass, reached by the Greenleaf Trail, is a narrow
rocky cleft between Mt. Lafayette and Eagle Cliff that merits exploration [rt: 3.0 mi., 1000 ft., 2:00]. **Lonesome
Lake,** a very popular objective, offers fine views of the
Franconia Range [rt: 3.2 mi., 1000 ft., 2:05]. The Kinsman
Ridge Trail provides access to a fine broad ledge on the
east peak of Cannon that commands a spectacular view
across the notch [rt: 3.0 mi., 1800 ft., 2:25]; you can easily
extend the trip to the tourist trap on the summit [rt: 4.4 mi.,
2100 ft., 3:15]. **Indian Head,** offering an excellent outlook
from a prowlike cliff, is reached from the Flume Visitor
Center by the Mount Pemigewasset Trail [rt: 3.6 mi., 1200
ft., 2:25]. **Bridal Veil Falls,** one of the more attractive
waterfalls in the White Mtns., is reached by the Coppermine Trail [rt: 5.0 mi., 1000 ft., 3:05].

Moderate Trips

Cherry Mtn., located north of Twin Mountain village, has
some good views from the summit, where a fire tower used
to stand; but the most interesting viewpoint by far is the
ledge on Owl's Head, the lower north summit. Since the
Owl's Head Trail, the direct route [rt: 3.8 mi., 2100 ft.,
2:55], has parts with poor footing, it is probably easiest to
follow the Cherry Mountain Trail from NH 115 to the
main summit [rt: 3.8 mi., 2000 ft., 2:55], then follow
Martha's Mile to Owl's Head [rt: 5.4 mi., 2600 ft., 3:30], in
spite of the extra elevation gain. **Mt. Garfield** offers one of
the best views in the Whites from summit ledges perched
high above the Pemigewasset Wilderness; the Garfield
Trail, though long, is easier (except for the last 0.2 mi.)

than most mountain trails, with generally good footing and moderate grades [rt: 10.0 mi., 3000 ft., 6:30]. **North Kinsman** has a spectacular view out to the Franconia Range and almost straight down to picturesque Kinsman Pond at the foot of its cliffs; an interesting and varied trip can be made using the Mount Kinsman Trail from NH 116 and including the spur paths to Kinsman Flume and Bald Knob and a side trip to Kinsman Pond [rt: 9.4 mi., 3600 ft., 6:30]. South Kinsman, with its fine views particularly to the south, can be added to this trip [rt: 11.2 mi., 4200 ft., 7:35].

Though virtually everyone agrees that there is too much traffic on the **Franconia Ridge**, it is hard to imagine a serious hiker with enough resolve to forego one of the most spectacular walks in the East. The standard loop via the Old Bridle Path and Falling Waters Trail is probably unbeatable [lp: 7.9 mi., 3900 ft., 5:55]; it is a good trip in either direction, but most people will prefer the excuse to rest while ascending that is offered by the excellent outlook ledges on the Bridle Path, and appreciate the cold brooks for soaking heads and feet on the descent of the Falling Waters Trail. Nearby **Mt. Liberty** offers equally good summit views but much less open ridge walking, the Liberty Spring Trail is the usual route [rt: 8.0 mi., 3200 ft., 5:35].

MOOSILAUKE REGION
Easy Trips

An interesting **loop through a region of ponds and swamps** can be made via the Three Ponds Trail, Mount Kineo Trail, and Donkey Hill Cutoff [lp: 5.1 mi., 500 ft., 2:50]; the trip can be lengthened as much as desired by walking on the Three Ponds Trail or Mount Kineo Trail beyond the loop. **Black Mtn.** in the Benton Range is a fine viewpoint reached by the attractive Chippewa Trail [rt: 3.6 mi., 1600 ft., 2:35]. **Rattlesnake Mtn.** is easily climbed, and the new loop trail offers interesting views of the Baker River Valley [lp: 2.5 mi., 1000 ft., 1:45]. **Mt. Cube** is a very attractive small mountain in the Connecticut Valley; it can be ascended most easily via the South Cube Trail [rt: 3.0 mi., 1500 ft., 2:15], and it is worthwhile to include the trip on the spur trail to the viewpoints on the north peak [rt: 3.8 mi., 1600 ft., 2:40].

Moderate Trips

Mt. Moosilauke is the dominating peak of this region. Unless the brook at the start is high, the Benton Trail on the west side is probably the most attractive route [rt: 7.2 mi., 3200 ft., 5:10]. Another good choice is the Gorge Brook Trail on the east side, newly relocated to eliminate steep sections on the former route and include several excellent viewpoints [rt: 7.4 mi., 2600 ft., 5:00]. A good long loop with a wide variety of scenery can be made via the Glencliff, Tunnel Brook, and Benton trails [lp: 13.3 mi., 4000 ft., 8:40]. The trip on the Wachipauka Pond Trail (a part of the Appalachian Trail) to Wachipauka Pond and the spectacular cliff-edge outlook on **Webster Slide Mtn.**, in an area just to the west of Moosilauke, is particularly appealing [rt: 6.0 mi., 1800 ft., 3:55].

WATERVILLE VALLEY REGION

Easy Trips

Hikers interested in very short trips should obtain a map of the WVAIA trail system and make use of it. One of the most popular objectives in this region is the **Greeley Ponds,** easily reached from the Kancamagus Highway by the Greeley Ponds Trail [rt: 4.4 mi., 600 ft., 2:30]. However, the trip from the Waterville Valley side [rt: 6.8 mi., 800 ft., 3:50] is more interesting and permits exploration of some of the side paths to local attractions such as the Scaur, Goodrich Rock, and the flume on Flume Brook. Hikers should be aware that the trail to Mt. Osceola from Greeley Ponds is one of the steepest and roughest in the mountains; Mt. Osceola can be ascended fairly easily from the high point on Tripoli Rd. [rt: 6.4 mi., 2000 ft., 4:10]. The loop trip including both **East Pond and Little East Pond** [lp: 5.0 mi., 1300 ft., 3:10] is a pleasant walk, but finding the trailhead is often a problem due to lack of a sign—the trails themselves are easy to follow. The loop over **Welch Mtn.** and **Dickey Mtn.** [lp: 4.4 mi., 1900 ft., 3:10] is a local favorite, offering a great deal of open ledge walking. **Mt. Israel,** located south of the main peaks of the Sandwich Range, offers an impressive view of its higher neighbors; its ascent via the Guinea Pond and Mead trails provides a pleasant, varied walk [rt: 6.6 mi., 1100 ft., 3:50].

Moderate Trips

Sandwich Mtn. at the south end of the Waterville Valley has a good view, but is upstaged by the little rock peak called Jennings Peak on its north ridge. You can follow the Sandwich Mountain Trail to Jennings Peak [rt: 6.0 mi., 2000 ft., 4:00], then decide whether to continue to the main summit [rt: 8.2 mi., 2600 ft., 5:25]. For a direct ascent of Sandwich, the Algonquin Trail is an extremely scenic route [rt: 9.0 mi., 3000 ft., 6:00]. **Tripyramid** is a tempting objective, not because of its summit views, which are good but limited, but because of its rugged architecture. By any route Tripyramid makes a strenuous trip, but the loop by the Mount Tripyramid Trail up the North Slide and down the South Slide is a White Mtn. classic [lp: 11.0 mi., 3000 ft., 7:00], though it is definitely not for everyone. For those who enjoy steep ledges and using their hands it is a satisfying challenge, but those who do not find such climbing exhilarating would do well to avoid it.

SOUTHERN NEW HAMPSHIRE

Easy Trips

South of the main ranges there are a number of desirable small peaks, and one of their important advantages is that they are often free of snow and ice in late fall or early spring, when winter still lies heavy on the mountains to the north.

In the Lakes Region, **West Rattlesnake,** with its fine, easily attained view over Squam Lake, is one of New Hampshire's most popular peaks. Hikers using the most popular route, the Old Bridle Path [rt: 1.8 mi., 400 ft., 1:05], may find that they have to walk farther from their parking spot to the trailhead than from the trailhead to the summit; the Pasture Trail is a good alternative [rt: 1.2 mi., 600 ft, 0:55]. Directly across NH 113, the loop hike over **Mt. Percival** and **Mt. Morgan** via the Mount Percival, Crawford-Ridgepole, and Mount Morgan trails offers exceptional views for the effort required [lp: 5.1 mi., 1600 ft., 3:20]. **Red Hill** offers fine views north to the Sandwich Range; the Red Hill Trail, being an old jeep road, has much easier grades and footing than most mountain trails, making it suitable for hikers with limited agility [rt: 3.4 mi., 1300 ft., 2:20]; the Eagle Cliff Trail provides a more interesting route, but it is much steeper and rougher, particularly in the vicinity of the cliff [rt: 5.2 mi., 1800 ft., 3:30].

Mt. Major, ascended by the Mount Major Trail, is a small, bare-topped mountain with excellent views of Lake Winnipesaukee, but in season its blueberries draw as many visitors as its views [rt: 3.0 mi., 1100 ft., 2:05]. **North Pawtuckaway,** with practically no view from its true summit, is visited for the outlooks and the rugged rock formations one passes on the way, and for the geologically noteworthy collection of huge boulders at its foot [rt: 3.0 mi., 600 ft., 1:50].

West of the Merrimack, three major isolated peaks dominate the region south of the White Mtns. **Cardigan** can be climbed most easily from the west side, using the West Ridge Trail alone [rt: 3.0 mi., 1100 ft., 2:05] or in combination with the South Ridge Trail [lp: 3.6 mi., 1200 ft., 2:25]. However, there is far greater variety of possible routes on the east side. For direct routes to the summit from the AMC Cardigan Lodge, hikers can choose between the relatively easy ascent by the Holt, Cathedral Forest, and Clark trails [ow: 2.6 mi., 1800 ft., 2:10], or stay on the Holt Trail [ow: 2.2 mi., 1800 ft., 2:00] for a sporty ascent of the rather airy ledges near the summit. A good loop hike combines one of the direct ascents with the Mowglis Trail to Firescrew (the north peak) and the Manning Trail back to the lodge [lp: 5.6 mi., 1900 ft., 3:45]. Another good loop can be made by pairing a direct route with a return over Orange Mtn. via the South Ridge, Skyland, and Vistamont trails [lp: 7.2 mi., 2000 ft., 4:35]. For those willing to forego the thrills of the Holt Trail ledges, a good longer loop combines the aforementioned routes over Orange Mtn. and Firescrew [lp: 7.6 mi., 2100 ft., 4:50]. While in the area, one should not miss **Welton Falls,** easily reached from the lodge via the Manning Trail [rt: 2.6 mi., 300 ft., 1:25].

Mt. Kearsarge, a very prominent peak despite its low elevation due to the lack of significant neighbors, has only two routes: the Warner Trail from Rollins State Park [rt: 2.2 mi., 1100 ft., 1:40], and the Wilmot Trail from Winslow State Park [rt: 1.2 mi., 300 ft., 0:45].

Mt. Monadnock receives such heavy use that a major part of climbing strategy is avoiding the crowds. The White Arrow, White Cross, and White Dot trails receive particularly heavy traffic due to their short distances and easily accessible trailheads. The long, strenuous, but very scenic Pumpelly Trail [rt: 8.8 mi., 2100 ft., 5:25] is probably the most attractive of the major trails, but the Dublin Trail [rt: 4.4 mi., 1700 ft., 3:05] and the Marlboro Trail [rt: 4.4 mi., 1900 ft., 3:10] are also worthy of serious consideration. The secondary trails that form a network on the south and east sides of the mountain will amply reward anyone who takes the time to explore them and become familiar with their beauty and variety.

Index

Note: Trails marked by an asterisk do not have a separate description, but are discussed or mentioned in groups or within other trails' descriptions. **Boldface** denotes trail name.